Praise for the First Edition

This is the EJB book to read! Don't miss its practical advice.

—Jeanne Boyarsky, JavaRanch.com

A technical book that is surprisingly entertaining.

—King Y. Wang, Oracle Canada

Great book—covers everything relating to EJB 3.

—Awais Bajwa, Expert Group Member
JSR 243 Java Data Objects

Well-written, easy, and fun.

—Patrick Dennis, Management Dynamics Inc.

Written with a wide audience in mind ... not just a recitation of the EJB specification ... includes a lot of practical advice. Has a light, humorous, and accessible style of writing and all the concepts are illustrated with examples.

—One Minute Review from javalobby.org

Broad coverage of EJB 3 with a very simple and excellently crafted case study. The book starts lightly on this complex subject and slowly dives into the details of advanced concepts like interceptors, transactions, security, JPA, and performance issues, developing each scenario in the case study. Overall, a very good book and a very smooth read.

—Amazon.com reader

This edition has been published by arrangement with the **Manning Publications Co., USA.** and published in India by **Dreamtech Press, 19-A, Ansari Road, Daryaganj, New Delhi-110002.**

ISBN: 978-93-5119-917-5

Edition : 2016

Printed at : *Radha Offset, Delhi*

EJB 3 in Action
Second Edition

DEBU PANDA
REZA RAHMAN
RYAN CUPRAK
MICHAEL REMIJAN

MANNING

Published by:
dreamtech PRESS

brief contents

contents

preface

In its early days, EJB was inspired by the distributed computing ideas of technologies such as CORBA and was intended to add scalability to server-side applications. EJB and J2EE enjoyed some of the greatest buzz in the industry during the dot.com boom.

The initial goal for EJB was to provide a simpler alternative to CORBA through the benefits of a standard development framework and reusable components. By the time EJB 2 was released, it became apparent that the EJB framework could become the new standard for server-side development. The framework provided Enterprise developers with everything they needed—remoting, transaction management, security, state maintenance, persistence, and web services—but it was heavyweight, requiring developers to focus more on the framework itself than on the requirements of their business applications. Because EJB was loaded with more features, its inventors failed to address its growing complexity.

As the community became disenchanted with the limitations of EJB 2, innovative open source tools emerged. These tools were signs of the increasing discontent with the complexities of Java EE. Though well-intentioned, these tools made Enterprise development even more complex since they deviated from the standards of the application server they were to run in. It was time for the Java Community Process (JCP) and expert groups to work on the simplification of Java EE development. That was the sole motivation behind Java EE 5 and the goal of the EJB 3 expert group.

For a technology with a wide deployment base, the changes that came with EJB 3 were nothing short of stunning. EJB 3 successfully melds innovative techniques to make component development as easy as possible. These techniques include the use of annotations, metadata programming, dependency injection, AspectJ-like interceptors, and intelligent defaulting. The heavyweight inheritance-based programming model was abandoned in favor of Plain Old Java Object (POJO) programming, and the verbose XML descriptor was now out of the developer's way.

The changes to the persistence model were particularly dramatic. EJB 3 left behind the flawed EJB 2 Entity Beans model in favor of the lightweight Java Persistence API (JPA). Unlike Entity Beans, JPA is not container-based. It has more in common with open source object relational mapping (ORM) tools that emerged in the community in response to Entity Beans complexity. JPA can be used either inside or outside a Java Enterprise server and is now the de facto persistence standard for Java. Its Java Persistence Query Language (JPQL) standardizes object relational queries but also supports native SQL queries if the need arises.

The changes made in EJB 3 have been well received in the Java community. Its simplified specification has led to its wide adoption in new projects. More and more companies are giving the once "ugly" EJB technology another look and they like what they see. With the release of EJB 3.2, the adoption will continue to grow. EJB 3.2 has made support for EJB 2 optional so that older technology can finally be sunset and innovations in EJB 3 can continue to grow. EJB 3.2 has also seen major enhancements to message-driven beans (MDBs), making messaging much easier. EJB 3.2 made improvements to stateful session bean passivation and session bean local interfaces, as well as dramatic improvements to the timer services. All this and more await you in EJB 3.2.

Since EJB is POJO-based, every Java developer can easily become an EJB developer. Simple annotations give your business logic safe transaction management, security, and exposure as web services for easy interoperability in your company. We strive to keep our book different from other books on EJB by providing practical examples, best practices, and tips for performance tuning. We highlight what's new in the EJB 3.2 specification, which gives you more tools for your development. We hope this revised edition will help you to quickly learn how to use EJB 3 effectively in your next Enterprise application.

acknowledgments

Authoring a book requires great effort and it's difficult to list everyone who helped us during this project. First and foremost we'd like to thank everyone at Manning for their encouragement and support, especially publisher Marjan Bace, associate publisher Michael Stephens, and our editor Nermina Miller. We'd also like to thank others at Manning who worked on different stages of the project: review editor Olivia Booth; project editor Jodie Allen; development manager Maureen Spencer; technical proofreader Deepak Vohra, who performed a final review of the book shortly before it went to press; Linda Recktenwald and Melody Dolab, who edited, proofread, and polished our prose; and typesetter Dennis Dalinnik, who converted our Word documents into a real book! Thanks also to all of those who worked behind the scenes to help get our book published.

Many reviewers spent their valuable time reading the manuscript at various stages of its development, and their feedback greatly improved the quality of the book. We'd like to thank Artur Nowak, Aziz Rahman, Bob Casazza, Christophe Martini, David Strong, Jeet Marwah, John Griffin, Jonas Bandi, Josef Lehner, Jürgen De Commer, Karan Malhi, Khalid Muktar, Koray Güclü, Luis Peña, Matthias Agethle, Palak Mathur, Pavel Rozenblioum, Rick Wagner, Sumit Pal, Victor Aguilar, Wellington Pinheiro, and Zorodzayi Mukuya.

Finally, thanks to the readers of Manning's Early Access Program (MEAP), who read our chapters as they were being written and posted comments and corrections in the book's online forum. Your input has made this a better book.

DEBU PANDA

I'd like to thank my wife, Renuka, for her immense support and continuous encouragement and for her patience with all the late nights, early mornings, and weekends that I spent on the first edition of the book. I'd also like to thank my kids, Nistha and Nisheet, who had to share their bapa with the computer during that time.

Many thanks to my coauthors Reza Rahman, Ryan Cuprak, and Michael Remijan, who worked hard on the second edition of the book.

REZA RAHMAN

A journey of a thousand miles begins with a single step.

—Lao-tzu

When I decided to take on writing the first edition of this book, I don't think any of the authors were certain how successful the book was going to be or where it might take us personally. Today I have the luxury of hindsight in saying the book has been a resounding success and that writing it was the first step of a whirlwind journey over the past few years that I could have never foreseen. I must confess I continue to enjoy every minute of it. Since finishing the first edition, I've become increasingly more engaged with the Java community. I've contributed to various Java EE expert groups, including the EJB expert group, had the once-in-a-lifetime opportunity to write an open source EJB container almost from scratch, and now find myself at the forefront of the Java EE evangelism team at SunOracle.

One casualty of all of this has been my own personal bandwidth, which was more abundant when I wrote the first edition. This is a large part of why we had to skip a Java EE 6 and EJB 3.1 edition of this book. I do think it's all for the best since Java EE 7 is an even stronger and more compelling platform, as this edition will demonstrate. I'm extremely grateful to Michael and Ryan for taking ownership of the book and being instrumental in producing a worthy second edition. I'm also grateful to the many folks like you in the Java EE community that I've had the privilege to serve and work with. Lastly, I'm ever thankful to my wife Nicole and daughter Zehra for allowing me to pursue my passion without reservation. And so the journey continues.

RYAN CUPRAK

Writing this book would not have been possible without the support of family and friends. I'd especially like to thank the love of my life, Elsa, who has supported and encouraged me throughout the long, arduous process and the many long nights I was hunched over the computer. Finally, I'd like to thank Reza for recruiting me to this project and encouraging me to take a second look at Java EE many years ago.

MICHAEL REMIJAN

My wonderful wife Kelly and my daughter Sophia are the first people I need to thank when it comes to writing this book. It's one of many adventures we've shared together, and without their support while I worked early mornings, late nights, and weekends, I wouldn't have been able to do the research and writing necessary for a project this big. Kelly is my best friend, who encourages me in all I do, and is the perfect one for me—I love her dearly. I'm blessed with a remarkable family.

My coauthors Debu, Ryan, and Reza are next, and many thanks go to them. This book was a team effort. EJB is a great technology with many, many features; hence the size of this book. It'd be a monumental task for one person to write it on their own, so the collaboration among us was essential for delivering this book. It was a great opportunity to work with such talented colleagues.

Finally, thanks to all the people at Manning who did countless reviews and kept the book on track, especially Maureen Spencer and Jodie Allen. Christina Rudloff originally recruited me into the project, and without her I wouldn't have gotten involved.

about this book

EJB 3 is meant to recast Java server-side development into a mold you might not expect. Therefore, we've tried to make this an EJB book you might not anticipate.

Most server-side Java books tend to be serious affairs—heavy on theory, slightly preachy, and geared toward the advanced developer. While we easily fit the stereotype of geeks and aren't the funniest comedians or entertainers, we've tried to add some color to our writing to keep this book as lighthearted and down-to-earth as possible. The tone is intended to be friendly, conversational, and informal. We made a conscious effort to drive the chapter content with examples that are close to the real-world problems you deal with every day. In most cases, we introduce a problem that needs to be solved, show you the code to solve it using EJB 3, and explore features of the technology using the code.

We cover theory when it is necessary. We try to avoid theory for theory's sake and to make the discussion as lively as we can. The goal of this book is to help you learn EJB 3 quickly and effectively, not to be a comprehensive reference book. We don't cover features you're unlikely to use. Instead, we provide deep coverage of the most useful EJB 3 features and its related technologies. We discuss various options so you can make educated choices, warn you about common pitfalls, and tell you about battle-hardened best practices.

If you've picked up this book, it's unlikely you're a complete newcomer to Java. We assume you've done some work in Java, perhaps in the form of web development using a presentation-tier technology like JSF, Struts, JSP, or Servlets. We assume you're familiar with database technologies such as JDBC and have at least a casual familiarity with SQL. You don't need any experience with EJB 2.x to pick up this book; EJB 3 is completely new. We don't assume you know any of the Java EE technologies that EJB is dependent on, such as the Java Naming and Directory Interface (JNDI), Java Remote Method Invocation (RMI), and Java Messaging Service (JMS). In fact, we assume you're not familiar with middleware concepts like remoting, pooling, concurrent programming, security, and distributed transactions. This book is ideally suited for a Java developer with a couple of years' experience who is curious about EJB 3.

You might find this book different from others in one more important way. EJB is a server-side middleware technology. This means that it doesn't live in a vacuum and must be integrated with other technologies to fulfill its mission. Throughout the book, we talk about how EJB 3 integrates with technologies like JNDI, JMS, JSF, JSP, Servlets, AJAX, and even Swing-based Java SE clients.

This book is about EJB 3 as a standard, not a specific application server technology. For this reason, we avoid tying our discussion to any specific application server implementation. Instead, the code samples in this book are designed to run with any EJB 3 container or persistence provider. The website accompanying this book at www.manning.com/EJB3inActionSecondEdition will tell you how you can get the code up and running in GlassFish and Oracle Application Server 10g. Maintaining the application server–specific instructions on the publisher's website instead of in the book will allow us to keep the instructions up to-date with the newest implementation details.

Roadmap

This book is divided into four parts.

Part 1 provides an overview of EJB. Chapter 1 introduces EJB 3 and EJB types, makes the case for EJB 3, and provides an overview of changes introduced with EJB 3.2. Chapter 2 gives you a first taste of EJB, building EJB as you build your first solution using EJB technology.

Part 2 covers working with EJB components to implement your business logic. Chapter 3 dives into the details of session beans and outlines best practices. Chapter 4 gives a quick introduction to messaging and JMS and covers MDB in detail. Chapter 5 covers advanced topics such as the EJB context, JNDI, resource and EJB injection, AOP interceptors, and the application client container. Chapter 6 discusses transaction and security. Chapter 7 introduces timers and new scheduling options. Chapter 8 exposes EJB business logic as SOAP and RESTful web services.

Part 3 provides in-depth coverage of EJB 3's relationship with JPA and CDI. Chapter 9 introduces domain modeling and how to map JPA entities to your domain. Chapter 10 covers managing JPA entities through CRUD operations. Chapter 11 introduces JPQL and covers retrieval of data in-depth. Chapter 12 is an introduction to CDI and how it complements EJB development.

Part 4 provides guidelines for putting EJB 3 into action in your enterprise. Chapter 13 discusses packaging EJBs and entities for deployment to a server. Chapter 14 introduces web sockets, their relationship to EJBs, and asynchronous business logic execution using the EJB concurrency utilities. Chapter 15 covers unit and integration testing without the need for deployment to a running server.

The book has three appendixes. Appendix A is a reference on the ejb-jar.xml deployment descriptor. Appendix B contains step-by-step instructions on downloading and installing the Java EE 7 SDK, which includes Java SE 7, GlassFish 4, and NetBeans. Appendix C provides information on Oracle's EJB certification process and the EJB certification exam.

Source code downloads

Appendix B provides step-by-step instructions on installation of the Java EE 7 SDK. The source code for this book is available from http://code.google.com/p/action-bazaar/. From here you can either clone the Git repository to get a copy of all of the examples or you can download a prepared ZIP file that has all the code in it. The code was developed primarily in NetBeans, but all the examples are built with Maven, so they should run in your favorite IDE.

A zip file with the source code is also available for download from the publisher's website at www.manning.com/EJB3inActionSecondEdition.

Source code conventions

Because of the example-driven style of this book, the source code was given a great deal of attention. Larger sections of code in the chapters are presented as their own listings. All code is formatted using `fixed-width Courier font like this` for visibility. All inside code, such as XML element names, method names, Java type names, package names, variable names, and so on, are also formatted using Courier font. Some code is formatted as **`Courier Bold`** to highlight important sections. Code annotations are also sometimes used to point out important concepts. In some cases, we've abbreviated the code to keep it short and simple. In all cases, the full version of the abbreviated code is contained in the downloadable zip files. We encourage you to set up your development environment for each chapter before you begin reading it.

Author Online

Purchase of *EJB 3 in Action, Second Edition* includes free access to a private web forum run by Manning Publications where you can make comments about the book, ask technical questions, and receive help from the authors and other users. To access the forum and subscribe to it, point your web browser to www.manning.com/EJB3inActionSecondEdition. This Author Online (AO) page provides information on how to get on the forum once you're registered, what kind of help is available, and the rules of conduct on the forum.

Manning's commitment to our readers is to provide a venue where a meaningful dialog among individual readers and between readers and the authors can take place.

It's not a commitment to any specific amount of participation on the part of the authors, whose contribution to the AO remains voluntary (and unpaid). We suggest you try asking the authors some challenging questions, lest their interest stray!

The AO forum and the archives of previous discussions will be accessible from the publisher's website as long as the book is in print.

About the title

By combining introductions, overviews, and how-to examples, the *In Action* books are designed to help you learn and remember. According to research in cognitive science, the things people remember are things they discover during self-motivated exploration.

Although no one at Manning is a cognitive scientist, we're convinced that for learning to become permanent, it must pass through stages of exploration, play, and, interestingly, retelling of what's being learned. People understand and remember new things—that is, they master them—only after actively exploring them. Humans learn in action. An essential part of an *In Action* guide is that it's example-driven. It encourages the reader to try things out, play with new code, and explore new ideas.

There is another, more mundane, reason for the title of this book: our readers are busy. They use books to do a job or solve a problem. They need books that allow them to jump in and jump out easily and learn just what they want just when they want it. They need books that aid them in action. The books in this series are designed for such readers.

about the authors

DEBU PANDA is a seasoned product manager, technologist, and community leader. He has authored more than 50 articles on Enterprise Java, Cloud, and SOA technologies and two books on Enterprise middleware. Follow Debu on Twitter @debupanda.

REZA RAHMAN is a former long-time independent consultant and is now officially a Java EE/GlassFish evangelist at Oracle. Reza is a frequent speaker at Java user groups and conferences worldwide. He is an avid contributor to industry journals like *JavaLobby/DZone* and *TheServerSide*. Reza has been a member of the Java EE, EJB, and JMS expert groups. He implemented the EJB container for the Resin open source Java EE application server.

RYAN CUPRAK is an e-formulation analyst at Dassault Systèmes (DS), author of the *NetBeans Certification Guide* from McGraw-Hill, and president of the Connecticut Java Users Group since 2003. He's also a JavaOne 2011 Rockstar Presenter. At DS he's focused on developing data integrations to convert clients' data, as well as user interface development. Prior to joining DS, he worked for a startup distributed-computing company, TurboWorx, and Eastman Kodak's Molecular Imaging Systems group, now part of Carestream Health. At TurboWorx he was a Java developer and a technical sales engineer supporting both presales and professional services. Cuprak earned a BS in computer science and biology from Loyola University Chicago. He is a Sun-certified NetBeans IDE specialist.

MICHAEL REMIJAN is an operations manager and technical lead at BJC Hospital. Michael started working with Java EE in the late 1990s. He has developed Enterprise systems for B2C and B2B commerce, manufacturing, astronomy, agriculture, telecommunications, national defense, and healthcare. He earned a BS in computer science and mathematics from the University of Illinois in Urbana-Champaign and an MBA in technology management from the University of Phoenix. He has numerous Sun Microsystem certifications and has published articles with *Java Developer's Journal* and *JavaLobby/DZone*. His technology blog is mjremijan.blogspot.com.

about the cover illustration

The figure on the cover of *EJB 3 in Action, Second Edition* is captioned "Russian girl with fur," taken from a French travel book, *Encyclopedie des Voyages* by J. G. St. Saveur, published in 1796. Travel for pleasure was a relatively new phenomenon at the time and travel guides such as this one were popular, introducing both the tourist as well as the armchair traveler to the inhabitants of other regions of France and abroad.

The diversity of the drawings in the *Encyclopedie des Voyages* speaks vividly of the uniqueness and individuality of the world's towns and provinces just 200 years ago. This was a time when the dress codes of two regions separated by a few dozen miles identified people uniquely as belonging to one or the other. The travel guide brings to life a sense of isolation and distance of that period and of every other historic period except our own hyperkinetic present.

Dress codes have changed since then and the diversity by region, so rich at the time, has faded away. It is now often hard to tell the inhabitant of one continent from another. Perhaps, trying to view it optimistically, we've traded a cultural and visual diversity for a more varied personal life. Or a more varied and interesting intellectual and technical life.

We at Manning celebrate the inventiveness, initiative, and fun of the computer business with book covers based on the rich diversity of regional life two centuries ago brought back to life by the pictures from this travel guide.

Part 1

Overview of the EJB landscape

This book is about Enterprise Java Beans (EJB) 3, and covers up to the EJB 3.2 specification. The goal of EJB 3.2 is to continue to evolve the EJB specification to be a complete solution for all Enterprise business needs and to improve the EJB architecture by reducing its complexity from the developer's point of view.

Part 1 presents EJB 3 as a powerful, highly usable platform worthy of its place as the business component development standard for mission-critical Enterprise development. We'll introduce the Java Persistence API (JPA 2.1), a Java EE technology that aims to standardize Java ORM and works hand-in-hand with EJB 3. We'll also take a quick look at Contexts and Dependency Injection for Java (CDI 1.1), the next-generation generic type-safe dependency injection technology for Java EE.

In chapter 1 we introduce the pieces that make up EJB 3, touching on the unique strengths EJB has as a development platform and the new features that promote productivity and ease of use. We even throw in a "Hello World" example.

In chapter 2 we provide more realistic code samples and introduce the ActionBazaar application, an imaginary Enterprise system developed throughout the book. We'll try to give you a feel for how EJB 3 looks as quickly and easily as possible. Be ready for a lot of code!

1 What's what in EJB 3

This chapter covers

- The EJB container and its role in Enterprise applications
- The different types of Enterprise Java Beans (EJBs)
- Closely related technologies such as the Java Persistence API (JPA)
- The different EJB runtime environments
- Innovations started with EJB 3
- New changes with EJB 3.2

One day, when God was looking over his creatures, he noticed a boy named Sadhu whose humor and cleverness pleased him. God felt generous that day and granted Sadhu three wishes. Sadhu asked for three reincarnations—one as a ladybug, one as an elephant, and the last as a cow. Surprised by these wishes, God asked Sadhu to explain himself. The boy replied, "I want to be a ladybug so that everyone in the world will admire me for my beauty and forgive the fact that I do no work. Being an elephant will be fun because I can gobble down enormous amounts of food without being ridiculed. I'll like being a cow the best because I'll be loved by all and useful to mankind." God was charmed by these answers and allowed Sadhu to live through the three incarnations. He then made Sadhu a morning star for his service to humankind as a cow.

EJB too has lived through three major incarnations. When it was first released, the industry was dazzled by its innovations. But like the ladybug, EJB 1 had limited functionality. The second EJB incarnation was almost as heavy as the largest of our beloved pachyderms. The brave souls who couldn't do without its elephant power had to tame the awesome complexity of EJB 2. And finally, in its third incarnation, EJB has become much more useful to the huddled masses, just like the gentle bovine that's sacred for Hindus and respected as a mother whose milk feeds us well.

A lot of hard work from a lot of good people made EJB 3 simple and lightweight without sacrificing Enterprise-ready power. EJB components can now be Plain Old Java Objects (POJOs) and look a lot like code in a "Hello World" program. In the following chapters we'll describe a star among frameworks with increasing industry adoption.

We've strived to keep this book practical without skimping on content. The book is designed to help you learn EJB 3 quickly and easily without neglecting the basics. We'll also dive into deep waters, sharing all the amazing sights we've discovered and warning about any lurking dangers.

In the Java world EJB is an important and uniquely influential technology radically transformed in version 3. We'll spend little time with EJB 2. You probably either already know earlier versions of EJB or are completely new to it. Spending too much time on previous versions is a waste of time. EJB 3 and EJB 2 have very little in common, and EJB 3.2 now makes support for EJB 2 optional. But if you're curious about EJB 2, we encourage you to pick up one of the many good books on the previous versions of EJB.

In this chapter we'll tell you what's what in EJB 3, explain why you should consider using it, and outline the significant improvements the newest version offers, such as annotations, convention-over-configuration, and dependency injection. We'll build on the momentum of this chapter by jumping into code in chapter 2. Let's start with a broad overview of EJB.

1.1 EJB overview

The first thing that should cross your mind while evaluating any technology is what it really gives you. What's so special about EJB? Beyond a presentation-layer technology like JavaServer Pages (JSP), JavaServer Faces (JSF), or Struts, couldn't you create your web application using the Java language and some APIs like Java Database Connectivity (JDBC) for database access? You could—if deadlines and limited resources weren't realities. Before anyone dreamed up EJB, this is exactly what people did. The resulting long hours proved that you'd spend a lot of time solving very common system-level problems instead of focusing on the real business solution. These experiences emphasized that there are common solutions for common development problems. This is exactly what EJB brings to the table. EJB is a collection of "canned" answers to common server application development problems, as well as a roadmap to common server component patterns. These canned solutions or services are provided by the EJB container. To access these services, you build specialized components using declarative and programmatic EJB APIs and deploy them into the container.

1.1.1 EJB as a component model

In this book, EJBs refer to server-side components that you can use to build the business component layer of your application. Some developers associate the term *component* with developing complex and heavyweight CORBA or Microsoft COM+ code. In the brave new world of EJB 3, a component is what it ought to be—nothing more than a POJO with some special powers. More importantly, these powers stay invisible until they're needed and don't distract from the real purpose of the component. You'll see this firsthand throughout this book, especially starting in chapter 2.

To use EJB services, your component must be declared to be a recognized EJB component type. EJB recognizes two specific types of components: session beans and message-driven beans. Session beans are further subdivided into stateless session beans, stateful session beans, and singletons. Each component type has a specialized purpose, scope, state, lifecycle, and usage pattern in the business logic tier. We'll discuss these component types throughout the rest of the book, particularly in part 2. For data CRUD (create, read, update, delete) operations in the persistence tier, we'll talk about JPA entities and their relationship with EJBs in detail in part 3. As of EJB 3.1, all EJBs are managed beans. Managed beans are basically any generic Java object in a Java EE environment. Contexts and Dependency Injection (CDI) allows you to use dependency injection with all managed beans, including EJBs. We'll explore CDI and managed beans further in part 3.

1.1.2 EJB component services

As we mentioned, the canned services are the most valuable part of EJB. Some of the services are automatically attached to recognize components because they make a lot of sense for business logic-tier components. These services include dependency injection, transactions, thread safety, and pooling. To use most services, you must declare you want them using annotations/XML or by accessing programmatic EJB APIs. Examples of such services include security, scheduling, asynchronous processing, remoting, and web services. Most of this book will be spent explaining how you can exploit EJB services. We can't explain the details of each service in this chapter, but we'll briefly list the major ones in table 1.1 and explain what they mean to you.

Table 1.1 EJB services

Service	What it means for you
Registry, dependency injection, and lookup	Helps locate and glue together components, ideally through simple configuration. Lets you change component wiring for testing.
Lifecycle management	Lets you take appropriate actions when the lifecycle of a component changes, such as when it's created and when it's destroyed.

Table 1.1 EJB services *(continued)*

Service	What it means for you
Thread safety	EJB makes all components thread-safe and highly performant in ways that are completely invisible to you. This means that you can write your multi-threaded server components as if you were developing a single-threaded desktop application. It doesn't matter how complex the component is; EJB will make sure it's thread-safe.
Transactions	EJB automatically makes all of your components transactional, which means you don't have to write any transaction code while using databases or messaging servers via JDBC, JPA, or Java Message Service (JMS).
Pooling	EJB creates a pool of component instances that are shared by clients. At any point in time, each pooled instance can only be used by a single client. As soon as an instance is done servicing a client, it's returned to the pool for reuse instead of being frivolously discarded for the garbage collector to reclaim. You can also specify the size of the pool so that when the pool is full, any additional requests are automatically queued. This means that your system will never become unresponsive trying to handle a sudden burst of requests. Similar to instance pooling, EJB also automatically pools threads across the container for better performance.
State management	The EJB container manages the state transparently for stateful components instead of having you write verbose and error-prone code for state management. This means that you can maintain the state in instance variables as if you were developing a desktop application. EJB takes care of all the details of session/state maintenance behind the scenes.
Memory management	EJB steps in to optimize memory by saving less frequently used stateful components into the hard disk to free up memory. This is called *passivation*. When memory becomes available again and a passivated component is needed, EJB puts the component back into memory. This is called *activation*.
Messaging	EJB 3 allows you to write message processing components without having to deal with a lot of the mechanical details of the JMS API.
Security	EJB allows you to easily secure your components through simple configuration.
Scheduling	EJB lets you schedule any EJB method to be invoked automatically based on simple repeating timers or cron expressions.
Asynchronous processing	You can configure any EJB method to be invoked asynchronously if needed.
Interceptors	EJB 3 introduces AOP (aspect-oriented programming) in a lightweight, intuitive way using *interceptors*. This allows you to easily separate out crosscutting concerns such as logging and auditing, and to do so in a configurable way.
Web services	EJB 3 can transparently turn business components into Simple Object Access Protocol (SOAP) or Representational State Transfer (REST) web services with minimal or no code changes.
Remoting	In EJB 3, you can make components remotely accessible without writing any code. In addition, EJB 3 enables client code to access remote components as if they were local components using dependency injection (DI).
Testing	You can easily unit- and integration-test any EJB component using embedded containers with frameworks like JUnit.

1.1.3 *Layered architectures and EJB*

Enterprise applications are designed to solve a unique type of problem and therefore share many common requirements. Most Enterprise applications have some kind of user interface, implement business processes, model a problem domain, and save data into a database. Because of these shared requirements, you can follow a common architecture or design principle for building Enterprise applications known as *patterns*.

For server-side development, the dominant pattern is *layered architectures*. In a layered architecture, components are grouped into tiers. Each tier in the application has a well-defined purpose, like a section of a factory assembly line. Each section of the assembly line performs its designated task and passes the remaining work down the line. In layered architectures, each layer delegates work to a layer underneath it.

EJB recognizes this fact and thus isn't a jack-of-all-trades, master-of-none component model. Rather, EJB is a specialist component model that fits a specific purpose in layered architectures. Layered architectures come in two predominant flavors: traditional four-tier architectures and domain-driven design (DDD). Let's take a look at each of these architectures and where EJB is designed to fit in them.

TRADITIONAL FOUR-TIER LAYERED ARCHITECTURE

Figure 1.1 shows the traditional four-tier server architecture. This architecture is pretty intuitive and enjoys a good amount of popularity. In this architecture, the *presentation layer* is responsible for rendering the graphical user interface (GUI) and handling user input. The presentation layer passes down each request for application functionality to the business logic layer. The *business logic layer* is the heart of the application and contains workflow and processing logic. In other words, business logic–layer components model distinct actions or processes that the application can perform, such as billing, search, ordering, and user account maintenance. The business logic layer retrieves data from and saves data into the database by utilizing the persistence

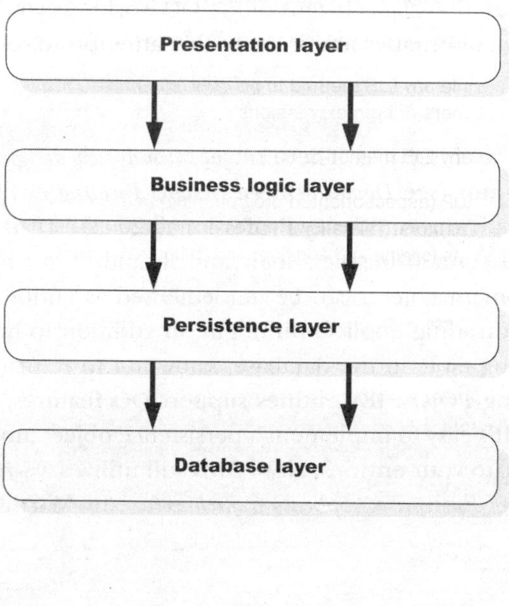

Figure 1.1 Most traditional Enterprise applications have at least four layers: the presentation layer is the actual user interface and can either be a browser or a desktop application; the business logic layer defines the business rules; the persistence layer deals with interactions with the database; and the database layer consists of a relational database such as Oracle database that stores the persistent objects.

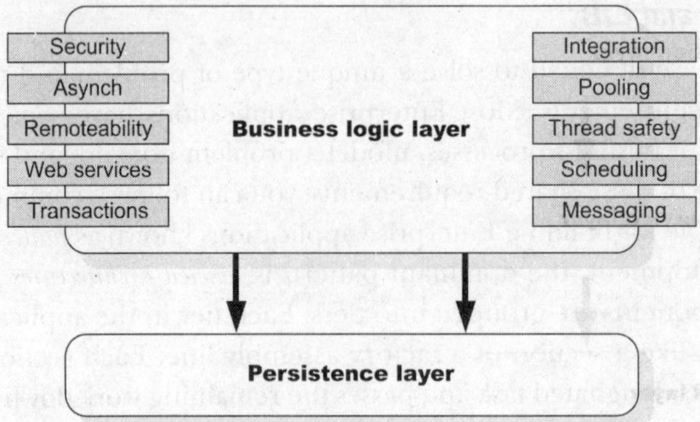

Figure 1.2 The component services offered by EJB 3 at the supported application layer. Note that each service is independent of the others, so you are (for the most part) free to pick the features important for your application.

tier. The *persistence layer* provides a high-level object-oriented (OO) abstraction over the database layer. The *database layer* typically consists of a relational database management system (RDBMS) like Oracle database, DB2 database, or SQL Server database.

EJB isn't a presentation layer or persistence-layer technology. It's all about robust support for implementing business logic-layer components for Enterprise applications. Figure 1.2 shows how EJB supports these layers via its services.

In a typical Java EE-based system, JSF and CDI will be used at the presentation tier, EJB will be used in the business layer, and JPA and CDI will be used in the persistence tier.

The traditional four-tier layered architecture isn't perfect. One of the most common criticisms is that it undermines the OO ideal of modeling the business domain as objects that encapsulate both data and behavior. Because the traditional architecture focuses on modeling business processes instead of the domain, the business logic tier tends to look more like a database-driven procedural application than an OO one. Because persistence-tier components are simple data holders, they look a lot like database record definitions rather than first-class citizens of the OO world. As you'll see in the next section, DDD proposes an alternative architecture that attempts to solve these perceived problems.

DOMAIN-DRIVEN DESIGN

Figure 1.3 shows domain-driven architecture. The term *domain-driven design* may be relatively new but the concept is not (see *Domain-Driven Design: Tackling Complexity in the Heart of Software*, by Eric Evans [Addison-Wesley Professional, 2003]). DDD emphasizes that domain objects should contain business logic and shouldn't just be dumb replicas of database records. Domain objects can be implemented as entities in JPA. With DDD, a `Catalog` object in a trading application might, in addition to having all the data of an entry in the catalog table in the database, know not to return catalog entries that aren't in stock. Being POJOs, JPA entities support OO features, such as inheritance and polymorphism. It's easy to implement a persistence object model with the JPA and to add business logic to your entities. Now, DDD still utilizes a *service layer* or *application layer* (see *Patterns of Enterprise Application Architecture*, by Martin Fowler

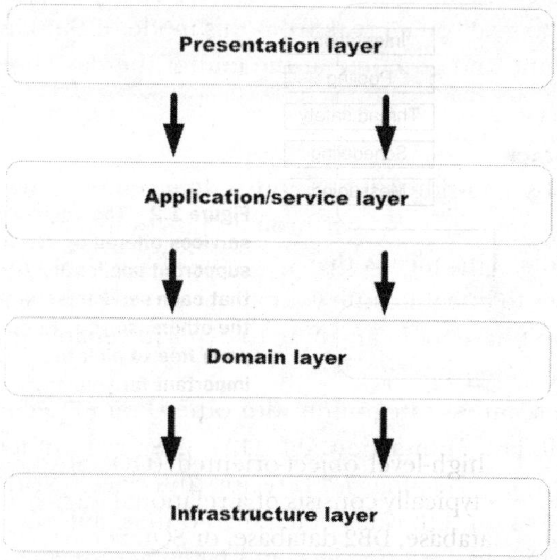

Figure 1.3 Domain-driven design typically has four or more layers. The presentation layer is responsible for the user interface and for interaction with the application/service layer. The application/service layer is typically very light and only allows communication between the presentation layer and the domain. The domain layer is the complex expression of your application data model consisting of entities, value objects, aggregates, factories, and repositories. The infrastructure layer gets to the database and other similar technology.

[Addison-Wesley Professional, 2002]). The application layer is similar to the business logic layer of the traditional four-tier architecture but much thinner. EJB works well as the service-layer component model. Whether you use the traditional four-tier architecture or a layered architecture with DDD, you can use entities to model domain objects, including modeling state and behavior. We'll discuss domain modeling with JPA entities in chapter 7.

Despite its impressive services and vision, EJB 3 isn't the only act in town. You can combine various technologies to more or less match EJB services and infrastructure. For example, you could use Spring with other open-source technologies such as Hibernate and AspectJ to build your application, so why choose EJB 3? Glad that you asked....

1.1.4 Why choose EJB 3?

At the beginning of this chapter, we hinted at EJB's status as a pioneering technology. EJB is a groundbreaking technology that raised the standards of server-side development. Just like Java itself, EJB changed things in ways that are here to stay and inspired many innovations. Up until a few years ago, the only serious competition to EJB came from the Microsoft .NET framework. In this section, we'll point out a few of the compelling EJB 3 features that we feel certain will have this latest version at the top of your short list.

Ease of use

Thanks to the unwavering focus on ease of use, EJB 3 is probably the simplest server-side development platform around. The features that shine the brightest are POJO programming, annotations in favor of verbose XML, heavy use of sensible defaults, and avoidance of complex paradigms. Although the number of EJB services is significant, you'll find them very intuitive. For the most part, EJB 3 has a practical outlook on things and doesn't demand that you understand the theoretical intricacies. In fact, most EJB services are designed to give you a break from this mode of thinking so you can focus on getting the job done and go home at the end of the day knowing you accomplished something.

Complete, integrated solution stack

EJB 3 offers a complete stack of server-side solutions, including transactions, security, messaging, scheduling, remoting, web services, asynchronous processing, testing, dependency injection, and interceptors. This means that you won't have to spend a lot of time looking for third-party tools to integrate into your application. These services are also just there for you—you don't have to do anything to explicitly enable them. This leads to near-zero configuration systems.

In addition, EJB 3 provides seamless integration with other Java EE technologies, such as CDI, JPA, JDBC, JavaMail, Java Transaction API (JTA), JMS, Java Authentication and Authorization Service (JAAS), Java Naming and Directory Interface (JNDI), Remote Method Invocation (RMI), and so on. EJB is also guaranteed to seamlessly integrate with presentation-tier technologies like JSP, Servlets, and JSF. When needed, you can integrate third-party tools with EJB using CDI.

Open Java EE standard

EJB is a critical part of the Java EE standard. This is an extremely important concept to grasp if you're to adopt EJB. EJB 3 has an open, public API specification and compatibility test kit that organizations are encouraged to use to create a container implementation. The EJB 3 standard is developed by the Java Community Process (JCP), consisting of a nonexclusive group of individuals driving the Java standard. The open standard leads to broader vendor support for EJB 3, which means you don't have to depend on a proprietary solution.

Broad vendor support

EJB is supported by a large and diverse variety of independent organizations. This includes the technology world's largest, most respected, and most financially strong names, such as Oracle and IBM, as well as passionate and energetic open-source groups like JBoss and Apache. Wide vendor support translates to three important advantages for you. First, you're not at the mercy of the ups and downs of a particular company or group of people. Second, a lot of people have concrete long-term interests in keeping the technology as competitive as possible. You can essentially count on being able to take advantage of the best-of-breed technologies both in and outside the Java world in a competitive timeframe. Third, vendors have historically competed against one another by providing value-added nonstandard features. All of these factors help keep EJB on the track of continuous healthy evolution.

Clustering, load balancing, and failover

Features historically added by most application server vendors are robust support for clustering, load balancing, and failover. EJB application servers have a proven track record of supporting some of the largest high-performance computing (HPC)–enabled server farm environments. More importantly, you can use such support with no changes to code, no third-party tool integration, and relatively simple configuration (beyond the inherent work in setting up a hardware cluster). This means that you can rely on hardware clustering to scale up your application with EJB 3 if you need to.

PERFORMANCE AND SCALABILITY

Enterprise applications have a lot in common with a house. Both are meant to last, often much longer than anyone expects. Being able to support high-performance, fault-tolerant, scalable applications is an upfront concern for the EJB platform instead of being an afterthought. Not only will you be writing good server-side applications faster, you can also expect your platform to grow as needed. You can support a larger number of users without having to rewrite your code; these concerns are taken care of by EJB container vendors via features like thread safety, distributed transactions, pooling, passivation, asynchronous processing, messaging, and remoting. You can count on doing minimal optimization or moving your application to a distributed, clustered server farm by doing nothing more than a bit of configuration.

We expect that by now you're getting jazzed about EJB and you're eager to learn more. So let's jump right in and see how you can use EJB to build the business logic tier of your applications, starting with the beans.

1.2 Understanding EJB types

In EJB-speak, a component is a *bean*. If your manager doesn't find the Java "coffee bean" play on words cute either, blame Sun's marketing department. Hey, at least you get to hear people in suits use the words "Enterprise" and "bean" in close sequence as if it were perfectly normal.

As we mentioned, EJB classifies beans into two types based on what they're used for:

- Session beans
- Message-driven beans

Each bean type serves a purpose and can use a specific subset of EJB services. The real purpose of bean types is to safeguard against overloading them with services that cross wires. This is kind of like making sure the accountant in the horn-rimmed glasses doesn't get too curious about what happens when you touch both ends of a car battery terminal at the same time. Bean classification also helps you understand and organize an application in a sensible way; for example, bean types help you develop applications based on a layered architecture. Let's start digging a little deeper into the various EJB component types, starting with session beans.

1.2.1 Session beans

A session bean is invoked by a client to perform a specific business operation, such as checking the credit history of a customer. The name *session* implies that a bean instance is available for the duration of a unit of work and doesn't survive a server crash or shutdown. A session bean can model any application logic functionality. There are three types of session beans: *stateful, stateless,* and *singleton.*

A stateful session bean automatically saves the bean state between invocations from a single, unique client without your having to write any additional code. The typical example of a state-aware process is the shopping cart for a web merchant like Amazon. Stateful session beans are either timed out or end their lifecycle when the client requests it. In contrast, stateless session beans don't maintain any state and model application services that can be completed in a single client invocation. You could build stateless session beans for implementing business processes such as charging a credit card or checking a customer's credit history. Singleton session beans maintain the state, are shared by all clients, and live for the duration of the application. You could use a singleton bean for a discount processing component since the business rules for applying discounts are usually fixed and shared across all clients. Note that singleton beans are a new feature added in EJB 3.1.

A session bean can be invoked either locally or remotely using Java RMI. A stateless or singleton session bean can also be exposed as a SOAP or REST web service.

1.2.2 Message-driven beans

Like session beans, message-driven beans (MDBs) process business logic. But MDBs are different in one important way: clients never invoke MDB methods directly. Instead, MDBs are triggered by messages sent to a messaging server, which enables sending asynchronous messages between system components. Some typical examples of messaging servers are HornetQ, ActiveMQ, IBM WebSphere MQ, SonicMQ, Oracle Advanced Queueing, and TIBCO. MDBs are typically used for robust system integration and asynchronous processing. An example of messaging is sending an inventory-restocking request from an automated retail system to a supply-chain management system. Don't worry too much about messaging right now; we'll get to the details later in this book.

1.3 Related specifications

EJB has two closely related specifications that we'll cover in this book. The first is JPA, which is the persistence standard for Java EE and CDI, and provides dependency injection and context management services to all Java EE components including EJB.

1.3.1 Entities and the Java Persistence API

EJB 3.1 saw JPA 2 moved from an EJB 3 API to a completely separate Java EE specification. But JPA has some specific runtime integration points with EJB because the specifications are so closely related. We'll say just a few things about JPA here because we have chapters dedicated to it.

Persistence is the ability to have data contained in Java objects automatically stored into a relational database like Oracle database, SQL server database, and DB2 database. Persistent objects are managed by JPA. It automatically persists Java objects using a technique called object-relational mapping (ORM). ORM is the process of mapping data held in Java objects to database tables using configuration or declaratively using annotations. It relieves you of the task of writing low-level, boring, and complex JDBC code to persist objects into a database.

An ORM framework performs transparent persistence by making use of ORM metadata that defines how objects are mapped to database tables. ORM isn't a new concept and has been around for a while. Oracle TopLink is probably the oldest ORM framework in the market; open-source framework JBoss Hibernate popularized ORM concepts within the mainstream developer community. Because JPA standardizes ORM frameworks for the Java platform, you can plug in an ORM product like JBoss Hibernate, Oracle TopLink, or Apache OpenJPA as the underlying JPA "persistence provider" for your application.

JPA isn't just a solution for server-side applications. Persistence is a problem that even a standalone Swing-based desktop application has to solve. This drove the decision to make JPA 2 a cleanly separated API in its own right that can be run outside an EJB 3 container. Much like JDBC, JPA is intended to be a general-purpose persistence solution for any Java application.

ENTITIES

Entities are the Java objects that are persisted into the database. While session beans are the "verbs" of a system, entities are the "nouns." Common examples include an `Employee` entity, a `User` entity, and an `Item` entity. Entities are the OO representations of the application data stored in the database. Entities survive container crashes and shutdown. The ORM metadata specifies how the object is mapped to the database. You'll see an example of this in the next chapter. JPA entities support a full range of relational and OO capabilities, including relationships between entities, inheritance, and polymorphism.

ENTITYMANAGER

Entities tell a JPA provider how they map to the database, but they don't persist themselves. The `EntityManager` interface reads the ORM metadata for an entity and performs persistence operations. The `EntityManager` knows how to add entities to the database, update stored entities, and delete and retrieve entities from the database.

JAVA PERSISTENCE QUERY LANGUAGE

JPA provides a specialized SQL-like query language called Java Persistence Query Language (JPQL) to search for entities saved into the database. With a robust and flexible API such as JPQL, you won't lose anything by choosing automated persistence instead of handwritten JDBC. In addition, JPA supports native, database-specific SQL, in the rare cases where it's worth using.

1.3.2 Contexts and dependency injection for Java EE

Java EE 5 had a basic form of dependency injection that EJB could use. It was called *resource injection* and allowed you to inject container resources, such as data sources, queues, JPA resources, and EJBs, using annotations like `@EJB`, `@Resource`, and `@PersistenceContext`. These resources could be injected into Servlets, JSF backing beans, and EJB. The problem was that this was very limiting. You weren't able to inject EJB into Struts or JUnit, and you couldn't inject non-EJB DAOs (data access objects) or helper classes into EJB.

CDI is a powerful solution to the problem. It provides EJB (as well as all other APIs and components in the Java EE environment) best-of-breed, next-generation, generic dependency injection and context management services. CDI features include injection, automatic context management, scoping, qualifiers, component naming, producers, disposers, registry/lookup, stereotypes, interceptors, decorators, and events. Unlike many older dependency injection solutions, CDI is completely type-safe, compact, futuristic, and annotation-driven. We'll cover CDI in detail in chapter 12.

1.4 EJB runtimes

When you build a simple Java class, you need a Java Virtual Machine (JVM) to execute it. In a similar way (as you learned in section 1.3), to execute session beans and MDBs you need an EJB container. In this section we give you a bird's-eye view of the different runtimes that an EJB container may contain inside.

Think of the container as an extension of the basic idea of a JVM. Just as the JVM transparently manages memory on your behalf, the container transparently provides EJB component services such as transactions, security management, remoting, and web services support. You might even think of the container as a JVM on steroids, of which the purpose is to execute EJB. In EJB 3, the container provides services applicable only to session beans and MDBs. The task of putting an EJB 3 component inside a container is called *deployment*. Once an EJB is successfully deployed in a container, it can be used in your applications.

In the Java world, containers aren't limited to the realm of EJB 3. You're probably familiar with a web container, which allows you to run web-based applications using Java technologies such as Servlets, JSP, and JSF. A *Java EE container* is an application server solution that supports EJB 3, a web container, and other Java EE APIs and services. Oracle WebLogic server, GlassFish server, IBM WebSphere application server, JBoss application server, and Caucho Resin are examples of Java EE containers.

1.4.1 Application servers

Application servers are where EJBs have been traditionally deployed. Application servers are Java EE containers that include support for all Java EE APIs, as well as facilities for administration, deployment, monitoring, clustering, load balancing, security, and so on. In addition to supporting Java EE-related technologies, some application servers can also function as production-quality HTTP servers. Others support modularity via technologies like OSGi. As of Java EE 6, application servers can also come in a scaled-down, lightweight *Web Profile* form. The Web Profile is a smaller subset of Java EE APIs specifically geared toward web applications. Web Profile APIs include JSF 2.2, CDI 1.1, EJB 3.2 Lite (discussed in section 1.4.2), JPA 2.1, JTA 1.2, and bean validation. At the time of writing, GlassFish and Resin provided Java EE 7 Web Profile offerings. Note that Java EE 7 Web Profile implementations are free to add APIs as they wish. For example, Resin adds JMS, as well as most of the EJB API including messaging, remoting, and scheduling (but not EJB 2 backward compatibility). Figure 1.4 shows how the Web Profile compares with the complete Java EE platform.

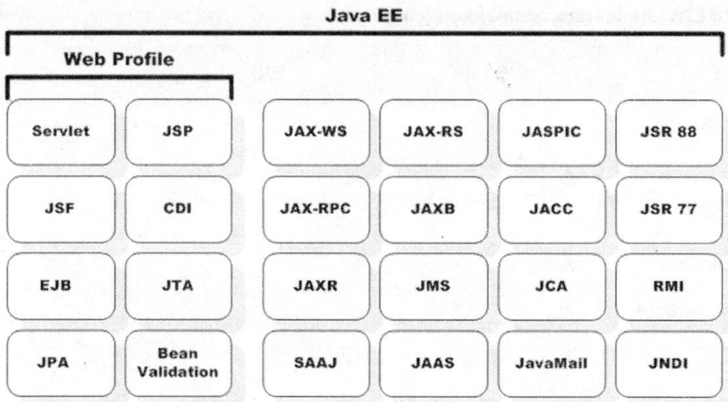

Figure 1.4 Java EE Web Profile versus full Java EE platform

The Web Profile defines a complete stack on which to build a modern web application. Web applications are now rarely written from the ground up using raw Servlets, but instead sit on top of JSF and make use of the various EE technologies.

1.4.2 *EJB Lite*

Similar to the idea of the Java EE 7 Web Profile, EJB 3.2 also comes in a scaled-down, lighter-weight version called EJB 3.2 Lite. EJB Lite goes hand-in-hand with the Web Profile and is intended for web applications. Just as with the Web Profile, any vendor implementing the EJB 3.2 Lite API is free to include EJB features as they wish. From a practical standpoint, the most important thing that EJB 3.2 Lite does is remove support for EJB 2 backward compatibility. This means that an EJB container can be much more lightweight because it doesn't have to implement the old APIs in addition to the lightweight EJB 3 model. Because EJB 3.2 Lite also doesn't include support for MDBs and remoting, it can mean a lighter-weight server if you don't need these features. For reference, table 1.2 compares the major EJB and EJB Lite features.

Table 1.2 EJB and EJB Lite feature comparison

Feature	EJB Lite	EJB
Stateless beans	☑	☑
Stateful beans	☑	☑
Singleton beans	☑	☑
Message-driven beans		☑
No interfaces	☑	☑
Local interfaces	☑	☑
Remote interfaces		☑
Web service interfaces		☑

Table 1.2 EJB and EJB Lite feature comparison *(continued)*

Feature	EJB Lite	EJB
Asynchronous invocation	✓	✓
Interceptors	✓	✓
Declarative security	✓	✓
Declarative transactions	✓	✓
Programmatic transactions	✓	✓
Timer service	✓	✓
EJB 2.x support		✓
CORBA interoperability		✓

1.4.3 *Embeddable containers*

Traditional application servers run as a separate process that you deploy your applications into. Embedded EJB containers, on the other hand, can be started through a programmatic Java API inside your own application. This is very important for unit testing with JUnit as well as using EJB 3 features in command-line or Swing applications. When an embedded container starts, it scans the class path of your application and automatically deploys any EJBs it can find. Figure 1.5 shows the architecture of an embedded EJB 3 container.

Embeddable containers have been around for a while. OpenEJB, EasyBeans, and Embedded JBoss are examples. Embeddable containers are only required to support EJB Lite, but most implementations are likely to support all features. For example, the embedded versions of GlassFish, JBoss, and Resin support all the features available on the application server. We'll discuss embedded containers in detail in chapter 15 on testing EJB 3.

1.4.4 *Using EJB 3 in Tomcat*

Apache Tomcat, the lightweight, popular Servlet container, doesn't support EJB 3, because unlike application servers, Servlet containers aren't required to support EJB. But you can easily use EJB 3 on Tomcat through embedded containers. The Apache

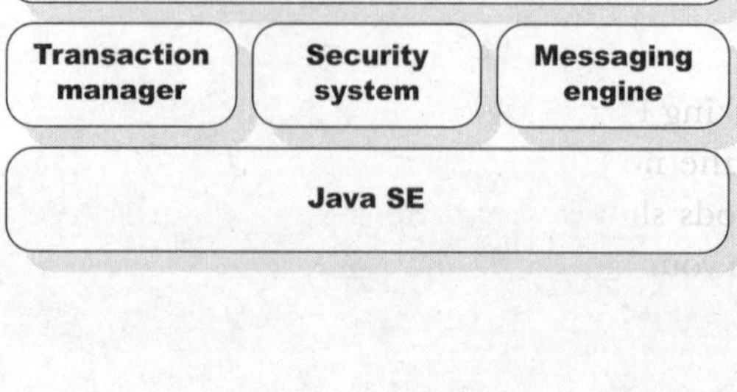

Figure 1.5 EJB 3.1 embedded containers run directly inside Java SE and provide all EJB services such as transactions, security, and messaging.

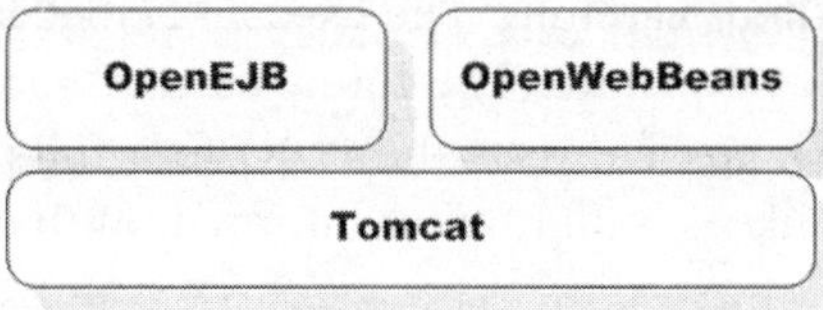

Figure 1.6 You can use OpenEJB and OpenWebBeans to enable both EJB and CDI on Tomcat.

OpenEJB project has specific support for enabling EJB 3 on Tomcat. As shown in figure 1.6, you can also enable CDI on Tomcat using Apache OpenWebBeans. OpenWebBeans and OpenEJB are closely related projects and work seamlessly together. In this way, you can use a majority of Java EE 7 APIs on Tomcat if you wish.

1.5 Brave new innovations

From this point onward, let's start getting a little down and dirty and seeing what the brave new world of EJB 3 looks like in code. We'll note the primary distinguishing features of EJB 3 along the way.

1.5.1 "Hello User" example

"Hello World" examples have ruled the world since they first appeared in *The C Programming Language* by Brian Kernighan and Dennis Ritchie (Prentice Hall PTR, 1988). "Hello World" caught on and held ground for good reason. It's very well suited to introducing a technology as simply and plainly as possible. The code samples for this book will use Maven, and if you're using Eclipse, you'll find it useful to have the m2eclipse plug-in installed to integrate Eclipse with Maven.

In 2004, one of the authors, Debu Panda, wrote an article for the TheServerSide.com in which he stated that when EJB 3 was released, it would be so simple you could write a "Hello World" in it using only a few lines of code. Any experienced EJB 2 developer knows that this couldn't be done easily in EJB 2. You had to write a home interface, a component interface, a bean class, and a deployment descriptor. Well, let's see if Debu was right in his prediction, as shown in the following listing.

Listing 1.1 `HelloUser` session bean

```
package ejb3inaction.example;
import javax.ejb.Stateless;

@Stateless
public class HelloUserBean implements HelloUser {
    public String sayHello(String name) {
        return String.format("Hello %s welcome to EJB 3.1!",name);
    }
}
```

❶ Stateless annotation

❷ HelloUserBean POJO

This listing is a complete and working EJB! The bean class is a POJO ❶, without even an interface. EJB 3.1 introduced the no-interface view. Before this, EJB required an interface to indicate which methods should be visible. The no-interface view essentially says that all public methods in your bean will be available for invocation. It's easy to use, but you need to pick your public methods carefully. The `exposeAllTheCompanys-DirtySecrets()` method should probably be private. The funny `@Stateless` symbol in listing 1.1 is a metadata annotation ❷ that converts the POJO to a full-powered stateless EJB. In effect, they're "comment-like" configuration information that can be added to Java code.

EJB 3 enables you to develop an EJB component using POJOs that know nothing about platform services. You can apply annotations to these POJOs to add platform services such as remoteability, web services support, and lifecycle callbacks as needed.

To execute this EJB, you have to deploy it to the EJB container. If you want to execute this sample, download the actionbazaar-snapshot-2.zip from https://code.google.com/p/action-bazaar/, extract "chapter1 project" to build, and install it using Maven and the embedded GlassFish server.

We're going to analyze a lot of code in this book—some just as easy as this. You could trigger the hello as a web service by simply adding the `@WebService` annotation. You could inject a resource, like a helper bean that will translate hello into foreign languages, with `@Inject`. What do you want to do with EJB? If you keep reading, we'll probably tell you how to do it.

1.5.2 Annotations versus XML

Prior to annotations (introduced in Java SE 5), XML was the only logical choice for application configuration because there were no other viable options around, except for tools like XDoclet, which was popular in many relatively progressive EJB 2 shops.

The problems with XML are myriad. XML is verbose, not that readable, and extremely error-prone. XML also takes no advantage of Java's unique strength in strong type safety. Lastly, XML configuration files tend to be monolithic and they separate the information about the configuration from the Java code that uses them, making maintenance more difficult. Collectively, these problems are named XML Hell and annotations are specifically designed to be the cure.

EJB 3 was the first mainstream Java technology to pave the way for annotation adoption. Since then, many other tools like JPA, JSF, Servlets, JAX-WS, JAX-RS, JUnit, Seam, Guice, and Spring have followed suit.

As you can see in the code example in listing 1.1, annotations are essentially property settings that mark a piece of code, such as a class or method, as having particular attributes. When the EJB container sees these attributes, it adds the container services that correspond to it. This is called *declarative-style programming*, where the developer specifies what should be done and the system adds the code to do it behind the scenes.

In EJB 3, annotations dramatically simplify development and testing of applications. Developers can declaratively add services to EJB components when they need to. As figure 1.7 depicts, an annotation basically transforms a simple POJO into an EJB, just as the `@Stateless` annotation does in the example.

Figure 1.7 EJBs are regular Java objects that may be configured using metadata annotations.

While XML has its problems, it can be beneficial in some ways. It can be easier to see how the system components are organized by looking at a centralized XML configuration file. You can also configure the same component differently per deployment or configure components whose source code you can't change. Configuration that has little to do with Java code is also poorly expressed in annotations. Examples of this include port/URL configuration, file locations, and so on. The good news is that you can use XML with EJB 3. You can even use XML to override or augment annotation-based configuration. Unless you have a very strong preference for XML, it's generally advisable to start with annotations and use XML overrides where they're really needed.

1.5.3 Intelligent defaults versus explicit configuration

EJB takes a different approach to default behavior than most frameworks such as Spring. With Spring, for example, if you don't ask, you don't get. You have to ask for any behavior you want to have in your Spring components. In addition to making the task of configuration easier via annotations, EJB 3 reduces the total amount of configuration altogether by using sensible defaults wherever possible. For example, the "Hello World" component is automatically thread-safe, pooled, and transactional without you having to do anything at all. Similarly, if you want scheduling, asynchronous processing, remoting, or web services, all you need to do is add a few annotations to the component. There's no service that you'll need to understand, explicitly enable, or configure—everything is enabled by default. The same is true of JPA and CDI as well. Intelligent defaulting is especially important when you're dealing with automated persistence using JPA.

1.5.4 Dependency injection versus JNDI lookup

EJB 3 was reengineered from the ground up for dependency injection. This means that you can inject EJBs into other Java EE components and inject Java EE components into EJBs. This is especially true when using CDI with EJB 3. For example, if you want to access the HelloUser EJB in listing 1.1 from another EJB, Servlet, or JSF backing bean, you could use code like this:

```
@EJB                                         <-- ❶ EJB injection
private HelloUserBean helloUser;

void hello(){
    helloUser.sayHello("Curious George");
}
```

Isn't that great? The `@EJB` annotation ❶ transparently "injects" the `HelloUserBean` EJB into the annotated variable. The `@EJB` annotation reads the type and name of the

EJB and looks it up from JNDI under the hood. All EJB components are automatically registered with JNDI while being deployed. Note that you can still use JNDI lookups where they're unavoidable. For example, to dynamically look up your bean, you could use code like this:

```
Context context = new InitialContext();
HelloUserBean helloUser = (HelloUserBean)
    context.lookup("java:module/HelloUserBean");
helloUser.sayHello("Curious George");
```

We'll talk in detail about EJB injection and lookup in chapter 5.

1.5.5 CDI versus EJB injection

EJB-style injection predates CDI. Naturally, this means that CDI injection adds a number of improvements over EJB injection. Most importantly, CDI can be used to inject almost anything. EJB injection, on the other hand, can only be used with objects stored in JNDI, such as EJB, as well as some container-managed objects like the EJB context. CDI is far more type-safe than EJB. Generally speaking, CDI is a superset of EJB injection. For example, you can use CDI to inject the EJB as follows:

```
@Inject                                  <-- EJB injection via CDI
private HelloUserBean helloUser;

void hello(){
    helloUser.sayHello("Curious George");
}
```

It might seem that CDI should be used for all Java EE injections, but it currently has a limitation. Although CDI can retrieve an EJB by type, it doesn't work with remote EJBs. EJB injection (`@EJB`) will recognize whether an EJB is local or remote and return the appropriate type. You should use CDI for injection when possible.

1.5.6 Testable POJO components

Because all EJBs are simply POJOs, you can easily unit test them in JUnit for basic component functionality. You can even use CDI to inject EJBs directly into unit tests, wire mock objects, and so on. Thanks to embedded containers, you can even perform full integration testing of EJB components from JUnit. Projects like Arquillian focus specifically on integrating JUnit with embedded containers. The following listing shows how Arquillian allows you to inject EJBs into JUnit tests.

Listing 1.2 EJB 3 unit testing with Arquillian

```
package ejb3inaction.example;

import javax.ejb.EJB;
import org.jboss.arquillian.api.Deployment;
import org.jboss.arquillian.junit.Arquillian;
import org.jboss.shrinkwrap.api.Archive;
import org.jboss.shrinkwrap.api.ShrinkWrap;
import org.jboss.shrinkwrap.api.spec.JavaArchive;
```

```
import org.junit.Assert;
import org.junit.Test;
import org.junit.runner.RunWith;

@RunWith(Arquillian.class)                                  <-- Running JUnit with Arquillian
public class HelloUserBeanTest {
    @EJB
    private HelloUser helloUser;                            <-- Injecting bean to be tested

    @Deployment
    public static Archive<?> createDeployment() {
        return ShrinkWrap.create(JavaArchive.class, "foo.jar")
        .addClasses(HelloUserBean.class);
    }

    @Test
    public void testSayHello() {
        String helloMessage = helloUser.sayHello("Curious George");   <-- Using EJB in unit test
        Assert.assertEquals(
          "Hello Curious George welcome to EJB 3.1!",helloMessage);
    }
}
```

We've dedicated chapter 15 in its entirety to testing EJB components.

1.6 Changes in EJB 3.2

The goal of 3.2 is to continue to evolve the EJB specification to be a complete solution for all Enterprise business needs and to improve the EJB architecture by reducing its complexity from the developer's point of view. In this section we'll briefly talk about the particular changes in EJB 3.2.

1.6.1 Previous EJB 2 features now optional

Support for EJB 2 has been made optional by EJB 3.2. This means a fully compliant Java EE 7 application server no longer needs to support EJB 2-style entities beans. EJB QL and JAX-RPC have also been made optional.

1.6.2 Enhancements to message-driven beans

In EJB 3.2, MDBs have been given a major overhaul. The update to JMS 2.0 brings a simplified API as well as integration with advances to Java in other areas such as dependency injection with CDI. It also makes using the `javax.jms.MessageListener` interface optional, giving you the ability to create an MDB with a no-methods listener interface, which makes public methods of the class message listener methods. Here's a quick look at the simplified API for MDB.

Send a message:

```
@Inject @JMSConnectionFactory("jms/QueueConnectionFactory")
private JMSContext context;                                 <-- Injects JMSContext

@Resource(lookup="jms/MessageQueue")
private Queue queue;                                        <-- Injects destination
```

```
public void sendMessage(String txtToSend) {
    context.createProducer().send(queue, txtToSend);    <-- Uses simplified API to send message
}
```

Receive a message:

```
@MessageDriven(mappedName="jms/BidQueue")    <-- Annotated as an MDB for the container, listen on "jms/BidQueue"
public class BidMdb implements MessageListener {    <-- Class implements MessageListener to receive JMS messages
  @Resource
  private MessageDrivenContext mdc;    <-- Injects a MessageDrivenContext if needed

  public void onMessage(Message inMessage) {    <-- Method implements MessageListener and handles message
    // handle message
  }
}
```

1.6.3 *Enhancements to stateful session beans*

In EJB 3.2, session beans haven't changed dramatically, at least not as dramatically as MDBs. A few enhancements have been made to stateful session beans concerning passivation and transaction support. Here's a quick look at these enhancements.

DISABLE PASSIVATION

Prior to EJB 3.2, stateful beans needed all objects in them to implement `Serializable` so that the EJB container could passivate a bean without error. If one object in your stateful bean wasn't serializable, passivation would fail and the EJB container would destroy the bean, losing the state. Although it's highly advisable to make sure your stateful beans are serializable so the EJB container can provide you with services like passivation and clustered failover, sometimes it's not possible. To prevent the container from attempting to passivate a stateful bean you don't want to passivate, use the `passivationCapable` element:

```
@Stateful(passivationCapable=false)    <-- Prevents EJB container from passivating stateful bean
public class BiddingCart {
}
```

TRANSACTION SUPPORT TO LIFECYCLE CALLBACKS

Prior to EJB 3.2, stateful session beans had lifecycle callback methods, but it was undefined how transactions were supported during these method calls. So the new API adds transactional support to the lifecycle callback methods by introducing the ability to annotate the lifecycle callback methods with `@TransactionalAttribute(REQUIRES_NEW)`. `REQUIRES_NEW` is the only valid value for stateful lifecycle callback methods:

```
@Stateful    <-- Stateful session bean
public class BiddingCart {
  @PostConstruct
  @TransactionAttribute(REQUIRES_NEW)
  public void lookupDefaults() { }    <-- @PostConstruct lifecycle method lookupDefaults is run in its own transaction
}
```

1.6.4 Simplifying local interfaces for stateless beans

Prior to 3.2, if interfaces weren't marked as `@Local` or `@Remote`, then the implementing bean was forced to define them. Here's what the pre-3.2 interface and bean looked like:

```
public interface A {}
public interface B {}

@Stateless
@Local({A.class, B.class})
public class BidServicesBean implements A, B {}
```

Interfaces A and B don't specify @Local or @Remote

❶ Prior to EJB 3.2, @Local must be used to define both A and B as local interfaces

Now EJB 3.2 has more intelligent defaults. By default, all interfaces that don't specify `@Local` or `@Remote` automatically become local interfaces by the container. So you can skip line ❶ and rewrite the code like this:

```
@Stateless
public class BidServicesBean implements A, B {}
```

Container will now default A and B to local interfaces

1.6.5 Enhancements in TimerService API

The TimerService API has been enhanced to expand the scope of where and how timers may be retrieved. Prior to EJB 3.2, the `Timer` and `TimerHandler` objects could only be accessed by the bean that owned the timer. This restriction has been lifted, and a new API method called `getAllTimers()` has been added that will return a list of all active timers in the EJB module. This allows any code to view all timers and have the ability to alter them.

1.6.6 Enhancements in EJBContainer API

For EJB 3.2, a couple of changes have been made to the embeddable EJBContainer API. First, the API now implements `AutoCloseable` so it may be used with a `try-with-resources` statement:

```
try (EJBContainer c = EJBContainer.createEJBContainer();) {
  // work with container
}
```

Second, the embeddable `EJBContainer` object is required to support the EJB Lite group of the EJB API. EJB API groups will be discussed further in the next section.

1.6.7 EJB API groups

Because EJB technology is the backbone of Enterprise Java development, EJBs need to be able to provide a large number of services to fulfill business needs. These services include but aren't limited to transactions, security, remote access, synchronous and asynchronous execution, and state tracking, and the list goes on. Not all Enterprise solutions require all the services EJBs are able to provide. To help streamline usage, EJB API groups were created for EJB 3.2. EJB API groups are well-defined subsets of the capabilities of EJBs created for specific purposes. The groups defined in the EJB 3.2 specification are these:

- EJB Lite
- Message-driven beans
- EJB 3.x Remote
- Persistent EJB timer services
- JAX-WS Web Service endpoints
- Embeddable EJB container (optional)
- EJB 2.x API
- Entity beans (optional)
- JAX-RPC Web Service endpoints (optional)

Except for the few groups that are optional, a full EJB container is required to implement all of the groups. The most important of these is the EJB Lite group. The EJB Lite group consists of the minimum number of EJB features that's still powerful enough to handle the majority of business transactions and security needs. This makes an EJB Lite implementation ideal to embed into a Servlet container like Tomcat to give the container some Enterprise features, or you can embed it into your Android tablet application to handle its data needs.

Now that we've looked at some of the new features and changes made to EJB 3.2, let's see how EJB technology compares with other frameworks in the marketplace that are also attempting to provide solutions for Enterprise Java software development.

1.7 Summary

You should now have a good idea of what EJB 3 is, what it brings to the table, and why you should consider using it to build server-side applications. We gave you an overview of the new features in EJB 3, including these important points:

- EJB 3 components are POJOs that are configurable through simplified metadata annotations.
- Accessing EJB from client applications and unit tests has become very simple using dependency injection.
- EJB provides a powerful, scalable, complete set of Enterprise services out-of-the-box.

We also provided a taste of code to show how EJB 3 addresses development pain points. Armed with this essential background, you're probably eager to look at more code. We aim to satisfy this desire, at least in part, in the next chapter. Get ready for a whirlwind tour of the EJB 3 API that shows just how easy the code really is.

2 A first taste of EJB

This chapter covers

- The ActionBazaar application
- Stateless and stateful session beans in ActionBazaar
- Integrating CDI and EJB 3
- Persisting objects with JPA 2

In the age of globalization, learning a new technology by balancing a book on your lap while hacking away at a business problem on the keyboard has become the norm. Let's face it—somewhere deep down you probably prefer this "baptism by fire" to trudging the same old roads over and over again. This chapter is for the brave pioneer in all of us, eager to peek over the horizon into the new world of EJB 3.

The first chapter gave you a 20,000-foot view of the EJB 3 landscape from a hypersonic jet. We defined EJB, described the services it offers and the EJB 3 architectural blueprint, and described how EJB 3 is related to CDI and JPA 2. This chapter is a low-altitude flyover with a reconnaissance airplane. Here we'll take a quick look at the code for solving a realistic problem using EJB 3, JPA 2, and CDI. The example solution will use some of the EJB 3 component types, a layered architecture, and some of the services we discussed in chapter 1. You'll see firsthand exactly how easy and useful EJB 3 is and how quickly you could pick it up.

If you aren't a big fan of views from heights, don't worry. Think of this chapter as that first day at a new workplace, shaking hands with the strangers in the neighboring cubicles. In the chapters that follow, you'll get to know more about your new coworkers' likes, dislikes, and eccentricities, and you'll learn how to work around these foibles. All you're expected to do right now is put names to faces.

Running the example code

At this point, we encourage you to start exploring the code examples for this book. You can peek at the entire solution by downloading the zip file containing the code examples from www.manning.com/panda2. We highly recommend that you set up your favorite development environment with the code. That way, you can follow along with us and even tinker with the code on your own, including running it inside a container.

The problem you'll solve in this chapter utilizes an essential element of this book—ActionBazaar. ActionBazaar is an imaginary enterprise system around which we'll weave most of the material in this book. In a sense, this book is a case study of developing the ActionBazaar application using EJB 3. Let's take a quick stroll around the ActionBazaar application to see what it's all about.

2.1 Introducing the ActionBazaar application

ActionBazaar is a simple online auctioning system like eBay. Sellers dust off the treasures hidden away in basement corners, take a few out-of-focus pictures, and post their item listings on ActionBazaar. Eager buyers get in the competitive spirit and put exorbitant bids against each other on the hidden treasures with the blurry pictures and misspelled descriptions. Winning bidders pay for the items. Sellers ship sold items. Everyone is happy, or so the story goes.

As much as we'd like to take credit for it, the idea of ActionBazaar was first introduced in *Hibernate in Action* by Christian Bauer and Gavin King (Manning, 2004) as the CaveatEmptor application. *Hibernate in Action* primary dealt with developing the persistence layer using the Hibernate object-relational mapping (O/R mapping) framework. The idea was later used by Patrick Lightbody and Jason Carreira in *WebWork in Action* (Manning, 2005) to discuss the open source presentation-tier framework. We thought this was a pretty good idea to adopt for *EJB 3 in Action*.

This section will introduce you to the ActionBazaar application. You'll start with a subset of the architecture of ActionBazaar, and then you'll design a solution based on EJB 3. After this section, the rest of the chapter explores some of the important features of these technologies, using examples from the ActionBazaar application to introduce you to some of the EJB bean types and show how they're used with CDI and JPA 2.

Let's begin by taking a look at the requirements and design of the example.

2.1.1 Starting with the architecture

For the purposes of introducing EJB 3, let's focus on a small subset of ActionBazaar functionality in this chapter—starting from bidding on an item and ending with ordering the item won. This set of application functionality is shown in figure 2.1.

The functionality represented in figure 2.1 encompasses the essentials of ActionBazaar. The major functionalities not covered are posting an item for sale, browsing items, and searching for items. We'll save these pieces of functionality for later. This includes presenting the entire domain model, which we'll discuss in chapter 9 when we start talking about domain modeling and persistence using JPA 2.

The chain of actions in figure 2.1 starts with the user deciding to place a bid on an item. The user, Jenny, spots the perfect Christmas gift for her grandpa and quickly puts down a starting bid of $5.00. After the timed auction ends, the highest bidder wins the item. Jenny gets lucky and no one else bids on the item, so she wins it for the grand sum of $5.00. As the winning bidder, Jenny is allowed to order the item from the seller, Joe. An order includes all the items you've come to expect from online merchants—shipping information, billing details, a total bill with calculated shipping and handling costs, and so on. Persuasive Jenny gets her mom to foot the bill with her credit card and has the order shipped directly to her grandpa's address. Not unlike many e-businesses, such as Amazon.com and eBay, ActionBazaar doesn't make the user wait for the billing process to finish before confirming an order. Instead, the order is confirmed as soon as it's received and the billing process is started in parallel in the background. Jenny gets an order confirmation as soon as she clicks the Order button. Although Jenny doesn't realize it, the process to charge her mom's credit card starts in the background as she's receiving the confirmation. After the billing process is finished, both Jenny and Joe are sent email notifications. Having been notified of the

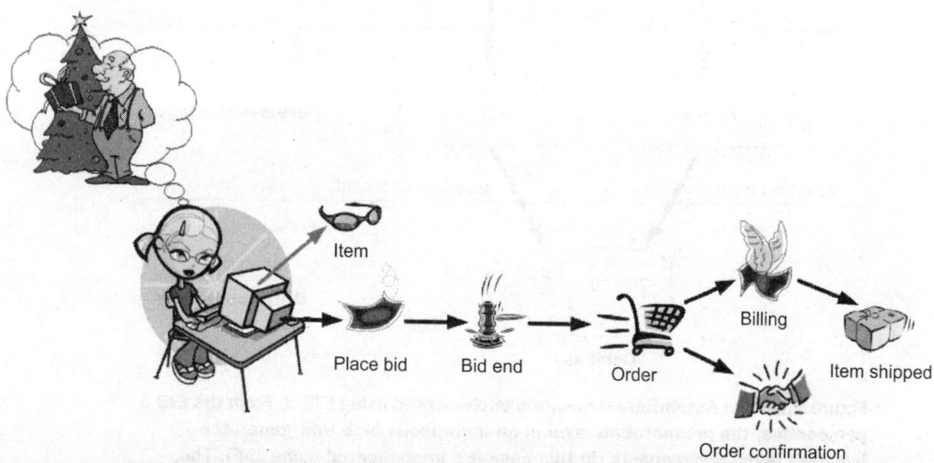

Figure 2.1 A chain of representative ActionBazaar functionality used to examine a cross-section of EJB 3. The bidder bids on a desired item, wins the item, orders it, and instantaneously receives confirmation. Parallel with the order confirmation, the user is billed for the item. Upon successful receipt of payment, the seller ships the item.

receipt of the money for the order, Joe ships the item, just in time for Jenny's grandpa to get it before Christmas!

In the next section, you'll see how the business logic components for this set of actions can be implemented using EJB 3. Before peeking at the solution diagram in the next section, you should try to visualize how the components might look with respect to an EJB-based layered architecture. How do you think session beans, CDI, entities, and the JPA 2 API fit into the picture, given our architectural discussion in chapter 1?

2.1.2 An EJB 3–based solution

Figure 2.2 shows how the ActionBazaar scenario in the previous section can be implemented using EJB 3 in a traditional four-tier layering scheme utilizing a domain model.

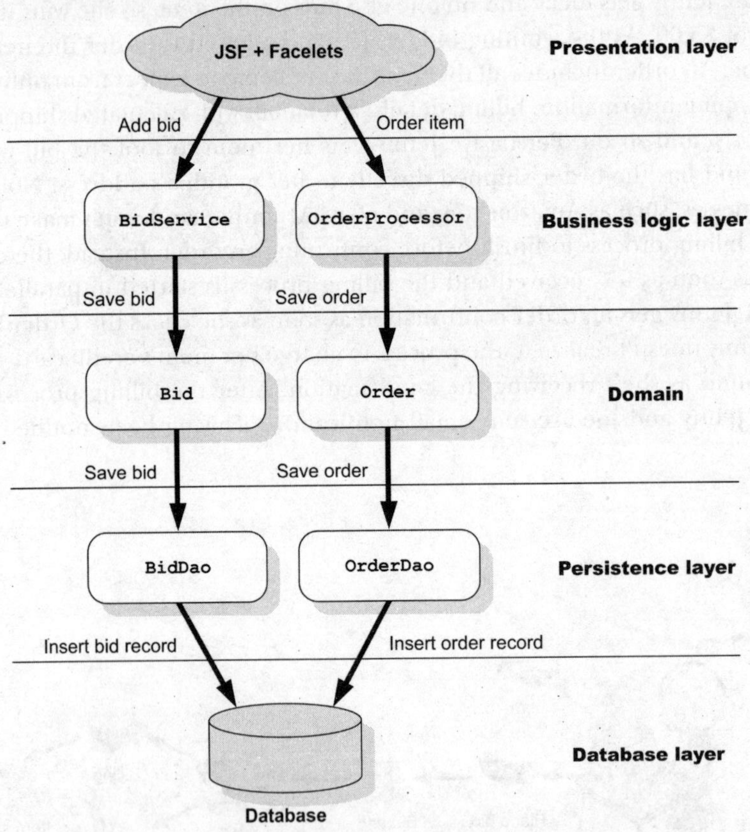

Figure 2.2 The ActionBazaar scenario implemented using EJB 3. From the EJB 3 perspective, the presentation layer is an amorphous blob that generates business logic–tier requests (in this case it's implemented using JSF). The business logic–tier components match up with the distinct processes in the scenario—putting a bid on an item and ordering the item won. The business logic–tier components use JPA entities to persist the application state into the database via persistence-layer DAO components.

If you examine the scenario in figure 2.2, you'll see that only two processes are triggered by the user: adding a bid to an item and ordering items won. As you might be able to guess from figure 2.2, the bidding and ordering processes are implemented as session beans (`BidService` and `OrderProcessor`) in the business logic tier.

Both of the business processes persist data. The `BidService` needs to add a bid record to the database. Similarly, the `OrderProcessor` must add an order record. These database changes are performed through two entities in the JPA-managed persistence tier—the `Bid` and `Order` entities. Whereas the `BidService` uses the `Bid` entity, the `OrderProcessor` uses the `Order` entity. The business-tier components use `BidDao` and `OrderDao` persistence-tier components. Note that the DAOs need not be EJBs because there's no need to use EJB services directly at the persistence layer. Indeed, as you'll soon see, the DAOs are minimalistic Java objects managed by CDI that use no services other than dependency injection. Recall that although JPA 2 entities contain ORM configuration, they don't persist themselves. As you'll see in the actual code, the DAOs have to use the JPA 2 `EntityManager` API to add, delete, update, and retrieve entities.

If your mental picture matches up with figure 2.2 pretty closely, it's likely the code we're going to present next will seem intuitive too, even though you don't know EJB 3.

2.2 Building business logic with EJB 3

Let's start exploring the solution from the business logic tier, just like you would in a real-world application. EJB 3 session beans are ideal for modeling the bidding and ordering processes in your scenario. By default they're transactional, thread-safe, and pooled—all characteristics you need to build the business logic tier of an enterprise application. Session beans are the easiest but most versatile part of EJB 3, so they're a great place to start.

Recall that session beans come in three flavors: stateful, stateless, and singleton. You'll use stateless beans and stateful beans in the examples, but not singleton beans. You'll also save message-driven beans for later. You'll take on stateless session beans first, primarily because they're simpler.

2.2.1 Using stateless session beans

Stateless session beans are used to model actions or processes that can be done in a single method call, such as placing a bid on an item in your ActionBazaar scenario. A vast majority of your business-tier components are likely to be stateless. The `addBid` bean method in listing 2.1 is called from the ActionBazaar web tier when a user decides to place a bid. The parameter to the method, the `Bid` object, represents the bid to be placed. The `Bid` object contains the bidder placing the bid, the item being bid on, and the bid amount. As you know, all the method needs to do is save the passed-in `Bid` data to the database. As you'll see toward the end of the chapter, the `Bid` object is really a JPA 2 entity.

Listing 2.1 BidService stateless session bean code

```
@Stateless
public class DefaultBidService implements BidService {
    @Inject
    private BidDao bidDao;
    ...
    public void addBid(Bid bid) {
        bidDao.addBid(bid);
    }
    ...
}
@Local
public interface BidService {
    ...
    public void addBid(Bid bid);
    ...
}
```

Marks POJO as stateless session bean

Injects non-EJB DAO

Marks interface as local

The first thing that you've probably noticed is how plain this code looks. The `DefaultBidService` class is just a Plain Old Java Object (POJO) and the `BidService` interface is a Plain Old Java Interface (POJI). There's no cryptic interface to implement, class to extend, or confusing naming convention to follow. The only notable features in listing 2.1 are the three annotations—`@Stateless`, `@Local`, and `@Inject`:

- `@Stateless`—The `@Stateless` annotation tells the EJB container that `DefaultBidService` is a stateless session bean. This means that the container automatically makes sure that the bean is completely thread-safe, transactional, and pooled. Thread-safe and transactional mean that you can use any back-end resources such as a database or message queue without writing any concurrency or transaction code yourself. Pooling ensures that the service will perform well even under a very heavy load. You can add additional EJB services to the component, such as security, scheduling, or interceptors, on an as-needed basis.
- `@Local`—The `@Local` annotation on the `BidService` interface tells the container that the `BidService` EJB can be accessed locally through the interface. Because EJBs and components that use them are typically collocated in the same application, this is probably perfect. If you want, you can omit the `@Local` annotation and the interface will still count as a local EJB interface. Alternatively, you could have marked the interface with the `@Remote` or `@WebService` annotations. Remote access through the `@Remote` annotation is provided under the hood by Java Remote Method Invocation (RMI), so this is the ideal means of remote access from Java clients. If the EJB needs to be accessed by non-Java clients like Microsoft .NET or PHP applications, SOAP–based remote access can be enabled using the `@WebService` annotation applied either on the interface or on the bean class. Note also that an EJB need not have an interface at all.
- `@Inject`—As you know, the bid service depends on the bid DAO for persistence. The `@Inject` CDI annotation injects the non-EJB DAO into the `BidService`

instance variable. If you're not familiar with dependency injection, you may think that what the `@Inject` annotation is doing is a little unusual—in a nifty, black-magic kind of way. You might have been wondering if the `bidDao` private variable is even usable because it's never set! If the container didn't intervene, you'd get the infamous `java.lang.NullPointerException` when you tried to call the `addBid` method in listing 2.1 because the `bidDao` variable would still be null. One interesting way to understand dependency injection is to think of it as "custom" Java variable instantiation. The `@Inject` annotation in listing 2.1 makes the container "instantiate" the `bidDao` variable with the right DAO implementation before the variable is available for use.

UNDERSTANDING STATELESSNESS

As long as calling the `addBid` method results in the creation of a new bid record each time, the client doesn't care about the internal state of the bean. There's absolutely no need for the stateless bean to guarantee that the value of any of its instance variables will be the same across any two invocations. This property is what statelessness means in terms of server-side programming.

The `BidService` session bean can afford to be stateless because the action of placing a bid is simple enough to be accomplished in a single step. The problem is that not all business processes are that simple. Breaking down a process into multiple steps and maintaining the internal state to glue together the steps is a common technique to present complex processes to the user in a simple way. Statefulness is particularly useful if what the user does in a given step in a process determines what the next step is. Think of a questionnaire-based setup wizard. The user's input for each step of the wizard is stored behind the scenes and is used to determine what to ask the user next. Stateful session beans make maintaining a server-side application state as easy as possible.

That's all we're going to say about stateless session beans and the bid service for now. Let's now turn our attention to the stateful order processor. A little later, we'll take a look at how the bid service is actually used by JSF, as well as what the DAO code looks like.

2.2.2 Using stateful beans

Unlike stateless session beans, stateful session beans guarantee that a client can expect to set the internal state of a bean and count on the state being maintained between any number of method calls. The container makes sure this happens by doing two important things behind the scenes: maintaining the session and implementing the solution.

MAINTAINING THE SESSION

First, the container ensures that a client can reach a bean dedicated to it across more than one method invocation. Think of this as a phone switchboard that makes sure it routes you to the same customer service agent if you call a technical support line more than once in a given time period (the time period is the session).

Second, the container ensures that bean instance variable values are maintained for the duration of a session without your having to write any session maintenance code. In the customer service example, the container makes sure that your account information and call history in a given time period automatically appear on your agent's screen when you call technical support. The ActionBazaar ordering process is a great example for stateful session beans because it's broken up into four workflow-like steps, each of which roughly corresponds to a screen presented to the user:

1. Picking the item to the order—The user starts the ordering process by clicking the Order Item button on the page displaying an item won, and the item is automatically added to the order.
2. Specifying shipping information, including the shipping method, shipping address, insurance, and so on—The user can have one or more previous shipping details saved in the history, including a default one. The user can view and use the saved history to enter shipping information. The available history is filtered to only show options appropriate for the current item (for example, an item/seller can support only a limited number of shipping methods/ locations). Once shipping options are specified, the shipping cost is automatically calculated.
3. Adding billing information, such as credit card data and the billing address—The billing data supports a history/defaulting/filtering feature similar to the shipping data.
4. Confirming the order after reviewing the complete order, including total cost.

Figure 2.3 depicts these ordering steps. With a stateful bean, the data the user enters at each workflow step can be cached into bean variables until the ordering workflow completes, including any hidden workflow state that the bean client doesn't need to be aware of.

Now that you know what you want, let's see how you can implement it.

IMPLEMENTING THE SOLUTION

The next example shows a possible implementation of the ActionBazaar ordering workflow using a bean named `DefaultOrderProcessor`. As you can see, `DefaultOrderProcessor` roughly models a workflow. You've ordered the methods so that you can easily visualize how the component might be invoked from a set of JSF pages, each implementing a stage of the ordering process. The `setBidder` and `setItem` methods are invoked by the presentation tier at the very beginning of the workflow, presumably when the user clicks the Order button. The bidder is likely the currently logged-in user, and the item is likely the current item selected to be ordered. In the `setBidder` method, the component retrieves the shipping and billing histories of the bidder and stores them away behind the scenes along with the bidder. In the `setItem` method, the shipping and billing choices are filtered down to what's applicable to the current item. The current item is also stored away into an instance variable for use farther down the workflow.

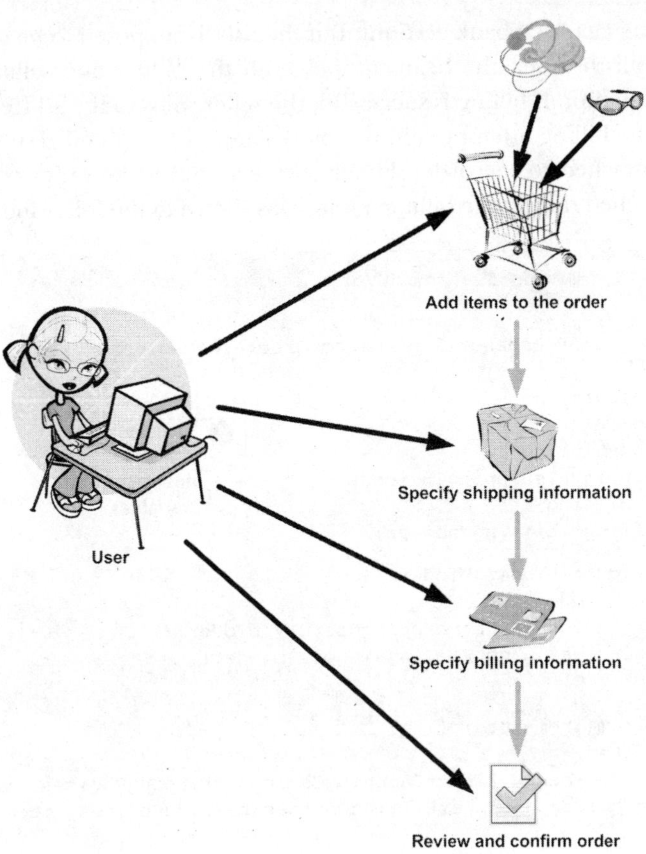

Figure 2.3 To make an otherwise involved process manageable, the ActionBazaar ordering process is broken down into several steps. The first step is to pick an item to order, the second step is to specify shipping information for the order, and the third step is to specify the billing information. Reviewing and confirming the order finishes the ordering process.

The next thing the JSF layer does is to prompt the user to enter the shipping details for the order. As an ease-of-use feature, the presentation tier will allow the user to reuse any applicable shipping details entered in the recent past. The shipping history is retrieved by invoking the `getShippingChoices` method. When the user selects a shipping history entry or enters new shipping information, it's passed back to the order processor by invoking the `setShipping` method. When the shipping details are set, the bidder's shipping history is also updated if needed. The order processor also immediately calculates the shipping cost and updates the shipping details internally. The JSF layer can get and display the updated shipping details by invoking the `getShipping` method. Similar to the shipping details, the JSF layer can get the billing history using the `getBillingChoices` method and set the billing details using the `setBilling` method.

The `placeOrder` method is invoked at the very end of the workflow, likely when the user has reviewed the order details and clicked the Confirm Order button. The `placeOrder` method actually creates and populates the `Order` object and attempts to bill the bidder for the total cost of the order, including the cost of the item, shipping, insurance, and so on. The customer can be billed in a number of ways—perhaps by charging a credit card or crediting against a bank account. But the user is supposed to be charged; after attempting to bill the user, the bean notifies both the bidder and seller of the results of the billing attempt. If billing is successful, the seller ships to the address specified in the order. If the billing attempt fails, the bidder must correct and resubmit the billing information attached to the order. Finally, the bean saves the order record to reflect whatever happened during the billing attempt, as shown in the following listing.

Listing 2.2 OrderProcessor stateful session bean

```
@Stateful
public class DefaultOrderProcessor implements OrderProcessor {     ❶ Marks POJO as stateful
   ...
   private Bidder bidder;
   private Item item;
   private Shipping shipping;                                       ❷ Defines stateful
   private List<Shipping> shippingChoices;                             instance variables
   private Billing billing;
   private List<Billing> billingChoices;

   public void setBidder(Bidder bidder) {
      this.bidder = bidder;
      this.shippingChoices = getShippingHistory(bidder);
      this.billingChoices = getBillingHistory(bidder);
   }

   public void setItem(Item item) {
      this.item = item;
      this.shippingChoices = filterShippingChoices(shippingChoices, item);
      this.billingChoices = filterBillingChoices(billingChoices, item);
   }

   public List<Shipping> getShippingChoices() {
      return shippingChoices;
   }

   public void setShipping(Shipping shipping) {
      this.shipping = shipping;
      updateShippingHistory(bidder, shipping);
      shipping.setCost(calculateShippingCost(shipping, item));
   }

   public Shipping getShipping() {
      return shipping;
   }

   public List<Billing> getBillingChoices() {
      return billingChoices;
   }

   public void setBilling(Billing billing) {
      this.billing = billing;
      updateBillingHistory(bidder, billing);
   }                                                                ❸ Asynchronous method

   @Asynchronous
   @Remove                                                          ❹ Remove method
```

```
    public void placeOrder() {
        Order order = new Order();
        order.setBidder(bidder);
        order.setItem(item);
        order.setShipping(shipping);
        order.setBilling(billing);

        try {
            bill(order);
            notifyBillingSuccess(order);
            order.setStatus(OrderStatus.COMPLETE);
        } catch (BillingException be) {
            notifyBillingFailure(be, order);
            order.setStatus(OrderStatus.BILLING_FAILED);
        } finally {
            saveOrder(order);
        }
    }
    ...
}
```

As you can see, there's little difference between developing a stateless and a stateful bean. From a developer's perspective, the only difference is that the `DefaultOrderProcessor` class is marked with the `@Stateful` annotation instead of the `@Stateless` annotation ❶. As you know, though, under the hood this makes a huge difference in how the container handles the bean's relationship to a client and the values stored in the bean instance variables ❷. The `@Stateful` annotation also serves to tell the client-side developer what to expect from the bean if behavior isn't obvious from the bean's API and documentation.

The `@Asynchronous` annotation ❸ placed on the `placeOrder` method makes the method asynchronously invokable. This means that the bean will return control back to the client as soon as the innovation happens. The method is then executed as a lightweight background process. This is an important piece of functionality in this case, because the billing process can potentially take a long time. Instead of making the user wait for the billing process to finish, the `@Asynchronous` annotation means that the user gets an immediate order placement confirmation while the final step of the ordering process can finish in the background.

It's also important to note the `@Remove` annotation ❹ placed on the `placeOrder` method. Although this annotation is optional, it's critical from a server performance standpoint. The `@Remove` annotation marks the end of the workflow modeled by a stateful bean. In this case, you're telling the container that there's no longer a need to maintain the bean's session with the client after the `placeOrder` method is invoked. If you didn't tell the container what method invocation marked the end of the workflow, the container could wait for a long time until it could safely time out the session. Because stateful beans are guaranteed to be dedicated to a client for the duration of a session, this could mean a lot of orphaned state data consuming precious server resources for long time periods!

2.2.3 Unit testing EJB 3

The ability to use EJB 3 in a Java SE environment is one of the most exciting developments in EJB 3.1. As we discussed in chapter 1, this is done through EJB 3 containers that can be embedded into any Java runtime. Although you could do this using nonstandard embedded containers like OpenEJB since Java EE 5, EJB 3.1 makes it required for all implementations.

Embedded containers are most useful in unit testing EJB 3 components with frameworks like JUnit or TestNG. Allowing for robust EJB 3 unit testing is the primary focus of projects like Arquillian. The following listing shows how the `OrderProcessor` stateful session bean can be easily tested inside a JUnit test. The unit test mimics the workflow that would be implemented by the presentation tier using a test item and bidder.

Listing 2.3 Stateful session bean client

```
@RunWith(Arquillian.class)                                    ❶ Integrating Arquillian with JUnit
public class OrderProcessorTest {
    @Inject                                                   ❷ Injects an instance of stateful bean
    private OrderProcessor orderProcessor;
    ...
    @Test                                                     ❸ Test to run
    public void testOrderProcessor {
              // Test bidder
              Bidder bidder = (Bidder) userService.getUser(new
      Long(100));

              // Test item
        Item item = itemService.getItem(new Long(200));

        orderProcessor.setBidder(bidder);
        orderProcessor.setItem(item);

        // Get the shipping history of the test bidder
        List<Shipping> shippingChoices = orderProcessor.getShippingChoices();

        // Choose the first one in the list
        orderProcessor.setShipping(shippingChoices.get(0));

        // Get the billing history of the test bidder
        List<Billing> billingChoices = orderProcessor.getBillingChoices();

        // Choose the first one in the list
        orderProcessor.setBilling(billingChoices.get(0));

        // Finish the workflow and end the stateful session
        orderProcessor.placeOrder();

        // Wait some time for the order to be placed in a separate process
    }
}
```

The `@RunWith` annotation ❶ tells JUnit to run Arquillian as part of the test. Arquillian controls the lifecycle of the embedded EJB container behind the scenes—it starts the container before the unit test starts and shuts it down when the unit test ends. Arquillian then deploys the components under testing to the embedded container—we've omitted the code that makes the deployment happen, but you can find it in the code samples. Arquillian is also responsible for injecting the ordering processor into the test ❷, along with any other required dependencies.

The test itself ❸ isn't that hard to grasp. First, you look up a test bidder and item (using a couple of other likely stateless EJB services). In unit testing parlance, the bidder and item are parts of the test data set. You then set the item and bidder as part of the workflow. You also simulate retrieving the shipping and billing history of the bidder and setting the shipping and billing details. In both cases, you're choosing the first item in the history. Finally, you finish the workflow by actually placing the order. The stateful session bean begins its lifecycle when it's injected into the test and ends its lifecycle when the `placeOrder` method finishes executing as a background process. In a real-world unit test, you'd also retrieve the order placed asynchronously and make sure the database saved the results that you expected it to save through a series of assertions.

2.3 Using CDI with EJB 3

As we noted in chapter 1, CDI plays a vital role by providing robust, next-generation, annotation-driven dependency injection to all Java EE components, including EJB 3. In this section, we'll show you some of the most common ways CDI is used with EJB 3—namely, as a more robust replacement to JSF-managed beans and complementing EJB with components that aren't in the business tier and don't need to use EJB services directly.

2.3.1 Using CDI with JSF 2 and EJB 3

To see how CDI can be used as the superglue between JSF and EJB 3, let's get back to the `BidService` stateless session bean example. Recall that `BidService` allows you to save bids into the database. Clearly, the `addBid` functionality would likely be used on a page that allows the bidder to place a bid on an item. If you're familiar with auction sites, this page could look something like figure 2.4.

Most of the page displays details of the item, bids, seller, and bidder, such as the item title, description, highest bid, current bidders, seller information, and so on. The

Figure 2.4 ActionBazaar auction page

part you're most interested in is the text box to enter a bid amount and the button to place a new bid. The JSF 2 code for these two page elements will look like the following listing.

Listing 2.4 JSF page to add bid

```
<!DOCTYPE html PUBLIC "-//W3C//DTD XHTML 1.0 Transitional//EN"
  "http://www.w3.org/TR/xhtml1/DTD/xhtml1-transitional.dtd">
<html xmlns="http://www.w3.org/1999/xhtml"
      xmlns:h="http://java.sun.com/jsf/html"
      xmlns:f="http://java.sun.com/jsf/core"
      xmlns:ui="http://java.sun.com/jsf/facelets">
<h:body>
    ...
    <h:form id="bid-form">
        ...
        <h:inputText id="input-bid" value="#{bid.amount}"/>
        ...
        <h:commandButton id="place-bid-button"
                         value="Place Bid!"
                         action="#{bidManager.placeBid}"/>
        ...
    </h:form>
    ...
</h:body>
</html>
```

❶ Binding expressions to CDI-managed beans

As you can see, both the `inputText` field and the button are bound to underlying beans using binding expressions ❶. The `inputText` field is bound to the `amount` field of a bean named `bid`. This means that the text field displays the value of the bound bean field and any value entered into the text field is automatically set into the bean field. The Place Bid button is bound to the `placeBid` method of a bean named `bidManager`. This means that the bound method is automatically invoked when the button is clicked. The next listing shows code that the JSF page elements are bound to.

Listing 2.5 `BidManager` CDI-managed bean

```
@Named
@RequestScoped
public class BidManager {
  @Inject
  private BidService bidService;

  @Inject
  @LoggedIn
  private User user;

  @Inject
  @SelectedItem
  private Item item;

  private Bid bid = Bid();
```

❶ Names BidManager CDI-managed bean

❷ BidManager is request scoped

❸ Injects BidService EJB

❹ Injects currently logged-in user

❺ Injects currently selected item

```
    @Produces
    @Named
    @RequestScoped
    public Bid getBid() {
        return bid;
    }

    public String placeBid() {
        bid.setBidder(user);
        bid.setItem(item);
        bidService.addBid(bid);
        return "bid_confirm.xhtml";
    }
}
```

6 **Produces a request-scoped CDI-managed bean named bid**

The `BidManager` component isn't an EJB but simply a CDI-managed bean. This means that other than lifecycle, dependency injection, and context management, no enterprise services such as transaction management are available directly to the `BidManager` component. This is perfectly fine in this case because the `BidManager` simply acts as the glue between the JSF page and transactional EJB service tier.

As such, the `BidManager` is probably fairly self-explanatory even with the various CDI annotations. The `@Named` CDI annotation **1** on the `BidManager` names the component. By default, the component is named because the simplified class name is camel-case. In the case of the `BidManager` component, the name assigned will be `bidManager`. Naming a component is necessary to reference it from JSF EL. As you've seen, the `BidManager.placeBid` method is bound to the Place Bid button via an EL binding expression. The `@RequestScoped` CDI annotation **2** specifies the scope of the `BidManager`. Because the `BidManager` is request-scoped, the bean will be created when the JSF page is loaded and destroyed when the user navigates to another page.

A number of other beans are injected into the `BidManager` component as dependencies. The first is the `BidService` stateless session bean **3** you're already familiar with. The injections for the bidder **4** and item **5** are a bit more interesting. The `@LoggedIn` and `@SelectedItem` annotations are CDI user-defined qualifiers. We'll discuss CDI qualifiers in great detail in chapter 12. For now, what you should understand is that qualifiers are user-defined metadata used to specify that you want a specific type of bean injected. For example, in the case of injecting the user into the `BidManager`, you're specifying that you want a special kind of user—namely, the currently logged-in user. The code assumes that CDI has a reference to a suitable user instance in some known accessible scope. Most likely, the `User` bean corresponding to the logged-in user is in the session scope and was placed there as part of the login process. Similarly, the `BidManager` code uses the `@SelectedItem` qualifier to specify that it depends on the item that the user has currently selected. The selected `Item` bean was likely placed into the request scope when the user clicked the link to view the item details.

The `@Produces`, `@RequestScoped`, and `@Named` annotations **6** placed on the `getBid` method are very interesting as well. As you may have guessed, the `@Produces` annotation is a key piece of functionality. The `@Produces` annotation tells CDI that the getBid method returns a Bid object that it should manage. The @Named and @RequestScoped annotations on the getBid method tell CDI that the returned Bid object should be named and should be in the request scope. Because the Bid object is named, it can be referenced in EL just as you did in the JSF page. We'll take a look at the Bid object in detail in a few sections. For now, you should know that a JPA 2 entity holds all bid data, including the bid amount that's bound by EL to the input text field on the JSF page. Because the BidManager creates and holds a reference to the Bid object, it automatically has access to all the bid data entered via the JSF page.

When the placeBid method is invoked in response to the button click on the JSF page, the BidManager uses all the data that it has reference to and properly populates the Bid object. It then uses the BidService stateless session bean to enter the bid into the database. Finally, the user is redirected to a page that confirms the bid.

That's all that we need to say about using CDI with EJB 3 at the presentation tier at the moment. CDI is used with EJB 3 in a number of other ways, including at the persistence tier to implement DAOs. Let's take a look at that next.

2.3.2 Using CDI with EJB 3 and JPA 2

In Java EE 7–based systems, the DAO layer is often implemented as EJB 3 beans. This technique makes a certain amount of sense especially if the DAO is marked with the transaction-required attribute (we'll discuss this transaction management attribute in detail in chapter 6). This forces all clients who use the DAOs to handle transactions and is a great safeguard because DAOs often utilize resources that require transactions, such as the database. But for in-house applications where the service and DAO layers are often developed by the same team, these safeguards aren't always needed. It's possible to develop DAOs using plain CDI-managed beans and inject them into EJBs at the service tier. To see how the code looks, let's quickly revisit the BidService stateless session bean in the following listing.

Listing 2.6 BidService stateless session bean code

```
@Stateless
public class DefaultBidService implements BidService {    // Marks POJO as stateless session bean
    @Inject                                               // Injects non-EJB DAO
    private BidDao bidDao;
    ...
    public void addBid(Bid bid) {
        bidDao.addBid(bid);
    }
    ...
}

@Local                                                    // Marks interface as local
public interface BidService {
    ...
    public void addBid(Bid bid);
    ...
}
```

The `BidDao` injected into the EJB is a CDI-managed bean with an interface. The DAO relies on the transaction and thread-safety context of the EJB and doesn't need to have any services other than basic dependency injection offered by CDI. Any other services, like security and asynchronous processing, are also likely best applied at the service tier rather than the persistence tier. The next listing shows the code for the DAO.

Listing 2.7 `BidDao` CDI-managed bean

```
public class DefaultBidDao implements BidDao {
    @PersistenceContext
    private EntityManager entityManager;
    ...
    public void addBid(Bid bid) {
        entityManager.persist(bid);
    }
    ...
}

public interface BidDao {
    ...
    public void addBid(Bid bid);
    ...
}
```

Injects JPA 2 entity manager

The DAO is very simple. Some of you might be surprised that neither the DAO class nor the interface has any annotations on it at all. This is normal in the CDI world because CDI-managed beans truly are bare POJOs. When CDI sees the `@Inject` annotation in the `BidService` EJB, it looks for any object that implements the `BidDao` interface and injects it. It's important to note that the `BidDao` is "nameless"—it doesn't have an `@Named` annotation. This is because the DAO doesn't need to be referenced by name anywhere. The DAO also doesn't have a defined scope. When this happens, CDI assumes that the bean belongs in the default scope. By default, CDI creates a brand-new instance of the bean and injects it into the dependent component—basically the same behavior as a "new" operator at the injection point. Notice also that the `BidDAO` itself can request injection. In the example, CDI injects a JPA 2 entity manager into the DAO that's used to save the `Bid` entity into the database. We'll talk more about JPA 2 in the next section.

The CDI features you saw in this section are truly the tip of the iceberg. CDI has a vast array of other features like stereotypes, events, interceptors, and decorators, some of which we'll look at in chapter 12. For now, let's turn our attention to the last piece of the EJB 3 puzzle: JPA 2.

2.4 Using JPA 2 with EJB 3

JPA 2 is the de facto persistence solution for the Java EE platform and is a closely related API to EJB 3. In Java EE 5, JPA was part of EJB 3. If you're familiar with Hibernate, TopLink, or JDO, you'll be right at home with JPA 2. Most of these tools now strongly support the JPA 2 standard.

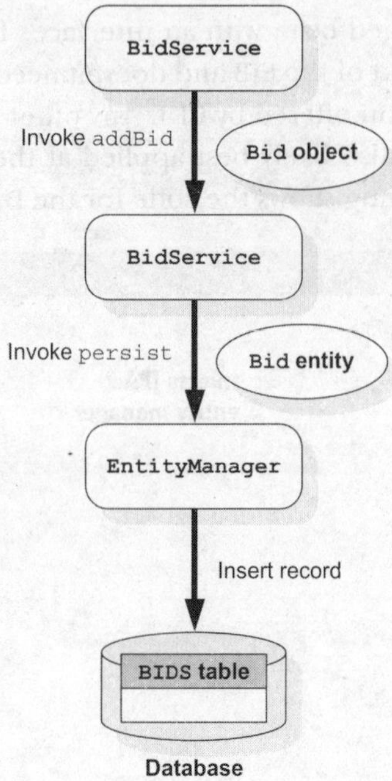

Figure 2.5 The `BidService` EJB invokes the `addBid` method of `BidDao` and passes a `Bid` object. The `BidDao` invokes the persist method of `EntityManager` to save the `Bid` entity into the database. When the transaction commits, you'll see that a corresponding database record in the `BIDS` table will be stored.

As you'll see shortly, the JPA `EntityManager` interface defines the API for persistence operations, whereas JPA entities specify how application data is mapped to a relational database. Although JPA takes a serious bite out of the complexity of saving enterprise data, O/R mapping–based persistence is still a nontrivial topic. We'll devote chapters 9, 10, and 11 of this book to JPA.

In almost every step of the ActionBazaar scenario, data is saved into the database using JPA 2. It's neither necessary nor very interesting to go over every one of those scenarios at the moment. Instead, you'll see what JPA 2 looks like by revisiting the `BidDAO`. As a brief visual reminder, figure 2.5 depicts the various components that interact with one another when a bidder creates a bid in ActionBazaar. We'll first take a look at how the `Bid` entity is mapped to the database and then take a close look at how the `BidDAO` uses the JPA 2 entity manager.

2.4.1 Mapping JPA 2 entities to the database

So far you've seen how the `Bid` object is used by the various layers of the application and that the object is a JPA 2 entity. We haven't shown you the actual code for the `Bid` entity, and this is a great time to do exactly that to start exploring how JPA 2 entities are mapped to the underlying database. The following listing shows the `Bid` entity.

Listing 2.8 `Bid` entity

```
@Entity                            // ❶ Marks POJO as entity
@Table(name="BIDS")                // ❷ Specifies table mapping
public class Bid {
```

```
    private Long id;
    private Item item;
    private Bidder bidder;
    private Double amount;                     ❸ Specifies ID field

    @Id                                        ❹ Generates ID value
    @GeneratedValue
    @Column(name="BID_ID")
    public Long getId() {                      ❺ Specifies column mappings
        return id;
    }

    public void setId(Long id) {
        this.id = id;
    }
                                               ❻ Specifies many-to-one relationship
    @ManyToOne
    @JoinColumn(name="BIDDER_ID", referencedColumnName="USER_ID")
    public Bidder getBidder() {                ❼ Specifies relationship mapping
        return bidder;
    }

    public void setBidder(Bidder bidder) {
        this.bidder = bidder;                  ❽ Specifies many-to-one relationship
    }

    @ManyToOne
    @JoinColumn(name = "ITEM_ID", referencedColumnName = "ITEM_ID")
    public Item getItem() {                    ❾ Specifies relationship mapping
        return item;
    }

    public void setItem(Item item) {
        this.item = item;
    }

    @Column(name="BID_AMOUNT")
    public Double getAmount() {                ❿ Specifies column mappings
        return amount;
    }

    public void setAmount(Double amount) {
        this.amount = amount;
    }
}
```

You probably have a pretty good idea of exactly how O/R mapping in JPA 2 works just by glancing at listing 2.8, even if you have no familiarity with ORM tools such as Hibernate. Think about the annotations that mirror relational concepts such as tables, columns, foreign keys, and primary keys.

The `@Entity` annotation signifies the fact that the `Bid` class is a JPA entity ❶. The `@Table` annotation tells JPA that the `Bid` entity is mapped to the `BIDS` table ❷. Similarly, the `@Column` annotations (❺ and ❿) indicate which `Bid` properties map to which `BIDS` table fields. The `@Id` annotation is somewhat special. It marks the `Id` property as the primary key for the `Bid` entity ❸. Just like a database record, a primary key uniquely identifies an entity instance. The `@GeneratedValue` annotation ❹ is used to indicate that the persistence provider should automatically generate the primary key when the entity is saved into the database. The `Bid` entity is related to a number of other JPA entities by holding direct object references, such the `Bidder` and `Item` entities. JPA allows such object reference–based implicit relationships to be elegantly mapped to the database. In the example, this is exactly what the `@ManyToOne` (❻ and ❽) and `@JoinColumn` (❼ and ❾) annotations do. In both cases, the `@ManyToOne` annotation indicates the nature of the relationship between the entities. In relational terms, this means that the `BIDS` table holds foreign-key references to the tables holding the `Item` and `Bidder` entities. The `@JoinColumn` annotation specifies what these foreign-key references are. In the case of the bid–item relationship, the foreign key stored in the `BIDS` table is `ITEM_ID`, which references a key named `ITEM_ID` that's likely the primary key of the `ITEMS` table. In the case of the bid–bidder relationship, the foreign key is `BIDDER_ID` and it references the `USER_ID` column. Having looked at the `Bid` entity, let's now turn our attention to how the entity winds up in the database through the `BidDao` bean.

2.4.2 Using the EntityManager

You've probably noticed that the `Bid` entity doesn't have a method of saving itself into the database. The JPA `EntityManager` performs this bit of heavy lifting by reading the O/R mapping configuration and providing entity persistence operations through an API-based interface. The `EntityManager` knows how to store a POJO entity into the database as a relational record, read relational data from a database and turn it into an entity, update entity data stored in the database, and delete data mapped to an entity instance from the database. The `EntityManager` has methods corresponding to each of these CRUD (create, read, update, delete) operations, in addition to support for the robust Java Persistence Query Language (JPQL).

Let's take a more detailed look at the `BidDao` in the next listing to see how some of these `EntityManager` operations work.

Listing 2.9 `EntityManager` operations in the `BidDao`

```
public class DefaultBidDao implements BidDao {
    @PersistenceContext                              ❶ Injects EntityManager
    private EntityManager entityManager;

    public void addBid(Bid bid) {
        entityManager.persist(bid);                  ❷ Persists entity instance
    }

    public Bid getBid(Long id) {
        return entityManager.find(Bid.class, id);    Retrieves entity instance
    }

    public void updateBid(Bid bid) {
        entityManager.merge(bid);                    Updates entity instance
    }
```

```
    public void deleteBid(Bid bid) {
        entityManager.remove(bid);     <-- Deletes entity instance
    }
}
```

The true magic of the code in this listing lies in the `EntityManager` interface. One interesting way to think about the `EntityManager` interface is as an interpreter between the object-oriented and relational worlds. The manager reads the O/R mapping annotations like `@Table` and `@Column` on the `Bid` entity and figures out how to save the entity into the database. The `EntityManager` is injected into the `DefaultBidDao` bean through the `@PersistenceContext` annotation ❶.

In the `addBid` method, the `EntityManager` `persist` method is called to save the `Bid` data into the database ❷. After the `persist` method returns, an SQL statement much like the following is issued against the database to insert a record corresponding to the bid:

```
INSERT INTO BIDS (BID_ID, BIDDER_ID, BID_AMOUNT, ITEM_ID)
VALUES (52, 60, 200.50, 100)
```

It might be instructive to look back at listing 2.7 now to see how the `EntityManager` figures out the SQL to generate by looking at the O/R mapping annotations on the `Bid` entity. Recall that the `@Table` annotation specifies that the bid record should be saved in the `BIDS` table, while each of the `@Column` and `@JoinColumn` annotations in listing 2.7 tells JPA which `Bid` entity field maps to which column in the `BIDS` table. For example, the `Id` property maps to the `BIDS.BID_ID` column, the `amount` property maps to the `BIDS.BID_AMOUNT` column, and so on. As we discussed earlier, the `@Id` and `@GeneratedValue` value annotations specify that the `BID_ID` column is the primary key of the `BIDS` table and that the JPA provider should automatically generate a value for the column before the `INSERT` statement is issued (the `52` value in the SQL sample). This process of translating an entity to columns in the database is exactly what O/R mapping and JPA is all about.

In a similar vein to the `persist` method, the `find` method retrieves an entity by the primary key, the `merge` method updates an entity in the database, and the `remove` method deletes an entity.

This brings us to the end of this brief introduction to the Java Persistence API—and to the end of this whirlwind chapter. At this point, it should be clear to you how simple, effective, and robust EJB 3 is, even from a bird's-eye view.

2.5 Summary

As we stated in the introduction, the goal of this chapter wasn't to feed you the "guru pill" for EJB 3 but rather to show you what to expect from this new version of the Java Enterprise platform.

This chapter introduced the ActionBazaar application, a central theme to this book. Using a scenario from the ActionBazaar application, we showed you a cross-section of EJB 3 functionality, including stateless session beans, stateful session beans,

CDI, JSF 2, and JPA 2. You learned some basic concepts such as metadata annotations, dependency injection, and O/R mapping.

You used a stateless session bean to implement the business logic for placing a bid for an item in an auctioning system. You then saw a stateful session bean that encapsulated the logic for ordering an item. You saw how EJB 3 components can be unit-tested via JUnit and how JSF 2, CDI, and EJB 3 work together seamlessly across application tiers. Finally, we examined the entity for storing bids, and you used the `EntityManager` API to manage the entity in the database.

In the next chapter, we'll shift to a lower gear and dive into the details of session beans.

Part 2

Working with EJB components

In this part of the book you'll learn how to work with EJB components to implement your business logic. Up first is chapter 3, where we'll dive into the details of session beans and outline best practices. Then chapter 4 gives a quick introduction to messaging, including sending and receiving messages, and JMS and it covers MDB in detail. Chapter 5 moves to more advanced topics such as the EJB context, using JNDI to look up EJBs and other resources, resource and EJB injection, the basics of AOP interceptors, and the application client container. Chapter 6 discusses transactions and security in terms of development, including when to use transactions and how to use groups and roles in security. The basics of EJB Timer Service are covered in chapter 7, as well as the different types of timers. In chapter 8, we'll delve into exposing Enterprise Java Beans via web services using either SOAP or REST.

Building business logic with session beans

This chapter covers

- Stateless session beans
- Stateful session beans
- Singleton beans
- Asynchronous beans

At the heart of any enterprise application is its business logic. In an ideal world, application developers should mainly be concerned with implementing business logic, while concerns like presentation, persistence, and integration should largely be window dressing. From this perspective, session beans are the most important part of the EJB technology because their purpose in life is to model high-level business processes.

If you think of a business system as a horse-drawn chariot carrying the Greco-Roman champion to battle, session beans are the driver. Session beans utilize data and system resources (the chariot and horses) to implement the goals of the user (the champion) using business logic (the skills and judgment of the driver). For this and other reasons, sessions beans, particularly stateless session beans, have been popular, even despite the problems of EJB 2. EJB 3 makes this vital bean type much easier to use and adds some important functionality.

In chapter 1 we briefly introduced session beans. In chapter 2 you saw simple examples of these beans in action. In this chapter, we'll discuss session beans in much greater detail, focusing on their purpose, the different types of session beans, how to develop them, and some of the advanced session bean features available to you, including asynchronous processing and concurrency management with singleton beans.

We start this chapter by exploring some basic session bean concepts and then discuss some fundamental characteristics of session beans. We then cover each type—stateful, stateless, singleton, and the asynchronous processing support that can be used with each one of these beans—in detail.

3.1 Getting to know session beans

A typical enterprise application will have numerous business activities or processes. For example, the ActionBazaar application has processes like creating a user, adding an item for auctioning, bidding for an item, ordering an item, and many more. Session beans are used to encapsulate the business logic for each process. To best understand session beans, you have to first understand the concept of a session.

The theory behind session beans centers on the idea that each request by a client to complete a distinct business process is completed in a session. So what is a session? For an example of a session, you can look to Microsoft's Remote Desktop. With Remote Desktop, you can establish a connection to a remote machine which you can then control. You get to see the desktop as if you were sitting right in front of the machine. You can access volumes on the remote computer, launch applications, and, if the machine is on a separate network, access resources available only on that network. When you're finished with the session you disconnect to terminate it. In this case, your local computer is the client and the remote computer is the server. Simply put, a *session* is a connection between a client and a server that lasts a finite amount of time.

Not all sessions are equal. Sessions last for different durations with some being short and others long. Instead of the remote desktop example, let's take a look at day-to-day conversations. A conversation can be thought of as a form of a session between two people. A short conversation would be a simple question and response to a stranger about the current time: "What time is it?" "It's noon." A longer conversation would be a discussion between two friends as they banter about a basketball game. In the short conversation, the conversation ends once the person responds with the time. You can categorize these two conversations as stateless and stateful sessions, respectively—conveniently corresponding to session bean types we'll discuss soon.

The concept of stateless and stateful sessions is seen throughout software development. In the ActionBazaar application, some application processes are stateful whereas others are stateless. For example, registering a new bidder involves multiple steps as the person sets up an account, sets a password, and creates a profile. Bidding on an item is an example of a stateless process. The request includes the user ID, item number, and amount. The server responds with either a success or failure. This all happens in one step.

Besides stateful and stateless beans, the third type of session bean is a *singleton*. You can think of a singleton bean as being like a conductor on a train. The conductor knows the fares, stops, arrival times, and times of connecting trains. Passengers can ask the conductor questions but generally only one at a time. The conductor can, however, accept tickets while answering a question. There's generally only one conductor and they are shared by all of the passengers on the train. This is analogous to a singleton bean. There's only one instance of a singleton bean in the application.

Regardless of the type of conversation, session beans are optimally designed to be directly invoked by all the clients of the application's business service API. A client can be just about anything, such as a web application component (servlet, JSF, and so on), a command-line application, another EJB application, or even a JavaFX/Swing GUI application. A client can even be a Microsoft .NET application using web services or an application written for iOS or Android. Session beans are incredibly powerful and can be used to build scalable back-end systems for all of these clients.

At this point you should be wondering what makes session beans so special. After all, each of the three types of session beans sounds simple enough that you could code them yourself without a container, right? Session bean concepts transcend the EJB technology itself. Chapter 1 mentioned that besides simply modeling the application business API, the container provides a number of important services to session beans, such as dependency injection, lifecycle management, thread safety, transactions, security, and pooling. The next section should help to make it clear why you should use session beans and when you should use them.

3.1.1 When to use session beans

Session beans are much more than a simple abstraction for partitioning business logic. The container manages session beans and provides them with a number of important services. These services include injection, transaction management, concurrency control, security, remoting, scheduling (timer), and interceptors. If used appropriately, session beans form the foundation of highly scalable, reliable applications. Session beans can be abused—if everything is a session bean, then performance will suffer due to container overhead. Container overhead isn't a bad thing per se, however. If you weren't using the container or EJBs, you'd still have to implement not only your business logic but also the services being provided by the container and would probably do a worse job in terms of performance and reliability. If you're using the services that EJB offers for what they're really intended for, then there really isn't any overhead.

By default, all session beans are transactional and completely thread-safe. In addition, many containers pool stateless session beans for scalability (we'll discuss pooling in greater detail in section 3.2). So application components that these services are best applied to should be session beans. Prime candidates are business logic/service-tier components that directly or indirectly make use of back-end resources like database connections that require transactions and thread safety (for a more detailed discussion on EJB thread safety, see the sidebar "Do EJBs need to be thread-safe?"). Session beans are also the de facto delivery mechanisms for container services like security, scheduling, asynchronous processing, remoting, and web services. Components that might need these services should be session beans (usually these services are applied at the business application API layer anyway).

Just as important as knowing where to use session beans is realizing when session beans aren't appropriate. Making utility classes session beans isn't terribly useful. A utility method for formatting phone numbers or parsing tab-delimited input doesn't benefit from the services being offered by an EJB container. A utility method doesn't use security, transactions, or remoting. Making a utility class a session bean would add overhead without any clear benefit. Although EJB provides dependency injection, lifecycle management, and interceptors, plain CDI-managed beans can use these services too. A utility API should probably just use CDI and not EJB. The same is also true for DAO/repository classes. Although these objects rely on thread safety and transactions, they don't need to be session beans themselves because they'll likely be used through the EJB application service layer. As a result, making DAOs session beans simply adds needless overhead.

As of Java EE 6, technically you can use EJBs directly as JSF-backing beans. Although this is possible and might be useful for rapid prototyping, this is generally an approach we recommend that you avoid. Session beans shouldn't be used for page navigation or processing the request parameters from a web form. These are tasks best suited for JSF-backing beans or plain CDI-managed beans. Putting this logic in a session bean pushes the session bean up into the UI layer. Mixing UI logic and business logic makes for messy code that's hard to maintain in the long run.

> **Do EJBs need to be thread-safe?**
>
> We're using JDBC for simplicity only because we haven't introduced the EJB 3 Persistence API (JPA) in any detail yet. We don't want to assume that you already understand ORM. Using JDBC also happens to demonstrate dependency injection of resources and the stateless bean lifecycle callbacks. In general, you should avoid using JDBC in favor of JPA once you're comfortable with it.

3.1.2 Component state and session bean types

As we alluded to earlier, component state is the fundamental distinguishing characteristic of the three different types of session beans. The closest parallel to how stateless session beans manage state is the original connectionless, sessionless HTTP web server request/response cycle. The web browser requests a page and the server serves up the page and ends the connection. The particular contents of the page might change from one request to the other, but the browser doesn't expect the web server to maintain any client-, request-, or session-specific information on the server side. This doesn't mean, however, that the web server doesn't utilize state for its own internal

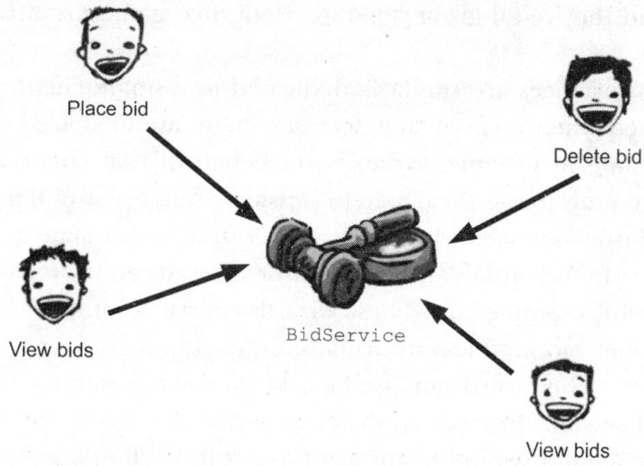

Figure 3.1 The `BidService` class is stateless

functioning. For example, the web server might keep an open connection to a remote file server, maintain an in-memory file cache, and so on.

Stateless session bean clients similarly can't be expected to maintain state on behalf of a client. A client can't even expect to be interacting with the same session bean instance across invocations, and all stateless session bean invocations are atomic. With or without pooling, clients are almost guaranteed to be talking to a different session bean instance across each invocation. Even though a stateless session bean doesn't hold state specific to a single client, it can and usually does internally make use of reusable resources like database connections. Stateless session beans are ideal for business services that have atomic, fire-and-forget API methods. The vast majority of Enterprise application services fall under this category, so a majority of your session beans are likely to be stateless. In terms of ActionBazaar, the `BidService` class is a prime candidate for a stateless session bean. As figure 3.1 shows, it contains APIs to add, get, and remove bids (all operations that can be completed in a single method call).

An online solitaire game, shown in figure 3.2, is a good analogy for how stateful session beans handle state. For the duration of a game, the game server holds state specific to a player and game in memory. Each game is essentially an extended session enforced through an underlying persistent connection between the client (player) and the server. Multiple players can be playing solitaire at the same time, but none

Figure 3.2 Online solitaire is analogous to stateful sessions.

share the same game and they're all given separate, dedicated game instances, each with its own state.

Stateful session bean instances are similarly dedicated to a single client. Stateful bean instances are created when a client first accesses them, aren't shared with any other clients, maintain state in instance variables on behalf of that client, and are destroyed when the client ends the session. Stateful session beans are useful in modeling workflow-based multistep services where the service must hold state from one workflow state to the other. In ActionBazaar, the bidder or seller Account Creator wizard services are ideal for stateful session beans. These wizards consist of multiple steps like entering login information, biographical information, geographic information, billing information, and so on. The wizard can also be cancelled at any stage of the workflow, ending the stateful session. In most applications, stateful services are relatively rare; bona fide cases for stateful session beans are rarer still. We'll talk about this in greater detail in section 3.2.

If online solitaire is a good analogy for stateful session beans, online multiplayer games, especially massively multiplayer online role-playing games (MMORPGs), as shown in figure 3.3, are a great analogy for singleton beans. Multiplayer games are concurrently accessed by all players and store the shared state common to all players. There's only one live instance of the game that all players connect to. In essence, all clients share a single extended session.

Similarly, there's only ever one instance of an EJB singleton session bean that's shared across all clients. Conceptually, it's the descendant of the Gang of Four's singleton pattern. But instead of using a private constructor and a factory method for creating the singleton, the container instantiates the singleton and ensures that only one instance is created. The container also helps to properly manage concurrent access to the bean by multiple clients. All clients share the internal state of the singleton,

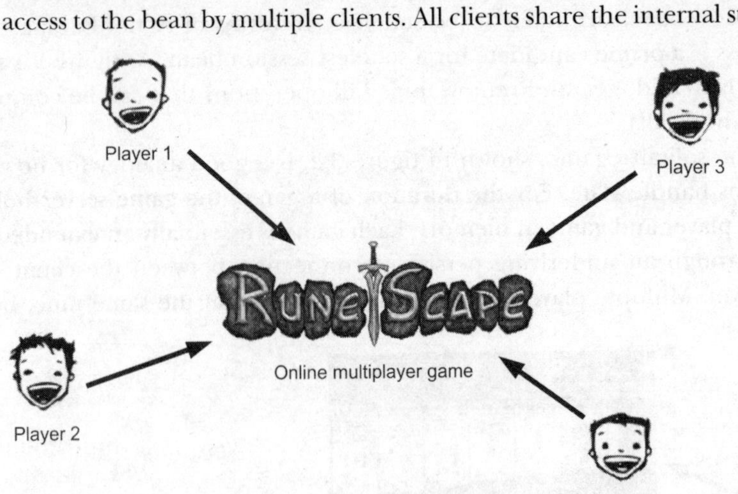

Figure 3.3 Multiplayer games like RuneScape maintain state in the same way EJB singletons do.

and the singleton is expected to hold and pass on a state change that one client makes across all other clients via its current state. Singletons are intended to model services that utilize state stored in a shared cache. In ActionBazaar, a singleton could be used for a service to get all current system alerts, such as fraud alerts. Singletons are relatively uncommon in Enterprise applications but are a very important use-case when they're needed.

Now that you have a rough sense of component state and session bean types, it's time to cover each of the bean types in more detail. Because stateless session beans are the most commonly used session bean, we'll start with them.

3.2 Stateless session beans

As we noted, a stateless session bean doesn't maintain any conversational state, and service tasks must be completed in a single method call. This certainly doesn't limit a stateless session bean to containing only one method. On the contrary, stateless session beans usually group together several closely related business service API methods. Of the session bean types, stateless session beans have the best performance characteristics.

In this section you'll learn more about developing stateless session beans. You'll implement some key pieces of the ActionBazaar application using stateless session beans. This will help reinforce key features of session beans and provide you with some practical code to use. You'll learn how to use the `@Stateless` annotation and the various types of business interfaces and lifecycle callbacks supposed by stateless session beans.

3.2.1 When to use stateless session beans

The obvious case for stateless session beans is stateless business API services. There are a few other scenarios where stateless session beans might make sense. Generally, you don't need the DAO/repository layer to be an EJB. But in some cases you might want to take advantage of pooling, security, or transactions at the DAO layer. As we'll discuss in the next section, pooling can be an important scalability technique applied not just at the service tier but also at the DAO tier for greater resilience. For many applications developed using rapid application development (RAD), there isn't an immediate need for the service tier because the UI layer accesses data repositories directly. In this case, DAO/repository objects can be stateless session beans so that they're thread-safe and transactional. As we also mentioned earlier, you can directly use stateless session beans as JSF-backing beans with CDI.

Like other EJBs, stateless session beans should be used sparingly. For example, it doesn't make much sense to use stateless session beans for utilities. You should also avoid stateless session beans if your API requires any state maintenance. In theory, it's possible to roughly simulate singletons by using static fields in stateless session beans. The problems with this are two-fold. First, although individual stateless session bean instances are thread-safe, static fields wouldn't be safe because stateless beans can be used by multiple concurrent clients at once. In contrast, there's only one singleton bean instance and it's accessed in a thread-safe manner by all concurrent clients. The second problem occurs when a cluster is introduced. In a cluster, stateless session beans on different clustered machines would have different static field values.

3.2.2 Stateless session bean pooling

EJB pooling is a complex, seldom documented, and poorly understood topic, so it deserves proper coverage here, particularly stateless session bean pooling. The basic idea behind instance pooling is to reuse a predefined number of bean instances to service incoming requests. Whenever a request arrives for a bean, the container allocates a bean. When the stateless session bean's method returns, the bean is placed back into the pool. Thus, a bean is either servicing a request or waiting for a request in the pool. Pools have an upper bound. If the number of concurrent requests for a stateless session bean exceeds the size of the pool, the requests that can't be handled are placed in a queue. As soon as instances become available in the pool, they're assigned to a request in the queue. No instances can hang around the pool forever—they're eventually timed out if they sit idle for too long. A pool can also have a lower bound to specify the minimum number of instances it must always have.

The pool provides several important benefits. Having a minimum set of beans in the pool ensures that there are objects ready to service a request when one arrives. This reduces the overall time to service a request by creating beans beforehand. Reusing bean instances when possible instead of frivolously discarding them also means less total object creation and destruction for the application, which saves time for the JVM garbage collector. Lastly, specifying an upper limit of the pool acts as an effective bandwidth-throttling mechanism. Without an effective bandwidth-throttling mechanism, a machine could be easily overwhelmed with a sudden burst of concurrent requests. Bandwidth throttling ensures that the server performs gracefully even under heavy load. Dynamic pools, bandwidth throttling, and request queuing are essential elements of the proven staged event-driven architecture (SEDA) model central to highly concurrent, well-conditioned, dependable, scalable, modern internet services.

Pooling isn't a standard feature mandated by the EJB specification. Like clustering, pooling is left optional but most application servers support it. Containers compete on scalability and performance-tuning features, so each container provides slightly different parameters for pooling as well as different defaults. For example, these are some of the pooling settings available in the GlassFish server:

- *Initial and minimum pool size*—The minimum number of beans to appear in the pool. The default is 0.
- *Maximum pool size*—The maximum number of beans that can be present in the pool. The default is 32.
- *Pool resize quantity*—The number of beans to be removed when the pool idle time-out expires. The default is 8.

- *Pool idle time-out*—The maximum number of seconds that a bean can reside in the pool without servicing a request before it's released for garbage collection. The default is 600.

These are only a few of the pool settings—there are many more. Each application is different and it's important to tune pool settings to truly match your needs.

In modern JVMs, object construction is very cheap. Most modern JVMs also support generational garbage collection, which makes it efficient to destroy short-lived objects. Generational garbage collection is the default for the HotSpot VM. This means that it's typically not necessary to specify a minimum size for a pool. It's all right for bean instances to be created on the fly and destroyed after the idle time-out expires (unless a subsequent request uses the bean again). This is why the default minimum pool size for most modern application servers like GlassFish, WebLogic 12c, and JBoss 7 is set to zero. But you should definitely specify a sensible minimum pool size if you're not using generational garbage collection (for example, to reduce garbage collection overhead or minimize garbage collection pauses) or if your JVM doesn't support generational garbage collection. In such cases, caching and reusing objects will significantly boost garbage collection performance. You should also utilize minimum pool sizes for objects that are particularly heavyweight, slow to construct, or use resources that aren't pooled like raw TCP-based connections.

It's almost always a good idea to specify a maximum pool size to safeguard against resource starvation caused by sudden bursts of concurrent requests. The typical default value of maximum pool sizes is between 10 and 30. As a general rule of thumb, you should set a maximum pool size matching the highest normally expected number of concurrent users you have for a given service. Too low a number will make the application appear unresponsive with long wait queues, whereas too high a number will risk resource starvation under heavy load. (Similarly, you should specify a database pool size matching the total expected concurrent users for a system or the capacity of your database server.) Fast services should have a lower maximum pool limit, and slower services should have a higher pooling limit. If you truly have very high server capacity and must support a very large number of concurrent users, it's possible to disable the upper limits of pools.

It's important to properly tune pooling for your individual application. Most application servers will allow you to monitor the state of bean pools at runtime to help you with tuning. Now that you have a handle on when to use stateless session beans and how they're pooled, let's look at some code and then dive into their mechanics.

3.2.3 BidService example

Bidding on an item is a critical piece of ActionBazaar functionality. Users can bid on an item and view the current bids. ActionBazaar administrators and customer service representatives can view and remove bids depending on the circumstances. Figure 3.4 depicts these bid-related actions.

Because all of these bid-related functions are simple, single-step processes, a stateless session bean can be used to model all of them. The `DefaultBidService` presented

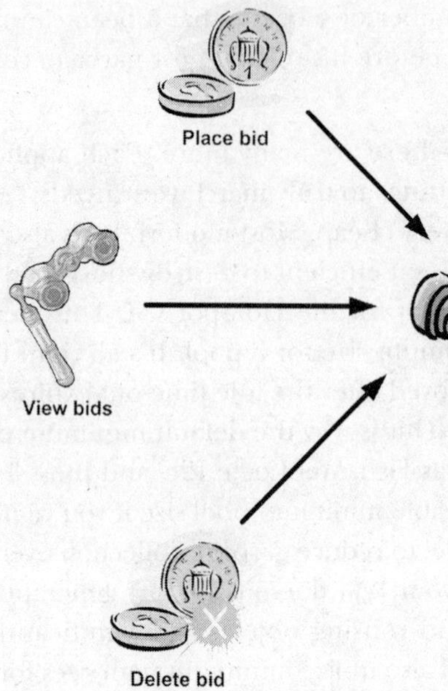

Figure 3.4 Some ActionBazaar bid-related actions. Bidders can place bids and view the current bids on an item, but administrators can remove bids when needed. All of these actions can be modeled with a single stateless session bean.

in listing 3.1 contains methods for adding, viewing, and cancelling bids. This is essentially an enhanced version of the basic `PlaceBid` EJB you saw earlier. The complete code is available for download from http://code.google.com/p/action-bazaar/.

> **NOTE** We're using JDBC for simplicity because we haven't introduced JPA in any detail yet. We don't want to assume that you already understand ORM. Using JDBC also demonstrates dependency injection of resources and the stateless bean lifecycle callbacks. In general, you should avoid using JDBC once you're comfortable with JPA.

Listing 3.1 Stateless session bean example

```
@Stateless(name = "BidService")                              ❶ Marks as a
public class DefaultBidService implements BidService {          stateless bean
  private Connection connection;
  @Resource(name = "jdbc/ActionBazaarDB")                    ❷ Injects data
  private DataSource dataSource;                                source
  @PostConstruct
  public void initialize() {                                 ❸ Receives
    try {                                                       PostConstruct
      connection = dataSource.getConnection();                  callback
    } catch (SQLException sqle) {
      sqle.printStackTrace();
    }
  }

  public void addBid(Bid bid) {
    Long bidId = getBidId();
```

```
    try {
      Statement statement = connection.createStatement();
      statement.execute("INSERT INTO BIDS "
     + " (BID_ID, BIDDER, ITEM_ID, AMOUNT) VALUES( "
     + bidId
     + ", "
     + bid.getBidder().getUserId()
     + ", "
     + bid.getItem().getItemId()
     + ", "
     + bid.getBidPrice() + ")");
    } catch (Exception sqle) {
   sqle.printStackTrace();
    }
  }

  private Long getBidId() {
    ...Code for generating a unique key...
  }

  public void cancelBid(Bid bid) {
    ...
  }

  public List<Bid> getBids(Item item) {
    ...
  }                                              ❹ Receives
                                                   PreDestroy
  @PreDestroy                                  <-  callback
  public void cleanup() {
    try {
   connection.close();
   connection = null;
    } catch (SQLException sqle) {
      sqle.printStackTrace();
    }
  }
}                                              ❺ Designates
...                                              remote business
@Remote                                       <- interface
public interface BidService {
  void addBid(Bid bid);
  void cancelBid(Bid bid);
  List<Bid> getBids(Item item);
}
```

As you've seen before, the `@Stateless` annotation marks the POJO as a stateless session bean ❶. The `DefaultBidService` class implements the `BidService` interface, which is marked `@Remote` ❺. The `@Resource` annotation is used to perform injection of a JDBC data source ❷. The `PostConstruct` ❸ and `PreDestroy` ❹ callbacks are used to manage a JDB database connection derived from the injected data source. If a client will be accessing remotely, you define a remote interface using the `@Remote` annotation ❺. We'll start exploring the features of EJB stateless session beans by analyzing this code next, starting with the `@Stateless` annotation.

3.2.4 Using the @Stateless annotation

The `@Stateless` annotation marks the `DefaultBidService` POJO as a stateless session bean. Believe it or not, other than marking a POJO to make the container aware of its purpose, the annotation doesn't do much. The specification of the `@Stateless` annotation is as follows:

```
@Target(value = {ElementType.TYPE})
@Retention(value = RetentionPolicy.RUNTIME)
public @interface Stateless {
    public String name() default "";
    public String mappedName() default "";
    public String description() default "";
}
```

The `name` parameter specifies the name of the bean. Containers use this parameter to bind the EJB to the global JNDI tree. JNDI is essentially the application server's managed resource registry. All EJBs automatically get bound to JNDI as soon as the container discovers them. We'll discuss EJB naming and JNDI in detail in chapter 5. You'll also see the `name` parameter used again in chapter 14 when we discuss deployment descriptors. In listing 3.1, the bean name is specified as `BidService`. As the annotation definition shows, the `name` parameter is optional. You could easily omit it as follows:

```
@Stateless
public class DefaultBidService implements BidService {
```

If the `name` parameter is omitted, the container assigns the unqualified name of the class to the bean. In this case, the container would assume the bean name to be `DefaultBidService`. The `mappedName` field is a vendor-specific name that you can assign to your EJBs; some containers use this name to assign the JNDI name for the EJB. Generally, you won't be using the `mappedName` field.

3.2.5 Bean business interfaces

Clients of session beans have three different ways of invoking these beans. The first is through the local interface within the same JVM. The second is through a remote interface using RMI. The third way that stateless session beans can be invoked is via SOAP or REST web services. The same session bean may be accessed by any number of these methods.

These three methods of accessing a stateless session bean are denoted using annotations. Each of these three annotations must be placed on an interface that the bean then implements. Let's take a look at these annotations in more detail.

LOCAL INTERFACE

A *local interface* is designed for clients of a stateless session bean collocated in the same container (JVM) instance. You designate an interface as a local business interface by using the `@Local` annotation. The following code could be a local interface for the `DefaultBidService` class in listing 3.1:

```
@Local
public interface BidLocalService {
    void addBid(Bid bid);
    void cancelBid(Bid bid);
    List<Bid> getBids(Item item);
}
```

Local interfaces are the easiest to define and use. They're also by far the most common type of EJB interface and are the default type of interface for EJBs. This means that you can omit the `@Local` annotation and the interface will still be treated as a local interface. Note that in EJB 3.1 it's not necessary to define a local interface. You can't define a bean interface at all; instead, you access the bean by its implementation class directly. For example, you can redefine the `BidService` and remove all interfaces as follows:

```
@Stateless
public class BidService {
  ...
  @PostConstruct
  public void initialize() {
    ...
  }

  public void addBid(Bid bid) {
    ...
  }

  public void cancelBid(Bid bid) {
    ...
  }

  public List<Bid> getBids(Item item) {
    ...
  }
  @PreDestroy
  public void cleanup() {
    ...
  }
}
```

In this case, it's possible to locally access the bid service by injecting a `BidService` instance by a concrete class instead of an interface. Note that all bean methods are available if a local interface isn't explicitly defined.

REMOTE INTERFACE

Clients residing outside the container's JVM instance must use some kind of *remote interface.* If the client is also written in Java, the most logical and resource-efficient choice for remote EJB access is Java RMI. RMI is a highly efficient, TCP/IP-based binary remote communication API that automates most of the work needed for calling a method on a Java object across a network. EJB 3 enables a session bean to be made accessible via RMI through the `@Remote` annotation. The `BidService` business interface in the example uses the annotation to make the bean remotely accessible:

```
@Remote
public interface BidService extends Remote {
  ...
}
```

A remote business interface may extend `java.rmi.Remote` as you've done here, although this is strictly optional. Remote business methods aren't required to throw `java.rmi.RemoteException` unless the business interface extends the `java.rmi.Remote` interface. Remote business interfaces have one special requirement: all parameters and return types of the interface methods *must* be `Serializable`. This is because only `Serializable` objects can be sent across the network using RMI.

The example code for this chapter makes use of a remote client. The example code includes a simple JavaFX interface that invokes methods on a remote bean.

WEB SERVICE ENDPOINT INTERFACE

In addition to local and remote interfaces, session beans can also have web service interfaces. In Java EE 7 two different web service technologies are supported: SOAP via JAX-WS and REST via JAX-RS. With both JAX-WS and JAX-RS, annotations can be placed either on a separate interface or on the bean implementation class itself.

The following code is a REST adaptation of the bid service. The class is a stateless session bean and delegates to the injected `BidService` instance:

```
@Stateless
@Path("/bid")
public class BidRestService {
  @EJB
  private BidService bidService;
  ...
  @GET
  @Produces("text/xml")
  public Bid getBid(@QueryParam("id") Long id) {
    return bidService.getBid(id);
  }
  ...
  @DELETE
  public void deleteBid(@QueryParam("id") Long id) {
    Bid bid = bidService.getBid(id);
    bidService.deleteBid(bid);
  }
}
```

Marks stateless session bean as exposed via REST with a root URI of /bid

getBid method will be invoked with HTTP GET

getBid method will return bid object translated to XML

Bid identifier is mapped from an HTTP query parameter to a method parameter

deleteBid method will be invoked with HTTP DELETE

This REST web service is invoked via http://<hostname>:<port>/actionbazaar/rest/bid. Query parameters can be passed in as needed. For example, the URL for getting a bid would be http://<hostname>:<port>/actionbazaar/rest/bid?id=1010.

As you'll see in detail in chapter 8, the reason you created the adapter layer for REST is because HTTP methods don't map well to Java service method calls directly. SOAP, on the other hand, maps to Java method calls much better, so existing EJBs can usually be exported as is via JAX WS.

For traditional SOAP-based web services, Java EE 6 includes JAX-WS. Like JAX-RS, JAX-WS uses annotations. To expose an existing stateless bean as a web service, simply

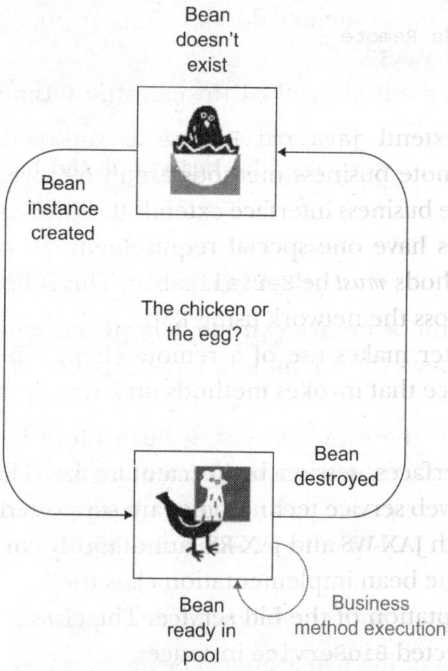

Figure 3.5 Chicken or the egg—the stateless session bean lifecycle has three states: doesn't exist, idle, or busy. As a result, there are only two lifecycle callbacks corresponding to bean creation and destruction

create a new interface and add the `@javax.jws.WebService` annotation. The following code snippet demonstrates this for the `BidService`:

```
@WebService
public interface BidSoapService {
  List<Bid> getBids(Item item);
}
```

As this interface demonstrates, it's possible to selectively hide methods you don't want to expose via web services. This interface omitted the `cancelBid` and `addBid` methods; these methods are thus not available via SOAP web services. They're still available via the local and remote interfaces. The `@WebService` annotation doesn't place any special restrictions on either the interface or the implementing bean. We'll discuss EJB web services in great detail in chapter 8.

3.2.6 Lifecycle callbacks

Stateless session beans have a very simple lifecycle—they either exist or they don't. This lifecycle is shown in figure 3.5. Once a bean is created, it's placed in a pool to service client requests. Eventually a bean is destroyed, either when the load on the server decreases or when the application is shutdown. The container does the following:

1. Creates bean instances using the default constructor.
2. Injects resources such as JPA providers and database connections.
3. Put instances of the bean in a managed pool (if the container supports pooling).
4. Pulls an idle bean out of the pool when an invocation request is received from the client. At this point, the container may have to instantiate additional beans

to handle additional requests. If the container doesn't support pooling, bean instances are simply created on demand.

5 Executes the requested business method invoked through the business interface by the client.
6 When the business method finishes executing, the bean is placed back in the "method-ready" pool (if the container supports pooling). If the container doesn't support pooling, the bean is discarded.
7 As needed, the container retires beans from the pool.

As mentioned previously, stateless session beans are extremely performance-friendly. A relatively small number of bean instances can handle a large number of virtually concurrent clients when pooling is used.

If you look carefully, you'll see that the stateless session bean lifecycle ensures that all bean instances are accessed only by one request thread at a time. This is why stateless session beans are completely thread-safe and you don't have to worry about synchronization concerns at all, even though you're running in a highly concurrent server environment!

A stateless session bean has two callbacks with the following annotations:

- `@PostConstruct`—This is invoked immediately after a bean instance is created and set up and all resources are injected.
- `@PreDestroy`—This is invoked right before the bean instance is retired.

If needed, multiple methods in a bean class can be annotated with these lifecycle callbacks. Listing 3.1 uses both the `@PostConstruct` and `@PreDestroy` callbacks in the `initialize` and `cleanup` methods, respectively. These callbacks are typically used for allocating and releasing injected resources that are used by business methods. This is exactly what's happening in listing 3.1—you open and close connections to the database using the injected JDBC data source. The question might arise as to why you can't perform both of these operations using the constructor and the `finalize` method. Well, when the constructor is instantiated none of the resources have been injected yet, so all of the references will be null. As for the `finalize` method, its use is actively discouraged and it's meant more for closing out low-level resources such as JNI references. It's never to be used for closing out database connections. The `finalize` method is invoked long after the bean has left the pool and is in the process of being garbage collected.

Recall that the `addBid` method in listing 3.1 inserted the new bid submitted by the user. The method created a `java.sql.Statement` from an open JDBC connection and used the statement to insert a record into the `BIDS` table. The JDBC connection object used to create the statement is a classic heavy-duty resource. It's expensive to open and should be shared across calls whenever possible. Because it can hold a number of native resources, it's important to close when it's no longer needed.

In listing 3.1, the JDBC data source from which the connection is created is injected using the `@Resource` annotation. We'll explore injecting resources using the

`@Resource` annotation in chapter 5; for now, this is all that you need to know. Let's take a close look at how you use the callbacks in listing 3.1.

PostConstruct callback

After injecting all of the resources, the container scans the bean class for methods annotated with `@PostConstruct`. If there are any methods, the methods are invoked before the bean instance is ready for use. In this case, you mark the initialize method in listing 3.1 with the `@PostConstruct` annotation:

```
@PostConstruct
public void initialize () {
  ...
  connection = dataSource.getConnection();
  ...
}
```

In the initialize method, you create a `java.sql.Connection` from the injected data source and save it into the connection instance variable used in `addBid` each time the client method is invoked.

PreDestroy callback

At some point the container decides that your bean should be destroyed. The `PreDestroy` callback gives the bean a chance to cleanly tear down bean resources before this is done. In the cleanup method marked with the `@PreDestroy` annotation in listing 3.1, you tear down the open database connection resource before the container retires your bean:

```
@PreDestroy
public void cleanup() {
  ...
  connection.close();
  connection = null;
  ...
}
```

3.2.7 *Using stateless session beans effectively*

Like all technologies, EJB and stateless session beans have best practices to follow and anti-patterns to avoid. In this section we'll mention some of these points.

Tune pooling

As we discussed in section 3.2.2, tuning pooling correctly is a critical part of getting the most out of stateless session beans. Generally, the defaults of most application servers are good enough, but tuning can truly optimize your application and prime it for performance under pressure. The importance of taking advantage of the EJB monitoring features built into most application servers also can't be understated. Making use of monitoring will truly help you understand the runtime patterns of your application.

Don't abuse remoting

Recall that the default interface type is local. While remote interfaces are very useful when they're needed, they can be a serious performance killer if used otherwise. The issue is that if you accidentally use the `@Remote` annotation instead of the `@Local` annotation, you'll still be able to transparently inject the remote EJB using `@EJB` as though it were a local EJB without realizing it. This is why it's very important that you avoid the `@Remote` annotation unless it's really needed.

USE INTERFACES

Although it's technically possible to avoid using interfaces with EJB 3.1, we recommend that you use interfaces anyway unless you're developing a prototype or using session beans as JSF-backing beans. If you're developing a service, it's best to maintain loose coupling through an interface for easier testability as well as future flexibility.

PROPERLY DESIGN REMOTE INTERFACES

When using remote interfaces, make sure the methods that you include in the interface are really supposed to be remotely exposed. You can have a local interface and a remote interface that expose completely different methods.

REMOTE OBJECTS AREN'T PASSED BY REFERENCE

Remote method parameters and return types must be serializable. Furthermore, objects are exchanged by copying over the network. This means that you can't pass an object to a remote stateless method and expect your local reference to mirror changes made by the method. For example, if you pass a list of objects to a remote stateless session bean, you won't see any changes made to the list unless it's returned by the remote method. Although this may work for beans being accessed locally in the same application and Java Virtual Machine (JVM), this obviously doesn't work for remote beans.

AVOID FINE-GRAINED REMOTE CALLS

Remote calls are expensive—beans accessed locally can be finer grained, whereas remote beans should naturally be very coarse-grained. On a remote service you want to avoid repeatedly contacting the server for different bits of information to fulfill a request because each call exacts a charge that in aggregate might be unacceptable. For example, if the user interface (UI) provided a UI that enabled multiple bids to be cancelled, it wouldn't make sense to call the `BidService.cancel()` method in a loop—that would be horribly inefficient. Instead you should add an additional method that takes a list of bids to be cancelled.

3.3 Stateful session beans

Recall that unlike stateless session beans, stateful session beans maintain their state over multiple method invocations. Supporting a conversational state opens up new opportunities, such as long-running database transactions. Programmatically, stateful session beans aren't that different from their stateless counterparts. The only real difference is in terms of how the container manages its lifecycle. The container ensures that each method invocation is on the same bean instance, whether it's local or remote. This is done behind the scenes. Figure 3.6 shows this behavior graphically.

In addition to ensuring that the same bean is used for all invocations from a given client, the container also ensures that only one thread is accessing the bean at a time.

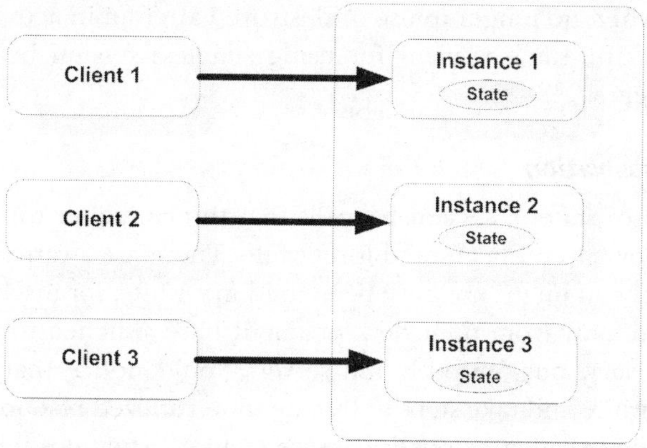

Figure 3.6 A bean instance is reserved for each client for the duration of the bean. The bean is thus able to store client state information until the bean is removed by the client or times out.

This means that you don't have to worry about enforcing synchronization yourself—multiple threads can access the bean and the container will ensure that the bean isn't in an inconsistent state. But by giving up some control, you also lose some flexibility—only one thread at a time—no exceptions.

The one-to-one mapping between a client and a bean instance makes saving a bean conversational state in a useful manner possible. But this one-to-one correlation comes at a price. Bean instances can't be readily returned to a pool and reused for another client. Instead, a bean instance must be squirreled away in memory to wait for the next request from the client owning the session. As a result, stateful session bean instances held by a large number of concurrent clients can have a significant memory footprint. An optimization technique called *passivation*, which we'll discuss in section 3.3.2, is used to alleviate this problem.

3.3.1 When to use stateful session beans

Stateful session beans are ideal for multistep, workflow-oriented business processes. To understand what this means, think of the new envelope wizard in Microsoft Word. If you want to create a new envelope, the wizard will guide you through the steps to select a particular style of envelop and enter the destination address and return address. Real business workflows are a great deal more complex with conditional steps and additional requests to back-end databases and message queues.

Multistep, workflow-oriented business processes don't necessarily require stateful session beans. For example, you can use plain CDI managed beans at the web tier to manage state. As we'll discuss in chapter 12, CDI and JSF have a rich set of scopes that's unmatched in EJB. As a rule of thumb, you should use stateful session beans if your workflow contains business logic that's not appropriate for the web tier. Like other EJBs, stateful session beans bring a few important features to the table. Stateful session beans are thread-safe and participate in transactions as well as container security. Stateful session beans can also be accessed remotely via RMI and SOAP as well as REST. Finally, the container manages them for you—stateful session beans are automatically passivated when no longer in use or destroyed after an in-activity time-out is triggered. Many of the same reasons for using stateless session beans also apply to stateful session beans.

3.3.2 Stateful session bean passivation

One of the great benefits of stateful session beans is that the container will archive stateful session beans if they haven't been used for a while. There are a variety of reasons why a stateful session bean might not have been used in a while; for instance, the user might have wandered away from their desk or might have switched to another application. The reasons vary, but obviously the server should notice that a bean hasn't been accessed in a while and take steps to free up underutilized resources. The container employs a technique called *passivation* to save memory when possible.

Passivation means moving a bean instance from memory to disk. The container accomplishes this task by serializing the entire bean instance. Activation is the opposite of passivation and is done when the bean instance is needed again, as shown in figure 3.7. The container activates a bean instance by retrieving it from permanent storage and deserializing it. As a result, all bean instance variables must either be a Java primitive, implement `java.io.Serializable`, or be marked as `transient`.

As you'll see in section 3.3.7, stateful session beans provide hooks for executing logic right before passivation and right after activation. Using these hooks, you can write data out to the database and perform any last-minute operations. Note that just like pooling, passivation isn't mandated by the EJB specification. But most application servers support passivation. Just like pooling, it's possible to tune and monitor stateful session bean passivation.

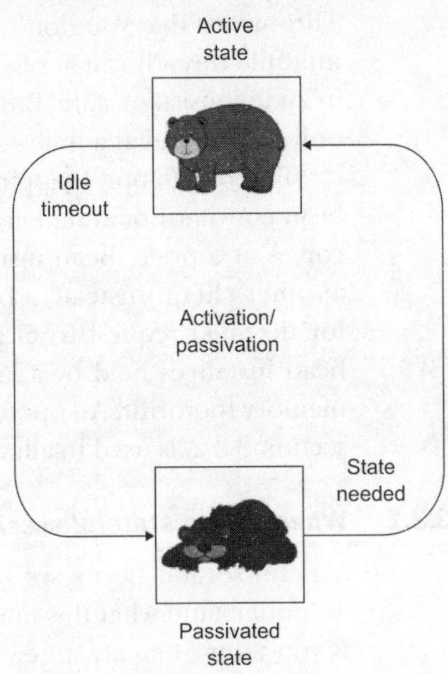

Figure 3.7 Passivation and activation are critical optimization techniques for stateful session beans.

3.3.3 Stateful session bean clustering

Although the EJB specification doesn't require it, most application servers cluster stateful session beans. This means that the state of the bean is replicated across all machines participating in the application server cluster. Even if the machine that your stateful session bean currently resides in crashes, a clustered, load-balanced, and failed-over set of servers means that you'll be transparently rerouted to the next available machine on the cluster and it'll still have the up-to-date state of the bean. Clustering is an essential feature for mission-critical systems that must guarantee reliability.

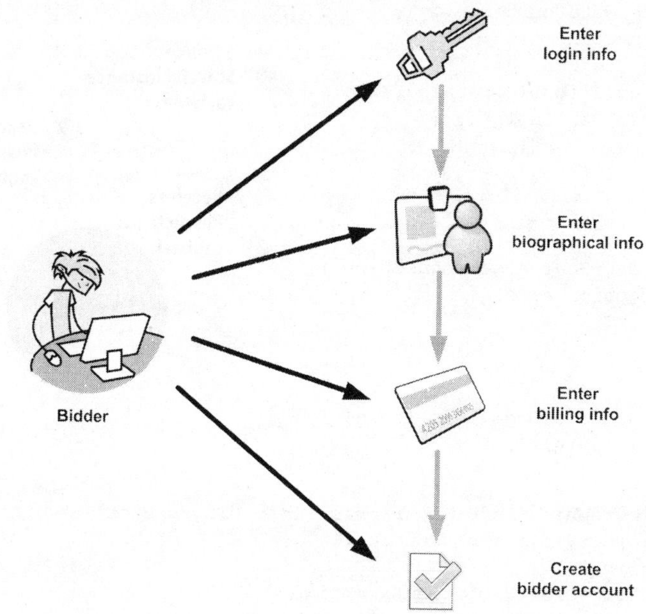

Figure 3.8 The ActionBazaar bidder account creation process is broken up into multiple steps. Each step is a separate method call, and the stateful session bean maintains the state between method invocations.

3.3.4 *Bidder account creator bean example*

The process to create an ActionBazaar bidder account is too involved to be implemented as a single-step action. As a result, account creation is implemented as a multistep process. At each step of the workflow, the bidder enters digestible units of data. For example, the bidder may enter username/password information first; then the biographical information such as a name, address, and contact information; then billing information such as credit card and bank account data; and so forth. At the end of the workflow, the bidder account is created or the entire task is abandoned. This workflow is depicted in figure 3.8.

Each step of the workflow is implemented as a method of the `BidderAccountCreator` presented in listing 3.2. Data gathered in each step is incrementally cached into the stateful session bean in instance variables. Calling either the `cancelAccountCreation` or `createAccount` method ends the workflow. The `createAccount` method creates the bidder account in the database and it concludes the workflow. The `cancelAccountCreation` method, on the other hand, prematurely terminates the process when called by the client and nothing is saved to the database. The `cancelAccountCreation` method can be called at any point during the workflow. The full code listing is available on the book's website.

Listing 3.2 Stateful session bean example

Marks POJO stateful (1)

```
@Stateful(name="BidderAccountCreator")
public class DefaultBidderAccountCreator implements BidderAccountCreator {
  @Resource(name = "jdbc/ActionBazaarDataSource")
```

```
    private DataSource dataSource;
    private Connection connection;
    private LoginInfo loginInfo;
    private BiographicalInfo biographicalInfo;
    private BillingInfo billingInfo;

    @PostConstruct
    @PostActivate
    public void openConnection() {
      try {
        connection = dataSource.getConnection();
      } catch (SQLException sqle) {
        sqle.printStackTrace();
      }
    }

    public void addLoginInfo(LoginInfo loginInfo) {
      this.loginInfo = loginInfo;
    }

    public void addBiographicalInfo(BiographicalInfo biographicalInfo)
      throws WorkflowOrderViolationException {
      if (loginInfo == null) {
        throw new WorkflowOrderViolationException(
          "Login info must be set before biographical info");
      }
      this.biographicalInfo = biographicalInfo;
    }

    public void addBillingInfo(BillingInfo billingInfo)
      throws WorkflowOrderViolationException {
      if (biographicalInfo == null) {
        throw new WorkflowOrderViolationException(
          "Biographical info must be set before billing info");
      }
      this.billingInfo = billingInfo;
    }

    @PrePassivate
    @PreDestroy
    public void cleanup() {
      try {
        connection.close();
        connection = null;
      } catch (SQLException sqle) {
        sqle.printStackTrace();
      }
    }

    @Remove
    public void cancelAccountCreation() {
      loginInfo = null;
      biographicalInfo = null;
      billingInfo = null;
    }

    @Remove
    public void createAccount() {
```

2 Stateful instance variables

3 Receives PostConstruct callback

4 Receives PostActivate callback

5 Receives PrePassivate callback

6 Receives PreDestroy callback

7 Designates the remove methods

```
        try {
          Statement statement = connection.createStatement();
          String sql = "INSERT INTO BIDDERS("
                                 ...
                                 + "username, "
                                 ...
                                 + "first_name, "
                                 ...
                                 + "credit_card_type"
                                 ...
                             + ") VALUES ("
                                 ...
                                 + "'" + loginInfo.getUsername() + "', "
                                 ...
                                 + "'" + biographicalInfo.getFirstName() + "', "
                                 ...
                                 + "'" + billingInfo.getCreditCardType() + "'"
                                 ...
                             + ")";
          statement.execute(sql);
          statement.close();
        } catch (SQLException sqle) {
          sqle.printStackTrace();
        }
      }
    }

    public interface BidderAccountCreator {
      void addLoginInfo(LoginInfo loginInfo);
      void addBiographicalInfo(BiographicalInfo biographicalInfo)
        throws WorkflowOrderViolationException;
      void addBillingInfo(BillingInfo billingInfo)
        throws WorkflowOrderViolationException;
      void cancelAccountCreation();
      void createAccount();
    }
```

As we mentioned earlier, it should be surprising that the stateful session bean code has much in common with the stateless session bean code in listing 3.1.

> **NOTE** We're using JDBC for simplicity in this example. The completed code for this book will use JPA, but we didn't want to distract you at this point with JPA code. We'll cover JPA in chapter 9.

The `@Stateful` annotation was placed on `DefaultBidderAccountCreator` to mark the POJO as a stateful session bean ❶. Other than the annotation name, this annotation behaves exactly like the `@Stateless` annotation, and we'll discuss it briefly in the next section. The bean implements the `BidderAccountCreator` business interface. Just like listing 3.1, a JDBC data source is injected using the `@Resource` annotation. Both the `PostConstruct` ❸ and `PostActivate` ❹ callbacks prepare the bean for use by opening a database connection from the injected data source. On the other hand, both the `PrePassivate` ❺ and `PreDestroy` ❻ callbacks close the cached connection.

The `loginInfo`, `biographicalInfo`, and `billingInfo` instance variables are used to store a client conversational state across business method calls ❷. Each of the business methods models a step in the account-creation workflow and incrementally populates the state instance variables. We didn't include it, but each of the steps could have had elaborate business logic as well as database access (perhaps for validation). The workflow is terminated when the client invokes either of the `@Remove` annotated methods ❼.

3.3.5 Using the @Stateful annotation

The `@Stateful` annotation marks the `DefaultBidderAccountCreator` POJO as a stateful session bean. Other than marking a POJO to make the container aware of its purpose, the annotation doesn't do much. The specification of the `@Stateful` annotation is as follows:

```
@Target(value = {ElementType.TYPE})
@Retention(value = RetentionPolicy.RUNTIME)
public @interface Stateless {
    public String name() default "";
    public String mappedName() default "";
    public String description() default "";
}
```

As you can see, the stateful annotation matches the stateless annotation verbatim. The `name` parameter specifies the name of the bean. In listing 3.2, the bean name is specified to be `BidderAccountCreator`. As the annotation definition shows, the `name` parameter is optional and defaults to an empty string. You could easily omit it as follows:

```
@Stateful
public class DefaultBidderAccountCreator implements BidderAccountCreator {
```

If the `name` parameter is omitted, the container assigns the name of the class to the bean. In this case, the container assumes the bean name is `DefaultBidderAccountCreator`. The `mappedName` field is a vendor-specific name that you can assign to your EJBs; some containers, such as GlassFish, use this name to assign the global JNDI name for the EJB. For the most part, this is how a legacy field with EJB names is standardized in Java EE 6 (we'll discuss EJB names in chapter 5). As we noted, the `DefaultBidderAccountCreator` implements a business interface name of `BidderAccountCreator`. Let's look at the business interfaces for stateful session beans and the limitations as compared to stateless session beans.

3.3.6 Bean business interfaces

Specifying stateful session bean business interfaces works in almost exactly the same way as it does for stateless beans, with a couple of exceptions. Stateful session beans support local and remote invocations through the `@Local` and `@Remote` annotations. But a stateful session bean can't have a web service endpoint interface. This means that a stateful session bean can't be exposed using JAX-RS or JAX-WS. This is because web service interfaces are inherently stateless in nature.

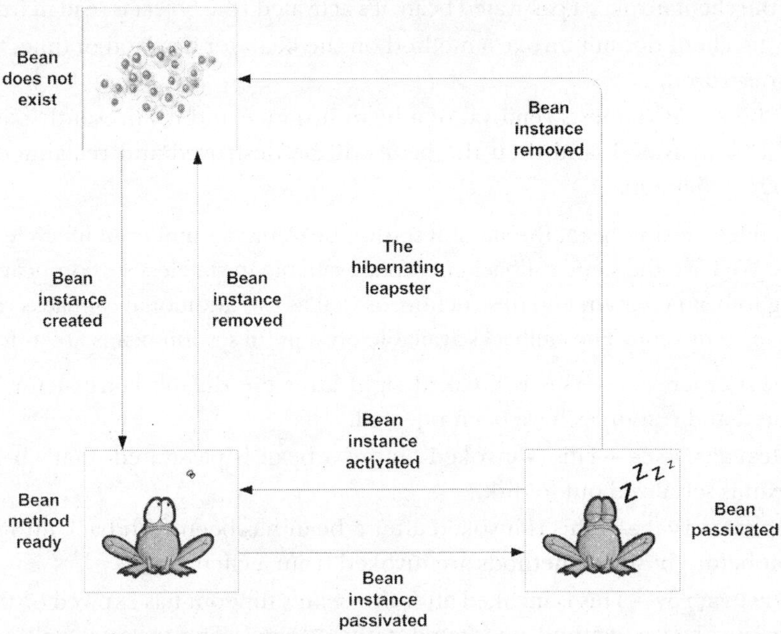

Figure 3.9 The lifecycle of a stateful session bean. A stateful bean maintains the client state and cannot be pooled. It may be passivated when the client isn't using it and must be activated when the client needs it again.

A business interface should always include a `@Remove` annotated method. Multiple methods can have this annotation. This annotation signals that the client has finished with the bean. In the next sections we'll dive into the lifecycle, and the reason for always providing a `@Remove` method will become clear.

3.3.7 *Lifecycle callbacks*

The lifecycle callbacks on a stateful session bean are more complicated than those of a stateless session bean. The difference is for two reasons: stateful session beans are tied to a particular client and stateful session beans can be passivated. Let's start by looking at the lifecycle in figure 3.9. The container follows these steps:

1. The container always creates a new bean instance using the default constructor whenever a new client session is started.
2. After the constructor has completed, the container injects the resources such as JPA contexts, data sources, and other beans.
3. An instance is stored in memory awaiting method invocations.
4. A client executes a business method through the business interface.
5. The container waits for subsequent method invocations and executes them.
6. If the client remains idle for a period of time, the container passivates the bean instance (if the container supports passivation). The bean gets serialized out to disk.

7. If the client invokes a passivated bean, it's activated (the object is read in from disk).
8. If the client doesn't invoke a method on the bean for a period of time, the bean is destroyed.
9. If the client requests removal of a bean instance and it's presently passivated, it'll be activated, and then the bean will be destroyed and reclaimed by garbage collection.

Like a stateless session bean, the stateful session bean has a number of lifecycle callback methods. We have the same callback methods available in stateless session beans, corresponding to bean creation and destruction, as well as two additional callbacks related to passivation/activation. The callbacks available on stateful session beans are as follows:

- `@PostConstruct`—This is invoked right after the default constructor has executed and resources have been injected.
- `@PrePassivate`—This is invoked before a bean is passivated; that's before the bean is serialized out to disk.
- `@PostActivate`—This is invoked after a bean has been read back into memory but before business methods are invoked from a client.
- `@PreDestroy`—This is invoked after the bean's timeout has expired or the client has invoked a method annotated with `@Remove`. The instance will be subsequently released to the garbage collector.

These callback annotations may be placed on multiple methods—you're not limited to one per class. The point of the `PrePassivate` callback is to give the bean a chance to prepare for serialization. This may include copying nonserializable variable values into serializable variables and clearing unneeded data out of those variables to save disk space. Most often the prepassivation step consists of releasing heavy-duty resources like open databases, messaging, and socket connections that can't be serialized. A well-behaved bean should ensure that heavy-duty resources are both closed and explicitly set to null before the actual passivation (serialization) takes place.

From the perspective of a bean instance, there isn't much of a difference between being passivated and being destroyed. Very often one method is annotated with both the `@PrePassivate` and `@PreDestroy` annotations. The same thing is often done for `@PostConstruct` and `@PostActivate`. In the case of both of these annotations, heavy-duty resources are being either established or reestablished. Listing 3.2 is a good example because the `java.sql.Connection` object can't be serialized and must be reinstated during activation.

One caveat: you're not responsible for reestablishing connections of injected resources. When a bean is activated, the container will reinject all of the resources. Also, any references to other stateful session beans will be reestablished. In these callback methods, you need to install or break down only the resources that you're manually managing.

In addition to these callbacks, one or more methods can be annotated with `@Remove`. This annotation informs the container that when the method exits, the stateful session bean is to be released. The client no longer needs and will no longer access the stateful session bean. If the client attempts to access the bean afterward, an exception will be thrown. As in the case of the `BidderAccountCreator`, multiple methods will most likely be annotated with `@Remove`. One method commits the contents of the workflow, whereas the other method cancels the changes. Failure to remove stateful beans will have a serious impact on server performance. The problem might not be apparent with a small number of clients, but it will become critical as more people request stateful session beans over time.

3.3.8 Using stateful session beans effectively

There's little doubt that stateful session beans provide extremely robust business logic–processing functionality if maintaining a conversational state is an essential application requirement. In addition, EJB 3 adds extended persistence contexts specifically geared toward stateful session beans (discussed in chapter 10). This significantly increases their capabilities. Nonetheless, there are a few things to watch out for while using stateful session beans. First, most of the best practices for stateless session beans apply to stateful session beans. In addition, stateful beans have the following factors that you should consider.

Choosing session data appropriately

Stateful session beans can become resource hogs and cause performance problems if they're not used properly. Because the container stores session information in memory, if you have thousands of concurrent clients for your stateful session bean, you may run out of memory or cause excessive *disk thrashing* as the container passivates and activates beans. Consequently, you have to closely examine what kind of data you're storing in the conversation state and make sure the total memory footprint for the stateful bean is as small as possible. For example, be careful of storing objects with very deep dependency graphs, byte arrays, or character arrays.

If you cluster stateful session beans, the conversational state is replicated between different instances of the EJB container. State replication uses network bandwidth. Storing a large object in the bean state may have a significant impact on the performance of your application because the container will spend an excessive amount of time replicating objects to other instances to ensure high availability. We'll discuss EJB clustering further in chapter 15.

Tuning passivation

The rules for passivation are generally implementation-specific. Improper use of passivation policies (when passivation configuration is an option) may cause performance problems. For example, the Oracle Application Server passivates bean instances when the idle time for a bean instance expires, when the maximum number of active bean instances allowed for a stateful session bean is reached, and when the threshold for JVM memory is reached. You have to check the documentation for your EJB container and appropriately set passivation rules. For example, if you set the maximum number of active instances allowed for a stateful session bean instance to 100 and you usually have 150 active clients, the container will continue to passivate and activate bean instances, thus causing performance problems.

REMOVE STATEFUL SESSION BEANS

You can go a long way toward solving potential memory problems by explicitly removing the bean instances that are no longer required rather than depending on the container to time them out. Thus, each stateful session bean should have at least one method annotated with `@Remove` and then invoke this method at the end of the bean's workflow.

Now that you have a handle on stateful session beans, let's delve into singleton beans.

3.4 Singleton session beans

Singleton session beans were added in EJB 3.1. As their name suggests, only one instance is created during the lifecycle of an enterprise application. Thus, all clients access the same bean, as shown in figure 3.10. Singleton beans solved two architectural problems that had long plagued Java EE applications: how to initialize at server startup and also have only a single instance of a bean. Solutions prior to EJB 3.1 involved the use of "startup servlets" or JCA connectors. Countless applications undoubtedly violated the Java EE specification and used static variables or nonmanaged objects. At best these were inelegant solutions, but many solutions were undoubtedly unsound.

Singleton session beans are very similar to stateless session beans. Singleton beans support the same callbacks as stateless session beans but come with some unique features, including the ability to control concurrent access to the bean as well as the ability to chain singleton bean instantiation. Chaining instantiation means that one bean can depend on another bean. As already mentioned, singleton beans can be marked to start when the application is deployed with the added semantics that application launch isn't complete until the startup beans have successfully completed. Just like stateless and stateful beans, singleton beans also support injection, security, and transaction management.

3.4.1 When to use singleton session beans

Prior to EJB 3.1 most developers of applications with a web front-end probably used a "startup servlet" to fulfill the role of an EJB singleton bean. The servlet was configured

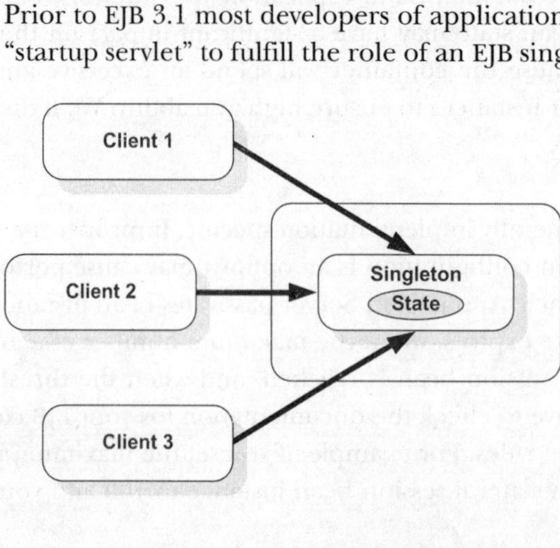

Figure 3.10 A single bean instance is created that all clients then use.

to eagerly start by the web container via settings in web.xml. The startup logic was placed in the `init` method of the servlet. Common tasks such as configuring logging, initializing database connections, and caching frequently accessed data in memory were implemented here. Cached data was then placed in the application session scope of the web application container. Special constructs were then necessary to synchronize updating of the cached data, which could be especially tricky if the application was load-balanced across multiple servers. This wasn't an optimal solution.

Singleton beans enable you to get around having to use custom solutions, such as startup servlets, POJOs with static fields, and various other derivations. Thus, you use singleton beans when you want to have a shared state that's application-global or a single chokepoint for a specific task. Let's look at these in more detail, and also, more importantly, see when you shouldn't use a singleton session bean.

STARTUP TASKS

Very often when an application is deployed, you want to perform a couple of operations before the application is accessible to external users and other systems. When the application starts up, you may want to check the database for consistency or verify that an external system is up and running. Very often there are race conditions with startup processes—although LDAP might be configured to start before GlassFish, GlassFish might successfully deploy an application before LDAP is ready to accept connections. A singleton bean marked annotated to launch on startup could repeatedly poll for LDAP and thus ensure that the application isn't accessible until all of the external services are ready to accept connections.

CENTRALIZED CLEARINGHOUSE

Although centralized chokepoints are the anathema to writing scalable software, there are times when this is necessary. Perhaps the bean is interacting with a legacy system that's limited in its connectivity. More likely you'll have situations where you want to cache a value once and control its value while making it available to multiple clients. With the concurrency control, you can enable concurrent reads while enforcing synchronization on the writes. So, for instance, you may want to cache a value in memory so that each web visit results in a database hit.

COUNTERPOINT

Singleton session beans should be used to solve problems that call for a singleton and require services of the container. For example, a singleton bean shouldn't be used to implement logic that verifies a phone number. That doesn't need to be a singleton nor does it require any services from a container. It's a utility method. If the bean isn't caching or guarding state from concurrent access or modification, then it shouldn't be a singleton session bean. Because singleton beans can be a bottleneck if used incorrectly, a large application should be weighted primarily toward stateless session beans, some stateful session beans, and a handful of singleton beans if necessary.

You should never use singletons as stateless services; rather, use stateless session beans instead. Most stateless services aren't read-only and require database interaction

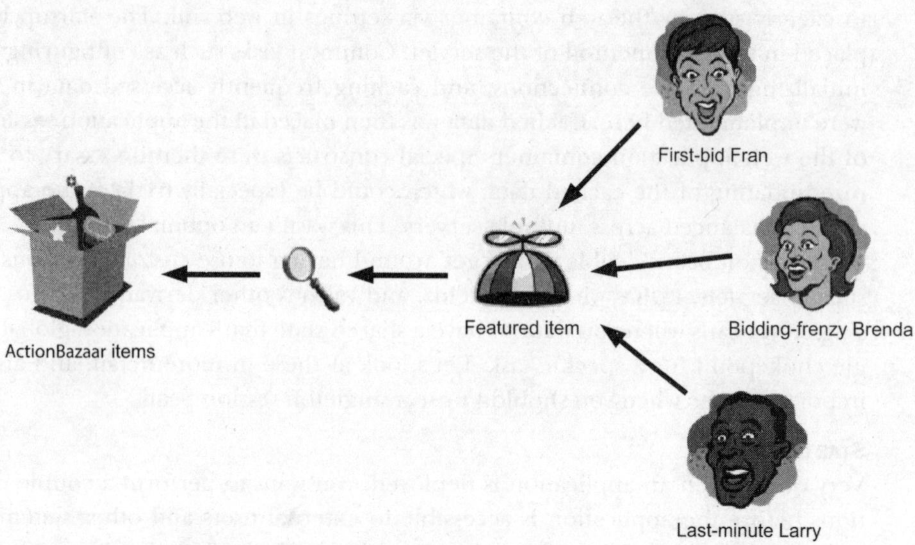

Figure 3.11 Action Bazaar's featured item is a good candidate for a singleton session bean.

through non-thread-safe APIs like the JPA entity manager. Using a thread-safe singleton in such a case doesn't scale because there's only one instance of a bean that must be shared by all concurrent clients. Now that you have a basic grasp of singleton session beans, let's dive into a code example.

3.4.2 *ActionBazaar featured item example*

Each day ActionBazaar Company spotlights a particular item or featured deal, as shown in figure 3.11. Shortly after midnight the site is refreshed to reflect the new deal. A couple of years ago the logic for the hot deal could have resided in the web tier, because there was only one interface to the application. But ActionBazaar now sports native iPhone and Android apps that use a restful web service along with a dedicated mobile website. This logic is thus pushed down into the business layer. Because this information is essentially static, it doesn't make any sense to load it each time someone visits the website. Hitting the database each time would needlessly waste database and network resources. One of the tricks to scalability is caching this frequently accessed data.

Each of these different clients gets the same spotlighted item from a singleton bean. The singleton bean caches the value on startup and then updates the value at midnight. The following listing contains the code for this bean. Not shown is the `SystemInitializer` bean that configures logging and performs other startup operations; it's included in the zip file containing the chapter's source code.

Listing 3.3 Singleton session bean example

```
@Singleton                            // 1 Marks POJO as being a singleton session bean
@Startup                              // 2 Instantiates bean on startup
@DependsOn("SystemInitializer")       // 3 Defines a bean dependency
```

```
public class DefaultFeaturedItem implements FeaturedItem {
  private Connection connection;

  @Resource(name = "jdbc/ActionBazaarDataSource")
  private DataSource dataSource;

  private Item featuredItem;

  @PostConstruct                                         <-- 4 Code to be run immediately after creation
  public void init() {
    try {
      connection = dataSource.getConnection();
    } catch (SQLException sqle) {
      sqle.printStackTrace();
    }

    loadFeaturedItem();
  }

  @Schedule(dayOfMonth="*",dayOfWeek="*",hour="0",minute="0",second="0")  <-- 5 Schedules featured item to be reloaded at midnight regularly
  private void loadFeaturedItem() {
    featuredItem = ... load item from the database ...
  }

  @Override
  public Item getFeaturedItem() {
    return featuredItem;
  }
}
...
@Remote
public interface FeaturedItem {
  public Item getFeaturedItem();
}
```

The @Singleton annotation marks this POJO as being a singleton bean ❶. It implements the FeaturedItem business interface. The @Startup annotation informs the container that the bean should be eagerly created on startup ❷. But although the bean should be eagerly created, it shouldn't be instantiated until the SystemInitializer singleton bean has been created ❸. Once the SystemInitializer is created, then DefaultFeaturedItem is instantiated, resource injection is performed, and the init method is called per the @PostConstruct annotation ❹. An EJB timer is created and will run once every day at midnight to load the featured item ❺. The EJB timer will be covered in chapter 5—it isn't specific to singleton beans.

As you can see, singleton session beans are very similar to stateless session beans. The one difference is that only one instance is created and that one instance serves all clients. Let's take a closer look at the @Singleton annotation.

3.4.3 Using the @Singleton annotation

The @Singleton annotation marks the DefaultFeaturedItem POJO as a singleton session bean. Other than marking a POJO to make the container aware of its purpose, the annotation doesn't do much. The specification of the @Singleton annotation is as follows:

```
@Target(value = {ElementType.TYPE})
@Retention(value = RetentionPolicy.RUNTIME)
public @interface Stateless {
    public String name() default "";
    public String mappedName() default "";
    public String description() default "";
}
```

The definition of this annotation is no different from stateless and stateful session beans. The name parameter specifies the name of the bean. Containers use this parameter to bind the EJB to the global JNDI tree. The name field is optional and will default to the simplified name of the bean if not specified. The mappedName field is a vendor-specific name that you can assign to your EJBs; some containers, such as GlassFish, use this name to assign the global JNDI name for the EJB. The description is for documenting the bean for use by tools and containers.

3.4.4 Singleton bean concurrency control

Because multiple consumers access singleton beans at the same time, concurrency is of paramount performance. Singleton concurrency support comes in two flavors: container-managed concurrency and bean-managed concurrency. The default setting if none is specified is container-managed concurrency. With container-managed concurrency, the container synchronizes method calls. Annotations are provided so that you can mark methods as either read or write and also specify time-out for methods that may block. With bean-managed concurrency, it's up to you to use Java's concurrency features such as the synchronized and volatile primitives or the java.util.concurrent API to manage concurrent access and ensure correctness.

An annotation is used to specify which concurrency management approach is being used. If no annotation is provided, container-managed concurrency is assumed. This was the case in listing 3.3. The annotation/parameter combinations are as follows for each concurrency management method:

- @ConcurrencyManagement(ConcurrencyManagementType.BEAN)—Bean concurrency management
- @ConcurrencyManagement(ConcurrencyManagementType.CONTAINER)—Container concurrency management

The @ConcurrencyManagement annotation is to be placed on the bean class, not the business interface:

```
@Target(value = {ElementType.TYPE})
@Retention(value = RetentionPolicy.RUNTIME)
  public @interface ConcurrencyManagement {
  public ConcurrencyManagementType value() default
      ConcurrencyManagementType.CONTAINER;
}
```

CONTAINER-MANAGED CONCURRENCY

Container-managed concurrency is the default setting for singleton session beans. By default, all bean methods are serialized via write locks. In the case of the `DefaultFeaturedItem` in listing 3.3, only one thread may execute the `getFeaturedItem` method at a time. This is obviously not what you want: if a thousand clients are hitting the site at the same time, making each one of them wait to see the featured item isn't a good idea for performance, not to mention sales. Two annotation combinations are provided by the EJB specification, enabling you to tell the container what type of locking behavior you really want:

- `@Lock(LockType.READ)`—This method can be accessed concurrently while no one holds a write lock on the bean.
- `@Lock(LockType.WRITE)`—Place a write lock on the bean when the method is invoked so that only the current thread gets access.

If you don't specify either, `@Lock(LockType.WRITE)` is essentially assumed. These annotations may be placed on methods either in the business interface or on the bean itself. The XML deployment file for the bean can override the annotations placed on the code, although it's probably not a good idea to override concurrency handling at deployment. Because a singleton method call potentially locks out callers, a mechanism is provided to time out the callers so that they don't block forever. If the time-out is exceeded, a `javax.ejb.ConcurrentAccessTimeoutException` is thrown. This is a runtime exception, meaning that a caller doesn't have to catch it. The `@AccessTimeout` annotation is used to specify lock time-outs. The annotation is defined as follows:

```
@Target(value = {ElementType.METHOD, ElementType.TYPE})
@Retention(value = RetentionPolicy.RUNTIME)
public @interface AccessTimeout {
  public long value();
  public TimeUnit unit() default TimeUnit.MILLISECONDS;
}
```

As you can see from this definition, you specify the time duration (value) and a time unit. The time unit defaults to milliseconds (1 second = 1,000 milliseconds). The available time units are these:

- Nanoseconds
- Microseconds
- Milliseconds
- Seconds
- Minutes
- Hours
- Days

Most applications will probably use either milliseconds, seconds, or, at the upper extreme, minutes. The timer on the computer system, especially Windows, may not be able to resolve nanoseconds, and hours and days are a little extreme. Let's update your business interface for the `DefaultFeaturedItem` to enable concurrent access and time-out after one minute:

```
public interface FeaturedItem {
  @Lock(LockType.READ)
  @AccessTimeout(value=1,unit=TimeUnit.MINUTES)
  public Item getFeaturedItem();
}
```

BEAN-MANAGED CONCURRENCY

Bean-managed concurrency puts you completely in charge of managing the concurrency of your singleton bean. To do this, you use the Java concurrency primitives, such as synchronized, volatile, wait, notify, and so on, or Doug Lea's fabled `java.util.concurrent` API. If you decide to go this route, you should make sure that you're very familiar with concurrent programming and with the concurrency constructs in Java (there are many good books on the topic). Troubleshooting concurrency problems is a challenge, but troubleshooting concurrency issues in a container is even more challenging. In the real world, you should opt for bean-managed concurrency only if you need more complex or finer-grained concurrency than what container-managed concurrency offers, which is a pretty rare case for most enterprise applications. The following listing synchronizes access on the `DefaultFeaturedItem` so that only one thread may access the bean at a time. Obviously this is very dangerous for performance reasons and not something you'll likely want to do in a real application.

Listing 3.4 Bean-managed concurrency

```
@Singleton
@Startup
@DependsOn("SystemInitializer")
@ConcurrencyManagement(ConcurrencyManagementType.BEAN)          <-- Bean will manage its concurrency
public class DefaultFeaturedItem implements FeaturedItem {
  private Connection connection;

  @Resource(name = "jdbc/ActionBazaarDataSource")
  private DataSource dataSource;

  private Item featuredItem;

  @PostConstruct
  private synchronized void init() {          <-- Limit access to one thread at a time
    try {
     connection = dataSource.getConnection();
    } catch (SQLException sqle) {
      sqle.printStackTrace();
    }
    loadFeaturedItem();
  }

  @Schedule(dayOfMonth="*",dayOfWeek="*",hour="0",minute="0",second="0")
  private synchronized Item loadFeaturedItem() {
    ...
  }
```

```
  @Override
  public synchronized Item getFeaturedItem() {
    return featuredItem;
  }
}
```

Now that you have a grasp of concurrent programming with singleton beans, let's briefly look at singleton session bean business interfaces.

3.4.5 Bean business interface

Singleton session beans have the same business interface capabilities as stateless session beans. You can have remote, local, and web service (both SOAP and REST) business interfaces. Each of these three methods of accessing a singleton session bean is denoted using the annotations `@Local`, `@Remote`, and `@WebService`, respectively. All three of these interfaces are covered in section 3.2.5.

The only real difference between singleton and stateless session bean business interfaces is that you can annotate a singleton session bean interface's methods with the following annotations:

- `@Lock(LockType.READ)`
- `@Lock(LockType.WRITE)`
- `@AccessTimeout`

All three of these annotations have an effect only if container-managed concurrency is being used; otherwise they have no effect. It's possible that the web service interface specifies different concurrency behavior than the local interface (although this is unlikely). As is the case with both stateless and stateful session beans, it isn't necessary to provide a local interface.

3.4.6 Lifecycle callbacks

The lifecycle of singleton session beans is the simplest of all of the beans. Once they're instantiated, they're not destroyed until the application terminates. Complexity in their lifecycle comes into play only if there are dependencies between beans. During application deployment, the container iterates over the singleton beans checking for dependencies. We'll discuss dependency specification in a minute. In addition, a bean can also be marked to auto-instantiate on application deployment. This enables business logic to auto-execute when an application is started. Let's start by looking at the lifecycle in figure 3.12:

1. The container starts by creating a new instance of the singleton bean. The bean may be instantiated on startup (`@Startup`) or as a result of another bean being instantiated (`@DependsOn`). Normally, beans are instantiated lazily as they're first accessed.
2. After the constructor has completed, the container injects the resources such as JPA contexts, data sources, and other beans.

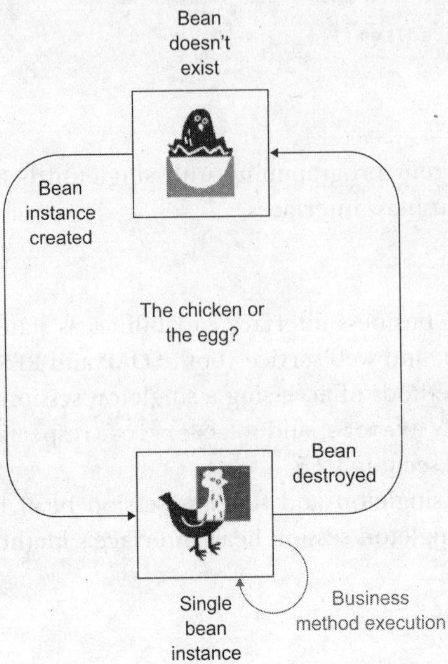

Figure 3.12 Lifecycle of singleton session beans

3. The @PostConstruct annotated method is invoked. The bean isn't accessible until it completes successfully.
4. The instance is stored in memory awaiting method invocations.
5. The client executes a business method through the business interface.
6. The container is informed that it must shut down.
7. The @PreDestroy callback is invoked prior to the application terminating.

The singleton session bean has the same lifecycle callbacks as the stateless session bean. These callbacks enable you to run code after resources have been injected but before the class receives method invocations and before the bean is handed off to garbage collection. The callbacks are as follows:

- `@PostConstruct`—This is invoked right after the default constructor has executed and resources have been injected.
- `@PreDestroy`—This is invoked before the bean is destroyed. The instance will subsequently be released to the garbage collector.

The most important thing to remember about these callbacks is that they're invoked once at most. A singleton bean, as its name implies, is instantiated only once and it's destroyed only once.

A singleton bean may be annotated with a `@DependsOn` annotation. This annotation enables a bean to depend on another bean. When a bean is instantiated, any of its dependencies will also be instantiated. The expectation is that when a bean depends on another bean, that other bean will have done something to set the state of the application. The following is the definition of the `@DependsOn` annotation:

```
@Target(value = {ElementType.TYPE})
@Retention(value = RetentionPolicy.RUNTIME)
public @interface DependsOn {
  public String[] value();
}
```

This annotation is placed on the bean class and takes one or more names of singleton session beans that must be instantiated first. The order of the dependencies in the list isn't maintained—this means that if a bean is annotated with `@DependsOn(A,B)`, you can't depend on `A` being instantiated before `B`. `B` should have its own `@DependsOn` annotation and specify that it expects `A` to be instantiated. The `@DependsOn` annotation ties nicely into the `@Startup` annotation.

3.4.7 @Startup annotation

One of the key features of singleton session beans is the ability to have them auto-start when the application is deployed. To mark a singleton session bean as being auto-instantiated, all you need to do is add the `@Startup` annotation to the bean. The annotation is defined as follows:

```
@Target(value = {ElementType.TYPE})
@Retention(value = RetentionPolicy.RUNTIME)
  public @interface Startup {
}
```

The annotation itself has no parameters. This is merely a marker that the container examines. When the container goes to instantiate a singleton bean with this annotation, it first instantiates any singleton beans on which the bean depends. There are some ramifications to this that we discuss in the next section.

3.4.8 Using stateful singleton session beans effectively

Stateful singleton session beans are an incredibly useful feature of EJB 3.1. Before you run off and put them to use, there are some important things to remember about them. First, because there's only one instance, they can be a performance bottleneck if they're used incorrectly. Second, using container-managed concurrency doesn't absolve you from configuring the concurrency behavior. Just as garbage collection doesn't free you from managing memory (RAM isn't limitless), container-managed concurrency isn't a magical solution to a hard problem. Third, there are some caveats to creating a startup singleton. Finally, exception handling with singleton beans is a bit different.

CHOOSING CORRECT CONCURRENCY TYPE

When you create a new singleton bean, one of the most important decisions is choosing the correct concurrency type for your bean. For the vast majority of beans, container-managed concurrency makes the most sense. With container-managed concurrency, you're delegating synchronization to the container. The container gives you the option of marking methods either `@Lock(LockType.READ)` or `@Lock(LockType.WRITE)`. A lock type of `READ` enables multiple threads to access the bean concurrently, whereas the

`WRITE` lock grants exclusive access. If you go with the bean-managed approach, it's up to you to manage concurrent access via `synchronized`, `volatile`, and other Java constructs. This approach makes sense if you require finer-grained locking than simply read–write locks. Alternatively, if you're storing and retrieving data from a concurrent `HashMap`, you won't need the container concurrency features.

CONFIGURING CONTAINER-MANAGED CONCURRENCY

One of the dangers with container-managed concurrency is that the container by default uses the write lock if you don't specify otherwise. The write lock limits access to the class to only one method at a time. Each business method in the class is effectively marked with the synchronized keyword. This will adversely affect performance of the singleton—only one client will be serviced at a time. If a request takes one second to service, then 1,000 clients will result in a total wait of about 17 minutes. The wait times per client will vary—some will have one second whereas others might wait for a bit longer. A singleton thus needs to be divided into write (`@Lock(LockType.WRITE)`) and read (`@Lock(LockType.READ)`) methods. The write method updates data and thus requires the exclusive lock. The read method doesn't require an exclusive lock and thus multiple clients can concurrently access the data. If a write method may take a long time, it should be annotated `@AccessTimeout` if you don't want the code waiting for an indeterminate amount of time. This annotation can also be used to enforce a certain level of service—if the method is taking too long, an exception raising the method as a problem can go a long way toward resolving performance issues.

MANAGING STARTUP SINGLETONS

Startup singletons can be used to auto-run business logic on application startup and cache data for the application. A singleton class marked with the startup annotation will be instantiated during application deployment. It must be stressed that this is during application deployment. Containers, such as GlassFish, will throw a `java.lang.IllegalAccessException` if your bean tries to access a stateless/stateful session bean from the `@PostConstruct` method. So other beans may not be available yet, but you'll have access to JPA and can manipulate the database. If multiple startup beans are used, the `@DependsOn` annotation should be used to control the startup sequence. Without the `@DependsOn` annotation, there's no guarantee that the singleton will be instantiated—a changing random order should be assumed. It's also important that you don't create circular dependencies of startup singletons.

HANDLING EXCEPTIONS

Exceptions generated from a singleton bean are treated differently than exceptions from a stateless or stateful session bean. An exception thrown from the `PostConstruct` method of a singleton causes the instance to be discarded. If the exception is thrown from the `PostConstruct` method of a startup bean, the application server may choose not to deploy the application. An exception thrown by a business method doesn't result in the bean being discarded—the bean will be discarded only when the application terminates. What this means is that your application logic should take this into account. Also, because a singleton bean is in existence for the entire life of the application, you might have to take care when dealing with external resources. If the application is left running for weeks, you must take care to ensure that there's appropriate error handling and recovery code in place. If the bean opens up a socket connection to another system, at some point that socket connection will be closed—watch out for time-outs.

3.5 Asynchronous session beans

New to EJB 3.1 is support for asynchronous beans with the `@Asynchronous` annotation. This isn't a new type of session bean but rather a new functionality that you can use with stateless, stateful, and singleton session beans. This new functionality enables methods invoked by the client on methods contained in the business interface to be executed asynchronously on a separate thread. Prior to this, the only avenue for parallelization in Java EE was via MDBs. Using and coordinating activities between MDBs and stateless/stateful session beans is a pretty heavyweight solution that for simple tasks is overkill and adds unnecessary complexity.

The title *asynchronous session beans* is somewhat of a misnomer. The beans aren't asynchronous in themselves; rather, their methods are asynchronous. With the `@Asynchronous` annotation, a method or an entire class can be marked as being asynchronous. When an asynchronous method or method on an asynchronous class is invoked, the container spawns a separate thread for execution.

3.5.1 Basics of asynchronous invocation

An asynchronous method is just like any other business method on a bean class—it can return a value, throw exceptions, and accept parameters. The return type for an asynchronous method is either `void` or `java.util.concurrent.Future<V>`. This enables two usage patterns: fire and forget (using `void`) or fire and check back later for an answer (`Future<V>`). Only methods with a declared return type of `Future<V>` can declare an exception. If an exception is thrown by the asynchronous method, the exception will be caught and rethrown when `get()` is called on the `Future` object. The original exception will be wrapped in an `ExecutionException`. Runtime exceptions thrown by an asynchronous method with no return type will be lost and the original caller will not be notified.

One important caveat of asynchronous method invocation is that transactions aren't propagated to the asynchronous method—a new transaction will be started for the asynchronous method. But unlike transactions, the security principle will be propagated. We'll cover transactions and security in great detail in chapter 6.

When an asynchronous method is invoked, the call returns to the client before the method is invoked on the bean. If no value is returned from the method (the return type is `void`), the operation is a fire-and-forget task from the perspective of the client. If you might need the result of asynchronous processing or might have to potentially cancel the operation, a `Future` object should be returned by the business method. In both circumstances, the execution proceeds on a separate thread. This is incredibly powerful; the next section will explain the ground rules for when and where you should add asynchronous processing to an application.

3.5.2 When to use asynchronous session beans

Asynchronous session beans should be used only under two circumstances:

- You have a long-running operation that you want to start and then continue something else, regardless of what happens with this operation.
- You have a long-running operation for which you want to start and then check back later to see what the result is after doing something. You may also want to cancel this operation.

Prior to EJB 3.1, the only way to do either of these was to multithread your client. Because the container controlled concurrency, there was no way to notify a bean that a long-running operation should be cancelled. Remember, the container controls concurrency, so each method was synchronized on the bean, meaning that only one thread could invoke a method at a time. EJB 3.1 is thus a point release with additional major functionality.

Asynchronous session beans are intended to be lightweight, so they don't provide any reliability guarantees. This means that if a container crashes while an asynchronous method is getting executed, the method won't recover. Asynchronous beans are also not loosely coupled, which means that a client holds a direct reference to the asynchronously invoked session bean. If you require reliability and loose coupling and not just asynchronous processing, you should consider message-driven beans.

3.5.3 ProcessOrder bean example

To put asynchronous methods in context, let's return to the ActionBazaar application. There are two order-processing tasks that are candidates for parallelization: sending out the confirmation email and debiting the credit card. Sending out the email is a fire-and-forget task; therefore, there's no return value. Processing the credit card, on the other hand, may take a while, but you need to know that the card was debited before continuing. If there's an error, you want to stop the process and immediately notify the bidder that the transaction couldn't be completed. Both of these asynchronous tasks started by the `ProcessOrder` stateless session bean are shown in the next listing.

Listing 3.5 `ProcessOrder`

```
@Stateless(name = "processOrder")
public class OrderService {

    private String CONFIRM_EMAIL = "actionbazaar/email/confirmation.xhtml";

    @EJB
    private EmailService emailService;
```

```
    @EJB
    private BillingService billingService;

    public void processOrder(Order order) {
        String content;
        try {
            URL resource = OrderService.class.getResource(CONFIRM_EMAIL);
            content =  resource.getContent().toString();
            emailService.sendEmail(order.getEmailAddress(),     <-- Asynchronously send confirmation email
                "Winning Bid Confirmation",content);
Asynchronously debit credit card -->  Future<Boolean> success =
              billingService.debitCreditCard(order);
              // Perform other tasks such as updating the database
              if(!success.get()) {
                  // handle failure
              }
        } catch (IOException ex). {
            Logger.getLogger(OrderService.class.getName()).log(Level.SEVERE,
     null, ex);
        }
    }
}
```

The `EmailService` class will handle sending out confirmation emails. The confirmation email includes an order number for tracking the shipping, as well as information about the payment method used and a summary of the item to be shipped. Sending out an email may take some time because a connection with the mail server must be established and domain names and addresses resolved. The code for this class is shown in the following listing.

Listing 3.6 Asynchronous email notification

```
@Stateless(name = "emailService")
public class EmailService {

    Logger logger = Logger.getLogger(AuthenticateBean.class.getName());

    @Resource(name="config/emailSender")
    private String emailSender;

    @Resource(name = "mail/notification")
    private Session session;
                                            Asynchronous annotation signals container to run method in another thread
    @Asynchronous                       <--
    public void sendEmail(String emailAddress, String subject,   <-- No return parameters—fire and forget
      String htmlMessage) {
        try {
            MimeMessage message = new MimeMessage(session);
            message.setFrom(new InternetAddress(emailSender));
            InternetAddress[] toAddress = new InternetAddress[] {
                new InternetAddress(emailAddress)};
            message.setRecipients(Message.RecipientType.TO, toAddress);
            message.setSubject(subject);
            message.setContent(createHtmlMessage(htmlMessage));
            Transport.send(message);
        } catch (Throwable t) {
```

```
            logger.log(Level.SEVERE, null,t);
        }
    }
    ...
}
```

The BillingService, shown in listing 3.7, debits the credit card. The asynchronous annotation on the class means that all public methods will be executed on a separate thread. The SessionContext is injected so that calls to success.cancel(true) will be honored. Chapter 5 will cover SessionContext in more depth.

Listing 3.7 BillingService

```
@Stateless(name="billingService")
@Asynchronous                                          <-- Marks class as asynchronous
public class BillingService {

    @Resource
    private SessionContext sessionContext;             <-- Injects SessionContext for honoring cancel

    public Future<Boolean> debitCreditCard(Order order) {   <-- Returns a value wrapped in Future<Boolean>
        boolean processed = false;
        if(sessionContext.wasCancelCalled()) {         <-- Checks to see if cancelled
            return null;
        }
        // Debit the credit card
        return new AsyncResult<Boolean>(processed);    <-- Wraps result in convenience implementation of Future
    }
}
```

Now that you have a handle on a simple example, let's look at the annotation and then the Future interface.

3.5.4 Using the @Asynchronous annotation

The @Asynchronous annotation is one of the simplest annotations covered in this chapter. It has no parameters and can be placed either on the class or on individual methods. If it's placed on the class, all of the methods within the class are invoked asynchronously. Placing the annotation on individual methods enables fine-grained control over which methods are invoked asynchronously. This annotation can be used with any of the bean types described in this chapter: stateless, stateful, and singleton. The annotation is defined as follows:

```
@Target(value = {ElementType.METHOD, ElementType.TYPE})
@Retention(value = RetentionPolicy.RUNTIME)
public @interface Asynchronous {
}
```

The use of this annotation on a class was demonstrated in listing 3.5 and on individual methods in listing 3.6. The annotation is the simple part; things start to get complicated when we look at the Future interface.

3.5.5 Using the Future interface

Unless your method is a fire and forget, you'll probably be interested in the results of the method call. To work with results from an asynchronous method, you must return an object implementing the `java.util.concurrent.Future` interface. The `Future` interface has the following methods:

- `boolean cancel(boolean mayInterruptIfRunning)`—This cancels the operation.
- `V get()`—This returns the value and blocks until the result is available.
- `V get(long timeout, TimeUnit unit)`—This returns the result or null if the result isn't available in the specified time limit.
- `boolean isCancelled()`—This returns true if this task was cancelled.
- `boolean isDone()`—This returns true if the task has completed.
- With the `Future` interface you can do the following tasks:
  - Cancel the operation.
  - Retrieve the value of the computation, optionally with a time-out if you don't want to wait.
  - Check to see if the operation has either been cancelled or has completed.

The `javax.ejb.AsyncResult` class was added in Java EE 6 as a convenience class for wrapping the result to be returned so that you don't have to provide your own implementation of `Future`. An asynchronous method creates an instance of `AsyncResult` and passes in the "payload" that will be returned to the caller, as you can see in listing 3.7. While the bean is performing the long-running operation, it can find out if the task has been cancelled via the `Future` interface by calling the static `SessionContext.wasCancelCalled()` method. If the operation has been cancelled, the method should bail at this point, because the result of the operation will be ignored. The `AsyncResult` class makes passing back asynchronous data easy.

3.5.6 Using asynchronous session beans effectively

The `@Asynchronous` annotation is very powerful and potentially dangerous. Using this annotation too liberally will have a detrimental impact on performance. Threads have a large resource footprint and thus there's an upper limit to the number of threads. Either the limit may be operating system-dependent or the application container may limit the number of threads via a thread pool. In either case, hitting the upper limit has negative consequences. Thus, this functionality should be used where it's truly needed. Pay special attention to thread leaks—if threads fail to terminate, they may loiter until the application terminates. There are two more important considerations with asynchronous methods: supporting cancel and handling exceptions.

SUPPORTING CANCEL

Asynchronous tasks that return results should support the cancel operation. Supporting cancel enables clients to terminate the operation at their discretion. This is especially important if the operation is long running. Within an asynchronous bean method, the `wasCancelCalled()` method on the `SessionContext` will report if the client, via the `Future` object, has requested the operation to be terminated. This method should be checked within a loop and before blocking operations are called.

HANDLING EXCEPTIONS

If an asynchronous task doesn't return a `Future` instance to a client, and the client never calls `get()` on the `Future` object, the client will never know if an asynchronous method failed. This approach should only be taken if the asynchronous operation is optional. Optional means that it doesn't matter if the method runs, succeeds, or fails. In a situation where it's necessary to know if the operation succeeded or if it failed, a `Future` object should be returned and the client code should check it and act upon the error. Remember, if you're using the fire-and-forget approach, the only way to find out if an asynchronous method failed is to look at the log file for the application server.

3.6 Summary

In this chapter we examined the various session bean types and how stateless session beans and stateful session beans differ. We also looked at singleton beans and the new asynchronous method support added in EJB 3.1. As you learned, stateless session beans have a simple lifecycle and can be pooled. Stateful beans require instances for each client, and for that reason they can have a significant impact on resource consumption. In addition, passivation and activation of stateful session beans can impact performance if they're used inappropriately. With singleton beans, only one instance is created. You have the option of either letting the container manage the concurrency or manually managing currency (bean-managed concurrency). Even with container-managed concurrency, you can pass hints to the container informing it whether a method is doing a read or a write; the default assumption is a write. With asynchronous session beans, you learned how you could annotate methods to cause them to be spawned into a separate thread. Using the `Future` interface you can defer retrieving resources until later. Asynchronous session beans aren't the fourth type but merely an annotation that you can use with stateless, stateful, and singleton session beans.

You learned about the different types of business interfaces. Stateless session beans support local, remote, and web services interfaces. Web services can be exposed via JAX-RPC (legacy), JAX-WS (SOAP), and JAX-RS (REST). We showed you that dependency injection simplifies the use of EJB and saves you from having to perform complex JNDI lookups.

At this point you know all of the basic pieces necessary to build the business logic portion of your application using stateless, stateful, and singleton beans. In the next chapter we'll discuss how you can build messaging applications with message-driven beans.

Messaging and developing MDBs

This chapter covers

- The basics of message-driven beans (MDBs)
- Sending and receiving messages
- `@JMSConnectionFactory` annotation
- `JMSContext`, `JMSConsumer`, and `JMSProducer` classes

In this chapter we'll take a closer look at developing message-driven beans (MDBs). We'll provide you with an overview of these powerful concepts and show in the context of the ActionBazaar application how they can be used to solve real-world problems. First, we'll introduce the fundamental concepts of messaging and then you'll explore the basics of the Java Messaging Service (JMS) by creating a message producer. We'll then take a look at MDBs and how EJB 3 simplifies the task of building message consumers.

It's important that you gain an understanding of messaging and JMS before diving into MDB for two reasons. First, most MDBs you'll see are really souped-up JMS message consumers implementing JMS interfaces (such as `javax.jms.MessageListener`) and using JMS APIs (such as `javax.jms.Message`). Second, for most solutions with MDB, your messaging will involve more than just processing incoming messages.

If you're comfortable with messaging and JMS, feel free to skip to the sections covering MDBs. But it's always good to reinforce what you know from time to time.

4.1 Messaging concepts

When we talk about messaging in the Java EE context, what we really mean is the process of sending loosely coupled, asynchronous messages that are transferred in a reliable fashion. Most communication between components—for example, between stateless session beans—is synchronous and tightly coupled. The caller directly invokes a method on the recipient bean and waits for the method to finish. Both ends must be present for the communication to be successful. Messaging is different in that the sender doesn't know when the message is received and doesn't even directly control who processes the message. In addition, Java EE messaging is reliable in the sense that you can be guaranteed that the message will not be lost en route from the sender to the receiver.

As an analogy, consider the process of contacting someone via phone. If the person answers the call, then it's synchronous communication. On the other hand, if the person doesn't answer the phone and you leave a voicemail message, it's an asynchronous communication. The message is stored so that the recipient can listen to it at their convenience. You don't know when the person will get the message or even who will initially check the message. The voicemail system can be thought of as a message-oriented middleware (MOM) service. It acts as a middleman between the message sender and receiver so that both don't have to be present simultaneously. In this section, we'll briefly introduce MOM, show how messaging is used in the ActionBazaar application, and examine three messaging models.

4.1.1 Message-oriented middleware

MOM is software that sends and receives messages reliably between disparate systems. It's used primarily to integrate different systems, often legacy systems. For example, MOM infrastructure software has been used to route messages from a web front end to a system written in COBOL and running on a mainframe. When a message is sent, the MOM software stores the message in a location specified by the sender and acknowledges the receipt. The message sender is called a *producer*, and the destination location where the message is stored is called a *destination*. At a later point in time, any software component interested in messages at that particular destination can retrieve the unread messages. The software components receiving the messages are called the *consumers*. Figure 4.1 depicts the various components of MOM.

MOM systems and vendors aren't a new concept—they've been around since the 1980s. MOMs evolved as a way to simplify system integration and reduce the amount of custom integration code. Systems written today must still interact with other systems—both legacy and new. There are many MOM products on the market today. All Java EE servers come with a messaging system.

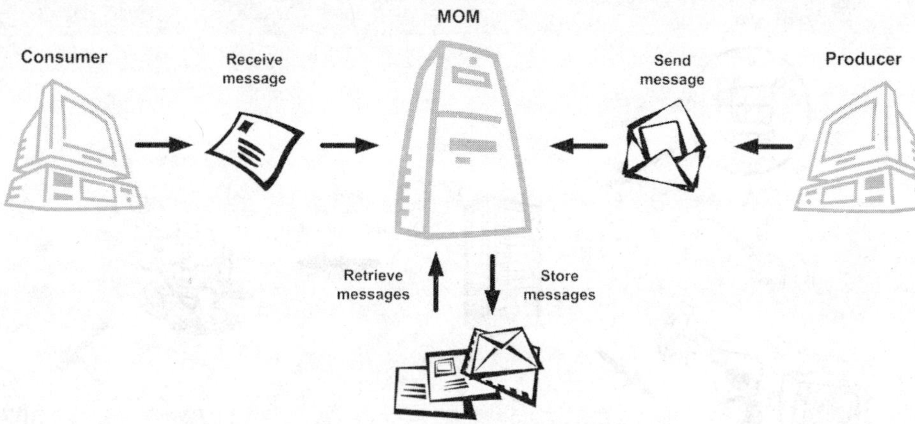

Figure 4.1 Basic MOM flow. When the producer sends a message to the middleware, it's stored immediately and later collected by the consumer.

To flesh out messaging concepts a bit more, let's explore a problem in the ActionBazaar application. You'll continue working on this problem as we progress through the rest of the chapter.

4.1.2 Messaging in ActionBazaar

ActionBazaar isn't a self-contained, end-to-end system. It excels at managing and tracking auctions. But other business functions like accounting and shipping are handled by separate dedicated systems provided by specialized vendors. ActionBazaar chooses to purchase and integrate with these vendor services instead of reinventing the services in-house. For example, ActionBazaar uses the Turtle Shipping Company to deliver items to winning bidders. When a bidder wins an auction, a shipment request is sent to Turtle's system via a business-to-business (B2B) connection. Initially, all external vendor systems were integrated in a synchronous fashion. Figure 4.2 shows how this integration looked and what the problems with it were.

In the synchronous communication model, the user waited for the shipment request submission to finish processing before an order was completed. The problem was that the B2B connection was often slow or unreliable. In addition, Turtle's systems were much slower and overloaded compared to ActionBazaar's servers. And sometimes Turtle's systems were dependent on other third-party systems. As you can imagine, this resulted in some unhappy customers!

The answer was to integrate all external vendor systems through asynchronous messaging. Figure 4.3 shows how this works. In this model, a MOM is put between ActionBazaar's and Turtle's systems. A message containing the shipment request is sent to the MOM asynchronously. This message is stored by the MOM until Turtle's system receives and processes the request at its own pace. In the meantime, the user is sent a confirmation of the order as soon as a message is successfully sent to the MOM, which is typically an instantaneous process.

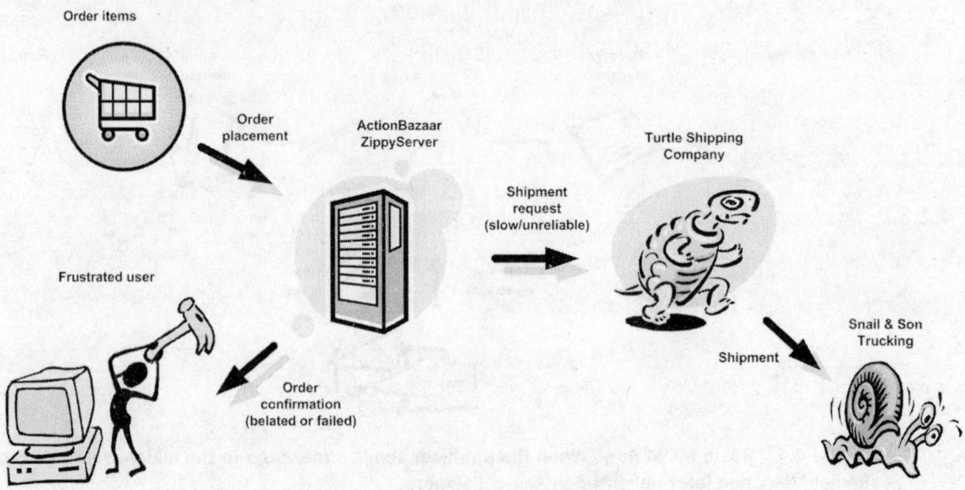

Figure 4.2 ActionBazaar ordering before MOM was introduced

In this situation, messaging is improving reliability by decoupling the order confirmation process from the actual processing of the shipping request. The reliability stems from the fact that ActionBazaar's and Turtle's servers don't have to be up and running at the same time. Also, the servers aren't expected to function at the same processing rate. Because MOM systems persist messages and will resend messages if a connection is lost midstream, shipping requests aren't lost if Turtle's servers suddenly become unreachable. In addition, MOM systems ensure additional reliability by incorporating transactions and acknowledgments for both message delivery and receipt.

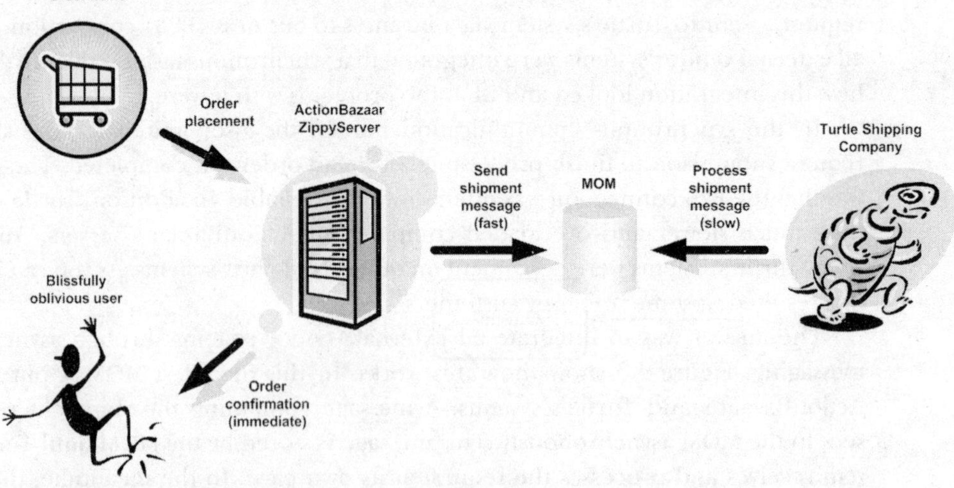

Figure 4.3 ActionBazaar ordering after MOM was introduced. Messaging enables both fast customer response times and reliable processing.

Looking toward future expansion, the decoupling achieved through messaging is useful in other ways as well. For example, other shipping providers could connect to ActionBazaar's MOM server instead of or in addition to Turtle. This reduces ActionBazaar's dependency on a single shipping company and orders can be processed by whatever shipping company is available at the time.

4.1.3 Messaging models

A *messaging model* is a pattern defining how senders and consumers exchange messages. JMS uses two standard models: point-to-point (PTP) and publish–subscribe. An application can use either one or both of these models—it all depends on how messages will be exchanged. We'll discuss each of these messaging models here.

POINT-TO-POINT

In the PTP scheme, a single message travels from a single producer (point A) to a single consumer (point B). There may be multiple producers and consumers, but only one consumer will process a given message. PTP message destinations are called *queues.* Producers write to the queue and consumers read from the queue. PTP doesn't guarantee that messages are delivered in any particular order—the term *queue* is more symbolic than anything else. If more than one potential consumer exists for a message, a random consumer is chosen, as shown in figure 4.4.

The classic message-in-a-bottle story is a good analogy for PTP messaging. The message in a bottle is set afloat by a lonely castaway (the producer). The ocean (the queue) carries the message to an anonymous beach dweller (the consumer). The message can be "found" only once.

The ActionBazaar shipping request forwarding was implemented using the PTP model. A request to ship a winning bid should be processed by only one shipper.

PUBLISH–SUBSCRIBE

Publish–subscribe (pub–sub) messaging is similar to a traditional home-delivered newspaper service. As shown in figure 4.5, a single producer generates a message

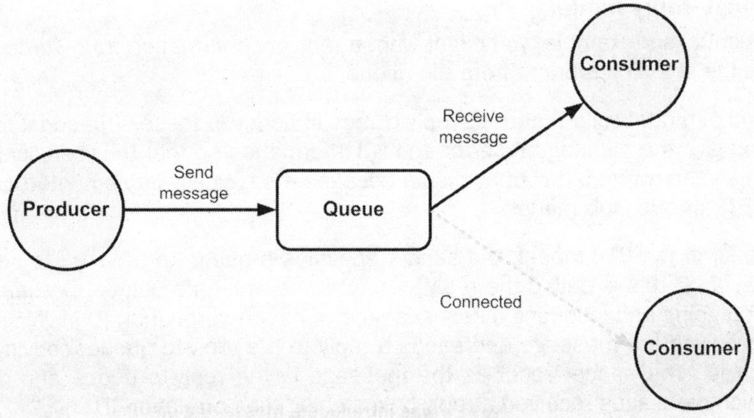

Figure 4.4 PTP messaging model with one producer and two consumers

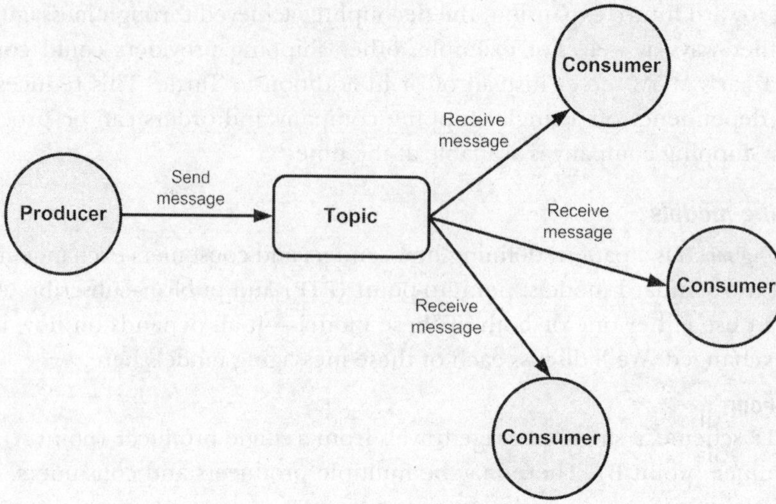

Figure 4.5 The pub–sub messaging model with one producer and three consumers. Each topic subscriber receives a copy of the message.

that's received by any number of consumers who happen to be connected to the destination at the time. The message destination in this model is called a *topic* and a consumer is called a *subscriber*. Pub–sub messaging works particularly well in broadcasting information across systems. For example, it could be used to broadcast a system maintenance notification several hours before an outage to all premium sellers whose systems are directly integrated with ActionBazaar and who are listening at the moment.

At this point, you have a basic understanding of messaging and are perhaps eager to see some code. In the next section we'll introduce JMS and you'll write some producer code that will be used by the ActionBazaar application to send the shipping messages.

The request–reply model

In the ActionBazaar example, you might want a receipt confirmation from Turtle once they have the shipping request from the queue.

A third kind of model called request–reply comes in handy in these situations. In this model, you give the message receiver enough information so that they can "call you back." This is known as an overlay model because it's typically implemented on top of either PTP or pub–sub models.

For example, in the PTP model, the sender specifies a queue to be used to send a reply to (in JMS, this is called the reply-to queue), as well as a unique ID shared by both the outgoing and incoming messages (known as the correlation ID in JMS). The receiver receives the message and sends a reply to the reply-to queue, copying the correlation ID. The sender receives the message in the reply-to queue and determines which messages received a reply by matching the correlation ID.

4.2 Introducing JMS

In this section we provide a brief overview of the JMS API by building a basic message producer. JMS is a deceptively small API to a very powerful technology. The JMS API is to messaging what the Java Database Connectivity (JDBC) API is to database access. JMS provides a standard way of accessing MOM in Java and is therefore an alternative to using product-specific APIs.

The easiest way to learn JMS is by looking at some code. We're going to explore JMS by developing the ActionBazaar code that sends out the shipping request. As we described in section 4.1.2, when a user places an order, a shipping request is sent to a queue shared between ActionBazaar and Turtle. The code in listing 4.1 sends the message out and could be part of a method in a simple service invoked by the ActionBazaar application. All relevant shipping information, such as the item number, shipping address, shipping method, and insurance amount, is packed into a message and sent out to the `ShippingRequestQueue`.

Listing 4.1 JMS code that sends out shipping requests from ActionBazaar

```
@Inject
@JMSConnectionFactory("jms/QueueConnectionFactory")
private JMSContext context;

@Resource(name="jms/ShippingRequestQueue")
private Destination destination;

ShippingRequest shippingRequest = new ShippingRequest();
shippingRequest.setItem("item");
shippingRequest.setShippingAddress("address");
shippingRequest.setShippingMethod("method");
shippingRequest.setInsuranceAmount(100.50);

ObjectMessage om = context.createObjectMessage();
om.setObject(shippingRequest);

JMSProducer producer = context.createProducer();
producer.send(destination, om);
```

(1) Basic CDI @Inject annotation
(2) The queue factory to use
(3) Simplified interface for JMS operations
(4) The queue to use
(5) ShippingRequest to send to queue
(6) JMSObjectMessage to send ShippingRequest
(7) JMSProducer to send message

As we explain each step of this code in the following sections, we'll go through a larger subset of the JMS API and note usage patterns. For simplicity, the code for exception handling has been removed.

RETRIEVING THE CONNECTION FACTORY AND DESTINATION

In JMS, message server resources are similar to JDBC `javax.sql.DataSource` objects. These resources are created and configured outside the code and stored in the server JNDI registry, usually through XML or an administrative console. JMS has two primary types of resources: `javax.jms.JMSContext` (3) and `javax.jms.Destination` (4), both of which are used in listing 4.1. You retrieve the `JMSContext` using dependency injection with the CDI `@Inject` (1) annotation and configure the `JMSContext` to connect to a connection factory with the `@JMSConnectionFactory` (2) annotation. The `JMSContext` wraps a `javax.jmx.ConnectionFactory` and `javax.jmx.Session` in one object. The

`JMSContext` was introduced with EE 7 to simplify JMS operations and also to make it easier to stick to the one-session-per-connection restriction in EE environments (this isn't a restriction in SE applications). You also inject the queue to forward the shipping request to, aptly named `ShippingRequestQueue`, using the `@Resource` annotation ❹.

This code example is from a servlet that uses the annotations for injection. The servlet container automatically looks up the resources registered in JNDI and injects them. Chapter 5 discusses dependency injection in greater detail.

PREPARING THE MESSAGE

In this example, you want to send the `Serializable` Java object `ShippingRequest` to Turtle. So you create a new instance of the object and set its data ❺. After doing this, you need to determine which JMS message type you need in order to send this object. The most appropriate message type is `javax.jms.ObjectMessage`. You use your `JMSContext` to create an `ObjectMessage` and set the `ShippingRequest` inside ❻. Now that you have your message ready to send, the only thing left to do is send it.

SENDING THE MESSAGE

A `JMSProducer` is used to send a message. As in preparing the message, the `JMSContext` is your source for the producer. Simply call the `createProducer` method and send the message you just created ❼. It doesn't get much simpler than that! After sending your message, you have one more thing to worry about. You need to clean up the resources you've used—or do you?

RELEASING RESOURCES

The great thing about using dependency injection in a managed environment is that the container can take care of a number of very important things for you. Releasing resources is one of them. The previous code example is from a Servlet, and because of this the `JMSContext` is a container-managed resource. That means the container will handle closing the resource for you. The `JMSContext` does have a close method, however. If you obtain a `JMSContext` from a nonmanaged environment—such as creating one from a `ConnectionFactory` in a Java SE application—you do need to manually clean things up by explicitly calling the `JMSContext.close()` method or else take advantage of the `AutoCloseable` interface introduced with Java SE 7.

If all goes well, a message containing the shipping request ends up in the queue. Before we look at the message consumer code that receives this message, let's discuss the `javax.jms.Message` object in a little more detail.

4.2.1 JMS Message interface

The `Message` interface standardizes the different types of messages that can be exchanged across different JMS providers. As figure 4.6 shows, a JMS message has the following parts: the message header, the message properties, and the message body, each of which is detailed in the following sections.

A good analogy for JMS messages is mailing envelopes. Let's see how this analogy fits.

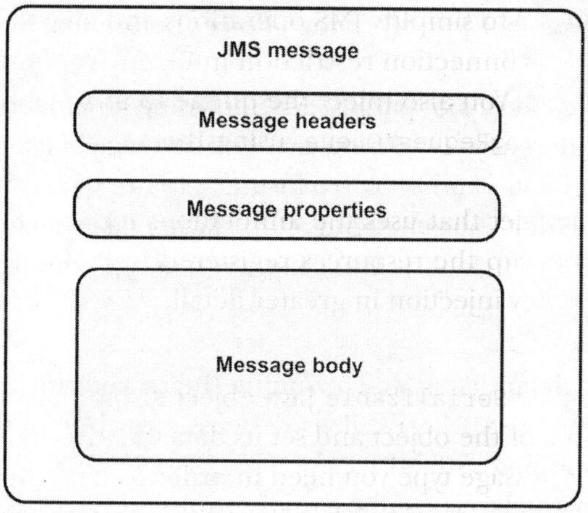

Figure 4.6 Anatomy of a JMS message

MESSAGE HEADERS

Headers are name–value pairs common to all messages. In the envelope analogy, the message header is the standard information found on the typical postal letter: the to and from addresses, postage, and postmark. For example, the JMS message version of a mail postmark is the `JMSTimestamp` header. MOM sets this header to the current time when the message is sent.

Here are some other commonly used JMS headers:

- `JMSCorrelationID`
- `JMSReplyTo`
- `JMSMessageID`

MESSAGE PROPERTIES

Message properties are similar to headers but are explicitly created by the application instead of being standard across messages. Continuing with the envelope analogy, if you decide to write "Happy Holidays" on the envelope to let the receiver know the envelope contains a gift or a note, the text is a property instead of a header. In the ActionBazaar example, one way to mark a shipping request as "Fragile" would be to add a `boolean` property `Fragile` and set it to `true`:

```
Message.setBooleanProperty("Fragile", true);
```

A property can be a `boolean`, `byte`, `double`, `float`, `int`, `long`, `short`, `String`, or `Object`.

MESSAGE BODY

The message body contains the contents of the envelope; it's the payload of the message. What you're trying to send in the body determines what message type you should use. In listing 4.1, `javax.jms.ObjectMessage` is used because you're sending out the `ShippingRequest` Java object. Alternatively, you could have chosen to send `BytesMessage`, `MapMessage`, `StreamMessage`, or `TextMessage`. Each of these message types has a slightly different interface and usage pattern. There are no hard-and-fast rules dictating the choice of message type. Explore all of the choices before making a decision for your application.

We just finished reviewing most of the major parts of JMS, including how to send a message, parts of a message, and the different types of messages. Full coverage of JMS is unfortunately beyond the scope of this chapter and book. To further explore JMS, visit http://docs.oracle.com/javaee/7/tutorial/doc/partmessaging.htm. Having taken a closer look at JMS messages, the time is right for us to look at Turtle's server message consumer.

4.3 Working with MDBs

We'll now explore MDBs in more detail. First, we'll examine the reasons for considering them and then dive into how to use MDBs. We'll also discuss some best practices as well as pitfalls to avoid when developing with MDBs.

MDBs are EJB components designed to consume asynchronous messages. Although MDBs are intended to handle many different kinds of messages (see the sidebar "JCA connectors and messaging"), we'll primarily focus on MDBs that process JMS messages because that's what MDBs are most commonly used for. You might ask why you'd need to employ EJBs to handle the task of consuming messages at all or why you need to use JMS messaging in the first place. We'll address this question next. You'll develop a simple message consumer application using MDBs and we'll show you how to use the `@MessageDriven` annotation. You'll also learn more about the `MessageListener` interface, activation configuration properties, and the MDB lifecycle.

JCA connectors and messaging

Although JMS is by far the primary messaging provider for MDBs, as of EJB 2.1 it's not the only one. Thanks to the Java EE Connector Architecture (JCA), MDBs can receive messages from any Enterprise information system (EIS), such as PeopleSoft or Oracle Manufacturing, not just MOMs that support JMS.

Suppose you have a legacy application that needs to send messages to an MDB. You can do this by implementing a JCA-compliant adapter/connector that includes support for message *inflow contract*. Once your JCA resource adapter or connector is deployed to a Java EE container, you can use the message inflow contract to have an asynchronous message delivered to an endpoint inside the container. A JCA endpoint is essentially the same as a JMS destination—it acts as a server proxy to an MDB (a message consumer/listener in JMS terms). As soon as a message arrives at the end point, the container triggers any registered MDBs listening to the endpoint and delivers the message to it.

For its part, the MDB implements a listener interface that's appropriate to the JCA connector/message type, passes activation configuration parameters to the JCA connector, and registers as a listener to the JCA connector (we'll discuss message listeners and activation configuration parameters shortly). JCA also enables MOM providers to integrate with Java EE containers in a standardized manager using a JCA-compliant connector or resource adapter. For more information, visit the JCA JSR for Java EE 7 at http://jcp.org/en/jsr/detail?id=322.

4.3.1 When to use messaging and MDBs

Messaging and MDBs are powerful concepts, but they're not right for every use case. As a rule of thumb, you should use MDBs only if you require asynchronous processing, loose coupling, *and* reliability—that is, unless you need all three of these characteristics, you probably don't need MDB.

If you simply need asynchronous processing and not reliability or loose coupling, you should opt to use the session bean `@Asynchronous` annotation described in chapter 3. The `@Asynchronous` annotation is obviously not loosely coupled because you invoke the asynchronous session bean method directly from the client code. It's less obvious that session bean asynchronous methods are also not reliable. If the container crashes in the middle of asynchronous processing, the session bean is lost. With MDBs, on the other hand, the JMS message isn't removed from the middleware until the MDB finishes processing the message. If the MDB suddenly crashes before finishing processing, the message is reprocessed later when the container is ready again.

Similarly, if all you need is loose coupling, you should take a close look at CDI events. As we'll discuss in chapter 12, CDI events allow message consumers and producers to be separated through elegant type-safe object-based events. Like session bean asynchronous processing, the CDI event bus isn't fault-tolerant and is also not asynchronous. Note that you can combine the `@Asynchronous` annotation with CDI events if you need to.

When you do need asynchronous processing, loose coupling, *and* reliability, MDBs are one of the best solutions around, which is why they're so popular for system integration. Let's take a closer look at why this is the case.

4.3.2 Why use MDBs?

Most Enterprise applications require some form of messaging, whether they know it or not. In this section we're going to look at some of the reasons you may need messaging in your application. You may discover that you've already fulfilled this need in another way, but now that you're learning about MDBs, you'll see that they're a much more elegant solution.

MULTITHREADING

Your business application may require multithreaded message consumers that can process messages concurrently and maximize message throughput. MDBs help you avoid complexity because they handle multithreading right out of the box, without any additional code. They manage incoming messages among multiple instances of beans (in a pool) that have no special multithreading code themselves. As soon as a new message reaches the destination, an MDB instance is retrieved from the pool to handle the message, as shown in figure 4.7. This is popularly known as *MDB pooling*, which you'll learn about when we discuss the MDB lifecycle later in this chapter.

SIMPLIFIED MESSAGING CODE

MDBs relieve you from coding the mechanical aspects of processing JMS messages—tasks like retrieving connection factories or destinations, creating connections, opening

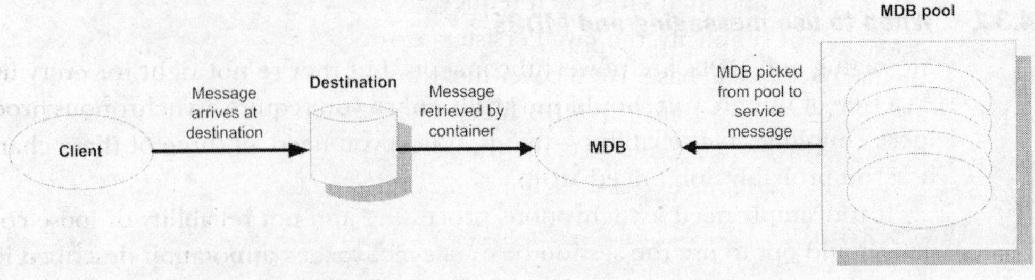

Figure 4.7 As soon as a message arrives at its destination, the container retrieves it and assigns a servicing MDB instance from the pool.

sessions, creating consumers, and attaching listeners. As you'll see when you build the Turtle message-consumer MDB, all these tasks are handled behind the scenes for you. In EJB 3, using sensible defaults for common circumstances eliminates most of the configuration. In the worst-case scenario, you'll have to supply configuration information using simple annotations or through the deployment descriptor.

ROBUST MESSAGE PROCESSING

As we mentioned earlier, reliability is a critical hallmark of MDBs. All MDBs use transactions and message acknowledgment by default. What this means is that messages aren't removed from the message server unless an MDB message listener method completes normally. If an unexpected error occurs during message processing, the transaction is marked for rollback and the message receipt isn't acknowledged. Because MDBs use JTA transactions, any database changes made during message listener processing are also automatically rolled back. As a result, the unacknowledged message can be reprocessed by the MDB cleanly without your having to do any work. In case of successful message processing, database changes are committed and the message is removed from the message server in an atomic fashion.

STARTING MESSAGE CONSUMPTION

To start picking up messages from the shipping request queue, someone needs to invoke the appropriate method in your code. In a production environment, it's not clear how this will be accomplished. Starting message consumption through a user-driven manual process obviously isn't desirable. In a server environment, almost every means of executing the method on server startup is highly system-dependent, not to mention awkward. The same is true about stopping message processing manually. On the other hand, registered MDBs would be bootstrapped or torn down gracefully by the container when the server is started or stopped.

We'll continue exploring these points shortly as we start investigating a real example of developing MDBs.

4.3.3 Developing a message consumer with MDB

Let's now explore developing an MDB by implementing the Turtle server message consumer. Listing 4.2 shows the MDB code that first retrieves shipping requests sent to the queue and then saves each request in Turtle's database table named SHIPPING_REQUEST. For simplicity, the Java Persistence API (JPA) is used in this example to persist the data to the database. We'll cover more about JPA starting with chapter 9. Using JPA also helps demonstrate the MDB lifecycle and transaction management; if there's a failure processing the message, the transaction is rolled back and neither the database data gets written nor is the message removed from the queue.

Listing 4.2 Turtle shipping request message bean

```
@MessageDriven(activationConfig = {
 @ActivationConfigProperty(propertyName = "destinationType",
   propertyValue = "javax.jms.Queue"),
 @ActivationConfigProperty(propertyName = "destinationLookup",
   propertyValue = "jms/ShippingRequestQueue")
})
public class TurtleShippingRequestMessageBean implements MessageListener{

 @PersistenceContext()
 EntityManager entityManager;

 @Override
 public void onMessage(Message message) {
  try {
    ObjectMessage om = (ObjectMessage) message;
    Object o = om.getObject();
    ActionBazaarShippingRequest sr = (ActionBazaarShippingRequest) o;
    Logger.getLogger(TurtleShippingRequestMessageBean.class.getName())
      .log(Level.INFO, String.format("Got message: %s", sr));

    TurtleShippingRequest tr = new TurtleShippingRequest();
    tr.setInsuranceAmount(sr.getInsuranceAmount());
    tr.setItem(sr.getItem());
    tr.setShippingAddress(sr.getShippingAddress());
    tr.setShippingMethod(sr.getShippingMethod());
    entityManager.persist(tr);
  } catch (JMSException ex) {
    Logger.getLogger(TurtleShippingRequestMessageBean.class.getName())
      .log(Level.SEVERE, null, ex);
  }
 }
}
```

❶ Configures bean with queue it listens on for messages

❷ Implements MessageListener interface for processing JMS messages

Injects EntityManager for saving data to database

❸ Implements onMessage method

❹ Retrieves ActionBazaar data

❺ Converts ActionBazaar data to Turtle data

❻ Persists shipping request to Turtle's database

The @MessageDriven annotation ❶ identifies this object as an MDB and specifies the MDB configuration, including the fact that you're listening on the jms/ShippingRequestQueue. Recall from the "JCA connectors and messaging" sidebar that MDBs may be configured to listen for notifications other than JMS messages on queues and topics. But in this example, Turtle's MDB implements the MessageListener interface, marking it a JMS MessageListener interface ❷. To implement the MessageListener interface, code is given for the onMessage method ❸. The body of this method is simple. First, the ActionBazaarShippingRequest is retrieved from the ObjectMessage ❹. Recall that the ActionBazaarShippingRequest object has the data sent by ActionBazaar to Turtle for fulfilling the shipping request. Next, the method converts the data in the ActionBazaarShippingRequest object into a TurtleShippingRequest ❺. Transforming data like this is very common and necessary to get the data into Turtle's database for processing. Finally, the EntityManager is used to save the data to Turtle's database ❻. Remember, you'll learn more about the EntityManager and JPA starting with chapter 9.

Next, we'll examine the major MDB features by analyzing this code in greater detail, starting with the @MessageDriven annotation.

4.3.4 Using the @MessageDriven annotation

MDBs are one of the simplest kinds of EJBs to develop, and they support the smallest number of annotations. The @MessageDriven annotation and the @ActivationConfigProperty annotation nested inside it are the only MDB-specific annotations. The @MessageDriven annotation in the example represents what you'll use most of the time. The annotation is defined as follows:

```
@Target(value = {ElementType.TYPE})
@Retention(value = RetentionPolicy.RUNTIME)
public @interface MessageDriven {
    String name() default "";
    Class messageListenerInterface default Object.class;
    ActivationConfigProperty[] activationConfig() default {};
    String mappedName();
    String description();
}
```

Notice that all three of the annotation's arguments are optional. If you're a minimalist, you can keep the annotation as simple as this and leave any details to be added elsewhere, such as in the deployment descriptor (or simply use the default values):

```
@MessageDriven
public class TurtleShippingRequestMessageBean
```

The first element, name, specifies the name of the MDB if you need to explicitly assign it. If the name element is omitted, the code uses the name of the class, TurtleShippingRequestMessageBean, in the example. The second parameter, messageListenerInterface, specifies which message listener the MDB implements. The third parameter, activationConfig, is used to specify listener-specific configuration properties. Let's take a closer look at these last two parameters.

4.3.5 Implementing the MessageListener

The container uses the MessageListener interface implemented by the MDB to register the MDB with the underlying JMS message provider. Once registered, the provider can pass along incoming messages by invoking the implemented methods on the MDB class. Using the messageListenerInterface parameter of the @MessageDriven annotation is just one way to specify the MessageListener interface. The following code shows how it's done:

```
@MessageDriven(
  messageListenerInterface="javax.jms.MessageListener")
public class ShippingRequestProcessor {
```

But most often you'll omit this parameter and specify the interface using the Java `implements` keyword, just as you did in listing 4.2 ❷.

Yet another option is to specify the `MessageListener` interface through the XML deployment descriptor and leave this detail out of the code altogether:

```
<ejb-jar...>
  <enterprise-beans>
    <message-driven>
      ...
      <messaging-type> javax.jms.MessageListener</messaging-type>
    </message-driven>
  </enterprise-beans>
</ejb-jar>
```

The approach you choose is largely a matter of taste. Next, we'll look at configuring your `MessageListener` interface.

4.3.6 Using ActivationConfigProperty

The `ActivationConfigProperty` of the `@MessageDriven` annotation allows you to provide messaging provider–specific configuration information through an array of `ActivationConfigProperty` instances. `ActivationConfigProperty` is defined as follows:

```
@Target(value = {})
@Retention(value = RetentionPolicy.RUNTIME)
public @interface ActivationConfigProperty {
  String propertyName();
  String propertyValue();
}
```

Each activation property is a name–value pair that the underlying messaging provider understands and uses to set up the MDB. The best way to grasp how this works is through an example. Here, we provide two of the most common JMS activation configuration properties: `destinationType` and `destinationLookup`:

```
@MessageDriven(activationConfig = {
  @ActivationConfigProperty(propertyName = "destinationType",
    propertyValue = "javax.jms.Queue"),
  @ActivationConfigProperty(propertyName = "destinationLookup",
    propertyValue = "jms/ShippingRequestQueue")
})
```

First, the `destinationType` property tells the container this JMS MDB is listening to a queue. If you were listening to a topic instead, the value could be specified as `javax.jms.Topic`. The `destinationLookup` parameter specifies that you're listening for messages arriving at a destination with the JNDI name of `jms/ShippingRequestQueue`.

There are a few other configuration properties for a JMS provider that handle JMS messages. Table 4.1 summarizes these properties.

Table 4.1 Activation properties for a JMS provider standardized by the JMS 2.0 spec

Activation property	Description
`destinationLookup`	The JNDI lookup of a `javax.jms.Queue` or a `javax.jms.Topic`.
`connectionFactoryLookup`	The JNDI lookup of a `javax.jms.ConnectionFactory`, `javax.jms.QueueConnectionFactory`, or `javax.jms.TopicConnectionFactory`.
`acknowledgeMode`	`Auto-acknowledge` (default) or `Dups-ok-acknowledge`.
`messageSelector`	A message select to filter the messages the MDB receives.
`destinationType`	`javax.jms.Queue` or `javax.jms.Topic`.
`subscriptionDurability`	Applies only to `destinationType=" javax.jms.Topic"`. Values are either `Durable` or `NonDurable` (default).
`clientId`	Sets the client identifier used when connecting to the JMS provider.
`subscriptionName`	Applies only to `destinationType=" javax.jms.Topic"`. The name of the durable or non-durable subscription.

It's important to remember that these configuration properties are defined in the JMS 2.0 specification for consuming JMS messages. If your MDB is going to consume different kinds of messages, the activation configuration properties will be specific for that provider and may not share any similarity to these configuration properties. Next, we're going to look at some of these additional activation configuration properties in more detail.

ACKNOWLEDGMENT MODE

Messages aren't actually removed from the underlying JMS queue until the consumer acknowledges them. There are many "modes" through which messages can be acknowledged. By default, the acknowledgement mode for the underlying JMS session is assumed to be `Auto-acknowledge`, which means that the session acknowledges messages on your behalf in the background. This is the case for the example (because you omitted this property). You could change the acknowledgement mode to `Dups-ok-acknowledge` by using the following code:

```
@ActivationConfigProperty {
        propertyName="acknowledgeMode"
        propertyValue="Dups-ok-acknowledge"
```

SUBSCRIPTION DURABILITY

If the MDB is listening on a topic, you can specify whether the topic subscription is durable or nondurable.

Recall that in the pub–sub domain, a message is distributed to all currently subscribed consumers. In general, this is much like a broadcast message in that anyone who isn't connected to the topic at the time doesn't receive a copy of the message. The exception to this rule is what is known as the *durable subscription.*

Once a consumer obtains a durable subscription on a topic, all messages sent to the topic are guaranteed to be delivered to the consumer. If the durable subscriber isn't connected to a topic when a message is received, the MOM retains a copy of the message until the subscriber connects and delivers the message. The following shows how to create a durable subscriber in plain JMS:

```
MessageConsumer orderSubscriber = session.createDurableSubscriber(
    orderTopic, "OrderProcessor");
```

Here, we're creating a durable subscription message consumer to the `javax.jms.Topic` `orderTopic` with a subscription ID of `OrderProcessor`. From now on, all messages to the topic will be held until a consumer with the subscription ID `OrderProcessor` receives them. You can remove this subscription with the following code:

```
session.unsubscribe("OrderProcessor");
```

If you want an MDB to be a durable subscriber, then `ActivationConfigProperty` would look like this:

```
@ActivationConfigProperty(
    propertyName="destinationType",
    propertyValue="javax.jms.Topic"),
@ActivationConfigProperty(
    propertyName="subscriptionDurability",
    propertyValue="Durable"
```

For nondurable subscriptions, explicitly set the value of the `subscriptionDurability` property to `NonDurable`. This is the default if no value is set.

MESSAGESELECTOR

The `messageSelector` property is the MDB parallel to applying a selector for a raw JMS consumer. The current code consumes all messages at the destination. If you prefer, you could filter the messages you retrieve by using a *message selector*—a criterion applied to the headers and properties of messages specifying which messages the consumer wants to receive. For example, you could specify in your MDB that you want to handle only fragile shipping requests as follows:

```
@ActivationConfigProperty
    propertyName="messageSelector"
    propertyValue="Fragile is TRUE")
```

As you might have noticed, the selector syntax is almost identical to the `WHERE` clause in SQL, but the selector syntax uses message header and property names instead of database column names. Selector expressions can be as complex and expressive as you need them to be. They can include literals, identifiers, whitespace, expressions, standard brackets, logical and comparison operators, arithmetic operators, and null comparisons. Table 4.2 summarizes the common message selector types.

Table 4.2 Common message selector types

Type	Description	Example

Literals	Can be strings, exact or approximate numeric values, or Booleans.	`BidManagerMDB`
		`100`
		`TRUE`

Identifiers	Can be a message property or header name; case sensitive.	`RECIPIENT`
		`NumOfBids`
		`Fragile`
		`JMSTimestamp`

Whitespace	Same as defined in the Java language specification: space, tab, form feed, and line terminator.	
Comparison operators	Comparison operators, such as =, >, >=, <=, <>.	`RECIPIENT='BidManagerMDB'` `NumOfBids>=100`
Logical operators	All three types of logical operators—NOT, AND, OR—are supported.	`RECIPIENT='BidManagerMDB'` AND `NumOfBids>=100`
Null comparison	`IS NULL` and `IS NOT NULL` comparisons.	`Firstname IS NOT NULL`
True/false comparison	`IS [NOT] TRUE` and `IS [NOT] FALSE` comparisons.	`Fragile is TRUE` `Fragile is FALSE`

4.3.7 Using bean lifecycle callbacks

As you'll recall from chapter 3, similar to stateless session beans, MDBs have a simple lifecycle (see figure 4.8 for a refresher). For each MDB, the container is responsible for the following:

- Creates MDB instances.
- Injects resources, including the message-driven context (discussed in chapter 5 in detail).
- Places instances in a managed pool (if the container supports pooling; if pooling isn't supported, new instances are created when needed).
- Pulls an idle bean out of the pool when a message arrives (the container may have to increase the pool size at this point).
- Executes the message listener method—for example, the `onMessage` method.
- When the `onMessage` method finishes executing, it pushes the idle bean back into the method-ready pool.
- As needed, retires (and destroys) beans out of the pool.

The MDB's two lifecycle callbacks are `PostConstruct`, which is called immediately after an MDB is created and set up and all the resources are injected, and `PreDestroy`, which is called right before the bean instance is retired and removed from the pool. These callback methods can be used for any kind of operations you want, but typically

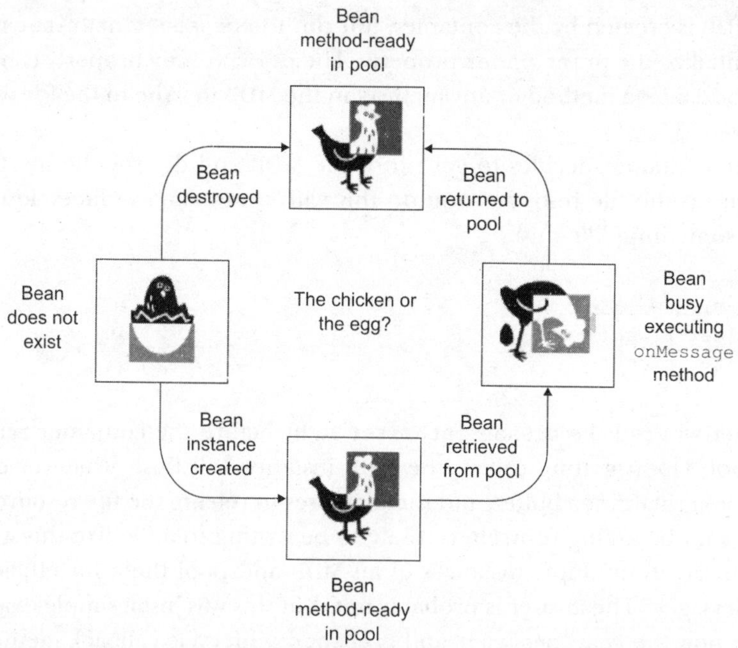

Figure 4.8 The MDB lifecycle has three states: doesn't exist, idle, and busy. There are only two lifecycle callbacks corresponding to bean creation and destruction; you can use `PostConstruct` and `PreDestroy` to receive these callbacks.

they're used for creating and cleaning up resources used by the MDB. As a simple example, let's suppose your MDB needs to write a file on the file system. To do this, a `PrintWriter` is first needed. You can easily define a `PrintWriter` in the MDB class like this:

```
PrintWriter printWriter;
```

Now you need to initialize the `printWriter` property, which you do by using a `PostConstruct` lifecycle method, which may look like the following:

```
@PostConstruct
void createPrintWriter() {
  File f = new File(new File(System.getProperty("java.io.tmpdir"))
    , "ShippingMessages.txt");
  try {
    printWriter = new PrintWriter(f);
  } catch (Throwable t) {
    throw new RuntimeException(t);
  }
  Logger.getLogger(TurtleShippingRequestMessageBean.class.getName())
    .log(Level.INFO,
    String.format("Write to file: %s", f.getAbsolutePath()));
}
```

When the MDB is created by the container, it'll run the `createPrintWriter` method, which will initialize the `printWriter` property. The `printWriter` property can now be used by the `onMessage` method or any method in the MDB to write to the file while the MBD is active.

When the container decides to get rid of the MDB and destroy the instance, it's time to clean up the file resource. You do this with a `PreDestroy` lifecycle method, which looks something like this:

```
@PreDestroy
void closePrintWriter() {
  printWriter.flush();
  printWriter.close();
}
```

The container will call the `closePrintWriter` right before the container removes it from the pool. Upon getting called, the MDB instance will flush whatever contents may be in the `PrintWriter` buffer, and then it closes to release the file resources.

Now you may be asking yourself, is it safe to be writing to a file like this when the container can create multiple instances of an MDB and pool them for efficient processing of messages? The answer is probably not. But this was just a simple example to demonstrate how the `PostConstruct` and `PreDestroy` lifecycle callback methods may be used in an MDB.

An MDB is great for receiving and processing messages. We've just finished covering the basics of this. But can an MDB also send messages? The answer is yes, and you may find yourself doing this more often than you'd think. We'll explore how MDBs can send JMS messages next.

4.3.8 Sending JMS messages from MDBs

Somewhat ironically, a task you find yourself performing time and time again in an MDB is sending JMS messages. As a simple example, suppose that you have an incomplete shipping request and you need to communicate that back to ActionBazaar from the `ShippingRequestProcessor`. The easiest way to handle this notification is via JMS messages sent to an error queue that ActionBazaar is monitoring. Fortunately, you've already seen how to send a JMS message in listing 4.1. You inject the queue named `jms/ShippingErrorQueue` and the connection factory named `jms/QueueConnectionFactory`:

```
@Inject
@JMSConnectionFactory("jms/QueueConnectionFactory")
private JMSContext context;

@Resource(name="jms/ShippingErrorQueue")
private Destination errorQueue;
```

Turtle can then send the error message back to ActionBazaar:

```
Message m = context.createTextMessage(
  String.format("Item in error %s",tr.getItem()));
```

```
JMSProducer producer = context.createProducer();
producer.send(destination, om);
```

Although we didn't explicitly show it in the example, there's one more MDB feature you should know about: MDB transaction management. We'll discuss EJB transactions in general in much more detail in the next chapter, so here we'll give you the "bargain-basement" version.

4.3.9 Managing MDB transactions

By default, the container will start a transaction before the onMessage method is invoked and will commit the transaction when the method returns, unless the transaction was marked as rollback through the message-driven context or an unhandled runtime exception is thrown in the onMessage method. You'll learn more about EJB transactions in chapter 6, but this happens because the container assumes that a transaction is required by the MDB. You can specify this explicitly using the following code:

```
@MessageDriven
@TransactionAttribute(TransactionAttributeType.REQUIRED)
public class TurtleShippingRequestMessageBean
```

If you want, you can also tell the container that the MDB shouldn't use transactions at all. In this case, you need to ensure database and message acknowledgment reliability yourself. The message is acknowledged regardless of whether the message listener finishes normally or not. Generally, we don't recommend this approach. But you can do it as follows:

```
@MessageDriven
@TransactionAttribute(TransactionAttributeType.NOT_SUPPORTED)
public class TurtleShippingRequestMessageBean
```

This very brief discussion of transaction management concludes our analysis of the basic features that MDBs offer. We've discussed how you can use MDBs to use the power of messaging without dealing with the low-level details of the messaging API. As you've seen, MDBs provide a host of EJB features for free, such as multithreading, resource injection, lifecycle management, and container-managed transactions. You've formulated the code samples so that you can use them as templates for solving business problems.

4.4 MDB best practices

Like all technologies, MDBs and asynchronous methods have some pitfalls to watch out for and some best practices that you should keep in mind. This is particularly true in demanding environments where messaging is typically deployed.

Choose your messaging models carefully. Before you wade knee deep in code, consider your choice of messaging model carefully. You might find that PTP will solve your problem 9 times out of 10. In some cases, though, the pub–sub approach is better, especially if you find yourself broadcasting the same message to more than one receiver (such as the system outage notification example). Luckily, most messaging code is domain-independent, and you should strive to keep it that way. For the most part, switching domains should be just a matter of configuration.

Don't overuse MDBs. Many tasks are better suited for session bean asynchronous methods or CDI events. If you simply need to spawn another task to perform an operation, queuing up a JMS message is probably overkill. An asynchronous method is much simpler. The container will manage the threads for you, and you'll be able to pass values back without developing a complex message-passing sequence with error handling. Similarly, use CDI events if all that you're looking for is looser coupling.

Remember modularization. Because MDBs are so similar to session beans, it's natural to start putting business logic right into the message listener methods. Business logic should be decoupled and modularized away from messaging-specific concerns. An excellent practice (but one that would have made this chapter unnecessarily complicated) is to put business logic in session beans and invoke them from the `onMessage` method.

Make good use of message filters. There are some valid reasons for using a single messaging destination for multiple purposes. Message selectors come in handy in these circumstances. For example, if you're using the same queue for both shipping requests and order cancellation notices, you can have the client set a message property identifying the type of request. You can then use message selectors on two separate MDBs to isolate and handle each kind of request.

Conversely, in some cases, you might dramatically improve performance and keep your code simple by using separate destinations instead of using selectors. In the example, using separate queues and MDBs for shipping requests and cancellation orders could make message delivery much faster. In this case, the client would have to send each request type to the appropriate queue.

Choose message types carefully. The choice of message type isn't always as obvious as it seems. For example, it's a compelling idea to use XML strings for messaging. Among other things, this tends to promote loose coupling between systems. In the example, Turtle's server would know about the format of the XML messages and not the `ActionBazaarShippingRequest` object itself.

The problem is that XML tends to bloat the size of the message, significantly degrading MOM performance. In certain circumstances, it might even be the right choice to use binary streams in the message payload, which puts the least amount of demand on MOM processing as well as memory consumption.

Be wary of poisoned messages. Imagine that a message is handed to you that your MDB wasn't able to consume. Using the example, let's assume that you receive a message that's not an `ObjectMessage`. As you can see from this code snippet, if this happens, the cast in `onMessage` will throw a `java.lang.ClassCastException`:

```
try {
   ObjectMessage om = (ObjectMessage) message;     <-- Wrong message type fails cast
```

```
    Object o = om.getObject();
    ActionBazaarShippingRequest sr = (ActionBazaarShippingRequest) o;
    . . .
  } catch (JMSException ex) {
    Logger.getLogger(TurtleShippingRequestMessageBean.class.getName())
       .log(Level.SEVERE, null, ex);
  }
```

Because onMessage won't complete normally, the container will be forced to roll back the transaction and put the message back on the queue instead of acknowledging it. The problem is, because you're still listening on the queue, the same message will be delivered to you again and you'll be stuck in the accept/die loop indefinitely! Messages that cause this all-too-common scenario are called *poisoned messages.*

The good news is that many MOMs and EJB containers provide mechanisms that deal with poisoned messages, including redelivery counts and dead-message queues. If you set up the redelivery count and dead-message queue for the shipping request destination, the message delivery will be attempted for the specified number of times. After the redelivery count is exceeded, the message will be moved to a specifically designated queue for poisoned messages called the dead-message queue. The bad news is that these mechanisms aren't standardized and are vendor-specific.

Configure MDB pool size. Most EJB containers let you specify the maximum number of instances of a particular MDB the container can create. In effect, this controls the level of concurrency. If there are five concurrent messages to process and the pool size is set to three, the container will wait until the first three messages are processed before assigning any more instances. This is a double-edged sword and requires careful handling. If you set your MDB pool size too small, messages will be processed slowly. At the same time, it's desirable to place *reasonable* limits on MDB pool size so that many concurrent MDB instances don't choke the machine. Unfortunately, at the time of this writing, setting MDB pool sizes isn't standardized and is provider-specific.

Consider nonpersistent messages, duplicate-OK acknowledgment, and nontransactional MDBs. If you want, you can specify a JMS message to be nonpersistent. This means that the message server doesn't back up the message to the disk. As a result, if the message server crashes, the message is lost forever. The benefit to using nonpersistent messages is that they're much faster to process, but at the cost of reliability. Similarly, specifying the message acknowledgment mode to DUPS_OK_ACKNOWLEDGE can also reduce overhead and increase performance, as does using nontransactional MDBs. You should be very careful when using these optimization techniques and make sure the business case can tolerate the relative lack of reliability.

4.5 Summary

In this chapter, we covered basic messaging concepts, JMS, and MDBs. Messaging is an extremely powerful technology for the enterprise, and it helps build loosely integrated reliable systems. JMS allows you to use MOM from Enterprise Java applications without being bound to vendor-specific APIs. Using the JMS API to build a message consumer application can be time consuming, and MDBs make using MOM in a standardized manner through Java EE extremely easy and robust.

A few major EJB features we touched on in this chapter are JNDI, dependency injection, EJB contexts, and transactions. We'll discuss these concepts in the following chapters.

5 EJB runtime context, dependency injection, and crosscutting logic

This chapter covers

- The basics of the `EJBContext`
- Using JNDI to look up EJBs and other resources
- The `@EJB` annotation
- EJBs in the application client and embedded containers
- The basics of AOP interceptors

In the previous two chapters we focused on developing session beans and message-driven beans (MDBs). In this chapter we build on that material and introduce some advanced concepts applicable to MDBs and session beans. We begin by discussing how containers provide services behind the scenes and how to access the runtime environment. We then move on to advanced uses of dependency injection, JNDI lookups, and EJB interceptors. As you'll learn, EJB 3 largely relieves you of these system-level concerns while providing extremely robust and flexible functionality when you need it.

5.1 EJB context

EJB components are generally meant to be agnostic of the container. This means that in the ideal case, EJB components should merely hold business logic and never access the container or use container services directly. But in rare cases it's necessary for the bean to explicitly use container services in code. For example, it may be necessary to manually roll back a transaction or create a timer to execute a business process at some point in the future. These are the situations the EJB context is designed to handle. The `javax.ejb.EJBContext` interface is your backstage entrance into the mystic world of the container. In this section, we define the `EJBContext`, explain its use, and show you how to use dependency injection to retrieve the `EJBContext`.

5.1.1 Basics of EJB context

As you can see in the following listing, the `EJBContext` interface allows direct programmatic access to services such as transaction, security, and timers, which are typically specified through configuration and managed completely by the container.

Listing 5.1 `javax.ejb.EJBContext` interface

```
public interface EJBContext {
    public Principal getCallerPrincipal();                  // Bean-managed security
    public boolean isCallerInRole(String roleName);

    public boolean getRollbackOnly();                       // Transaction management
    public UserTransaction getUserTransaction();
    public void setRollbackOnly();

    public TimerService getTimerService();                  // Access to timer service

    public Object lookup(String name);                      // JNDI lookup
    public Map<String, Object> getContextData();            // Interceptor context data

    public EJBHome getEJBHome();                            // EJB 2 compatibility
    public EJBLocalHome getEJBLocalHome();
}
```

Let's look briefly at what each of these methods does (table 5.1). We'll save a detailed analysis for later, when we discuss the services that each of the methods is related to. For now, you should note the array of services offered through the EJB context, as well as the method patterns.

Table 5.1 You can use `javax.ejb.EJBContext` to access runtime services

Methods	Description
`getCallerPrincipal` `isCallerInRole`	These methods are useful when using bean-managed security. We discuss these two methods further in chapter 6 when we discuss programmatic security.

Table 5.1 You can use `javax.ejb.EJBContext` to access runtime services *(continued)*

Methods	Description
`getEJBHome` `getEJBLocalHome`	These methods are used to obtain the bean's "remote home" and "local home" interfaces respectively. Both are optional for EJB 3 containers and are hardly used beyond legacy EJB 2.1 beans. We won't discuss these methods beyond this basic introduction. They're mainly provided for backward compatibility.
`getRollbackOnly` `setRollbackOnly`	These methods are used for EJB transaction management in the case of container-managed transactions. We discuss container-managed transactions in greater detail in chapter 6.
`getUserTransaction`	This method is used for EJB transaction management in the case of bean-managed transactions. We discuss bean-managed transactions in greater detail in chapter 6.
`getTimerService`	This method is used to get access to the EJB timer service. We discuss EJB timers in chapter 7.
`lookup`	This method is used to get references to objects stored in the JNDI registry. With dependency injection, direct JNDI lookup has been rendered largely unnecessary. But there are some edge cases that dependency injection can't handle. This method proves handy in such circumstances. We'll discuss this topic later in this chapter.
`getContextData`	This method allows the EJB to get access to context data from an interceptor. We'll discuss interceptors in greater detail later in this chapter.

5.1.2 EJB context interfaces

Both session and message-driven beans have their own subclasses of the `javax.ejb.EJBContext` interface. As shown in figure 5.1, the session bean–specific subclass is `javax.ejb.SessionContext`, and the MDB-specific subclass is `javax.ejb.MessageDrivenContext`.

Each subclass is designed to suit the particular runtime environment of each bean type. As a result, they either add methods to the superclass or invalidate methods not suited for the bean type.

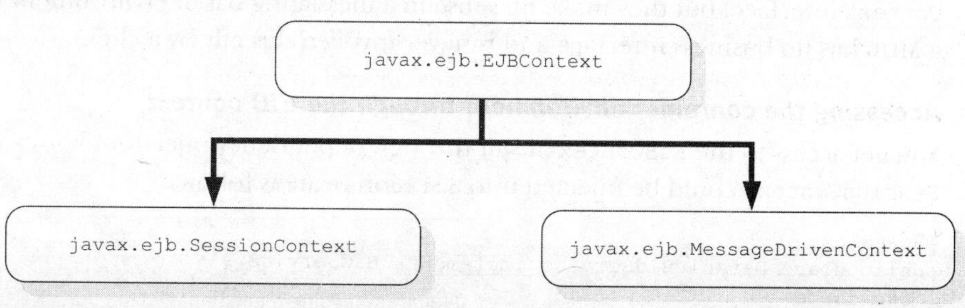

Figure 5.1 `EJBContext` interface has a subclass for each session and message-driven bean type.

SESSIONCONTEXT

SessionContext is an implementation that adds methods specific to the session bean environment. Table 5.2 describes these methods. Although these methods have their use cases, they're rarely used.

Table 5.2 Additional methods added by javax.ejb.SessionContext

Methods	Description
getBusinessObject	Get an object as either the current bean's no-interface view or as one of its business interfaces (local or remote).
getEJBLocalObject getEJBObject	Get the local or remote object for the current bean instance. Only valid for use with EJB 2 beans. An exception is generated if used with EJB 3.
getInvokedBusinessInterface	The interface or no-interface view used to invoke the business method for the current bean.
getMessageContext	If the bean is accessed through a web service, this method returns the MessageContext associated with that request.
wasCancelCalled	Get if the user wants to cancel a long-running asynchronous method call.

The wasCancelCalled() method was added for EJB 3.1. It works with asynchronous method calls discussed in chapter 3. When an asynchronous method call occurs, a Future<V> object is returned. The client may then call the Future<V>.cancel() method to stop the long-running process. It's good practice for long-running processes to regularly check a sentinel value to determine if the process should terminate. Your EJB can use wasCancelCalled() as a sentinel value to determine if the user decided to stop the process.

MESSAGEDRIVENCONTEXT

MessageDrivenContext is an implementation specifically for the MDB environment. Unlike SessionContext, this implementation adds no new methods. Instead, it overrides the following methods, throwing exceptions if they're called: isCallerInRole, getEJBHome, or getEJBLocalHome. Recall that these methods are part of the SessionContext interface, but they make no sense in a messaging-based environment because a MDB has no business interface and is never invoked directly by a client.

5.1.3 *Accessing the container environment through the EJB context*

You get access to the EJBContext itself through dependency injection. For example, a SessionContext could be injected into a session bean as follows:

```
@Stateless
public class DefaultBidService implements BidService {
  @Resource
  SessionContext context;
  ...
}
```

In this code snippet, the container detects the `@Resource` annotation on the `context` variable and figures out that the bean wants an instance of its session context. A more detailed discussion of the `@Resource` annotation will be described later in the chapter.

Much like a session context, a `MessageDrivenContext` can be injected into a MDB as follows:

```
@MessageDriven
public class OrderBillingProcessor {
@Resource
MessageDrivenContext context;
  ...
}
```

> **NOTE** It's illegal to inject a `MessageDrivenContext` into a session bean or a `SessionContext` into an MDB.

This is all the time we need to spend on the EJB context right now. Now let's turn our attention to a vital part of EJB 3—dependency injection (DI). We provided a brief overview of DI in chapter 2 and have been seeing EJB DI in action in the last few chapters. It's time we take a closer look.

5.2 Using EJB DI and JNDI

With Java EE 5, the `@EJB` annotation was added to the specification to make it easier for container-managed components to get reference to EJBs. Following the inversion of control best practice, the container uses the DI pattern to wire up beans. Although JNDI is still used in the background, those details are hidden from the developer by the `@EJB` annotation. Prior to EE5, JNDI was used exclusively. The key difference is it was the developer's responsibility to wire up beans manually using a JNDI implementation of the service locator pattern instead of having the container do it through dependency injection. In this section we'll first review the basics of JNDI to gain an understanding of what's happening behind the scenes. Then we'll look at the `@EJB` annotation in more detail, demonstrating how and when to use the annotation and how it may also be used in conjunction with JNDI.

> **Inversion of control (IoC)**
>
> Inversion of control is a general programming best practice in the object-oriented world. It describes that dependencies between objects should be loosely coupled through the use of interfaces and concrete implementations determined at runtime. The service locator (SL) pattern and dependency injection pattern follow this best practice.
>
> **Dependency injection pattern**
>
> DI follows a "push" model. An object's dependencies are configured in some way (XML, annotations, and so on), and it's the responsibility of a container to create concrete implementations of these dependencies at runtime and then push the dependencies into the objects. This is the core technology of CDI (discussed later in the chapter).

> ***(continued)***
>
> **Service locator pattern**
>
> SL follows a "pull" model. Objects are registered inside a central location service. It's then the responsibility of the objects to use this central location service to look up or pull whatever dependencies the object needs into itself. JNDI provides this central location service, and objects use JNDI lookups to pull in their dependencies.

5.2.1 *JNDI primer for EJB*

In essence, JNDI is the JDBC of naming and directory services. Just as JDBC provides a standard Java API to access all kinds of databases, JNDI standardizes naming and directory service access. If you've ever used your computer's file system, you already know what a naming and directory service is. A computer's file system is a basic directory service. You can use the file system to browse and look up a file you have on your desktop. If you've ever used a Lightweight Directory Access Protocol (LDAP) or Microsoft Active Directory (AD) server, you're familiar with a more robust naming and directory service.

As figure 5.2 shows, JNDI provides a uniform abstraction over a number of different naming services, such as LDAP, Domain Naming System (DNS), Network Information Service (NIS), Novell Directory Services (NDS), remote method invocation (RMI), Common Object Request Broker Architecture (CORBA), and so on. Once you get an instance of a JNDI context, you can use it to locate resources in any underlying naming service available to the context. Under the hood, JNDI negotiates with each available naming service, giving the service the name of the resource; then the service uses that name to figure out where the resource actually resides.

As an analogy, think of JDBC. An SQL `SELECT` statement is the resource name. The database server is the naming service, and JDBC is the standard API. When the SQL `SELECT` is executed, the database server uses it to find the real resource (the data), which may really reside in a linked table on a completely separate database server.

JNDI plays a vital role in Java EE, although it's largely hidden behind the scenes. JNDI is used as the central repository for resources managed by the container. As a result, every bean managed by the container is automatically registered with JNDI. In

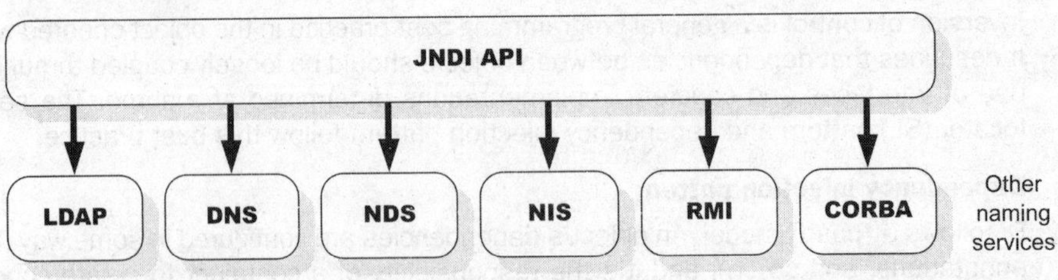

Figure 5.2 JNDI provides a single unified API to access various naming services such as LDAP, DNS, NDS, NIS, RMI, and CORBA. Any naming service with a JNDI SPI provider can be plugged into the API seamlessly.

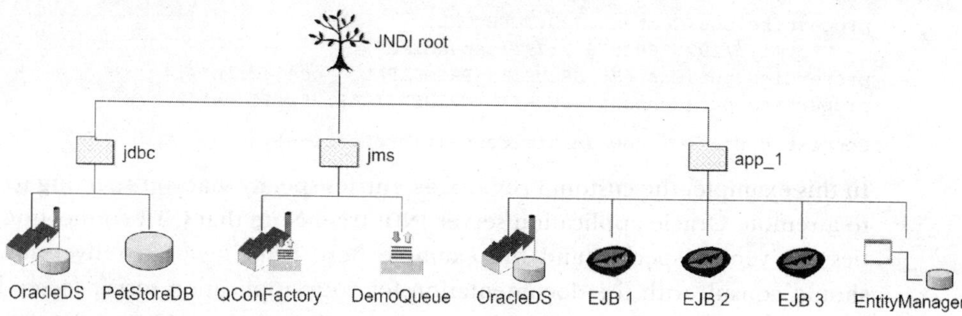

Figure 5.3 An example JNDI tree for an application server. All global resources, such as JDBC and JMS, are bound to the root context of the JNDI tree. Each application has its own application context and EJBs, and other resources in the application are bound under the application context.

addition, a typical container JNDI registry will also store JDBC data sources, JMS queues, JMS connection factories, JPA entity managers, JPA entity manager factories, JavaMail sessions, and so on. Whenever a client (such as an EJB) needs to use a managed resource, it can get hold of JNDI and look up the resource by its unique name. Figure 5.3 shows how a typical JNDI tree for a Java EE application server might look.

As you can see from figure 5.3, resources are stored in a JNDI tree in a hierarchical manner. This means that JNDI resource names look very much like your computer's file system with folders and filenames. Resources also sometimes start with a protocol specification such as `java:`, much like using `C:\` for your computer's main drive and `S:\` for a mapped network drive. After you get a handle to a resource from a JNDI context, you can use it as though it were a local resource.

INITIALIZING A JNDI CONTEXT

To use a resource stored in the JNDI context, a client has to initialize the context and look up the resource. Despite the robustness of the JNDI mechanism itself, the code to do so is pretty simple. It's similar to the configuration for a JDBC driver to connect to a database.

First and foremost, to connect to any naming or directory service, you need to obtain the JNDI libraries provided by that service. This is no different than getting the right JDBC driver to connect to your database. If you want to connect to LDAP, DNS, or your computer's file system, you need the LDAP, DSN, and file system service providers, respectively.

When you're working in a Java EE environment, the Enterprise server already has the libraries loaded that are needed to connect to the Enterprise server's JNDI environment. Outside of a Java EE environment, you need to configure your application so it knows which JNDI libraries it needs to use. One way to do this is to create a `Properties` object and then pass this to `InitialContext`:

```
Properties properties = new Properties();
properties.put(Context.INITIAL_CONTEXT_FACTORY
  ,"oracle.j2ee.rmi.RMIInitialContextFactory");
```

```
properties.put(Context.PROVIDER_URL,
    "ormi://192.168.0.6:23791/appendixa");
properties.put(Context.SECURITY_PRINCIPAL, "oc4jadmin");
properties.put(Context.SECURITY_CREDENTIALS, "welcome1");

Context context = new InitialContext(properties);
```

In this example, the custom `Properties` entries specify that you're trying to connect to a remote Oracle application server JNDI tree. Note that JNDI connection properties are vendor-specific and the example here can't be used universally, so you should consult with the documentation for your application server to see how you can connect to it remotely.

Another way to do the configuration is to create a `jndi.properties` file and put this file anywhere in your application's `CLASSPATH`. The same name/value pairs used with the `Properties` object are put into the `jndi.properties` file. With this configuration, you simply need to create a new `InitialContext`:

```
Context context = new InitialContext();
```

In this example, the `jndi.properties` file is found on the `CLASSPATH` for the configuration. Most application servers will make a default `jndi.properties` automatically available in the `CLASSPATH`. As a result, in most cases your JNDI context initialization code inside an application server will look no more complex than the simple object creation via the `new` operator with a default constructor.

Table 5.3 describes the most common JNDI properties required to connect to a remote JNDI service provider interface (SDI).

Table 5.3 Common JNDI properties for connecting to a remote JNDI Java EE environment

Property name	Description	Example value
`java.naming.factory.initial`	The name of the factory class that will be used to create the context	`oracle.j2ee.rmi.RMIInitialContextFactory`
`java.naming.provider.url`	The URL for the JNDI service provider	`ormi://localhost:23791/chapter1`
`java.naming.security.principal`	The username or identity for authenticating the caller in the JNDI service provider	`oc4jadmin`
`java.naming.security.credentials`	The password for the username/principal being used for authentication.	`welcome1`

LOOKUP JNDI RESOURCES

After you've connected to your JNDI provider, the `Context` interface provides the functionality to interact with the provider and get resources. For this primer, we'll concentrate on the `lookup` method and leave the rest for you to explore on your own. Table 5.4 describes this method.

Table 5.4 Context lookup method

Method	Description
`Object lookup(String name)`	Returns the named resource, which must be typecast to the type you need. A new `Context` instance is returned if the resource name is empty.

So to look up a resource, you need to know the resource's name. Suppose the `BidService` EJB is bound in JNDI at `"/ejb/bid/BidService"`. To look up the `BidService`, you can look it up directly:

```
Context context = new InitialContext();
BidService service = (BidService) context.lookup("/ejb/bid/BidService");
```

Or you can chain lookups together:

```
Context newContext = new InitialContext();
Context bidContext = (Context) newContext.lookup("/ejb/bid/");
BidService service = (BidService) bidContext.lookup("BidService");
```

Although these lookup code examples look pretty harmless, don't be taken by appearances. JNDI lookups were one of the primary reasons for EJB 2.x complexity. First of all, you had to do lookups to access any resource managed by the container, even if you were only accessing data sources and EJBs from other EJBs located in the same JVM. Given that most EJBs in an application depend on other EJBs and resources, imagine the lines of repetitive JNDI lookup code littered across an average business application! To make matters worse, before Java EE 6, JNDI resources didn't have standard lookup names with every Enterprise server binding resources in JNDI with different names. So JNDI lookup names weren't portable across servers and the JNDI names of resources weren't always that obvious to figure out, especially for local resources that used the arcane `java:comp/env/` prefix.

The good news is that except for certain corner cases, you won't have to deal with JNDI directly in EJB 3. EJB 3 hides the mechanical details of JNDI lookups behind metadata-based DI. DI does such a great job in abstraction that you won't even know that JNDI lookups are happening behind the scenes, even for remote lookups. This abstraction is possible in part to standard JNDI lookup names, especially for EJBs, which are portable across all EE servers. In the next section we'll look at this standard and see how EJB names are assigned.

5.2.2 *How EJB names are assigned*

To make EJB JNDI lookups portable across all Java EE servers, the following portable JNDI name has been standardized:

```
java:<namespace>/[app-name]/<module-name>/<bean-name>[!fully-qualified-
    interface-name]
```

Where `<namespace>`, `<module-name>`, and `<bean-name>` are required and always present, `[app-name]` and `[!fully-qualified-interface-name]` may be optional. Let's take a look at each part of this portable JNDI name and see how they get their values.

<NAMESPACE>

The Java EE server's naming environment is divided into four namespaces, with each namespace representing a different scope. Table 5.5 describes these namespaces.

Table 5.5 Java EE naming environment namespaces

Namespace	Description
`java:comp`	Lookups in this namespace are scoped per component. For example, an EJB is a component, so each EJB in a JAR file gets its own unique `java:comp` namespace. This means both `AccountEJB` and `CartEJB` can look up `java:comp/LogLevel` and get different values. For backward compatibility, this isn't true for the web module. All components deployed as part of a WAR share the same `java:comp` namespace. It's unlikely you'll use this namespace very often. It's mostly there for backward compatibility. Prior to Java EE 6, `java:comp` was really the only standard namespace.
`java:module`	Lookups in this namespace are scoped per module. All components in the module share the `java:module` namespace. An EJB-JAR file is a module, as is a WAR file. For backward compatibility, the `java:comp` and `java:module` namespaces are treated identically in web modules and refer to the same namespace. You should favor the use of `java:module` over `java:comp` when possible.
`java:app`	Lookups in this namespace are scoped per application. All components in all modules in the application share the `java:app` namespace. An EAR is an example of an application. All WARs and EJBs deployed from the EAR would share this namespace.
`java:global`	Lookups in this namespace are global and shared by all components in all modules in all applications.

[APP-NAME]

The `[app-name]` value is optional and only present if the EJBs are deployed to the server inside of an EAR. If an EAR isn't used, then the `[app-name]` value will be absent from the EJBs' portable JNDI name.

The default value for `[app-name]` is the name of the EAR file without the .ear extension. The application.xml file is able to override this default value, however.

<MODULE-NAME>

The `<module-name>` value is required and will always be present. The value for `<module-name>` depends on how the modules containing the EJBs are deployed.

For EJBs deployed as standalone EJB-JAR files (JAR files deployed directly), the default value for `<module-name>` is the name of the EJB-JAR file without the .jar extension. This default name can be overridden using the `module-name` element of the META-INF/ejb-jar.xml configuration file.

For EJBs deployed as part of a standalone web module (WAR file), the default value for `<module-name>` is the name of the WAR file without the .war extension. This default name can be overridden using the `module-name` element of the WEB-INF/web.xml configuration file.

For EJBs deployed as part of an Enterprise application (EAR file), the default value for `<module-name>` will be determined differently depending on whether the EJB is part of an EJB-JAR or WAR in the EAR. Inside a WAR, the default name follows the standalone web module rules. Use WEB-INF/web.xml to change this default. In an EJB-JAR, the default name is the fully qualified path (directory) of the EJB-JAR inside the EAR plus the name of the EJB-JAR file without the .jar extension. Use the EJB-JAR's META-INF/ejb-jar.xml to change this default.

<BEAN-NAME>

The `<bean-name>` value is required and will always be present. For EJBs defined using the `@Stateless`, `@Stateful`, or `@Singleton` annotations, the default value for `<bean-name>` is the *unqualified* name of the bean class. This default value can be overridden using the annotation `name()` attribute. For EJBs defined using ejb-jar.xml the `bean-name` element sets the value for the bean name.

[!FULLY-QUALIFIED-INTERFACE-NAME]

The `[!fully-qualified-interface-name]` is required, and a binding with a value for this part of the portable EJB name will always exist in JNDI. But the EE server is also required to create a binding in JNDI with this value missing. This "shortcut" binding is useful when the EJB can only be accessed through one interface (or has no interface at all). The following examples will make this clearer. The values for `[!fully-qualified-interface-name]` are the fully qualified names of each local, remote, EJB 2 local home, or EJB 2 remote home interface or the fully qualified name of the bean class if the bean class implements no interfaces.

EXAMPLES

This is a stateless EJB implementing a single interface:

```
package com.bazaar;
@Stateless
public class AccountBean implements Account { ... }
```

If it's deployed as accountejb.jar, it'll have the following JNDI bindings:

```
java:global/accountejb/AccountBean
java:global/accountejb/AccountBean!com.bazaar.Account

java:app/accountejb/AccountBean
java:app/accountejb/AccountBean!com.bazaar.Account

java:module/AccountBean
java:module/AccountBean!com.bazaar.Account
```

If it's deployed as accountejb.jar inside accountapp.ear, it'll have the following JNDI bindings:

```
java:global/accountapp/accountejb/AccountBean
java:global/accountapp/accountejb/AccountBean!com.bazaar.Account
```

```
java:app/accountejb/AccountBean
java:app/accountejb/AccountBean!com.bazaar.Account

java:module/AccountBean
java:module/AccountBean!com.bazaar.Account
```

If it's deployed as accountweb.war, it'll have the following JNDI bindings:

```
java:global/accountweb/AccountBean
java:global/accountweb/AccountBean!com.bazaar.Account

java:app/accountweb/AccountBean
java:app/accountweb/AccountBean!com.bazaar.Account

java:module/AccountBean
java:module/AccountBean!com.bazaar.Account
```

Now that you know how the portable JNDI names for EJBs are assigned, we'll look at the `@EJB` annotation, which takes away the complexity of JNDI lookups and allows the EE server to inject EJBs as needed.

5.2.3 *EJB injection using @EJB*

The `@EJB` annotation was introduced to allow injection of EJBs into client code without the client code needing to perform JNDI lookups. Although the portable JNDI names for EJBs make the look-up of beans easier, lookups still put the responsibility on the developer to get the dependencies your code needs. By using the `@EJB` annotation, that responsibility is now part of the EE server, and the EJB container will inject the dependencies for you. The following listing shows the `@EJB` annotation.

Listing 5.2 `javax.ejb.EJB` annotation

```
@Target({TYPE, METHOD, FIELD}) @Retention(RUNTIME)
  public @interface EJB {
    String name() default "";
    Class beanInterface() default Object.class;
    String beanName() default "";
    String lookup() default "";
}
```

All three of the `@EJB` elements are optional, and for the most part, the EE server will be able to figure what bean to inject without any trouble simply by type. The elements are there to handle edge cases that aren't encountered very often. Table 5.6 describes the elements.

Table 5.6 `@EJB` annotation elements

Element	Description
`name`	Besides performing injection, the `@EJB` annotation implicitly creates a binding referring to the injected EJB in the `java:comp` namespace. This is primarily done for backward compatibility. This attribute allows you to specify the name that's used for the implicit binding. This is equivalent to the `<ejb-ref-name>` element in deployment descriptors used extensively in EJB 2.

Table 5.6 `@EJB` annotation elements *(continued)*

Element	Description
`beanInterface`	This helps narrow the type of EJB references when needed, which can be a local business interface, a remote business interface, or the bean class if it implements no interfaces.
`beanName`	This refers to either the `name` element of the `@Stateless` or `@Stateful` annotations or the `<ejb-name>` tag of the deployment descriptor for the bean. Like `beanInterface`, this helps to narrow down the specific bean to inject in cases where multiple beans implement the same interface.
`lookup`	This is the actual JNDI lookup name of the EJB to be injected. This is likely the attribute you'll use the most.
`mappedName`	A vendor-specific name for the bean.
`description`	A description of the EJB.

5.2.4 When to use EJB injection

It's a good idea to always use EJB injection when you can. But the `@EJB` annotation is specifically intended for injecting session beans into client code and injection is only possible within managed environments. This annotation only works inside another EJB, in code running inside an application-client container (ACC), or in components registered with the web container (such as a Servlet or JSF-backing bean). If you need an EJB in any other code, you'll need to use JNDI directly and perform a lookup.

5.2.5 @EJB annotation in action

The `@EJB` annotation is very easy to put into action. It is also very powerful because it has smart defaults which allows you to quickly wire EJB injection with very little effort but it also has the flexibility to handle unique situations where the defaults are not enough and you need to provide some customization for your injections. What follows next are some examples showing how to put the `@EJB` annotation into action.

DEFAULT INJECTION

Suppose you have the following local interface and implementing bean:

```
@Local
public interface AccountLocal {
  public void Account getAccount(String accountId);
}

@Stateless(name="accountByDatabase")
public class AccountByDatabaseEjb implements AccountLocal {. . .}
```

To inject this bean into a container-managed resource, such as a Servlet, you can use the `@EJB` annotation without any of the optional elements and let the container figure out the DI:

```
@EJB
AccountLocal accountInfo;
```

In this example, the container will detect the @EJB annotation and see that the injected bean needs to implement the AccountLocal interface. The container will look through its registered beans and inject an instance of AccountByDatabaseEjb because that bean implements the required interface.

INJECTION USING BEANNAME

Now suppose your code base has more than one implementation of the AccountLocal interface. The previous example shows an implementation using a database; now let's add an implementation that uses Active Directory:

```
@Stateless(name="accountByActiveDirectory")
public class AccountByActiveDirectoryEjb implements AccountLocal {. . .}
```

With multiple beans now implementing the AccountLocal interface, you need to give the @EJB annotation a little help so the container knows which implementation should be injected:

```
@EJB(beanName="accountByActiveDirectory")
AccountLocal accountInfo;
```

In this example, the container detects the @EJB annotation, and the value for beanName narrows down what implementation to inject. The container will find the bean with the name accountByActiveDirectory, check that the bean implements the AccountLocal interface, and inject an instance of the AccountByActiveDirectoryEjb into the accountInfo variable.

INJECTION USING BEANINTERFACE

In many cases, you'll have a common interface that you'll want to expose locally and remotely. Your classes may resemble this structure:

```
public interface AccountServices {
    public Account getAccount(String accountId);
}

@Local
public interface AccountLocal extends AccountServices {}

@Remote
public interface AccountRemote extends AccountServices {}

@Stateless
public class AccountEjb implements AccountLocal, AccountRemote {. . .}
```

The @EJB annotation is configured using the beanInterface property to tell the container to inject either the remote or the local interface:

```
@EJB(beanInterface="AccountLocal.class")
AccountServices accountServices;
```

In this example, the container detects the @EJB annotation, and the value for beanInterface narrows down what to inject. The container will find a bean with AccountLocal.class as an interface. When the bean is injected, it's type-casted to AccountServices. Injecting like this tells the container you want to use a local bean but interact with it through AccountServices. This is good practice if you want to have both remote and local interactions to stay the same.

INJECTION USING BEANNAME

Now suppose your code base has more than one implementation of the AccountLocal interface. The previous example shows an implementation using a database; now let's add an implementation that uses Active Directory:

```
@Stateless(name="accountByActiveDirectory")
public class AccountByActiveDirectoryEjb implements AccountLocal {. . .}
```

With multiple beans now implementing the AccountLocal interface, you need to give the @EJB annotation a little help so the container knows which implementation should be injected:

```
@EJB(beanName="accountByActiveDirectory")
AccountLocal accountInfo;
```

In this example, the container detects the @EJB annotation, and the value for beanName narrows down what implementation to inject. The container will find the bean with the name accountByActiveDirectory, check that the bean implements the AccountLocal interface, and inject an instance of the AccountByActiveDirectoryEjb into the accountInfo variable.

INJECTION USING LOOKUP

Using the lookup attribute takes all the guesswork out of EJB injection. Instead of the container trying to resolve the correct bean, you can tell the container exactly which bean you want by specifying the actual JNDI name:

```
@EJB(lookup="java:module/DefaultAccountService")
AccountServices accountServices;
```

In this example, the container detects the @EJB annotation and the value for lookup narrows down what to look up from JNDI and inject. You can use any naming scope that makes sense.

Using the @EJB annotation is very powerful and allows the container to do the work of looking up beans and injecting them into classes instead of you having to do the JNDI lookups yourself. The @EJB annotation is a special subset of DI that only handles EJBs. There are other resources, such as JDBC data sources, JMS queues, and email sessions, which the container manages and your code needs to get at. In the next session we'll discuss the @Resource annotation for injecting these other resources.

Injection using proxy objects

When a container injects an EJB, what really gets injected? The answer is a proxy object. The container creates a proxy object for your bean and injects the proxy, not the bean class itself. The container does this so it can properly manage all the services that EJBs provide, such as transactions and thread safety. The proxy also makes

(continued)

sure the correct underlying bean is being accessed through the proxy. For example, suppose you have the following simple stateless session bean:

```
@Stateless
public class BidService {
}
```

Because all references to this bean are assigned the same object identity by the container, the proxy ensures the correct object is returned. You can use the `equals()` method to check if this is true:

```
@EJB
BidService bid1;
@EJB
BidService bid2;
. . .
bid1.equals(bid2);  // this will return true
```

On the other hand, suppose you have the following simple stateful session bean:

```
@Stateful
public class ShoppingCart {
}
```

In this case, the container is required to assign different identities to different stateful session bean instances. The proxy handles this as well, so the `equals()` method can check that these are two different carts:

```
@EJB
ShoppingCart cart1;
@EJB
ShoppingCart cart2;
. . .
cart1.equals(cart2); // this is required to be false
```

5.2.6 *Resource injection using @Resource*

The `@Resource` annotation is by far the most versatile mechanism for resource injection in EJB 3. In most cases the annotation is used to inject JDBC data sources, JMS resources, and EJB contexts. But the annotation can also be used for anything in the JNDI registry. The following listing shows the `@Resource` annotation.

Listing 5.3 `javax.annotation.Resource` annotation

```
@Target({TYPE, FIELD, METHOD}) @Retention(RUNTIME)
  public @interface Resource {
    String name() default "";
    String lookup() default "";
    Class type() default java.lang.Object.class;
    AuthenticationType authenticationType()
      default AuthenticationType.CONTAINER;
    boolean shareable() default true;
}
```

All of the @Resource elements are optional. Just as in the case of EJBs, the EE server can usually figure out what resource to inject by the resource type. But this isn't always the case, so the elements are there to help the container figure it out. For example, you may want to inject a DataSource, but if your EE server is configured with multiple data sources, you'll need to use the name or lookup elements to narrow down which one to inject. Table 5.7 describes the elements.

Table 5.7 @Resource annotation elements

Element	Description
name	Besides performing an injection, the @Resource annotation implicitly creates a binding referring to the injected resource in the java:comp namespace. This is primarily done for backward compatibility. This attribute allows you to specify the name that's used for the implicit binding. This is equivalent to the <res-ref-name> element in deployment descriptors used extensively in EJB 2.
lookup	This is the actual JNDI lookup name of the resource to be injected. This is likely the attribute you'll use the most.
type	The type of the resource. If the @Resource annotation is on a field, the default is the type of the field. If the annotation is on a setter method, the default is the type of the method's element.
authenticationType	This can have the value AuthenticationType.CONTAINER or AuthenticationType.APPLICATION. This is only used for connection factory–type resources like data sources.
shareable	This indicates if this resource can be shared between other components. This is only for connection factory type resources like data sources.
mappedName	A vendor-specific name for the bean.
description	A description of the EJB.

The @Resource annotation attributes are used in the same fashion as in the @EJB annotation.

5.2.7 When to use resource injection

The @Resource annotation is used to inject container-managed resources into code that the container also manages. This annotation works only inside an EJB, an MDB, in code running inside an application-client container (ACC), or in components registered with the web container (such as a Servlet or JSF-backing bean). Resources range from a simple integer value to a complex DataSource, but as long as the resource is container-managed, the @Resource annotation can be used to inject it into your code.

5.2.8 @Resource annotation in action

Let's take a brief look at injecting DataSource, JMS, EJBContext, email, timer, and environment entry resources. We'll start with a familiar JDBC DataSource example to explain the basic features of the `@Resource` annotation before moving on to the more involved cases.

INJECTING DATASOURCE

The following code injects a `DataSource` into the `DefaultBidService` bean:

```
@Stateless
public class DefaultBidService implements BidService {
  ...
  @Resource(lookup="java:global/jdbc/ActionBazaarDB")
  private DataSource dataSource;
```

The `lookup` element allows for direct JNDI lookup, and this code assumes the EE server has been configured with a `DataSource` bound to this location. If this name is changed or if the `DataSource` is bound to a different location in a different EE server, the injection will fail.

INJECTING JMS RESOURCES

Recall the discussion on messaging and MDBs in chapter 4. If your application has anything to do with messaging, it's likely going to need to use JMS resources such as `javax.jms.Queue`, `javax.jms.Topic`, `javax.jms.QueueConnectionFactory`, or `javax.jms.TopicConnectionFactory`. Just like a JDBC `DataSource`, these resources are stored in the application server's JNDI context and can be injected through the `@Resource` annotation. As an example, the following code injects a `Queue` bound to the name `"java:global/jms/ActionBazaarQueue"` to the `queue` field:

```
@Resource(lookup="java:global/jms/ActionBazaarQueue")
private Queue queue;
```

INJECTING EJBCONTEXT

Earlier we discussed the `EJBContext`, `SessionContext`, and `MessageDrivenContext` interfaces. One of the most common uses of resource injection is to gain access to the `EJBContext`. The following code, used in the `DefaultBidService` session bean, injects the EJB type–specific context into the `context` instance variable:

```
@Resource
private SessionContext context;
```

Note that the injected session context isn't stored anywhere in JNDI. In fact, it would be incorrect to try to specify JNDI lookup parameters in this case at all, and servers will probably ignore the element if specified. Instead, when the container detects the `@Resource` annotation on the `context` variable, it figures out that the EJB context specific to the current bean instance must be injected by looking at the variable data type, `javax.ejb.SessionContext`. Because `DefaultBidService` is a session bean, the result of the injection would be the same if the variable were specified to be the parent class, `EJBContext`. In the following code, an underlying instance of `javax.ejb.SessionContext` is still injected into the `context` variable, even if the variable data type is `javax.ejb.EJBContext`:

```
@Resource
private EJBContext context;
```

Using this code in a session bean would make a lot of sense if you didn't plan to use any of the bean type–specific methods available through the `SessionContext` interface anyway.

INJECTING ENVIRONMENT ENTRIES

If you've been working with Enterprise applications for any length of time, it's likely you've encountered situations where some parameters of your application change from one deployment to another (customer site information, product version, and so on). It's overkill to save this kind of "semi-static" information in the database. This is exactly the situation environment entry values are designed to handle.

For example, in the ActionBazaar application, suppose you want to set the censorship flag for certain countries. If this flag is on, the ActionBazaar application checks items posted against a censorship list specific to the country the application deployment instance is geared toward. You can inject an instance of an environment entry as follows:

```
@Resource
private boolean censorship;
```

Environment entries are specified in the deployment descriptor and are accessible via JNDI. The ActionBazaar censorship flag could be specified like this:

```
<env-entry>
  <env-entry-name>censorship</env-entry-name>
  <env-entry-type>java.lang.Boolean</env-entry-type>
  <env-entry-value>true</env-entry-value>
</env-entry>
```

Environment entries are essentially meant to be robust application constants and support a relatively small range of data types. Specifically, the values of the `<env-entry-type>` tag are limited to these Java types: `String`, `Character`, `Byte`, `Short`, `Integer`, `Long`, `Boolean`, `Double`, and `Float`. Because environment entries are accessible via JNDI they can be injected by name. As you might gather, the data types of the environment entry and the injected variable must be compatible. Otherwise, the container throws a runtime exception while attempting injection. Note that if you have complex DI-based configuration needs, you should most likely look into CDI. CDI is covered in more depth in section 5.3.8.

INJECTING EMAIL RESOURCES

In addition to JDBC data sources and JMS resources, the other heavy-duty resource Enterprise application often used is the JavaMail API `javax.mail.Session`. JavaMail sessions abstract the email server configuration and are stored in the application server JNDI registry. The `Session` can be injected into an EJB with the `@Resource` annotation and used to send email. In the ActionBazaar application, this is useful for sending the winning bidder a notification after bidding on an item is over. The code to inject the mail `Session` looks like this:

```
@Resource(lookup="java:global/mail/ActionBazaar")
private javax.mail.Session mailSession;
```

We'll leave the deployment descriptor configuration of a mail session as an exercise. You can find the one-to-one mapping between annotations and deployment descriptors in appendix A.

INJECTING THE TIMER SERVICE

The container-managed timer service gives EJBs the ability to schedule tasks in a simple way (you'll learn more about timers in chapter 7). You inject the container timer service into an EJB using the `@Resource` annotation:

```
@Resource
private javax.ejb.TimerService timerService;
```

Just as with the EJB context, the timer service isn't registered in JNDI, but the container resolves the resource by looking at the data type of the injection target.

As useful as `@Resource` is, it can't solve every problem. There are some cases where you must programmatically look up resources from a JNDI registry yourself. We'll talk about some of these cases next, as well as show you how to perform programmatic lookups.

Field injection versus setter injection

In the vast majority of cases, resources and EJBs are injected into fields. In DI parlance this is called field injection. But besides field injection, EJB also supports setter injection (on the other hand, EJB doesn't support constructor injection, whereas CDI does). To see how it works, transform the data source example to use setter injection:

```
@Stateless
public class DefaultBidService implements BidService {
  ...
  private DataSource dataSource;
  ...
  @Resource(lookup="java:global/jdbc/ActionBazaarDB")
  public void setDataSource(DataSource dataSource) {
    this.dataSource = dataSource;
}
```

Just as in field injection, the container inspects the `@Resource` annotation on the `setDataSource` method before a bean instance becomes usable, looks up the data source from JNDI using the lookup element value, and calls the `setDataSource` method using the retrieved data source as the parameter.

Whether or not to use setter injection is largely a matter of taste. Although setter injection might seem like a little more work, it provides a couple of distinct advantages. First, it's easier to unit test by invoking the public setter method from a testing framework like JUnit. Second, it's easier to put initialization code in the setter if you need it.

In this case, you can open a database connection in the `setDataSource` method as soon as injection happens, as follows:

```
private Connection connection;
...
@Resource(lookup="java:global/jdbc/ActionBazaarDB")
public void setDataSource(DataSource dataSource) {
  this.connection = dataSource.getConnection();
}
```

5.2.9 *Looking up resources and EJBs from JNDI*

Although you can use the `@EJB` or `@Resource` annotations to inject resource instances, you may still need to look up items from JNDI in several advanced cases. There are two ways of using programmatic lookups—with either the `EJBContext` or a JNDI `InitialContext`. We'll look at both methods.

EJBCONTEXT LOOKUP

Recall from an earlier discussion that you're able to look up any object stored in JNDI using the `EJBContext.lookup()` method (including session bean references). This technique can be used to accomplish something extremely powerful: building lookups so resources can be changed dynamically during runtime. Injection, though powerful, does constrain you to using static configuration that can't be changed programmatically.

Building lookups to dynamically get different resources at runtime is similar to dynamically building SQL statements. The difference is that instead of performing a query on a database, you perform a lookup on JNDI. All you have to do is pass the dynamically generated name to the lookup method to retrieve a different resource. As a result, program logic driven by data and/or user input can determine dependencies instead of deploy-time configuration. The following code shows the `EJBContext.lookup()` method in action:

```
@Stateless
public class DefaultDiscountService implements DiscountService {
  @Resource
  private SessionContext sessionContext;
  ...
  DiscountRateService discountRateService
      = (DiscountRateService) sessionContext.lookup(
          "java:app/ejb/HolidayDiscountRateService");
  ...
  long discount = discountRateService.calculateDiscount(...);
```

This example shows how to look up a `DiscountRateService` using the `SessionContext`. Notice that the JNDI lookup string is part of the code and can easily be dynamically changed to look up different implementations of `DiscountRateService` based on any business rules. In this example, the EJB must be mapped to the `java:app` namespace and the `/ejb/HolidayDiscountRateService` path.

INITIALCONTEXT LOOKUP

Although both DI and lookup using `EJBContext` are relatively convenient, the problem is that the `EJBContext` is available only inside the Java EE or application client container. For POJOs outside a container, you're limited to the most basic method of looking up JNDI references—using a JNDI `InitialContext`. The code to do this is a little mechanical, but it isn't too complex:

```
Context context = new InitialContext();
BidService bidService = (BidService)
        context.lookup("java:app/ejb/DefaultBidService");
```

```
...
bidService.addBid(bid);
```

The `InitialContext` object can be created by any code having access to the JNDI API. Also, the object can be used to connect to a remote JNDI server, not just a local one. Note that although this code probably looks harmless enough, you should avoid it if at all possible. Mechanical JNDI lookup code was one of the major pieces of avoidable complexity in EJB 2, particularly when these same bits of code were repeated hundreds of times across an application.

5.2.10 When to use JNDI lookups

For the majority of cases, the `@EJB` and `@Resource` annotations will be able to inject the resources you need into your classes and you'll not need to use JNDI lookups directly. There are, however, cases when JNDI lookups will be needed.

Classes not managed by the container will need to use JNDI lookups. The `@EJB` and `@Resource` annotations are available only to classes managed by the Java EE or application client container. This includes objects like EJBs, MDBs, Servlets, and JSF-backing beans. Any nonmanaged class will need to use JNDI lookups through the `InitialContext` to get access to the server's resources.

Resource access isn't always static, and as a consequence, it may not be possible to use the `@EJB` or `@Resource` annotations to inject a static resource into your object. If your resource lookup is dynamic, you'll need to use JNDI lookups. If this dynamic behavior occurs in a container-managed resource such as an EJB, you're able to inject an `EJBContext` into your EJB (using `@Resource`, of course) and then use `EJBContext.lookup()` to dynamically look up the resource you need. If your dynamic behavior occurs in a non-container-managed resource, such as a utility class, you'll need to use the `InitialContext`.

5.2.11 Application client containers

So far you've been learning about EJB and resource injection for applications that are deployed inside an EE server and run inside the EE server as well. But what about SE applications that run outside the EE server that need to access the EJBs and other resources the server manages? This is where the application client container (ACC) comes in.

The ACC is a hidden gem in the EE world. It's a mini Java EE container that can be run from the command line. Think of it as a souped-up Java Virtual Machine (JVM) with some Java EE juice added. You can run any Java SE client such as a Swing application inside the ACC as if you were using a regular JVM. The beauty of it is that the ACC will recognize and process most Java EE annotations such as the `@EJB` annotation. Among other things, the ACC can look up and inject EJBs on remote servers, communicate with remote EJBs using RMI, provide authentication, perform authorization, publish and subscribe to JMS resources, and so forth. The ACC really shines if you need to use EJBs in an SE application or would like to inject real resources into your POJO during unit testing.

Any Java class with a main method can be run inside the ACC. Typically, you package your application as a JAR and define the `MainClass` in `META-INF/MANIFEST`. Optionally, the JAR may contain a deployment descriptor (`META-INF/application-client.xml`) and a `jndi.properties` file that contains the environment properties for connecting to a remote EJB container. As a quick example, if the ActionBazaar EE application had a remote bid service EJB, an SE application would simply use a static property to inject it, as follows:

```
@EJB
private static BidService remoteBidService;

public class BidServiceClient {
  public static void main(String[] args) {
        System.out.println("result = " + remoteBidService.addBid(bid));
    }
```

Once you've created your SE application, the process of running it in the ACC is EE server–specific. Let's take a quick look at how to do this with GlassFish. Assume you packaged up your SE application in a JAR file named bidservice-client.jar. Using Sun Microsystems's GlassFish application server, you could launch your SE application inside the ACC as follows:

```
appclient -client bidservice-client.jar
```

You'll need to consult the documentation for your EE server to get the details on using its ACC.

5.2.12 *Embedded containers*

Although the Java EE specification is intended for an Enterprise application running inside of an EE server, not all applications are intended to run that way. Nevertheless, most applications will need common services like DI and container-managed transactions, which EE servers happen to provide. This is where embedded containers come in. An *embedded container* is an in-memory EJB container that an SE application (or unit tests) can start and run within its own JVM. The SE application can then take advantage of most of the power and convenience provided by EJBs.

You may think the ACC and embedded containers are the same, but they're quite different. An ACC is all about an SE application connecting to a remote EE server to gain access to its resources, so all of the resources are remote. For an embedded container, all of the resources are local because the SE application starts its own in-memory EJB container and becomes its own little EE server.

CREATING AN EMBEDDED CONTAINER

The `javax.ejb.embeddable.EJBContainer` is an abstract class that EE servers may choose to implement—it's not a requirement. A static method bootstraps its creation:

```
EJBContainer ec = EJBContainer.createEJBContainer();
```

An SE application may then use `EJBContainer` to interact with the EJB container. The SE may perform operations such as lookups to get EJB instances. Table 5.8 defines `EJBContainer`'s methods.

Table 5.8 Methods of `EJBContainer`

Method	Description
`close()`	Shuts down the in-memory EJB container.
`createEJBContainer()`	Creates an `EJBContainer` using default properties.
`createEJBContainer(Map<?,?>)`	Creates an `EJBContainer` providing values for some properties.
`getContext()`	Returns `javax.naming.Context`.

REGISTERING EJBS

When using the default `createEJBContainer()` bootstrap method, the application's class path will be scanned for EJBs. If you don't want the entire class path scanned, or if for some reason you want only specific EJBs loaded, use `createEJBContainer(java.util.Map<?,?>)` and configure the map with names of the modules you want loaded. For example, this configuration will scan for EJBs only in the bidservice.jar and accountservice.jar files; there may be other EJBs in other modules but they'll be ignored.

```
Properties props = new Properties();
props.setProperty(
  EJBContainer.MODULES, new String[]{"bidservice","accountsevice"});
EJBContainer ec = EJBContainer.createEJBContainer(props);
```

When an EJB is found, the embedded container will bind the EJB to JNDI using the portable global JNDI name, the same as a full EE server. For example, suppose on the class path there's bidservice.jar, which has an `@Local com.bazaar.BidServiceLocal` interface with an `@Stateless com.bazaar.BidServiceEjb` implementation. The embedded container will bind the following:

```
java:global/bidservice/BidServiceEjb
java:global/bidservice/BidServiceEjb!com.bazaar.BidServiceLocal
```

EJBs with `@Local` interfaces or no-interface EJBs are allowed in the embedded container. `@Remote` beans aren't supported by the embedded container.

PERFORMING EJB LOOKUPS

EJB lookups are the same as any other JNDI lookup. For classes not managed by the embedded container, use the `Context` provided by `EJBContainer.getContext()` to perform the lookup. For example, get the `BidServiceLocal` EJB as follows:

```
Context ctx = ec.getContext();
BidServiceLocal bsl = ctx.lookup("java:global/bidservice/BidServiceEjb");
```

Of course, for EJBs managed by the embedded container, use the `@EJB` and `@Resource` annotations and have the embedded container perform the DI.

CLOSING

When your application is finished with the embedded container, use `ec.close()` to close it and release its resources. Closing the embedded container doesn't mean the SE application is closing as well. The SE application may decide to close the embedded container for any number of reasons. Once closed, the standalone application is free to bootstrap a new one if needed.

The embedded container has also been updated to implement the `AutoCloseable` interface. Because of this, you can use the `try-with-resource` statement and have the embedded container closed for you automatically. Using the `try-with-resource` statement looks like this:

```
try (EJBContainer ec = EJBContainer.createEJBContainer())
{
    // do what you want with the embedded container
} catch (Throwable t) {
    t.printStackTrace();
}
```

5.2.13 Using EJB injection and lookup effectively

Using the `@EJB` annotation to inject bean instances into your code is the quickest, easiest, and safest way for you to wire your application together. For the majority of cases, the EJB container will be able to determine what bean to create and inject by either the bean's interface or the bean class itself. But a lookup becomes necessary for `@EJB` injection if multiple beans implement the same interface and you're referencing the bean by that interface. CDI injection has a more elegant solution, which we'll look at next.

5.2.14 EJB versus CDI injection

The `@EJB` annotation is a fast, easy, and powerful way to have the EE server inject EJBs into managed resources for you. The `@EJB` annotation was a great step forward for simplifying Enterprise development and introducing DI to the EJB container. But `@EJB` is limited to injecting only EJBs and only into managed resources like other EJBs, JSF-backing beans, and Servlets. CDI, on the other hand, is much more powerful and `@Inject` can inject just about anything into anything else. This includes the ability for `@Inject` to inject EJBs. Because `@Inject` is more powerful and can inject EJBs, why use `@EJB`?

For simple cases, `@EJB` and `@Inject` are interchangeable. Suppose ActionBazaar's `SimpleBidService` is a stateless no-interface EJB, which is as simple as you can get:

```
@Stateless
public class SimpleBidService {
  ...
}
```

In this case, @EJB and @Inject can be used exactly the same way and produce exactly the same results:

```
@Inject
SimpleBidService bidService;

@EJB
SimpleBidService bidService;
```

But anything beyond this simple example and CDI starts to have a few problems. For example, suppose BidService becomes an interface with multiple implementations:

```
public interface BidService { ... }

@Stateless(name="defaultBids")
public class DefaultBidService implements BidService { ... }

@Stateless(name="clearanceBids")
public class ClearanceBidService implements BidService { ... }
```

@EJB handles this nicely in a few ways, but the easiest is to use the beanName parameter:

```
@EJB(beanName="clearanceBids")
BidService clearanceBidService;
```

@Inject works a bit differently and requires more work to narrow down which implementation of BidService to inject. @Inject requires the creation of a producer class, which follows the factory pattern:

```
public class BidServiceProducer {
    @Produces
    @EJB(beanName="defaultBids")
    @DefaultBids
    BidService defaultBids;

    @Produces
    @EJB(beanName="clearanceBids")
    @ClearanceBids
    BidService clearanceBids;
}
```

@Inject can now be paired with the qualifiers used in BidServiceProducer to inject the right instance of the BidService EJB:

```
@Inject @ClearanceBids
BidService clearanceBidService;
```

Ultimately, to get an EJB beyond the most simple cases, even CDI needs to rely on the @EJB annotation in its producer classes so @Inject will get the right instances of the EJBs.

5.3 AOP in the EJB world: interceptors

Have you ever been in a situation where your requirements changed toward the end of the project and you were asked to add some common missing feature to the EJBs in your application, such as logging or auditing? Adding logging code in each of your EJB classes would be time consuming, and this common type of code also causes maintainability issues and requires you to modify a number of Java classes. Well, EJB 3 interceptors solve this problem. In this section, we'll demonstrate how to create a simple logging interceptor that does the logging. We'll also show how this interceptor can be made the default interceptor for your application, executing any time a bean method is executed. In this section, you'll learn how interceptors work.

5.3.1 What is AOP?

It's very likely you've come across the term *aspect-oriented programming* (AOP). The essential idea behind AOP is that for most applications, common code that doesn't necessarily solve the core business problem and is repeated across components is considered an infrastructure concern and shouldn't be part of the core business logic. The common term used to describe these cases is *crosscutting concerns*—concerns that cut across application logic.

CROSSCUTTING CONCERNS

The most commonly cited example of this is logging, especially at the basic debugging level. To use the ActionBazaar example, let's assume that you log the entry into every method in the system. This would mean adding logging statements at the beginning of every single method in the system to log the action of "entering method XX"! This logic would be copied and pasted everywhere and have little to do with actual business logic. Some other common examples of crosscutting logic are auditing, profiling, and statistics.

An AOP system allows the separation of crosscutting concerns into their own modules. Logging, auditing, profiling, and statistics would all become their own modules. These modules are then applied across the relevant cross-sections of application code, such as the beginning and end of every method call. EJB 3 supports crosscutting functionality by providing the ability to intercept business methods and lifecycle callbacks. We'll now jump into world of EJB 3 interceptors. You'll learn what interceptors are and how to build both business method and lifecycle callback interceptors.

5.3.2 Interceptor basics

To understand the basics of EJB interceptors, let's first briefly look at the basic concepts defined by AOP.

First is the *concern* (or crosscutting concern). The concern, so named, defines what you're concerned about. For example, I'm concerned about adding logging to all of my business methods, or I'm concerned about making sure all numbers are consistently rounded to a certain number of decimal points.

Second is the *advice*. The advice is the actual code you develop to handle whatever concern you have. For example, if your concern is to log method entry events to a database, your advice is the code that connects to the database and executes the query to insert the data.

Third is a *pointcut*. A pointcut describes a point in your application where you want to run the code of your *advice*. Common pointcuts include before entry into a method and after exiting from a method.

Fourth is an *aspect*. An aspect is a combination of a pointcut and advice. Your AOP implementation uses the aspect to weave in your advice and run it at the pointcuts.

An EJB 3 interceptor is the most general form of interception—it's an around-invoke advice. Interceptors are triggered at the entry into a method pointcut. The interceptor is still around when the method returns, so the interceptor can inspect the method return value. The interceptor can also catch any exceptions thrown by the method. Interceptors can be applied to session and message-driven beans.

Although EJB 3 interceptors provide sufficient functionality to handle most common crosscutting concerns, they don't try to provide the level of functionality that a full-scale AOP package such as AspectJ offers. On the flip side, EJB 3 interceptors are also generally a lot easier to use. Now that you know the basics of interceptors, let's take a look at when to use them.

5.3.3 When to use interceptors

EJB 3 interceptors are designed to be used with session beans and MDBs. EJB 3 interceptors are an invoke-around aspect for methods, so you can use interceptors to perform some kind of crosscutting concern logic before a method is executed, examine a return value from an executed method, and catch any exceptions that a method may throw. When an interceptor performs logic before a method is executed, it's usually for an auditing concern (logging, statistic, and so on) or to verify and optionally change parameter values before they're sent to the method. When an interceptor performs logic after the method returns a value, it's again usually for an auditing concern or to alter the return value before actually returning. When an interceptor catches and handles exceptions thrown by the method, again auditing is the most common concern, but the interceptor may also attempt to recall the method or take a different execution path. Now that you know when to use interceptors, let's look at how a basic logging interceptor is implemented.

5.3.4 How interceptors are implemented

Implementing an EJB 3 interceptor requires only two annotations. The first is `@AroundInvoke`. This annotation is placed on the method of a class that you want to serve as the interceptor's advice. Remember, an advice is the actual code you want to weave into your session bean or MDB business methods. The following listing is a quick example. We'll go into more detail about what this code is doing in section 5.3.6.

Listing 5.4 Annotate method with `@AroundInvoke`

```
@Interceptor
public class SayHelloInterceptor {
  @AroundInvoke
  public Object sayHello(InvocationContext ctx) throws Exception {
```

```
        System.out.println("Hello Interceptor!");
        return ctx.proceed();
    }
}
```

The second annotation is `@Interceptors`. This annotation is used in the EJB or MDB class and defines how interceptors are applied to the methods of the class. The next listing shows the `@Interceptors` annotation applied to an individual method.

Listing 5.5 Annotate EJB method with `@Interceptors`

```
@Stateless
public class OrderBean {
  @Interceptors(SayHelloInterceptor.class)
  public Order findOrderById(String id) { return null; }
}
```

The following listing shows the `@Interceptors` annotation applied to the EJB class itself.

Listing 5.6 Annotate EJB class with `@Interceptors`

```
@Stateless
@Interceptors(SayHelloInterceptor.class)
public class OrderBean {  }
```

The combination of `@AroundInvoke` and `@Interceptors` makes providing powerful crosscutting concerns to your application using EJB 3 interceptors simple and easy. This was just a quick taste of how EJB 3 interceptors are implemented to get you going. In section 5.3.6 we'll provide a more comprehensive example and explanation of EJB 3 interceptor features. But first we'll talk more about the different options available in EJB 3 for specifying interceptors.

5.3.5 *Specifying interceptors*

Now that you know the annotations involved for interceptors, you'll learn how to use them. Like a lot of annotations, `@Interceptors` can be used at both a method and a class level. So you'll see examples of this. Annotations are not all-powerful, however. In some cases annotations cannot do the job. This is true for `@Interceptors`, and you'll see an example of this where you'll need to abandon annotations and use the ejb-jar.xml file again.

METHOD- AND CLASS-LEVEL INTERCEPTORS

The `@Interceptors` annotation allows you to specify one or more interceptor classes for a method or class. In listing 5.5 a single interceptor is attached to the `findOrderById()` method. In this example, the `sayHello()` method of `SayHelloInterceptor` will be called before `findOrderById()` is called:

```
@Interceptors(SayHelloInterceptor.class)
public Order findOrderById(String id) { ... }
```

In listing 5.6 a single interceptor is attached to the entire `OrderBean` class. When you attach an interceptor to a class, the interceptor is triggered if any of the target class's methods are invoked. In this example the `sayHello()` method of `SayHelloInterceptor` will be called before any of the methods in `OrderBean` are called:

```
@Stateless
@Interceptors(SayHelloInterceptor.class)
public class OrderBean { ... }
```

The `@Interceptors` annotation is fully capable of attaching more than one interceptor at either a class or a method level. All you have to do is provide a comma-separated list as a parameter to the annotation. For example, add two interceptors to `OrderBean` at the class level:

```
@Stateless
@Interceptors({SayHelloInterceptor.class, SayGoodByeInterceptor.class})
public class OrderBean { ... }
```

DEFAULT-LEVEL INTERCEPTOR

Besides specifying method- and class-level interceptors, you can create what is called a default interceptor. A default interceptor is a catchall mechanism that attaches to all the methods of every bean in the module.

It's important to understand that the scope of default interceptors is limited to the module the interceptor resides in. If the interceptor is in an EJB-JAR file, it's applied only to beans in that EJB-JAR file and no other EJB-JAR files in the EJB container. If the interceptor is inside of a JAR that's part of the library of a WAR, the interceptor is applied to only those beans in the JAR, not to the entire WAR.

To define a default interceptor for a module, you have to use the ejb-jar.xml file. No corresponding annotation exists. Consider an example of a default interceptor for an EJB-JAR module. The following listing shows how to configure two default interceptors for an ActionBazaar module.

Listing 5.7 Configure default interceptors

```
<ejb-jar...>
  <interceptors>                                        <- Declare your interceptor classes
    <interceptor>
      <interceptor-class>com.bazaar.DefaultInterceptor1</interceptor-class>
    </interceptor>
    <interceptor>
      <interceptor-class>com.bazaar.DefaultInterceptor2</interceptor-class>
    </interceptor>
  </interceptors>
  <assembly-descriptor>
    <interceptor-binding>
      <ejb-name>*</ejb-name>                            <- Use * to indicate all EJBs in module
      <interceptor-class>
        com.bazaar.DefaultInterceptor2
      </interceptor-class>
      <interceptor-class>
        com.bazaar.DefaultInterceptor1
      </interceptor-class>
```

List all interceptors to apply to all EJBs in module; the order listed here is the order in which the interceptors are executed.

```
    </interceptor-binding>
  </assembly-descriptor>
</ejb-jar>
```

ORDERING INTERCEPTORS

An interesting question that might have already crossed your mind is what would happen if there are default-, class-, and method-level interceptors all defined at the same time (yes, this is perfectly legal). In which order do you think the interceptors will be triggered?

Interceptors are called from the most general level to the most specific level. That is, the default-level interceptor is triggered first, then any class-level interceptors in the order in which they're listed in the `@Interceptors` annotation on the class, and finally the method-level interceptors in the order in which they're listed in the `@Interceptors` annotation on the method. This is the default ordering of interceptors.

To change the default ordering of interceptors, you use the ejb-jar.xml file to configure the order. The next listing shows how to override any default-level and class-level interceptors on the `OrderBean`.

Listing 5.8 Overriding default- and class-level interceptors

```
<ejb-jar...>
  <interceptors>
    <interceptor>
      <interceptor-class>com.bazaar.MyInterceptor</interceptor-class>
    </interceptor>
  </interceptors>
  <assembly-descriptor>
    <interceptor-binding>
      <ejb-name>OrderBean</ejb-name>
      <interceptor-order>                                    ← 1 Overrides default- and class-level annotations
        <interceptor-class>com.bazaar.MyInterceptor</interceptor-class>   ← 2 Fully qualified name of interceptor class
      </interceptor-order>
    </interceptor-binding>
  </assembly-descriptor>
</ejb-jar>
```

Using the `<interceptor-order>` tag ❶, any default-level interceptors will be overridden as well as any class-level interceptors defined by the `@Interceptors` annotation. The ejb-jar.xml in this example configures the `MyInterceptor` ❷ to be executed instead.

If your bean also has methods annotated with `@Interceptors`, the ejb-jar.xml can be used to override and reorder those interceptors as well. The following listing shows how this is done.

Listing 5.9 Overriding default-, class-, and method-level interceptors

```
<ejb-jar...>
  <interceptors>
    <interceptor>
      <interceptor-class>com.bazaar.MyInterceptor</interceptor-class>
```

```
    </interceptor>
  </interceptors>
  <assembly-descriptor>
    <interceptor-binding>
      <ejb-name>OrderBean</ejb-name>
      <interceptor-order>
         <interceptor-class>com.bazaar.MyInterceptor</interceptor-class>
      </interceptor-order>
      <method>                                        <- Overrides default-,
        <method-name>placeOrder</method-name>            class-, and method-
      </method>                                          level annotations
    </interceptor-binding>
  </assembly-descriptor>
</ejb-jar>
```

Here the example is almost the same as before, but now the `<method>` tag has been added. This ejb-jar.xml file configuration will override any default-, class-, and method-level annotations when the `placeOrder()` method is called. Instead, `MyInterceptor` will be executed.

Defining interceptors with the `@Interceptors` annotation and using the ejb-jar.xml file to either configure interceptors as well or to override the annotations is all about enabling interceptors, and that's only part of the story. Sometimes it's necessary to disable interceptors. We'll look at this next.

DISABLING INTERCEPTORS

In some cases, it may be necessary to disable interceptors. There are two annotations you can use to disable interceptors at either the default or class levels if you need to. Applying the `@javax.interceptor.ExcludeDefaultInterceptors` annotation on either a class or a method disables all default interceptors on the class or method. Similarly, the `@javax.interceptor.ExcludeClassInterceptors` annotation disables class-level interceptors for a method. For the following example, both default- and class-level interceptors are disabled for the `findOrderById()` method, but the `SayHelloInterceptor` will be applied because the method is specifically annotated to use it:

```
@Interceptors(SayHelloInterceptor.class)
@ExcludeDefaultInterceptors
@ExcludeClassInterceptors
public Order findOrderById(String id) { ... }
```

Now that you know how interceptors are implemented and how to specify them, we'll take an in-depth look at the interceptor classes themselves and see them in action.

5.3.6 *Interceptors in action*

Let's implement a basic logging interceptor on `BidServiceBean` from chapter 2. Listing 5.10 contains the code for the interceptor. The interceptor attached to the `addBid()` method will print a log message to the console each time the method is invoked. In a real-world application, this could be used as debugging information (and perhaps printed out using `java.util.logging` or Log4J).

Listing 5.10 EJB business method interceptors

```
@Stateless
public class BidServiceBean implements BidService {
    @Interceptors(ActionBazaarLogger.class)
    public void addBid(Bid bid) {
    }
}

public class ActionBazaarLogger {
    @AroundInvoke
    public Object logMethodEntry(
    InvocationContext invocationContext)
        throws Exception {
    System.out.println("Entering method: "
        + invocationContext.getMethod().getName());
    return invocationContext.proceed();
    }
}
```

❶ Attaching interceptor

❷ Specifying interceptor method

Let's take a bird's-eye view of this code before analyzing each feature in detail in the coming sections. The interceptor class, `ActionBazaarLogger`, is attached to the `addBid()` method of the `PlaceBidBean` stateless session bean using the `@Interceptors` annotation ❶. The `ActionBazaarLogger` object's `logMethodEntry()` method is annotated with `@AroundInvoke` ❷. When the `addBid()` method is called, the method call will be intercepted by `ActionBazaarLogger` and the `logMethodEntry()` method will be invoked before the `addBid()`. The `logMethodEntry()` method prints a log message to the system console and uses `InvocationContext` to include the method name being entered. Finally, the `InvocationContext.proceed()` method is called to signal to the container that the `addBid()` invocation can proceed normally.

Interceptors can be implemented either in the bean class itself or in separate classes. We recommend that you create interceptor methods external to the bean class because that approach allows you to separate crosscutting concerns from business logic and you can share the methods among multiple beans. After all, isn't that the whole point of AOP?

AROUND-INVOKE METHODS

It's important to realize that an interceptor must always have only one method that's designated as the around-invoke (`@AroundInvoke`) method. Around-invoke methods must not be business methods, which means that they shouldn't be public methods in the bean's business interface(s).

An around-invoke method is automatically triggered by the container when a client invokes a method that has designated it to be its interceptor. In listing 5.10, the triggered method is marked with the `@AroundInvoke` annotation:

```
@AroundInvoke
public Object logMethodEntry(InvocationContext invocationContext)
throws Exception {
    System.out.println("Entering method: "
```

```
        + invocationContext.getMethod().getName());
    return invocationContext.proceed();
}
```

In effect, this means that the `logMethodEntry()` method will be executed whenever the `ActionBazaarLogger` interceptor is triggered. As you might gather from this code, any method designated `@AroundInvoke` must follow this pattern:

```
Object <METHOD>(InvocationContext) throws Exception
```

The `InvocationContext` interface passed in as the single parameter to the method provides a number of features that make the AOP mechanism extremely flexible. The `logMethodEntry()` method uses just two of the methods included in the interface. The `getMethod().getName()` call returns the name of the method being intercepted—`"addBid"` in this case.

The call to the `proceed()` method is extremely critical to the functioning of the interceptor. This tells the container it should proceed to the next interceptor in the execution chain or call the intercepted business method. On the other hand, not calling the `proceed()` method will bring processing to a halt and prevent the business method (and any other interceptor down the execution chain) from being called.

This feature can be extremely useful for procedures like security validation. For example, the following interceptor method prevents the intercepted business method from being executed if security validation fails:

```
@AroundInvoke
public Object validateSecurity(InvocationContext invocationContext)
throws Exception {
    if (!validate(...)) {
        throw new SecurityException("Security cannot be validated. " +
            "The method invocation is being blocked.");
    }
    return invocationContext.proceed();
}
```

THE INVOCATIONCONTEXT INTERFACE

The following listing shows that the `javax.interceptor.InvocationContext` interface has a number of other useful methods.

Listing 5.11 `javax.interceptor.InvocationContext` interface

```
public interface InvocationContext {
    public Object getTarget();
    public Method getMethod();
    public Object[] getParameters();
    public void setParameters(Object[]);
    public java.util.Map<String,Object> getContextData();
    public Object proceed() throws Exception;
}
```

The `getTarget()` method retrieves the bean instance that the intercepted method belongs to. This method is particularly valuable for checking the current state of the bean through its instance variables or accessor methods.

The `getMethod()` method returns the method of the bean class for which the interceptor was invoked. For `@AroundInvoke` methods, this is the business method on the bean class; for lifecycle callback interceptor methods, `getMethod()` returns null.

The `getParameters()` method returns the parameters passed to the intercepted method as an array of objects. The `setParameters()` method, on the other hand, allows you to change these values at runtime before they're passed to the method. These two methods are helpful for interceptors that manipulate bean parameters to change behavior at runtime. An interceptor in ActionBazaar that transparently rounds off all monetary values to two decimal places for all methods across the application could use the `getParameters()` and `setParameters()` methods to accomplish its task.

The key to understanding the need for the `InvocationContext.getContextData()` method is the fact that contexts are shared across the interceptor chain for a given method. As a result, data attached to an `InvocationContext` can be used to communicate between interceptors. For example, assume that the security validation interceptor stores the member status into invocation context data after the user is validated:

```
invocationContext.getContextData().put("MemberStatus", "Gold");
```

As you can see, the invocation context data is simply a map used to store name/value pairs. Another interceptor in the invocation chain can now retrieve this data and take specific actions based on the member status. For example, a discount calculator interceptor can reduce the ActionBazaar item listing charges for a Gold member. The code to retrieve the member status would look like this:

```
String memberStatus =
    (String) invocationContext.getContextData().get("MemberStatus");
```

The following is the `@AroundInvoke` method of the `DiscountVerifierInterceptor` that actually uses the invocation context as well as most of the methods we discussed earlier:

```
@AroundInvoke
public Object giveDiscount(InvocationContext context)
throws Exception {
    System.out.println("*** DiscountVerifier Interceptor"
        + " invoked for " + context.getMethod().getName() + " ***");

    if (context.getMethod().getName().equals("chargePostingFee")
        && (((String) (context.getContextData().get("MemberStatus")))
            .equals("Gold"))) {
        Object[] parameters = context.getParameters();
        parameters[2] = new Double((Double) parameters[2] * 0.99);
        System.out.println(
            "*** DiscountVerifier Reducing Price by 1 percent ***");
            context.setParameters(parameters);
    }
    return context.proceed();
}
```

You can throw or handle a runtime or checked exception in a business method interceptor. If a business method interceptor throws an exception before invoking the proceed method, the processing of other interceptors in the invocation chain and the target business method will be terminated.

This covers how interceptors are trigged for business methods. But recall that an EJB is more than just business methods—it has an entire lifecycle. This isn't readily obvious, but lifecycle callbacks are a form of interception as well. Lifecycle callbacks are triggered when a bean transitions from one lifecycle state to another. Although this wasn't the case in the previous lifecycle examples, in some cases such methods can be used for crosscutting concerns (for example, logging and profiling) that can be shared across beans. For this reason, you can define lifecycle callbacks in interceptor classes in addition to business method interceptors. Let's take a look at how to do this.

LIFECYCLE CALLBACK METHODS IN THE INTERCEPTOR CLASS

The `@PostConstruct`, `@PrePassivate`, `@PostActivate`, and `@PreDestroy` annotations can be applied to bean methods to receive lifecycle callbacks. When applied to interceptor class methods, lifecycle callbacks work in exactly the same way. Lifecycle callbacks defined in an interceptor class are known as lifecycle callback interceptors or lifecycle callback listeners. When the target bean transitions lifecycles, the annotated methods in the interceptor class are triggered.

The following interceptor class logs when ActionBazaar beans allocate and release resources when beans instances are constructed and destroyed:

```
public class ActionBazaarResourceLogger {

    @PostConstruct
    public void initialize(InvocationContext context) {
        System.out.println("Allocating resources for bean: "
            + context.getTarget());
        context.proceed();
    }

    @PreDestroy
    public void cleanup(InvocationContext context) {
        System.out.println("Releasing resources for bean: "
            + context.getTarget());
        context.proceed();
    }
}
```

As the code sample shows, lifecycle interceptor methods can't throw checked exceptions (it doesn't make sense because there's no client for lifecycle callbacks to bubble a problem up to).

Note that a bean can have the same lifecycle callbacks both in the bean itself as well as in one or more interceptors. That's the whole point of calling the `InvocationContext.proceed()` method in lifecycle interceptor methods as in the resource logger code. This ensures that the next lifecycle interceptor method in the invocation chain or the bean lifecycle method is triggered. There's absolutely no difference between applying an interceptor class with or without lifecycle callbacks. The resource logger, for example, is applied as follows:

```
@Interceptors({ActionBazaarResourceLogger.class})
public class PlaceBidBean { ... }
```

You might find that you'll use lifecycle callbacks as bean methods to manage resources a lot more often than you use interceptor lifecycle callbacks to encapsulate crosscutting concerns such as logging, auditing, and profiling. But interceptor callbacks are extremely useful when you need them.

As a recap, table 5.9 contains a summary of both business method interceptors and lifecycle callbacks.

Table 5.9 Differences between lifecycle and business method interceptors. Lifecycle interceptors are created to handle EJB lifecycle callbacks. Business method interceptors are associated with business methods and are automatically invoked when a user invokes the business method.

Supported feature	Lifecycle callback methods	Business method interceptor
Invocation	Gets invoked when a certain lifecycle event occurs.	Gets invoked when a business method is called by a client.
Location	In a separate Interceptor class or in the bean class.	In the class or an interceptor class.
Method signature	`void <METHOD>(InvocationContext)`—in a separate interceptor class. `void <METHOD>()`—in the bean class.	`Object <METHOD>(InvocationContext) throws Exception`
Annotation	`@PreDestroy, @PostConstruct, @PrePassivate, @PostActivate`	`@AroundInvoke`
Exception handling	May throw runtime exceptions but must not throw checked exceptions. May catch and swallow exceptions. No other lifecycle callback methods are called if an exception is thrown.	May throw application or runtime exception. May catch and swallow runtime exceptions. No other business interceptor methods or the business method itself are called if an exception is thrown before calling the `proceed` method.
Transaction and security context	No security and transaction context. Transaction and security are discussed in chapter 6.	Share the same security and transaction context within which the original business method was invoked.

Clearly, interceptors are extremely important to EJB. It's likely that the AOP features in future releases of EJB will grow more and more robust. Interceptors certainly have the potential to evolve into a robust way of extending the EJB platform itself, with vendors offering new out-of-the-box interceptor-based services.

5.3.7 *Using interceptors effectively*

To use interceptors effectively, you have to keep in mind what interceptors are used for. Interceptors are used to implement crosscutting concern logic before or after a business method is executed. To effectively use interceptors, keep their use limited to these crosscutting concerns like auditing, metrics, logging, error handling, and so on. Although interceptors have the ability to examine and even change a return value from an executed method, try to avoid doing this. Changing a return value usually involves a business requirement and, as such, belongs in the bean itself as part of the bean's business logic.

Everything we've covered so far has been about EJB interceptors. Though extremely useful and powerful, EJB interceptors are a simple implementation meant to be used only with Enterprise beans. Next, we'll look at how EJB interceptors compare to the more powerful CDI interceptors.

5.3.8 *CDI versus EJB interceptors*

EJB interceptors are very powerful, but they provide only a basic framework for implementing interceptors. CDI takes this a step further by providing type-safe interceptor bindings that can be combined in a number of different ways to provide much more advanced options when implementing interceptors. We'll look at how to use these interceptor bindings, and you'll immediately be able to see the advantages over plain EJB interceptors.

CREATING INTERCEPTOR BINDINGS

Let's suppose ActionBazaar has some kind of auditing concern and you want to use a CDI interceptor to handle this. The first step is to create an interceptor binding. An interceptor binding is a type-safe link between an interceptor and your EJB. Its name should indicate what the interceptor binding does. In the example you have an auditing concern, so you'll create an interceptor binding named `@Audited`:

```
@InterceptorBinding
@Target({TYPE, METHOD})
@Retention(RUNTIME)
public @interface Audited {}
```

As you can see, an interceptor binding is a custom annotation declared with `@javax.interceptor.InterceptorBinding`. The `@Audited` interceptor binding may now be used in your code as a go-between to link interceptors with beans. To perform this link, the interceptor binding must be applied to both the interceptor and the bean. Let's first look at how to apply the interceptor binding to the interceptor.

DECLARING BINDINGS FOR AN INTERCEPTOR

When creating a CDI interceptor class (the *advice* in the AOP world), you must declare that the class is an interceptor and declare what interceptor bindings are on the class. Continuing with the auditing example, create the `AuditInterceptor`:

```
@Audited @Interceptor
public class AuditInterceptor {
```

```
    @AroundInvoke
    public Object audit(InvocationContext context) throws Exception {
        System.out.print("Invoking: "
            + context.getMethod().getName());
        System.out.println(" with arguments: "
            + context.getParameters());
        return context.proceed();
    }
}
```

The @Interceptor annotation declares this class to be an interceptor. The @Audited annotation links this interceptor to your interceptor binding. All CDI interceptors require an interceptor binding. If you were using regular EJB interceptors (see ActionBazaarLogger in listing 5.10), then you wouldn't need these annotations. Then, of course, there's the familiar @AroundInvoke annotation that tells CDI what method of this class will be called when the interceptor is invoked. Now that you have an interceptor binding and you've applied the binding to an interceptor, it's time to finish by linking the interceptor to an EJB.

LINKING AN INTERCEPTOR TO A BEAN

To link an interceptor to an EJB, you use the interceptor binding either on the bean class or on methods within the bean. Suppose BidService of the ActionBazaar application needs to be audited. You can easily audit all methods of the EJB by annotating the class:

```
@Stateless
@Audited
public class BidService {
    ...
}
```

Or you can audit just the addBid() method:

```
@Stateless
public class BidService {
    @Audited
    public void addBid(Bid bid) {
        bidDao.addBid(bid);
    }
    ...
}
```

In each case you use the @Audited interceptor binding. The @Audited interceptor binding is declared for either target (@Target({TYPE, METHOD})), so you use it for both cases. You can declare interceptor bindings that may be used only at the class or method level. Because @Audited is linked to AuditInterceptor, when the addBid() method is called, the invocation will be intercepted and the audit() method will be called first.

This is a simple example showing how CDI interceptors work. CDI interceptors can become much more powerful with interceptor bindings including other bindings, and interceptors declaring multiple bindings. We'll explore this next.

BEANS.XML

Recall that when using CDI, your bean archive JAR file needs a META-INF/beans.xml file for CDI to look in your JAR files for beans. In addition, when using CDI interceptors, all the interceptors you want to activate must be listed in beans.xml. So the final step is to add the `AuditInterceptor` to bean.xml:

```
<beans
   xmlns="http://java.sun.com/xml/ns/javaee"
   xmlns:xsi="http://www.w3.org/2001/XMLSchema-instance"
   xsi:schemaLocation="
      http://java.sun.com/xml/ns/javaee
      http://java.sun.com/xml/ns/javaee/beans_1_0.xsd">
   <interceptors>
      <class>com.bazaar.AuditInterceptor</class>
   </interceptors>
</beans>
```

It may seem like an unnecessary step to have to list your interceptors in beans.xml, but the `AuditInterceptor` example is simple with only one interceptor binding. What makes CDI interceptors powerful are their ability to make new interceptor bindings on top of existing ones and to have both interceptors and beans use multiple bindings. Throw EJB interceptors into the mix as well and the necessity of having interceptors listed in beans.xml becomes clear. Next we'll look at multiple interceptor bindings.

MULTIPLE BINDINGS

When creating a new interceptor binding, existing bindings may be used to make the new one more powerful. Suppose ActionBazaar has some EJB business logic that's secure. It's accessible only if certain strict security criteria are met. To meet this concern, a `@Secured` interceptor binding may be created. But when discussing this new binding, someone points out that part of being secure is also auditing this business logic. So it's decided that auditing may happen to business logic that's not secure, but secure business logic is required also to be audited without fail. This is a perfect use case for interceptor binding. Let's take a look at what the `@Secured` interceptor binding will look like:

```
@InterceptorBinding                      <-- ❶ An interceptor binding
@Target({TYPE, METHOD})
@Retention(RUNTIME)
@Audited                                 <-- ❷ With an additional interceptor binding
public @interface Secured {}
```

When defining the `@Secured` interceptor, use `@InterceptorBinding` ❶ to make it an interceptor binding. Then use `@Audited` as well ❷ to add an additional interceptor binding to `@Secured`. This means that the interceptors linked to `@Secured` and the interceptors linked to `@Audited` will both be applied when the `@Secured` interceptor binding is used on an EJB class or method. For example, consider the following `SecurityCheckInterceptor`:

```
@Secured @Interceptor
public class SecurityCheckInterceptor {
    @AroundInvoke
    public Object checkSecurity(InvocationContext context)
    throws Exception {
        // Check security here, proceed if OK
        return context.proceed();
    }
}
```

Now apply this interceptor binding to the `removeBid()` method of the `BidService` bean—a method that should never be executed without very specific security, and should also be audited if needed for verification purposes later:

```
@Stateless
public class BidService {
    ...
    @Secured
    public void removeBid(Bid bid) {
        bidDao.removeBid(bid);
    }
}
```

When the `removeBid()` method is called, the `@Secured` interceptor binding will intercept the call. `@Secured` is bound to `SecurityCheckInterceptor`, and `@Audited` is bound to `AuditInterceptor`. Because `@Audited` is used to define `@Secured`, when the `removeBid()` method is called, both `SecurityCheckInterceptor` and `AuditInterceptor` are called before `removeBid()`. This satisfies the concern that secure business logic is also required to be audited without fail.

Because there are two interceptors bound to the two bindings, you may be asking yourself which interceptor will be executed first. When using EJB interceptors, the order was very clear (see section 5.3.5). But how does CDI interceptor ordering work?

The answer is the beans.xml file. When listing interceptors, you not only tell CDI what interceptors are active but also what order they're to be executed in. For `removeBid()` it's probably a good idea to audit any calls to this method first before the security check is performed. Listing `AuditInterceptor` first guarantees it'll be called before `SecurityCheckInterceptor`:

```
<beans
  xmlns="http://java.sun.com/xml/ns/javaee"
  xmlns:xsi="http://www.w3.org/2001/XMLSchema-instance"
  xsi:schemaLocation="
     http://java.sun.com/xml/ns/javaee
     http://java.sun.com/xml/ns/javaee/beans_1_0.xsd">
  <interceptors>
     <class>com.bazaar.AuditInterceptor</class>
     <class>com.bazaar.SecurityCheckInterceptor</class>
  </interceptors>
</beans>
```

If CDI interceptors are mixed with EJB interceptors, the EJB interceptors go first, followed by the CDI ones. So the order of interceptor execution would be as follows:

1. Interceptors in the `@Interceptors` annotation
2. Interceptors in ejb-jar.xml
3. List of CDI interceptors in beans.xml

In addition to creating new interceptor bindings with additional interceptor bindings, the beans themselves may annotate several interceptor bindings. For example, you can audit, profile, and keep statistics on the `addBid()` method by adding those annotations to `BidService`:

```
@Stateless
@Audited
public class BidService {
    @Profiled @Statistics
    public void addBid(Bid bid) {
        bidDao.addBid(bid);
    }
    ...
}
```

`BidService` is annotated in such a way that every method in `BidService` will be audited because `@Audited` is annotated at the class level. In addition to being audited, statistics will be collected on calls to `addBid()` by `@Statistics`, and the `addBid()` method will also be profiled by `@Profiled`. Again, the listing of the interceptors in beans.xml determines the interceptor execution order.

Binding multiple interceptors to a bean is fairly straightforward. The bindings are associated with one or more interceptors, so there's a collection of interceptor calls before getting to the bean's method. Interceptors themselves may be bound to multiple bindings as well, and when interceptors have multiple bindings, it really changes how they get executed. The best way to explain this is with an example. Suppose ActionBazaar secure business processes require additional auditing. The auditing provided by `@Audited` is good, but more is needed. To fulfill this requirement, a new interceptor is created:

```
@Secured @Audited @Interceptor
public class SecuredAuditedInterceptor {
    @AroundInvoke
    public Object extraAudit(InvocationContext context)
    throws Exception {
        ...
        return context.proceed();
    }
}
```

This interceptor has multiple bindings. It's bound to both `@Secured` and `@Audited`. This means that this interceptor will only be called if both the `@Secured` and `@Audited` are applied to the method. If you go back and look at `removeBid()`, you'll see that it won't trigger the `SecuredAuditedInterceptor` because only the `@Secured` annotation is applied to the method. But add `@Audited` to the method:

```
@Stateless
public class BidService {
    ...
    @Secured @Audited
    public void removeBid(Bid bid) {
        bidDao.removeBid(bid);
    }
}
```

In this example, both annotations are added to `removeBid()` so the `SecuredAudited-Interceptor` will now be invoked. Now move `@Audited` to the class level:

```
@Stateless
@Audited
public class BidService {
    ...
    @Secured
    public void removeBid(Bid bid) {
        bidDao.removeBid(bid);
    }
}
```

In this example, `SecuredAuditedInterceptor` will still be invoked because `@Audited` will be applied to every method in `BidService`, which includes `removeBid()`. Because `remove-Bid()` is also annotated with `@Secured`, `SecuredAuditedInterceptor` will be called.

5.4 Summary

In this chapter we covered the EJB context, how to use the `@EJB` and `@Resource` annotations for dependency injection, and how and when JNDI must be used to manually look up EJBs and resources. We introduced aspect-oriented programming and showed how EJB interceptors can be used to implement crosscutting concerns on EJB business logic. Finally, we compared EJB interceptors with the more powerful CDI interceptors.

6 Transactions and security

This chapter covers

- The basics of transactions in EJBs
- When to use transactions
- Container-managed versus bean-managed transactions
- The basics of authentication and authorization in EJBs
- Using groups and roles in security

Transactions and security are the cornerstones upon which an Enterprise application is built. In terms of development, transactions and security are probably the hardest to implement correctly and nearly impossible to retrofit into an application once it's built. Both are system-level concerns that crosscut through an application and are intrinsically assumed by the business logic. EJB tackles both of these concerns and provides a framework for building robust applications while enabling you to focus on the business logic.

If you're already familiar with the basics of JDBC, EJB provides another layer on top of JDBC. This additional layer introduces abstractions that you'd otherwise have to invent. JDBC is an abstraction for talking to a database generically using SQL; it's not a framework. Building a scalable application that uses transactions involves much more than simply setting auto-commit to `false`. Building a framework to manage transactions isn't a trivial task, and there are many ways to do it wrong. In this chapter you'll learn how to use transactions in EJB and also how to secure your application.

This chapter is split into two parts, with the first half tackling transactions and the second half delving into security. Our coverage of transactions starts off by first reviewing the basics and then looking at the two approaches that can be taken. Topics that we'll cover include database transactions, two-phase commit with multiple databases, and declarative security and programmatic security.

6.1 Understanding transactions

A *transaction* is a grouping of tasks that must be processed atomically. If any of the tasks fail, the changes made by any of the successful tasks are rolled back. A failure results in the system returning to its original unmodified state. A task in the context of EJB refers to an SQL statement or the processing of a JMS message. To put this in perspective, when you transfer money from a checking account to a savings account, you want both operations to succeed. If the deposit in the savings account fails for any reason, such as power loss, disk failure, or networking failure, the withdrawal of money to the checking account should be rescinded. Transactions are thus an integral part of your daily life whether you realize it or not. You don't want to arrive at the airport to discover that although you've paid for a flight and have a printed boarding pass, the airline has no reservation.

Transaction support is an integral component of the EJB architecture. As you'll see, you have the choice of two transaction models when working with EJBs: programmatic and declarative. Programmatic transactions, known as *bean-managed transactions* (BMTs), place the onus on the developer to explicitly start, commit, and roll back transactions. Declarative transactions, known as *container-managed transactions* (CMTs), manage the commit and rollback transactions with configuration settings specified by the developer. Both models can be used within the same application, although there are certain situations where they're incompatible; these will be covered later in the chapter. If not specified, the default for a bean is CMTs.

Stateful, stateless, singleton, and message-driven beans all support both BMTs and CMTs. Note the inclusion of BMTs—transaction support also extends to JMS messaging. It's possible to implement Java Connector Architecture (JCA) connectors that talk to Enterprise information systems as well as legacy systems and also participate in transactions. Systems such as databases, JMS message queues, and external systems accessed via JCA are all resources, and a *resource manager* controls access. To put everything in context, let's review the basic properties of transactions and then work our way from Java SE to Java EE.

6.1.1 Transaction basics

Transactions are an exceedingly complex subject and are the focal point of much ongoing research. Entire books have been devoted to the subject and for good reason. In this section we'll give you a brief overview of the core concepts. This overview will be enough to make you dangerous if you're new to transactions and give you a foundation on which to dive into the subject further. If you're already familiar with transactions, this section can either be skipped or used as a basic refresher.

Earlier a transaction was defined as being an atomic task. It's a task that's composed of multiple steps that you want to execute as a single operation. If you're updating five different records in a database—maybe in the same table or different tables—you want the operations to either all succeed or all fail. Transactions can also be distributed; if you're talking to two different systems, you also want the same semantics. For example, in ActionBazaar, if a credit card operation fails, you also want the request to the inventory management system to be rolled back. So besides being atomic, what are the other properties of transactions? Many eons ago, Jim Gray coined the acronym ACID: atomicity, consistency, isolation, and durability.

ATOMICITY

As we've discussed, transactions are atomic in nature—they either commit or roll back. In coding terms, if you band together an arbitrary body of code under the umbrella of a transaction, an unexpected failure will result in all changes made by that block of code being undone. The system is thus left in its original state. If the code completes without any failures, the changes become permanent.

CONSISTENCY

This is the trickiest of the four properties because it encompasses more than just writing code. Consistency refers to the validity of the system—before and after a transaction executes, the system should be consistent with the business rules of the application. It's the responsibility of the developer to ensure consistency through the use of transactions. The underlying system, such as a database, doesn't have enough information to know what constitutes a valid state. Whether a transaction succeeds or fails is immaterial—the system will be in a valid state.

While a transaction is in progress, the system doesn't need to be in a valid state. You can think of a transaction as a sandbox or sanctuary—you're temporarily protected from the rules while inside it. But when you go to commit the work done in the sandbox, the system should be in a valid state that complies with the business rules of the application. Putting this in the context of ActionBazaar, it's fine to charge a customer even though you haven't removed the item from bidding while in a transaction. This is safe because the results of the code will have no impact on the system until and unless the transaction finishes successfully. Database constraints help ensure that a database conforms to the rules, but constraints can't encode all semantic rules.

ISOLATION

If there were only one transaction executing at a time, then isolation wouldn't be a concern. In a given system, any number of transactions can be concurrently manipulating overlapping data. Some of these operations are changing the data, whereas other operations are simply retrieving it for presentation or analyzing it for decision making. There are many shades of gray—for instance, a transaction can be aware of changes being made by another transaction or work in total isolation. The degree to which a transaction is isolated determines its performance characteristics. The more restrictive isolation levels have poorer performance.

Within the Java universe there are four isolation levels, each with different characteristics:

- *Read uncommitted*—A transaction can see uncommitted changes from other transactions. This would be the equivalent of grabbing code off a developer's machine during the day—you have no idea whether it'll compile or even run.
- *Read committed*—A transaction can see only committed changes, not changes made by other transactions that are still in progress. It's important to note that if a transaction re-reads the data, there's no guarantee that the data hasn't been changed.
- *Repeatable read*—Within a transaction, a read operation may be performed multiple times and each time it'll return the same result. The transaction won't see changes made by other transactions even if they commit before this transaction completes. The transaction is essentially working with its own copy of the data.
- *Serializable*—Only one transaction can operate on the data at a given time. This significantly degrades performance because only one transaction can be accessing the data at a time.

As the isolation level increases, the performance decreases. This means that the serializable level would have the worst performance characteristics—only one transaction could execute at a time. Selecting the correct isolation level is an important decision. Performance and correctness must both be taken into account. For example, in the ActionBazaar application, serializable doesn't make sense when retrieving the list of items for the main welcome page. By the time the user reads through the page, the data is already out of date. Using the most restrictive setting would severely limit the scalability of the application. Also, isolation-level support varies by database vendor and version.

DURABILITY

With durability, state changes made by a transaction are permanently stored. Once an owner of a transaction has been informed that the transaction has succeeded, any changes made by the transaction will survive system failure. This is typically accomplished with a transaction log—each of the changes is recorded and can be "replayed" to re-create the state that existed prior to the failure. To put this in context, once the client has been notified that the database transaction has completed, the data is safe even if the power plug is pulled on the database. In the next two sections we'll tie transactions and these characteristics back to the Java SE and EJB.

6.1.2 *Transactions in Java*

You now have a basic grasp of transactions and their importance. Transactions are a necessity; otherwise the transient state would be exposed to other users and failures could wreak havoc on data integrity. Lacking transactional support, you'd be forced to implement your own locking, synchronization, and rollback logic. Such an effort would be exceedingly complex, and working with transactions is complicated enough; therefore, implementing a transaction system would be an epic endeavor. But practically all databases today support transactions and are ACID-compliant. Let's now transition from the theoretical discussions of transactions to the practical and see how you make transactions in Java against a database.

To execute SQL and store procedures against a database, you use JDBC. JDBC abstracts connectivity to databases so that you aren't forced to use a separate API for each database vendor. Thus, you use the same Java code to execute an SQL statement against Oracle as you would against DB2; the SQL obviously might be different. When working with JDBC, you use the `java.sql.DriverManager` class to create a `java.sql.Connection` object. The `Connection` object represents a physical connection to the database. On the connection object, you have a number of methods for executing calls against the database. The following code demonstrates a sequence of SQL statements executed against the ActionBazaar database:

```
Class.forName("org.postgresql.Driver");
Connection con =
    DriverManager.getConnection("jdbc:postgresql:actionbazaar","user","pw");
Statement st = con.createStatement();
st.executeUpdate("insert into item ( item_id, bidstartdate, createddate ,
    initialprice , itemname ) values ( 0 , current_date, current_date,
    100.50 , 'Apple IIGS')");
st.executeUpdate("insert into item ( item_id, bidstartdate, createddate ,
    initialprice , itemname ) values ( 1 , current_date, current_date,
    100.50 , 'Apple IIE')");
st.executeUpdate("insert into item ( item_id, bidstartdate, createddate ,
    initialprice , itemname ) values ( 1 , current_date, current_date,
    100.50 , 'Apple IIC')");
```

This code has one important flaw: as each SQL statement is executed, the changes are committed to the database. The field `item_id` is a primary key, which means that it must be unique. When the third state attempts to execute, it fails because a record with the same `item_id` has already been inserted and committed. To make all of these statements execute within a transaction, you can turn off auto-commit and then explicitly commit and roll back the changes if an error occurs. This is demonstrated in the following improved code snippet:

```
Class.forName("org.postgresql.Driver");
Connection con =
    DriverManager.getConnection("jdbc:postgresql:actionbazaar","user","pw");
con.setAutoCommit(false);
try {
  Statement st = con.createStatement();
```

```
    st.executeUpdate("insert into item ( item_id, bidstartdate, createddate ,
        initialprice , itemname ) values ( 0 , current_date, current_date,
        100.50 , 'Apple IIGS')");
    st.executeUpdate("insert into item ( item_id, bidstartdate, createddate ,
        initialprice , itemname ) values ( 1 , current_date, current_date,
        100.50 , 'Apple IIE')");
    st.executeUpdate("insert into item ( item_id, bidstartdate, createddate ,
        initialprice , itemname ) values ( 1 , current_date, current_date,
        100.50 , 'Apple IIC')");
    con.commit();
} catch (Throwable t) {
    con.rollback();
    t.printStackTrace();
}
```

At some point, practically every Java developer has written similar code. With this code, you're directly managing the connection to the database. It's easy to make a mistake and not correctly handle a failure or omit a commit. If the connection object is being passed between multiple objects that are performing operations as a part of a transaction, things can become unmanageable. Design considerations aside, managing the connections directly precludes this code from coordinating operations among multiple resources such as JMS.

6.1.3 Transactions in EJB

Java EE, of which EJB is a component, was developed to make our lives easier. The code snippets in the previous section are deceptively simple. When confronted with the alphabet soup in Java EE, you may pine for simpler times. Thus far in this book you've seen JDBC and JPA. If you've downloaded the source to the book, you've probably been confronted with configuring the `DataSource` interface in your application server. You might be wondering how these various acronyms and technologies are related.

Let's start by defining some of the common acronyms that you'll come across and how they relate back to persistence and transactions:

- *JPA*—Java Persistence API is an API that defines how Java objects can be mapped to relational structures and how these objects are queried, retrieved, persisted, and deleted. Consider a simple Java object that represents a person. JPA provides annotations for documenting how a `Person` class is mapped to an entity within a database. JPA also provides classes and methods for accessing instances stored in a database.
- *JDBC*—Java Database Connectivity is an API that defines how a client can access a database. This ensures that you don't have to write Java code that's database-specific. This is relatively low-level—you're working directly with SQL that's database-specific. When you retrieve data from a database, you have to turn the retrieved data into an object-graph that can then be used by the application.
- *JTA*—Java Transaction API is an API for managing transactions. It's based on the *distributed transaction processing* (DTP) model from the Open Group. If you're

doing programmatic transaction or bean-managed persistence, then you're using JTA interfaces.

- *JTS*—Java Transaction Service is a specification for building a transaction service. JTA may rest upon JTS. As an EJB developer, you'll practically never touch JTS. JTS is defined in CORBA and is part of Object Services.
- `DataSource`—A replacement interface for the `java.sql.DriverManager` (see the code example in the previous section), it's used for retrieving connections to a database and can be registered in JNDI.
- *XA*—The Java mapping of the Open Group's DTP specification. You'll see classes such as `javax.transaction.xa.XAResource`, `javax.transaction.xa.XAConnection`, and so on. Remember that the DTP specification is provided by JTA. You'll use XA resources and connections when transactions cross multiple databases or resources such as JMS.

EJB manages transactions either programmatically or via annotations. This will be covered in subsequent sections. When managing transactions programmatically—that is, bean-managed persistence—you're using APIs defined by JTA. Within the EJB container, connections to resources such as databases are provided via `DataSource`, and very often these `DataSources` support the XA protocol. The XA protocol enables transactions to span multiple resources such as databases and containers. `DataSources` are retrieved via JNDI either programmatically or via the `@Inject` annotation. Optionally, you can use JPA to shuttle your data between the database and Java objects—JPA will use the `DataSource` under the hood and participate in transactions configured by EJB. The transaction manager implements the JTS interface and provides the implementation of JTA.

Configuration of isolation levels isn't specified by the Java EE standard and is thus container-specific. Generally, isolation levels are configured when defining the `DataSource`. As a result, the isolation level is global and affects all connections and transactions. Although it's possible to programmatically change the isolation level on a connection acquired from a `DataSource`, this is dangerous. First, if this connection ends up back in the pool without its original setting, it'll impact other transactions. Second, countermanding configuration settings from the container obfuscates application behavior.

If you're limited to setting the transaction isolation level on the `DataSource`, which isolation level should you choose? The read uncommitted is dangerous because you'd see changes from other transactions that haven't been committed and aren't necessarily valid. This could cause unexpected rollbacks and leave the database in a contorted state. Repeatable read suffers from phantom reads—for instance, a query when executed twice returns different results due to changes made by other transactions. Serializable, on the other hand, scales poorly because locks must be acquired on the data. For situations where read committed isn't acceptable, there are several approaches. One is to create a data source for each isolation level you need. Another approach is to use version columns and optimistic locking.

6.1.4 When to use transactions

Transactions are an integral part of EJB. By default, EJBs will use CMTs and the bean will either participate in an existing transaction, if already started, or start a new transaction. This is the behavior of EJBs if you don't provide any additional configuration. As you've seen, transactions are extremely important for ensuring data integrity. The more apt question is this: when would you not want to use transactions? You wouldn't use transactions in situations where you're accessing a resource manager that doesn't support transactions. This would be a resource manager that would throw an exception if a transaction had been started. Generally, situations where this might occur are few and far between.

Disabling transactions where you're using a resource manager that supports transactions may have unintended consequences. In the case of a database, the connection might revert to auto-commit or an exception might be thrown. Even if you're just retrieving data from a database, that operation is still performed in the context of a transaction. The semantics of what will happen aren't well defined and will undoubtedly vary. Don't disable transactions in an attempt to improve performance—they probably aren't the performance bottleneck.

If you were indeed using a resource manager that doesn't support transactions, you'd annotate the class as in the following hypothetical code snippet. These annotations will be discussed in more detail later in the chapter. If a transaction is already started when a method on this bean is invoked, the transaction will be suspended:

```
@TransactionManagement(TransactionManagementType.CONTAINER)
@TransactionAttribute(TransactionAttributeType.NOT_SUPPORTED)
public class BidServiceBean implements BidService {
...
}
```

In summary, EJBs are by their nature transactional. Disable transactions only if you're using a resource manager that doesn't support them. Next, let's get a sense of how transactions are implemented.

6.1.5 How EJB transactions are implemented

Your primary concern in writing Enterprise applications is with the correct usage of transactions. The heavy lifting of implementing transaction support is provided by cooperation of the container and resource managers. Ultimately, everything that you do in code translates into low-level database operations, such as locking and unlocking rows or tables in a database, beginning a transaction log, committing a transaction by applying log entries, or rolling back a transaction by abandoning a transaction log. In Enterprise transaction management, the component that takes care of transactions for a particular resource is called a resource manager. Remember that a resource isn't just a database system like Oracle or PostgreSQL. It could also be a message server like IBM MQSeries or an Enterprise information system (EIS) like PeopleSoft CRM.

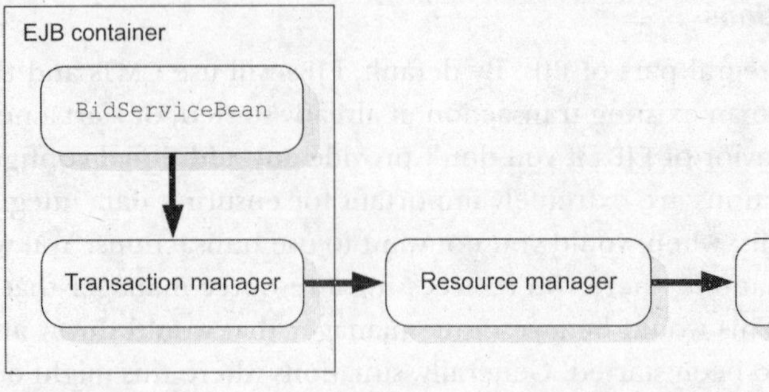

Figure 6.1 Transaction implementation—beans to the database

Figure 6.1 shows the overall relationship of your bean to the underlying database. The aptly named transaction manager handles transaction management. The transaction manager interacts with one or more resource managers that ultimately communicate with the underlying database. In the case of an Oracle database, the resource manager is the JDBC driver provided by Oracle. The transaction manager can be either part of the container or a separate process. You may have run across this in documentation for configuring a JTA provider for Tomcat when configuring a JPA provider.

An EJB's interaction with the transaction manager is done via JTA. JTA is based on the distributed transaction processing (DTP) model and is defined by Open Group. JTA was introduced in 1999 and hasn't changed much since. JTA supports only synchronous communication between the application and the resource (database). DTP breaks up its interfaces into two parts: TX, the transaction manager, and XA, the interface between the transaction manager and the resource manager. XA is often used as a prefix on classes, such as `javax.transaction.xa.XAConnection`. You may have heard someone ask if a particular driver supported XA. When using declarative transaction support (a.k.a. BMT), you'll use `javax.transaction.UserTransaction` to initiate, commit, and roll back transactions. The `UserTransaction` interface is part of the TX portion of the DTP.

Thus far you may be questioning the need for a transaction manager. Some Enterprise applications involve only a single resource. A transaction that uses a single resource is called a *local transaction.* But many Enterprise applications use more than one resource. It's not uncommon for an application to communicate with multiple databases and legacy systems. This is where the transaction manager comes into play—it coordinates transactions that span multiple resources. For example, in the ActionBazaar application, the `OrderProcessorBean` must update the inventory records in ActionBazaar's database and also persist the credit information in the billing database, as shown in figure 6.2.

From the application's perspective, the transaction manager is an external component that provides simplified transaction services. The `OrderProcessorBean` asks the transaction manager to start, commit, and roll back transactions. The transaction manager coordinates these requests among the two resource managers. If the update

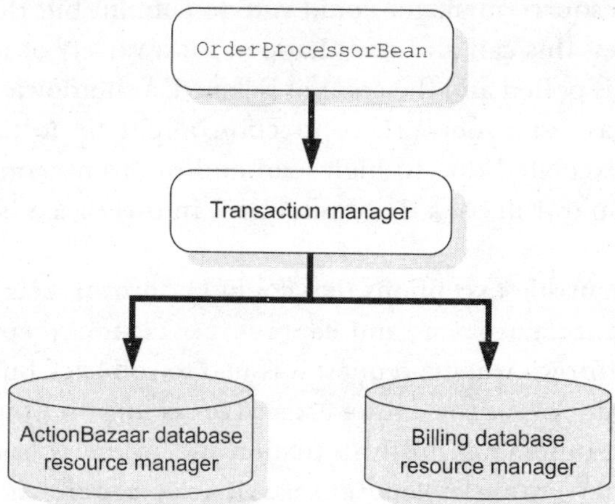

Figure 6.2 Distributed transaction management. The application program delegates transaction operations to the transaction manager, which coordinates between resource managers.

to the billing database fails, the transaction manager will ensure that changes made to the inventory in the ActionBazaar database are reverted. Coordination between two or more resources is accomplished via the use of the two-phase commit.

6.1.6 *Two-phase commit*

The two-phase commit protocol is used in situations where a transaction spans multiple resources. As its name suggests, a two-phase commit has two phases. In the first phase the transaction manager polls the resource managers asking them if they're ready to commit. If all of the resource managers reply affirmatively, the transaction manager then issues a commit message to each resource manager, as shown in figure 6.3. If any one of the resource managers responds negatively, the transaction is rolled back. Each resource manager is responsible for maintaining a transaction log so that if anything happens, the transaction can be recovered.

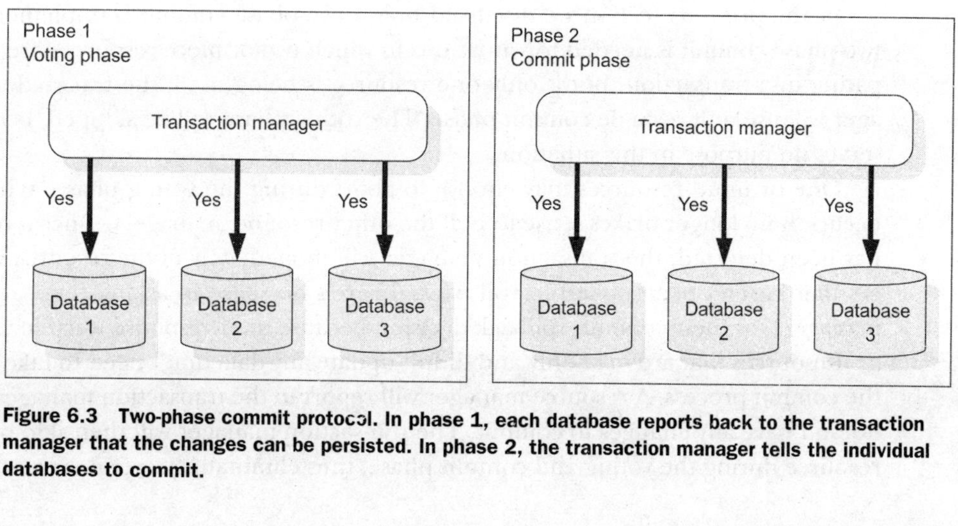

Figure 6.3 Two-phase commit protocol. In phase 1, each database reports back to the transaction manager that the changes can be persisted. In phase 2, the transaction manager tells the individual databases to commit.

You might be wondering if a resource manager could vote to commit but then subsequently fail. The answer is yes; this can and does happen for a variety of reasons. Between the time that the data is polled and the commit is issued, a shutdown request might be issued to the database or a network connection might be lost. Often, though, a time-out might be exceeded due to high load and the transaction manager makes a unilateral decision to roll back the transaction. In this case a heuristic exception is thrown.

There are three different heuristic exceptions that could be thrown: `HeuristicCommitException`, `HeuristicMixedException`, and `HeuristicRollbackException`. A `HeuristicCommitException` is thrown when a request is issued to roll back but a heuristic decision is made to commit. A `HeuristicMixedException` is thrown when some resource managers commit but others fail. In this situation the system is now in an invalid state that will require intervention. A `HeuristicRollbackException` is thrown when a heuristic decision is made and all of the resources have been rolled back. With this exception, the client should resubmit the request. These exceptions need to be caught and handled by the application.

One important thing to remember is that failures can happen on any end. The container with the transaction manager may fail (system shutdown), leaving the resource managers hanging. In this case, the individual resource managers may make a decision on their own to roll back—they can't keep resources locked forever. When the transaction manager comes back up, it'll attempt to complete the transaction.

6.1.7 *JTA performance*

JTA is designed to perform optimally whether you're using a single resource or a dozen. There are a number of common optimizations that are implemented by every transaction manager. These optimizations help ensure that JTA won't be a bottleneck for your application. These optimizations can be summarized as one-phase, presumed abort, and read-only.

In the previous section we discussed how a two-phase commit is implemented. A two-phase commit is needed for situations in which two or more resources are participating in a transaction. But if only one resource is being used, the transaction manager will use only a single commit phase. The voting phase will be skipped, because it serves no purpose in this situation.

One or more resources may choose to abort during the voting phase. When this occurs, it no longer makes sense to poll the other resource managers. Once a rollback has been detected, the transaction manager will immediately notify resource managers that haven't been polled to roll back. There's no sense in asking these resource managers for their commit/rollback decision because their response is irrelevant.

Resources that are read-only and didn't update any data don't need to take part in the commit process. A resource manager will report to the transaction manager that it doesn't have any changes to commit. The transaction manager will then skip over the resource during the voting and commit phase, thus eliminating several extra steps.

In addition to these three optimizations, during both the voting and commit phases, the transaction manager may execute the calls concurrently to the resource managers. If there are three databases and each database takes 10 ms to respond, then the entire voting phase will take only 10 ms and not 30 ms as in the case where each resource manager was polled sequentially.

6.2 Container-managed transactions

In a CMT, the container starts, commits, and rolls back a transaction on your behalf. Transaction boundaries in declarative transactions are always marked by the start and end of EJB business methods. More precisely, the container starts a JTA transaction before a method is invoked, invokes the method, and, depending on what happened during the method call, either commits or rolls back the managed transaction. All you have to do is tell the container how to manage the transaction by using either annotations or deployment descriptors and informing the transaction manager when the transaction needs to be rolled back. As mentioned previously, the container assumes that you'll be using CMT on all business methods.

This section dives into the nuts and bolts of CMT. You'll learn how to use the `@TransactionManagement` and `@TransactionAttribute` annotations. In addition you'll learn how to roll back a transaction using the `EJBContext` and how to handle application exceptions.

6.2.1 Snag-it ordering using CMT

Some items on ActionBazaar have a "snag-it" ordering option. This option enables a user to purchase an item on bid at a set price before anyone else bids on it. With this feature, buyers and bidders alike don't have to wait for bidding to finish. As soon as the user clicks the Snag-It button, the ActionBazaar application makes sure no bids have been placed on the item, validates the buyer's credit card, charges the buyer, and removes the item from bidding. It's important that this operation takes place within the context of a transaction. Obviously, the buyer would be upset if they were billed for an item that never shipped, and the seller would be upset if the item was shipped but no money collected.

To implement snag-it ordering, you'll add a `placeSnagItOrder` to the `OrderManagerBean`, which is a stateless session bean. The code for this method is shown in the following listing. The bean first checks to see if there are any bids on the item, and if there are none, it validates the customer's credit card, charges the customer, and removes the item from bidding. To keep the code sample as simple as possible, most of the business logic is omitted.

Listing 6.1 Implementing snag-it ordering using CMT

```
@Stateless(name = "BidManager")
@TransactionManagement(TransactionManagementType.CONTAINER)      <-- 1 Uses CMT
public class BidManagerBean implements BidManager {
  @Inject
```

```
    private CreditCardManager creditCardManager;
    @Inject
    private SessionContext context;                          ❷ Injects EJB context
    @Inject
    private CreditCardManager creditCardManager;             ❸ Defines Transaction attribute for method
    @TransactionAttribute(TransactionAttributeType.REQUIRED)
    @Override
    public void placeSnagItOrder(Item item, Bidder bidder, CreditCard card) {
      try {
        if(!hasBids(item)) {
          creditCardManager.validateCard(card);
          creditCardManager.chargeCreditCard(card,item.getInitialPrice());
          closeBid(item,bidder,item.getInitialPrice());
        }
      } catch (CreditProcessingException ce) {
        logger.log(Level.SEVERE,"An error ocurred processing the order.",ce);
        context.setRollbackOnly();
      } catch (CreditCardSystemException ccse) {                ❹ Rolls back on exception
        logger.log(Level.SEVERE,"Unable to validate credit card.",ccse);
        context.setRollbackOnly();
      }
    }
  }
```

First, you tell the container that it should manage the transactions for this bean ❶. This is optional for this bean because the container assumes CMT by default. The EJB context is injected into the bean ❷. A transaction is required for the `placeSnagItOrder` method ❸, and the container should start one when needed. If an exception stops you from completing the snag-it order, you ask the container to roll back the transaction using the injected `EJBContext` object's `setRollbackOnly` method ❹. It's your responsibility to roll back the exception in the event of an application error. Let's take a closer look at the `TransactionManagement` annotation.

6.2.2 @TransactionManagement annotation

The `@TransactionManagement` annotation specifies whether CMT or BMT is to be used for a particular bean. In this case, you specify the value `TransactionManagementType.CONTAINER`—meaning that the container should manage transactions on the bean's behalf. If you wanted to manage the transaction programmatically instead, you'd specify `TransactionManagementType.BEAN` for the `TransactionManagement` value. Notably, although you've explicitly included the annotation in the example, if you leave it out the container will assume CMT anyway. When we explore BMT, it'll be more obvious why CMT is the default and usually the best choice. Next, we'll look at the second transaction-related annotation in listing 6.1: `@TransactionAttribute`.

6.2.3 @TransactionAttribute annotation

Although the container does most of the heavy lifting in CMT, you still need to tell the container how it should manage transactions. To understand what this means, consider the fact that your `placeSnagItOrder` could be called from another bean with a transaction already in progress. In this case, do you want it to suspend that transaction, join it, or fail? In the case of this method, it's being called from the web tier and there's no transaction in progress, so obviously a new transaction should be started. The `@TransactionAttribute` gives you the control to determine what the container should do in relation to transactions.

Looking at the code in listing 6.1 you'll notice that this is calling `chargeCreditCard` on the `CreditCardManager` bean. The code for this method is shown in listing 6.2. In this listing you can see that the method is marked with a transaction attribute of `MANDATORY`. This means that the method can only join transactions already in progress—it can't create a new transaction. Logically, when would you debit money from an account if it wasn't associated with another operation such as processing a winning bid? When this method is invoked, it'll participate in the transaction started by `placeSnagItOrder`. If an error occurs in the `CreditCardManagerBean`, any changes made in the `placeSnagItOrder` method will also be rolled back. It doesn't matter if the `CreditCardManagerBean` is using the database or even the same JDBC connection. Note that you didn't have to pass exception objects around to get this behavior nor write any code to ensure that a transaction was already in progress and fail otherwise.

Listing 6.2 Implementing a method requiring an existing transaction

```
@Stateless(name="CreditCardManager")
@TransactionManagement(TransactionManagementType.CONTAINER)
public class CreditCardManagerBean implements CreditCardManager {
  @TransactionAttribute(TransactionAttributeType.MANDATORY)
  public void chargeCreditCard(CreditCard creditCard, BigDecimal amount)
    throws CreditProcessingException {
    // debit the credit card...
  }
}
```

The `@TransactionAttribute` annotation tells the container how to handle transactions, including when to start a new transaction, when to join an existing transaction, and so on. The annotation can be applied to either an individual CMT bean method or to the entire bean. If the annotation is applied at the bean level, all business methods in the bean inherit the transaction attribute value specified by it. In listing 6.1, you specify that the value of `@TransactionAttribute` annotation for the `placeSnagItOrder` method should be `TransactionAttribute.REQUIRED`. There are six choices for this annotation defined by the enumerated type `TransactionAttributeType`. Table 6.1 summarizes their behavior.

Table 6.1 Effects of transaction attributes on EJB methods

Transaction attribute	Caller transaction exists?	Effect
REQUIRED	No	Container creates a new transaction.
	Yes	Method joins the caller's transaction.

Table 6.1 Effects of transaction attributes on EJB methods *(continued)*

Transaction attribute	Caller transaction exists?	Effect
`REQUIRES_NEW`	No	Container creates a new transaction.
	Yes	Container creates a new transaction and the caller's transaction is suspended.
`SUPPORTS`	No	No transaction is used.
	Yes	Method joins the caller's transaction.
`MANDATORY`	No	`javax.ejb.EJBTransactionRequiredException` is thrown.
	Yes	Method joins the caller's transaction.
`NOT_SUPPORTED`	No	No transaction is used.
	Yes	The caller's transaction is suspended and the method is called without a transaction.
`NEVER`	No	No transaction is used.
	Yes	`javax.ejb.EJBException` is thrown.

Let's take a look at what each value means and where each is applicable.

REQUIRED

`REQUIRED` is the default and most commonly applicable transaction attribute value. This value specifies that the EJB method must always be invoked within a transaction. If the method is invoked from a nontransactional client, the container will start a transaction before the method is called and finish it when the method completes. On the other hand, if the caller invokes the method from a transactional context, the method will join the existing transaction. In case of transactions propagated from the client, if your method indicates that the transaction should be rolled back, the container will not only roll back the whole transaction but will also throw a `javax.transaction.RollbackException` back to the client. This lets the client know that the transaction it started has been rolled back by another method. Your `placeSnagItOrder` method is invoked from the nontransactional web tier. Therefore, the `REQUIRED` value in the `@TransactionAttribute` annotation will cause the container to create a new transaction for you. If all the other session bean methods you invoke from your bean are also marked `REQUIRED`, when you invoke them they'll join the transaction created for you. This is fine for your problem because you want the entire ordering action to be covered by one "umbrella" transaction. In general, you should use the `REQUIRED` value if you're modifying any data in your EJB method and you aren't sure whether the client will start a new transaction before calling your method.

REQUIRES_NEW

The `REQUIRES_NEW` value indicates that the container must always create a new transaction to invoke the EJB method. If the client already has a transaction, it's temporarily *suspended* until your method returns. This means that the success or failure of your new transaction has no effect on the existing client transaction.

From the client's perspective,

1. Its transaction is paused.
2. The method is invoked.
3. The method either commits or rolls back its own transaction.
4. The client's transaction is resumed as soon as the method returns.

The `REQUIRES_NEW` attribute is of limited use in most applications. It should be used in situations where you need a transaction but don't want a transaction rollback to affect a client and vice versa. Logging is a great example of where this transaction attribute could be used. Even if the parent transaction rolls back, you still want the log message recorded. On the flip side, if creating the logging message fails, you don't want the operation it was logging to also fail.

SUPPORTS

The `SUPPORTS` attribute means that the method is ambivalent to the presence of a transaction. If a transaction has been started, the method will join the existing transaction. If no transaction has been started, then the method will execute without a transaction. The `SUPPORTS` attribute is typically useful for methods that perform read-only operations such as retrieving a record from a database table. In the snag-it example, the method for checking whether a method has a bid is annotated with `SUPPORTS` because it modifies no data.

MANDATORY

`MANDATORY` means that the method requires an existing transaction to already be in progress for this method to join. We briefly alluded to this when we talked about the `CreditCardManager` bean. When the container goes to invoke the method, it'll check to make sure that a transaction is already in progress. If a transaction hasn't previously been started, an `EJBTransactionRequiredException` will be thrown. Thus, in the `CreditCardManager` bean, if the method is invoked without a transaction, an exception will be thrown.

NOT_SUPPORTED

When assigning `NOT_SUPPORTED` as the transaction attribute, the EJB method can't be invoked in a transactional context. If a caller with an associated transaction invokes the method, the container will suspend the transaction, invoke the method, and then resume the transaction when the method returns. This attribute is typically only useful for an MDB supporting a JMS provider in nontransactional, auto-acknowledge mode. In this case, the message is acknowledged as soon as it's successfully delivered and the MDB has no capability or apparent need to support rolling back message delivery.

NEVER

In a CMT, NEVER means that the EJB method can never be invoked from a transactional client. If such an attempt is made, a `javax.ejb.EJBException` is thrown. This is probably the least-used transaction attribute value. It's possibly useful if your method is changing a nontransactional resource (such as a text file) and you want to make sure the client knows about the nontransactional nature of the method. Note that you aren't supposed to directly access the file system from an EJB.

TRANSACTION ATTRIBUTES AND MDBs

As discussed in chapter 4, MDBs don't support all six transaction attributes. MDBs support only REQUIRED or NOT_SUPPORTED. Remember that no client ever invokes MDB methods directly—they're invoked when a message is delivered to the bean from the queue. There's no existing transaction to suspend or join when a message is delivered; therefore, REQUIRES_NEW, SUPPORTS, and MANDATORY make no sense. NEVER is illogical because you don't need a strong guard against the container. The two options you have available are REQUIRED if you want a transaction or SUPPORTS if you don't need a transaction.

You now have a handle on how to mark a bean as using CMTs and how to demarcate or join an existing transaction. The successful conclusion of a transactional method results in the transaction being committed. Let's next look at how you can mark a transaction for rollback.

6.2.4 *Marking a CMT for rollback*

Sometimes in the course of a transaction it's determined that the changes need to be rolled back. The rollback could be due to an error, an invalid credit card number, or a result of a business decision. CMT provides the capability for the bean to signal that the transaction must be rolled back. The rollback doesn't take place immediately—a flag is set, and at the end of the transaction the container will perform the rollback. Let's revisit the code from listing 6.1 to see how this is done:

```
@Resource
private SessionContext context;
public void placeSnagItOrder(Item item, Bidder bidder, CreditCard card) {
  try {
  } catch (CreditProcessingException ce) {
    logger.log(Level.SEVERE,"An error ocurred processing the order.",ce);
    context.setRollbackOnly();
  }
  ...
}
```

As this snippet shows, calling `setRollbackOnly` on `javax.ejb.EJBContext` marks the transaction for rollback when there's an error processing the credit card. If you didn't mark the transaction for rollback, then any changes made would actually be committed. This is an important point to remember—it's your responsibility to tell the container what to do in the event of an application exception.

The `setRollbackOnly` method on the `EJBContext` can only be used in methods that have a transaction attribute type of `REQUIRED`, `REQUIRED_NEW`, or `MANDATORY`. If a transaction hasn't been started, as in the case of `SUPPORTED` or `NEVER`, a `java.lang.IllegalStateException` will be thrown.

As we stated earlier, when a transaction is marked for rollback, the transaction doesn't immediately end. The method doesn't return when the transaction is marked for rollback. Instead, the method will continue as if nothing happened. The `EJBContext` provides a method that enables you to determine whether a transaction has been marked for rollback: `getRollbackOnly()`. Using this method, you can then decide whether you want to engage in a long-running operation that isn't going to be persisted. You could tweak the code from listing 6.1 to skip closing a bid if the `chargeCreditCard` operation fails:

```
public void placeSnagItOrder(Item item, Bidder bidder, CreditCard card) {
  try {
    if(!hasBids(item)) {
    creditCardManager.chargeCreditCard(card,item.getInitialPrice());
    if(!context.getRollbackOnly()) {
      closeBid(item,bidder,item.getInitialPrice());
    }
}
```

NOTE The `setRollbackOnly` and `getRollbackOnly` methods can only be invoked in an EJB using CMT with these transaction attributes: `REQUIRED`, `REQUIRES_NEW`, or `MANDATORY`. Otherwise, the container will throw an `IllegalStateException`.

If having to catch exceptions just to call `setRollbackOnly` seems a little cumbersome and repetitious, then you're in luck. EJB 3 has a simpler approach to using annotations. We'll examine exception handling in transactions next.

6.2.5 Transaction and exception handling

Exceptions happen and you must deal with them. Very often exceptions happen when you least expect them, like in a production system while demoing features to a high-level executive. Because exceptions aren't supposed to occur regularly, it's easy to handle them incorrectly and not realize it until it's too late. In listing 6.1 there are two exceptions, and in both cases a rollback is triggered. Let's review the code:

```
public void placeSnagItOrder(Item item, Bidder bidder, CreditCard card) {
  try {
    if(!hasBids(item)) {
      creditCardManager.validateCard(card);
      creditCardManager.chargeCreditCard(card,item.getInitialPrice());
      closeBid(item,bidder,item.getInitialPrice());
    }
  } catch (CreditProcessingException ce) {
    logger.log(Level.SEVERE,"An error ocurred processing the order.",ce);
    context.setRollbackOnly();
  } catch (CreditCardSystemException ccse) {
```

```
        logger.log(Level.SEVERE,"Unable to validate credit card.",ccse);
        context.setRollbackOnly();
    }
}
```

As you can see, the CreditProcessingException and CreditCardSystemException both trigger a rollback. To avoid this all-too-common mechanical code, EJB 3 introduces the idea of controlling a transactional outcome from an exception using the @javax.ejb.ApplicationException annotation. The best way to see how this works is through an example. The following listing reimplements the placeSnagItOrder method using the @ApplicationException mechanism to roll back CMTs.

Listing 6.3 Using @ApplicationException to roll back CMTs

```
@TransactionAttribute(TransactionAttributeType.REQUIRED)
public void placeSnagItOrder(Item item, Bidder bidder, CreditCard card)
  throws CreditProcessingException, CreditCardSystemException {       ❶ Declares exceptions on throws clause
  if(!hasBids(item)) {
    creditCardManager.validateCard(card);                              ❷ Throws exceptions from method bodies
    creditCardManager.chargeCreditCard(card,item.getInitialPrice());
    closeBid(item, bidder, item.getInitialPrice());
  }
}
...
@ApplicationException(rollback=true)                                   ❸ Specifies ApplicationException
public class CreditProcessingException extends Exception {
...
@ApplicationException(rollback=true)                                   ❹ Marks RuntimeEx as ApplicationExc
public class CreditCardSystemException extends RuntimeException {
```

The first change from listing 6.1 you'll notice is the fact that the try-catch block has been removed and replaced by a throws clause in the method declaration ❶. But it's a good idea for you to gracefully handle the application exceptions in the client and generate the appropriate error messages. The various nested method invocations still throw two exceptions listed in the throws clause ❷. The most important thing to note, however, is the two @ApplicationException annotations on the exception classes. The @ApplicationException annotation ❸ identifies a Java checked or unchecked exception as an *application exception.*

> **NOTE** An application exception is an exception that a client of an EJB is expected to handle. When thrown, such exceptions are passed directly to the method invoker. By default, all checked exceptions except for java.rmi.RemoteException are assumed to be application exceptions. All exceptions that inherit from either java.rmi.RemoveException or java.lang.RuntimeException (unchecked) are assumed to be system exceptions. In EJB, it's not assumed that the client expects system exceptions. When encountered, such exceptions aren't passed to the client but are wrapped in a javax.ejb.EJBException instead.

In listing 6.3, the `@ApplicationException` annotation on `CreditProcessingException` doesn't change the behavior of the exception—the exception is passed up to the client. But the application exception annotation ❹ changes the behavior of the `CreditCardSystemException` that would normally be wrapped as an `EJBException` because it would be interpreted as a system exception. Applying the `@ApplicationException` annotation causes it to be treated as an application exception instead.

You may have noticed the rollback attribute on the `@ApplicationException` annotation. By default, application exceptions don't cause an automatic CMT rollback because the rollback element is defaulted to `false`. But setting the element to `true` tells the container that it should roll back the transaction before the exception is passed to the client. In listing 6.3, this means that both `CreditProcessingException` and `CreditCardSystemException` will result in a rollback before the exception is delivered. If the container catches a system exception, such as an `ArrayIndexOutOfBounds` or a `NullPointerException` that isn't caught, the container will still issue a rollback for these system exceptions. But in such cases the container will assume that the bean is in an inconsistent state and destroy it.

6.2.6 Session synchronization

The session synchronization interface enables stateful session beans to be notified of container transaction boundaries. This interface is defined as `javax.ejb.SessionSynchronization`. To take advantage of this interface, implement this interface as a part of your bean. This interface defines three methods:

- `void afterBegin()`—Called right after the container creates a new transaction and before the business method is invoked.
- `void beforeCompletion()`—Invoked after a business method returns but right before the container ends a transaction.
- `void afterCompletion(boolean committed)`—Called after the transaction finishes. The Boolean `committed` flag indicates whether a transaction was committed or rolled back.

The first two methods are executed within the transactional context so you can read and write data to the database. For example, you could use the `afterBegin()` to load cached data into the bean and the `beforeCompletion()` to write data out to the bean.

6.2.7 Using CMT effectively

CMTs are straightforward and much easier to use as compared to BMTs. If you don't annotate your beans or provide a deployment descriptor, your beans will execute with CMTs and a transaction attribute of `REQUIRED`. This is a "safe" setting. Your application should work without any additional effort provided application exceptions aren't thrown. There are a couple of things that you can do to more effectively use CMTs and ensure that your application is logically correct and easy to maintain.

For maintainability, you generally want to identify the logical transactions that are taking place and assign a method as being responsible for the transaction. This method is responsible for two things: catching application exceptions and setting the rollback flag. Handling of application exceptions should be uniform and not distributed throughout a set of beans that are participating in a transaction. If an application exception fails to roll back or doesn't cause a rollback, it's often hard to pinpoint the problem spot if exception handling is distributed and handled nonuniformly. Regarding rollbacks, rollback logic should be centralized, preferably in the method that serves as a gateway for the transaction. As in the application exceptions, the more distributed the handling of rollbacks, the harder the code becomes to verify, test, and maintain. Also, prior to performing long-running tasks, make sure to check `getRollbackOnly()` to find out if it's worth proceeding. There's no sense in performing a long-running operation if it's just going to be reverted.

When setting the transaction attributes on methods in a class as well as at the class level, set the most restrictive level required by a method of the class. This minimizes the chance that a method that requires a more stringent transaction attribute isn't accidently executed with a lesser one. For example, it would be bad if you set the class level as `SUPPORTS` and then added a new method that required a `REQUIRED` but forgot to annotate it. This method would then essentially execute in auto-commit mode. It's better to use a transaction when you don't need to than fail to use a transaction when it's critical.

Correctly handling application exceptions is critical, because the container doesn't automatically roll back when an application exception is thrown. If you catch an application exception that requires a rollback, make sure it's handled in the `catch`. Where possible, attempt to annotate application exceptions with `@ApplicationException`. This can greatly reduce the number of places where a forgotten `setRollbackOnly()` could trip your application.

Finally, make use of the `@TransactionAttribute`. If a method always requires a transaction and never starts it, mark it with `MANDATORY`. If a block of code must execute in a transaction but should never trigger a rollback on the transaction of a caller, use `REQUIRES_NEW`.

CMTs are great, but there are situations where you want more explicit control over a transaction. Let's take a look at BMTs.

6.3 Bean-managed transactions

The greatest strength of a CMT is also its greatest weakness. Using a CMT, you're limited to having the transaction boundaries set at the beginning and end of business methods and relying on the container to determine when a transaction starts, commits, or rolls back. A BMT, on the other hand, allows you to specify these details programmatically, using semantics similar to the JDBC transaction model. But even in this case, the container helps you by actually creating the physical transaction, as well as taking care of a few low-level details. With BMT, you must be much more aware of the underlying JTA transaction API, primarily the `javax.transaction.UserTransaction` interface that we mentioned earlier. Let's revisit the snag-it ordering code from listing 6.1 and reimplement it using BMT. In the process, you'll learn how to use BMT.

6.3.1 *Snag-it ordering using BMT*

Listing 6.4 reimplements the code in listing 6.1 using BMT. The core business logic is the same as in the CMT code listing. It checks to see if there are any bids, validates the card, charges the card, and finally closes out the bid by shipping the item. Fundamentally the code hasn't changed.

Listing 6.4 Implementing snag-it ordering using BMT

```
@Stateless(name = "BidManager")
@TransactionManagement(TransactionManagementType.BEAN)
public class BidManagerBean implements BidManager {
  @Resource
  private UserTransaction userTransaction;
  public void placeSnagItOrder(Item item, Bidder bidder, CreditCard card) {
    try {
      userTransaction.begin();
      if(!hasBids(item)) {
        creditCardManager.validateCard(card);
        creditCardManager.chargeCreditCard(card,item.getInitialPrice());
        closeBid(item,bidder,item.getInitialPrice());
      }
      userTransaction.commit();
    } catch (CreditProcessingException ce) {
      logger.log(Level.SEVERE,"An error ocurred processing the order.",ce);
      context.setRollbackOnly();
    } catch (CreditCardSystemException ccse) {
      logger.log(Level.SEVERE,"Unable to validate credit card.",ccse);
      context.setRollbackOnly();
    } catch (Exception e) {
      logger.log(Level.SEVERE,"An error ocurred processing the order.",e);
    }
}
```

❶ Uses BMT
❷ Injects UserTransaction
❸ Starts transaction
❹ Commits transaction
❺ Rolls back transaction on exception

Scanning the code, you'll notice that the `@TransactionManagement` annotation specifies the value `TransactionManagementType.BEAN` as opposed to `TransactionManageMent-Type.CONTAINER`, indicating that BMT is used this time ❶. The `TransactionAttribute` annotation is missing altogether because it's applicable only for CMT. A `User-Transaction`, a JTA interface, is injected ❷ and used explicitly to `begin` ❸, `commit` ❹, or `rollback` ❺ a transaction. The transaction boundary is much simpler than the entire method and includes only calls that really need to be atomic. The sections that follow discuss the code in greater detail, starting with getting a reference to a `javax.transaction.UserTransaction` instance.

6.3.2 *Getting a UserTransaction*

The `UserTransaction` interface encapsulates the basic functionality provided by the Java EE transaction manager. JTA has a few other interfaces used under different circumstances. We won't cover them here, because most of the time you'll be dealing with `UserTransaction`. As you might expect, the `UserTransaction` interface is too intricate to be instantiated directly and must be obtained from the container. Listing 6.4

used the simplest way of getting a UserTransaction: injecting it through the @Resource annotation. There are a couple of other ways to do this: using JNDI lookups or through the EJBContext.

JNDI LOOKUPS

The application server binds the UserTransaction to the JNDI name java:comp/UserTransaction. You can look it up directly using JNDI with this code:

```
Context context = new InitialContext();
UserTransaction userTransaction = (UserTransaction)context.lookup("java:comp/
    UserTransaction");
userTransaction.begin();
// Perform transacted tasks.
userTransaction.commit();
```

This method is typically used outside of EJBs—for example, if you need to use a transaction in a helper or nonmanaged class in the EJB or web tier where dependency injection isn't supported. If you find yourself in this situation, you might want to consider another approach. It's much better to have that code in an EJB with greater access to abstractions.

EJBCONTEXT

You can also acquire a UserTransaction by invoking the getUserTransaction method on EJBContext. This approach is useful if you're using a SessionContext or MessageDrivenContext for some other purpose anyway, and a separate injection to get a transaction instance would clutter the code. Note that you can use the getUserTransaction method only if you're using BMT. Calling this in a CMT environment will cause the context to throw an IllegalStateException. The following code shows the getUserTransaction method in action:

```
@Resource
private SessionContext context;
...
UserTransaction userTransaction = context.getUserTransaction();
userTransaction.begin();
// Perform transacted tasks...
userTransaction.commit();
```

It's important to note that the EJBContext.getRollbackOnly() and setRollbackOnly() methods will throw an IllegalStateException if you call them while in BMT. These methods can only be called while you're in CMT. Next, let's see how the obtained UserTransaction interface is used.

6.3.3 Using user transactions

You've already seen the UserTransaction interface's most frequently used methods: begin, commit, and rollback. The UserTransaction interface has a few other useful methods you should take a look at as well. Let's take a look at the entire interface:

```
public interface UserTransaction {
  public void begin() throws NotSupportedException, SystemException;
```

```
  public void commit() throws RollbackException,
    HeuristicMixedException,HeuristicRollbackException, SecurityException,
    IllegalStateException, SystemException;
  public void rollback() throws IllegalStateException,
    SecurityException,SystemException;
  public void setRollbackOnly() throws IllegalStateException,
    SystemException;
  public int getStatus() throws SystemException;
  public void setTransactionTimeout(int seconds) throws SystemException;
}
```

The `begin` method creates a new low-level transaction behind the scenes and associates it with the current thread. You might be wondering what would happen if you called the `begin` method twice before calling `rollback` or `commit`. Perhaps it's possible to create a nested transaction using this approach. In reality, the second invocation of `begin` would throw a `NotSupportedException` because Java EE doesn't support nested transactions. The `commit` and `rollback` methods, on the other hand, remove the transaction attached to the current thread by the `begin` method. Whereas `commit` sends a "success" signal to the underlying transaction manager, `rollback` abandons the current transaction. The `setRollbackOnly` method on this interface might be slightly counterintuitive as well. After all, why bother marking a transaction as rolled back when you can roll it back yourself?

To understand why, consider the fact that you could call a CMT method from your BMT bean that contains a length calculation and checks the transactional flag before proceeding. Because your BMT transaction would be propagated to the CMT method, it might be programmatically simpler, especially in a long method, to mark the transaction as rolled back using the `setRollbackOnly` method instead of writing an involved `if-else` block to avoid such conditions. The `getStatus` method is a more robust version of `getRollbackOnly` in the CMT world. Instead of returning a Boolean, this method returns an integer-based status of the current transactions, indicating a more fine-tuned set of states that a transaction could possibly be in. The `javax.transaction.Status` interface defines exactly what these states are, and they're listed in table 6.2.

Table 6.2 The possible values of `javax.transaction.Status` interface. These are the status values returned by the `UserTransaction.getStatus` method.

Status	Description
`STATUS_ACTIVE`	The associated transaction is in an active state.
`STATUS_MARKED_ROLLBACK`	The associated transaction is marked for rollback, possibly due to invocation of the `setRollbackOnly` method.
`STATUS_PREPARED`	The associated transaction is in the prepared state because all resources have agreed to commit. (Refer to the section on two-phase commit.)
`STATUS_COMMITTED`	The associated transaction has been committed.

Table 6.2 The possible values of `javax.transaction.Status` interface. These are the status values returned by the `UserTransaction.getStatus` method. *(continued)*

Status	Description
`STATUS_ROLLBACK`	The associated transaction has been rolled back.
`STATUS_UNKNOWN`	The status for the associated transaction isn't known.
`STATUS_NO_TRANSACTION`	There's no associated transaction in the current thread.
`STATUS_PREPARING`	The associated transaction is preparing to be committed and awaiting response from subordinate resources. (Refer to the section on two-phase commit.)
`STATUS_COMMITTING`	The transaction is in the process of committing.
`STATUS_ROLLING_BACK`	The transaction is in the process of rolling back.

The `setTransactionTimeout` method specifies the time (in seconds) in which a transaction must finish. The default transaction time-out value is set to different values for different application servers. For example, JBoss has a default transaction time-out value of 300 seconds, whereas Oracle Application Server 10g has a default transaction time-out value of 30 seconds. You might want to use this method if you're using a long-running transaction. Typically, it's better to simply set the application server–wide defaults using vendor-specific interfaces. At this point, you're probably wondering how to set a transaction time-out when using CMT instead. Only containers using either an attribute in the vendor-specific deployment descriptor or vendor-specific annotation support this.

6.3.4 *Using BMT effectively*

CMT is the default transaction type for EJB transactions. In general, BMT should be used sparingly because it's verbose, complex, and difficult to maintain. There are some concrete reasons to use BMT, however. BMT transactions need not begin and end in the confines of a single method call. If you're using a stateful session bean and need to maintain a transaction across method calls, BMT is your only option. But things get complicated because you can't call a bean that uses CMT, and one BMT bean can't pass one programmatic context to another bean. In addition, it's easy to ignore exceptions and not roll back or commit a transaction. This is illustrated in listing 6.3 where the last exception doesn't issue a `rollback` method.

One argument for BMT is that you can fine-tune your transaction boundaries so that the data held by your code is isolated for the shortest time possible. Our opinion is that this idea indulges in premature optimization and you're better off refactoring your methods to be smaller and more specific. Now that you have a firm grasp of transactions, let's turn our attention to security.

6.4 EJB security

It's hard to overemphasize the importance of security in an Enterprise application. Whether the application is hidden behind a corporate firewall or accessible via the web, someone is always interested in causing mischief or worse. Security falls into two modes: making sure users have access only to data and operations for which they're credentialed and ensuring that hackers can't circumvent application security mechanisms.

Security must be approached from both the view and the business layer. Just because a user can't access a page doesn't mean that the business logic couldn't be invoked. Hackers have successfully queried many AJAX web services that were meant only for restricted pages or for users with different roles. One of the benefits of EJB is that it has an elegant and flexible security model. Using this security model, you can not only lock down the view but also ensure that methods on an EJB are restricted.

The approach taken with EJB security is similar to the one taken with transactions: you can choose from either declarative or programmatic security. It's not a binary decision; you can use a mix with declarative for some beans and programmatic for others. Let's start by examining one of the fundamental concepts: authentication and authorization.

> **NOTE** The Open Web Application Security Project (OWASP) is a nonprofit organization focused on improving web application security. They have many excellent resources documenting how to secure and verify the security of your Java EE applications. They also provide an example Java EE application, WebGoat, which demonstrates how not to write a web application. This application is open source and includes documentation explaining the various security mistakes in the application and how they're exploited and fixed.

6.4.1 Authentication versus authorization

Securing an application invokes two primary functions: authentication and authorization. Authentication must be done before authorization can be performed, but as you'll see, both are necessary aspects of application security.

AUTHENTICATION

Authentication is the process of verifying user identity. By authenticating, you prove you are who you claim to be. In the real world, this is usually accomplished through visual inspection/identity cards, signatures/handwriting, fingerprints, or DNA tests. In the computing realm, authentication is usually accomplished through a username and password.

AUTHORIZATION

Authorization is the process of determining whether a user should have access to a particular resource or operation. Authorization is preceded by authentication—only after a user is authenticated can you check their authorization. In an open system, an authenticated user can access any resource or operation. Most systems, however, restrict access to resources based on user identity. Although there might be some resources in a system that are accessible to all, most resources are restricted to a small subset of users. Both authentication and authorization are closely tied to users, groups, and roles, which we'll look at next.

6.4.2 User, groups, and roles

Users, groups, and roles are three interrelated concepts that form the basic building blocks of EJB security. We've already mentioned users, so let's start with groups. To simplify, administration users are divided into groups as shown in figure 6.4. *Groups* are a logical partition for the application to identify users who should have access to different functions—for example, to administrative functions, customer service support, and so on. All users in the Administrator group can reset accounts and check account activity, whereas users in the Customer Service group can only change the status of an order. The application checks to see if the user is a member of the group before performing an operation. User/group functionality with EJB security is thus analogous to groups in the Unix file system, which simplifies the management of access lists for individual resources.

A role is closely related to the concept of a group. A *role* is an application container's abstraction of a group. A mapping is typically created to associate application groups to Enterprise application roles. This separation enables applications to be coded independently of their deployment environment. An application might be developed with more fine-grained access controls than presently supported, or it might be purchased from an external vendor that obviously isn't familiar with the company's internal roles. Thus, this abstraction dissociates groups from the actual group names used in production. An application might have an Administrator group, whereas a company's LDAP directory has a role Department Head that is equivalent. The mapping between the two is application server-specific—many containers can automatically make associations if the group and role names match.

6.4.3 How EJB security is implemented

Java EE security is largely based on the Java Authentication and Authorization Service (JAAS). JAAS separates the authentication system from the Java EE application by using

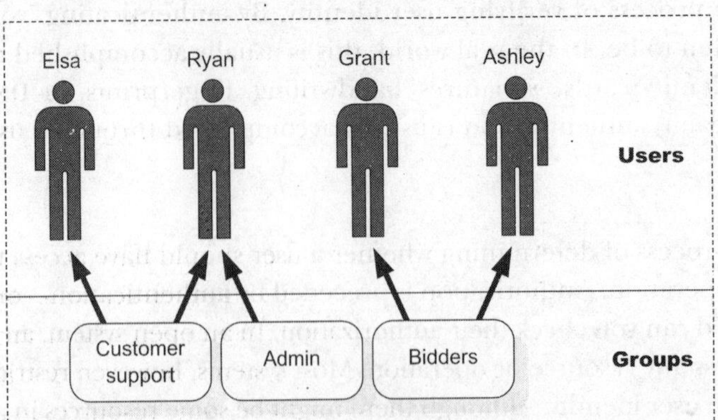

Figure 6.4 Users and groups

a well-defined, pluggable API. The Java EE application interacts only with the JAAS API. The application isn't responsible for the low-level details of user authentication, such as working with SHA-256 (password encryption) or communicating with the external authenticating service, such as Microsoft's Active Directory or the LDAP. The vendor plug-in that's configured in the application container handles the details for you and can be changed as needed. In addition to authentication, the container implements authorization in both the web and EJB tiers using JAAS.

JAAS is designed so that both the authentication and authorization steps can be performed at any Java EE tier, including the web and EJB tiers. Realistically, though, most Java EE applications are web-accessible and share an authentication system across tiers, if not across the application server. JAAS fully uses this reality once a user is authenticated at any Java EE tier. Once authenticated, the authentication context is passed through the tiers wherever possible, instead of repeating the authentication step. The `Principal` object we already mentioned represents this sharable, validated authentication context. Figure 6.5 depicts this common Java EE security management scenario.

As shown in figure 6.5, a user enters the application through the web tier. The web tier gathers authentication information from the user and authenticates the supplied credentials using JAAS against an underlying security system. A successful authentication results in a valid user `Principal`. At this point, the `Principal` is associated with one or more roles. For each secured web/EJB tier resource, the application server checks to see if the principal/role is authorized to access the resource. The `Principal` is transparently passed from the web tier to the EJB tier as needed.

A detailed discussion of web tier authentication and authorization is beyond the scope of this book, as is the extremely rare scenario of standalone EJB authentication using JAAS. But we'll give you a basic outline of web-tier security to serve as a starting point for further investigation before diving into authorization management in EJB 3.

WEB-TIER AUTHENTICATION AND AUTHORIZATION

The web-tier servlet specification (http://java.sun.com/products/servlet) successfully hides many low-level details for both authentication and authorization. As a developer,

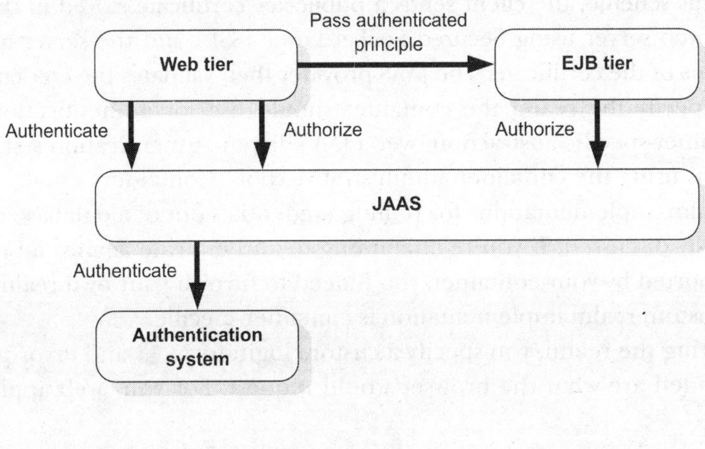

Figure 6.5 Most common Java EE security management scenario using JAAS

you simply need to tell the servlet container what resources you want secured and how they're secured—that is, what roles can view secured resources. The servlet container takes care of the rest.

Web-tier security is configured using the `login-config` and `security-constraint` elements of the web.xml file. The following listing shows how the administrative pages within the ActionBazaar application are secured.

Listing 6.5 Sample web.xml elements to secure order cancelling and other functionality

```
<login-config>
  <auth-method>FORM</auth-method>                              ❶
  <realm-name>ActionBazaarRealm</realm-name>                   ❷
  <form-login-config>
    <form-login-page>/login.faces</form-login-page>            ❸
    <form-error-page>/login_error.faces</form-error-page>      ❹
  </form-login-config>
</login-config>

<security-constraint>
  <web-resource-collection>
    <web-resource-name>
      Action Bazaar Administrative Component
    </web-resource-name>
    <url-pattern>/admin/*</url-pattern>                        ❺
  </web-resource-collection>
  <auth-constraint>
    <role-name>CSR</role-name>                                 ❻
  </auth-constraint>
</security-constraint>
```

❶ Sets authentication to FORM
❷ Security realm used for authentication
❸ Form used for authentication
❹ Error page if validation fails
❺ URL pattern to be locked down
❻ Role required for access to resource collection

This listing specifies how the web container should gather and validate authentication. In this case, a custom form for authentication is used, so authentication is set to `FORM` ❶. With form-based authentication, you supply a custom login form as well as a custom error form. There are two other options: `BASIC` and `CLIENT-CERT`. With `BASIC`, the web browser will display a generic dialog prompting for a username and password. `CLIENT-CERT` is an advanced form of authentication that bypasses username/password prompts altogether. In this scheme, the client sends a public-key certificate stored in the client browser to the web server using Secured Socket Layer (SSL) and the server authenticates the contents of the certificate. The JAAS provider then validates the credentials.

Next, you specify the realm the container should use for authentication ❷. A realm is a container-specific abstraction over a JAAS-driven authentication system. You configure realms using the container administrative tools. Containers usually provide several basic realm implementations for pulling credentials out of a database or LDAP like we previously discussed. If you're attempting to authenticate against an external system not supported by your container, you'll need to furnish your own realm implementation. A custom realm implementation is container-specific.

After specifying the realm, you specify a custom login form ❸ and error page ❹. The URLs provided are what the browser would request. For your web application,

XHTML pages are processed as JSF pages by appending the `*.jsf` extension. Depending on how you configure your application, this may vary.

With the next two elements, you specify which pages you want secured ❺ and what role is required to access these pages ❻. The URL pattern you provide, `/admin/*`, results in all files under the admin directory being secured. The role name must be mapped to a group name from the realm.

The login page is shown in the next listing. When the form is posted, the username and password will be extracted from the request parameters by the container and authentication performed.

Listing 6.6 Sample custom authentication form for ActionBazaar

```
<!DOCTYPE HTML PUBLIC "-//W3C//DTD HTML 4.01 Transitional//EN"
  "http://www.w3.org/TR/html4/loose.dtd">
<HTML xmlns:f=http://java.sun.com/jsf/core
  xmlns:h="http://java.sun.com/jsf/html">
  <h:head>
    <title>ActionBazaar Admin Login</title>
  </h:head>
  <h:body>
    <form action="j_security_check" method="POST">          ❶ Sets action for the form
      <h:panelGrid columns="2">
        <f:facet name="header">
          Authentication
        </f:facet>
        <h:outputText value="Username"/>
        <input type="text" name="j_username" size="25"/>      ❷ Sets username
        <h:outputText value="Password"/>
        <input type="password" size="15" name="j_password"/>  ❸ Sets password
        <h:panelGroup>
          <input type="submit" value="Submit"/>
          <input type="reset" value="Reset"/>
        </h:panelGroup>
      </h:panelGrid>
    </form>
  </h:body>
</HTML>
```

The container requires a form action of `j_security_check` ❶. The username ❷ and password ❸ fields both used are predefined. Using a `FORM` approach instead of a `BASIC` enables you to provide a customized login screen instead of the generic modal dialog that's displayed by the browser when `BASIC` is used. Next, let's take a quick look at EJB authentication and authorization.

EJB AUTHENTICATION AND AUTHORIZATION

Although it's not commonly done, it's possible to authenticate from a standalone client such as a swing desktop application. But this is a daunting task requiring you to implement all of the security mechanisms being provided by the container. Many application containers provide a JAAS login module for performing this task. Because this book is about the EJB and not specific implementation features available from different containers, we don't attempt to cover it. It's a moving topic that's vendor- and version-specific.

Now that we've covered how authentication is performed, let's look at authorization. We'll start by examining declarative security.

6.4.4 EJB declarative security

Declarative security is somewhat analogous to CMTs. You tell the container what you expect through annotation or configuration files, and the container takes care of the heavy lifting. Conveniently, both the annotations and/or configuration files can apply to either an entire class or an individual method. The container looks at the converts of the server container's role into an application group and then checks against the list of valid roles to determine whether a particular method on a bean can be invoked. If it can't be invoked, then an exception is thrown.

To put this discussion of security into context, let's look at a security problem in ActionBazaar. Customer service representatives (CSRs) are allowed to cancel a user's bid under certain circumstances—for example, if a seller discloses something in an answer to a bidder that should have been mentioned in the listing. But in the original implementation of the cancel bid operation, there was no check to ensure that the action was being performed by a CSR.

A clever hacker analyzes the logical naming conventions used in the forms and links. After some trial and error, he finally bangs out some Perl script that constructs a `POST` request that will cancel a bid. The hacker then uses his utility to engage in "shell bidding" in an attempt to incite users to overpay for an item. The hacker posts items for sale and uses a friend's account to incite a bidding war. Once the genuine bidders stop bidding, the hacker removes the fake bid using his knowledge of HTML post requests. No one has any clue that this is happening.

After a while, customer service discovers the scheme as a result of questions from observant bidders who are surprised that they've won a bid after being outbid. Protections are put in place using EJB security so that only CSRs can cancel a bid. An implementation using declarative security is shown in the following listing.

Listing 6.7 Securing bid cancellation using declarative security management

```
@DeclareRoles({"BIDDER", "CSR", "ADMIN"})        // ❶ Declares roles for bean
@Stateless(name = "BidManager")
public class BidManagerBean implements BidManager {
  @RolesAllowed({"CSR","ADMIN"})                 // ❷ Specifies roles with access to method
  public void cancelBid(Bid bid) {
    ...
  }
  @PermitAll                                     // ❸ Permits all system roles access to method
  public List<Bid> getBids(Item item) {
    return item.getBids();
  }
}
```

This listing includes some of the most commonly used security annotations defined in JSR-250, including `javax.annotation.security.DeclarRoles`, `javax.annotation.security.RolesAllowed`, and `javax.annotation.security.PermitAll`. Two other annotations that we haven't used but will discuss are `javax.annotation.security.DenyAll` and `javax.annotation.security.RunAs`. Let's start our analysis of the code and security annotations with the `@DeclareRoles` annotation.

@DeclareRoles annotation

The `@DeclareRoles` annotation lists the security roles used in an EJB. It can only be placed on a class. If it isn't provided, then the container looks through the `@RolesAllowed` annotations and builds up a master list for the class. If a bean extends another bean, the list of roles is concatenated. In the case of listing 6.5, the `BidManagerBean` is marked as using roles `BIDDER`, `CSR`, and `ADMIN` ❶.

@RolesAllowed annotation

The `@RolesAllowed` annotation ❷ is the crux of declarative security management. This annotation can be applied to either an EJB business method or an entire class. When applied to an entire EJB, it tells the container which roles are allowed to access any EJB method. On the other hand, you can use this annotation on a method to specify the authentication for that particular method. The tremendous flexibility offered by this annotation becomes evident when you consider the fact that you can override class-level settings by reapplying the annotation at the method level. For example, the `BidManagerBean` could be restricted to only administrators and specific methods opened up for nonadministrators such as `getBids`. But using a mixture of security roles on a class can quickly become convoluted. It's perhaps better to use a separate bean.

@PermitAll and @DenyAll annotations

The `@PermitAll` and `@DenyAll` annotations are self-explanatory—either everyone has access or no one does. The `@PermitAll` annotation is used in listing 6.7 ❸ to instruct the container that any user can retrieve the current bids for a given item. You should use this annotation sparingly, especially at the class level, because it's possible to inadvertently leave security holes if it's used carelessly.

The `@DenyAll` annotation renders either a class or method completely inaccessible by any role. This annotation isn't terribly useful because blocking all access to a method makes the method unusable. But using the equivalent `@DenyAll` XML configuration would enable you to disable methods for all roles without altering a line of code. This is useful after you've deployed the application and want to disable functionality.

@RunAs

The `@RunAs` annotation is similar to the `sudo` command on Unix systems. On a Unix system you'd use `sudo` to execute a command as another user; very often that other user is an administrator. This enables tasks to be executed with a different set of privileges. These other sets of privileges may be more or less restrictive. For example, the cancelBid method in listing 6.7 might need to invoke a statistics-tracking EJB that manages historical records and removes a record that had been created. In this hypothetical situation, the statistics-tracking EJB requires an ADMIN role. By using the @RunAs annotation, you can temporarily assign a CSR an ADMIN role so that the statistics-tracking EJB thinks an administrator is invoking the method:

```
@RunAs("ADMIN")
@RolesAllowed({"CSR"})
public void cancelBid(Bid bid, Item item) {…}
```

This annotation should be used sparingly. Like the @PermitAll annotation, it can open up unforeseen security holes in the software. Now that you understand declarative security, let's investigate programmatic security.

6.4.5 *EJB programmatic security*

Declarative security is powerful but there are situations where you need more control over security. For example, you might want to alter the behavior of a method based on the user's role or even the username. In addition, you may want to check whether the user is the member of two groups or make sure that a user is in one group but not in another group. With programmatic security, you can handle such use cases. Before we delve into it, it should be noted that programmatic security and declarative security aren't mutually exclusive. Unlike transaction management, a class isn't marked as using either declarative or programmatic security as was the case with transaction management.

Programmatic security is accessed via the SessionContext. From this you can retrieve the Principal and/or check whether the caller to a method is executing in a specific role. The next listing contains the bid-cancelling scenario we discussed in the last section, except it's reimplemented using programmatic security.

Listing 6.8 Securing bid cancellation using programmatic security

```
@Resource
private SessionContext context;
public void cancelBid(Bid bid) {
  if(!context.isCallerInRole("CSR") && !context.isCallerInRole("ADMIN"))
  {
    throw new SecurityException(
      "You do not have permission to cancel an order.");
    …
  }
}
```

❶ Injects EJB context

❷ Checks authorization

❸ Throws exception on violation

The listing first injects the EJB context ❶. The isCallerInRole method of the EJB-Context is used to see if the underlying authenticated principal has the CSR role ❷. If it does not, you throw a java.lang.SecurityException notifying the user about the authorization violation ❸. Otherwise, the bid-cancellation method is allowed to proceed normally. Next we'll discuss both of the the security management–related methods provided in the EJB context, namely isCallerInRole and getCallerPrincipal.

ISCALLERINROLE AND GETCALLERPRINCIPAL

Programmatic security is relatively straightforward. It's composed of the two security-related methods that you access via the `javax.ejb.EJBContext` interface as follows:

```
public interface EJBContext {
  ...
  public java.securityPrincipal getCallerPrincipal();
  public boolean isCallerInRole(java.lang.String roleName);
  ...
}
```

You've already seen the `isCallerInRole` method in action; it's fairly self-explanatory. Behind the scenes, the EJB context retrieves the `Principal` associated with the current thread and checks if any of its roles match the name you provided. The `getCallerPrincipal` method gives you direct access to the `java.security.Principal` representing the current authentication context. The only method of interest in the `Principal` interface is `getName`, which returns the name of the principal. Most of the time, the name of the principal is the login name of the validated user. This means that just in case of a homemade security framework, you could validate the individual user if you needed to.

For example, assume that you decided to allow bidders to cancel their orders if the cancellation was performed within five minutes. This is in addition to allowing CSRs to cancel bids. You'd implement this using `getCallerPrincipal` method as follows:

```
public void cancelBid(Bid bid) {
  if(!context.isCallerInRole("CSR") &&
      !context.isCallerInRole("ADMIN") &&
      (!bid.getBidder().getUsername().equals(
      context.getCallerPrincipal().getName()) &&
      bid.getBidDate().getTime() >= (new Date().getTime() - 60*1000))) {
    throw new SecurityException("You do not have permission to cancel an
     order.");
    ...
  }
}
```

One thing to note is that there's no guarantee exactly what `Principal` name might return. In some environments, it can return the role name, group name, or any other arbitrary string that makes sense for the authentication system. Before you use the `Principal.getName` method, you should check the documentation of your particular security environment. As you can see, the one great drawback of programmatic security management is the intermixing of security code with business logic, as well as the potential hardcoding of role and principal names. In previous versions of EJB, there was no way of getting around these shortfalls. But in EJB 3 you can alleviate this problem somewhat by using interceptors. Let's see how to accomplish this next.

USING INTERCEPTORS FOR PROGRAMMATIC SECURITY

In EJB 3 you can set up interceptors that are invoked before and after (around) any EJB business method. This facility is ideal for crosscutting concerns that shouldn't be duplicated in every method. You could reimplement listing 6.8 using interceptors instead of hardcoding security in the business method, as in the following listing.

Listing 6.9 Using interceptors with programmatic security

```
public class SecurityInterceptor {
  @Resource
  private SessionContext sessionContext;
  @AroundInvoke                                              <- 1 Marks intercepted invocation
  public Object checkUserRole(InvocationContext context)
    throws Exception {
    if(!sessionContext.isCallerInRole("CSR")) {             <- 2 Accesses EJBContext from InvocationContext
      throw new SecurityException("No permission to cancel bid.");
    }
    return context.proceed();
  }
}

@Stateless
public class BidManagerBean implements BidManager {
  @Interceptors(SecurityInterceptor.class)                  <- 3 Specifies interceptor for method
  public void cancelBid(Bid bid) {…}
}
```

The `SecurityInterceptor` class method `checkUserRole` is designated as `AroundInvoke`, meaning it would be invoked whenever a method is intercepted ❶. In the method you check to see if the `Principal` is CSR ❷. If the role isn't correct, you throw a `SecurityException`. The `BidManagerBean`, on the other hand, specifies the `SecurityInterceptor` class as the interceptor for the `cancelBid` method ❸.

Note that although using interceptors helps matters a bit in terms of removing hardcoding from business logic, there's no escaping the fact that there's still a significant amount of hardcoding. Basically you've moved the hardcoding from the business method to the interceptors. Moreover, unless you're using a simple security scheme where most EJB methods have similar authorization rules and you can reuse a small number of interceptors across the application, things could become complicated very quickly. In effect, you'd have to resort to writing ad hoc interceptors for method-specific authentication combinations. Contrast this to the relatively simple approach of using the declarative security management annotations or deployment descriptors.

6.4.6 Using EJB security effectively

As with the case of transactions, declarative transactions are the recommended approach to take when implementing security. You should avoid working with specific users or accessing `Principal.getName()`. As mentioned, the `getName` method returns a value that's dependent on the authentication system being used. Although you may not be concerned about portability between application servers, coding to a specific authentication system will only cause problems in the future. Declarative security is also much easier to analyze and less prone to errors than programmatic. With declarative security, a class can be annotated and then individual methods override the security settings where necessary. With programmatic security, forgetting to check the credentials or mistyping credentials can open security holes that go unnoticed. With transactions, inconsistencies show up in a database that can be analyzed. Security failures, on the other hand, are silent and don't show up as system failures. As you saw with ActionBazaar, users of a system are often the first ones to discover that the system has been breached and they've been affected.

Container-managed security should always be used. The web container will automatically forward the security context to the EJB container. This ensures continuity between the web and the business tiers. In addition, security checks should exist at the presentation level (WAR) and at the business logic level (EJB). Security shouldn't be implemented using obscurity—don't be fooled into believing that a user won't figure out how to generate a form posting that deletes records or calls up records for which the user isn't credentialed, because someone will always try.

6.5 Summary

In this chapter, we discussed the basic theory of transactions management using CMT and BMT, basic security concepts, and programmatic and declarative security management. Both transactions and security are crosscutting concerns that ideally shouldn't be interleaved with business logic. The EJB 3 take on security and transaction management tries to reflect exactly this belief. Minimizing crosscutting concerns in business logic simplifies the code and reduces errors that invariably arise when the same logic must be replicated in multiple spots.

Out of the box, EJBs default to container-managed persistence with a transaction encompassing a method invocation. On the security front, there are no security constraints on beans. By default, the web tier can call any bean and any bean can invoke any other bean on behalf of any user. The best approach for both managing transactions and security is to use declarative transactions (CMT) and declarative security. Declarative security can be mixed with the programmatic approach, but CMT and BMT can't be mixed in the same bean, and using BMT for one bean and CMT for another bean will cause complications quickly if one bean uses the other. With both transactions and security, additional configuration of the application container will be necessary.

The discussion on security and transactions wraps up our coverage of session and message-driven beans. In the next chapter we'll delve into scheduling and timers.

7 Scheduling and timers

This chapter covers

- The basics of the EJB Timer Service
- The basics of cron
- Different types of timers
- Declaring cron timers
- Using ad hoc timers

So far in our study of EJBs, actions performed by beans must be initiated either on startup or as a result of an external action such as a method invocation from the web tier or to handle a message delivered via JMS. A user must click something in a web page or a JMS message must be delivered for an EJB method to be invoked and the application to do something. While most of the behavior in an application is prompted by user actions, there are times when you want the application to do something on its own either at a specific interval or at specific times. For example, you may want the application to send out an email reminder a day in advance, batch process records at night, or scan a legacy database looking for records to process every 15 minutes. To implement such behaviors you need the EJB Timer Service. Using the Timer Service, you can build Enterprise applications that schedule operations.

The EJB Timer Service underwent a major upgrade with the 3.1 release, which added support for cron-like scheduling. Prior to EJB 3.1, only delayed (performed in 10 minutes) and interval (executed every 20 minutes) operations were supported. If you were interested in scheduling operations for specific times or dates, you had to look outside the EJB specification to third-party solutions. Although these solutions were powerful, they added an extra layer of unnecessary complexity. Full cron-like scheduling is a core requirement for many applications, and support should be standardized and available in all containers.

In this chapter we'll delve into how timers can be created both declaratively and programmatically. We'll also examine how timers interact with transactions and EJB security. But first, let's explore the basics of scheduling.

7.1 Scheduling basics

This chapter is concerned with scheduling method invocations on EJB using the EJB Timer Service. The concept of the Timer Service isn't that different from the timer on your kitchen stove. When the timer goes off, you either pull the cookies out of the oven or stir another ingredient into the pot. Putting this in the context of the container, when a timer is created by an application—either from configuration files or programmatically—a timer is set. When the timer goes off, a bean is plucked from the method-ready pool (unless it's a singleton bean), and the specified method is invoked, as shown in figure 7.1. In the case of a singleton bean, the existing singleton instance is used. The method is invoked just as if a user accessing it from a web interface invoked it. The container will perform dependency injection, and no special setup or logic is required on your part. If the timer is a reoccurring timer (every 10 minutes, for example), another timer is set to go off in 10 minutes.

In the upcoming sections we'll define time-outs and look at cron functionality, the timer interface, and finally the different types of timers. This section has quite a bit of material for you to digest, but all we're really covering is an egg timer on steroids. Let's start by looking at the core features of the Timer Service.

7.1.1 Timer Service features

Let's now turn our attention and examine the fundamental features of the EJB Timer Service. Using the EJB Timer Service, tasks can be scheduled at specific dates and times, for specific intervals, or after an elapsed duration. Although the Timer Service is robust and timers will survive server restarts/failures, the Timer Service doesn't support real-time scheduling. This means that you shouldn't use the EJB scheduling capabilities for situations where you must respond to real-world events within a

Figure 7.1 Timer Service in a nutshell

measureable timeframe. A measurable timeframe is a period of time in which you absolutely must process a request or provide a response. The EJB Timer Service is applicable in situations that aren't mission-critical (where something bad happens if you're late by a nanosecond). For example, sending out an email broadcast at midnight with bid statuses is a good fit for the Timer Service. Using the Timer Service to monitor the pilot tubes on an airplane and calculate engine thrust would be a bad solution.

We'll now examine the types of beans that support timers, fault tolerance, and methods for creating timers. After we've talked about these features in the abstract, we'll dive into code.

SUPPORTED BEAN TYPES

As of EJB 3.1, the EJB Timer Service can be used with stateless session beans, singleton beans, and message-driven beans. Stateful session beans aren't supported—perhaps in a future revision support will be added, but it doesn't exist today. What this means is that unless you're using a singleton bean, it's your responsibility to persist state between timer invocations. Each time a timer fires, a potentially different stateless session bean will be retrieved and invoked, as shown in figure 7.2. Singleton beans can be used where state needs to be maintained between timer invocations with one caveat: too many timers on a singleton bean can result in complications as timers clash attempting to execute on the same method at the same time or different methods at the same time. Let's turn our attention toward fault tolerance.

FAULT TOLERANCE

With any timer, the question of fault tolerance is an important one. Even the most basic alarm clocks include battery backup so that if the power is lost the clock continues to track time and remembers your wake-up time. Thus, you can sleep through the night, and an intermittent power failure—provided it doesn't occur when the alarm is supposed to sound—won't result in you being late for work or missing that important flight to Hawaii. If the power is out when the alarm is supposed to sound, there's not much the alarm clock can do. With the EJB Timer Service, alarms will survive server restarts and failures with no additional effort on your part.

When a method is scheduled, the container creates a timer that will execute the specified method at the designated time. When the timer fires, the time condition has been met, and the method is either called in the case of a singleton bean or an

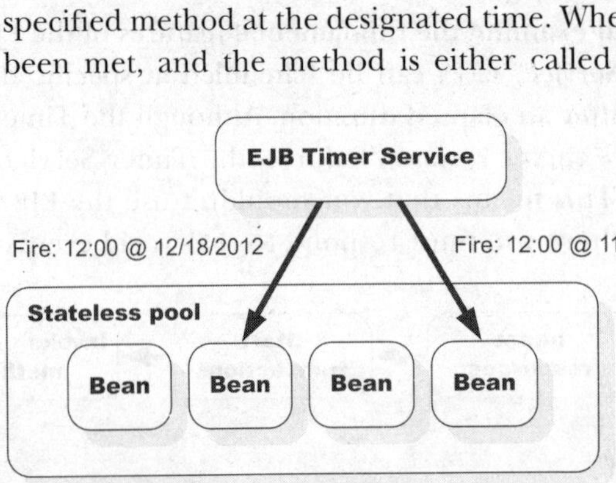

Figure 7.2 Timer Service and the stateless pool

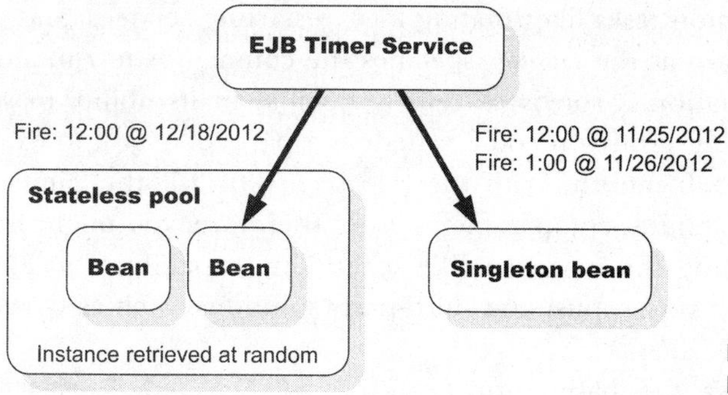

Figure 7.3 Timers on stateless beans versus singleton beans

instance is plucked from the method-ready pool and executed in the case of a stateless singleton bean. This is illustrated in figure 7.3. Note that singleton beans aren't serialized between server restarts, so it's important that beans persists their state. Timers aren't supported with stateful beans.

TIMER CREATION

The scheduling of the execution can be done via configuration, programmatically, or by using annotations. Each approach fulfills a different need. Timers created via configuration are typically scheduled processes that execute on a fixed schedule. An example would be a nightly process for deleting temporary files or collecting performance data. Timers created programmatically are typically end user–driven and are an integral part of a business process. For example, an application might enable an administrator to send out an email broadcast at a specified date and time. This is an ad hoc task—not something an application should be redeployed for so that an updated configuration file can be reloaded. As you'll see in this chapter, scheduling is fairly straightforward.

7.1.2 *Time-outs*

At first glance, a time-out might conjure images of being sent to the corner in grade school for an infraction. But EJB time-outs bear no relation to elementary school punishments. A time-out is simply an action, or method, that's invoked when a timer fires. A timer firing is analogous to an alarm going off—you configure a timer and specify the time-out action. The action can be either an implementation of the `ejbTimeout` method defined in the `javax.ejb.TimedObject` interface or a method marked with the `@Scheduled` annotation. Time-outs can also be configured via XML configuration files. A time-out is associated with a timer. We'll go deeper into timers and the implementation details of time-outs as we go through the rest of the chapter.

> **NOTE** A time-out is an action that's performed when the timer operation completes.

7.1.3 *Cron*

Cron refers to a job scheduler available on many Unix systems including Mac OS X, Linux, and Solaris, among others. It launches applications or scripts at specific times to perform common tasks like rotating logs, restarting services, and so on. A configuration file, known as the *crontab*, specifies the commands to run along with the scheduling information. Cron is extremely flexible in its ability to schedule tasks. For example, using cron you could schedule a particular task to execute on the first Saturday of each month. With the release of EJB 3.1, the Timer Service gained scheduling capabilities comparable to cron; therefore, you might have seen articles or blogs extolling the new cron-like scheduling capabilities in EJB. Previously, scheduling wasn't very robust and third-party solutions, such as Quartz, were used to fill in the gaps.

Figure 7.4 specifies the basic format of the crontab file. There are five setting positions that configure the scheduler followed by the command to execute. An asterisk signifies that all possible values are matched. For example, placing an asterisk in the first column matches every minute. This gives you considerable flexibility in configuring the execution of scripts. Although this isn't as powerful as a batch-queuing system, it's suitable for many everyday problems.

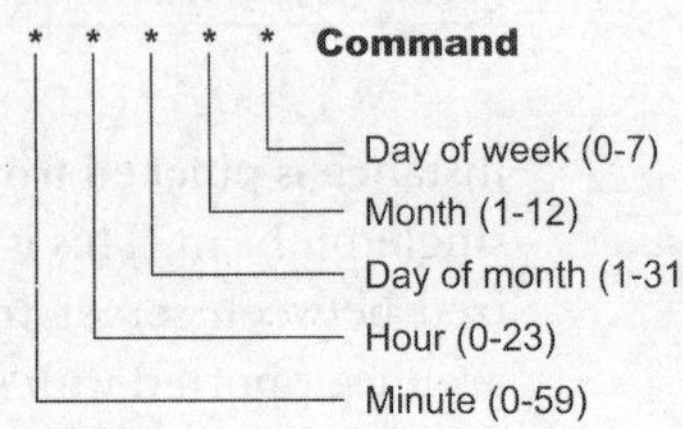

Figure 7.4 Format of the crontab file

If you aren't familiar with cron, the following snippet will give you a taste. This is a cron file from the CentOS Linux distribution. In it, tasks that must run hourly, daily, weekly, or monthly are split up into separate files. The cron.hourly script will execute on the hour and so on:

```
20 * * * * root run-parts /etc/cron.hourly
25 1 * * * root run-parts /etc/cron.daily
50 3 * * 0 root run-parts /etc/cron.weekly
43 4 16 * * root run-parts /etc/cron.monthly
```

Both time-outs and cron are key to understanding the EJB Timer Service, which we'll delve into next.

7.1.4 Timer interface

When you schedule a delayed invocation on a bean, you're creating a timer. A timer knows when it's going to go off and what method it's going to invoke. Therefore, when you create timers, you provide the container with two pieces of information: a configuration setting defining when you want the timer to complete and a method, known as a time-out, to invoke when the timer completes. The container uses this information to create a timer. How the timer is implemented is up to the container provider—implementing timers robustly is obviously not trivial.

As you'll see, there are three ways to configure timers: with annotations, programmatically, or via configuration files. Individual timers can be manipulated via the `javax.ejb.Timer` interface shown in listing 7.1. This interface provides you with one operation, `cancel`, and several methods for retrieving various pieces of information about the timer. To get a representation of a timer that can be serialized, use the `getHandle()` method. This method returns a `javax.ejb.TimerHandle`, which can be used to retrieve the timer instance. The `TimerHandle` is valid only within the container—it can't be passed to remote code. Information on the timer, passed in when creating the timer, can be retrieved with the `getInfo()` method. This can be any serialized object but will be a string if you're using the `info` attribute on the `Schedule` annotation. The `getNextTimeout()` will return a `Date` object with the time of the next time-out. Note that by the time you check it, the timer may have already fired. The `getSchedule()` returns a `javax.ejb.ScheduleExpression` with the scheduling information for cron-based timers. The `getTimeRemaining()` returns the number of milliseconds that will elapse before the timer fires again. The `isCalendarTimer()` returns true if this timer is a cron-based timer. Finally, the last method on the interface, `isPersistent()`, returns true if this timer will survive server restarts/failures.

Listing 7.1 Specification for the `Timer` interface

```
public interface Timer {
  void cancel();
  TimerHandle getHandle();
  Serializable getInfo();
  Date getNextTimeout();
  ScheduleExpression getSchedule();
  long getTimeRemaining();
  boolean isCalendarTimer();
  boolean isPersistent();
}
```

Timer instances are obtained from the `javax.ejb.TimerService`. The `TimerService` contains numerous methods for programmatically creating timers, as well as a method for retrieving all running timers. It's important to note that the list of timers is transient—a timer retrieved from this interface may be invalid by the time you get around to inspecting it. Subsequent sections will cover the `TimerService` in more detail because it's primarily used for creating timers programmatically.

Two topics we haven't yet touched on are transactions and security with regard to timers. The topic of transactions is two-fold: how timer creations are impacted by transactions and how a time-out method participates within the context of a transaction. To answer the first question, see the following code snippet. If the call to the `entityManager` fails, the transaction will be marked for rollback, and this will result in the timer being cancelled provided that it hasn't already executed. This also applies to timer cancellation: if a method that cancels a timer is subsequently rolled back, so is the request to cancel the timer.

```
public void addBid(Bid bid) {
  timerService.createTimer(15*60*1000,15*60*1000,bid);
  entityManager.persist(bid);
  ...
}
```

A time-out method is invoked within the context of a transaction. If the transaction is rolled back, the container retries the time-out. This happens in the case of a bean with container-managed transactions and with the time-out method marked with `REQUIRED` or `REQUIRES_NEW`.

With security, the time-out method is invoked with no security context. This means that if the `getCallerPrincipal` is invoked, it'll return the container's representation of an unauthenticated user. Thus, if the time-out method attempts to call any methods that have security requirements, the method invocation will fail. Remember that timers can be configured via configuration files and thus might have no connection with any user. Now that we've covered the basics of timers, it's time to look at the different types of timers.

7.1.5 Types of timers

There are two types of timers for EJBs: time-delayed timers and calendar-based timers. The time-delayed timers were added in EJB 2.1 and can be thought of as sophisticated egg timers. You can specify that you want a method to execute at regular intervals, at a specific point in time, once after an elapsed time, and so on. For example, time-delayed timers could be used to refresh cached pick lists in a singleton bean every 20 minutes. These timers are useful but not as flexible or as powerful as the calendar-based timers.

Calendar-based timers are based on the cron scheduling concepts we covered earlier. With calendar-based timers, complex execution schedules can be constructed. Cron-based scheduling is very powerful and simplifies support for a wide variety of temporal business progresses. For example, a data synchronization process can be scheduled to start during the middle of the night and pause before people arrive in the morning so as to not negatively affect system performance during the workday.

Looking at timers based on whether they're time-delayed or calendar-/cron-based is one approach to understanding the Timer Service. This approach enables you to compare the services available prior to EJB 3.1 and afterward. If you're working with an existing EJB 3 system, this puts using external libraries such as Quartz into perspective.

Another approach to decomposing the functionality available with the Timer Service is to break down timers by how they're created. Timers can be created either declaratively or programmatically. Declarative timers are built into the application and can be changed only via configuration, which requires an application restart. Programmatic timers can be created at runtime to implement time-based business processes. Let's start by looking at declarative timers.

7.2 Declarative timers

Either placing annotations on bean methods or declaring them in an application configuration file creates declarative timers. Timers created programmatically are best used for routine maintenance tasks or business processes that really don't change. For example, declarative timers are a good fit for recalculating performance of a portfolio every night, or, in the case of ActionBazaar, downloading the latest UPS tracking information to know what shipments have been received. Because timer configuration files are container-specific, we'll focus this section on the `@Schedule` annotation. This annotation was added with EJB 3.1 and configures calendar-/cron-based timers. To create time-delayed timers, you need to use the programmatic API discussed in section 7.3.

7.2.1 @Schedule annotation

Placing the `@Schedule` annotation on the method to be used as the time-out creates a declarative timer. The annotation can only be used in singleton beans, stateless session beans, and message-driven beans. The following code shows the definition of the annotation. If no attributes are specified, the timer will fire at midnight every day. The `info` attribute can be used to provide descriptive text that can be retrieved at runtime—it has no effect on the execution of the timer:

```
@Target(value=METHOD)
@Retention(value=RUNTIME)
public @interface Schedule {
  String dayOfMonth() default "*";
  String dayOfWeek() default "*";
  String hour() default "0";
  String info() default "";
  String minute() default "0";
  String month() default "*";
  boolean persistent() default true;
  String second() default "0";
  String timezone() default "";
  String year() default "*";
}
```

The method on which the `@Schedule` annotation can be placed has the same requirements as the `@Timeout` annotation. The method can't return a value and arguments are limited to the `javax.ejb.Timer` object discussed earlier. Thus, the following time-outs are legal method prototypes:

```
void <METHOD>()
void <METHOD>(Timer timer)
```

With declarative cron timers, multiple timers can be registered for a single method. This is accomplished via the `@Schedules` annotation. This annotation takes an array of `@Schedule` annotations. Remember that a timer isn't associated with a specific instance so it doesn't matter if two or more timers are registered for the same method—both fire at the same time and each will operate on a completely different instance. When a timer fires, a new instance will be pulled from the pool; there isn't a one-to-one correspondence between a timer and a bean.

7.2.2 @Schedules annotation

The `@Schedules` annotation is used to create multiple calendar-based timers on a single time-out method. It only accepts an array of `@Schedule` annotations. It's straightforward to use:

```
@Target({METHOD})
@Retention(RUNTIME)
public @interface Schedules {
  javax.ejb.Schedule[] value();
}
```

Before we look at an example, let's backtrack and look at the parameters of the `@Schedule` annotation.

7.2.3 @Schedule configuration parameters

A cron timer is specified using a calendar expression that's very similar to the format used by the cron utility. The calendar expression comprises seven attributes: `second`, `minute`, `hour`, `dayOfMonth`, `month`, `dayOfWeek`, and `year`. For each of these attributes, there's a well-defined set of values and syntax rules for building expressions that include specific ranges, lists, and increments. Table 7.1 summarizes the attributes along with the default values for each.

Table 7.1 EJB cron scheduling attributes

Attribute	Allowable values	Default
second	[0,59]	0
minute	[0,59]	0
hour	[0,23]	0
dayOfMonth	[1,31]	*
month	[1,12] or {"Jan," "Feb," "Mar," "Apr," "May," "Jun," "Jul," "Aug," "Oct," "Nov," "Dec"}	*
dayOfWeek	[0,6] or {"Sun," "Mon," "Tue," "Wed," "Thu," "Fri," "Sat"}	*
year	A four-digit calendar year	*

It should be noted that by default timers operate within the time zone where the server is running. To specify a different time zone, you'd use the `timezone` attribute and specify a value from the IANA Time Zone Database. The valid values are specified in the Zone Name column. You can also query the `java.util.TimeZone` class to find the string representation. To put this in perspective, let's put declarative timers to use in ActionBazaar.

7.2.4 Declarative timer example

Let's explore the features of the declarative cron timer by using it to send out monthly and holiday newsletters. The monthly newsletter highlights items that attracted heavy bidding along with similar items and profiles of select sellers. In addition, a holiday newsletter will be broadcast to coincide with major holidays and special events such as Black Friday. Both tasks will make use of declarative cron timers.

To implement this feature, you'll add a new stateless session bean, `Newsletter`, to ActionBazaar. The method skeleton is shown in listing 7.2. The `Newsletter` class will use container-managed persistence. Because requesting the list of users is restricted to administrative users, the `Newsletter` bean will run as an administrator so that a security violation exception isn't thrown. Remember that timer methods execute as the nonauthenticated user.

One important use case to consider is what happens in the event of a container crash while the `Newsletter` bean is in the process of sending out newsletters. The container will attempt to reexecute the method when the container is restarted. Emailing a large distribution list will take a long time and the email service isn't transactional. To get around this limitation, you can use JMS. As the service iterates over the users to be emailed, a new JMS message is inserted into the queue. If for any reason the method fails, no emails are sent and the transaction is rolled back. Additionally, with JMS beans sending out the actual emails, the email load can be load-balanced with multiple message-driven bean instances processing email requests. The code for this advanced behavior isn't shown in the following listing but is available online. This demonstrates how the various aspects of EJB thus covered can be used to build a robust service.

Listing 7.2 Scheduling newsletters and reminders

```
@RunAs("Admin")                                    <- Methods will be executed with Admin role
@Stateless
public class NewsletterBean {
  @PersistenceContext
  private EntityManager em;

  @Schedule(second="0", minute="0", hour="0", dayOfMonth="1",   <- Monthly newsletter scheduled to be sent at midnight the first of each month
    month="*", year="*")
  public void sendMonthlyNewsletter() {
    ...
  }

  @Schedules({                                      <- @Schedules enables multiple timers to be created
    @Schedule(second="0", minute="0", hour="12",
      dayOfMonth="Last Thu", month="Nov", year="*"),   <- Timer created for last Thursday of November at noon
    @Schedule(second="0", minute="0", hour="12",
      dayOfMonth="18", month="Dec", year="*")          <- Timer created for December 18 at noon
})
  @TransactionAttribute(TransactionAttributeType.REQUIRES_NEW)   <- Method marked as requiring a new transaction
  public void sendHolidayNewsletter() {
    ...
  }
  ...
}
```

In this listing, the `NewsletterBean` class is first declared as running as an administrator. This enables the bean to retrieve the list of users that's restricted for security reasons. Next, the `sendMonthlyNewsletter` method is annotated with a schedule annotation specifying that the newsletter should be sent out on the first of each month. The sendHolidayNewsletter uses the @Schedules annotation to configure a broadcast for Thanksgiving and Christmas.

Now that you have a basic grasp of declarative timers, let's dig into the syntax to see what's truly possible. The example in listing 7.2 only scratches the surface.

7.2.5 Cron syntax rules

The syntax rules for calendar-based scheduling are straightforward. Table 7.1 documents the attributes along with the valid values and the default values. But that table isn't the complete story. You may have noticed that the second, minute, and hour attributes on the @Schedule annotation are typed as strings and not integers. This is because you can provide expressions to attributes for constructing complex schedules. For example, you could create a timer that executes only Monday through Friday or a timer that executes every other week. If you were limited to single values or the scheduling capabilities prior to EJB 3.1, you wouldn't be able to easily implement this functionality. The attributes support the following syntax forms: single value, wildcard, list, ranges, and increments.

SINGLE VALUE

Single values are the most straightforward and easiest to understand. Table 7.1 lists the valid values that can be used for each attribute. The values are case-insensitive. For some attributes, there are two representations—either numeric or text—as in the case of days of the week where Monday can be represented as either "Mon" or "0". The following are some examples of setting an attribute to a single value:

```
@Schedule(second="0", minute="1", hour="23", dayOfMonth="1", month="Apr",
    dayOfWeek="Mon", year="2015")
```

In this example, a timer is created that will execute on at 11:01:00 on the first day of April and the first Monday of April if the year is 2015. This expression is somewhat deceiving because the dayOfMonth and dayOfWeek are combined using an or, whereas the other attributes are combined using a logical and. Thus, this expression will fire on April 1, 2015, and April 6, 2015.

WILDCARD

The wildcard * matches all possible values for a given attribute. If you've used either ls on Unix or dir on Windows, this should be familiar. The wildcard is used in situations where you want the expression for an attribute to match all possible values but you don't want to list all of the values. The wildcard can be used on all attributes but in most circumstances it's not advisable to use it on second and minute. Running a task every second or every minute will have an adverse impact on system performance. Frequent polling in an Enterprise application reduces scalability and responsiveness. Let's look at an example using the wildcard:

```
@Schedule(second="*", minute="*", hour="*", dayOfMonth="*", month="*",
    dayOfWeek="*", year="*")
```

In this example, the timer will fire on every second of every minute, of every day, of every month, of every year. This example isn't terribly useful but shows that each attribute supports the wildcard.

LIST

The list expression is composed of single values separated by a comma. The list can contain duplicate entries but they're simply ignored. Whitespace between commas and the values are also ignored. A list can't contain a wildcard, sublists, or increments. But a list can contain a range; for instance, you could specify Monday through Tuesday and Thursday through Friday. The following is an example:

```
@Schedule(second="0,29", minute="0,14,29,59", hour="0,5,11,17",
     dayOfMonth="1,15-31",year="2011,2012,2013")
```

This timer will execute for the years 2011, 2012, and 2013 on the first and for days 15–31, every 6 hours, every 15 minutes of those hours, and every 30 seconds. The timer will thus fire on 0:0:0 1, 2011, as well as 0:0:29 1, 2011, and so on. Note that `dayOfWeek` was omitted to simplify the already complex example.

RANGE

You've already seen examples of ranges in the example on lists. A range enables you to specify an inclusive set of values. A single value is separated by a dash (`-`), where the value preceding the dash is the start value and the value after the dash is the end value. A range may not contain the wildcard, lists, or increments. Here's a simple example using ranges:

```
@Schedule(hour="0-11",dayOfMonth="15-31",dayOfWeek="Mon-Fri",month="11-12",
     year="2010-2020")
```

In this example the timer is going to execute for years 2011–2020, for the months of November and December, for days Monday through Friday of the last half of the month, and from midnight until noon. Ranges can also be used for the `minutes`, `seconds`, and `dayOfWeek` attributes, but this would have made this example too complex.

INCREMENTS

Increment support enables the creation of timers that execute at fixed intervals. It's composed of a forward slash, where the value preceding the slash specifies the starting point and the value after the slash specifies the interval. Increments can be used only with `second`, `minute`, and `hour` attributes. The increment executes until it hits the next unit—if the increment is set on the second, the increment will terminate once the next minute is reached. Ditto for minute and hour. Wildcards may be used when specifying the starting position but not following the slash. Let's look at a simple example:

```
@Schedule(second="30/10", minute="*/20", hour="*/6")
```

In this example, the timer will fire every 10 seconds, after a delay of 30 seconds, every 20 minutes, within every sixth hour. Thus, starting the timer at midnight would result in it firing at 06:20:40, 6:40:30, 12:20:40, 12:40:30, and so on. None of the other attributes were specified, because they don't support increments.

7.3 Using programmatic timers

In the previous section you were introduced to declarative timers using the `@Schedule` and `@Schedules` annotations. Declarative timers are useful when the task to be scheduled and its scheduling parameters are known. Declarative cron timers are useful for tasks such as log rotation, batch processing of records off-hours, and other well-known schedulable business processes. Ad hoc timers, on the other hand, aren't known in advance and are created dynamically at runtime as required. Using the ActionBazaar newsletter example, hardcoding holiday newsletter broadcasts into the application isn't flexible. Because ActionBazaar is used in different countries, additional holiday broadcasts will be required. Obviously recompiling the application for additional holidays would be excessive. A superior approach is to use ad hoc timers and let a marketing administrator schedule newsletter broadcasts at runtime.

Ad hoc timers are thus created programmatically at runtime. Functionally they're every bit as powerful as the declarative timers. The only difference is that ad hoc timers are created programmatically at runtime and each bean is limited to one time-out because only one method can be annotated with `@Timeout`. As you'll see, there's a variety of different methods to choose from when creating a programmatic timer.

7.3.1 Understanding programmatic timers

Ad hoc timers are created via the `javax.ejb.TimerService`. The `TimerService` can either be injected via the `@Resource` annotation or acquired from the `javax.ejb.SessionContext`. Once acquired, `TimerService` has numerous `createTimer` variations that simplify timer creation. Two types of timers can be created with the `TimerService`: interval timers and calendar timers. Calendar timers are also known as cron-based timers and were covered earlier. Interval timers made their appearance in EJB 2.1 and are also supported.

Listing 7.3 contains the `TimerService` interface. With the exception of the `getTimers()` method, all other methods are responsible for creating timers. Each method returns a `javax.ejb.Timer` object. The `Timer` object can be used for retrieving basic information about the timer, such as whether it's persistent, the time remaining until it fires, and a method for cancelling the timer. The `getHandle()` method returns a `javax.ejb.TimerHandle`, which supports serialization. The `javax.ejb.Timer` object can't be serialized and thus shouldn't be stored in a member variable of a stateful session bean, JPA entity, and so on. The `javax.ejb.TimerHandle` provides a method enabling the current `Timer` instance to be returned.

Listing 7.3 `TimerService` interface

```
public interface TimerService {
  Timer createCalendarTimer(ScheduleExpression schedule)
    throws IllegalArgumentException, IllegalStateException,
    EJBException;                                                   ❶ Calendar-/
  Timer createCalendarTimer(ScheduleExpression schedule,              cron-like
    TimerConfig timerConfig) throws IllegalArgumentException,         scheduling
    IllegalStateException, EJBException;
```

```
  Timer createIntervalTimer( Date initialExpiration,
    long intervalDuration, TimerConfig timerConfig ) throws
    IllegalArgumentException, IllegalStateException, EJBException;
  Timer createIntervalTimer( long initialDuration,
    long intervalDuration, TimerConfig timerConfig ) throws
    IllegalArgumentException, IllegalStateException,
    EJBException;
  Timer createTimer( long duration, Serializable info )
    throws IllegalArgumentException, IllegalStateException,
    EJBException;
  Timer createTimer( long initialDuration, long intervalDuration,
    Serializable info ) throws IllegalArgumentException,
    IllegalStateException, EJBException;
  Timer createTimer( Date expiration, Serializable info )
    throws IllegalArgumentException, IllegalStateException,
    EJBException;
  Timer createTimer( Date initialExpiration, long intervalDuration,
    Serializable info ) throws IllegalArgumentException,
    IllegalStateException, EJBException;
  Timer createSingleActionTimer( Date expiration,
    TimerConfig timerConfig ) throws IllegalArgumentException,
    IllegalStateException, EJBException;
  Timer createSingleActionTimer(long duration, TimerConfig timerConfig)
    throws IllegalArgumentException, IllegalStateException,
    EJBException;
  Collection<Timer> getTimers() throws IllegalStateException, EJBException;
}
```

❷ EJB 2.1 interval scheduling

❸ Single action timers

The methods for creating a calendar-based timer ❶ accept a `javax.ejb.ScheduleExpression` and optionally a `javax.ejb.TimerConfig` object. The `ScheduleExpression` specifies when the timer should fire and has methods for configuring dates, times, and so on. The second block of methods ❷ creates the interval-based timers, which are timers that execute after a fixed period of time and possibly repeatedly. The third block ❸ creates single-action timers, which are timers that fire only once after a specified time period. Many of the methods optionally accept an `info` object that can be null if you don't wish to use it. The only requirement on the object passed in is that it must implement the `java.io.Serializable` interface; otherwise everything else is up to you. The `info` object is a container for you to pass information to the timer when it executes—whatever information you choose.

Not mentioned in the discussion is the `getTimers()` method, which returns a collection of all outstanding timers. You can iterate over this list, cancel outstanding timers, and find out when the next timer will execute. One thing to keep in mind is that the timers may execute by the time you retrieve them from the `TimerService`—be careful not to introduce race conditions by depending on your ability to reach in and cancel timers before they execute.

Listing 7.3 referenced two additional classes: `javax.ejb.ScheduleExpression` and `javax.ejb.TimerConfig`. The `ScheduleExpression` class is used to specify when the timer should fire. It has a no-argument constructor and methods for setting the day of the week, month, year, hour, second, and so on. Each method returns the same

ScheduleExpression instance enabling chaining so that the schedule can be defined on a single line. The TimerConfig object is a container for additional timer configuration information. It encapsulates the info object to be passed back to a time-out method along with a flag indicating whether the timer is persistent and thus should survive server restarts.

When scheduling using the TimerService, the bean invoking the schedule methods must have a time-out method. When using the TimerService, you're specifying an alarm for the current bean into which the TimerService was injected—you can't specify another bean. The bean must either have a method annotated with @TimeOut or implement the TimedObject interface. This will be demonstrated in the ad hoc timer example.

The TimerService participates in transactions. When a new timer is created within the context of a transaction, the timer is cancelled if the transaction is rolled back. The time-out method can be executed within the context of a transaction. If the transaction fails, the container will make sure the changes made by the failed method don't take effect and will retry the time-out method. Now that you have a basic handle on ad hoc timers, let's take a look at an example from ActionBazaar.

7.3.2 Programmatic timer example

Marketing frequently has the need to send out flyers advertising items for sale on ActionBazaar and enticing potential bidders and sellers to check out the site. Timing is critical for the flyer. Send it out toward the end of the workday and people will probably forget about the notice by the time they get home. Send it out before a long holiday weekend and it'll stay buried in people's inboxes. As a result, when the flyer is approved and ready to be sent isn't necessarily the time that it should be sent. When uploading a flyer for distribution, ActionBazaar prompts for the date and time the email blast should be sent. This is similar to the previous newsletter example except that it's an ad hoc email blast not done with any regularity. The scheduling information specified by the marketing person is packaged up into a ScheduleExpression, and the scheduleFlyer on the FlyerBean is invoked. The code for this bean is shown in the following listing.

Listing 7.4 FlyerBean implementation

```
@Stateless
public class FlyerBean {

  private static final Logger logger = Logger.getLogger("FlyerBean");

  @Resource
  private TimerService timerService;                          // ❶ Inject timer service

  public List<Timer> getScheduledFlyers() {
    Collection<Timer> timers = timerService.getTimers();      // ❷ Retrieve list of timers associated with this bean
    return new ArrayList<Timer>(timers);
  }
```

```
  public void scheduleFlyer(ScheduleExpression se, Email email) {
    TimerConfig tc = new TimerConfig(email,true);                    // 3
    Timer timer = timerService.createCalendarTimer(se,tc);           // 4
    logger.info("Flyer will be sent at: "+ timer.getNextTimeout());  // 5
  }

  @Timeout                                                           // 6
  public void send(Timer timer) {
    if(timer.getInfo() instanceof Email) {                           // 7
      Email email = (Email)timer.getInfo();
      // Retrieve bidders/sellers and email…
    }
  }
}
```

❸ Create a new TimerConfig object encapsulating email
❹ Schedule flyer broadcast
❺ Log scheduled time for email
❻ Annotate timeout callback method
❼ Retrieve flyer to be broadcasted

The `FlyerBean` in this listing is responsible for scheduling the flyer for delivery and also sending the email when the timer expires. The `TimerService` is injected via an annotation ❶. The method `getScheduledFlyers` has been implemented to drive a web page enabling someone in marketing to see which flyers have been scheduled for delivery ❷. The `scheduleFlyer` method is responsible for scheduling the flyer. The user interface constructs an instance of `ScheduleExpression` that will ultimately be passed off to the `TimerService`. A `TimerConfig` instance is created to encapsulate the flyer and also specify that this timer should survive server restarts ❸. A `Timer` is created inside the `TimerService` using the scheduling from the `ScheduleExpression` and the configuration from the `TimerConfig` ❹. Once a `Timer` is created, information about it may be retrieved, such as the next time the timer will time out ❺. The `send` method is annotated with `@TimeOut` ❻ to mark it as the method responsible for executing the task with the timer completes.

This example is straightforward. The `TimerService` creates timers that are associated with the current bean. The method to be invoked when the timer expires can either be marked with the `@TimeOut` annotation or by implementing the `javax.ejb.TimedObject` interface.

One important snippet of code that you've not yet seen is how to construct a `ScheduleExpression`. `ScheduleExpression`, as mentioned earlier, supports method chaining, thus reducing the number of lines of code necessary to specify a time. To construct an expression for sending out a flyer on Valentine's day right before lunch, the following code snippet would construct the appropriate `ScheduleExpression`:

```
ScheduleExpression se = new ScheduleExpression();
se.month(2).dayOfMonth(14).year(2012).hour(11).minute(30); // 2/14/2012 @
    11:30
```

Using programmatic timers is thus relatively easy. You have the Timer Service injected into the bean, annotate a method in the bean with the `javax.ejb.TimeOut`, and schedule the method using one of the methods on the `javax.ejb.TimerService` object. This couldn't be any easier!

7.3.3 Using EJB programmatic timers effectively

Programmatic timers enable operations to be scheduled programmatically at runtime. They're great for user-driven operations like the example of scheduling a flyer. These are operations where you can't predict when something will be scheduled. Another example in ActionBazaar would be the conclusion of bidding on an item. A programmatic timer could be used to close out bidding and mail the winning bidder notification of their triumph. When bidding is first opened, a new timer is created that will fire when the bidding is scheduled to conclude. Programmatic timers thus are versatile, and, unlike declarative timers, they're fluid and can be created and changed at runtime without editing a configuration file or recompiling. In contrast, declarative timers should be used for operations that are known in development and perform an application maintenance task such as purging inactive accounts on a monthly basis.

When using programmatic timers, it's important to consider how the timers are being persisted by the application container. Redeploying an application may wipe existing timers. This would probably be an unintended side effect if you were merely deploying a patch to fix a bug in production. Therefore, it's important to understand how timer persistence is impacted by more than just server restarts/failures. What happens when an application is redeployed or migrated to another server? Application server developers have already tackled many of these issues, so it's just a matter of investigating your container and precisely defining and understanding how the application will respond to different events besides just server restarts.

In addition to issues surrounding server restarts, one other consideration is making sure that the EJB scheduling facilities aren't overused. It's important to consider the granularity of the task. In the ActionBazaar application, the email address specified when creating a new account must be verified. If account verification doesn't occur within 24 hours, the account is deleted—you don't want the system polluted with unactivated accounts. Whether the cleanup of unactivated accounts happens at exactly at 24 hours, 24:30 hours, or even 25 hours later isn't important. Thus, it would be overkill to use programmatic timers on each new account creation because deleting the account exactly at the specified time isn't important. Instead, a better solution would be to use a declarative timer that fires every hour or every day and deletes accounts that haven't been activated within the past 24 hours. Multiple accounts can be deleted within the same transaction, and the server isn't busy tracking dozens of scheduled timers.

7.4 Summary

In this chapter we've delved into EJB's scheduling capabilities. EJB 3.1 was a major leap forward from EJB 3 in terms of scheduling. With 3.1, EJB gained cron-like scheduling. Prior to EJB 3.1, serious scheduling requirements necessitated the use of third-party solutions such as Quartz. Bolting on external libraries is fraught with code complications and potential legal problems depending on the acceptability of the license. Thus, the new scheduling features are a major improvement.

As you've seen, the EJB scheduling capabilities can be broken down into declarative and programmatic. With declarative, annotations are placed on methods within stateless session beans to specify when the method should be executed and how often. Programmatic scheduling is done at runtime via the `javax.ejb.TimerService` object. Both declarative and programmatic scheduling support calendar-/cron-based scheduling in addition to the interval-based scheduling present in previous releases. Which approach is used depends on the task and whether it's hardwired into the application or driven at runtime. In the next chapter we'll switch gears and look at web services.

8 Exposing EJBs as web services

This chapter covers

- The basics of web services
- The basics of SOAP (JAX-WS)
- Exposing EJBs as SOAP web services
- The basics of REST (JAX-RS)
- Exposing EJBs as RES web services

In this chapter we're going to delve into exposing Enterprise Java Beans via web services using either SOAP or REST. Web services have become an industry standard for application-to-application (A2A) and business-to-business (B2B) integration. They're key to developing software according to SOA principles where functionality is exposed as interoperable services that are loosely coupled.

What do web services have to do with EJB 3? You can think of web services as a way to expose your stateless session beans to clients written in both Java and other programming languages on different platforms. Web services can be thought of as an alternative method of exposing beans to remote applications that doesn't require RMI or the use of Java. The client could thus have code written in Objective-C on an iPhone, a .NET application running on a server, or a web application written in PHP and JavaScript—the possibilities are endless. Your EJBs are your reusable business services and web services are a technology stack for abstractly defining your services and providing a generic method of invoking the services that's language- and platform-independent.

This chapter assumes that you're familiar with web services, so in-depth coverage of web service development isn't provided. Entire books have been devoted to this subject and it would be impossible to replicate those efforts within the span of a single chapter. For an introduction and deep-dive coverage of REST and SOAP, consult *Restlet in Action* by Jerome Louvel (Manning, 2012) and *SOA Patterns* by Arnon Rotem-Gal-Oz (Manning, 2012). In this chapter we'll start off by reviewing the basics of web services—both SOAP and REST. We'll then tie this understanding back in to Enterprise Java and specifically to stateless EJBs. Along the way, we'll put web services to use in ActionBazaar and discuss best practices for using web services effectively.

8.1 What is a web service?

It's very difficult to arrive at a single definition of web services that all camps will agree on. Simply put, a *web service* is a standard platform that provides interoperability between networked applications. For most developers, this means XML messages that are transmitted via HTTP/HTTPS. Both XML and HTTP/HTTPS are standard and pervasive in enabling the service to be used by a multitude of different clients built with different technologies. For example, if you build a web service using Java EE, you can invoke that client from any number of applications—including those written in C#, Python, C++, and Objective-C—without having to make any changes. This is shown in figure 8.1, where web services enable a multitude of applications to exchange data with a Java Enterprise application.

8.1.1 Web service properties

When a web service is invoked, ultimately a method ends up handling the request and generating a response. Thinking in terms of Java methods, the parameters to the request can be a Java primitive or an objective graph—the same is true of the response. As its name implies, a web service is a service—that is, it performs a business operation. Examples of web services include operations to place an order, check the status of an order, cancel an order, and so on. A web service wouldn't be used to implement accessor/mutator methods like `setName()`, `setPhoneNumber()`, and so on. These are

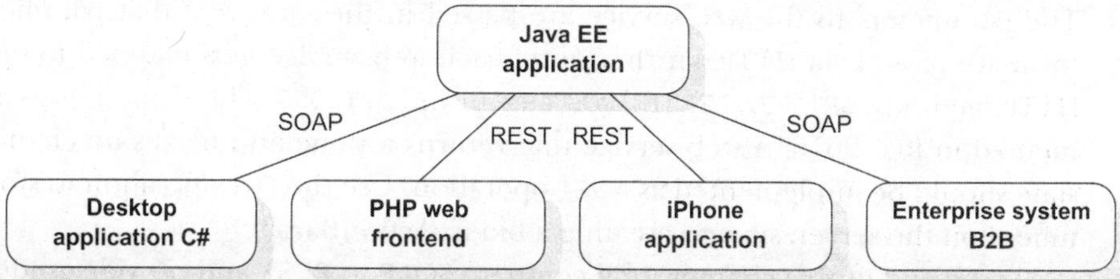

Figure 8.1 Web services provide interoperability between networked applications, like the Java EE application and a PHP web front end.

too granular and web service calls are stateless. Let's expound upon the last point: web services deal with services and not objects. With web services there's no concept of sessions and therefore subsequent method calls are completely independent. This is different from something like Java's RMI where you have a proxy representing a remote object and can invoke remove methods. Besides being stateless, web service invocations are also synchronous. A client must wait for the web service to complete and return a response.

8.1.2 Transports

Web services typically use HTTP or HTTPS to exchange messages. HTTP and HTTPS are usually used because of their ubiquity. Using established ports and protocols simplifies web service deployment because firewalls and routers are already configured for this traffic. It's not necessary to open additional ports, which in some environments isn't possible. It also simplifies development because existing web servers can host the web services. Web services, specifically SOAP-based services, can also use other transports such as SMTP and FTP. These other transports are beyond the scope of this chapter.

8.1.3 Web service types

The two big web service standards are SOAP and REST. With SOAP, messages are defined using the Web Services Description Language (WSDL) and the message is encoded in a well-defined XML format called a SOAP message. The WSDL defines the structure of an incoming request and also the structure of the response. Given a WSDL document, code-generation tools can produce code that will invoke a web service and process the response. These tools exist for practically every language and platform. For example, if you're attempting to invoke a web service from a .NET application, Microsoft provides tools and APIs that make creating a client painless. The wsdl.exe application generates C# client code from a WSDL file. The developer doesn't need to write the code that processes the XML request or generate the response. Similar tools exist for other languages including C++, Python, PHP, and so on.

Representational State Transfer (REST), like SOAP, uses XML and the HTTP protocol. RESTful web services take a much different and arguably simpler approach from that of SOAP. The basic idea behind REST is that a unique URL identifies each service. The parameters to the web service are passed in the same way that parameters to a form are passed via HTTP. Furthermore, each web service gets mapped to one of the HTTP methods: `GET`, `PUT`, `DELETE`, `POST`, `HEAD`, and `OPTIONS`. These operations are documented in RFC 2616. A web service that returns a value and makes no change to the state should be implemented as a `GET` operation. Use the `PUT` operation to store a document on the server, such as creating a bid in ActionBazaar.

At the end of this chapter we'll compare SOAP to REST and provide guidelines for choosing a technology after we explore each.

8.1.4 Java EE web service APIs

In this chapter we'll delve into the nuts and bolts of exposing EJBs via SOAP and RESTful web services. When looking over the Java EE specification or browsing articles online, you'll be confronted with an alphabet soup of acronyms. JAX-WS (JSR 224) and JAX-RS (JSR 399) in Java EE 7 define the standard APIs for creating SOAP and RESTful web services, respectively. These are specifications for which there are different implementations. Because Java EE 7 mandates JAX-WS and JAX-RS, you won't need to worry about picking an implementation unless you choose to deviate from the one provided by your container. Some implementations available are Metro (http://metro.java.net/), which is included with GlassFish, and Apache Axis 2 (http://axis.apache.org/).

As you peruse the Java EE documentation, you may come across JAX-RPC. JAX-RPC was the forerunner to JAX-WS in J2EE 1.4. JAX-RPC is a legacy technology and should be replaced whenever possible. JAX-WS is much easier to use with many more features. The complexity of JAX-RPC gave web services in Java a bad reputation.

In addition to JAX-WS and JAX-RS, JAXB will also be covered. JAXB is the Java architecture for XML binding. As its name implies, it's responsible for converting a Java object graph into XML and back again. JAXB can be used to generate your data model from an XML schema, which can then be persisted to XML, or you can annotate your code; the latter approach is what we'll take in this chapter. Comprehensive coverage of JAXB is beyond the scope of this chapter—we'll cover enough to give you an introduction.

New to Java EE 7 is JSON support (JSR 353). JSON stands for JavaScript object notation and it's a compact encoding of data. You'll use JSON when we cover the RESTful web services. RESTful web services often use JSON as the response. This is useful if you're building a website that's heavily interactive with lots of JavaScript code. XML is very verbose, consumes bandwidth, and also consumes resources on both the client and server. When using an interactive web application that uses AJAX, JSON is definitely the approach to take.

8.1.5 Web services and JSF

You might have started reading this chapter in the hope of mastering web services so that you can construct a user interface that uses AJAX and therefore web services. JSF has its own built-in support for AJAX and handles marshaling information between the client and server. JSF has its own JavaScript functions and server support code that make building AJAX-enabled web pages trivial. Discussing JSF in more detail is out of the scope of this book. Now that we've explored the basics of web services, let's dig into the traditional SOAP-based web services using JAX-WS.

8.2 Exposing EJBs using SOAP (JAX-WS)

Starting with Java EE 7 onward, JAX-WS 2.2 is the specification standardizing SOAP web services on the Java EE platform. Developing SOAP-based web services using JAX-WS is straightforward and easy. Using the annotations, a web service can be written and deployed within minutes. SOAP web service support on the Java platform has come a long way since the early days. Before we start looking at code, we'll briefly review the basics of SOAP-based web services.

8.2.1 Basics of SOAP

SOAP is a distributed protocol similar to COBRA and Java RMI. It enables applications to talk to each other by exchanging messages over a network protocol, most commonly HTTP/HTTPS. Communication is exchanged via a well-defined XML message format. The message format is defined using a WSDL and XML schema. The use of HTTP to exchange well-defined XML messages has resulted in the widespread adoption of SOAP to connect disparate systems written in different languages on different platforms. For example, using SOAP you can expose EJBs to an application written in Python, C#, Objective-C, and the like. In addition, because SOAP is well defined, both the server and client code can be auto-generated. Thus, SOAP-based web services have enjoyed enormous popularity.

Microsoft originally developed SOAP in 1998 and the W3C now manages the specification. At the time of writing, the current SOAP specification is 1.2. Just as important as the SOAP specification are the WS-I profiles. The WS-I (www.ws-i.org) is an industry consortium that defines interoperability standards for web services. Although SOAP is language-agnostic, issues do arise in how SOAP implementations interpret the specifications. The WS-I produces profiles and sample applications that provide clear guidance in developing web services that are truly compatible. The profiles pertinent to this chapter are as follows:

- *WS-I basic profile*—Defines a narrow set of valid services for SOAP, WSDL, and UDDI to support interoperability.
- *WS-I basic security profile*—Guide for defining secure and interoperable web services.
- *Simple SOAP binding profile*—Support profile for the WS-I basic profile. It binds operations to a specific transport protocol SOAP.

The major JAX-WS implementations, including Metro, JBossWS (used by GlassFish), and Apache Axis, are WS-I-compliant. WS-I conformance is important when building web services that are going to be consumed from implementations on other platforms. Now that you have a little background on the history of SOAP and some of the specifications surrounding it, let's take a look at a real SOAP message and examine its structure.

SOAP MESSAGE STRUCTURE

The structure of a SOAP message is relatively simple, as shown in figure 8.2. The outer element is an envelope that contains a header and a body. The header is optional and contains content not related to the content of the message. The web server usually processes the content of the header. The body contains the main payload—the XML data that the web service will process.

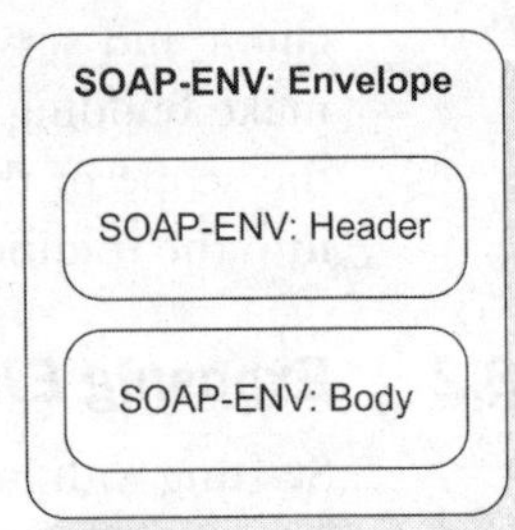

Figure 8.2 SOAP message structure

An SOAP message example from ActionBazaar is shown in the following listing. This message doesn't contain a header. The HTTP information is included—as you can see, the SOAP message will be delivered to the service residing at `/BidService/MakeBid`.

Listing 8.1 ActionBazaar bid SOAP message

```
POST /BidService/MakeBid HTTP/1.1
Content-type: text/xml;charset="utf-8"
Soapaction: ""
Accept: text/xml,multipart/related, text/html, image/gif, image/jpeg,
  *; q=.2, */*;q=.2
User-Agen: JAX-WS RI 2.1.6 in JDK 6
Host: localhost:8090
Connection: keep-alive
Content-Length: 230

<S:Envelop xmlns:S="http://schemas.xmlsoap.org/soap/envelope/">
  <S:Body>
    <bid xmlns="http://com.actionbazaar/bid">
      <bidPrice></bidPrice>
      <itemId></itemId>
      <bidderId></bidderId>
    </bid>
  </S:Body>
</S:Envelop>
```

HTTP header information that's processed by web server and SOAP implementation

SOAP XML message processed by web service

WEB SERVICE STYLES

There are two primary types of web service styles: RPC-oriented and document-oriented. Although RPC-oriented implies remote procedure call, it has nothing to do with the programming model. Instead, it has to with how the XML is structured. The RPC style of web services was popular initially, but more recently the pendulum has swung in the direction of document-oriented web services.

Document-oriented web services essentially mean that you're "exchanging" documents. You should use this if you're exchanging industry-standard XML documents or even custom-developed XML documents. With the document style, you can structure the message however you want. RPC, on the other hand, corresponds to a method invocation, so the XML will be structured with a method name and set of parameters. To see the differences, play with the `SOAPBinding` annotation described later in this chapter and examine the WSDL that's generated automatically by JAX-WS.

With either document or RPC, you'll have to choose one of the two encoding options: literal or encoded. With document you should use literal and with RPC you should use encoded. Choose document literal if you're writing web services that interoperate with other platforms and languages, especially .NET. Don't use document encoded—no one uses it and it has practically no support.

WSDL STRUCTURE

The WSDL is central to SOAP-based web services because it provides a complete blueprint of a service. It provides such a complete description of a web service that both the client and server code can be automatically generated. The code that's generated

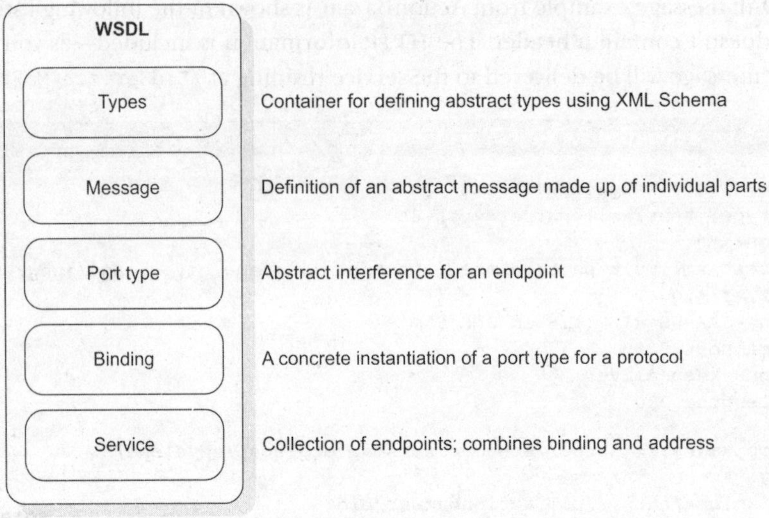

Figure 8.3 Structure of a WSDL document

will handle marshaling of the message and actually sending it. The structure of a WSDL file is shown in figure 8.3, and an example WSDL document for the `BidService` can be found later in listing 8.4.

In the types section, the data types composing the messages to be exchanged are defined. These are defined using an XML schema. The message part defines the messages that the service supports. A message is made up of one or more parts, which can serve as either input or output. The port type defines a group of operations (think interface). Each operation must have a unique name and contain a combination of input and output elements and reference the message elements. The binding section connects the port types (interfaces) with an actual protocol such as SOAP. The service section exposes the bindings as services and defines the endpoints.

Don't worry if this doesn't make sense initially. There are multiple levels of abstraction. After writing a couple of WSDL documents, it'll make much more sense.

WEB SERVICE STRATEGIES

When implementing a new web service, you must write two artifacts: a WSDL file defining the service and a Java class implementing the service. If complex data is being exchanged, a schema file defining the data constructs must also be created and referenced from the WSDL. With the WSDL and schema file, a client for the web service can be auto-generated by tools. For example, Java's `wsimport` can generate the Java code necessary to invoke a web service given a WSDL from Java. Similar tools exist for other languages and platforms—creating a SOAP client is a fairly standard task.

Focusing on the two main artifacts—WSDL and the Java implementation—you can take several different approaches. The approach taken can be made for each web service

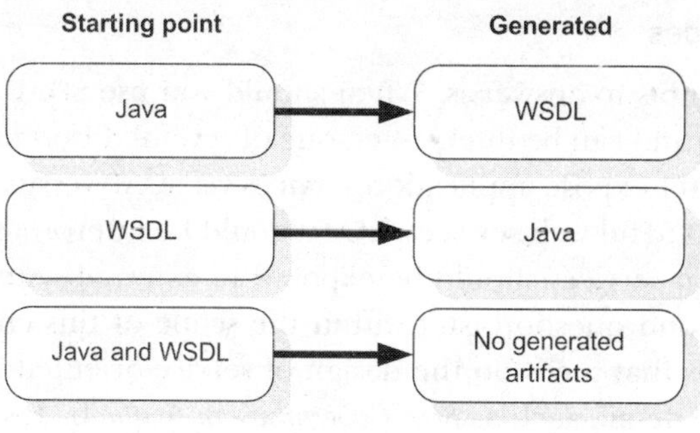

Figure 8.4 Approaches to build a web service

independently—it's not a binary decision for an entire project. The approaches are illustrated in figure 8.4.

When starting from Java, you use JAX-WS's ability to generate a WSDL from Java code. This approach saves you from digging into the intricacies of WSDL and XML schemas. Simply annotate a class with `@WebService` and add a `@WebMethod` annotation to configure a method, and a web service is born. Although this approach is expedient, it does have several drawbacks. The first is that the code generated can have unexpected dependencies on the Java language, such as depending on Java Generics. If the method parameters are objects, then the data-binding framework being used must generate a schema. The schema generated may be optimal and might not be portable across languages.

Instead of starting from Java, another approach is to start from the WSDL. Code the WSDL and then use Java's built-in tools to generate the server-side implementation of the service. This approach is slightly more laborious because it requires an in-depth knowledge of WSDL. The `wsimport` tool can be used to generate the server-side implements (it can do both client and server). The tool generates interfaces for which you then provide the implementation classes. After the code is initially generated, the challenge will be keeping the interfaces and implementation files synchronized. In addition, the code generated for complex objects that are passed around may not be optimal.

The third approach is to write both the WSDL and the corresponding Java code. This offers the best of both worlds: a well-written WSDL file and clean Java code. This gets around the issue of having the tools generate either a nonportable WSDL file or messy Java code. This is the most technically challenging approach, because both the WSDL and the Java code must match. For services targeted at other languages and platforms with a long-term life expectancy, this is definitely the best choice.

All three of these solutions require the use of a data-binding framework. In most environments, JAXB (JSR 222) is the default data-binding framework. The data-binding framework is responsible for converting the XML into Java objects that are then passed into your service. For example, consider the bid service that has a `placeBid` method. This method takes a `Bid` object as a parameter.

We'll touch on these approaches later when we examine best practices. Let's first answer the question of when SOAP should be used.

8.2.2 When to use SOAP web services

The question this section attempts to answer is, When should you use SOAP web services? This is a loaded question and can be interpreted one of several different ways. It could be interpreted as "Should I expose application services via SOAP versus another technology like Java's RMI or RESTful web services?" Or it could be interpreted as the question of whether application services should be exposed to external systems via a technology like SOAP. The second question isn't within the scope of this chapter. It can be best addressed by books that focus on the design of service-oriented architectures (SOA) and SOAP in more detail, such as *SOA Governance in Action* by Jos Dirksen (Manning, 2012). We'll focus on the first question.

When looking at exposing business functionality to other systems, the Java EE 7 stack provides several different technologies to choose from, including SOAP. You can also choose to expose business services via Java RMI, JMS, and RESTful web services. Each one of these technologies has benefits and trade-offs depending on your requirements.

Java Remote Method Invocation (RMI) is the original Java technology for exposing business services. Java RMI makes EJB possible, and beans are available by default via RMI. Java RMI is optimal in situations where the client is a Java application. RMI has much lower overhead as compared to SOAP-based web services. But if the services are to be exposed to applications written in other languages, Java RMI isn't a suitable solution because it isn't cross-platform. SOAP is a cross-platform solution that can be easily used from C# and C++ environments to COBOL, Python, and so on.

Another avenue for exposing services is via JMS. Although many developers probably wouldn't associate JMS and SOAP, both technologies fundamentally focus on message exchange. Messaging middleware has a long history that predates web services. The JMS approach to messaging is asynchronous message passing using store-and-forward, whereas SOAP is focused on synchronous message invocations. SOAP provides a well-documented interface in which tools can then be used to automatically generate client code. This isn't possible with JMS. JMS is a better solution when integrating two systems, not providing an external interface to one system.

We should also point out that SOAP-based web services, unlike either Java RMI or JMS, could easily work with corporate firewalls. SOAP messages are usually delivered using the pervasive HTTP/HTTPS. Let's next look at when you'd use EJBs with SOAP.

8.2.3 When to expose EJBs as SOAP web services

JAX-WS allows both regular Java classes (POJOs) and stateless or singleton EJBs to be exposed as web services. If you examine the source code for a POJO-based web service versus an EJB web service, there isn't a big difference. The EJB web service will have an additional `@Stateless/@Singleton` annotation and maybe an annotation or two for other EJB features that we've covered thus far, such as the timer service or transaction management. Both a POJO web service and an EJB web service support dependency injection and lifecycle methods such as `@PostConstruct` and `@PreDestroy`, but you gain several important benefits from exposing EJB as web services.

First, with EJB web services you automatically gain the benefits of declarative transaction and security management available only to EJB components. These are both big features that drive the use of EJBs over POJOs. You can use interceptors and a timer service if your application needs them, without any additional work.

Second, and most importantly, exposing an EJB via web services enables business logic to be exposed without any additional effort or code duplication. An EJB web service is no different than exposing an EJB via RMI—you use `@WebService` instead of `@Remote`. A stateless/singleton bean can be exposed both as a web service and also via RMI. Exposing core business logic has never been easier.

Table 8.1 compares EJB-backed web services versus POJO web services. There are some distinct advantages to EJB web services versus POJO web services.

Table 8.1 Feature comparison of Java web services to EJB web services

Feature	POJO web service	EJB web service
POJO	Yes	Yes
Dependency injection including resources, persistence units, and so on	Yes	Yes
Lifecycle methods	Yes	Yes
Declarative transactions	No	Yes
Declarative security	No	Yes

Now that we've reviewed the basics of SOAP web services and also discussed where they're appropriate, let's take a look at how ActionBazaar uses web services.

8.2.4 SOAP web service for ActionBazaar

Let's dive into two EJB 3 examples demonstrating how EJBs can be exposed as web services. We'll use two different examples to demonstrate the combination of EJB 3 and JAX-WS. The first example will provide a simple introduction with the container automatically generating the WSDL. In the second example, we'll show you how to write the WSDL as well as the JAXB schema file, generate JAXB beans, and write code that implements the WSDL. You can use these examples as a starting point for further exploration. The second one will definitely be useful as you dig deeper.

PLACEBID SERVICE

In the first example you'll expose the `PlaceBid` bean as a web service. This will enable clients written in other languages to submit bits. This EJB will be exposed as an RPC-encoded SOAP web service. The WSDL will be automatically generated by the JAX-RS runtime.

The following listing contains the code for the `PlaceBid` web service. There are two parts to this code: the interface for the web service and the stateless session bean.

Listing 8.2 PlaceBid

```
@WebService                                                    ❶ Exposes web service
@SOAPBinding(style=SOAPBinding.Style.RPC,                      ❷ Defines binding style
   use=SOAPBinding.Use.ENCODED)
public interface PlaceBidWS {
  public long submitBid(long userId, long itemId, double bidPrice);
}

@Stateless                                                     ❸ Specifies endpoint
@WebService(endpointInterface = "com.actionbazaar.ws.PlaceBidWS")
public class PlaceBid implements PlaceBidWS{

  @Override
  public long submitBid(long userId, long itemId, double bidPrice) {   ❹ Method implementation exposed
    ...
  }

  public List<Bid> getBids() {                                 ❺ Method not exposed
    ...
  }
}
```

In this listing, the `@WebService` annotation ❶ defines the interface as exposing a web service. It also specifies the SOAP binding style: RPC encoded ❷. The implementation of the class also has the `@WebService` annotation with the `endpointInterface` referencing the web service interface ❸; the bean also implements that interface. The class then implements the method being exposed ❹. Note that the `getBids` method ❺ isn't exposed because it doesn't appear in the interface.

If you have the ActionBazaar deployed in GlassFish, you can view the generated WSDL at http://localhost:8080/PlaceBidService/PlaceBid?wsdl. Using the `wsimport` utility provided by Java, you could generate a client that you can then use to invoke the service programmatically. In the next example we'll explore the annotations in more depth.

USERSERVICE

In this example you'll expose a new `createUser` method on the `UserService` stateless session bean. But instead of starting with Java objects, you'll start with the WSDL and XSD files.

The existing `createUser` method on `UserService` takes a `com.actionbazaar.account.User` object as input. This object is abstract; has subclasses `Bidder`, `Employee`, and `SellerI`; and also has references to other objects. Auto-generating a web service from such a complicated object may produce a WSDL with unexpected dependencies and may be incompatible with other programming languages.

To avoid these problems, the new `createUser` method on `UserService` will use a data transfer object (DTO). A DTO is a simplified version of your domain model objects created specifically for interoperable data transfer. Because DTOs don't have complicated object graphs, tools can handle them more easily. In this case, you'll start by creating the XSD schema for a `UserDTO` object in the following listing.

Listing 8.3 Creating UserDTO.xsd

```
<?xml version="1.0" encoding="UTF-8"?>
<xs:schema
  version="1.0"
  targetNamespace="http://com.actionbazaar/user"
  xmlns:xs="http://www.w3.org/2001/XMLSchema"
  xmlns:tns="http://com.actionbazaar/user"
  elementFormDefault="qualified">
  <xs:element name="user" type="tns:UserDTO"/>
  <xs:element name="createUserResponse" type="tns:CreateUserResponse"/>
  <xs:complexType name="UserDTO">
    <xs:sequence>
      <xs:element id="firstName" name="firstName" type="xs:string"
        minOccurs="1" maxOccurs="1" nillable="false"/>
      <xs:element id="lastName" name="lastName" type="xs:string"
        minOccurs="1" maxOccurs="1" nillable="false"/>
      <xs:element id="birthDate" name="birthDate" type="xs:date"
        minOccurs="1" maxOccurs="1" nillable="false"/>
      <xs:element id="username" name="username" type="xs:string"
        minOccurs="1" maxOccurs="1" nillable="false"/>
      <xs:element id="password" name="password" type="xs:string"
        minOccurs="1" maxOccurs="1" nillable="false"/>
      <xs:element id="email" name="email" type="xs:string"
        minOccurs="1" maxOccurs="1" nillable="false"/>
    </xs:sequence>
  </xs:complexType>
  <xs:complexType name="CreateUserResponse">
    <xs:sequence>
      <xs:element name="userId" type="xs:integer"/>
    </xs:sequence>
  </xs:complexType>
</xs:schema>
```

In addition to the `UserDTO`, the schema includes a `CreateUserResponse`. The response is used to communicate the ID of the new user back to the client for subsequent web service invocations.

Now that the schema is created, you use the JAXB generator tool provided by the JDK to turn the schema into real Java objects:

```
xjc -d <base directory>/ActionBazaar-ejb/src/main/java/ -p
     com.actionbazaar.ws.dto UserDTO.xsd
```

After the real Java objects are created, you can turn your attention to the WSDL of the web service. The WSDL file is shown in listing 8.4. The WSDL file should be placed in META-INF/wsdl. Because the WSDL references the UserDTO.xsd file, UserDTO.xsd should be placed in the same directory. The UserService.wsdl file defines one service, `createUser`, which will be implemented in the code.

Listing 8.4 Creating UserService.wsdl

```
<?xml version="1.0" encoding="UTF-8"?>
<definitions
```

```
xmlns:soap="http://schemas.xmlsoap.org/wsdl/soap/"
xmlns:xsd="http://www.w3.org/2001/XMLSchema"
xmlns:tns="http://com.actionbazaar/user"
xmlns="http://schemas.xmlsoap.org/wsdl/"
targetNamespace="http://com.actionbazaar/user"
name="UserService" xmlns:xsi="http://www.w3.org/2001/XMLSchema-instance">
<types>
  <xsd:schema>
    <xsd:import namespace="http://com.actionbazaar/user"
      schemaLocation="UserDTO.xsd"/>              <-- Imports user schema
  </xsd:schema>
</types>
<message name="createUserRequest">
  <part name="user" element="tns:user"/>      <-- UserDTO
</message>
<message name="createUserResponse">
  <part name="response" element="tns:createUserResponse"/>   <-- Response DTO
</message>
<portType name="CreateUser">
  <operation name="createUser">
    <input message="tns:createUserRequest"/>
    <output message="tns:createUserResponse"/>
  </operation>
</portType>
<binding name="UserPortBinding" type="tns:CreateUser">
  <soap:binding transport="http://schemas.xmlsoap.org/soap/http"
    style="document"/>
  <operation name="createUser">
    <soap:operation soapAction=""/>
    <input>
      <soap:body use="literal"/>
    </input>
    <output>
      <soap:body use="literal"/>
    </output>
  </operation>
</binding>
<service name="UserService">                  <-- Exposes UserService
  <port name="UserPort" binding="tns:UserPortBinding">
  <soap:address
    location="http://localhost:8080/UserService/CreateUser"/>
  </port>
</service>
</definitions>
```

The WSDL shown in this listing is fairly straightforward. Consult the discussion of WSDL earlier in the chapter for a breakdown of the elements. Using this WSDL document, a client for the web service can be auto-generated. The code in the following listing implements the web service and provides the services described in the WSDL.

Listing 8.5 `UserService` interface and implementation

```
@WebService(
 name="CreateUser",
```

```
  serviceName="UserService",
  targetNamespace="http://com.actionbazaar/user",      <- Namespace from schema
  portName = "UserPort",                               <- WSDL port reference
  wsdlLocation= "UserService.wsdl")                    <- References WSDL—must be in meta-inf/wsdl
@SOAPBinding(style=SOAPBinding.Style.DOCUMENT)
public interface UserServiceWS {
  @WebMethod(operationName="createUser")               <- Operation to method mapping
  @SOAPBinding(style=SOAPBinding.Style.DOCUMENT,
    use=SOAPBinding.Use.LITERAL,
    parameterStyle = SOAPBinding.ParameterStyle.BARE)
    public @WebResult(name="response",                 <- Maps response to schema
      targetNamespace="http://com.actionbazaar/user")
       CreateUserResponse
        createUser(
          @WebParam(name="user", mode= WebParam.Mode.IN,   <- Maps parameter to schema
           targetNamespace="http://com.actionbazaar/user")
            UserDTO user);
      }

@Stateless(name="UserService")
@WebService(endpointInterface = "com.actionbazaar.ws.UserServiceWS")   <- Endpoint specification
public class UserServiceBean implements UserService, UserServiceWS {   <- Implements service interface
  ...
  @Override
  public CreateUserResponse createUser(UserDTO user) {   <- Service implementation
    ...
  }
}
```

The code in this listing implements the web service and provides the services described in the WSDL. This is much more complicated than the first example. Using annotations, you must map the parameters and return value to the entities defined in the schema. In addition, you must map the method to entries in the WSDL. This example will make more sense as we go through the annotations.

> **Client generations**
>
> To generate a Java client for this service, use the `wsimport` command. This command generates all of the classes specified in the UserDTO.xsd file along with a stub that you can call to invoke the web service. You can use `wsimport` to quickly test services that you create.

With these two web service examples out of the way, let's dive deeper into the annotations.

8.2.5 *JAX-WS annotations*

Now that you've seen a basic example of a SOAP-based web service in ActionBazaar, we'll explore the annotations in more depth. Entire books have been written on SOAP and JAX-WS. This section will serve as a basic introduction. SOAP is a complicated set of technologies and specifications.

To get a SOAP web service up and running, you'll need at the minimum the following two annotations:

- `@javax.jws.WebService`—Marks an interface or a class as being a web service
- `@javax.jws.soap.SOAPBinding`—Configures the style (document/rpc) along with the encoded (document encoded/literal)

With these two annotations, you can build a simple SOAP web service. Let's examine each of the annotations individually.

USING THE @WEBSERVICE ANNOTATION

The `@WebService` annotation is used on a bean or an interface class. If you use this annotation on the bean class, the annotation processor or EJB container will generate the interface for you. If you already have a bean interface, then you can mark the `@WebService` annotation on the interface and the bean class will look like this:

```
@Retention(RetentionPolicy.RUNTIME)
@Target({ElementType.TYPE})
public @interface WebService {
  String name() default "";
  String targetNamespace() default "";
  String serviceName() default "";
  String portName() default "";
  String wsdlLocation() default "";
  String endpointInterface() default "";
}
```

USING THE @WEBMETHOD ANNOTATION

The `@javax.jws.WebMethod` annotation is used to configure a method being exposed as a web service. By default, on a class all methods are exposed as web services, so you'd use this annotation to either exclude a method or configure properties of the exposed method such as the operation name or SOAP action. The full definition of this annotation is as follows:

```
@ Retention(RetentionPolicy.RUNTIME)
@ Target({ElementType.METHOD})
public @interface WebMethod {
  String operationName() default "";
  String action() default "";
  boolean exclude() default false;
}
```

The `operationName` and `action` properties on the `@WebMethod` annotation specify the operation and SOAP action, respectively. The following example shows their use:

```
@WebMethod(operationName = "addNewBid",
           action = http://actionbazaar.com/NewBid)
public Long addBid(…) {
   …
}
```

The operationName will result in the following WSDL being generated:

```
<portType name="PlaceBidBean">
    <operation name = "addNewBid">
    ...
    </operation>
</portType>
```

Notice how the actual method name is addBid but the method name exposed in the web service is addNewBid. You can use this to help map the service contract to the actual implementation. Even if the implementation changes over time, the contract remains intact. If the operationName isn't specified, it'll default to the implementation name of the method. This can also be used in situations where the WSDL file is created separately and for some reason the method name shouldn't be exposed.

Similarly, the action element you defined earlier will be used for generating the SOAPAction in the WSDL as follows:

```
<operation name ="addNewBid">
    <soap:operation soapAction = "http://actionbazaar.com/NewBid"/>
</operation>
```

The SOAPAction element determines the header element in the HTTP request message. The web service client uses it when communicating with the web service using SOAP over HTTP. The content of the SOAPAction header field is used by the endpoint to determine the true intended destination rather than having to parse the SOAP message body to find the information. Now that you have a firm grasp of the @WebMethod annotation, let's dig into the @WebParam, which is naturally related.

USING THE @WEBPARAM ANNOTATION

The @javax.jws.WebParam annotation is used to customize a parameter for the web service part message generated in the WSDL document. This annotation is placed on the arguments to a method being exposed as a web service. The full definition for this annotation is as follows:

```
@Retention(RetentionPolicy.RUNTIME)
@Target({ElementType.PARAMETER})
public @interface WebParam {
  String name() default "";
  String partName() default "";
  String targetNamespace() default "";
  Mode mode() default Mode.IN;
  boolean header() default false;
  static final enum Mode {
    public static final  IN, public static final  OUT, public static final
     INOUT;
  }
}
```

The following code snippet demonstrates how this annotation is used. As you'll see, parameters can be used to pass data into a web service, return a result from a web service, or both:

```
@WebMethod
public Long addBid(
  @WebParam(name="user", mode= WebParam.Mode.IN) String userId) {
...
}
```

The name property specifies the name parameter for the message in the WSDL. If a name isn't specified, the default value generated will be the same as the name of the argument.

The targetNamespace property is used to customize the XML namespace for the message part. If a targetNamespace isn't specified, the server will use the namespace of the web service.

The mode property specifies the type of the property with valid options being IN, OUT, and INOUT (both). This property determines the direction of the parameter: whether a value is being passed in or is being passed back, or if the value is being passed in and also returned. You can think of INOUT like pointers in C++ where an argument to a method can be a pointer, thus enabling a method to return more than just one result. If the mode is either OUT or INOUT, it must be of the Holder type javax.xml.ws.Holder<T>. Further discussion of the Holder type is outside the scope of this book; for more details consult the JAX-WS specification.

The header property determines whether the parameter is pulled from the header of the message or the body. Setting the property to true means the parameter is pulled from the header. This is used in situations where an intermediary needs to do something with the SOAP message before passing it on, like routing it to the correct server. Intermediaries only examine the contents of the header. Setting the header to true generates the following WSDL:

```
<operation name = "addNewBid">
 <soap:operation soapAction="urn:NewBid"/>
  <input>
    <soap:header message="tns:PlaceBid_addNewBid" part="user" use="literal"/>
      <soap:body use="literal" parts="parameters"/>
  </input>
</operation>
```

The partName property controls the generated name element of the wsdl:part or the XML schema element of the parameter, if the web service binding style is RPC, or if the binding style is document and the parameter style is BARE. If name isn't specified for an RPC-style web service and the partName is specified, the server will use the partName to generate the name of the element.

USING THE @WEBRESULT ANNOTATION

The @WebResult annotation is very similar to the @WebParam annotation. It operates in conjunction with the @WebMethod to control the generated name for the message return value in the WSDL, as illustrated here:

```
@WebMethod
@WebResult(name="bidNumber"
public Long addBid(...) {}
```

The `@WebResult` annotation specification resembles the `@WebParam` annotation minus support for the mode:

```
@Retention(value = RetentionPolicy.RUNTIME)
@Target(value = {ElementType.METHOD})
public @interface WebResult {
  public String name() default "";
  public String partName() default "";
  public String targetNamespace() default "";
  public boolean header() default false;
}
```

As expected, the `name` element specifies the name of the value returned in the WSDL. The `targetNamespace` element customizes the XML namespace for the returned value. This works for document-style web services where the return value binds to an XML namespace.

If the `header` element is set to `true`, the value is returned as a part of the message header. As with the `@WebParam` annotation, the `partName` property is used to customize the name of the value returned from an operation.

USING @ONEWAY AND @HANDLERCHAIN

The web service metadata annotation specification defines two more annotations: `@OneWay` and `@HandlerChain`. We'll briefly introduce these two annotations, but further exploration is outside the scope of this book.

The `@OneWay` annotation is used to define a web service that doesn't return a value. The method's return type is void. For example, consider the following method:

```
@WebMethod
@OneWay
public void pingServer() {
...
}
```

In this case, `pingServer` doesn't return anything. The `@OneWay` annotation optimizes the message to reflect that no value is returned.

The `@HandlerChain` annotation is used to define a set of handlers that are invoked in response to a SOAP message. Logically, handlers are similar to EJB interceptors. There are two types of handlers:

- Logical handlers (`@javax.xml.ws.handler.LogicalHandler`), which operate on the message context properties and message payload
- Protocol handlers (`@javax.xml.ws.handler.soap.SOAPHandler`), which operate on the message context properties and protocol-specific messages

Now that we've covered the basic JAX-WS annotations, let's review how to effectively use SOAP from EJB.

8.2.6 Using EJB SOAP web services effectively

The combination of JAX-WS and EJB makes it almost too easy to expose business logic as web services. After reading this section, you might be tempted to expose every bean via SOAP. But there are many pitfalls that you must be careful of. Just like sprinkling `synchronize` throughout your code base won't make your code thread-safe, decorating your classes with `@WebService` won't turn your application into an overnight SOA success. Let's look at how you should approach EJB and SOAP.

The first consideration should be to determine whether it's necessary to expose beans to external systems and then determine whether the external systems require interoperability. If not, JMS or Java RMI is probably a better alternative. These technologies have much less overhead—both in terms of network traffic and in terms of processing the messages. XML is expensive to transmit and process. If you're providing services to third parties, then SOAP is a good solution; if you need to connect to Java systems internally, use RMI or JMS.

If you choose to expose services using SOAP, expose only the method that needs to be exposed. If you have a fairly rich object graph, you'll probably want to pass back DTOs and limit the amount of data exchanged via web services. You don't want JAXB serializing most of your database into an XML document. In the case of ActionBazaar, a web service request for an item shouldn't retrieve the list of all of the bidders along with the bidders' usernames and passwords.

Analyze whether you need RPC-oriented or document-oriented web services. You can use the `@SOAPBinding` annotation to control the style for your EJB web service. RPC-style web services may perform better than document-style web services. But document-style web services provide more flexibility because you can use XML schemas to define the messages. Similarly, avoid using message encoding because it makes your services less interoperable, as well as less portable between SOAP implementations. Document/literal is the recommended combination for an interoperable web service.

Design your EJB web service so that it creates minimal network traffic. Avoid sending large objects over the wire. It's best to send an ID or reference to an object instead of sending the entire object. All objects sent via SOAP are serialized into XML. The XML representation of data can be quite large, making SOAP messages much more expensive than retrieving the object in the target location. In addition, if your EJB involves a long-running transaction, avoid exposing it as a web service, or mark it as not returning a value so that it can be invoked in a more asynchronous manner.

Use JAX-WS data types as the method parameters for your web service to give it interoperability with heterogeneous web services. Suppose you have an object graph involving `Collections`, `HashMaps`, and `Lists` as web service parameters. Using these data types in the WSDL makes your application less interoperable. Test your application to make sure it complies with the WS-I Basic Profile if interoperability is important for your application.

There are several mechanisms to secure your web services. You must weigh your security requirements against performance, because security comes with a high cost. The performance costs of end-to-end security are commonly higher than the initial perceived costs. This is true in general of system/application security, but even more so with regard to web services that are designed to be shared with unknown client applications. Now that you're familiar with JAX-WS, let's shift gears and dig into RESTful web services using JAX-RS.

8.3 Exposing EJBs using REST (JAX-RS)

In the first half of the chapter we examined SOAP-based web services. In this half we switch gears and dive into RESTful web services. The last few years have seen RESTful web services explode dramatically and with good reason. The RESTful approach has a feeling of "back to the basics" when compared with SOAP. SOAP has been out for over a decade and thus has expanded far beyond its humble beginnings as a simple and standard approach for exchanging XML messages. SOAP used to officially stand for Simple Object Access Protocol, but now it's officially referred to as SOAP with the full title having been dropped from the specifications, and it's definitely no longer simple.

The concept of RESTful web services originated in Dr. Roy Fielding's dissertation titled "Architectural Styles and the Design of Network-based Software Architectures." In his paper, Dr. Fielding examined how the architecture of the web emerged and formulated a set of architectural principles, which he called representational state transfer (REST). These principles derive from his work on the HTTP 1.0 and 1.1 specifications, of which he was one of the principal authors. Unlike SOAP, REST isn't a standard.

RESTful web services fully use the HTTP protocol and URIs (uniform resource identifiers), which aren't fully exploited by SOAP. SOAP primarily uses HTTP as a transport mechanism because it's ubiquitous and can easily drill through firewalls. RESTful web services map the basic HTTP operations—`DELETE`, `GET`, `HEAD`, `OPTIONS`, `POST`, and `PUT`—to URIs. The HTTP operations thus provide the basic CRUD functionality. The payload for these messages can be anything—XML, graphics, text, and so on. Unlike SOAP, where the contents of the SOAP message determine the operation, a unique URL is used to call the RESTful web service. Parameters are passed in using a query. All of these were unused or underutilized with SOAP.

On the Java EE platform, JAX-RS defines the APIs for building a RESTful web service. JAX-RS has no dependence on EJBs and can be used to expose POJOs as RESTful web services. But as you've seen several times already, EJBs offer a number of advantages including integration with transactions. Exposing EJBs as REST is conceptually no different than exposing the beans as SOAP. Let's review the basics of REST.

8.3.1 Basics of REST

SOAP-based web services use HTTP as a transport mechanism. An HTTP `POST` or `GET` invocation is performed and a block of XML is uploaded to the server and ultimately processed. The request URI identifies the service, but it's the actual contents of the XML exchanged that determines what action is performed and what is returned to the client. Looking at the request URI, you can't necessarily tell what the operation does or whether there has been a state change on the server. REST, however, fully uses HTTP.

Let's consider the case of an HTTP form submission from the browser using HTTP GET. You fill out the form and then click Submit. In the browser URL bar you see something like the following:

```
http://localhost:8080/wse/join.html?firstname=Ryan&lastname=Cuprak&container=seller
```

The URL has the following structure:

```
<scheme>:<port>/<resource id>
```

So in this case the scheme, port, and resource ID are

- Scheme: `http`
- Port: `8080`
- Resource ID: `/wse/join.html?firstname=Ryan&lastname=Cuprak&container=seller`

Everything needed to service your request is included with the request. If you sniff the connection between the browser and the server, you'll see slightly more data being exchanged that's hidden. This information is put together and sent to the server to help the server process the request. The server will thus know whether the client is an iPhone handset, mobile browser, or full browser and can then respond with the appropriate content. The raw content on the wire is as follows:

```
GET /wse/join.html?firstname=Ryan&lastname=Cuprak&container=seller HTTP/1.1
Host: localhost:8090
User-Agent: Mozilla/5.0 (Macintosh; Intel Mac OS X 10_7_4) AppleWebKit/534.57.2
      (KHTML, like Gecko) Version/5.1.7 Safari/534.57.2
Accept: text/html,application/xhtml+xml,application/xml;q=0.9,*/*;q=0.8
Referer: http://localhost:8090/wse/join.html
Accept-Language: en-us
Accept-Encoding: gzip, deflate
Cookie: __utma=111872281.1889907053.1320526418.1320526418.1320526418.1; treeForm_tree-
      hi=treeForm:tree:configurations:default-config:loggerSetting;
      JSESSIONID=ba0e0c6c96fa10944cbf7d69309d
Connection: keep-alive
```

Debugging web service invocations

When working with web services, it's often necessary to debug the messages being exchanged. Tools such as tcpmon (http://ws.apache.org/commons/tcpmon/) enable you to capture both the request and the response. Using this tool you can see exactly what is being requested and the content of the response. You might discover that a proxy server is intercepting the request in an Enterprise environment (common at large corporations) or that the initial request is malformed. IDEs such as NetBeans have built-in support for tcpmon so that you can debug both the request to the server and the server's handling of the request.

We won't go into detail about the content of the request. HTTP is defined in RFC 2616 and can be read at www.w3.org. Full knowledge of this specification isn't necessary to create or consume RESTful web services, but you'll find yourself digging deeper as you implement more services or work with different toolkits on other platforms. This will be especially important if you're architecting new services.

The request that was issued previously used the `GET` method. Each HTTP call to a server must specify one of eight different methods. The method determines how the request will be processed and what the request should do. We'll only concern ourselves with six of these methods because the other two—`TRACE` and `CONNECT`—aren't relevant to RESTful web services. The methods are as follows:

- `GET`—Read-only operation that doesn't change anything on the server.
- `DELETE`—Deletes a specific resource. Performing this operation multiple times has no effect. Once the resource is deleted, all subsequent operations have no effect.
- `POST`—Changes the data/state on the server. The change request may or may not include a data payload and may or may not return data.
- `PUT`—Stores data sent in the message payload under the resource identified by the URL. Performing this operation multiple times has no effect because you're updating the same resources.
- `HEAD`—Returns only a response code and any headers associated with the request.
- `OPTIONS`—Represents a request for information about the communication options available on the request/response chain identified by the request URI.

With these methods there are two important properties to be aware of: safety and idempotence. Safe methods are methods that do nothing other than retrieve data. Methods that retrieve data are `GET` and `HEAD`. Idempotent methods have the same effect no matter how many times they're invoked. Methods that are idempotent are `GET`, `HEAD`, `PUT`, and `DELETE`. The other methods are neither safe nor idempotent. RESTful web services should respect these semantics. Invoking a RESTful web service in ActionBazaar using HTTP `DELETE` shouldn't delete an existing bid and place a new bid. This isn't what a consumer of the service would expect. Even if this is documented, it still violates the spirit of REST.

In addition to HTTP methods, you should also be aware of HTTP status codes. These are defined in the RFC as well and are returned with each HTTP invocation. You've undoubtedly run into these codes many times. For example, you might have copied and pasted an address for a website and gotten an error page with text similar to "HTTP Status 404—the requested resource isn't available." Status codes are defined in the RFC and will be returned for RESTful web services calls—you can think of them as analogous to a SOAP fault. If an exception is thrown while processing a RESTful web service request, a status code of 500 for an internal server error will most likely be returned.

Up to this point we've focused on HTTP. You might be wondering how exactly this discussion relates to RESTful web services. RESTful web services use the basic HTTP operations in combination with URLs. With a SOAP web service, you create an

XML document and then transmit it to a web service. The web service deconstructs the content of the XML document and then figures out what code needs to be invoked. With RESTful web services, a URL like the one examined previously is invoked using a specific HTTP method like GET, DELETE, or PUT. There's no XML document to be processed—the method and the URL contain everything. Parameters to the web service are encoded within the URL, just like HTML web forms. Content, which can include Microsoft Word documents, XML documents, video clips, and so on, are included in the content of the request—that is, multipart MIME requests that are streamed.

RESTful web services are thus a "back to the basics" approach. Invoking a RESTful web service is as simple as invoking a URL in a web browser. Parameters are URL-encoded and aren't embedded within an XML document. The output from a service can be anything—graphics, raw text, XML, JSON, and so on. If the web service is being consumed by an HTML 5 application, you can return the output formatted in compact JSON. Browser JavaScript implementations process JSON an order of magnitude more efficiently than a SOAP message.

These are the URLs for potential RESTful web services in the ActionBazaar application:

- (DELETE): http://actionbazaar.com/deleteBid?bidId=25
- (PUT): http://actionbazzar.com/placeBid?item=245&userId=4243&amount=5.66

These are much more compact and self-documenting than their would-be SOAP counterparts. The code to process these requests could easily have been written using a Servlet over 10 years ago. RESTful web services are thus not new—instead of requesting and returning HTML content, HTTP is being used to implement services. This is something it could do all along but was never fully exploited.

JAX-RS eliminates the redundant Servlet coding that you'd have to implement and directly invokes your methods with parameters provided by the URL, marshaling data where needed. Let's next take a look at where and when it makes sense to use REST before diving into code.

8.3.2 When to use REST/JAX-RS

The simplicity of RESTful web services means that they're extremely easy to implement and consume. No special tools are needed, and most platforms and languages already have libraries that can be used to invoke a RESTful web service without requiring additional tooling. Third-party libraries and implementation details make SOAP much more complicated. When implementing a SOAP service using Java, it's possible to code the service in a way that causes problems for a client written in C#. The WS-I Profiles attempt to reduce the chances of this happening, but it still can be an issue. Note that writing a custom socket protocol would be much more complicated than using SOAP; minor cross-platform issues aren't an indictment of the platform because no solution is perfect.

Because RESTful web services can return just about anything, the response can be tailored to the targeted client. SOAP-based messages are exceedingly verbose and are encumbered with a significant amount of overhead to process the XML request and generate the response. This contrasts with RESTful web services; they use HTTP and URLs to encode the request and the response can be just about anything. The request is compact and takes minimal effort to process. The response can be compact and tailored for the client. For example, a RESTful web service could return JSON to a Web 2.0 application; the response can be used immediately, and no complex code must be generated or custom code developed to process an XML document written.

A compact request and response are extremely important where latency and processing power are limiting factors. The larger the SOAP message, the longer it takes to send and the more computing power is required to process it. RESTful web services offer many more opportunities for optimizing the request and response for situations where performance is a driving factor. For example, the latest releases of iOS (iOS 5) include APIs for RESTful web services, but there's no built-in support for SOAP. Even though iPhones and iPads are very powerful, every little bit of optimization reduces the load on the battery.

Now that we've identified some of the key reasons for using SOAP, you must next decide when you should directly expose EJBs via REST.

8.3.3 When to expose EJBs as REST web services

The issue you're trying to decide in this section is when you should directly expose an EJB as a RESTful web service. As you've seen already, EJBs provide a number of useful services over POJOs. If your web service needs these facilities, such as transaction management, then the EJB should be exposed via REST. But there are some architectural points to take into account. First, only stateless session beans should be considered as RESTful service providers. Second, RESTful web services are much closer to the wire format than their SOAP counterparts; SOAP is a higher-level abstraction. You must take care that the interface of the services doesn't become warped to support REST. We'll now look at each one of these points in more detail.

Because RESTful web services are stateless, the combination of REST and EJBs makes sense only within the context of stateless EJBs. Stateful and message-driven beans aren't compatible with the stateless behavior of REST, nor would their combination make logical sense. Singleton beans could be used with REST, but this combination would have poor performance characteristics because only one bean would be servicing requests at a time. In summary, REST should only be used on stateless session beans.

But the EJB layer should be agnostic to the type of client. In the ActionBazaar application, the `BidManager` bean should return a list of bids for a user represented as a `java.util.List` of bids—not a JSON-structured string. JSON is a specific representation of the data that's targeted at a web client. The danger with RESTful services is that they're tied more finely to the underlying transport.

Another consideration with RESTful web services is the data types the service will handle. Exposing an EJB via REST is appropriate if the methods are fine-grained and accept and return primitives or string content. EJBs that exchange complex objects aren't ideal. While JAX-RS uses JAXB for serialization, SOAP (with its ability to define schemas) makes it much easier to generate clients that exchange complex XML documents.

Finally, you must consider the issue of packaging. If the application is deployed as an EAR with separate web and EJB modules, there might be issues in deploying the services. Containers might not scan the EJB module looking for RESTful web services. This is something you should verify with your target container to make sure it behaves as expected.

There are a number of issues to consider when deciding whether to expose an EJB as a RESTful web service. Although RESTful web services are much easier to use and are definitely lightweight, additional planning and thought must go into their development.

8.3.4 REST web service for ActionBazaar

The ActionBazaar application exposes some of its key services as RESTful web services. One of the key stateless beans exposed via JAX-RS is the `BidService` bean that you've seen several times throughout this book. It contains operations for adding, removing, and updating bids. Given the proliferation of smartphones like the iPhone, it makes sense to expose the core services in ActionBazaar via RESTful web services so that a native client can be easily implemented on these devices. SOAP would require a significant amount of processing and bandwidth. Although smartphones are more than capable of handling a SOAP request, a RESTful implementation is more appropriate.

To start the development process, you'll formulate the URI for the basic operations in the `BidService`:

- List the bids for a given user for a category over a date range:

  `/bidService/list/{userId}/{category}?startDate=x&endDate=x`

- Add a new bid and accepts XML as input:

  `/bidService/addBid`

- Retrieve a bid instance as XML or JSON:

  `/bidService/getBid/{bidId}`

- Cancel a bid using the `Bid` ID:

  `/bidService/cancel/{bidId}`

A sample invocation of one of these services would look like this:

```
http://actionbazaar.com:8080/bidService/getBid/83749
```

Executing this line from a web browser would render an XML representation, generated by JAXB, of the `Bid` object.

To implement the RESTful web service, you annotate the local interface with the JAX-RS annotations. This keeps the implementation clean of the JAX-RS details and also makes the implementation much more readable. Besides being good design, the interfaces ensure that the code doesn't become overrun with annotations. The class diagram is shown in figure 8.5.

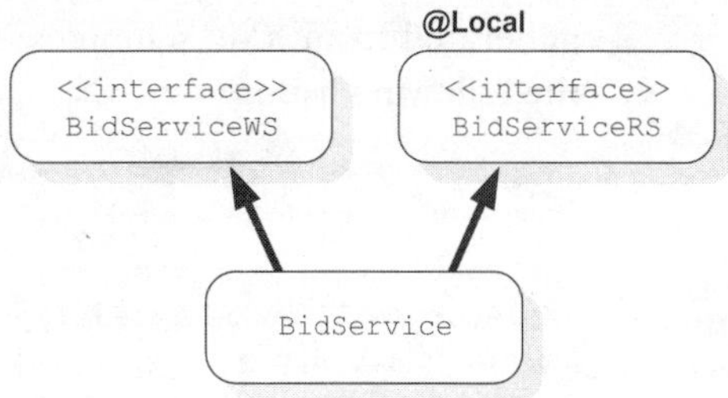

Figure 8.5 `BidService` **class structure**

The code for the `com.actionbazaar.buslogic.BidService` class is shown in listing 8.6. There are a total of four methods exposed via REST. This code example illustrates the annotations we'll cover in this chapter. After comparing the code to the URLs in section 8.3.4, it should be obvious how the annotations expose the methods as services. As you can see, exposing an EJB as a RESTful web service is straightforward. In addition, the service can be easily tested with a web browser—there's no need to generate a client.

Listing 8.6 `BidServiceRS` **RESTful interface**

```
@Local @Path("/bidService")
public interface BidServiceRS {

    @POST
    @Path("/addBid")
    @Consumes("application/xml")
    public void addBid(Bid bid);

    @GET
    @Path("/getBid/{bidId}")
    @Produces({"application/json","application/xml"})
    public Bid getBid(@PathParam("bidId") long bidId);

    @DELETE
    @Path("delete/{bidId}")
    public void cancelBid(@PathParam("bidId") long bidId);

    @GET
    @Produces("text/plain")
    @Path("/list/{userId}/{category}")
    public String listBids(
            @PathParam("category")String category,
            @PathParam("userId")long userId,
            @QueryParam("startDate") String startDate,
            @QueryParam("endDate") String endDate);
}
```

Annotations:
- Marks class as containing a RESTful web service; value is root of service
- Invoked via HTTP POST
- Full path / bidService/addBid
- Bid serialized as XML
- Invoked via HTTP GET
- JSON or XML output
- bidId is method parameter
- Invoked via HTTP DELETE
- Extract query parameters

Two of the methods in this listing either consumed or produced an XML representing a `Bid`. The `Bid` instance is actually a DTO—you don't want the `Item` and `Bidder` references accidently serialized. JAXB is responsible for the marshaling. Because the class is a fairly simple DTO, JAXB annotations are coded manually—the object wasn't generated from XML schema as is typically done. The code for this DTO is shown in the following listing.

Listing 8.7 `Bid` DTO class using JAXB annotations

```
@XmlRootElement(name="Bid")
@XmlAccessorType(XmlAccessType.FIELD)
public class Bid {

   @XmlElement
   private XMLGregorianCalendar bidDate;

   @XmlAttribute
   private Long bidId;

   @XmlElement
   private double bidPrice;

   @XmlElement
   private long itemId;

   @XmlElement
   private long bidderId;

   public Bid() {
   }

   // Setter and getter methods not shown.
}
```

Defines ROOT XML element

Nonstatic, nontransient field will be serialized

Field will be serialized to its own element

Use a cross-platform Date object compatible with .NET

Serializes field as attribute on root element

The DTO shown in listing 8.7 will result in the output shown in the next listing when the `getBid` method is invoked and XML is returned. This should give you a good idea of how the JAXB annotations drive the XML generation.

Listing 8.8 `Bid` DTO XML output example

```
<Bid bidId="10">
  <bidDate>2012-05-15T20:01:35.088-04:00</bidDate>
  <bidPrice>10.0</bidPrice>
  <itemId>45</itemId>
  <bidderId>77</bidderId>
</Bid>
```

If the client informs the `getBid` service that it wants JSON as the response instead, the output in the following listing will be returned instead of the XML. The JSON output is ideal for use by Web 2.0 applications written in JavaScript or for smartphones. When it gets read in by the client, the client will access it as a hash map, which is much easier to work with than XML.

Listing 8.9 JSON `Bid` DTO encoding

```
{
  "@bidId":"10",
  "bidDate":"2012-05-15T21:52:58.771-04:00",
  "bidPrice":"10.0",
```

```
  "itemId":"45",
  "bidderId":"77"
}
```

If you attempt to run this code, the JAX-RS implementation will most likely complain that it doesn't know how to instantiate `BidServiceRS`, which is an interface. To associate the stateless session bean with the service, you'll need to implement a `javax.ws.rs.core.Application` and return instances for all JAX-RS annotated interfaces. The `Application` instance, shown in the next listing, is then registered with the JAX-RS servlet in `web.xml` (not shown). This will work for the reference implementation Metro, but other JAX-RS implementations may have different mechanisms.

Listing 8.10 Configuring JAX-RS interface instances

```
public class SystemInit extends Application {
    public Set<Class<?>> getClasses() {
        return Collections.emptySet();
    }

    public Set<Object> getSingletons() {
        Set<Object> classes = new HashSet<Object>();
        try {
            InitialContext ctx = new InitialContext();
            Object bidServiceRS =
              ctx.lookup("java:global/WebServiceExperiment/BidService");
            classes.add(bidServiceRS);
        } catch (Throwable t) {
            t.printStackTrace();
        }
        return classes;
    }
}
```

Now that you've seen a basic example of a JAX-RS service, let's review the annotations in more depth.

8.3.5 JAX-RS annotations

In this section we're going to examine a key subset of the JAX-RS annotations. These will cover the basic cases and the code from ActionBazaar we just examined. Entire books have been written on JAX-RS, so if you choose to expose EJBs as RESTful web services, further investigation will be required. Implementing RESTful web services is still much simpler than SOAP.

To get a RESTful web service up and running, you'll need at least the following annotations:

- `@javax.ws.rs.Path`—This annotation must appear on the class providing the RESTful web service.
- `@javax.ws.rs.GET/POST/PUT/DELETE`—One of these annotations must be placed on a method. HTTP method annotations are uppercase and take no parameters.

With @Path on a class and an HTTP method annotating a class method, a simple RESTful web service is up and running. Let's examine the key annotation starting with @GET. Note that we won't cover every JAX-RS annotation—that's beyond the scope of this chapter.

USING THE @GET ANNOTATION

The @javax.ws.rs.GET annotation is a marker annotation for signaling that the web service is invoked via an HTTP GET. The following code snippet is all there is to the GET annotation:

```
@Target(value = {ElementType.METHOD})
@Retention(value = RetentionPolicy.RUNTIME)
@HttpMethod(value = "GET")
public @interface GET {}
```

If you're passing in parameters via GET, you should be aware that there's an upper limit on the size of the request URI. The HTTP specification doesn't define a limit so it would be dependent on the browser. Web browsers have traditionally limited the URI to anywhere from 4 KB to 8 KB.

USING THE @POST ANNOTATION

The @javax.ws.rs.POST annotation is a marker annotation and signals that the web service is invoked using the HTTP POST method. The following code snippet is all there is to the POST annotation:

```
@Target(value = {ElementType.METHOD})
@Retention(value = RetentionPolicy.RUNTIME)
@HttpMethod(value = "POST")
public @interface POST {}
```

An HTTP POST method is used for pushing data up to the server—for example, adding a picture of an item to ActionBazaar. The content of the message contains the new record or an annotation of an existing record on the server. Note that the operation doesn't necessarily result in a new resource that can be identified by a URI. In a given POST request, multiple attachments can be uploaded if the message is encoded as a multipart mime message; see, for example, the @Consumes annotation.

USING THE @DELETE ANNOTATION

The @javax.ws.rs.DELETE annotation is a marker annotation that signals that the web service is invoked using the HTTP DELETE method. The resource identified by the URI should be deleted with any subsequent operations using the same URI but doing nothing—the resource has already been deleted:

```
@Target(value = {ElementType.METHOD})
@Retention(value = RetentionPolicy.RUNTIME)
@HttpMethod(value = "DELETE")
public @interface DELETE {}
```

USING THE @PATH ANNOTATION

The @javax.ws.rs.Path annotation can be placed on both a class and a method. When it's placed on a class, it designates the class as a JAX-RS service. A class that's exposing RESTful web services must have this annotation. If the annotation is placed on a method, the method is exposed as a RESTful web service.

The value pass into the `@Path` annotation is the relative URI for the service. The URI provided in a method annotation, as you saw previously, is combined with the URI on the class to define the full path to the RESTful web service. The annotation is defined as follows:

```
@Target(value = {ElementType.TYPE, ElementType.METHOD})
@Retention(value = RetentionPolicy.RUNTIME)
public @interface Path {
  public String value();
}
```

Parameters can be encoded within the URI using curly brackets (`{}`). The parameters are bound to method parameters using `@java.ws.rs.PathParam`; we'll cover this annotation next. There can be as many curly brackets containing annotations that will be passed into the web service as needed.

USING THE @PATHPARAM ANNOTATION

The `@javax.ws.rs.PathParam` annotation maps the parameters specified by the `@javax.ws.rs.Path` annotation to actual parameters of the Java method. The JAX-RS implementation will perform type conversion when invoking your methods. The annotation is defined as follows:

```
@Target(value = {ElementType.PARAMETER, ElementType.METHOD,
     ElementType.FIELD})
@Retention(value = RetentionPolicy.RUNTIME)
public @interface PathParam {
  public String value();
}
```

Consider the following example that has two parameters encoded within the URI, `userId` and `category`:

```
@GET
@Path("/list/{userId}/{category}")
public List<Item> listBids(
        @PathParam("category")String category,
        @PathParam("userId")long userId
     ) {
  ...
}
```

In this example, `category` and `userID` are mapped from the request URI to the parameters. Assuming the class is annotated with `@Path("/bidService")`, an example invocation would look like this:

```
http://localhost:8080/actionbazaar/bidService/list/14235/cars
```

This assumes that the application was deployed under ActionBazaar context. This service could easily be tested from the web browser.

USING THE @QUERYPARAM ANNOTATION

The @javax.ws.rs.QueryParam annotation enables you to extract query parameters and map them to parameters on a method. The annotation is defined as follows:

```
@Target(value = {ElementType.PARAMETER, ElementType.METHOD,
    ElementType.FIELD})
@Retention(value = RetentionPolicy.RUNTIME)
public @interface QueryParam {
  public String value();
}
```

The following example demonstrates the use of this annotation:

```
@Path("/bidService")
@Stateless(name="BidService")
public class BidServiceBean {
  @GET @Produces("text/plain")
  @Path("/list/{userId}/{category}")
  public String listBids(
    @PathParam("category")String category,
    @PathParam("userId")long userId,
    @QueryParam("startDate") String startDate,
    @QueryParam("endDate") String endDate
   ) {
      ...
   }
}
```

This service can be invoked with the following URL from the web browser: http://localhost:8080/wse/bidService/list/3232/cars?startDate=10252012&endDate=10302012. The query parameters startDate and endDate will be mapped to the start and end date method parameters.

> **Type conversions**
>
> You might have noticed in this sample code that the start and end dates were passed in as java.lang.Strings. There's no compatible constructor on the java.util.Date object that accepts a string. Some implementations, such as Apache CFX, have extensions for registering handlers to deal with problems like this. This is where you want to make sure that the interfaces on your EJBs aren't driven by limitations within JAX-RS.

USING THE @PRODUCES ANNOTATION

The @javax.ws.rs.Produces annotation specifies the Multipurpose Internet Mail Extensions (MIME) types the service can produce and return to the client. One or more types can be returned to the client. The service should check the header values with the request to determine which one the client supports. The annotation is defined as follows:

```
@Inherited
@Target(value = {ElementType.TYPE, ElementType.METHOD})
```

```
@Retention(value = RetentionPolicy.RUNTIME)
public @interface Produces {
  public String[] value() default {"*/*"};
}
```

The following example demonstrates the use of this annotation with a method that can return either XML or JSON depending on the client:

```
@GET
@Path("/getBid/{bidId}")
@Produces({"application/json","application/xml"})
public Bid getBid(@PathParam("bidId") long bidId) {
  ...
}
```

If you invoke this from the web browser, you'll see either XML or JSON. The JAX-RS implementation can either generate XML using JAXB or generate JSON output.

Common MIME types, which might be produced by a method, include the following:

- `application/xml`—XML
- `application/json`—JSON-structured text
- `text/plain`—Raw text
- `text/html`—HTML output
- `application/octet-stream`—Arbitrary binary data

This isn't an exhaustive list but a sampling of some of the common ones you'll use.

USING THE @CONSUMES ANNOTATION

The `@javax.ws.rs.Consumes` annotation is similar to the `@Produces` annotation. The only difference is that it specifies the MIME type representations the service can accept. This annotation is used in situations where the method accepts different types of input. The annotation is defined as follows:

```
@Inherited
@Target(value = {ElementType.TYPE, ElementType.METHOD})
@Retention(value = RetentionPolicy.RUNTIME)
public @interface Consumes {
  public String[] value() default {"*/*"};
}
```

Consider the following example code demonstrating this annotation:

```
@POST @Path("/addBid")
@Consumes("application/xml")
public void addBid(Bid bid) {
  ...
}
```

This method accepts an XML representation of a `Bid`. The JAX-RS implementation will use JAXB to convert the XML document into a `com.actionbazaar.dto.Bid` instance. Note that a DTO used as a `com.actionbazaar.persistence.Bid` instance has references to the `Item` and `Bidder`—you don't want an entire serialized object graph.

As mentioned earlier, this is only a sampling of the annotation capabilities provided by JAX-RS. A full discussion of JAX-RS requires a separate book. A good book that covers just REST and Java is *Restlet in Action* by Jerome Louvel (Manning, 2012).

In the next section we'll look at how EJB and RESTful web services can be used effectively. Using REST effectively is a much larger topic.

8.3.6 Using EJB and REST web services effectively

Exposing stateless session beans via REST requires planning ahead and carefully crafting the external interface. Unlike SOAP-based web services, RESTful web services are much closer to the wire format. You must take care to avoid having client-related requirements, such as a requirement to return JSON structured data, drive the interface of the stateless session bean. Consequently, the stateless session beans that should be exposed should have relatively simple interfaces. As mentioned previously, these beans should primarily accept primitives or strings and return simple output.

The JAX-RS annotations should be placed on the local interface. Placing them directly on the stateless interface bean makes the implementation harder to read and also ties the bean directly to JAX-RS. The convoluted code will be harder to maintain and to read. In the future, it might be necessary to use the Adapter Pattern and split the bean off; therefore, having a separate interface will simplify such an architectural change.

In situations where the interface of the EJB must be adapted to support RESTful web services, the Adapter Pattern should be used. With the Adapter Pattern, the RESTful web service is implemented as a POJO. CDI (context and dependency injection) can be used to inject references to the EJB. CDI is covered in the next chapter. The adapter RESTful web service translates the request and response messages into forms that are acceptable to EJBs so that RESTful interface requirements don't infiltrate the business tier.

When using REST to expose an EJB, you should closely follow the semantics of REST. The operations on the EJB must be appropriately mapped to the HTTP methods. A method that removes a record should use an HTTP `DELETE`. In addition, an EJB method that retrieves data should use an HTTP `GET`. The principles of safety and idempotent methods are essential to building a well-architected solution. If you've worked mostly with SOAP-based web services, this can require a mental shift to adapt.

Above all, RESTful web services should be kept simple. RESTful web services are meant to be lightweight. A simple litmus test should be whether you could invoke your web services from the browser. If code is required to invoke the web service, then perhaps the service would be better implemented using SOAP. RESTful web services aren't XML-centric—if you find your services making extensive use of JAXB to handle marshaling and demarshaling of XML object graphs, then it's time to reconsider the design.

8.4 Choosing between SOAP and REST

This chapter discusses two different web service approaches: SOAP and REST. The first decision that you must make when exposing services is which approach to take. There's no simple answer to this question. You must weigh a number of factors that are application-specific. To start with, is your application already using exposing functionality via either SOAP or REST? If not, how well do the services map to either REST or SOAP? REST is much more stringent in terms of how the API should be structured. What types of clients are you expecting, and do you need to provide a self-documenting WSDL file so code can be auto-generated?

Popularity of a particular approach often factors into the decision. Currently, REST is the more popular approach for creating new web services. SOAP is complex and has significant overhead. This overhead and complexity often get in the way and make exposing simple services needlessly complex. As a result, REST is a "back to the basics" approach. REST's popularity has risen as a result of extremely popular RESTful services provided by Amazon, Flickr, and Google. If you're not locked into one approach or are considering switching, we'll look at the benefits and trade-offs of each.

Let's start with SOAP. A few of the chief benefits of SOAP are that it's self-documenting and has excellent tooling support, and there are multiple WS specifications that extend SOAP by adding layers for reliable messages, transactions, and security, among others. The self-documenting nature of SOAP through complex XML documents has resulted in a myriad of point-and-click tools that can auto-generate and invoke web services. A business analyst or system integrator can thus use a web service without necessarily understanding how the SOAP service works and what's happening under the hood. On the flip side, if you don't have good tools or don't know how to effectively use them, editing WSDL documents (if not using auto-generation) will be laborious. Because there's an emphasis on tooling and auto-generation, you must be aware of the limitation of the tools when supporting multiple platforms and how they interpret XML schema when generating code.

SOAP-based web services also support the ability to be routed through intermediate nodes. Each node can inspect the header, perform an operation, and then forward the message. This is a useful feature in complex environments.

REST is fairly simply: each REST operation maps to a URL and the HTTP method determines the type of operation performed. A RESTful web service should map to a CRUD operation. You must put thought into the HTTP method as well as the structure of the URL. The output from a RESTful web service doesn't need to be XML—it could be JSON, text, an image, and so on. Query parameters are used to pass parameters to the service. With the ability to use query parameters and return compact output, such as JSON, RESTful web services have low bandwidth requirements and require less resources for processing a message. Consequently, RESTful web services are more scalable.

Although REST is conceptually simpler, the tooling support isn't as good as for SOAP. Although WSDL now supports REST, it doesn't yet have wide market penetration. You can't auto-generate clients, but writing code to invoke a service is straightforward, and many platforms (for example, Java and iOS) have libraries that simplify the invocation of a RESTful service.

Table 8.2 is a decision matrix to aid you in deciding between SOAP and REST. Also factoring into your decision should be whether your application is already using web services. Tabulate the positives for both technologies and then compare the scores. Based on your needs, some factors might be more important than others.

Table 8.2 SOAP versus REST decision matrix

	SOAP	REST
Requires tooling support (auto-generate clients)	X	
Lacks tools for creating/editing WSDL		X
Low overhead		X
Limited bandwidth (many clients)		X
Operations map to CRUD		X
Processing XML documents	X	
Transactions, coordination, and the like	X	
Message routing/processing	X	X
Requires SMTP	X	
Non-XML output (JSON/text/graphics/etc.)		X
Point-to-point messages		X
Validates incoming/outgoing messages against schema	X	

Now that we've provided a baseline for helping you decide between technologies, let's summarize and move on to JPA.

8.5 Summary

In this chapter you learned how to expose a stateless session bean as either a SOAP or RESTful web service. The first half of this chapter focused on SOAP-based web services. SOAP-based web services are document-centric. We reviewed the basics of SOAP web services and covered the structure of WSDL and SOAP messages. We also talked about RPC versus document web services and the meaning of encoded versus literal. The basic JAX-WS annotations were covered along with a brief introduction to JAXB. In addition, we discussed the different approaches that can be taken when developing a web service—for instance, do you generate the server implementation from a WSDL or let the server generate the WDSL automatically? In the process, we discussed best practices.

In the second half of the chapter we dived into RESTful web services. A brief introduction was provided that contrasted RESTful web services with SOAP web services.

You saw how RESTful web services are much simpler and leverage the infrastructure already provided by HTTP. RESTful web services use the HTTP methods `GET`, `PUT`, `DELETE`, and so on to implement services—a service is tied to a particular HTTP method and must adhere to its semantics. A RESTful web service also uses the URI to define the service and incorporates URL-encoded form parameters. RESTful web services can return text, JSON, XML, and so on, enabling its output to be customized for the targeted clients. The JAX-RS annotations were covered along with best practices. In the next chapter we'll begin our exploration of JPA.

Part 3

Using EJB with JPA and CDI

In this section you'll get in-depth coverage of EJB 3's relationship with JPA and CDI. Chapter 9 introduces domain modeling and how to map JPA entities to your domain. Relationships between domain objects with JPAs are explained, as well as using inheritance with JPA domain objects. Chapter 10 covers managing JPA entities through CRUD operations. You'll learn about `EntityManager`, entity lifecycles, persisting and retrieving entities, and entity scopes. Chapter 11 introduces JPQL and covers retrieval of data in-depth. You'll learn how to create and execute standard JPQL queries, as well as how to use native SQL queries when needed. Chapter 12 is an introduction to CDI and how it complements EJB development. You'll also learn about web-specific extensions to CDL, specifically conversations that are vital for today's multitab browsers.

9 JPA entities

This chapter covers

- JPA and the impedance mismatch
- Domain models
- Implementing domain objects with JPA
- Defining relationships between domain objects with JPA
- Using inheritance with JPA domain objects

The Java Persistence API (JPA) is the Java standard to create, retrieve, update, and delete (CRUD) data from relational databases. Java has had the ability to access databases almost since its beginnings. The JDBC API gives developers direct access to the database for running SQL statements. Although powerful, JDBC is simple—it lacks many features. Because of this, many proprietary object-relational mapping (O/R mapping) tools have been developed on top of JDBC. JPA standardizes O/R mapping for both the Java SE and Java EE platforms. For developers, this means database applications created to these standards don't include proprietary classes in the code.

The goal of this chapter is to give an overview of the most common and often used features of JPA. First, we'll review how to turn any domain model POJO into an entity that JPA can manage. After that, we'll look at how to map the entity to the database tables and columns holding the data. Next, we'll examine the various strategies JPA has for specifying and generating database primary keys. Finally, we'll explore relationships between database tables (for example, multiple `Bids` on an `Item`) and how JPA manages mapping these relationships. Once you've learned how to do all of this, we'll discuss the `EntityManager` in the next chapter and look at the code that actually performs all of the CRUD operations.

9.1 Introducing JPA

JPA is the Java standard solution for a problem commonly known as object-relational mapping. Simply put, O/R mapping is a translator. Imagine two people wish to communicate. One speaks English and the other speaks French. They need a third party, a translator, who knows both languages to communicate. O/R mapping is exactly the same thing, except one language is your application's database and the other language is your application's Java domain model. The translator in this case will be JPA. It's the responsibility of JPA to move data back and forth between your database and Java domain model.

O/R mapping is a complicated job. Every possible database structure needs to be able to be mapped to every possible Java domain model. This mapping problem is commonly known as the impedance mismatch. In the next section, we'll begin a review of JPA by explaining the impedance mismatch and then continue on with the rest of the chapter to explain the key features JPA uses to solve it.

9.1.1 Impedance mismatch

The term *impedance mismatch* refers to the differences in the OO and relational paradigms and difficulties in application development that arise from these differences. The persistence layer, where the domain model resides, is where the impedance mismatch is usually the most apparent. The root of the problem lies in the differing fundamental objectives of both technologies.

When a Java object holds a reference to another object, the actual referred object isn't (typically) copied over into the referring object. In other words, Java accesses objects by reference and not by value. If this weren't the case, you'd probably store the identity of a referred object (perhaps in an `int` variable) instead and dereference the identity when necessary. On the other hand, relational databases have no concept of accessing objects by reference. Relational databases use identities almost exclusively. These identities point to where the real data resides, and database queries use the identities to dereference the data when needed.

Java also offers the luxury of inheritance and polymorphism that doesn't exist in the relational world. Lastly, Java objects include both data (instance variables) as well as behavior (methods). Databases tables, on the other hand, inherently encapsulate data in rows and columns but don't have behavior.

These differences highlight the impedance mismatch. Both relational databases and Java domain models attempt to solve the same conceptual problem, but they do so using completely different languages. An experienced database administrator (DBA) will efficiently store data in appropriately normalized database tables using primary keys, foreign keys, and constraints to maintain data integrity. An experienced Java developer will create a rich domain model using inheritance, encapsulation, and polymorphism to enable complex behavior and enforcement of business rules in an application. Table 9.1 summarizes some of the overt mismatches between the object and relational worlds.

Table 9.1 Impedance mismatch: differences between the object and relational worlds

Domain model (Java)	Relational model (database)
Objects, classes	Tables, rows
Attributes, properties	Columns
Identity	Primary key
Relationship/reference to other entity	Foreign key
Inheritance/polymorphism	Doesn't exist
Methods	Indirect parallel to SQL logic, stored procedures, triggers
Code is portable	Not necessarily portable, depending on vendor

For the remainder of this chapter, we'll look at how this impedance mismatch may be overcome, specifically using JPA as a translator between the relational and domain models. We'll look at how JPA maps relational database table rows and columns into Java object domain models.

9.1.2 *Relationship between EJB 3 and JPA*

Before we jump into JPA, let's look at its history and its relationship with EJBs. When Java EE 5 was released, the EJB container was completely rearchitected, moving to a lightweight POJO, annotation, and convention-over-configuration design. With EE 5 came the first introduction to the Java Persistence API. At the time, JPA was part of the EJB specification. This made sense because at that time JPA was tied heavily to EJBs, which are primarily responsible for enforcing business rules and maintaining data integrity for your applications. But as the JPA specification grew and become more feature-rich, it was eventually rolled into its own Java specification request (JSR).

JPA version 2.1 is specified in JSR-338 and is available at the Java Community Process website at http://jcp.org/en/jsr/detail?id=338. The exciting part of having its own specification is that JPA has been decoupled from the Java Enterprise Edition (Java EE) and can now be easily used within the Java Standard Edition (Java SE) applications as well. In other words, you no longer need to have a JAVA EE server or EJB container to take full advantage of the power that JPA brings to the data access layer of your application. This opens JPA for use in applications that it couldn't be used in before. But before using JPA in your application, you must determine what objects you'll need in your application to hold data and the relationships between those objects. This is known as domain modeling, and we'll discuss how you go about doing this next.

9.2 Domain modeling

Often the first step to developing an Enterprise application is creating the domain model—that is, listing the entities in the domain and defining the relationships between them.

In this section we'll present an introduction on domain modeling. Then we'll explore the ActionBazaar problem domain and identify actors in a domain model, such as objects, relationships, and cardinality. We'll provide a brief overview of how domain modeling is supported with the JPA and then build a simple domain object as a Java class.

9.2.1 Introducing domain models

A domain model is a conceptual image of the problem your application is trying to solve. The domain model is made up of Java objects representing your application's data and the relationships or associations among the data. Data may represent something physical like a customer or something conceptual like a customer preference. A relationship is a link between objects that need to know about one another. The critical thing to remember is that the domain model describes the objects and the relationships between them. The domain model doesn't describe how your application acts on the objects—that's the responsibility of the business rules of your EJBs and MDBs.

9.2.2 ActionBazaar domain model

We're going to develop the core functionality of the ActionBazaar application that's directly related to buying and selling items that are put up for bid online. To start we're going to look at the actions that are at the heart of the ActionBazaar application. As figure 9.1 shows, ActionBazaar centers on the following activities:

- Sellers post items on ActionBazaar.
- Items are organized into searchable and navigable categories.
- Bidders place bids on items.
- The highest bidder wins.

Looking at these activities, you can pick out the domain objects by scanning the list of activities and looking for nouns: seller, item, category, bidder, bid, and order. Your goal is to identify the domain objects or entities you want to persist in the database. In the real world, finding domain objects usually involves hours of work and numerous iterations spent analyzing the business problem. You'll make the initial diagram by randomly throwing together your objects as shown in figure 9.2.

Now that you have your model objects, you need to figure out how they interact with each other. By determining the links between objects that should know about

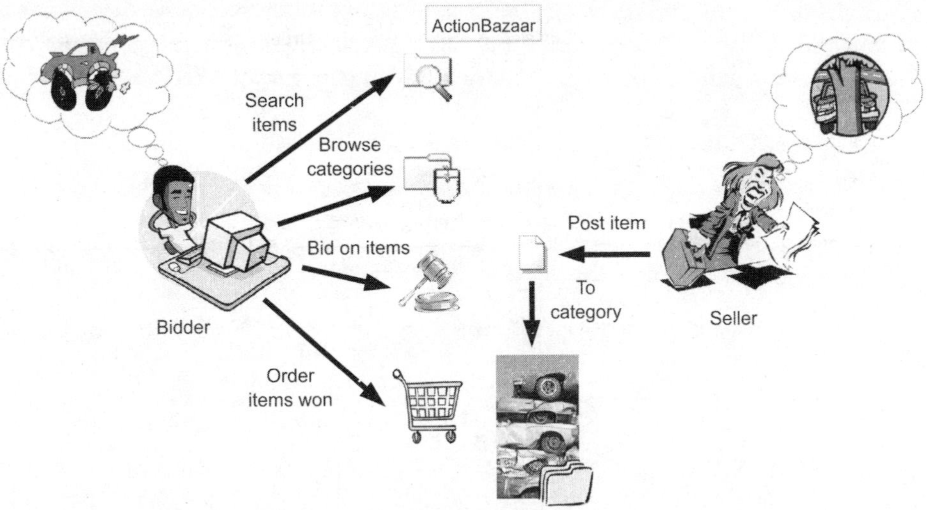

Figure 9.1 The core functionality of ActionBazaar. Sellers post items into searchable and navigable categories. Bidders bid on items, and the highest bid wins.

each other (these are the complex domain relationships) you complete the domain model. Figure 9.3 shows the relationships.

Figure 9.3 is pretty self-explanatory. For example, an item is sold by a seller, a seller may sell more than one item, the item is in one or more categories, each category may have a parent category, a bidder places a bid on an item, and so on. You should also note that although the domain model describes the possibilities for putting objects together, it doesn't describe the way in which the objects are manipulated. For instance, although you can see that an order consists of one or more items and is placed by a bidder, you're not told how or when these relationships are formed. By applying a bit of common sense, it's easy to figure out that an item won through a winning bid is put into an order placed by the highest bidder. These relationships are probably formed by the business rules after the bidding is over and the winner checks out the item won. Next, we'll take a look at how this domain model may be turned into Java classes.

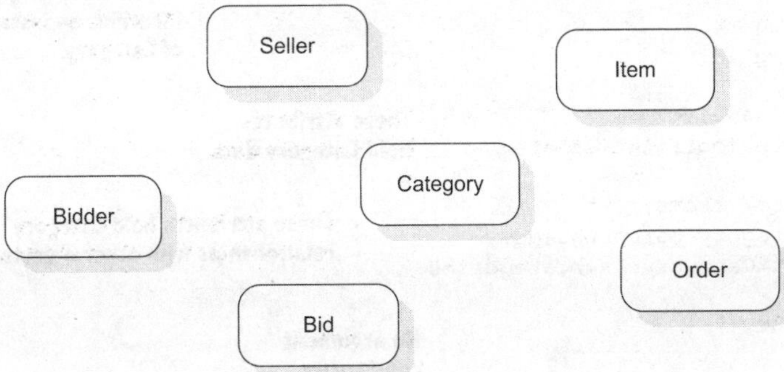

Figure 9.2 Entities in the ActionBazaar domain model

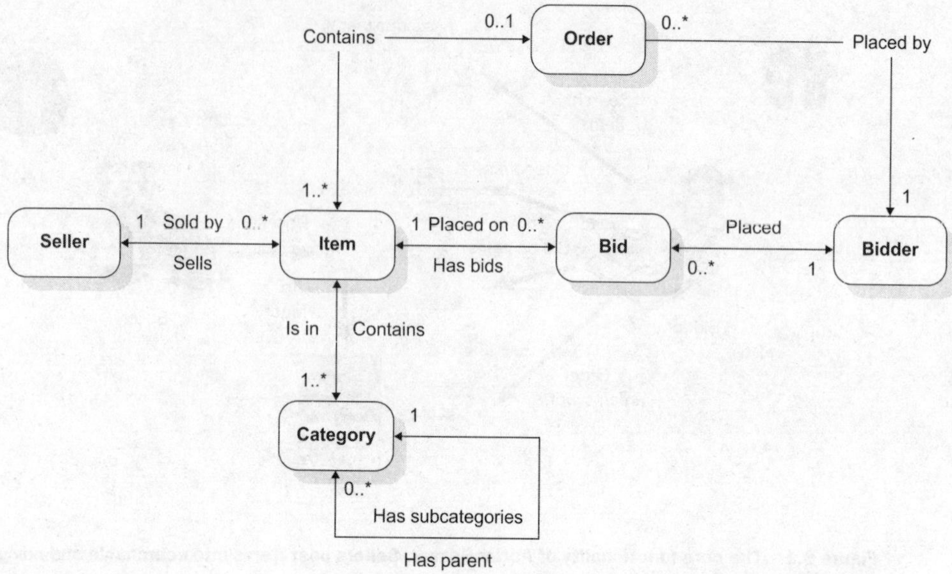

Figure 9.3 The ActionBazaar domain model complete with entities and relationships. Entities are related to one another and the relationship can be one-to-one, one-to-many, many-to-one, or many-to-many. Relationships can be either uni- or bidirectional.

DOMAIN OBJECTS AS JAVA CLASSES

Now let's get your feet wet by examining some JPA code. But before we get to JPA, we'll look at an ordinary POJO for the relatively complex domain object, `Category`. Listing 9.1 describes what the `Category` class will look like. You'll notice at this point that it's still a POJO with no JPA annotations. This is typically where you start when building your domain model. A POJO is only a *candidate* for becoming an entity and being persisted to the database.

Listing 9.1 `Category` domain object in Java

```
package com.actionbazaar.listing01;
import java.sql.Date;

public class Category {
    protected Long id;

protected String name;
    protected Date modificationDate;

protected Set<Item> items;
    protected Category parentCategory;
    protected Set<Category> subCategories;

    public Category() {
    }
```

Annotations:
- Category class is a regular POJO.
- id attribute uniquely identifies an instance of Category.
- These attributes hold Category data.
- These attributes hold Category relationships with other objects.
- No argument constructor.

```
    public Long getId() {
        return this.id;
    }

    public void setId(Long id) {
        this.id = id;
    }

    public String getName() {
        return this.name;
    }

    public void setName(String name) {
        this.name = name;
    }

    public Date getModificationDate() {
        return this.modificationDate;
    }

    public void setModificationDate(Date modificationDate) {
        this.modificationDate = modificationDate;
    }

    public Set<Item> getItems() {
        return this.items;
    }
    public void setItems(Set<Item> items) {
        this.items = items;
    }

    public Set<Category> getSubCategories() {
        return this.subCategories;
    }

    public void setSubCategories(Set<Category> subCategories) {
        this.subCategories = subCategories;
    }

    public Category getParentCategory() {
        return this.parentCategory;
    }

    public void setParentCategory(Category parentCategory) {
        this.parentCategory = parentCategory;
    }
}
```

The `Category` POJO has a number of protected instance variables, each with corresponding setters and getters that conform to JavaBeans naming conventions. Other than `name` and `modificationDate`, all the other properties have a specific role in domain modeling and persistence. The `id` property is used to store a unique number to identify the category. The `items` property holds all the items stored under a category and represents a many-to-many relationship between items and categories. The `parentCategory` property represents a self-referential many-to-one relationship between parent and child categories. The `subCategories` property maintains a one-to-many relationship between a category and its subcategories.

JAVABEANS JavaBeans rules state that all objects have a no-argument constructor and that instance variables should be nonpublic and made accessible via methods that follow the `getXX` and `setXX` pattern used in listing 9.1, where `XX` is the name of the property (instance variable).

The `Category` class as it stands in listing 9.1 is a perfectly acceptable Java implementation of a domain object. The problem is that it's still just a POJO. There's currently no way of distinguishing the fact that the `Category` class should be managed by JPA. There's also nothing that tells JPA how the `Category` class should be managed. For example, JPA has no idea the `id` property holds the unique identifier for the `Category`. Also, the relationship properties (`items`, `subCategories`) don't specify direction or multiplicity for the relationship. Next, you'll start solving some of these problems by updating the POJO with JPA annotations, starting with identifying the `Category` class as a domain object.

9.3 *Implementing domain objects with JPA*

In the previous sections you learned about domain modeling concepts and identified part of the ActionBazaar domain model. In this section, you'll see some of the JPA annotations in action as you implement part of the domain model using JPA. We'll start with the `@Entity` annotation that converts any POJO to an entity manageable by JPA. Then you'll learn about field- and property-based persistence and entity identity. Finally, we'll discuss embedded objects.

9.3.1 *@Entity annotation*

The `@Entity` annotation marks a POJO domain object as an entity that can be managed by JPA. You may think of the `@Entity` annotation as the persistence counterpart of the `@Stateless`, `@Stateful`, and `@MessageDriven` annotations. Mark the `Category` class as an entity as follows:

```
@Entity
public class Category {
    //...
    public Category() { /**/ }
    public Category(String name) { /**/ }
    //...
}
```

That's it! By using the `@Entity` annotation, JPA now knows this is an entity you wish it to manage during database interactions. As the code snippet demonstrates, all nonabstract entities must have either a public or a protected no-argument constructor. The constructor is used by JPA to create a new instance of the entity—you never manually create a new instance yourself when getting data through JPA.

A powerful feature of JPA is that because entities are POJOs, they support a full range of OO features like inheritance and polymorphism. You can have an entity extend to either another entity or even to a nonentity class. For example, figure 9.4 demonstrates

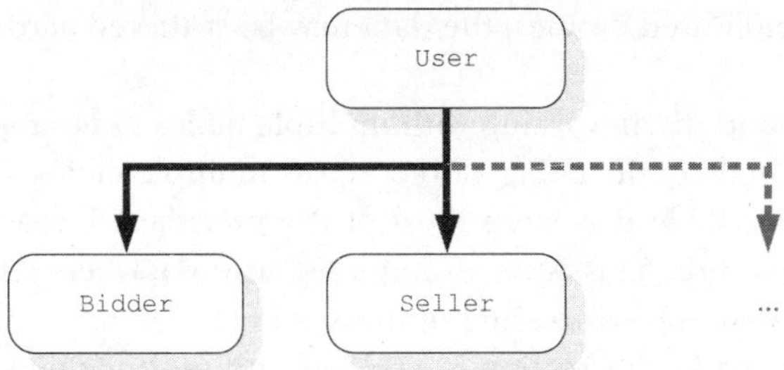

Figure 9.4 Inheritance support with entities. `Bidder` and `Seller` entities extend the `User` entity class.

good design to extend both the `Seller` and `Bidder` domain object classes from a common `User` class (the `User` class may or may not be annotated with `@Entity`). In the following listing, you'll declare the parent `User` class as an entity.

Listing 9.2 `User` entity

```
@Entity
public abstract class User {
    // ...
    String userId;
    String username;
    String email;
    byte[] picture;
    // ...
}

@Entity
public class Seller extends User { /**/ }

@Entity
public class Bidder extends User { /**/ }
```

All the `User` class fields (`userId`, `username`, `email`) are persisted when either the `Seller` or `Bidder` entity is saved. This wouldn't be the case if the `User` class weren't an entity itself. Rather, the value of the inherited properties would be discarded when either `Seller` or `Bidder` was persisted. This listing also demonstrates an interesting weakness—the `User` class could be persisted on its own, which isn't necessarily desirable or appropriate application behavior. One way to avoid this problem is to declare the `User` class abstract, because abstract entities are allowed but can't be directly instantiated or saved.

The ultimate goal of persistence is to save the properties of the entity into the database. The `@Entity` annotation is the beginning. Given the Java EE preference for convention over configuration, this may be all you need. But JPA has many more annotations to help specify how the data gets to the database. The next thing we'll look at is how JPA determines which table in your database holds the data for your entity.

9.3.2 Specifying the table

Data for the domain model will come from multiple tables in the database. For some entities, the mapping may be simple and all of the data for the entity will come from a single table. For more complicated entities, the data may be scattered across two or more tables.

It's important to understand when working with multiple tables *in this context* that we're discussing data for a single entity being stored across multiple tables. Consider user data as an example. One table may store most of the user data, but a separate table may store the user's picture. This is an example of user data being scattered across two tables. This is what we'll be discussing in this section.

What we won't be discussing in this section is working with multiple tables in the context of entity relationships. Consider user and address data as an example. A relationship exists between a single user and multiple addresses. We'll cover this starting in section 9.4 on entity relationships.

MAPPING AN ENTITY TO A SINGLE TABLE

`@Table` specifies the table containing the columns to which the entity is mapped. The `name` parameter is most important. By default all the persistent data for the entity is mapped to the table specified by the annotation's `name` parameter. As you can see from the annotation's definition, it contains a few other parameters:

```
@Target(TYPE)
@Retention(RUNTIME)
public @interface Table {
    String name() default "";
    String catalog() default "";
    String schema() default "";
    Index[] indexes() default {};
    UniqueConstraint[] uniqueConstraints() default {};
}
```

The `@Table` annotation is optional. By default, JPA will assume the name of the table is the name of the `@Entity` class itself. In the case of the `Category` class in listing 9.1, JPA will assume the name of the database table is `Category`. The `@Table` annotation allows you to override this conventional behavior. For example, if the database table is named `ITEM_CATEGORY`, use the `@Table` annotation to configure JPA:

```
@Table(name="ITEM_CATEGORY")
public class Category
```

The `catalog` and `schema` elements are there if you need to further specify the location of the table in the database. Schemas and catalogs are common database features and will not be discussed further. But as an example, suppose the `ITEM_CATEGORY` table was in the `ACTIONBAZAAR` schema. Use the `schema` parameter to configure JPA:

```
@Table(name="ITEM_CATEGORY", schema="ACTIONBAZAAR"))
public class Category
```

The `catalog` and `schema` elements aren't commonly used because those details are usually part of the data source configuration on your Java EE server. It's typically bad practice for your code to know too much about the database because changes would require a rebuild of your code instead of a reconfiguration of the EE server.

The `uniqueConstraints` element is also not commonly used. In addition, there's no guarantee this element will be used by your JPA implementation (persistence provider). Most persistence providers include a great developer-friendly feature known as automatic schema generation. The persistence provider will automatically create database objects for your entities when they don't exist in the database. This behavior isn't mandated by the JPA specification and is configured using vendor-specific properties. The `uniqueConstraints` element tells the persistence provider which columns on the auto-generated table should have a unique constraint. Again there's no guarantee the persistence provider will support auto-generation, and if it does, there's no guarantee the `uniqueConstraints` element will be applied.

Outside of a development environment for quick prototyping or unit testing, autogeneration of tables is almost never a good idea. But if you're working on an open-source project that requires a database, then auto-generation may allow the software community to get your application up and running quickly for evaluation purposes. Your application can configure JPA (using the `persistence.xml` discussed later) to use the EE server's default data source. This will allow others to deploy your application to their EE servers with little or no configuration. If you do use the default data source, expect an immediate request for instructions on configuring your application to use a different one.

> **Default data source**
>
> New to the Java EE 7 specification is a standardization of the JNDI location for the EE server's default data source. The standard location is defined as
>
> ```
> java:comp/DefaultDataSource
> ```
>
> This data source can easily be retrieved with the `@Resource` tag:
>
> ```
> @Resource(lookup="java:comp/DefaultDataSource")
> DataSource defaultDs;
> ```

The `@Table` annotation is limited to specifying a single table. But it's common for relational databases to store the data you want in multiple tables. Next, we'll look at how you use the `@SecondaryTable` annotation to work with two or more tables.

MAPPING AN ENTITY TO MULTIPLE TABLES

The `@SecondaryTables` (plural) and `@SecondaryTable` (singular) annotations allow JPA to handle the cases where an entity's data must come from two or more tables. In some rare situations, this is a very sensible strategy. Let's consider the `User` entity in listing 9.2. The `User` entity contains a byte array `picture` property. The DBA for ActionBazaar decided to store the data across the `USERS` and `USER_PICTURES` tables, as shown in figure 9.5.

This makes excellent sense because the `USER_PICTURES` table stores large binary images that could significantly slow down queries using the table. The `@SecondaryTable`

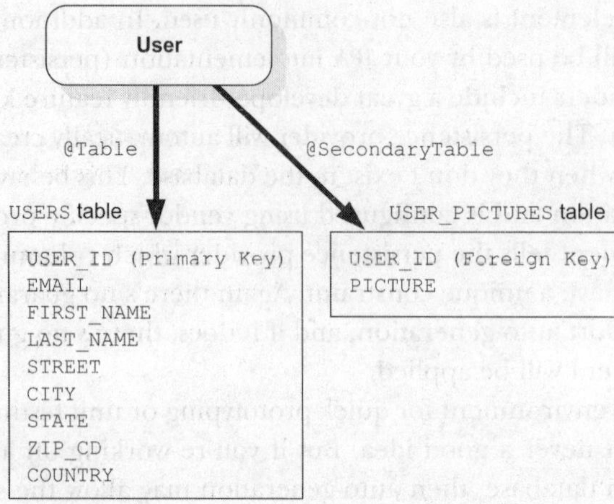

Figure 9.5 Storing user data across two tables

annotation enables you to get entity data from more than one table and is defined as follows:

```
@Target({ TYPE })
@Retention(RUNTIME)
public @interface SecondaryTable {
    String name();
    String catalog() default "";
    String schema() default "";
    PrimaryKeyJoinColumn[] pkJoinColumns() default {};
    UniqueConstraint[] uniqueConstraints() default {};
}
```

Notice that other than the `pkJoinColumns` element, the definition of the annotation is identical to the definition of the `@Table` annotation. This `pkJoinColumns` element is the key to how the annotation works. As an example, examine the following code implementing the `User` entity mapped to these two tables:

```
@Entity
@Table(name="USERS")
@SecondaryTable(name="USER_PICTURES",
    pkJoinColumns=@PrimaryKeyJoinColumn(name="USER_ID"))
public class User
```

The `pkJoinColumns=@PrimaryKeyJoinColumn(name="USER_ID")` configuration tells JPA that the primary key of the `USERS` table (how JPA determines the primary key of the `USERS` table is discussed in the next section when we look at the `@Id` annotation) is the same as the foreign key `USER_PICTURES.USER_ID` in the secondary table. JPA performs a join between the two tables to fetch the data for the `User` entity. This example involves only two tables. If more than two tables were involved, you'd use `@SecondaryTables` (plural) to specify all of the secondary tables.

Something you may be asking yourself about using `@SecondaryTable` is how JPA knows to map the columns from different tables to the correct Java object properties. After all, if you look at the `User` entity in listing 9.2, there's nothing to tell JPA the byte array picture property's data comes from the secondary table. To answer this question, we'll need to look at how JPA maps table columns.

9.3.3 Mapping the columns

Having learned how to map the database tables in the previous sections, it's now time to look at how to map the table columns. The @Column annotation maps a persisted object property to a table column. First, we're going to look at the basics of using the @Column annotation; then we'll look at some features added in JPA 2.0 that make mapping columns easier and more flexible for objects in your domain model. Finally, we'll discuss transient fields in more detail.

@COLUMN ANNOTATION

Let's start by looking at an example of how you'd map some properties from the User entity in listing 9.2, as shown in the following listing.

Listing 9.3 Mapping User entity properties

```
@Entity
@Table(name="USERS")
public class User {
    @Column(name="USER_ID")
    String userId;
    @Column(name="USER_NAME")
    String username;
    String email;
    //...Other getters and setters ommitted for brevity
    public String getEmail() {
        return email;
    }
    public void setFmail(String email) {
        this.email = email;
    }
}
```

1. userId property maps to "USER_ID" column
2. username property maps to "USER_NAME" column
3. email property is the same as "EMAIL" column so no @Column annotation needed
4. JavaBean getter and setter for email

This listing shows the @Column annotation specifying which column from the USERS table the property should map to. So, for the userId property, it's assumed a USER_ID column exists in the USERS table and JPA will store that database data in userId (1). The username property is similar—JPA assumes a USER_NAME column exists in USERS (2).

The email property is different. The email property doesn't have a @Column annotation (3). So how does JPA know how to map it? Remember the Java EE preference for convention over configuration? By convention, JPA saves all Java object properties that have JavaBeans-style public or protected setters and getters and by default assumes the column name is the same as the property name. The email property has the standard getter and setter methods, so JPA will, by default, automatically try to persist it (4). Because the name of the email property is "email," by default JPA assumes an EMAIL column exists in the USERS table. Because of this convention-over-configuration preference, if all of your object's property names match the name of the column they're persisted to, then you won't need to use the @Column attribute at all.

Listing 9.3 shows the `@Column` annotation in its simplest form. The next listing shows the other attributes of the annotation.

Listing 9.4 `@Column` attributes

```
@Target ({ METHOD, FIELD })
@Retention(RUNTIME)
public @interface Column {
    String name() default "";
    boolean unique() default false;
    boolean nullable() default true;
    boolean insertable() default true;
    boolean updatable() default true;
    String columnDefinition() default "";
    String table() default "";
    int length() default 255;
    int precision() default 0;
    int scale() default 0;
}
```

As you can see, there's a lot more to `@Column`, but these attributes aren't commonly used. The `insertable` and `updatable` attributes are most useful. If `insertable` is false, JPA won't include the Java object property in the SQL `INSERT` statement when persisting new data. Similarly, if `updatable` is false, JPA won't include the property in the SQL `UPDATE` statement when updating existing data. Why wouldn't you want to persist data? There can be any number of reasons, but a common one is that the data is generated by the database itself, usually through some kind of trigger. A table that uses a database-generated primary key is a good example.

The rest of the parameters (`unique`, `nullable`, `length`, `precision`, `scale`, `table`, and `columnDefinition`) are used by the persistence provider's vendor-specific automatic schema generation to create the tables in the database if they don't already exist. As discussed in section 9.3.2, this is almost never a good idea, so we'll leave you to further explore these attributes on your own.

Looking again at listing 9.3, you may be asking yourself why the `@Column` annotation was placed directly on the `User` object's properties. Does the annotation have to go there? Can the annotation be placed on the getter or setter methods instead? We'll explore this next when we discuss the difference between field- and property-based persistence.

FIELD- VERSUS PROPERTY-BASED PERSISTENCE

With JPA, you have a choice of where you place `@Column` annotations. Your first choice is to place the annotations on the variables of the class. This is known as field-based access. Here's an example:

```
@Column(name="USER_ID")
private Long id;
```

When you use field-based access, JPA will get and set the value directly by accessing the private variable. This may be acceptable if your domain model object is a simple bean with getters and setters that have no business logic. The other choice you have for the placement of your annotations is on the getter methods of the class (annotations on setter methods are ignored). This is known as property-based access. Here's an example:

```
@Column(name="USER_ID")
public Long getId() { return id; }
public Long setId(Long id) {
    this.id = (id <= 0) ? 0 : id;
}
```

In this example, notice that the annotation is on the getter method and that the setter method has some simple business logic. When you use property-based access, JPA will get the value by using the getter method and set the value by using the setter method. If you do have some business logic in your getter or setter methods, you should use property-based access so that JPA uses the getter and setter methods instead of accessing the private variable directly.

With JPA 1.0, you were limited to using either field-based access or property-based access and you couldn't mix and match the two within an object hierarchy. For example, ActionBazaar has a `User` superclass with `Seller` and `Bidder` child classes. With JPA 1.0, all three objects (`User`, `Seller`, `Bidder`) had to use either field-based access or property-based access. This has changed in JPA 2.0 with the introduction of the `@Access` annotation.

The `@Access` annotation must first be defined at the class level to set the default access type for the entire entity. The access types may be either `AccessType.FIELD` or `AccessType.PROPERTY`. Here's an example of setting the `User` entity access type to `FIELD`:

```
@Entity
@Access(FIELD)
public class User { ... }
```

You can now define the `Seller` entity and do some special things:

```
@Entity
@Access(FIELD)
public class Seller extends User {
  //...the rest of seller omitted for brevity

  @Transient
  private double creditWorth;

  @Column(name="CREDIT_WORTH")
  @Access(AccessType.PROPERTY)
  public double getCreditWorth() { return creditWorth; }
  public void setCreditWorth(double cw) {
    creditWorth = (cw <= 0) ? 50.0 : cw;
  }
}
```

Notice that the `Seller` entity uses the `@Access` annotation to set `FIELD` as the default for the class. But it uses `@Transient` and `@Access` to override field-based access for creditWorth in favor of property-based access. Everything else in Seller will be field-based access except for creditWorth. When performing an override like this, you always use @Transient and @Access together. This prevents JPA from basically trying to map creditWorth twice.

In the preceding example the default for Seller was field-based access and you performed an override for creditWorth to be property-based access. But this could just as easily have been the other way around. The default for Seller can be PROPERTY and the override for creditWorth can make it field-based access. Here's what that would look like:

```
@Entity
@Access(PROPERTY)
public class Seller extends User {
  //...the rest of seller omitted for brevity

  @Column(name="CREDIT_WORTH")
  @Access(Accesss.TypeFIELD)
  private double creditWorth;

  @Transient
  public double getCreditWorth() { return creditWorth; }
  public void setCreditWorth(double cw) {
    creditWorth = (cw <= 0) ? 50.0 : cw;
  }
}
```

The @Access annotation is a nice addition to JPA so that all the objects in your domain model hierarchy don't need to have either field- or property-based access. The @Access annotation allows for mixing the two access types. This is especially nice if objects in the domain model hierarchy are part of shared projects that can't be easily changed.

These examples introduced the @Transient annotation. This is another commonly used annotation in JPA, and it prevents JPA from managing whatever it annotates. We'll discuss the @Transient annotation in more detail next.

DEFINING A TRANSIENT FIELD

Because JPA will automatically attempt to persist a Java object property with standard JavaBeans getter and setter methods, is it possible to have a property in your object that JPA won't persist? The answer is yes. JPA follows the serialization model and has a @Transient annotation. The @Transient annotation is used to tell JPA to ignore a property completely. If a property is marked with @Transient, JPA won't try to select, insert, or update the property's value. Suppose you add the birthday and age properties to the User object as follows:

```
public class User {
    @Column(name="DATE_OF_BIRTH")
    Date birthday;
    @Transient
    int age;
    //...Other getters and setters ommitted for brevity
    public void setBirthday(Date birthday) {
```

```
        this.birthday = birthday;
        // calculate age...
    }
}
```

The setBirthday() method can automatically calculate the age. The application does this for convenience, but the age isn't something you want JPA to manage so you mark it as @Transient.

The @Column attribute is the starting point for mapping your Java object properties to database table columns. But JPA comes with a few more annotations to handle specific data requirements, such as primary keys, dates, timestamps, codes, and binary data. We'll start looking at examples of these kinds of data next.

9.3.4 Temporal types

Temporal types are all about dates and times. Most databases support a few different temporal data types with different granularity levels corresponding to DATE (storing day, month, and year), TIME (storing just time and not day, month, or year), and TIMESTAMP (storing time, day, month, and year). The @Temporal annotation specifies which of these data types you want.

JPA can map database data to either a java.util.Date or java.util.Calendar object property. When saving the data to the database, JPA will use only the relevant parts of the data stored in the property. This means if the database column is specified to store only time, then JPA will get the time out of the java.util.Date or java.util .Calendar property and ignore any date it holds.

JPA can also map to the java.sql.Date, java.sql.Time or java.sql.Timestamp Java types. Using these with @Temporal is a bit redundant because JPA will infer from the Java data type what kind of temporal data the database stores. It doesn't hurt to be explicit, though, and using the @Temporal annotation makes it clear how the data is to be handled.

As an example, suppose you store the date only, not the time, when data is created in the database. You can do this in either of the following ways:

```
@Temporal(TemporalType.DATE)
protected java.util.Date creationDate;

@Temporal(TemporalType.DATE)
protected java.util.Calendar creationDate;

// No annotation
protected javax.sql.Date creationDate;
```

9.3.5 Enumerated types

Referring back to figure 9.4, suppose the data model contains an enumeration that identifies the types of users in your application. The enumeration may look similar to the following:

```
public enum UserType { SELLER, BIDDER, CSR, ADMIN }
```

Because a relational database doesn't understand Java objects or type hierarchies, you can use this enumeration to persist data to the table to identify the type of user. A relational database doesn't understand `enum` types either, so the `UserType` will need to be converted into something the database can understand. This is where `@Enumerated` comes in. The `@Enumerated` annotation may be used in either of the following ways:

```
@Enumerated(EnumType.STRING)
protected UserType userType1;

@Enumerated(EnumType.ORDINAL)
protected UserType userType2;
```

The difference between the two is that one example uses `EnumType.STRING` and the other uses `EnumType.ORDINAL`. `EnumType` controls what data type is stored in the database for the enumeration.

Recall that each enumeration has an associated `String` representation. `UserType.SELLER` is represented by `SELLER`, `UserType.BIDDER` by `BIDDER`, and so on. When `@Enumerated(EnumType.STRING)` is used, JPA will persist this `String` representation to the database.

Recall also that each enumeration has an index representation as well. Given the order of the enumeration values in the preceding code snippet, `UserType.SELLER` is index 0 and may be retrieved from the enumeration by this index value by `UserType.values()[0];`. Similarly, `UserType.BIDDER` is index 1, `UserType.CSR` is index 2, and so on. When `@Enumerated(EnumType.ORDINAL)` is used, JPA will persist this index (or ordinal) representation to the database.

The JPA default is to save by ordinal value. So by default JPA will store `UserType.ADMIN` as the number 3, not the `String "ADMIN"`. It's also crucial to remember that once the data is persisted to the database, there's a disconnect between the data and your code. This means that if you change the `enum` in your code, there's no way for the database to know about it. If you change your code, you run the risk of your code no longer working with the data in the database. If JPA is persisting by ordinal and you change the order of your `enum` values, then users will suddenly become the wrong type. If JPA is persisting by `String` and you change the name of the `enum` value (from `BIDDER` to `BUYER`, for example), then you'll get a runtime exception because `BIDDER` exists in the database but no longer exists in your code.

9.3.6 Collections

So far you've been learning how to map the major types of single values from out of the database table columns to the Java domain object properties. But the domain model also deals with collections of data. For example, users on ActionBazaar may have multiple telephone numbers. The following listing shows an updated `User` entity that contains a `Collection` of telephone numbers.

Listing 9.5 User with a list of telephone numbers

```
@Entity
@Table(name="USERS")
public class User {
    private Collection<String> telephoneNumbers;
    //...
}
```

In this listing there's a `Collection` of `String` objects intended to hold telephone numbers. But you've yet to configure JPA with what it needs to know to get that data out of the database. This is where the `@ElementCollection` annotation comes in. To map a collection of basic types (`java.lang.String`, `java.util.Integer`, and so on) or embeddable types (more about embeddable types when we discuss the `@EmbeddedId` annotation in section 9.3.7), JPA 2.0 introduced the `@ElementCollection` annotation. Prior to JPA 2.0 it was still possible to map collections of objects, as you'll see in section 9.4 when we discuss entity relationships, but the addition of `@ElementCollection` has made mapping collections much easier. The next listing shows an updated `User` entity that maps the telephone numbers.

Listing 9.6 Mapping a collection of telephone numbers

```
@Entity
@Table(name="USERS")
public class User {
    @ElementCollection                                          ❶
    @CollectionTable(name="PHONE_NUMBERS",                      ❷
        joinColumns=@JoinColumn(name="USER_ID"))                ❸
    @Column(name="NUMBER")
    private Collection<String> telephoneNumbers;
    //...
}
```

❶ Used to specify a collection instead of a single value

❷ Name of collection table if default name needs to be overridden

❸ Name of column in collection table if default name needs to be overridden

The `@ElementCollection` annotation works with a collection table in the database, and you use it in your entity to tell JPA this property is going to be a collection, not just a single value ❶. This collection table is nothing more than another table in the database that holds the data you want. The default name for this collection table is a combination of the entity name and the property name. In the listing the default collection table name is `USER_TELEPHONENUMBER`, but you use the `@CollectionTable` annotation to override the default and use `"PHONE_NUMBERS"` instead ❷. The default name for the column in the collection table is the property name, which in this example would be `TELEPHONENUMBER`. But you use the `@Column` annotation to override the column name to be `"NUMBER"` instead ❸. And finally, you use the `joinColumns` attribute to tell JPA that the `PHONE_NUMBERS.USER_ID` column is the foreign key back to the primary key of the `USERS` table.

This listing shows an example using a `Collection` of `String` objects. But keep in mind that the `@ElementCollection` annotation can work with embeddable objects as well. We'll discuss embeddable objects more in section 9.3.7, but as a sneak peek, let's look at the classic embeddable object: the `Address`. An `Address` object may look like this:

```
@Embeddable
public class Address {
  @Column(name="HOME_STREET")
  private String street;
  @Column(name="HOME_CITY")
  private String city;
  @Column(name="HOME_STATE")
  private String state;
  @Column(name="HOME_ZIP")
  private String zipCode;
}
```

The `User` entity then has a `Collection` of `Address` objects:

```
@Entity
@Table(name="USERS")
public class User {
  @ElementCollection
  @CollectionTable(name="HOMES")
  private Set<Address> shippingAddresses;
}
```

When working with collections, database primary-key values become vital. It's through primary-key values that databases form relations. JPA can then use these relations to pull the correct data from other tables into collections for you. So next we're going to look at how JPA is configured to identify primary keys.

9.3.7 *Specifying entity identity*

When we talk about specifying an entity identity, what we're really talking about is how JPA identifies a database table's primary key. All database tables must have some way to uniquely identify a row in the table, so that when data needs to be updated only the data in that one row is changed and the rest of the data in the table remains unaffected. Likewise, when JPA pulls data out of the database and converts it to your Java object domain model, JPA needs to be able to uniquely identify the in-memory objects that hold the data from rows in your table. All this is done by configuring JPA so that it knows about your table's primary key. JPA has three ways of accomplishing this, and we'll look at how to use each one of them:

- Using the `@Id` annotation
- Using the `@IdClass` annotation
- Using the `@EmbeddedId` annotation

@ID ANNOTATION

When the primary key of your database table is a single column, you want to use the `@Id` annotation. Looking back at the `Category` object from listing 9.1, assume the `id` property holds the value of the primary-key column of the `CATEGORY` table in the database. You simply annotate the property to let JPA know it's to use that value to uniquely identify a `Category`. As the following examples show, you can annotate either the property

```
@Id
private long id;
```

or the getter method

```
@Id
public long getId() { return id; }
```

The value of the `@Id` property is used by JPA to uniquely identify a `Category`. This means if JPA wants to know if two `Category` objects are the same, it'll compare the `@Id` property values, and if the values are equal, then JPA thinks the two `Category` objects are the same. The `@Id` property can support primitives (`int`, `long`, `double`, and the like), and in these cases JPA performs a direct equality comparison. The `@Id` property also supports `Serializable` types (`String`, `Date`, and so on), and in these cases JPA will use the `equals()` method.

It's important to remember that the `@Id` annotation will work only if the primary key is a single column of the table. Most modern projects will add a column to the table for this very purpose. But legacy projects may not have a single-column primary key but instead rely on multiple columns to uniquely identify a row in the table. JPA has two ways of handling multiple column primary keys. We'll look at these next.

@IDCLASS ANNOTATION

The first way JPA handles multiple-column primary keys is with the `@IdClass` annotation. This allows you to mark multiple properties in your Java object with `@Id` (the columns of the table that make up the primary key) and then define a class that basically follows the comparator patterns and defines how those multiple `@Id` values are supposed to be compared to determine equality. Let's look at an example. Suppose the `CATEGORY` table is part of a legacy project and the table uses the category name and creation date as the primary key. The first thing you'll do in the following listing is define these two properties in the `Category` class and annotate them with `@Id` so JPA knows these two classes together uniquely identify the entity.

Listing 9.7 Category with two column primary keys

```
@Entity
public class Category {
    @Id @Column(name="CAT_NAME") private String name;          ❶
    @Id @Column(name="CAT_DATE") private java.util.Date createdDate;   ❷
    // ...
}
```

❶ name property is one part of primary key

❷ createdDate property is the other part of primary key

You now have the `name` property ❶ and the `createdDate` property ❷ both annotated with `@Id`, and this tells JPA that the two together uniquely identify the category. But what JPA doesn't know yet is how to use these two properties when comparing two

Category objects for equality. To do this, you introduce a new class, CategoryKey, as shown in the next listing.

Listing 9.8 CategoryKey

```
import java.io.Serializable;
import java.sql.Date;
public class CategoryKey implements Serializable {
  private static final long serialVersionUID = 1775396841L;
  String name;
  Date createDate;
  public CategoryKey(){}
  public boolean equals(Object other) {
    if (other instanceof CategoryKey) {
      final CategoryKey otherCategoryKey = (CategoryKey) other;
      return (otherCategoryKey.name.equals(name)
          &&
          otherCategoryKey.createDate.equals(createDate));
    }
    return false;
  }

  public int hashCode() {
    return super.hashCode();
  }
}
```

❶ JPA specification says this must be Serializable
❷ These two fields make up primary key
❸ Required no-argument constructor
❹ Required overridden equals method to perform comparison
❺ Required overridden hash code method

Let's take a look at CategoryKey in a little more detail. The JPA specification says classes like this should implement Serializable ❶, so the class does this and also defines a serialVersionUID. The two fields, name and createDate ❷, which compose the primary key, are duplicated here in CategoryKey. A no-argument constructor ❸ must be provided so JPA can create an instance of CategoryKey. An overridden equals() method ❹ is provided to perform the actual logic to compare the name and createDate properties. Finally, an overridden hashCode() method ❺ is required.

You're almost finished. The last thing you need to do is let Category know to use CategoryKey. Referring back to listing 9.7, you update the code for the Category class and add in the @IdClass annotation like this:

```
@Entity
@IdClass(CategoryKey.class)
public class Category {
    // ...
}
```

So how does this all fit together? When JPA retrieves data from the CATEGORY table and creates a Category object, the name and createdDate properties are set with data from their corresponding columns in the table. When the time comes for JPA to determine if two Category objects are the same, JPA will create a new instance of CategoryKey for each of the Category objects it's comparing. JPA will copy the name and createdDate property values from the Category objects into the CategoryKey objects. Finally, JPA will use the equals() method on CategoryKey to see if the two CategoryKey objects are the same. If they're equal, JPA then assumes the two Category objects are equal.

This is just one way JPA handles multiple-column primary keys when it maps the data to your Java domain model. Next, we look at another way JPA handles this with the @EmbeddedId annotation.

@EMBEDDEDID ANNOTATION

The second way JPA handles multiple-column primary keys is with the @EmbeddedId annotation. Using the @EmbeddedId is very similar to using @IdClass, but @EmbeddedId takes advantage of the @Embeddable annotation and turns your domain model object into a composite. Let's take a look at an example. Suppose the CATEGORY table is part of a legacy project and the table uses the category name and creation date as the primary key. To use @EmbeddedId to map this, the first thing you'll do in the following listing is create an @Embeddable CategoryId class to represent this primary key.

Listing 9.9 CategoryId

```
import java.sql.Date;
import javax.persistence.Embeddable;
@Embeddable                                        ❶ @Embeddable allows this object to be embedded into others
public class CategoryId {
    String name;                                   ❷ These two fields make up the primary key
    Date createDate;

    public CategoryId() {}                         ❸ Required no-argument constructor

    public boolean equals(Object other) {          ❹ Required overridden equals method to perform comparison
      if (other instanceof CategoryId) {
        final CategoryId otherCategoryKey = (CategoryId) other;
        return (otherCategoryKey.name.equals(name)
                &&
                otherCategoryKey.createDate.equals(createDate));
      }
      return false;
    }

    public int hashCode() {                        ❺ Required overridden hash code method
      return super.hashCode();
    }
    public String getName() {
        return name;
    }
    public Date getCreateDate() {
        return createDate;
    }
    // ...
}
```

As you can see, this listing is nearly identical to listing 9.8. The important difference is the use of the @Embeddable annotation ❶ in CategoryId. By using @Embeddable, you're telling JPA the CategoryId class can be put into or embedded into other classes. The name and createDate properties ❷ still make up the primary key. The

CategoryId class has a required no-argument constructor ❸. It overrides the equals() method ❹, which does the test for equality, and it has a required overridden hashCode() method ❺.

Although the CategoryId class of listing 9.9 isn't very different from the CategoryKey class of listing 9.8, changes to the Category class will be very different. When using @ClassId, the Category class retained the individual properties composing the CATEGORY table's primary key. This completely changes when using @EmbeddedId because those individual properties are now removed, replaced by the CategoryId class, and Category becomes a composite. The next listing shows these changes.

Listing 9.10 Category using @EmbeddedId

```
@Entity
public class Category {
    @EmbeddedId                                   ❶ @EmbeddedId defines an embedded object as primary key for this data
    private CategoryId categoryId;                ❷ CategoryId holds primary-key data
    // ...
    public String getName() {                     ❸ Getter methods wrap access to primary-key data
      return categoryId.getName();
    }
    public Date getCreateDate() {
      return categoryId.getCreateDate();
    }
}
```

Let's look at this more closely. First, you'll notice that the name and createDate properties no longer exist. They've been replaced by the categoryId property ❷, and the categoryId property is now annotated with @EmbeddedId ❶. This tells JPA that Category is now a composite object and it should create an instance of the CategoryId class to hold the CATEGORY table's primary key. Getter methods on Category are updated to use this embedded object ❸.

> **@Embeddable annotation**
>
> We introduced the @Embeddable annotation when discussing multicolumn primary keys and how JPA uses both @EmbeddedId and @Embeddable together as a solution for the primary-key mapping. It's important to note that the @Embeddable annotation isn't exclusive to primary keys. Any object may be annotated with @Embeddable and be used inside your Java domain model. An address is a good example. Multiple Java domain model objects may utilize address information, and instead of duplicating those properties, an @Embeddable Address object may be created and @Embedded used in your Java domain model. We invite you to further explore the @Embedded, @Embeddable, and @AttributeOverride annotations on your own.

Now that you know how to map primary keys to the Java domain model, let's take a look at how JPA can generate primary keys when inserting data into the database.

9.3.8 Generating primary keys

In the previous section you learned how to map database primary keys to the Java domain model. In the simplest case, you use the `@Id` annotation to map a single-column primary key. In more complicated cases, you use either `@IdClass` or `@EmbeddedId` to map multiple-column primary keys. But we've yet to discuss how the primary-key values are generated.

When generating primary keys, there are typically two schools of thought. The first is that primary keys should arise naturally from the data. For example, when storing user data it may be sufficient to say that a person's first name, last name, and telephone number are enough to uniquely identify a row in the table. Therefore, the primary key should consist of these three columns. The second school of thought is to introduce artificial data that's not related in any way to the data being stored and exists only to uniquely identify rows in the table. These are typically sequenced, numbered, single-column, primary keys.

Although there are pros and cons associated with each technique, in general, the introduction of artificial data to serve as the primary key is most conventional. There are five popular ways of generating primary-key values like this:

- Auto
- Identity
- Sequence
- Table
- Code

Next, we're going to introduce the `@GeneratedValue` annotation and see how it's used to generate primary keys in these different ways.

AUTO

The auto strategy is the JPA default and the simplest use of `@GeneratedValue`. Auto frees the developer from any special database work and leaves the generation of the primary key to whatever defaults are configured for the database. The next listing shows what the `User` object would look like using the auto strategy.

Listing 9.11 Auto strategy

```
@Entity
public class User {
    @Id
    @GeneratedValue(strategy=GenerationType.AUTO)      <-- Auto strategy
    @Column(name="USER_ID")
    protected Long userId;
}
```

IDENTITY

The identity strategy makes use of a special database column type that maintains its own auto-incrementing number to uniquely identify rows in the table. Most databases support this column type: Microsoft SQL Server, IDENTITY; MySQL, AUTO_INCREMENT; PostgreSQL, SERIAL; Oracle does have support for this column type. When data is inserted into the table, the identity field will automatically increment and store that value as the row's primary key. The following listing shows what the User object would look like using the identity strategy.

Listing 9.12 Identity strategy

```
@Entity
public class User {
    @Id
    @GeneratedValue(strategy=GenerationType.IDENTITY)    <-- Identity strategy
    @Column(name="USER_ID")
    protected Long userId;
}
```

SEQUENCE

The sequence strategy uses a database sequence to get auto-incrementing unique numbers. This strategy is most popular with Oracle because Oracle doesn't have the identity column type discussed in the previous section. To configure JPA to use a database sequence as the primary-key generator, first create the sequence. The following SQL shows how to create a sequence in Oracle:

```
CREATE SEQUENCE USER_SEQUENCE START WITH 1 INCREMENT BY 10;
```

Next, use @SequenceGenerator to configure a connection to the sequence; then configure @GeneratedValue to use this sequence generator. The following listing shows what the User object would look like using the sequence strategy.

Listing 9.13 Sequence strategy

```
@Entity
@SequenceGenerator(name="USER_SEQUENCE_GENERATOR",      <-- 1 Internal JPA name for sequence
    sequenceName="USER_SEQUENCE", initialValue=1, allocationSize=10)   <-- 2 Database name of sequence
public class User {
  @Id
  @GeneratedValue(strategy=GenerationType.SEQUENCE,     <-- 3 Sequence strategy
      generator="USER_SEQUENCE_GENERATOR")     <-- 4 Which internal JPA named sequence to use
  @Column(name="USER_ID")
  protected Long userId;
}
```

In this listing there's first a @SequenceGenerator with name set to USER_SEQUENCE_GENERATOR ❶. This is the internal JPA name for this sequence, and other JPA annotations will use this name when referring to the sequence. The sequenceName attribute is set to the actual name of the sequence in the database, which in this case is USER_SEQUENCE ❷. For the @GeneratedValue annotation, the strategy is set to Generation_Type.SEQUENCE ❸ and the generator is set to the internal JPA name of the sequence ❹.

A `@SequenceGenerator` is sharable across the entire persistence unit. This means a `@SequenceGenerator` doesn't need to be defined in the class it's used. Any `@SequenceGenerator` is shared among all entities, so keep that in mind when assigning internal JPA names to ensure they're unique.

TABLE

The table strategy uses a small database table to get auto-incrementing unique numbers. Typically the table has two columns in it. The first column is a unique name for a sequence. The second column is the sequence value. To configure JPA to use the table strategy, you first need a table:

```
CREATE TABLE SEQUENCE_GENERATOR_TABLE (
  SEQUENCE_NAME VARCHAR2(80) NOT NULL,
  SEQUENCE_VALUE NUMBER(15) NOT NULL,
  PRIMARY KEY (SEQUENCE_NAME));
```

Now that you have an empty table, the next step, shown in the following listing, is to manually insert a sequence and its initial value.

Listing 9.14 Insert the sequence name and initial value

```
INSERT INTO SEQUENCE_GENERATOR_TABLE
  (SEQUENCE_NAME, SEQUENCE_VALUE) VALUES ('USER_SEQUENCE', 1);
```

Insert 'USER_SEQUENCE' with a starting value of 1

Next, use `@TableGenerator` to configure a connection to the table, and then configure `@GeneratedValue` to use this sequence generator. The next listing shows what the `User` object would look like using the table strategy.

Listing 9.15 Table strategy

```
@Entity
@TableGenerator (name="USER_TABLE_GENERATOR",
  table="SEQUENCE_GENERATOR_TABLE",
  pkColumnName="SEQUENCE_NAME",
  valueColumnName="SEQUENCE_VALUE",
  pkColumnValue="USER_SEQUENCE")
public class User {
  @Id
  @GeneratedValue(strategy=GenerationType.TABLE,
       generator="USER_TABLE_GENERATOR")
  @Column(name="USER_ID")
  protected Long userId;
}
```

1. Internal JPA name for sequence
2. Database table name
3. Column of table holding sequence name
4. Column of table holding sequence value
5. Name of sequence (row in table) to use
6. Table strategy
7. Which internal JPA named sequence to use

In this listing, there's first a `@TableGenerator` with `name` set to `USER_TABLE_GENERATOR` (1). This is the internal JPA name for this sequence, and other JPA annotations will use this name when referring to the sequence. The `table` attribute is set to the name of the table (2). The `pkColumnName` attribute is the name of the column in the table that holds the names of the sequences (3). The `valueColumnName` attribute is the name of the column that holds the values of the sequences ❹. Finally, the `pkColumnValue` attribute ❺ is the name of the sequence you wish to use (see the insert statement of listing 9.14). For the `@GeneratedValue` annotation, the `strategy` is set to `GenerationType.TABLE` ❻ and the `generator` is set to the internal JPA name of the strategy ❼.

Remember that `@TableGenerator` is sharable across the entire persistence unit. This means a `@TableGenerator` doesn't need to be defined in the class it's used. Any `@TableGenerator` is shared among all entities, so keep that in mind when assigning internal JPA names to ensure they're unique.

> **Primary keys, equals(), and hashCode()**
>
> It's important to point out that the special relationship primary-key values have to the `equals()` and `hashCode()` methods. Typically these methods are overridden to compare Java domain model objects by primary-key values. But in *any* auto-generation key strategy, the primary-key value won't be known until the persistence manager inserts the data into the database. Before the insert happens, the primary-key value in your domain model object will be `NULL`. Therefore, `equals()` and `hashCode()` must be able to handle null values gracefully.

CODE

The code strategy is for situations when you don't want the database to auto-generate a primary key. Instead, you want to generate the primary key yourself in your application's code. This is achievable with JPA using various techniques, but the most popular one is to use the `@PrePersist` lifecycle annotation to set the value of the primary-key property before the data is inserted into the database. The following listing shows what the `User` object may look like using the code strategy.

Listing 9.16 Code-generated strategy

```
@Entity
public class User {
    @Id
    @Column(name = "USER_ID")
    protected String userId;

    @PrePersist                                    <-- ❶ JPA executes this method before insert
    public void generatePrimaryKey() {
        userId = UUID.randomUUID().toString();     <-- ❷ Generate a primary key for data
    }
}
```

In this listing you see a few changes to the `User` class. First, the `@GeneratedValue` annotation is no longer being used. This is because the primary key isn't being automatically generated anymore; you're instead generating the key yourself. Second, the `@PrePersist` annotation ❶ is introduced, which tells JPA to execute the `generatePrimaryKey()` method before data is inserted into the database. And third, the JDK `UUID` object is used as a simple example of a primary-key generation strategy ❷.

We've finished covering the basics of getting data into and out of individual database tables using JPA. Next, we'll look at the "relation" part of relational databases and see how JPA handles building object trees from related database data across multiple tables.

9.4 Entity relationships

Referring back to figure 9.3, the ActionBazaar domain model consists of a number of different entities that have relationships among them. Up until now, we've been concentrating on how JPA stores and retrieves data for a single entity. But now we're going to look at how JPA handles the relationships between entities. A relationship essentially means that one entity holds an object reference to another. For example, the `Bid` object holds a reference to the `Item` object the bid was placed on. Therefore, a relationship exists between the `Bid` and `Item` domain objects. Recall that relationships can be either uni- or bidirectional. The relationship between `Bidder` and `Bid` in figure 9.3 is unidirectional, because the `Bidder` object has a reference to `Bid` but the `Bid` object has no reference to the `Bidder`. The `Bid-Item` relationship, on the other hand, is bidirectional, meaning both the `Bidder` and `Item` objects have references to each other. Relationships can be one-to-one, one-to-many, many-to-one, or many-to-many. Each of these relationship types is expressed in JPA through an annotation. We'll discuss each of these relationships and their corresponding annotations in the next sections.

9.4.1 One-to-one relationships

The `@OneToOne` annotation is used to mark uni- and bidirectional one-to-one relationships. The ActionBazaar example in figure 9.3 has no one-to-one relationship. But you can imagine that the `User` domain object has a one-to-one relationship with a `BillingInfo` object. The `BillingInfo` object might contain billing data on a user's credit card, bank account, and so on. Let's start by seeing what a unidirectional relationship would look like.

UNIDIRECTIONAL ONE-TO-ONE

Let's assume the `User` object has a reference to the `BillingInfo` but not vice versa. In other words, the relationship is unidirectional, as shown in figure 9.6.

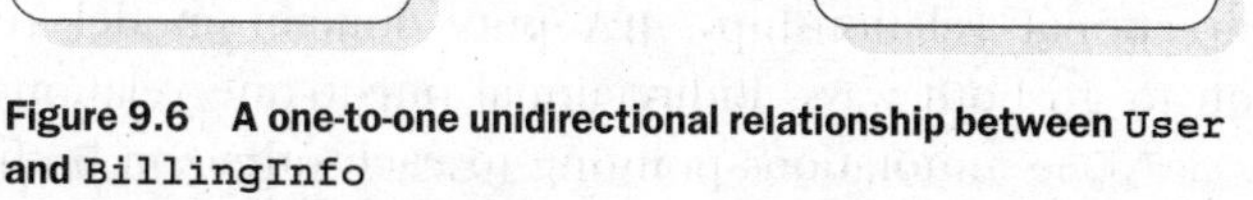

Figure 9.6 A one-to-one unidirectional relationship between `User` and `BillingInfo`

The following listing illustrates this relationship.

Listing 9.17 Unidirectional one-to-one relationship

```
@Entity
  public class User {
```

```
  @Id
  protected String userId;
  protected String email;
  @OneToOne
  protected BillingInfo billingInfo;
}

@Entity
public class BillingInfo {
  @Id
  protected Long billingId;
}
```

❶ Configure a one-to-one relationship between User and BillingInfo

❷ JPA entity in relationship with User

In this listing, the User class holds a BillingInfo reference in the billingInfo property. Because the billingInfo property holds only one instance of the BillingInfo class ❷, the relationship is one-to-one. The @OneToOne annotation configures JPA to maintain this relationship in the database ❶.

The @OneToOne annotation, like most JPA attributes, can be used on either a class's properties or on the getter methods. The @OneToOne annotation has a few configurable properties, but they're not often used. Table 9.2 briefly describes them.

Table 9.2 Attributes of the @OneToOne annotation

Attribute	Description
targetEntity	Class of the object to use in the relationship. Useful if the relationships are defined by interfaces and there are multiple implementing classes.
cascade	Database relationship changes that must be cascaded down to the related data.
fetch	Controls when the related data is populated.
optional	Specifies if the relationship is optional (see listing 9.18).
mappedBy	Specifies the entity that owns the relationship. This element is only specified on the non-owning side of the relationship (see listing 9.18).

BIDIRECTIONAL ONE-TO-ONE

In unidirectional relationships, navigating the domain model can be done only one way. In listing 9.17 the BillingInfo domain object can be reached through the User object, but you can't go the other way—you can't reach the User object through BillingInfo. In bidirectional relationships, JPA puts domain model references together to enable you to go both ways. Bidirectional one-to-one relationships are implemented using @OneToOne annotations pointing to each other on both sides of the relationship. Let's see how this works in the next listing by updating the code from listing 9.17.

Listing 9.18 Bidirectional one-to-one relationship

```
@Entity
  public class User {
```

```
  @Id
  protected String userId;
  protected String email;
  @OneToOne                                          ❶ Configure a one-to-one
  protected BillingInfo billingInfo;                    relationship
}

@Entity
public class BillingInfo {
  @Id
  protected Long billingId;                                ❷ Configure User.billingInfo
  protected String creditCardType;                            as the owner of this
  // ...                                                      one-to-one bidirectional
  @OneToOne(mappedBy="billingInfo", optional=false)           relationship
  protected User user;
}
```

In this listing, the `User` class has a relationship to the `BillingInfo` class through the `billingInfo` property ❶. This is no different than the unidirectional one-to-one relationship of listing 9.17. But in this example the relationship is bidirectional because the `BillingInfo` class also has a reference to the `User` class through the `user` property ❷. The `@OneToOne` annotation on the `user` property uses `mappedBy` and `optional`. The `mappedBy="billingInfo"` configuration tells JPA that the "owning" side of the relationship is the `User` class's `billingInfo` property. The `optional="false"` configuration tells JPA that `BillingInfo` can't exist without a `User`. This is interesting because the `@OneToOne` annotation in `User` doesn't have this configuration. This means a `User` may exist without a `BillingInfo` but a `BillingInfo` may not exist without a `User`.

9.4.2 *One-to-many and many-to-one relationships*

One-to-many and many-to-one relationships are the most common relationships in Enterprise systems. In this type of relationship, one entity will have two or more references of another. This usually means an entity has a collection-type property such as `java.util.Set` or `java.util.List` storing multiple instances of another entity. Also, if the association between two entities is bidirectional, one side of the association is one-to-many and the opposite side of the association is many-to-one.

Figure 9.7 shows the relationship between ActionBazaar `Item` and `Bid` entities. From the `Item` point of view, a single `Item` can contain multiple `Bid` entities; therefore the `Item-Bid` relationship is one-to-many. From the `Bid` point of view, multiple bids can be placed on a single `Item`; therefore the `Bid-Item` relationship is many-to-one.

The type of relationship is determined by the point of view. This is different from one-to-one relationships because in a one-to-one relationship there are only

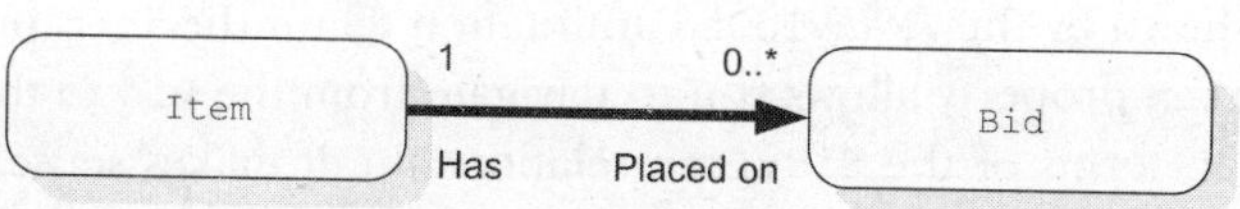

Figure 9.7 A single item may have multiple bids (one-to-many).

single instances of both entities. Similar to one-to-one relationships, one-to-many and many-to-one relationships do still have an owning side—all relationships have one side of the relationship that's the owner. The `mappedBy` attribute is used to specify the owning side. The following listing shows how to code the relationship between `Item` and `Bid`.

Listing 9.19 Bidirectional one-to-many and many-to-one relationships

```
import java.sql.Date;

import javax.persistence.Entity;
import javax.persistence.Id;
import javax.persistence.ManyToOne;
@Entity
public class Bid {
  @Id
  protected Long bidId;
  protected Double amount;
  protected Date timestamp;
  ...
  @ManyToOne                                   // 1 Configure a many-to-one relationship
  protected Item item;
  ...
}
import java.sql.Date;
import java.util.Set;

import javax.persistence.Entity;
import javax.persistence.Id;
import javax.persistence.OneToMany;

  @Entity
  public class Item {
  @Id
  protected Long itemId;
  protected String title;
  protected String description;
  protected Date postdate;
  ...
  @OneToMany(mappedBy="item")                  // 2 Configure a one-to-many relationship with Bid as the owner of the relationship
  protected Set<Bid> bids;
  ...
}
```

Remember, the type of relationship is determined by the point of view, so let's first look at this listing code example from the point of view of the `Bid`. From the `Bid` point of view, multiple bids are made on a single `Item`. Therefore, the `Bid-Item` relationship is many-to-one. This is shown by the `@ManyToOne` annotation ❶ on the `item` property of the `Bid` object. The `item` property allows you to navigate from the `Bid` to the `Item` the bid was placed on. In terms of the `Bid-Item` relationship, it makes sense for an `Item` to exist without a `Bid`, but a `Bid` can't exist without an `Item`. Because of this, the `Bid` is the owner of the relationship between `Bid` and `Item`. Remember, ownership is specified by using the `mappedBy` property on the entity that's owned, not on the entity that's the owner. Because `Bid` is the owner, you don't see `mappedBy` used on `@ManyToOne` ❶. In general, for bidirectional one-to-many relationships, the `@ManyToOne` side is always the owning side of the relationship.

Now let's take a look at this listing code example from the point of view of the `Item`. From the `Item` point of view, multiple bids will be placed on a single `Item`. Therefore, the `Item-Bid` relationship is one-to-many. This is shown by the `@OneToMany` annotation ❷ on the `bids` property of the `Item` object. This `bids` property allows you to look at all the bids placed on an `Item`. Because an `Item` can exist without a `Bid` but it doesn't make sense for a `Bid` to exist without an `Item`, the `Bid` is the owner of the relationship. The `@OneToMany` annotation on `Item.bids` configures the `mappedBy="item"` property to specify the `Bid.item` property as the owner.

Am I @ManyToOne or @OneToMany?

Working with `@ManyToOne` and `@OneToMany` can get confusing, especially when you're trying to decide which one to put on each entity of a relationship. Asking yourself these questions will be helpful.

Will "I" contain many of "You"? If the answer to this question is yes, then your class will contain a list or a set of entities and the relationship will be `@OneToMany`. (See the `Item` class in listing 9.19.)

Will many of "Me" be placed on "You"? If the answer to this question is yes, then your class will contain a single instance of the entity and the relationship will be `@ManyToOne`. (See the `Bid` class in listing 9.19.)

What gets interesting is if you answer yes to both of these questions. If so, you'll want to read more about the `@ManyToMany` relationship in the next section.

9.4.3 *Many-to-many relationships*

While not as common as one-to-many, many-to-many relationships occur quite frequently in Enterprise applications. In this type of relationship, both sides might have multiple references to related entities. In the ActionBazaar example, the relationship between `Category` and `Item` is many-to-many, as shown in figure 9.8.

In the `Item-Category` relationship, an `Item` can be placed on multiple categories, and at the same time a `Category` can contain multiple `Items`. With JPA, the `@ManyToMany` annotation is used to configure this relationship. Typically, many-to-many relationships are bidirectional. Listing 9.20 shows an example of a bidirectional many-to-many relationship between `Item` and `Category`.

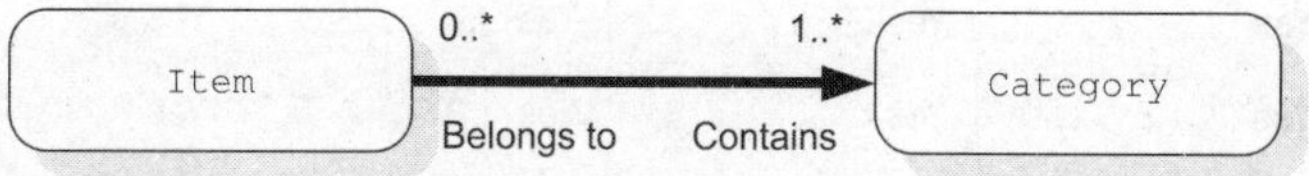

Figure 9.8 A many-to-many relationship between `Item` and `Category`

Listing 9.20 Bidirectional many-to-many relationship

```
import java.util.Set;

import javax.persistence.Entity;
import javax.persistence.Id;
import javax.persistence.ManyToMany;
@Entity
public class Category {
  @Id
  protected Long categoryId;
  protected String name;
  ...
  @ManyToMany                        <-- Configure a many-to-many relationship
  protected Set<Item> items;
  ...
}

import java.util.Set;

import javax.persistence.Entity;
import javax.persistence.Id;
import javax.persistence.ManyToMany;
@Entity
public class Item {
  @Id
  protected Long itemId;
  protected String title;
  ...
  @ManyToMany(mappedBy="items")      <-- Configure a many-to-many relationship with Category as the owner of the relationship
  protected Set<Category> categories;
  ...
}
```

In this listing, the `Category` object's `items` property is marked by the `@ManyToMany` annotation and is the owning side of the bidirectional association. In contrast, the `Item` object's `categories` variable signifies the subordinate bidirectional many-to-many association. As in the case of one-to-many relationships, the `@ManyToMany` annotation is missing the `optional` attribute. This is because an empty `Set` or `List` implicitly means an optional relationship, meaning that the entity can exist even if no associations do.

We've now covered all of the relationship annotations in JPA. With these annotations, you can configure your domain object relationships, whatever they may be. Table 9.3 provides a quick summary of the annotations and their attributes.

Table 9.3 Summary of JPA entity relationship annotations

Attribute	@OneToOne	@OneToMany	@ManyToOne	@ManyToMany
targetEntity	Yes	Yes	Yes	Yes
cascade	Yes	Yes	Yes	Yes
fetch	Yes	Yes	Yes	Yes

Table 9.3 Summary of JPA entity relationship annotations *(continued)*

Attribute	@OneToOne	@OneToMany	@ManyToOne	@ManyToMany
optional	Yes	No	Yes	Yes
mappedBy	Yes	Yes	No	Yes

This concludes our summary of mapping entity relationships. The automatic mapping of these relationships when retrieving data from the database is a powerful JPA feature. But as Java developers, we have other OO techniques that we use in our domain model that JPA also has to support. Building object hierarchies through inheritance is one of these features, so next we'll look at how JPA maps object inheritance.

9.5 Mapping inheritance

So far, you've learned how to get data into and out of tables using JPA and how to define relationships between entities. What we're going to look at next is a more detailed analysis of how Java object inheritance affects how database tables are designed. The easiest way to introduce this is with an example. Recall that in ActionBazaar there are two different kinds of users: bidders and sellers. From a Java domain model point of view, you use inheritance to keep properties common to both in a `User` object, and the `Bidder` and `Seller` objects have properties unique to those user types. Figure 9.9 shows this inheritance.

This is so common in OO design that most Java developers don't give it a second thought. It's obvious that `Bidder` and `Seller` should inherit from `User`. But for DBAs, this object inheritance is of great concern. Why? Because most databases don't support inheritance between tables (PostgreSQL has table inheritance, but this isn't common). So the question DBAs have to face is how to map an inheritance object hierarchy like that of figure 9.9 to relational database tables. There are three strategies for doing this:

- Single-table
- Joined-tables
- Table-per-class

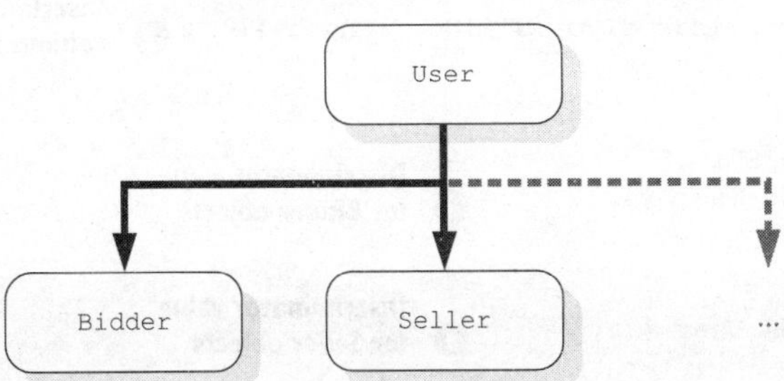

Figure 9.9 `Bidder` and `Seller` inherit shared properties from `User`.

	USER_ID	USERNAME		USER_TYPE	CREDIT_WORTH		BID_FREQUENCY
Bidder records	1	eccentric-collector	...	B	NULL	...	5.70
Bidder records	2	packrat	...	B	NULL	...	0.01
Seller records	3	snake-oil-salesman	...	S	$10,000.00	...	NULL

Figure 9.10 Store all user data in a single table.

9.5.1 *Single-table strategy*

In the single-table strategy, which is the default inheritance strategy for JPA, all classes in the domain model hierarchy are mapped to one table. This means a single table will store all data from all the objects in the domain model. Different objects in the domain model are identified using a special column called a *discriminator* column. In effect, the *discriminator* column contains a value unique to the object type in a given row (see section 9.3.5 on enumerated types). The best way to understand this scheme is to see it implemented. For the ActionBazaar schema, assume that all user types, including `Bidders` and `Sellers`, are mapped into the `USERS` table. Figure 9.10 shows how the table might look.

As figure 9.10 depicts, the `USERS` table contains data common to all users (`USER_IDD`, `USERNAME`). It also contains `Bidder`-specific data (`BID_FREQUENCY`) and `Seller`-specific data (`CREDIT_WORTH`). Records 1 and 2 contain `Bidder` records, whereas record 3 contains a `Seller` record. This is indicated by the `B` and `S` values in the discriminator column `USER_TYPE`. The `USER_TYPE` discriminator column will contain values corresponding to each user type of the ActionBazaar domain model. JPA maps each user type to the table by storing persistent data into relevant mapped columns, setting the `USER_TYPE` value correctly and leaving the rest of the values `NULL`. The next listing shows how to configure JPA using the single-table strategy.

Listing 9.21 Single-table strategy

```
@Entity
@Table(name="USERS")
@Inheritance(strategy=InheritanceType.SINGLE_TABLE)
@DiscriminatorColumn(name="USER_TYPE",
    discriminatorType=DiscriminatorType.STRING, length=1)
public abstract class User { ... }

@Entity
@DiscriminatorValue(value="B")
public class Bidder extends User {...}

@Entity
@DiscriminatorValue(value="S")
public class Seller extends User {...}
```

1. User entity maps to USERS table
2. Object domain model will use single-table strategy
3. Discriminator column and type
4. Discriminator value for Bidder objects
5. Discriminator value for Seller objects

The `@Inheritance` 2 and `@DiscriminatorColumn` 3 annotations are used to configure JPA to use the single-table strategy for this domain model. When configuring

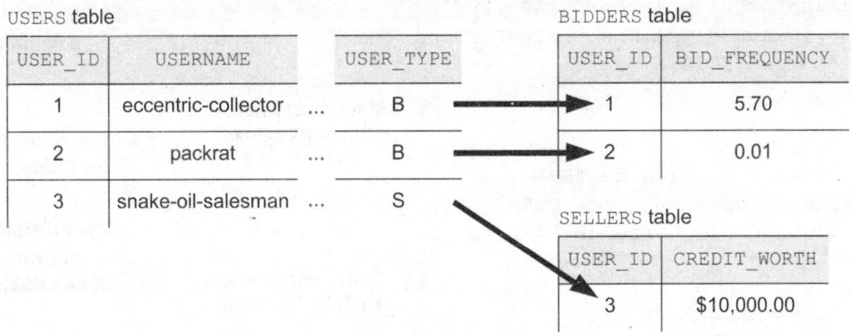

Figure 9.11 Store all user data using a one-to-one mapping from Java objects to tables.

JPA, the `@Inheritance` and `@DiscriminatorColumn` annotations must always be placed on the root object of the domain model. In this example it's the `User` object. Note that the `@Table(name="USERS")` ❶ annotation specifies the table name for `User` but the `Bidder` and `Seller` objects don't have `@Table` annotations of their own. This is because with the single-table strategy, there's only a single table, so bidder and seller data will be stored in the `USERS` table together. To tell the data apart, the `Bidder` class uses `@DiscriminatorValue` to configure JPA to store the value `"B"` in the `USERS` table discriminator column `USER_TYPE` ❹. `Seller` does the same thing for the value `"S"` ❺. Using `@DiscriminatorValue` is optional, and the default value will be the name of the class—that is, `Seller` for the `Seller` object.

9.5.2 *Joined-tables strategy*

In the joined-tables strategy, you use a one-to-one relationship between the domain model and the tables in the database. In effect, the joined-tables strategy involves creating separate tables for each entity in the domain model. Take a look at figure 9.11 to see how the joined-tables strategy works.

As figure 9.11 depicts, the `USERS` table is the parent table and it holds data common to all users (`USERNAME`). The `BIDDERS` and `SELLERS` tables are children of `USERS`. You can see that they're children because the `USER_ID` column in `BIDDERS` and `SELLERS` is a foreign key that points back to the `USER_ID` column in `USERS`. The `BIDDERS` table holds only bidder-specific data (`BID_FREQUENCY`), whereas the `SELLERS` table holds seller-specific data (`CREDIT_WORTH`). These tables have a one-to-one mapping back to the Java domain model. So the `User` entity maps to the `USERS` table, `Seller` to `SELLERS`, and `Bidder` to `BIDDERS`. The following listing shows how to configure JPA using the joined-tables strategy.

Listing 9.22 Joined-tables strategy

```
@Entity
@Table(name="USERS")
@Inheritance(strategy=InheritanceType.JOINED)
```

User entity maps to USERS table

❶ Object domain model will use joined-tables strategy

```
@DiscriminatorColumn(name="USER_TYPE",
    discriminatorType=DiscriminatorType.STRING, length=1)
public abstract class User { ... }

@Entity
@Table(name="BIDDERS")
@DiscriminatorValue(value="B")
@PrimaryKeyJoinColumn(name="USER_ID")
public class Bidder extends User {...}

@Entity
@Table(name="SELLERS")
@DiscriminatorValue(value="S")
@PrimaryKeyJoinColumn(name="USER_ID")
public class Seller extends User {...}
```

2 Discriminator column and type
3 Bidder entity maps to BIDDERS table
4 Discriminator value for Bidder objects
Use BIDDERS.USER_ID to join with USERS.USER_ID
5 Seller entity maps to SELLERS table
Discriminator value for Seller objects
6 Use SELLERS.USER_ID to join with USERS.USER_ID

This listing shows the `@DiscriminatorColumn` **2** and `@DiscriminatorValue` **1** annotations used in exactly the same way as the single-table strategy. The `@Inheritance` annotation's strategy element is specified as `JOINED`. In addition, the one-to-one relationships between parent and child tables are implemented through the `@PrimaryKeyJoinColumn` annotations in both the `Bidder` **4** and `Seller` **6** entities. In both cases, the `name` element specifies that `BIDDER.USER_ID` and `SELLER.USER_ID` are foreign keys back to `USER.USER_ID`. `Bidder` and `Seller` also use `@Table` to specify which table they map to (**3** and **5**).

The joined-tables strategy is probably the best mapping choice from a design perspective. From a performance perspective, it's worse than the single-table strategy because it requires the joining of multiple tables for polymorphic queries.

9.5.3 *Table-per-class strategy*

In the table-per-class strategy, each entity in the domain model gets its own table similar to the joined-tables strategy, but the big difference between the two strategies is that there's no relationship between the tables in the table-per-class strategy. All of the shared data of the joined-tables strategy isn't shared in the table-per-class strategy and is instead duplicated in each table. Take a look at figure 9.12 to see how the table-per-class strategy works.

`USERS` table

USER_ID	USERNAME
1	super-user

`SELLERS` table

USER_ID	USERNAME	CREDIT_WORTH
1	snake-oil-salesman	

`USERS` table

USER_ID	USERNAME	BID_FREQUENCY
1	eccentric-collector	5.70
2	packrat	0.01

Figure 9.12 Table-per-class strategy database tables with duplicate data

Looking at figure 9.12, you quickly see the difference in the table-per-class strategy. As before, the `User` entity maps to the `USERS` table, `Seller` to `SELLERS`, and `Bidder` to `BIDDERS`. But this strategy doesn't take advantage of the power of relational databases at all. The tables have no relationships among them so they're unable to share data. Consequently, shared data like `USER_ID` and `USERNAME` are duplicated in each table.

Because of the duplication of data, you have to be careful when saving data with the table-per-class strategy, especially if that data needs to be unique like the `USER_ID` and `USERNAME` columns. The data needs to be unique not only in the "child" table but in the "parent" table as well ("parent" and "child" are in quotes because no real relationship exists between the tables). For example, suppose you want to save a new bidder and this new bidder has the following data: `USER_ID = 10, USERNAME = "ActionBazaarUser123"`. These values may be unique in the `BIDDERS` table, but with the table-per-class strategy, the data will also be saved in the `USERS` table. In the `USERS` table, these values may not be unique because a seller may have already used them.

Configuring JPA to use the table-per-class strategy is the easiest of all the strategies. The following listing shows how to configure JPA using the table-per-class strategy.

Listing 9.23 The table-per-class stragegy

```
@Entity
@Table(name="USERS")                                          ❶ User entity maps to USERS table
@Inheritance(strategy=InheritanceType.TABLE_PER_CLASS)        ❷ Object domain model will use table-per-class strategy
public class User { ... }

@Entity
@Table(name="BIDDERS")                                        ❸ Bidder entity maps to BIDDERS table
public class Bidder extends User {...}

@Entity
@Table(name="SELLERS")                                        ❹ Seller entity maps to SELLERS table
public class Seller extends User {...}
```

This listing shows that the `@Inheritance` annotation's strategy element is specified as `TABLE_PER_CLASS` ❷. Of course, the `@DiscriminatorColumn` and `@Discriminator-Value` annotations are absent from this listing—they have no use because all the data for each entity is stored in its own table, so there's no need to distinguish which records are bidders and which are sellers. Finishing the code example, the `@Table` annotation is used to map each entity to its table (❶, ❸, and ❹).

This strategy is the hardest for a persistence provider to implement reliably. As a result, implementing this strategy has been made optional for the provider by the specification. We recommend that you avoid this strategy altogether.

This completes our analysis of the three strategies for mapping OO inheritance. Choosing the right strategy isn't as straightforward as you might think. Table 9.4 provides an overall comparison of each strategy.

Table 9.4 Summary of OO hierarchy inheritance mapping strategies

Feature	Single-table	Joined-tables	Table-per-class
Table support	One table for all classes in the entity hierarchy: ▪ Mandatory columns may be nullable. ▪ The table grows when more subclasses are added.	One for the parent class, and each subclass has a separate table to store polymorphic properties. Mapped tables are normalized.	One table for each concrete class in the entity hierarchy.
Uses discriminator column?	Yes	Yes	No
SQL generated for retrieval of entity hierarchy	Simple `SELECT`.	`SELECT` clause joining multiple tables.	One `SELECT` for each subclass or `UNION` of `SELECT`.
SQL for insert and update	Single `INSERT` or `UPDATE` for all entities in the hierarchy.	Multiple `INSERT`, `UPDATE`: one for the root class and one for each involved subclass.	One `INSERT` or `UPDATE` for every subclass.
Polymorphic relationship	Good	Good	Poor
Polymorphic queries	Good	Good	Poor

9.6 Summary

This concludes our introduction to JPA. Remember, JPA is rich in features and is now covered in its own JSR (JPA version 2.1 is specified in JSR-338 and is available at the Java Community Process website at http://jcp.org/en/jsr/detail?id=338). We encourage you to consider this chapter a brief introduction and to explore the many additional features of JPA on your own.

We started by explaining the challenges of mapping database data to a Java domain model. An impedance mismatch exists because each technology has completely separate views of data (which in a number of ways contradict each other), so a translator, JPA, is needed to bridge this gap. We continued by introducing you to a simple Java domain model for ActionBazaar. You gave names to the entities and defined the relationships between the entities. After this, we started exploring the rich JPA annotation set for configuring JPA to get data in and out of the database and to define relationships among data. We looked at `@Entity` to mark an object as an entity JPA should manage; `@Table` and `@SecondaryTable` to map entities to database tables; `@Column`, `@Transient`, `@Temporal`, and `@Enumerated` to map entity properties to table columns; `@Id`, `@IdClass`, and `@EmbeddedId` to identify primary keys; and `@GeneratedValue` for generating primary keys. Next, you saw how the relationships between entities are defined by looking at `@OneToOne`, `@ManyToOne`, `@OneToMany`, and `@ManyToMany`. Finally, you explored mapping inheritance strategies by learning the difference between single-table, joined-tables, and table-per-class strategies and how the strategies are configured using `@Inheritance`, `@DiscriminatorColumn`, `@DiscriminatorValue`, and `@PrimaryKeyJoinColumn`. In chapter 10 you're going to get an introduction to the `EntityManager` object and learn how to use the entities from this chapter and actually persist the data to the database.

10 Managing entities

This chapter covers

- `EntityManager`
- Entity lifecycle
- Persisting and retrieving entities
- Entity scopes

Chapter 9 introduced the basics of JPA entities. You saw how to implement the domain objects with JPA, define relationships between objects, and handle inheritance. In this chapter we're going to delve into `EntityManager` and show how to manage entities. We'll discuss what an `EntityManager` is and how to inject them into your EJB classes. You'll learn about the lifecycle of entities and how to use `EntityManager` to persist, find, merge, and remove entities—the `EntityManager` equivalent of the basic database CRUD (create, read, update, delete) operations. You'll also learn about the different scopes entities go through during their lifecycle.

Let's start this chapter by examining `EntityManager`. `EntityManager` is at the heart of JPA, and practically every operation you'll perform will depend on having an instance of `EntityManager`.

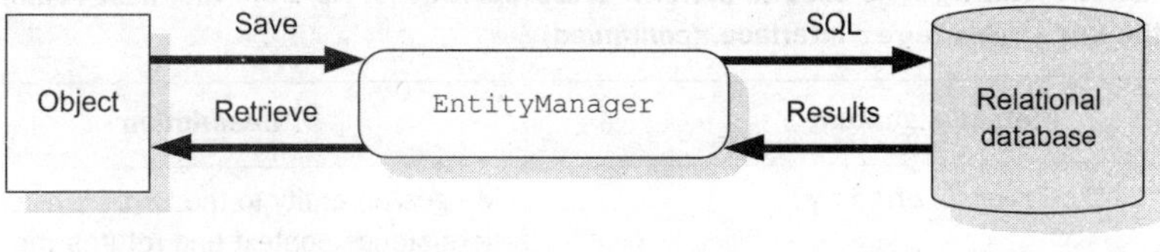

Figure 10.1 The `EntityManager` acts as a bridge between the OO and relational worlds. It interprets the O/R mapping specified for an entity and saves the entity in the database.

10.1 Introducing EntityManager

The `EntityManager` API is probably the most important and interesting part of the Java Persistence API. It manages the lifecycle of entities. In this section you'll learn about the `EntityManager` interface and its methods. We'll explore the entity lifecycle, and you'll also learn about persistence contexts and their types.

10.1.1 EntityManager interface

In a sense, the `EntityManager` is the bridge between the OO (object-oriented) and relational worlds, as depicted in figure 10.1. When you request that a domain entity be created, the `EntityManager` translates the entity into a new database record. When you request that an entity be updated, it tracks down the relational data that corresponds to the entity and updates it. Likewise, the `EntityManager` removes the relational data when you request that an entity be deleted. From the other side of the translation bridge, when you request that an entity be "found" in the database, the `EntityManager` creates the Entity object, populates it with relational data, and "returns" it to the OO world.

Besides providing these explicit SQL-like CRUD operations, the `EntityManager` also quietly tries to keep entities synched with the database automatically as long as they're *within the `EntityManager`'s reach* (this behind-the-scenes synchronization is what we mean when we talk about "managed" entities in the next section). The `EntityManager` is easily the most important interface in JPA and is responsible for most of the O/R (object-relational) mapping magic in the API.

Despite all this under-the-hood power, the `EntityManager` is a small, simple, and intuitive interface, especially compared to the mapping steps we discussed in the previous chapter and the query API, which we'll explore in the next chapter. Once we go over some basic concepts in the next few sections, the interface will seem almost trivial. You might already agree if you take a quick look at table 10.1. It lists some of the most commonly used methods defined in the `EntityManager` interface.

Table 10.1 `EntityManager` is used to perform CRUD operations. Here are the most commonly used methods of the `EntityManager` interface.

Method signature	Description
`public void persist(Object entity);`	Saves (persists) an entity into the database and makes the entity managed.

Table 10.1 `EntityManager` is used to perform CRUD operations. Here are the most commonly used methods of the `EntityManager` interface. *(continued)*

Method signature	Description
`public <T> T merge(T entity);`	Merges an entity to the `EntityManager`'s persistence context and returns the merged entity.
`public void remove(Object entity);`	Removes an entity from the database.
`public <T> T find(Class<T> entityClass, Object primaryKey);`	Finds an entity instance by its primary key. This method is overloaded and comes in different forms.
`public void flush();`	Synchronizes the state of entities in the `EntityManager`'s persistence context with the database.
`public void setFlushMode(FlushModeType flushMode);`	Changes the flush mode of the `EntityManager`'s persistence context. The flush mode may be `AUTO` or `COMMIT`. The default flush mode is `AUTO`, meaning that the `EntityManager` tries to automatically sync the entities with the database.
`public FlushModeType getFlushMode();`	Retrieves the current flush mode.
`public void refresh(Object entity);`	Refreshes (resets) the entities from the database. This method is overloaded and comes in different forms.
`public Query createQuery(String jpqlString);`	Creates a dynamic query using a JPQL statement. This method is overloaded and comes in different forms.
`public Query createNamedQuery(String name);`	Creates a query instance based on a named query on the entity instance. This method is overloaded and comes in different forms.
`public Query createNativeQuery(String sqlString);`	Creates a dynamic query using a native SQL statement. This method is overloaded and comes in different forms.
`public StoredProcedureQuery createStoredProcedureQuery(String procedureName);`	Creates a `StoredProcedureQuery` for executing a stored procedure. This method is overloaded and comes in different forms.
`public void close();`	Closes an application-managed `EntityManager`.
`public void clear();`	Detached all managed entities from the persistence context. All changes made to entities not committed will be lost.
`public boolean isOpen();`	Checks whether an `EntityManager` is open.

Table 10.1 `EntityManager` is used to perform CRUD operations. Here are the most commonly used methods of the `EntityManager` interface. *(continued)*

Method signature	Description
`public EntityTransaction getTransaction();`	Retrieves a transaction object that can be used to manually start or end a transaction.
`public void joinTransaction();`	Asks an `EntityManager` to join an existing JTA transaction.

Don't worry too much if the methods aren't immediately obvious. Except for the methods related to the query API (`createQuery`, `createNamedQuery`, and `createNativeQuery`), we'll discuss them in detail in the coming sections. The few `EntityManager` interface methods that we didn't cover are rarely used, so we won't spend time discussing them. Once you've read and understood the material in this chapter, though, we encourage you to explore the methods on your own. The EJB 3 Java Persistence API 2.1 final specification is available at http://jcp.org/en/jsr/detail?id=338.

Even though JPA isn't container-centric like session beans or MDBs, entities still have a lifecycle. This is because they're "managed" by JPA in the sense that the persistence provider keeps track of them under the hood and even automatically synchronizes the entity state with the database when possible. We'll explore exactly how the entity lifecycle looks in the following section.

10.1.2 *Lifecycle of an entity*

An entity has a pretty simple lifecycle. Making sense of the lifecycle is easy once you grasp a straightforward concept: the `EntityManager` knows nothing about a POJO, regardless of how it's annotated, until you tell the manager to start treating the POJO like a JPA entity. This is the exact opposite of POJOs annotated to be session beans or MDBs, which are loaded and managed by the container as soon as the application starts. Moreover, the default behavior of the `EntityManager` is to manage an entity for as short a time as possible. Again, this is the opposite of container-managed beans, which remain managed until the application is shut down.

An entity that the `EntityManager` is keeping track of is considered *attached* or *managed*. On the other hand, when an `EntityManager` stops managing an entity, the entity is said to be *detached*. An entity that was never managed at any point is called *transient* or *new*. Figure 10.2 summarizes the entity lifecycle.

Let's take a close look at the managed and detached states.

MANAGED ENTITIES

When we talk about managing an entity's state, what we mean is that the `EntityManager` makes sure that the entity's data is synchronized with the database. The `EntityManager` ensures this by doing two things. First, as soon as you ask an `EntityManager` to start managing an entity, it synchronizes the entity's state with the database. Second,

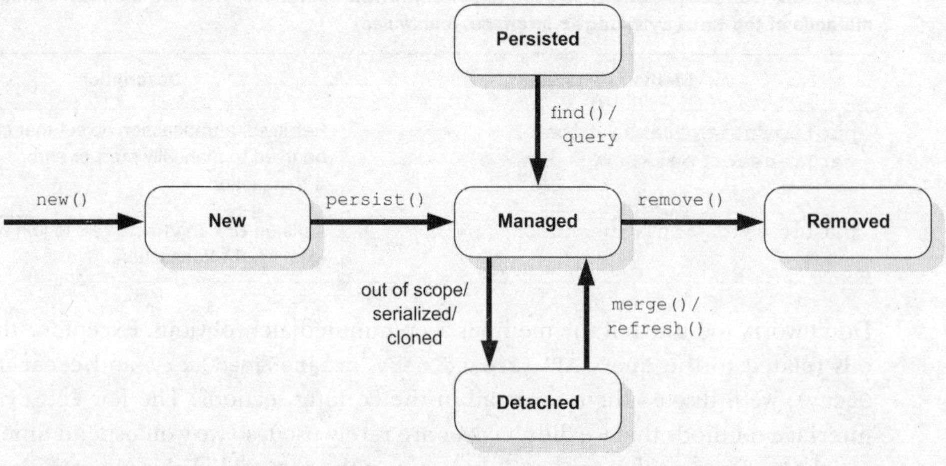

Figure 10.2 An entity becomes managed when you persist, merge, or retrieve it. A managed entity becomes detached when it's out of scope, removed, serialized, or cloned.

until the entity is no longer managed, the `EntityManager` ensures that changes to the entity's data (caused by entity method invocations, for example) are reflected in the database. The `EntityManager` accomplishes this feat by holding an object reference to the managed entity and periodically checking for data freshness. If the `EntityManager` finds that any of the entity's data has changed, it automatically synchronizes the changes with the database. The `EntityManager` stops managing the entity when the entity is either deleted or moves out of the persistence provider's reach.

An entity can become attached to the `EntityManager`'s context when you pass the entity to the `persist` or `merge` methods. An entity also becomes attached when you retrieve using the `find` method or a query within a transaction. The state of the entity determines which method you'll use. A managed entity can always be immediately refreshed with the latest database data by calling the `refresh` method.

When an entity is first instantiated, as in the following snippet, it's in the new or transient state because the `EntityManager` doesn't know it exists yet:

```
Bid bid = new Bid();
```

Therefore, the entity instance isn't managed yet. It'll become managed if the `EntityManager`'s `persist` method creates a new record in the database corresponding to the entity. This would be the most natural way to attach the `Bid` entity in the previous snippet to the `EntityManager`'s context:

```
manager.persist(bid);
```

A managed entity becomes detached when it's out of scope, removed, serialized, or cloned. For example, the instance of the `Bid` entity will become detached when the underlying transaction commits.

An entity retrieved from the database using the EntityManager's find method or one of the query methods is attached if retrieved within a transactional context. A retrieved instance of the entity becomes detached immediately if there's no associated transaction.

If you have a detached entity, you have two methods to reattach it. The first is by using the merge method. The merge method accepts a detached entity as a parameter and returns an attached entity. The merge method will use the detached entity parameter to find the database data again and create a new attached entity. It'll then copy any changes from the detached entity parameter into the new attached entity. The method then returns the new attached entity. Before the transaction is ended, any changes to this new attached entity are persisted to the database; therefore, the database gets updated with the new values from the detached entity parameter.

The second method is find. Use the primary key of your detached entity to query the database and return a new attached entity. Because we're talking about detached entities, we'll cover them in more detail next.

DETACHED ENTITIES

A detached entity is an entity that's no longer managed by the EntityManager and there's no guarantee that the state of the entity is in synch with the database. Detachment and merge operations become handy when you want to pass an entity across application tiers. For example, you can detach an entity and pass it to the web tier, then update it and send it back to the EJB tier, where you can merge the detached entity to the persistence context.

The usual way entities become detached is a little subtler. Essentially, an attached entity becomes detached as soon as it goes out of the EntityManager context's scope. Think of this as the expiration of the invisible link between an entity and the EntityManager at the end of a logical unit of work or a session. An EntityManager session could be limited to a single method call or span an arbitrary length of time. (Reminds you of session beans, doesn't it? As you'll soon see, this isn't entirely an accident.) For an EntityManager whose session is limited to a method call, all entities attached to it become detached as soon as a method returns, even if the entity objects are used outside the method. If this isn't crystal clear right now, it will be once we talk about the EntityManager's persistence context in the next section.

Entity instances also become detached through cloning or serialization. This is because the EntityManager quite literally keeps track of entities through Java object references. Because cloned or serialized instances don't have the same object references as the original managed entity, the EntityManager has no way of knowing they exist. This scenario occurs most often in situations where entities are sent across the network for session bean remote method calls.

In addition, if you call the clear method of EntityManager, it forces all entities in the persistence context to be detached. Calling the EntityManager's remove method will also detach an entity. This makes perfect sense because this method removes the data associated with the entity from the database. As far as the EntityManager is concerned, the entity no longer exists, so there's no need to continue managing it. For your `Bid` entity, this would be an apt demise:

```
manager.remove(bid);
```

A good way to remember the entity lifecycle is through a convenient analogy. Think of an entity as an aircraft and the `EntityManager` as the air traffic controller. When an entity is outside the range of air traffic control, it's "detached" or "new." But when it does come into range (managed), the traffic controller manages the aircraft's movement (state synchronized with database). Eventually, a grounded aircraft is guided into takeoff and goes out of airport range again (detached), at which point the pilot is free to follow their own flight plan (modifying a detached entity without the state being managed).

The *persistence context scope* is the equivalent of airport radar range. It's critical to understand how the persistence context works to use managed entities effectively. We'll examine the relationship between the persistence context, its scope, and the `EntityManager` in the next section.

10.1.3 Persistence context, scopes, and the EntityManager

The persistence context plays a vital role in the internal functionality of the `EntityManager`. Although you perform persistence operations by invoking methods on the `EntityManager`, the `EntityManager` itself doesn't directly keep track of the lifecycle of an individual entity. In reality, the `EntityManager` delegates the task of managing the entity state to the currently available persistence context.

In a very simple sense, a persistence context is a self-contained collection of entities managed by an `EntityManager` during a given persistence scope. The persistence scope is the duration of time a given set of entities remains managed.

The best way to understand this is to start by examining what the various persistence scopes are and what they do and then backtrack to the meaning of the term. We'll explain how the persistence context and persistence scope relate to the `EntityManager` by first exploring what the persistence scope is.

There are two different types of persistence scopes: *transaction* and *extended.*

TRANSACTION-SCOPED ENTITYMANAGER

An `EntityManager` associated with a transaction-scoped persistence context is known as a *transaction-scoped* `EntityManager`. If a persistence context is under transaction scope, entities attached during a transaction are automatically detached when the transaction ends. (All persistence operations that may result in data changes must be performed inside a transaction, no matter what the persistence scope is.) In other words, the persistence context keeps managing entities while the transaction it's enclosed by is active. Once the persistence context detects that a transaction has either been rolled back or committed, it'll detach all managed entities after making sure that all data changes until that point are synchronized with the database.

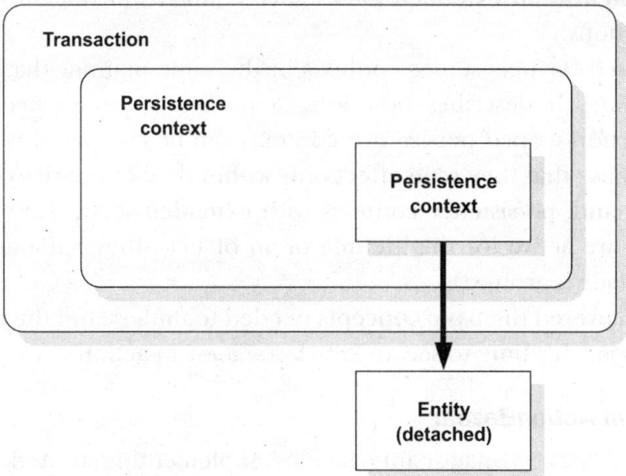

Figure 10.3 Transaction-scoped persistence contexts keep entities attached only within the boundaries of the enclosing transaction.

Figure 10.3 depicts this relationship between entities, the transaction persistence scope, and persistence contexts.

EXTENDED-SCOPED ENTITYMANAGER

The lifespan of the extended `EntityManager` lasts across multiple transactions. An extended-scoped `EntityManager` can only be used with stateful session beans and lasts as long as the bean instance is alive. Therefore, in persistence contexts with extended scope, how long entities remain managed has nothing to do with transaction boundaries. Once attached, entities stay managed as long as the `EntityManager` instance is around. As an example, for a stateful session bean, an `EntityManager` with extended scope will keep managing all attached entities until the `EntityManager` is closed as the bean itself is destroyed. As figure 10.4 shows, this means that unless explicitly detached through a `remove` method to end the life of the stateful bean

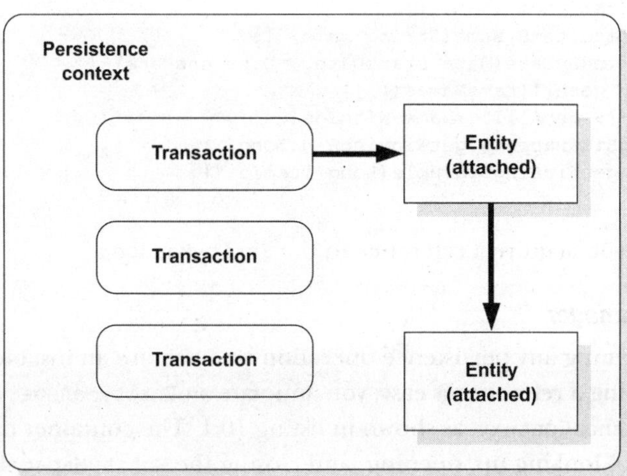

Figure 10.4 For an extended persistence context, once an entity is attached in any given transaction, it's managed for all transactions in the lifetime of the persistence context.

instance, entities attached to an extended persistence context will remain managed across multiple transactions.

The term *scope* is used for persistence contexts in the same manner that it's used for Java variable scoping. It describes how long a particular persistence context remains active. Transaction-scoped persistence contexts can be compared to method local variables, in the sense that they're in effect only within the boundaries of a transaction. On the other hand, persistence contexts with extended scope are more like instance variables that are active for the lifetime of an object—they hang around as long as the `EntityManager` is around.

At this point, we've covered the basic concepts needed to understand the functionality of the `EntityManager`. It's time to see an `EntityManager` in action.

10.1.4 Using EntityManager in ActionBazaar

You'll explore the EJB 3 `EntityManager` interface by implementing an ActionBazaar component. You'll implement the `ItemManagerBean` stateless session bean used to provide the operations to manipulate items. As listing 10.1 demonstrates, the session bean provides methods for adding, updating, and removing `Item` entities using the JPA `EntityManager`. This is a good bean on which to focus because items are at the heart of the ActionBazaar application. Users list items for auction and bid on items, and orders are generated for winning bids.

Listing 10.1 `ItemManager` performs basic CRUD operations for items

```
@Stateless
public class ItemManager {
  @PersistenceContext
  private EntityManager entityManager;
  public void addItem(String name, String description, byte[] picture,
    BigDecimal initialPrice, long sellerId){}
  public void saveItem(Item item) {}
  public void deleteItem(Item item) {}
  public Item updateItem(Item item) {}
  public List<Item> findItemByName(String name) {}
  public List<Item> findByDate(Date startDate , Date endDate) {}
  public List<String> getAllItemsNames() {}
  public List<Object[]> getAllItemNamesWithIds() {}
  public List<WinningBidWrapper> getWinningBid(Long itemId) {}
  public List<Tuple> getWinningBidTuple(Long itemId) {}
}
```

Inject an EntityManager

Let's next look at how you acquire a reference to the `EntityManager`.

10.1.5 Injecting the EntityManager

The first step to performing any persistence operation is to acquire an instance of the `EntityManager`. Acquiring a reference is easy; you annotate an `EntityManager` member variable with `@PersistenceContext`, as shown in listing 10.1. The container takes care of the mundane tasks of looking up, opening, and closing the `EntityManager` behind the scenes. In addition, unless specified, injected EntityManagers have transaction scope by default. To better understand how injection is performed, let's take a look at the annotation:

```
@Target(value = {ElementType.TYPE, ElementType.METHOD, ElementType.FIELD})
@Retention(value = RetentionPolicy.RUNTIME)
public @interface PersistenceContext {
  public String name() default "";
  public String unitName() default "";
  public PersistenceContextType type() default
     PersistenceContextType.TRANSACTION;
  public PersistenceProperty[] properties() default {};
}
```

The first element of the annotation, name, specifies the JNDI name of the persistence context. This element is used in the unlikely case that you must explicitly mention the JNDI name for a given container implementation to be able to look up an EntityManager. In most situations, leaving this element empty is fine, except when you use @PersistenceContext at the class level to establish a reference to the persistence context.

The unitName element specifies the name of the persistence unit. A persistence unit is a grouping of entities used in an application. The idea is useful when you have a large Java EE application and would like to separate it into several logical areas (think Java packages). For example, ActionBazaar entities could be grouped into general and admin units.

Persistence units can't be set up using code; you must configure them through the persistence.xml deployment descriptor. We cover configuration of persistence units in chapter 13. For now, all you need to understand is that to acquire an EntityManager for a specific persistence unit—for example, admin in ActionBazaar—you'd specify the unit as follows:

```
@PersistenceContext(unitName="admin")
EntityManager entityManager
```

In the event that a Java EE module has a single persistence unit, specifying the unitName might seem redundant. Most persistence providers will resolve the unit correctly if you don't specify a unitName. But it's good practice to specify the unitName because the specification isn't clear on the behavior if one isn't provided.

ENTITYMANAGER SCOPING

The element type specifies the EntityManager scope. As noted, for a container-managed EntityManager, scope can be either transaction or extended. If the type attribute isn't specified, the scope defaults to TRANSACTION. So, not surprisingly, the typical usage of the type element is to specify EXTENDED for an EntityManager. The code would like the following:

```
@PersistenceContext(type=PersistenceContexType.EXTENDED)
EntityManager entityManager;
```

You aren't allowed to use extended persistence scope for stateless session beans or MDBs. The reason is pretty obvious, because the purpose of the extended scope is to extend across method invocations on a bean, even if each method invocation is a separate transaction. Because neither stateless session beans nor MDBs are supposed to implement such functionality, it makes no sense to support extended scope for these bean types. On the other hand, extended persistence scope is ideal for stateful session beans. An underlying `EntityManager` with extended scope could be used to cache and maintain the application domain across an arbitrary number of method invocations from the client. More importantly, this can be done without giving up on method-level transaction granularity (most likely using CMT).

> **NOTE** The real power of container-managed `EntityManagers` lies in the high degree of abstraction they offer. Behind the scenes, the container instantiates `EntityManagers`, binds them to JNDI, injects them into beans on demand, and closes them when they're no longer needed (typically when a bean is destroyed).

It's difficult to appreciate the amount of menial code the container takes care of until you see the alternative. Keep this in mind when looking at the next section on directly accessing the `EntityManagerFactory`. Note that `EntityManagers` aren't thread-safe—this means that special care must be taken when injecting `EntityManagers` into CDI beans, servlets, JSF beans, and the like.

ENTITYMANAGERS AND THREAD SAFETY

`EntityManagers` aren't thread-safe and shouldn't be used in situations where more than one thread may access them. This means that it's dangerous to use `EntityManagers` in servlets or JSP pages. A servlet is instantiated once and handles multiple requests concurrently. Although the application may appear to work correctly in development or in light testing, once the application comes under increased load it may behave unpredictably. It's best to use `EntityManagers` from within EJBs. If you must access the `EntityManager` directly, you can use the following code snippet or access the `EntityManagerFactory`:

```
@PersistenceContext(name="pu/actionBazaar" unitName="ActionBazaar")
public class ItemServlet extends HttpServlet {
  @Resource
  private UserTransaction ut;
  public void service(HttpSerlvetRequest req, HttpServletResponse resp)
    throws ServletException, IOException {
    Context ctx = new InitialContext();
    EntityManager em = (EntityManager)ctx.lookup("java:comp/env/pu/
     actionBazaar");
    ...
    ut.begin();
    em.persist(item);
    ut.commit();
    ...
  }
}
```

The other alternative is to use an application-managed `EntityManager` with a JTA transaction. It's worth noting that `EntityManagerFactory` is thread-safe.

10.1.6 *Injecting the EntityManagerFactory*

In the previous section you saw how the container injects the `EntityManager`. When the container injects the `EntityManager`, you have very little control over the `EntityManager`'s lifecycle. In some situations you want fine-grained control over the lifecycle of the `EntityManager` as well as transaction management. For this reason, as well as to maintain flexibility, JPA provides injection support for the `EntityManagerFactory`. Using the `EntityManagerFactory`, you can get `EntityManager` instances that you can fully control. An example of the `ItemManager` controlling its `EntityManager` instance manually is shown in the following listing.

Listing 10.2 `ItemManager` using an application-managed `EntityManager`

```
@Stateless
public class ItemManager {
  @PersistenceUnit
  private EntityManagerFactory entityManagerFactory;      ❶ Injects EntityManagerFactory instance
  private EntityManager entityManager;

  @PostConstruct
  private void init() {
    entityManager = entityManagerFactory.createEntityManager();   ❷ Creates an EntityManager
  }

  public Item updateItem(Item item) {
    entityManager.joinTransaction();          Explicitly joins
    entityManager.merge(item);                a JTA transaction
    return item;
  }

  @PreDestroy
  private void cleanup() {
    if(entityManager.isOpen()) {             ❸ Closes EntityManager
      entityManager.close();
    }
  }
```

The code in this listing is straightforward. First, an `EntityManagerFactory` is injected ❶. You create an `EntityManager` using the injected `EntityManagerFactory` after the bean is constructed ❷ and lose it ❸ before the bean is destroyed. This mirrors what the container does automatically with a container-managed `EntityManager`.

The `EntityManagerFactory` annotation is defined as follows:

```
@Target({TYPE, METHOD, FIELD})
@Retention(RUNTIME)
public @interface PersistenceUnit {
  String name() default "";
  String unitName() default "";
}
```

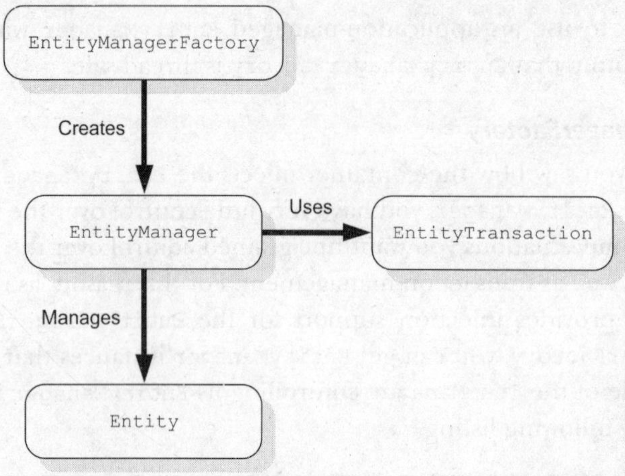

Figure 10.5 Relationships among the important JPA interfaces/classes when using an application-managed `EntityManager`

The `name` and `unitName` elements serve exactly the same purpose as they do for the `@PersistenceContext` annotation. Whereas the `name` element can be used to point to the JNDI name of the `EntityManagerFactory`, the `unitName` element is used to specify the name of the underlying persistence unit.

Figure 10.5 puts the relationship among the `EntityManagerFactory`, `EntityManager`, `EntityTransaction`, and `Entity` into context. We haven't discussed an `EntityTransaction`—it provides an API for fine-grained transaction management when you aren't delegating to the container.

As you can see in the listing, the `EntityManagerFactory` has a `createEntityManager` method for creating an application-managed `EntityManager`. Once you have a reference to an application-managed `EntityManager`, it's your responsibility to destroy it when you are finished; otherwise bad things can happen.

One thing to learn from this listing is that an application-managed `EntityManager` doesn't automatically participate in transaction management. Thus, you must use the `EntityTransaction` to join an existing transaction. Unless circumstances demand it, it's better to use the container-managed `EntityManager` because there are fewer manual steps—and fewer chances to misuse the API.

Now that you have a basic handle on the `EntityManager` and `EntityManagerFactory`, let's look at some of `EntityManager`'s persistence operations.

10.2 *Persistence operations*

The heart of the JPA API lies in the `EntityManager` operations, which we'll discuss in upcoming sections. As you might have noted in listing 10.1, although the `EntityManager` interface is small and simple, it's complete in its ability to provide an effective persistence infrastructure. In addition to the CRUD functionality introduced in listing 10.1, we'll cover a few less commonly used operations like flushing and refreshing.

Let's start our coverage in the most logical place: persisting new entities into the database.

10.2.1 Persisting entities

Recall that in listing 10.1 the `addItem` method persists an `Item` entity into the database. Because listing 10.1 was quite a few pages back, we'll repeat the `addItem` method body in the next listing. Although it isn't obvious, the code is especially helpful in understanding how entity relationships are persisted, which we'll look at in greater detail in a minute. For now, let's concentrate on the `persist` method itself.

Listing 10.3 Persisting entities

```
public void addItem(String name, String description, byte[] picture,
    BigDecimal initialPrice, long sellerId) {
  Item item = new Item();
  item.setItemName(name);
  item.setPicture(picture);
  item.setInitialPrice(initialPrice);
  BazaarAccount seller = entityManager.find(BazaarAccount.class,sellerId);
  item.setSeller(seller);
  entityManager.persist(item);          <-- Persists entity
}
```

A new `Item` entity corresponding to the record being added is first instantiated in the `addItem` method. All of the relevant `Item` entity data to be saved into the database, such as the item title and description, is then populated with the data passed in by the user. As you'll recall from chapter 9, the `Item` entity has a many-to-one relationship with the `Seller` entity. The related seller is retrieved using the `EntityManager`'s `find` method and set as a field of the `Item` entity. The `persist` method is then invoked to save the entity into the database, as shown in figure 10.6. Note that the `persist` method is intended to create new entity records in the database and not update existing ones. This means that you should make sure the identity or primary key of the entity to be persisted doesn't already exist in the database. If you try to persist an entity and the primary key already exists in the database, an `EntityExistsException` may be thrown either when the `persist` method is called or when the transaction is being committed.

If you try to persist an entity that violates another of the database's integrity constraints (such as an additional unique constraint), the persistence provider will throw an appropriate subclass of `javax.persistence.PersistenceException`, which wraps the database exception.

As noted earlier, the `persist` method also causes the entity to become managed as soon as the method returns. The `INSERT` statement (or statements) that creates the

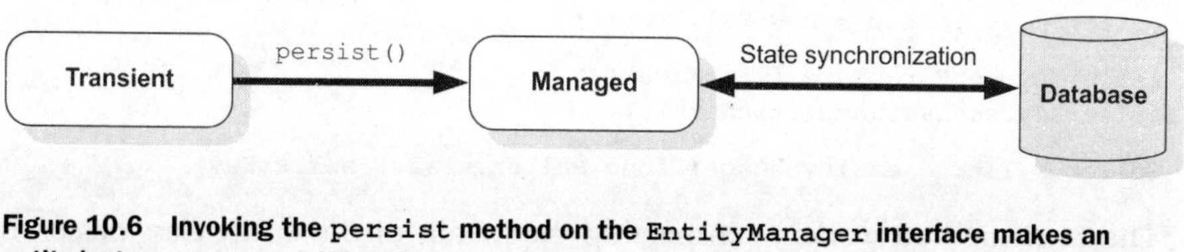

Figure 10.6 Invoking the `persist` method on the `EntityManager` interface makes an entity instance managed. When the transaction commits, the entity state is synchronized with the database.

record corresponding to the entity isn't necessarily issued immediately. For transaction-scoped `EntityManagers`, the statement is typically issued when the enclosing transaction is about to commit. In the example, this means the SQL statements are issued when the `addItem` method returns. For extended-scoped (or application-managed) `EntityManagers`, the `INSERT` statement is usually issued right before the `EntityManager` is closed. The `INSERT` statement can also be issued at any point when the `EntityManager` is flushed.

As mentioned earlier, all persistence operations that require database updates must be invoked within the scope of a transaction. If an enclosing transaction isn't present when the `persist` method is invoked, a `TransactionRequiredException` is thrown for a transaction-scoped entity manager. The same is true for the `EntityManager's` `flush`, `merge`, `refresh`, and `remove` methods.

10.2.2 Retrieving entities by key

JPA supports several ways to retrieve entity instances from the database. By far the simplest way is retrieving an entity by its primary key using the `find` method we introduced in listing 10.1. The other ways all involve using the query API and JPQL, which we'll discuss in chapter 11. Recall that the `find` method was used in the `addItem` method in listing 10.1 to retrieve the `Seller` instance corresponding to the `Item` to add:

```
Seller seller = entityManager.find(Seller.class, sellerId);
```

In this line of code, the first parameter of the `find` method specifies the Java type of the entity to be retrieved. The second parameter specifies the identity value for the entity instance to retrieve. Recall from chapter 9 that an entity identity can either be a simple Java type identified by the `@Id` annotation or a composite primary key class specified through the `@EmbeddedId` or `@IdClass` annotation. In the example in listing 10.1, the `find` method is passed a simple `java.lang.Long` value matching the `Seller` entity's `@Id` annotated identity, `sellerId`.

Although this isn't the case in listing 10.1, the `find` method is fully capable of supporting composite primary keys. To see how this code might look, assume for the sake of illustration that the identity of the `Seller` entity consists of the seller's first and last names instead of a simple numeric identifier. This identity is encapsulated in a composite primary key class annotated with the `@IdClass` annotation. The following listing shows how this identity class can be populated and passed to the `find` method.

Listing 10.4 Find by primary key using composite keys

```
SellerPK sellerKey = new SellerPK();

sellerKey.setFirstName(firstName);
sellerKey.setLastName(lastName);

Seller seller = entityManager.find(Seller.class, sellerKey);
```

The `find` method works by inspecting the details of the entity class passed in as the first parameter and generating a `SELECT` statement to retrieve the entity data. This generated `SELECT` statement is populated with the primary key values specified in the second parameter of the `find` method. For example, the `find` method in listing 10.1 could generate a `SELECT` statement that looks something like this:

```
SELECT * FROM SELLERS WHERE seller_id = 1
```

Note that if an entity instance matching the specified key doesn't exist in the database, the `find` method won't throw any exceptions. Instead, the `EntityManager` will return `null` or an empty entity, and your application must handle this situation. It isn't strictly necessary to call the `find` method in a transactional context. But the retrieved entity is detached unless a transaction context is available, so it's generally advisable to call the `find` method inside a transaction. One of the most important features of the `find` method is that it utilizes `EntityManager` caching. If your persistence provider supports caching and the entity already exists in the cache, then the `EntityManager` returns a cached instance of the entity instead of retrieving it from the database. Most persistence providers like Hibernate and Oracle TopLink support caching, so you can more or less count on this extremely valuable optimization.

There's one more important JPA feature geared toward application optimization—lazy and eager loading. The generated `SELECT` statement in the example attempts to retrieve all of the entity field data when the `find` method is invoked. In general, this is exactly what will happen for entity retrieval because it's the default behavior for JPA. But in some cases, this isn't desirable behavior. Fetch modes allow you to change this behavior to optimize application performance when needed.

ENTITY FETCH MODES

We briefly mentioned fetch modes in previous chapters but haven't discussed them in great detail. Discussing entity retrieval is an ideal place to fully explore fetch modes.

As we suggested, the `EntityManager` normally loads all entity instance data when an entity is retrieved from the database. In ORM-speak, this is called eager fetching, or eager loading. If you've ever dealt with application performance problems due to premature or inappropriate caching, you probably already know that eager fetching isn't always a good thing. The classic example we used in previous chapters is loading large binary objects (BLOBs), such as pictures. Unless you're developing a heavily graphics-oriented program such as an online photo album, it's unlikely that loading a picture as part of an entity used in a lot of places in the application is a good idea. Because loading BLOB data typically involves long-running, I/O-heavy operations, they should be loaded cautiously and only as needed. In general, this optimization strategy is called lazy fetching.

JPA has more than one mechanism to support lazy fetching. Specifying column fetch-mode using the `@Basic` annotation is the easiest one to understand. For example, you can set the fetch mode for the `picture` property on the `Item` entity to be lazy as follows:

```
@Column(name="PICTURE")
@Lob
@Basic(fetch=FetchType.LAZY)
```

```
    public byte[] getPicture() {
        return picture;
    }
```

A SELECT statement generated by the find method to retrieve Item entities won't load data from the ITEMS.PICTURE column into the picture field. Instead, the picture data will be automatically loaded from the database when the property is first accessed through the getPicture method.

Be advised, however, that lazy fetching is a double-edged sword. Specifying that a column be lazily fetched means that the EntityManager will issue an additional SELECT statement just to retrieve the picture data when the lazily loaded field is first accessed. In the extreme case, imagine what would happen if all entity data in an application is lazily loaded. This would mean that the database would be flooded with a large number of frivolous SELECT statements as entity data is accessed. Also, lazy fetching is an optional EJB 3 feature, which means not every persistence provider is guaranteed to implement it. You should check your provider's documentation before spending too much time figuring out which entity columns should be lazily fetched.

LOADING RELATED ENTITIES

One of the most intricate uses of fetch modes is to control the retrieval of related entities. Not surprisingly, the EntityManager's find method must retrieve all entities related to the one returned by the method. Let's take the ActionBazaar Item entity, an exceptionally good case because it has a many-to-one, a one-to-many, and two many-to-many relationships. The only relationship type not represented is one-to-one. The Item entity has a many-to-one relationship with the Seller entity (a seller can sell more than one item, but an item can be sold by only one seller), a one-to-many relationship with the Bid entity (more than one bid can be put on an item), and a many-to-many relationship with the Category entity (an item can belong to more than one category and a category contains multiple items). These relationships are depicted in figure 10.7.

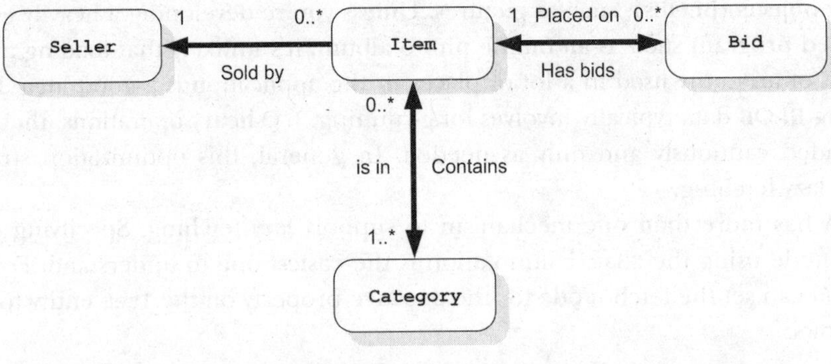

Figure 10.7 The Item entity is related to three other entities: Seller, Bid, and Category. The relationships to Item are many-to-one, one-to-many, and many-to-many, respectively.

When the find method returns an instance of an Item, it also automatically retrieves the Seller, Bid, and Category entities associated with the instance and populates them into their respective Item entity properties. As shown in listing 10.5, the single Seller entity associated with the Item is populated into the seller property, the Bid entities associated with an Item are populated into the bids list, and the Category entities the Item is listed under are populated into the categories property. It might surprise you to know some of these relationships are retrieved lazily.

All the relationship annotations you saw in chapter 9, including the @ManyToOne, @OneToMany, and @ManyToMany annotations, have a fetch element to control fetch modes, just like the @Basic annotation discussed in the previous section. None of the relationship annotations in the following listing specify the fetch element, so the default for each annotation takes effect.

Listing 10.5 Relationships in the Item entity

```
public class Item {
  @OneToMany(mappedBy = "item", cascade = CascadeType.ALL)      <-- One-to-many with Bids
  private List<Bid> bids;

  @ManyToOne                                                    <-- Many-to-one with sellers
  @JoinColumn(name = "SELLER_ID", referencedColumnName = "USER_ID")
  private BazaarAccount seller;

  @ManyToMany(mappedBy = "items")       <-- Many-to-many with categories
  private Set<Category> category;
  ...
}
```

By default, some of the relationship types are retrieved lazily and some are loaded eagerly. We'll discuss why each default makes sense as we go through each relationship retrieval case for the Item entity. The Seller associated with an Item is retrieved eagerly, because the fetch mode for the @ManyToOne annotation is defaulted to EAGER. To understand why this makes sense, it's helpful to understand how the EntityManager implements eager fetching. In effect, each eagerly fetched relationship turns into an additional JOIN tacked onto the basic SELECT statement to retrieve the entity. To see what this means, see how the SELECT statement for an eagerly fetched Seller record related to an Item looks in the following listing.

Listing 10.6 SELECT statement for eagerly fetched Seller related to an Item

```
SELECT
      *
FROM
      ITEMS
INNER JOIN               <-- Inner join for many-to-one
      SELLERS
ON
      ITEMS.SELLER_ID = SELLERS.SELLER_ID
WHERE ITEMS.ITEM_ID = 100
```

As the listing shows, an eager fetch means that the most natural way of retrieving the `Item` entity would be through a single `SELECT` statement using a `JOIN` between the `ITEMS` and `SELLERS` tables. It's important to note the fact that the `JOIN` will result in a single row, containing columns from both the `SELLERS` and `ITEMS` tables. In terms of database performance, this is more efficient than issuing one `SELECT` to retrieve the `Item` and issuing a separate `SELECT` to retrieve the related `Seller`. This is exactly what would have happened in a case of lazy fetching, and the second `SELECT` for retrieving the `Seller` will be issued when the `Item's` `seller` property is first accessed. Pretty much the same thing applies to the `@OneToOne` annotation, so the default for it is also eager loading. More specifically, the `JOIN` to implement the relationship would result in a fairly efficient single combined row in all cases.

LAZY VERSUS EAGER LOADING OF RELATED ENTITIES

In contrast, the `@OneToMany` and `@ManyToMany` annotations are defaulted to lazy loading. The critical difference is that for both of these relationship types, more than one entity is matched to the retrieved entity. Think about `Category` entities related to a retrieved `Item`, for example. `JOIN`s implementing eagerly loaded one-to-many and many-to-many relationships usually return more than one row. In particular, a row is returned for every related entity matched.

The problem becomes particularly obvious when you consider what happens when multiple `Item` entities are retrieved at one time (for example, as the result of a JPQL query, discussed in the next chapter). ($N_1 + N_2 + ... + N_x$) rows would be returned, where N_i is the number of related `Category` entities for the ith `Item` record. For non-trivial numbers of N and i, the retrieved result set could be quite large, potentially causing significant database performance issues. This is why JPA makes the conservative assumption of defaulting to lazy loading for `@OneToMany` and `@ManyToMany` annotations.

Table 10.2 lists the default fetch behavior for each type of relationship annotation.

Table 10.2 Behavior of loading an associated entity is different for each kind of association by default. You can change the loading behavior by specifying the `fetch` element with the relationship.

Relationship type	Default fetch behavior	Number of entities retrieved
One-to-one	`EAGER`	Single entity retrieved
One-to-many	`LAZY`	Collection of entities retrieved
Many-to-one	`EAGER`	Single entity retrieved
Many-to-many	`LAZY`	Collection of entities retrieved

The relationship defaults aren't right for all circumstances, however. Although the eager fetching strategy makes sense for one-to-one and many-to-one relationships under most circumstances, it's a bad idea in some cases. For example, if an entity contains a large number of one-to-one and many-to-one relationships, eagerly loading all of them would result in a large number of `JOIN`s chained together. Executing a relatively large number of JOINs can be just as bad as loading an $(N_1 + N_2 + ... + N_x)$ result set. If this proves to be a performance problem, some of the relationships should be loaded lazily. Here's an example of explicitly specifying the fetch mode for a relationship (it happens to be the familiar Seller property of the Item entity):

```
@ManyToOne(fetch=FetchType.LAZY)
public Seller getSeller() {
    return seller;
}
```

You shouldn't take the default lazy loading strategy of the @OneToMany and @ManyToMany annotations for granted. For particularly large data sets, this can result in a huge number of SELECTs being generated against the database. This is known as the $N+1$ problem, where 1 stands for the SELECT statement for the originating entity and N stands for the SELECT statement that retrieves each related entity. In some cases, you might discover that you're better off using eager loading even for @OneToMany and @ManyToMany annotations.

Unfortunately, the choice of fetch modes isn't cut and dried, and it depends on a whole host of factors, including the database vendor's optimization strategy, database design, data volume, and application usage patterns. In the real world, ultimately these choices are often made through trial and error. Luckily, with JPA, performance tuning just means a few configuration changes here and there as opposed to time-consuming code modifications.

Having discussed entity retrieval, we can now move into the third operation of the CRUD sequence: updating entities.

10.2.3 Updating entities

Recall that the EntityManager makes sure that changes made to attached entities are always saved into the database behind the scenes. This means that for the most part, the application doesn't need to worry about manually calling any methods to update the entity. This is perhaps the most elegant feature of ORM-based persistence because this hides data synchronization behind the scenes and truly allows entities to behave like POJOs. Take the code in the next listing, which updates an item that's being auctioned. Often after an item has been listed it's necessary to update its description or picture if the item fails to attract attention.

Listing 10.7 Transparent management of attached entities

```
@TransactionAttribute(REQUIRED)
public void updateItem(Long itemId, byte picture[],
    String description, StarRating starRating) {
  Item item = this.findItem(itemId);
  item.setPicture(picture);                    | Saves changes
  item.setDescription(description);            | to entity
  item.setStarRating(starRating);              | transparently
}
```

Other than looking up the item, little is done using the EntityManager in the updateItem method. After each method is invoked, the EntityManager ensures that the changes are persisted to the database. Typically, all changes are persisted when the transaction ends and the EntityManager attempts to commit all the changes. But you can force persistence at any time by using the EntityManager flush method. When flush is called, it applies to all entities managed in the persistence context. Flushing is controlled by the FlushModeType. FlushTypeMode.AUTO means to persist to the database at query execution time. FlushTypeMode.COMMIT will persist to the database when the transaction ends and is committed.

DETACHMENT AND MERGE OPERATIONS

Although managed entities are extremely useful, the problem is that it's difficult to keep entities attached at all times. Often the entities will need to be detached and serialized at the web tier where the entity is changed, outside the scope of the EntityManager. In addition, recall that stateless session beans can't guarantee that calls from the same client will be serviced by the same bean instance. This means that there's no guarantee an entity will be handled by the same EntityManager instance across method calls, thus making automated persistence ineffective.

This is exactly the model that the ItemManager session bean introduced in listing 10.1 assumes. The EntityManager used for the bean has TRANSACTION scope. Because the bean uses CMT, entities become detached when transactions end the method. This means that entities returned by the session bean to its clients are always detached, just like the newly created Item entity returned by the ItemManager's addItem method:

```
public Item addItem(String title, String description,
  byte[] picture, double initialPrice, long sellerId) {
  Item item = new Item();
  item.setTitle(title);
  ...
  entityManager.persist(item);
  return item;
}
```

At some point you'll want to reattach the entity to a persistence context to synchronize it with the database. The EntityManager's merge method is designed to do just that (see figure 10.8).

You should remember that like all attached entities, the entity passed to the merge method isn't necessarily synchronized with the database immediately, but it's guaranteed to be synchronized with the database sooner or later. You can use the merge method in the ItemManager bean in the most obvious way possible—to update the database with an existing Item:

```
public Item updateItem(Item item) {
  entityManager.merge(item);
  return item;
}
```

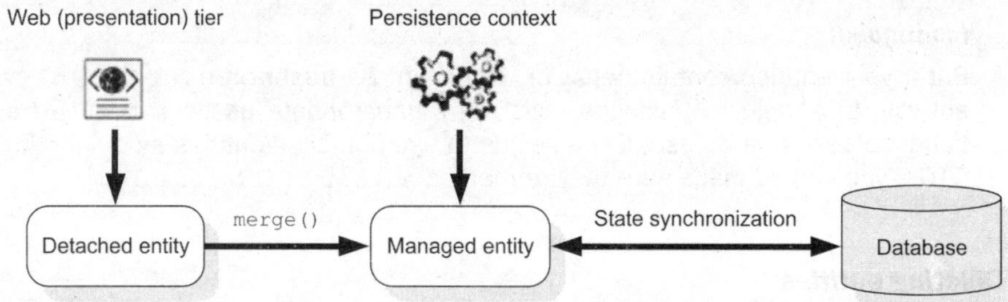

Figure 10.8 An entity instance can be detached and serialized to a separate tier where the client makes changes to the entity and sends it back to the server. The server can use a merge operation to attach the entity to the persistence context.

As soon as the `updateItem` method returns, the database is updated with the data from the `Item` entity. The `merge` method must only be used for an entity that exists in the database. An attempt to merge a nonexistent entity will result in an `IllegalArgumentException`. The same is true if the `EntityManager` detects that the entity you're trying to merge has already been deleted through the `remove` method, even if the `DELETE` statement hasn't been issued yet.

MERGING RELATIONSHIPS

By default, entities associated with the entity being merged aren't merged as well. For example, the `Seller`, `Bid`, and `Category` entities related to the `Item` aren't merged when the `Item` is merged in the previous code snippet. But this behavior can be controlled using the `cascade` element of the `@OneToOne`, `@OneToMany`, `@ManyToOne`, and `@ManyToMany` annotations. The `cascade` element is added to the annotation on the owning side of the relationship. If the `cascade` element is set to either `ALL` or `MERGE`, the related entities are merged. For example, the following code will cause the `Seller` entity related to the `Item` to be merged because the `cascade` element is set to `MERGE`:

```
public class Item {
    @ManyToOne(cascade=CascadeType.MERGE)
    public Seller getSeller() {
```

Note that as in most of the `EntityManager`'s methods, the `merge` method must be called from a transactional context or it'll throw a `TransactionRequiredException`. We'll now move on to the final element of the CRUD sequence: deleting an entity.

> **Detached entities and the DTO anti-pattern**
>
> If you've spent even a moderate amount of time using EJB 2, you're probably thoroughly familiar with the data transfer object (DTO) anti-pattern. In a sense, the DTO anti-pattern was necessary because of entity beans. The fact that EJB 3 detached entities are nothing but POJOs makes the DTO anti-pattern less of a necessity of life. Instead of having to create separate DTOs from domain data just to pass back and forth between the business and presentation layers, you may simply pass detached entities. This is exactly the model followed in this chapter.

> ***(continued)***
>
> But if your entities contain behavior, you might be better off using the DTO pattern anyway, to safeguard business logic from inappropriate usage outside a transactional context. In any case, if you decide to use detached entities as a substitute for DTOs, you should make sure they're marked `java.io.Serializable`.

10.2.4 Deleting entities

The `deleteItem` method in the `ItemManagerBean` in listing 10.1 deletes an `Item` from the database. An important detail to notice about the `deleteItem` method (repeated next) is that the `Item` to be deleted was first attached to the `EntityManager` using the `merge` method:

```
public void deleteItem(Item item) {
  entityManager.remove(entityManager.merge(item));
}
```

This is because the `remove` method can only delete currently attached entities and the `Item` entity being passed to the `deleteItem` method isn't managed. If a detached entity is passed to the `remove` method, it throws an `IllegalArgumentException`. Before the `deleteItem` method returns, the `Item` record will be deleted from the database using a `DELETE` statement like this:

```
DELETE FROM ITEMS WHERE item_id = 1
```

Just as with the `persist` and `merge` methods, the `DELETE` statement isn't necessarily issued immediately but is guaranteed to be issued at some point. Meanwhile, the `EntityManager` marks the entity as removed so that no further changes to it are synchronized (as we noted in the previous section).

CASCADING REMOVE OPERATIONS

Just as with merging and persisting entities, you must set the cascade element of a relationship annotation to either `ALL` or `REMOVE` for related entities to be removed with the one passed to the `remove` method. For example, you can specify that the `BillingInfo` entity related to a `Bidder` be removed with the owning `Bidder` entity as follows:

```
@Entity
public class Bidder {
  @OneToOne(cascade=CascadeType.REMOVE)
  public BillingInfo setBillingInfo() {
```

From a common usage perspective, this setup makes perfect sense. There's no reason for a `BillingInfo` entity to hang around if the enclosing `Bidder` entity it's related to is removed. When it comes down to it, the business domain determines if deletes should be cascaded. In general, you might find that the only relationship types where cascading removal makes sense are one-to-one and one-to-many. You should be careful when using the cascade delete because the related entity you're cascading the `delete` to may be related to other entities you don't know about. For example, assume there's a one-to-many relationship between the `Seller` and `Item` entities and you're using cascade delete to remove a `Seller` and its related `Items`. Remember the fact that other entities such as `Category` also hold references to the `Items` you're deleting, and those relationships would become meaningless!

HANDLING RELATIONSHIPS

If your intent was really to cascade-delete the `Items` associated with the `Seller`, you should iterate over all instances of `Category` that reference the deleted `Items` and remove the relationships first, as follows:

```
List<Category> categories = getAllCategories();
List<Item> items = seller.getItems();
for (Item item: items) {
  for (Category category: categories) {
    category.getItems().remove(item);
  }
}
entityManager.remove(seller);
```

The code gets all instances of `Category` in the system and makes sure that all `Items` related to the `Seller` being deleted are removed from referencing `Lists` first. It then proceeds with removing the `Seller`, cascading the remove to the related `Items`.

Not surprisingly, the `remove` method must be called from a transactional context or it'll throw a `TransactionRequiredException`. Also, trying to remove an already removed entity will raise an `IllegalArgumentException`.

Having finished the basic `EntityManager` CRUD operations, let's now move on to the two remaining major persistence operations: flushing data to the database and refreshing from the database.

10.3 Entity queries

Queries are as important as storing the data. Once you get the data into a database, you need a mechanism to query the data. With JPA you have several different options for querying data, ranging from JQL to the Criteria API, native SQL queries, and stored procedure queries. Each has its own advantages and disadvantages depending on what you're trying to do.

Up to this point you've retrieved entities using the `find` method on an `EntityManager` instance. The `find` method enables you to perform a query that retrieves an entity using its primary key. Although this is extremely useful, most of the time you want to search on something else. To do so, you need to make use of the `javax.persistence.Query` interface. This interface is used to define, bind parameters, execute, and paginate.

There are several different types of queries that we'll examine starting in this chapter and continuing in the next chapter:

- `javax.persistence.Query`—Represents either a JPQL or native SQL query. If a query is typed, a `javax.persistence.TypeQuery<T>` is returned, thus eliminating the need to cast results.

- javax.persistence.StoredProcedureQuery—Represents a query that invokes a stored procedure.
- javax.persistence.criteria.CriteriaQuery—Represents a query that's constructed using the meta-model.

In addition to these types of queries, you also have dynamic and named queries. Dynamic queries are queries created in code—the query is passed off to the EntityManager. A named query is a query that's either configured in an annotation or pulled from an ORM XML configuration file. A named query consolidates queries for reuse and keeps them from becoming buried in code. Let's examine both of these queries in more depth.

> **Query versus abstract query**
>
> We cover several different types of queries in this chapter including JPQL, SQL (native), and Criteria. javax.persistence.criteria.CriteriaQuery and javax.persistence.Query don't share a common ancestor despite the apparent similarity in their names. The two APIs are very different. As you'll see with the Criteria Query API, you construct queries using Java objects and not free-form strings that are interpreted at runtime.

10.3.1 *Dynamic queries*

Dynamic queries are created on the fly and embedded within the code. Dynamic queries are typically only used once—that is, the query isn't shared among multiple components in an application. If you're already using JDBC (Statements or PreparedStatements), this approach will look very familiar. Dynamic queries can contain either JPQL or native SQL. A simple example is as follows:

```
@PersistenceContext
private EntityManager entityManager;
public List<Category> findAllCategories() {
  TypedQuery<Category> query = entityManager.createQuery(
     "SELECT c FROM Category c",Category.class);
  return query.getResultList();
}
```

In this example the EntityManager provided by dependency injection is used. Then an instance of a TypedQuery is created, which leverages Java's Generics so that you don't have to cast the results. Once you have the query, the final step is to invoke getResultList() to execute and retrieve the results of the query. You can also use dynamic queries to execute both native SQL and stored procedure queries as well—with createNativeQuery and createStoredProcedureQuery, respectively.

10.3.2 *Named queries*

Unlike a dynamic query, a named query must be created before it can be used. It's defined in the entity using annotations or in the XML file defining O/R mapping metadata. A named query is accessed by its name, thus enabling its use across multiple components in an application. A named query is defined using the `@javax.persistence.NamedQuery` annotation:

```
@Entity
@NamedQuery(
  name = "findAllCategories",
  query = "SELECT c FROM Category c WHERE c.categoryName
    LIKE :categoryName ")
  public class Category implements Serializable {
    public List<Category> findAllCategories() {
      TypedQuery<Category> query =
       entityManager.createNamedQuery("findAllCategories",Category.class);
    }

  }
```

For a complex application, you'll probably have multiple named queries. In that case, you can use the `@javax.persistence.NamedQueries` annotation to specify multiple named queries like this:

```
@Entity
@NamedQueries({
  @NamedQuery(
    name = "findCategoryByName",
    query = "SELECT c FROM Category c WHERE c.categoryName
      LIKE :categoryName order by c.categoryId"
  ),
  @NamedQuery(
    name = "findCategoryByUser",
    query = "SELECT c FROM Category c JOIN c.user u
      WHERE u.userId = ?1"
)})
@Table(name = "CATEGORIES")
public class Category implements Serializable {
  ...
}
```

> **NOTE** Keep in mind that a named query is scoped with a persistence unit and therefore must have a unique name. We recommend that you devise a naming convention for your applications that will avoid duplicate names for named queries.

This was just a brief introduction to querying entities. With the `find`, `createQuery`, `createNativeQuery`, and `createStoredProcedureQuery` methods on `EntityManager`, you can get any entity filled with just about any data from your database that you need. Learning the ins and outs of JPQL, the JPA query language for entities, will be the topic of the next chapter. You'll learn exactly what you need to do to get the data you want.

10.4 Summary

In this chapter we covered the `EntityManager`. You learned how to use the `EntityManager` to persist, find, merge, and remove entities—the `EntityManager` equivalent of the basic database CRUD operations. We also discussed persistence contexts and scopes, new/detached objects versus managed objects, and the concept of merging objects. In addition, we briefly mentioned application-managed `EntityManager` that can be used for fine-grained control of persistence and transactions via the `EntityManagerFactory`. Following the discussion of the `EntityManager`, we briefly discussed querying—first discussing static versus dynamic queries and then covering basic JPA queries with simple JPQL, Criteria API, and native queries.

In the next chapter, we'll cover JPQL in depth. You'll learn the syntax you need to get entities with just the data you want. We'll also cover the Criteria API—a type-safe Java code approach to querying for entities.

11 JPQL

This chapter covers

- Creating and executing queries
- The Java Persistence Query Language
- Leveraging the criteria API
- Using SQL queries
- Invoking stored procedures

Chapter 10 introduced the basics of the `EntityManager` API. You saw how to get an instance of `EntityManager` from the container and use it to perform the basic CRUD operations (create, read, update, delete) on entities. Create, update, and delete are relatively simple operations that chapter 10 covered in full. Read, however, is much more complicated because of the variety of ways to query database data.

In this chapter we'll explore read in depth by looking at the Java Persistence Query Language (JPQL), the criteria API, and native SQL. Each method tackles the problem of querying objects in a relational database using a slightly different approach and addresses a different set of concerns and problems. We'll round out the chapter looking at support for invoking stored procedures—a new feature in Java EE 7. Let's start this chapter by diving right in to JPQL.

11.1 Introducing JPQL

The meat of this chapter covers the ins and outs of JPQL. We'll start with a definition of the language, provide numerous examples illustrating almost every aspect, and include some little-known tips along the way.

There was little debate among the EJB 3 Expert Group on which to use as the standard query language for JPA. They agreed to use JPQL. JPQL is an extension of EJB QL, the query language of EJB 2. It didn't make sense to invent yet another language for such a well-known domain, so the group voted unanimously to make EJB QL the query language of choice and to address all its previous limitations. The use of JPQL will make the migration of EJB 2 entity beans to EJB 3 persistence easier.

> **How is JPQL different from SQL?**
> JPQL operates on classes and objects (entities) in the Java space. SQL operates on tables, columns, and rows in the database space. Although JPQL and SQL look similar, they operate in two very different worlds.

The JPQL query parser or processor engine of a persistence provider, as shown in figure 11.1, translates the JPQL query into native SQL for the database being used by the persistence provider.

JPQL looks so much like SQL that it's easy to forget you're looking at JPQL when you're reviewing source code. Just remember that although JPQL may look like SQL, you'll need to be aware of the differences discussed in this chapter to effectively use and troubleshoot JPQL in your programs.

All this talk about JPQL queries has piqued your interest, hasn't it? What do you say to continuing this line of thinking by going over the types of statements JPQL supports? Then we'll discuss different elements of a JPQL statement, such as `FROM` and `SELECT` clauses, conditional statements, subqueries, and various types of functions. Finally, we'll take a look at update and delete statements.

11.1.1 Statement types

JPQL supports three types of statements, as shown in table 11.1. You can use JPQL to perform selects, updates, and deletes in your queries.

Let's first focus on retrieving entities using a `SELECT` statement with JPQL.

Figure 11.1 Each JPQL query is translated to an SQL query by the JPQL query processor and executed by the database. The query processor is supplied by the JPA provider, most likely the application server vendor.

Table 11.1 Statement types supported by JPQL

Statement type	Description
Select	Retrieves entities or entity-related data
Update	Updates one or more entities
Delete	Deletes one or more entities

DEFINING AND USING SELECT

Let's get jump-started with a simple JPQL query:

```
SELECT c
FROM Category c
WHERE c.categoryName LIKE :categoryName
ORDER BY c.categoryId
```

This JPQL query has (or can have) the following:

- A required SELECT clause specifying the object type, entity, or values being retrieved
- A required FROM clause specifying an entity declaration that's used by other clauses
- An optional WHERE clause to filter the results returned by the query
- An optional ORDER BY clause to order the results retrieved by the query
- An optional GROUP BY clause to perform aggregation
- An optional HAVING clause to perform filtering in conjunction with aggregation

DEFINING UPDATE AND DELETE

In the last chapter we discussed updating and removing entities using the EntityManager API. But these were limited to only one entity instance. What about when you want to remove more than one entity in a single call? Like SQL, JPQL also provides UPDATE and DELETE statements to perform updates and deletions of entities, and you can continue to specify a condition using a WHERE clause. These statements are quite similar to their SQL relatives. They're referred to as bulk updates or deletes, because you'll primarily use these to update or delete a set of entities matching a specific condition. In this section we'll limit our discussion to the JPQL syntax for update and delete statement types.

USING UPDATE

Only one entity type can be specified with an UPDATE statement, and you should provide a WHERE clause to limit the number of entities affected by the statement. Here's the syntax for the UPDATE statement:

```
UPDATE entityName indentifierVariable
SET single_value_path_expression1 = value1, ...
  single_value_path_expressionN = valueN
WHERE where_clause
```

You can use any persistence field and single-value association field in the SET clause of the UPDATE statement. Assume that you want to provide gold status and a commission rate of 10% to all sellers whose last name starts with Packrat. Start with the following JPQL statement:

```
UPDATE Seller s
SET s.status = 'G', s.commissionRate = 10
WHERE s.lastName like 'Packrat%'
```

It's clear from this statement that the WHERE clause of an UPDATE behaves exactly the same as the one you used in the SELECT statement. We'll return to a detailed discussion of the WHERE clause later in this chapter.

USING DELETE

Like UPDATE, DELETE in JPQL resembles its SQL cousin. You can specify only one entity type with a DELETE statement, and you should specify a WHERE clause to limit the number of entities affected by the statement. Here's the syntax for the DELETE statement:

```
DELETE entityName indentifierVariable
WHERE where_clause
```

For example, if you want to remove all instances of sellers with silver status, you'll use this:

```
DELETE Seller s
WHERE s.status = 'Silver'
```

11.1.2 FROM clause

The FROM clause of JPQL is by far the most important clause. It defines the domain for the query—that is, the names for the entities that will be used in the query. If your JPQL query is to get Category entities, you specify the FROM clause as follows:

```
FROM Category c
```

Category is the domain that you want to query, and here you have specified c as an identifier of type Category.

IDENTIFYING THE QUERY DOMAIN: NAMING AN ENTITY

You specify the entity name defined for the entity using the @Entity annotation as the domain type. You can define the name for an entity using the name element of the @Entity annotation. If you don't specify the name element, it defaults to the name of the entity class. The name of the entity must be unique within a persistence unit. In other words, you can't have two entities with the same name or the persistence provider will generate a deployment error. This makes sense because the persistence provider wouldn't be able to identify which entity domain to use if duplicate names for entities were allowed.

In the previous example, you're assuming the Category entity class that we discussed in earlier chapters doesn't define a name. If you assume that the Category class defines an entity name using the name element as follows

```
@Entity(name = "CategoryEntity")
public class Category
```

then you must change the FROM clause of the query as follows:

```
FROM CategoryEntity c
```

This change is required for JPQL to map the correct entity type as defined by the annotation.

IDENTIFIER VARIABLES

In the JPQL example, you defined an identifier variable named c, and you used that variable in other clauses, such as SELECT and WHERE. A simple identifier variable is defined using the following general syntax:

```
FROM entityName [AS] identificationVariable
```

The square brackets ([]) indicate that the AS operator is optional. The identifier variable (which isn't case sensitive) must be a valid Java identifier, and it must not be a JPQL reserved identifier. Table 11.2 lists all of the JPQL reserved identifiers for your convenience. Keep in mind that the identifier can't be the name of another entity packaged in the same persistence unit.

Table 11.2 JPQL keywords reserved by the specification. You're not allowed to give any of your variables these names.

Types	Reserved words
Statements and clauses	SELECT, UPDATE, DELETE, FROM, WHERE, GROUP, HAVING, ORDER, BY, ASC, DESC
Joins	JOIN, OUTER, INNER, LEFT, FETCH
Conditions and operators	DISTINCT, OBJECT, NULL, TRUE, FALSE, NOT, AND, OR,. BETWEEN, LIKE, IN, AS, UNKNOWN, EMPTY, MEMBER, OF, IS, NEW, EXISTS, ALL, ANY, SOME
Functions	AVG, MAX, MIN, SUM, COUNT, MOD, UPPER, LOWER, TRIM,POSITION, CHARACTER_LENGTH, CHAR_LENGTH, BIT_LENGTH, CURRENT_TIME, CURRENT_DATE, CURRENT_TIMESTAMP

Thus, you can't define the FROM clause like this

```
FROM Category User
```

or like this

```
FROM Category Max
```

because you already have an entity named User in the ActionBazaar application, and MAX is a reserved identifier.

You can define multiple identifiers in the FROM clause, and you'll see how to use them when we discuss joining multiple entities by association or field name later in this chapter.

WHAT IS A PATH EXPRESSION?

In the JPQL example you used expressions such as `c.categoryName` and `c.categoryId`. These are known as path expressions. A path expression is an identifier variable followed by the navigation operator (`.`) and a persistence or association field. You normally use a path expression to narrow the domain for a query by using it in a `WHERE` clause or order the retrieved result by using an `ORDER BY` clause.

An association field can contain either a single-value object or a collection. The association fields that represent one-to-many and many-to-many associations are collections of types, and such a path expression is a collection-value path expression. For example, if you have a many-to-many relationship between `Category` and `Item`, you can utilize a query to find all `Category` entities that have associated items as follows:

```
SELECT distinct c
FROM Category c
WHERE c.items isn't EMPTY
```

Here `c.items` is a collection type. Such expressions are known as collection-value expressions. If the association is either many-to-one or one-to-one, then the association fields are of a specific object type, and those types are known as single-value path expressions.

You can navigate further to other persistence fields or association fields using a single-value path expression. For example, say you have a many-to-one relationship between `Category` and `User`; you can navigate to a persistence field such as `firstName` using the association field `user` as follows:

```
c.user.firstName
```

You may also want to navigate to the association field `contactDetails` to use its email address:

```
c.user.contactDetails.email
```

While using path expressions, keep in mind that you can't navigate through the collection-value path expressions to access a persistence or association field as in the following example:

```
c.items.itemName or c.items.seller
```

This is due to the fact you can't access an element of a collection, and `items` is a collection of items. Using `c.items.itemName` in JPQL is similar to using `category.getItems().getItemName()`, and this isn't allowed. Next, you'll see how you can use path expressions in a `WHERE` clause.

FILTERING WITH WHERE

The `WHERE` clause in JPQL allows you to filter the results of a query. Only entities that match the query condition specified will be retrieved. Say you want to retrieve all instances of the `Category` entity; you can use a JPQL statement without a `WHERE` clause:

```
SELECT c
FROM Category c
```

Using this code will probably result in thousands of `Category` instances. But say you actually want to retrieve instances of a `Category` by a specific condition. To retrieve the `Category` instances that have a `categoryId` greater than 500, you'd have to rewrite the query like this:

```
SELECT c
FROM Category c
WHERE c.categoryId > 500
```

Almost all types of Java literals such as `boolean`, `float`, `enum`, `String`, `int`, and so forth are supported in the `WHERE` clause. You can't use numeric types such as octal and hexadecimals, nor can you use array types such as `byte[]` or `char[]` in the `WHERE` clause. Remember that JPQL statements are translated into SQL; SQL is actually imposing the restriction that BLOB and CLOB types can't be used in a `WHERE` clause.

PASSING PARAMETERS: POSITIONAL AND NAMED

Recall from our earlier discussion that JPQL supports two types of parameters: positional and named. Later in this chapter we'll show you how to set values for both named and positional parameters.

The value of the parameter isn't limited to numeric or string types; the value depends on the type of path expression used in the `WHERE` clause. The parameter can take more complex types, such as another entity type, but you're limited to using conditional expressions that involve a single-value path expression.

CONDITIONAL EXPRESSIONS AND OPERATORS

A condition in the `WHERE` clause that filters results from a query is known as a conditional expression. You can build a conditional expression using path expressions and operators supported by the language. JPQL can evaluate a path expression with numeric, string, or `boolean` values using relational operators. Here's an example of a conditional expression:

```
c.categoryName = 'Dumped Cars'
```

Table 11.3 lists the types of operators supported by JPQL, in order of precedence.

Table 11.3 Operator types supported by JPQL

Operator type	Operator
Navigational	`.`
Unary sign	`+, -`
Arithmetic	`*, /, +, -`
Relational	`=, >, >=, <, <=, <>, [NOT] BETWEEN, [NOT] LIKE, [NOT] IN, IS [NOT] NULL, IS [NOT] EMPTY, [NOT] MEMBER [OF]`
Logical	`NOT, AND, OR`

A complex conditional expression may include other expressions that are combined for evaluation using logical operators such as AND or OR. For instance, you can retrieve a category that meets either of these conditional expressions:

```
WHERE c.categoryName = 'Dumped Cars'
    OR  c.categoryName = 'Furniture from Garbage'
```

You can use all types of relational operators with numeric types of path expressions. String and Boolean operands can use the relational operators: equality (=) and non-equality (<>).

USING A RANGE WITH BETWEEN

You can use the BETWEEN operator in an arithmetic expression to compare a variable with a range of values. You can also use the BETWEEN operator in arithmetic, string, or date-time expressions to compare a path expression to a lower and upper limit using the following syntax:

```
path_expression [NOT] BETWEEN lowerRange and upperRange
```

Suppose you want to filter the results so that categoryId falls within a specified range. You can use a WHERE clause and named parameters for the range this way:

```
WHERE c.categoryId BETWEEN :lowRange AND :highRange
```

> **NOTE** The lower and upper range used in a BETWEEN operator must be the same data type.

USING THE IN OPERATOR

The IN operator allows you to create a conditional expression based on whether a path expression exists in a list of values. Here is the syntax for the IN operator:

```
path_expression [NOT] IN (List_of_values)
```

The list of values can be a static list of comma-separated values or a dynamic list retrieved by a subquery. Suppose you want to retrieve the results for userId that exist in a static list of userIds. This WHERE clause will do the trick:

```
WHERE u.userId IN ('viper', 'drdba', 'dumpster')
```

If you want to retrieve the information from users that don't exist in the same static list, then you can use this WHERE clause:

```
WHERE u.userId not IN ('viper', 'drdba', 'dumpster')
```

A subquery is a query within a query. A subquery may return a single value or multiple values. You'll learn more about subqueries in section 11.1.4. Let's review an example of a subquery with an IN operator:

```
WHERE c.user IN (SELECT u
                 FROM User u
                 WHERE u.userType = 'A')
```

In this expression you're trying to evaluate the `User` field with a list of users retrieved by the subquery. When a query contains a subquery, the subquery is executed first, and then the parent query is evaluated against the result retrieved by the subquery.

USING THE LIKE OPERATOR

The `LIKE` operator allows you to determine whether a single-value path expression matches a string pattern. The syntax for the `LIKE` operator is

```
string_value_path_expression [NOT] LIKE pattern_value_
```

Here `pattern_value` is a string literal or an input parameter. The `pattern_value` may contain an underscore (_) or a percent sign (`%`). The underscore stands for a single character. Consider the following clause:

```
WHERE c.itemName LIKE '_ike'
```

This expression will return `TRUE` when `c.itemName` has values such as `mike`, `bike`, and so forth. You should be able to extend this technique to embed a space into any search string, effectively making the space a wildcard. If you search for a single space, it'll only match a single character.

The percent sign (`%`) represents any numbers of characters. Whenever you want to search for all `Category` entities with a name that starts with `Recycle`, use this `WHERE` clause:

```
WHERE c.categoryName LIKE 'Recycle%'
```

The expression will return `TRUE` when `c.categoryName` has values such as `Recycle from Garbage`, `Recycle from Mr. Dumpster`, and `RecycleMania–the Hulkster strikes again!`.

Suppose you want to retrieve a result set in which a string expression doesn't match a literal. You can use the `NOT` operator in conjunction with the `LIKE` operator as in the following example:

```
WHERE c.categoryName NOT LIKE '%Recycle%'
```

The expression will return `FALSE` when `c.categoryName` has any values that include `Recycle` as any part of the return value, because in this example you used `%` before and after the filter string.

In most applications you probably want to supply a parameter for flexibility rather than use a string literal. You can use positional parameters as shown here to accomplish this:

```
WHERE c.categoryName NOT LIKE ?1
```

Here the result set will contain all `c.categoryNames` that aren't like values bound to the positional `parameter ?1`.

DEALING WITH NULL VALUES AND EMPTY COLLECTIONS

So far we've been able to avoid discussing null and how an expression deals with null values. Alas, now it's time to deal with this little mystery. You have to remember that null is different from an empty string, and JPQL treats them differently. But not all databases treat an empty string and null differently. You already know that JPQL is translated into SQL by the persistence provider. If the database returns `TRUE` when an empty string is compared with null, you can't rely on consistent results from your queries across two different databases. We recommend that you test this situation with your database.

When a conditional expression encounters a null value, the expression evaluates to `null` or `UNKNOWN`. A complex `WHERE` clause that combines more than one conditional expression with a Boolean operator such as `AND` may produce a result that's unknown. Table 11.4 is a truth table that lists the results of a conditional expression when it's compared with a null value.

Table 11.4 Truth table of Boolean value compared with null

Expression 1 value	Boolean operator	Expression 2 value	Result
TRUE	AND	null	UNKNOWN
FALSE	AND	null	FALSE
NULL	AND	null	UNKNOWN
TRUE	OR	null	TRUE
NULL	OR	null	UNKNOWN
FALSE	OR	null	UNKNOWN
	NOT	null	UNKNOWN

You can use the `IS NULL` or `IS NOT NULL` operator to check whether a single-value path expression contains null or not-null values. If a single-value path expression contains null, then `IS NULL` will return `TRUE` and `IS NOT NULL` will return `FALSE`. If you want to determine whether the single-value path expression isn't null, use the following `WHERE` clause:

```
WHERE c.parentCategory IS NOT NULL
```

You can't use the `IS NULL` expression to compare a path expression that's of type collection; in other words, `IS NULL` will not detect whether a collection type path expression is an empty collection. JPQL provides the `IS [NOT] EMPTY` comparison operator to check whether a collection type path expression is empty. The following `WHERE` clause will work when you want to retrieve all category entities that don't have any items:

```
WHERE c.items IS EMPTY
```

As we explained earlier, JPQL statements are translated to SQL statements by the persistence provider. There's no equivalent of the `IS EMPTY` clause in SQL. So you must be wondering what SQL statement is generated when `IS EMPTY` is used. The `IS EMPTY` clause is used with a collection-valued path expression that's typically an association field, and therefore the generated SQL statement will be determining whether the JOIN for the association retrieves any record in a subquery. To clarify, let's examine this JPQL query:

```
SELECT c
FROM Category c
WHERE c.items IS EMPTY
```

If you recall our discussions from chapter 9, a many-to-many relationship exists between Category and Item entities, with CATEGORIES_ITEMS as the intersection table. This means the persistence provider will generate the following SQL statement:

```
SELECT
  c.CATEGORY_ID, c.CATEGORY_NAME, c.CREATE_DATE,
  c.CREATED_BY, c.PARENT_ID
FROM CATEGORIES c
WHERE (
  (SELECT COUNT(*)
  FROM CATEGORIES_ITEMS ci, ITEMS i
  WHERE (
    (ci.CATEGORY_ID = c.CATEGORY_ID) AND
    (i.ITEM_ID = ci.ITEM_ID))) = 0)
```

From this generated SQL, you can see that the persistence provider uses a subquery to retrieve the number of associated items for a category by using the COUNT group function and then compares the result with 0. This means that if no items are found, the collection must be empty, and the IS EMPTY expression returns TRUE.

Have you ever had an occasion to detect the presence of a single value in a collection? Sure you have! In JPQL you can use the MEMBER OF operator for just that purpose. Let's take a look at how it works.

CHECKING FOR THE EXISTENCE OF AN ENTITY IN A COLLECTION

You can use the MEMBER OF operator to test whether an identifier variable, a single-value path expression, or an input parameter exists in a collection-value path expression. Here's the syntax for the MEMBER OF operator:

```
entity_expression [NOT] MEMBER [OF] collection_value_path_expression
```

The OF and NOT keywords are optional and can be omitted. Here's an example of using an input parameter with MEMBER OF:

```
WHERE :item MEMBER OF c.items
```

This condition will return TRUE if the entity instance passed (as:item) in the query exists in the collection of c.items for a particular category c.

WORKING WITH JPQL FUNCTIONS

JPQL provides several built-in functions for performing different kinds of operations. These functions can be used in either the WHERE or HAVING clause of a JPQL statement. You'll learn more about the HAVING clause when we cover aggregate functions later in this chapter. Right now we're going to explore the three kinds of JPQL functions:

- String functions
- Arithmetic functions
- Date-time functions

STRING FUNCTIONS

You can use string functions in the SELECT clause of a JPQL query; table 11.5 lists all string functions supported by JPQL. These functions are used to filter the results of the query. You have to use the functions available in the Java language if you want to perform any string manipulations on your data. The primary reason is that in-memory string manipulation in your application will be much faster than doing the manipulation in the database.

Table 11.5 JPQL string functions

String functions	Description
`CONCAT(string1, string2)`	Returns the value of concatenating two strings or literals together.
`SUBSTRING(string, position, length)`	Returns the substring starting at `position` that's `length` long.
`TRIM([LEADING | TRAILING | BOTH] [trim_character] FROM] string_to_trimmed)`	Trims the specified character to a new length. The trimming can be `LEADING`, `TRAILING`, or from `BOTH` ends. If no `trim_character` is specified, then a blank space is assumed.
`LOWER(string)`	Returns the string after converting to lowercase.
`UPPER(string)`	Returns the string after converting to uppercase.
`LENGTH(string)`	Returns the length of a string.
`LOCATE(searchString, stringToBeSearched[initialPosition])`	Returns the position of a given string within another string. The search starts at position 1 if `initialPosition` isn't specified.

Let's look at a couple of common string function examples. Suppose you want to compare the result of concatenating of two string expressions with a string literal. The following WHERE clause will perform the task well:

```
WHERE CONCAT(u.firstName, u.lastName) = 'ViperAdmin'
```

If the concatenation of u.firstName and u.lastName doesn't result in ViperAdmin, then the condition will return FALSE.

You can use the SUBSTRING function to determine if the first three letters of u.lastName start with VIP:

```
WHERE SUBSTRING(u.lastName, 1, 3) = 'VIP'
```

The name of each string function is a good indicator of the functional operation it can perform. The direct analog of string functions is arithmetic functions. We'll look at what JPQL supports in this area next.

ARITHMETIC FUNCTIONS

Although math is rarely used to perform CRUD operations, it's useful when trying to manipulate data for reports. JPQL supports only a bare minimum set of functions in this regard, and some vendors may choose to add functions to enhance their reporting capabilities. As with all vendor-specific features, be aware that using them will make your code less portable should you decide to change vendors in the future. You can use arithmetic functions in either the `WHERE` or `HAVING` clause of JPQL. Table 11.6 lists all arithmetic functions supported by JPQL.

Table 11.6 JPQL arithmetic functions

Arithmetic functions	Description
`ABS(simple_arithmetic_expression)`	Returns the absolute value of `simple_arithmetic_expression`
`SQRT(simple_arithmetic_expression)`	Returns the square root value of `simple_arithmetic_expression` as a `double`
`MOD(num, div)`	Returns the result of executing the modulus operation for `num, div`
`SIZE(collection_value_path_expression)`	Returns the number of items in a collection

Most of the arithmetic functions are self-explanatory, such as this example of `SIZE`:

```
WHERE SIZE(c.items) = 5
```

This expression will return `TRUE` when the `SIZE` of `c.items` is `5` and `FALSE` otherwise.

TEMPORAL FUNCTIONS

Most languages provide functions that retrieve the current date, time, or timestamp. JPQL offers the temporal functions shown in table 11.7. These functions translate into database-specific SQL functions, and the requested current date, time, or timestamp is retrieved from the database.

Table 11.7 JPQL temporal functions

Temporal functions	Description
`CURRENT_DATE`	Returns current date
`CURRENT_TIME`	Returns current time
`CURRENT_TIMESTAMP`	Returns current timestamp

Note that because JPQL time values are retrieved from the database, they may vary slightly from the time retrieved from your JVM if they aren't both running on the same server. This is an issue only if you have a time-sensitive application. You can resolve this issue by running a time service on all servers that are part of your environment. Next, we'll look at the SELECT clause of JPQL.

11.1.3 SELECT clause

Although you saw some examples of the SELECT clause at the beginning of this chapter, we avoided a detailed discussion of the SELECT clause until now. From the previous examples it's evident that the SELECT clause denotes the result of the query. Here's the JPQL syntax of a SELECT clause:

```
SELECT [DISTINCT] expression1, expression2, .... expressionN
```

A SELECT clause may have more than one identifier variable, one or more single-value path expressions, or aggregate functions separated by commas. Earlier you used an identifier in the SELECT clause as follows:

```
SELECT c
FROM Category AS c
```

You can also use one or more path expressions in the SELECT clause:

```
SELECT c.categoryName, c.createdBy
FROM Category c
```

The expressions used in the SELECT clause have to be single-value. In other words, you can't have a collection-value path expression in the clause. The path expressions can be an association field, as in the previous example, where c.createdBy is an association field of the Category entity.

The previous query may return duplicate entities. If you want the result to not contain duplicate data, use the DISTINCT keyword in this way:

```
SELECT DISTINCT c.categoryName, c.createdBy
FROM Category c
```

The following SELECT statement is invalid

```
SELECT c.categoryName, c.items
FROM Category
```

because c.items is a collection-type association field, and collection-value path expressions aren't allowed in a SELECT clause. We'll talk about using aggregate functions in the SELECT clause in the next section.

USING A CONSTRUCTOR EXPRESSION IN A SELECT CLAUSE

You can use a constructor in a SELECT clause to return one or more Java instances. This is particularly useful when you want to create instances in a query that are initialized with data retrieved from a subquery:

```
SELECT NEW actionbazaar.persistence.ItemReport (c.categoryID, c.createdBy)
FROM Category
WHERE categoryId.createdBy = :userName
```

The specified class doesn't have to be mapped to the database, nor is it required to be an entity.

USING AGGREGATIONS

JPQL provides these aggregate functions: AVG, COUNT, MAX, MIN, and SUM, as shown in table 11.8. Each function's name suggests its purpose. The aggregate functions are commonly used in creating report queries. You can only use a persistence field with the AVG, MAX, MIN, and SUM functions, but you can use any type of path expression or identifier with the COUNT function.

Table 11.8 Aggregate functions supported by JPQL

Aggregate functions	Description	Return type
AVG	Returns the average value of all values of the field it's applied to	Double
COUNT	Returns the number of results returned by the query	Long
MAX	Returns the maximum value of the field it's applied to	Depends on the type of the persistence field
MIN	Returns the minimum value of the field it's applied to	Depends on the type of the persistence field
SUM	Returns the sum of all values on the field it's applied to	May return either Long or Double

If you want to find the MAX value for the i.itemPrice field among all items, use the following query:

```
SELECT MAX(i.itemPrice)
FROM Item i
```

If you want to find out how many Category entities exist in the system, use COUNT like this:

```
SELECT COUNT(c)
FROM Category c
```

You've just seen some simple examples of aggregate functions. In the next section you'll learn how to aggregate results based on a path expression.

GROUPING WITH GROUP BY AND HAVING

In an Enterprise business application, you may need to group data by a persistence field. Assuming that there's a one-to-many relationship between User and Category, this query will generate a report that lists the number of Category entities created by each c.user:

```
SELECT c.user, COUNT(c.categoryId)
FROM Category c
GROUP BY c.user
```

As you can see, this code is grouped by an associated entity. You can group by a single-value path expression that's either a persistence or an association field. Only aggregate functions are allowed when you perform aggregation using `GROUP BY`. You can also filter the results of an aggregated query with a `HAVING` clause. Suppose you want to retrieve only the users who have created more than five `Category` entities. Simply modify the previous query as follows:

```
SELECT c.user, COUNT(c.categoryId)
FROM Category c
GROUP BY c.user
HAVING COUNT(c.categoryId) > 5
```

In addition, you can have a `WHERE` clause in a query along with a `GROUP BY` clause such as this:

```
SELECT c.user, COUNT(c.categoryId)
FROM Category c
WHERE c.createDate is BETWEEN :date1 and :date2
GROUP BY c.user
HAVING COUNT(c.categoryId) > 5
```

A `WHERE` clause in a query containing both the `GROUP BY` and `HAVING` clauses results in multistage processing. First, the `WHERE` clause is applied to filter the results. Then, the results are aggregated based on the `GROUP BY` clause. Finally, the `HAVING` clause is applied to filter the aggregated result.

11.1.4 *Ordering results*

A subquery is a query inside a query. You use a subquery in a `WHERE`, `HAVING`, or `GROUP BY` clause to filter the result set. Unlike SQL subqueries, EJB 3 subqueries aren't supported in the `FROM` clause. If you have a subquery in a JPQL query, the subquery will be evaluated first, and then the main query will be retrieved based on the result of the subquery.

Here's the syntax for the subquery:

```
[NOT] IN / [NOT] EXISTS / ALL / ANY / SOME (subquery)
```

From the syntax of the language, it's clear that you can use `IN`, `EXISTS`, `ALL`, `ANY`, or `SOME` with a subquery.

Let's look at some examples of subqueries in more detail.

USING IN WITH A SUBQUERY

We've already discussed using the `IN` operator when a single-value path expression is evaluated against a list of values. You can use a subquery to produce a list of results:

```
SELECT i
FROM Item i
WHERE i.user IN (SELECT c.user
                 FROM Category c
                 WHERE c.categoryName LIKE :name)
```

In this query, first the subquery (in parentheses) is executed to retrieve a list of users, and then the `i.item` path expression is evaluated against the list.

USING EXISTS

`EXISTS` (or `NOT EXISTS`) tests whether the subquery contains any result set. It returns `TRUE` if the subquery contains at least one result and `FALSE` otherwise. Here's an example illustrating the `EXISTS` clause:

```
SELECT i
FROM Item i
WHERE EXISTS (SELECT c
              FROM Category c
              WHERE c.user = i.user)
```

If you look carefully at the result of this subquery, you'll notice that it's the same as the query example used in the previous section with the `IN` operator. An `EXISTS` clause is generally preferred over `IN`, particularly when the underlying tables contain a large number of records. This is because databases typically perform better when using `EXISTS`. Again, this is due to the work of the query processor translating JPQL queries into SQL by the persistence provider.

USING ANY, ALL, AND SOME

Using the `ANY`, `ALL`, and `SOME` operators is similar to using the `IN` operator. You can use these operators with any numeric comparison operators, such as =, >, >=, <, <= and <>.

Here's an example of a subquery demonstrating the `ALL` operator:

```
SELECT c
FROM Category c
WHERE c.createDate >= ALL
             (SELECT i.createDate
              FROM Item i
              WHERE i.user = c.user)
```

If you include the `ALL` predicate, the subquery returns `TRUE` if all the results retrieved by the subquery meet the condition; otherwise, the expression returns `FALSE`. In the example the subquery returns `FALSE` if any item in the subquery has a `createDate` later than the `createDate` for the category in the main query.

As the name suggests, if you use `ANY` or `SOME`, the expression returns `TRUE` if any of the retrieved results meet the query condition. You can use `ANY` in a query as follows:

```
SELECT c
FROM Category c
WHERE c.createDate >= ANY
             (SELECT i.createDate
              FROM Item i
              WHERE i.seller = c.user)
```

`SOME` is just an alias (or a synonym) for `ANY`; therefore, it can be used anywhere `ANY` can be used.

11.1.5 Joining entities

If you've used relational databases and SQL, you must have some experience with the JOIN operator. You can use JOIN to create a Cartesian product between two entities. Normally you provide a WHERE clause to specify the JOIN condition between entities instead of just creating a Cartesian product.

You have to specify the entities in the FROM clause to create a JOIN between two or more entities. The two entities are joined based on either their relationships or any arbitrary persistence fields. When two entities are joined, you may decide to retrieve results that match the JOIN conditions. For example, suppose you join Category and Item using the relationships between them and retrieve only entities that match the JOIN condition. Such joins are known as inner joins. Conversely, suppose you need to retrieve results that satisfy the JOIN conditions but also include entities from one side of the domain that don't have matching entities on the other side. For example, you may want to retrieve all instances of Category even if there's no matching instance of Item. This type of join is called an outer join. Note that an outer join can be left, right, or both.

Let's first look at some examples of the most common types of joins: inner joins and outer joins. After this, we'll look at the less-commonly used (though sometimes useful) fetch and theta joins.

INNER JOINS

A common situation in applications is the need to join two or more entities based on something shared in their relationship. Here's the syntax for INNER JOIN:

```
[INNER] JOIN join_association_path_expression [AS]
  identification_variable
```

In ActionBazaar, Category and User entities have a many-to-one association. To retrieve all users who match a specific criterion, you could try this query:

```
SELECT u
FROM User u INNER JOIN u.Category c
WHERE u.userId LIKE ?1
```

The INNER clause is optional. Remember that INNER JOIN is the default when you use the JOIN operator by itself, without specifying INNER or OUTER. Now let's move to the other end of the spectrum: outer joins.

OUTER JOINS

Outer joins allow you to retrieve additional entities that don't match the JOIN conditions when associations between entities are optional. Outer joins are particularly useful in reporting. Assume that there's an optional relationship between User and Category and you want to generate a report that prints all the category names for the user. If the user doesn't have any categories, then you want to print NULL. If you specify the user on the left side of the JOIN, you can use either the LEFT JOIN or LEFT OUTER JOIN keyword phrases with a JPQL query as follows:

```
SELECT u
FROM User u LEFT OUTER JOIN u.Category c
WHERE u.userId like ?1
```

This will also retrieve `User` entities that don't have a matching `Category`, as well as those who do. It's worth noting that if an outer join isn't used, the query would only retrieve the users with the matching category but would fail to retrieve users that didn't have a matching category.

Although `INNER JOIN` and `OUTER JOIN` are the most common, are there any other types of `JOIN`s supported by JPQL? We're glad you asked! The answer is yes, and next we'll look at fetch and theta joins.

FETCH JOINS

In a typical business application, you may want to query for a particular entity but also retrieve its associated entities at the same time. For example, when you retrieve a `Bid` in the ActionBazaar system, you want to eagerly load and initialize the associated instance of `bidder`. You can use a `FETCH JOIN` clause in JPQL to retrieve an associated entity as a side effect of the retrieval of an entity:

```
SELECT b
FROM Bid b FETCH JOIN b.bidder
WHERE b.bidDate >= :bidDate
```

A fetch join is generally useful when you have lazy loading enabled for your relationship but you want to eagerly load the related entities in a specific query. You can use `FETCH JOIN` with both inner and outer joins.

THETA JOINS

Theta joins aren't very common, and are based on arbitrary persistence or association fields in the entities being joined, rather than the relationship defined between them. For example, in the ActionBazaar system you have a persistence field named `rating` that stores the rating for a category. The values for `rating` include `DELUXE`, `GOLD`, `STANDARD`, and `PREMIUM`. You also have a persistence field named `star` that you use to store a star rating for an item; the values for `star` also include `DELUXE`, `GOLD`, `STANDARD`, and `PREMIUM`. Assume that both persistence fields store some common values in these fields, such as `GOLD`, and you want to join these two entities based on the `rating` and `star` fields of `Category` and `Item`, respectively. To accomplish this, you use this query:

```
SELECT i
FROM Item i, Category c
WHERE i.star = c.rating
```

Although this type of join is less common in applications, it can't be ruled out.

Did you have any idea there was so much to JPQL? If you didn't know any better, you might think it was a whole other language.... Oh wait, it is! And it's just waiting for you to give it a test drive. We hope you were able to get your bearings so that you can get started with JPQL and put it to work in your applications.

We're in the home stretch of this chapter with only a couple of topics left. We still need to discuss native SQL queries, but first we'll talk about bulk updates and deletes.

11.1.6 Bulk updates and deletes

ActionBazaar categorizes its users by gold, platinum, and similar terms based on the number of successful trades in a year. At the end of the year, an application module is executed that appropriately sets the user status. You could run a query to retrieve the collection of `User` entities and then iterate through the collection and update the status. An easier way is to use a bulk `UPDATE` statement to update the collection of entities matching the condition, as in this example:

```
UPDATE User u
SET u.status = 'G'
WHERE u.numTrades >=?1
```

You've seen some examples of `DELETE` and `UPDATE` statements in JPQL in previous sections, but we avoided any in-depth discussion until now. Let's assume that ActionBazaar administrators need functionality to remove instances of entities such as `User` based on certain conditions. You start with the following code:

```
@PersistenceContext em;
. . .
// start transaction
Query query = em.createQuery("DELETE USER u WHERE u.status = :status ");
query.setParameter("status", 'GOLD');
int results = query.executeUpdate();
//end transaction
```

In this code, the use of `UPDATE` and `DELETE` statements is quite similar to using any other JPQL statements, except for two significant differences. First, you use the `executeUpdate` method of the Query interface to perform bulk updates and deletes instead of `getResultList` or `getSingleResult`. Second, you must invoke `executeUpdate` within an active transaction.

Because bulk updates and deletes involve many pitfalls, we recommend that you isolate any bulk operations to a discrete transaction, because they're directly translated into database operations and may cause inconsistencies between managed entities and the database. Vendors are required only to execute the update or delete operations and aren't required to modify any changes to the managed entities according to the specification. In other words, the persistence provider won't remove any associated entities when an entity is removed as a result of a bulk operation.

At this point, we've covered a lot of ground: queries, annotations, and JPQL. There's only one topic left to discuss in this arena: using regular SQL queries in EJB 3.

11.2 Criteria queries

Although JPQL is extremely powerful, it still depends on strings that are embedded within Java code and are evaluated only at runtime. This means that despite an application compiling and deploying successfully, it still may contain syntax errors. The only way to be sure that the queries are syntactically valid is to execute each and every query via either unit tests or integration tests. Ignoring regression testing, syntax errors are extremely expensive during development and are especially problematic if an application is large and takes a significant amount of time to compile, package, deploy, and then access the functionality that executes a problematic query. Starting with Java EE 6, the criteria queries were introduced to provide a type-safe mechanism for creating queries.

A type-safe API means that you'll build queries using real Java objects to represent the SQL statement. This is completely different than the traditional non-type-safe way, which is to build the SQL statement as a string and hope it has no syntactical errors. Using the type-safe API, it can be built entirely in code with no hardcoded strings. The queries are guaranteed to be syntactically correct, although they still may contain logical errors. Logical errors refer to human error, such as forgetting to provide a predicate expression on the `DELETE` because you were distracted by a phone call. The trade-off to this approach is that the code will be much more verbose and unwieldy for large complex queries. A single-line JPQL or SQL statement will span multiple lines when coded using the criteria API. Developing a domain-specific language (DSL) can be used to address this issue but is outside the scope of this book and chapter.

At this point, you might be wondering about mechanics and specifically how you can get static typing on properties. Obviously you need a data model to provide this support. This is where the *meta-model* comes in. The meta-model is a static representation of the data model. The compiler generates it for you using a JPA annotation processor. The meta-model is used in conjunction with the `CriteriaBuilder` to construct and execute a query. To put this discussion into context, let's examine a simple query to locate an item by name, as shown in the following listing.

Listing 11.1 Finding an item by name using criteria queries

```
public List<Item> findItemByName(String name) {
  CriteriaBuilder builder = entityManager.getCriteriaBuilder();
  CriteriaQuery<Item> query = builder.createQuery(Item.class);
  Root<Item> root = query.from(Item.class);
  Predicate condition = builder.like(root.get(Item_.itemName),name);
  query.where(condition);
  TypedQuery<Item> q = entityManager.createQuery(query);
  return q.getResultList();
}
```

Acquire the CriteriaBuilder from the EntityManager

Create new CriteriaQuery that will query for item class

Construct query using meta-model

This method, from `ItemManager`, creates a criteria query using a meta-model and then executes the query. Although verbose, the query will execute successfully at runtime because there are no strings that need to be dynamically evaluated. There's no chance that you incorrectly used `name` instead of `itemName`. Now that you have a basic understanding of criteria queries, let's dig into the meta-model API.

11.2.1 Meta-model API

The meta-model API provides a representation of the Java database entities as known by JPA. In some ways it's very similar to Java's reflection APIs and the metadata API of

JDBC. As with reflection, you can iterate over the attributes of each entity and get basic information, including the name and the Java data type. You can also determine relationships between entities such as whether there's a one-to-one relationship or a many-to-many, and so on. In some ways this is similar to the `DatabaseMetaData` API provided by JDBC. The API provided by JDBC provides low-level database schema information; the metadata model provides information about JPA-managed classes. The meta-model API provides introspection on the cached O/R mapping information.

The meta-model API is just part of the puzzle. To get static typing you need static objects representing the data model. These objects are created using an *annotation processor.* An annotation processor is a plug-in to the javac compiler that processes annotations at compile time. In the case of JPA, it processes the annotations as well as the `persistence.xml` configuration. The meta-model processor generates Java source files for each JPA-managed class. The generated source code files are ultimately compiled along with the project to provide the static meta-model used at runtime. IDEs can introspect the meta-model classes to provide code completion.

The steps for using a meta-model are as follows:

1. Annotate your POJOs using the JPA annotations.
2. Compile the code with the meta-model processor as part of the compile process.
3. Code criteria queries using the generated classes.
4. Repeat as the model changes.

> **Annotation processor**
>
> You'll have to configure your build process and possibly your IDE to use the meta-model processor. Consult the documentation for your JPA provider for more information. If you don't plan on using criteria queries, no action is needed on your part. The model will be automatically generated at deployment.

INTROSPECTION APIS

At the heart of the meta-model APIs is the `Metamodel` interface. You acquire a reference to the `Metamodel` implementation by calling `getMetamodel()` on the `EntityManager`. You can request a specific entity or get a list of all managed entities. Information on each entity is encapsulated in an `EntityType`. An `EntityType` has methods for getting additional information about the entity, including attribute information. If you've used Java reflection previously, this will be relatively straightforward.

The `Metamodel` interface is shown in the next listing. It leverages Java Generics to eliminate the need for casting.

Listing 11.2 `Metamodel` interface

```
public interface Metamodel {
  public <X extends Object> EntityType<X> entity(Class<X> type);
  public <X extends Object> ManagedType<X> managedType(Class<X> type);
```

Retrieves the EntityType for a managed entity

```
    public <X extends Object> EmbeddableType<X> embeddable(Class<X> type);
    public Set<ManagedType<?>> getManagedTypes();
    public Set<EntityType<?>> getEntities();                  <-- Retrieves all EntityTypes for all managed entities
    public Set<EmbeddableType<?>> getEmbeddables();
}
```

Using the `Metamodel` interface, you can then iterate over all managed classes. This is shown in the following listing.

Listing 11.3 Introspecting the `Metamodel` interface dynamically at runtime

```
Metamodel metaModel = entityManager.getMetamodel();                 <-- Acquire meta-model from the EntityManager
Set<EntityType<? extends Object>> types = metaModel.getEntities();   <-- Retrieve set of all managed classes for current persistence unit
for(EntityType<? extends Object> type : types) {
  logger.log(Level.INFO, "--> Type: {0}", type);                    <-- Display name of entity
  Set attributes = type.getAttributes();                             <-- Retrieve list of entity types on entity
  for(Object obj : attributes) {
    logger.log(Level.INFO, "Name: {0}", ((Attribute)obj).getName());   <-- Display name of attribute
    logger.log(Level.INFO, "isCollection: {0}",                     <-- Print TRUE if attribute is a collection
      ((Attribute)obj).isCollection());
  }
}
```

The meta-model API is extremely powerful. You can now retrieve a list of all managed entities and introspect them for their attributes and relationships. This is only one piece of the puzzle. The generated code is what you're after and what will provide you the static typing of your queries.

GENERATED CODE

The annotation processor will generate a meta-model class for each managed entity. The generated class will have the same name except for a _ that will be appended. The generated class will also be annotated with `@Static-Metamodel`. Table 11.9 documents the definition of attributes in the meta-model class instance. The table also documents the code generated for the different types of attributes. The `Metamodel` interface provides a mechanism for finding meta-model classes dynamically at runtime.

Table 11.9 Meta-model class attribute definitions

Meta-model declaration	Attribute type
`public static volatile SingularAttribute<X, Y> y;`	Noncollection attribute
`public static volatile CollectionAttribute<X, Z> z;`	`java.util.Collection`
`public static volatile SetAttribute<X, Z> z;`	`java.util.Set`
`public static volatile ListAttribute<X, Z> z;`	`java.utilList`
`public static volatile MapAttribute<X, K, Z> z;`	`java.util.Map`

The following listing shows the meta-model class generated by the annotation processor for the `Item` entity class in ActionBazaar.

Listing 11.4 Meta-model class produced by the meta-model annotation processor

```
package com.actionbazaar.model;
@Generated(value="EclipseLink-2.5.0.v20130321-rNA",
  date="2013-04-12T18:02:56")
@StaticMetamodel(Item.class)
public class Item_ {
  public static volatile SingularAttribute<Item, byte[]> picture;
  public static volatile SingularAttribute<Item, String> itemName;
  public static volatile SetAttribute<Item, Category> category;
  public static volatile SingularAttribute<Item, BigDecimal> initialPrice;
  public static volatile SingularAttribute<Item, Date> bidEndDate;
  public static volatile SingularAttribute<Item, String> description;
  public static volatile ListAttribute<Item, Bid> bids;
  public static volatile SingularAttribute<Item, Long> itemId;
  public static volatile SingularAttribute<Item, Date> createdDate;
  public static volatile SingularAttribute<Item, BazaarAccount> seller;
  public static volatile SingularAttribute<Item, Date> bidStartDate;
}
```

Annotations: Marks class as being part of static meta-model and maps it to its managed entity (@StaticMetamodel); Generated tag was automatically inserted; example generated using EclipseLink (@Generated); Name of managed entity has _ appended (Item_); Singular/simp attribute (picture); Many-to-m relationshi (category); One-to-ma relationshi (bids); Many-to-one relationship (seller).

The class in this listing has static properties that you'll use to provide static typing when building a query. The criteria query API makes extensive use of generics that when combined with the static class ensure that your queries are correct and will execute. Now it's time to start digging into the `CriteriaBuilder`.

11.2.2 CriteriaBuilder

The `CriteriaBuilder` is at the heart of the JPA criteria API. It's responsible for creating criteria queries, component selections, expressions, predicates, and orderings. It's the factory class that you'll use to construct your query leveraging the static meta-model. You acquire a reference to the `CriteriaBuilder` by calling the `getCriteriaBuilder()` on the `EntityManager` as you saw in listing 11.1. Table 11.10 lists the five different types of queries that can be created using the `CriteriaBuilder`.

Table 11.10 Create methods on `CriteriaBuilder`

Create method	Description
`createQuery()`	Creates a new criteria object
`createQuery(java.lang.Class<T> resultClass)`	Creates a new criteria object with a specific return type
`createTupleQuery()`	Creates a new criteria object that will return a tuple as its result
`createCriteriaDelete( Class<T> targetEntity)`	Creates a new criteria object for performing bulk delete operations
`createCriteriaUpdate( Class<T> targetEntity)`	Creates a new criteria object that will perform a bulk update operation

The type of the query indicates the expected return type. It need not be a managed entity. For example, you'd pass in `Long.class` if the result of the expression computed the average of all bids on a particular item. Alternatively, as you'll see when we cover the `SELECT` statement, you can specify a wrapper object that's not a managed entity at all but is instead populated from the results.

The `CriteriaBuilder` also provides factory methods for creating expressions, order statements, selection statements, and predicates. The methods are shown in table 11.11. We'll cover these in more detail in the subsequent sessions.

Table 11.11 `CriteriaBuilder` methods grouped by type

Type	Methods
Expression	`abs, all, any, avg, coalesce, concat, construct, count, countDistinct, currentDate, currentTime, currentTimestamp, diff, function, greatest, keys, least, length, literal, locate, lower, max, min, mod, neg, nullif, nullLiteral, parameter, prod, quot, selectCase, size, some, sqrt, substring, sum, sumAsDouble, sumAsLong, toBigDecimal, toBigInteger, toDouble, toFloat, toInteger, toLong, toString, trim, upper, values`
Selection	`array, construct, tuple`
Ordering	`asc, desc`
Predicate	`and, between, conjunction, disjunction, equal, exists, ge, greaterThan, greaterThanOrEqualTo, gt, in, isEmpty, isFalse, isMember, isNotEmpty, isNotMember, isNotNull, isNull, isTrue, le, lessThan, lessThanOrEqualTo, like, lt, not, notEqual, notLike, or`

11.2.3 CriteriaQuery

The `CriteriaQuery` object is the heart of the criteria API. It pulls together all the pieces of a query: `SELECT`, `FROM`, and the optional `WHERE` clause to create an object representation of an SQL query. Under the hood, JPA uses this object representation to generate an SQL statement. JPA executes this statement against the database and then repackages the result into the object form that you specified when you created the query. This isn't very different from JPQL except that you're building the object representation manually instead of having JPA validate and convert a freeform query into an object representation.

The `CriteriaBuilder` interface we discussed in the previous section is used to construct the `CriteriaQuery` instance. The `CriteriaBuilder` is also used to construct the various pieces of a query that you'll pass into the `CriteriaQuery` methods. You use the `CriteriaBuilder` as a factory to fabricate the selection, expression, predicates, and ordering statements you need. The key methods of the `CriteriaQuery` interface are shown in table 11.12 along with the object types that they accept.

Table 11.12 Core `CriteriaQuery` methods

Method	Parameter type	Description
`groupBy`	Expression	Constructs the SQL `groupBy` construct
`having`	Expression	Constructs the SQL `HAVING` construct
`multiselect`	Selection	Creates a query with multiple selections
`orderBy`	Order	Constructs the SQL `orderBy` statement
`select`	Selection	Creates a single selection
`where`	Predicate	Creates the SQL `WHERE` clause

11.2.4 Query root

The query root is a challenging abstraction to explain. A query root defines the origin for navigation—it's the entities you need as part of your query because they contain the properties you're going to use when constructing the SQL `WHERE`, `SELECT`, and `JOIN` expressions. A query may have zero or more query roots. If you're not joining on multiple tables, specifying specific properties you want to retrieve, or applying constraints to the values retrieved, it isn't necessary to create a query root. A query root is thus an object that you use to construct expressions.

To create a query root, you invoke the `from` method on the `CriteriaQuery` instance. Despite its name, invoking the `from` method doesn't mean that you're populating the SQL `FROM` clause; entities will only be added to the `FROM` clause if you actually use them in constructing an expression. The object that's returned is a `javax.persistence.criteria.Root`. You then subsequently use this object to build expressions.

To better understand how the query root is used, consider the simple example shown in the following listing.

Listing 11.5 Retrieving all item names using a query root

```
public List<String> getAllItemsNames() {
  CriteriaBuilder builder = entityManager.getCriteriaBuilder();
  CriteriaQuery<String> query = builder.createQuery(String.class);
  Root<Item> root = query.from(Item.class);
  query.select(root.get(Item_.itemName));
  TypedQuery<String> tq = entityManager.createQuery(query);
  return tq.getResultList();
}
```

Create CriteriaQuer result of query will be a string

Create a query root of type Item; will use this for navigating

Using Root object, select itemName property

The code in this listing will produce the following SQL query:

```
SELECT ITEM_NAME FROM ITEMS
```

Now that you know how to create a criteria root, let's look at predicate and join expressions.

EXPRESSIONS

Expressions are used in the SELECT, WHERE, and HAVING clauses. You use expressions to specify what you want returned by the query or how you want the query constrained. Expressions are all rooted by the javax.persistence.criteria.Expression<T> interface. There are several notable subinterfaces including Predicate, Join, and Path. To get an instance of an expression, you use utility methods on the CriteriaBuilder. You'll notice that in many situations you need an expression to create an expression. For example, consider the method signature on lessThanOrEqualTo of CriteriaBuilder:

```
Predicate lessThanOrEqualTo(Expression<? extends Y> x,
Expression<? extends Y> y)
```

You can see that this method takes two expressions and returns a predicate. Both expressions make use of generics whose type must match—if you're comparing Double, both must be Double and so on. To reference a column (property on an entity), you construct a Path. As mentioned previously, a Path is a type of expression and you use the query root to construct it by passing in the attribute from the metamodel. Because this can be a bit confusing, let's look at the findByDate method in the next listing.

Listing 11.6 Using expressions to retrieve items for a specific date range

```
public List<Item> findByDate(Date startDate , Date endDate) {
  CriteriaBuilder builder = entityManager.getCriteriaBuilder();
  CriteriaQuery<Item> query = builder.createQuery(Item.class);
  Root<Item> itemRoot = query.from(Item.class);
  Path<Date> datePath = itemRoot.get(Item_.createdDate);
  Predicate dateRangePred = builder.between(datePath,
    startDate, endDate);
  query.where(dateRangePred);
  TypedQuery<Item> q = entityManager.createQuery(query);
  return q.getResultList();
}
```

Construct query root referencing n objects.

Construct a Path expression that uses the metamodel to reference created date.

Construct a predicate that selects items with a created date in between two dates.

In this listing an expression is constructed that you'll use to retrieve Items with a createdDate between two dates. To do this, you use both the query root and the metamodel. The Item_.createDate ensures that you're referencing an attribute that exists and ensures, through the use of generics, that you use the appropriate types when you invoke the between method. The entire listing results in the following query going to the database:

```
SELECT ITEM_ID, BID_END_DATE, BID_START_DATE, CREATEDDATE, DESCRIPTION,
INITIAL_PRICE, ITEM_NAME, PICTURE, STARRATING, SELLER_ID FROM ITEMS WHERE
(CREATEDDATE BETWEEN ? AND ?)
```

This is a trivial example. But it demonstrates how the criteria API can be used to create type-safe queries programmatically that are checked for correctness by the Java compiler. Let's examine joins next.

JOINS

The criteria API supports joining of related classes using an inner join by default. A join is performed either on a Root object or a Join object. Both objects possess a join method that can take either a singular or collection-based attribute from the metamodel: SingularAttribute, CollectionAttribute, SetAttribute, ListAttribute, or MapAttribute, respectively. The first join has to be performed on a Root object and subsequent joins can be performed using returned Join objects.

To demonstrate this functionality, let's consider a summarization page within ActionBazaar that summarizes a winning bid. The information for this summarization is pulled from the Order, Item, Bid, and BazaarAccount entities. You could retrieve this information by traversing the object graph from the Order object to retrieve the Bid, Item, and BazaarAccount instances, respectively, but this is very inefficient. You'd perform multiple roundtrips to the database and thus give the database and network a needless workout. A better solution is to use the criteria-API JOIN functionality. The code sample in the following listing performs four joins.

Listing 11.7 A winning bid using joins to retrieve fields from multiple objects

```
public List<WinningBidWrapper> getWinningBid(Long itemId) {
  CriteriaBuilder builder = entityManager.getCriteriaBuilder();
  CriteriaQuery<WinningBidWrapper> query =
    builder.createQuery(WinningBidWrapper.class);
  Root<Item> itemRoot = query.from(Item.class);
  Root<Order> orderRoot = query.from(Order.class);
  Root<Bid> bidRoot = query.from(Bid.class);
  Root<BazaarAccount> userRoot = query.from(BazaarAccount.class);
  Join<Order,Bid> j1 = orderRoot.join(Order_.bid);
  Join<Order,Item> j2 = orderRoot.join(Order_.item);
  Join<Order,BazaarAccount> j3 = orderRoot.join(Order_.bidder);
  Path<Long> itemIdPath = itemRoot.get(Item_.itemId);
  Predicate itemPredicate = builder.equal(itemIdPath,itemId);
  query.where(itemPredicate);
  query.select(
    builder.construct(
      WinningBidWrapper.class,
      userRoot.get( BazaarAccount_.username ),
      bidRoot.get( Bid_.bidPrice ),
      itemRoot.get(Item_.itemName) ,
      itemRoot.get(Item_.description)
  ));
  TypedQuery<WinningBidWrapper> q = entityManager.createQuery(query);
  return q.getResultList();
}
```

Performs an inner join on Order and Bid entities

Performs an inner join on Order and Item entities

Performs an inner join on Order and BazaarAccount entities

Retrieves a Path object for use in a predicate to construct a WHERE clause that retrieves only item you're interested in

Constructs select structure to create a wrapper object using only fields you're using in summary

The code in this listing performs a join of the selected entities and creates a wrapper entity. A wrapper entity is a synthetic object that's used to encapsulate the fields you're retrieving—it is essentially a data transfer object (DTO). We'll cover wrappers in section 11.2.6 when we discuss the SELECT clause.

The code sample from ActionBazaar used an inner join. To specify an outer join, pass a JoinType to the join method. JoinType enumerates three types of join: INNER (default), RIGHT (outer), and LEFT (outer) join types.

Using the join object that's returned from the join method, you can specify an on-condition. The on-condition takes either an expression or a predicate, both of which are constructed using the CriteriaBuilder. The following is an example of an on-condition:

```
j2.on(builder.like(itemRoot.get(Item_.itemName),"boat"));
```

The criteria API also supports fetch joins, which are used to specify an association or attribute that's to be fetched as a part of the query. For example, an order contains a reference to a bid; to fetch both at the same time, you'd construct the following query:

```
orderRoot.fetch(Order_.bid,JoinType.INNER);
```

Now that you have a handle on the query root, let's take a closer look at the FROM clause.

11.2.5 FROM clause

The FROM clause is dynamically created by the criteria API taking into account your query roots and joins. There's no need to explicitly write a FROM clause—JPA will do all of the heavily lifting for you. JPA will look at both the query roots you've requested and the joins that you've specified and construct the FROM clause.

11.2.6 SELECT clause

The SELECT clause controls the output of the query. The SELECT clause is extremely flexible, providing several different approaches to retrieving data. It's configured using the select method on the CriteriaQuery object. The deceptively simple select method takes a Selection instance as its sole parameter. As you'll see, there are quite a few subclasses of Selection that you can use to construct complex queries. An entire chapter could be devoted to covering just the SELECT clause in more detail. Consequently, we'll only skim the surface.

The select method enables you to retrieve data in several different representations depending on your needs. You aren't limited to only retrieving JPA entities—far from it, in fact. You can retrieve entities, values, and multiple values, and as you saw earlier, you can synthesize new objects from the results of a query. You can also work with tuples, which is an ordered list of values, if you don't want to go through the trouble of creating a wrapper entity.

SELECTING AN ENTITY

The simplest usage of the select method is to select an entity. To select an entity, you pass the Root object for the entity into the select method. This is shown in the following code snippet:

```
CriteriaBuilder builder = entityManager.getCriteriaBuilder();
CriteriaQuery<Item> query = builder.createQuery(Item.class);
```

```
Root<Item> root = query.from(Item.class);
query.select(root);
TypedQuery<Item> tq = entityManager.createQuery(query);
```

This code snippet is self-explanatory. The `Root` object is passed into the `select` method—this coupled with the use of a `TypedQuery` means that a list of items is returned with no need to perform any casting.

SELECTING A VALUE

Using the `select` method, you can select a specific value to be retrieved. In listing 11.5 the `getAllItemsNames()` method retrieved a list of all item names. This was accomplished by using the query root to specifically request the `itemName` attribute. The slightly convoluted syntax, using the meta-model, ensures that you're requesting a value that's available in a query root. You can't request a username value if your query root is an item because an item doesn't have a username. The relevant lines of code from that earlier example are reprinted as follows:

```
Root<Item> root = query.from(Item.class);
query.select(root.get(Item_.itemName));
```

SELECTING MULTIPLE VALUES

Selecting multiple values is the next logical step. Often you want more than a single value—usually you need the value along with the key the value is associated with. To do this, you create a `CriteriaQuery` instance that's typed as an `Object[]`. You then use the `CritieriaBuilder` instance to construct a `CompoundSelection` instance and provide the values you're interested in retrieving. The values can come from any instance that you're retrieving—if you're doing a join on multiple tables, you can pluck the values you're interested in from the join. An array of objects is returned by the query, which can be slightly dangerous because coding errors in dealing with the resulting array are found only at execution time and not by the compiler. To get a better sense of this, the following code snippet returns the `itemId` along with the `itemName`—much more useful than just retrieving the name alone:

```
CriteriaQuery<Object[]> query = builder.createQuery(Object[].class);
Root<Item> root = query.from(Item.class);
query.select(builder.array(root.get(Item_.itemId),
  root.get(Item_.itemName)));
TypedQuery<Object[]> tq = entityManager.createQuery(query);
```

SELECTING WRAPPERS

Working with arrays of objects is problematic because you won't discover errors with the handling of the array until runtime. Furthermore, depending on the type of data you're dealing with, you might not discover that the array element is being accessed. For example, if you were retrieving bid start and end dates, you might not realize an error where you accidently grabbed the wrong date/time due to an off-by-one mistake. With wrappers, you can construct an object just to handle the results of the query. In the example earlier from ActionBazaar, you used a wrapper to collect all of the values returned by a `JOIN` expression into a single object that summarized a winning bid. The relevant code from the section on joining is shown again in the following listing.

Listing 11.8 Constructing `WinningBidWrapper` class from a complex query

```
query.select(
  builder.construct(
    WinningBidWrapper.class,                        <- Class to be instantiated for each row in result set
    userRoot.get( BazaarAccount_.username ),        <- First parameter to constructor
    bidRoot.get( Bid_.bidPrice ),                   <- Second parameter to constructor
    itemRoot.get(Item_.itemName) ,                  <- Third parameter to constructor
    itemRoot.get(Item_.description)                 <- Forth parameter to constructor
));
```

In this code excerpt you can see that the `CriteriaBuilder construct` method takes a class along with the columns to appear in the result set that will then be fed into the class's constructor. So the list of parameters following the class serves two purposes: to define the columns to be retrieved and to specify the parameters to the class's constructor. The class you provide is a regular POJO—it doesn't have to be a JPA entity.

SELECTING TUPLES

Wrapper classes are very convenient, but creating too many custom wrapper objects can clutter a code base. To get around this but still benefit from type-safety, the criteria API provides support for retrieving results as tuples. A tuple is an ordered list of elements—in this case, results. Using the meta-model, you specify what values are selected and then retrieve the values from the tuple. You can also retrieve values using a string key, identifier, and so on. The code in the following listing retrieves the same winning bid summary data, but it uses a tuple to report the results.

Listing 11.9 Selecting values and retrieving the result as a tuple

```
public List<Tuple> getWinningBidTuple(Long itemId) {
  CriteriaBuilder builder = entityManager.getCriteriaBuilder();
  CriteriaQuery<Tuple> query = builder.createTupleQuery();      <- Creates a new CriteriaBuilder instance typed as a tuple
  Root<Item> itemRoot = query.from(Item.class);
  Root<Order> orderRoot = query.from(Order.class);
  Root<Bid> bidRoot = query.from(Bid.class);
  Root<BazaarAccount> userRoot = query.from(BazaarAccount.class);
  Join<Order,Bid> j1 = orderRoot.join(Order_.bid);
  Join<Order,Item> j2 = orderRoot.join(Order_.item);
  Join<Order,BazaarAccount> j3 = orderRoot.join(Order_.bidder);
  Path<Long> itemIdPath = itemRoot.get(Item_.itemId);
  Predicate itemPredicate = builder.equal(itemIdPath,itemId);
  query.multiselect(                                            <- Selects attributes to be in tuple
    userRoot.get( BazaarAccount_.username ),
    bidRoot.get( Bid_.bidPrice ),
    itemRoot.get(Item_.itemName) ,
    itemRoot.get(Item_.description));
  TypedQuery<Tuple> q = entityManager.createQuery(query);       <- Creates a TypedQuery tuple
  query.where(itemPredicate);
```

```
  List<Tuple> results = q.getResultList();          <-- Executes query and
  for(Tuple result : results) {                          retrieves results as a tuple
    logger.log(Level.INFO, "Item: {0}",
      result.get(itemRoot.get(Item_.itemName)));   <-- Extracts a value
  }                                                      from tuple
  return q.getResultList();
}
```

From the code in this listing, you can see that using a tuple is relatively straightforward and not very different from a wrapped object. The elements in the tuple can be accessed using the meta-model, index, or string keys. For illustration, the item names are logged at the end of the method to demonstrate how values can be retrieved.

11.3 Native queries

Just what is native SQL? It's the SQL understood by the specific database server—Oracle, MySQL, Derby, and so on—that you're using. Up to this point, you've been constructing queries either in JPQL or via the criteria API, which are then converted into native SQL. This extra layer gives you database-independence and also enables you to work in terms of objects instead of the relational model. This extra layer of abstraction is a double-edged sword in that you can't use any database-specific features. Native queries allow for the direct use of database-specific SQL without the extra translation layer.

To see how native SQL is beneficial, suppose you want to generate a hierarchical list of categories, each showing its subcategories; it's impossible to do that in JPQL because JPQL doesn't support recursive joins, similar to databases like Oracle. This means you have to use native SQL.

Let's assume you're using an Oracle database and you want to retrieve all subcategories of a particular category by using recursive joins in the form of a `START WITH ... CONNECT BY ...` clause as follows:

```
SELECT CATEGORY_ID, CATEGORY_NAME
FROM CATEGORY
START WITH parent_id = ?
CONNECT BY PRIOR category_id = category_id
```

Ideally, you should limit your use of native SQL to queries that you can't express using JPQL (as in your Oracle database–specific SQL query). But for demonstration purposes, in the example in the next section we've used a simple SQL statement that can be used with most relational databases.

> **NOTE** A JPA provider just executes SQL statements as JDBC statements and doesn't track whether the SQL statement updated data related to any entities. You should avoid using SQL `INSERT`, `UPDATE`, and `DELETE` statements in a native query because your persistence provider will have no knowledge of such changes in the database, and it may lead to inconsistent/stale data if your JPA provider uses caching.

As in JPQL, you can use both dynamic queries and named queries with SQL. You have to remember the subtle differences between JPQL and SQL. JPQL returns an entity, or set, of scalar values, but a SQL query returns database records. Therefore, a SQL query may return more than entities, because you may join multiple tables in your SQL. Let's see how to use native SQL with both dynamic and native queries.

11.3.1 Using dynamic queries with native SQL

You can use the `createNativeQuery` method of the `EntityManager` interface to create a dynamic query using SQL as follows:

```
Query q = em.createNativeQuery("SELECT user_id, first_name, last_name "
          + " FROM users WHERE user_id IN (SELECT seller_id FROM "
          + "items GROUP BY seller_id HAVING COUNT(*) > 1)",
            actionbazaar.persistence.User.class);

return q.getResultList();
```

In this statement the `createNativeQuery` method takes two parameters: the SQL query and the entity class being returned. This will become an issue if the query returns more than one entity class, which is why JPA allows a `@SqlResultSetMapping` to be used with the `createNativeQuery` method instead of passing an entity class. A `@SqlResultSetMapping` may be mapped to one or more entities.

For example, if you want to create a `SqlResultSetMapping` for the `User` entity and use it in your native query, then you can use the `@SqlResultSetMapping` annotation as follows:

```
@SqlResultSetMapping(name = "UserResults",
  entities = @EntityResult(
    entityClass =  actionbazaar.persistence.User.class))
```

Then you can specify the mapping in the query as follows:

```
Query q = em.createNativeQuery("SELECT user_id, first_name, last_name "
          + " FROM users WHERE user_id IN (SELECT seller_id FROM "
          + "items GROUP BY seller_id HAVING COUNT(*) > 1)",
            "UserResults");

return q.getResultList();
```

This is useful when the SQL query returns more than one entity. The persistence provider will automatically determine the entities being returned based on the `SqlResultSetMapping`, instantiate the appropriate entities, and initialize those entities with values based on the O/R mapping metadata.

Once you create a query, it makes no difference whether you retrieve the results from a native SQL or a JPQL query.

11.3.2 Using a named native SQL query

Using a named native query is quite similar to using a named JPQL query. To use a named native query, you must first create it. You can use the `@NamedNativeQuery` annotation to define a named query:

```
public @interface NamedNativeQuery {
  String name();
```

```
  String query();
  QueryHint[] hints() default {};
  Class resultClass() default void.class;
  String resultSetMapping() default ""; // name of SQLResultSetMapping
}
```

You can either use an entity class or a result set mapping with the `@NamedNativeQuery` annotation. Suppose you want to convert the query that was used earlier to a named native query. The first step is to define the named native query in the `User` entity:

```
@NamedNativeQuery(
  name = "findUserWithMoreItems",
  query = "SELECT user_id , first_name , last_name,
             birth_date
   FROM   users
   WHERE user_id IN
  ( SELECT seller_id
   FROM items
   GROUP BY seller_id   HAVING COUNT(*) > ?)",
   hints = {@QueryHint(name = "toplink.cache-usage",
      value="DoNotCheckCache")},
  resultClass = actionbazaar.persistence.User.class)
```

Next, if your query returns more than one entity class, you must define `SqlResultSetMapping` in the entity class using `resultSetMapping` as follows:

```
@NamedNativeQuery(
  name = "findUserWithMoreItems",
  query = "SELECT user_id , first_name , last_name,
               birth_date
          FROM users
          WHERE user_id IN
             (SELECT seller_id
              FROM items
              GROUP BY seller_id
              HAVING COUNT(*) > ?)",
  resultSetMapping = "UserResults")
```

You can provide a vendor-specific hint using the `queryHint` element of the `NamedNativeQuery`. It's similar to the `hints` element for `NamedQuery` discussed in section 10.3.2.

> **NOTE** There's no difference in executing a named native SQL query and a JPQL named query, except that a named parameter in a native SQL query isn't required by the JPA spec.

To illustrate how similar the execution of JPQL and native SQL queries is, you'll execute the named native query `findUserWithMoreItems` (which you defined earlier in a session bean method):

```
return em.createNamedQuery("findUserWithMoreItems")
                    .setParameter(1, 5)
                    .getResultList();
```

This statement first creates a query instance for the named native query `findUser-WithMoreItems`. Next, you set the required positional parameter. Finally, you return the result set.

11.3.3 Using stored procedures

Java EE 7 introduced support for invoking stored procedures. A stored procedure is essentially a script that executes inside of the database. The language used to write the scripts is usually database-specific—Oracle has PL/SQL, SQL Server uses Transact-SQL, PostgreSQL supports its own pgSQL as well as pl/perl and pl/PHP, and so on. Some databases even support stored procedures written in Java including Oracle, Informix, and DB2. A stored procedure is basically a function that takes a set of parameters and can optionally return data. The data can be returned from the function or passed back via the parameters to the function. Parameters can be `IN`, `OUT`, or `INOUT`—`IN` being a parameter passed in, `OUT` being a parameter used to return a value, and `INOUT` being a parameter that's consumed and also returns a value.

Stored procedures are used for a myriad of reasons: faster performance, data logging, avoiding network traffic on complex queries, encapsulating business logic, handling permissions, and more. Stored procedures can either be invoked like a query or automatically executed in the case of a trigger. These two methods of invoking stored procedures are the most common, but several databases provide even more methods such as using HTTP to invoke the stored procedure. With JPA, you can invoke a stored procedure and process the results just like any other query.

With JPA's stored procedure support, you work with a `javax.persistence.Stored-ProcedureQuery` object. This class extends the `javax.persistence.Query` interface that you've seen throughout this chapter. To create a `StoredProcedureQuery`, you use one of the three methods on the `EntityManager`:

```
StoredProcedureQuery createStoredProcedureQuery(String procedureName);
StoredProcedureQuery createStoredProcedureQuery(
    String procedureName, Class... resultClasses);
StoredProcedureQuery createStoredProcedureQuery(
    String procedureName, String... resultSetMappings);
```

These methods take a procedure name as well as the result types or mappings. The procedure name is the name of the procedure in the database. Table 11.13 lists the important methods on the `StoredProcedureQuery` interface. You use these methods to configure the parameters that you'll send the procedure. As mentioned earlier, parameters can be used to pass in values (`IN`), retrieve data (`OUT`), or both pass in and retrieve data (`INOUT`)—referred to as the direction of the parameter. The `Parameter-Mode` is an enum that you pass in when you're defining the parameters.

To get a better idea of how to use stored procedures, let's look at a trivial example from ActionBazaar. An example stored procedure from ActionBazaar, written in pgSQL, is shown in listing 11.10. pgSQL is one of the scripting languages supported by

Table 11.13 Table key methods on the StoredProcedureQuery interface for setting parameters

Method	Description
setParameter(Parameter<T> param, T value)	Sets a parameter
setParameter(Parameter<Calendar> param, Calendar value, TemporalType temporalType)	Sets a parameter that's a calendar
setParameter(Parameter<Date> param, Date value, TemporalType temporalType)	Sets a parameter that's a date
setParameter(String name, Object value)	Sets a parameter via a string name
setParameter(String name, Calendar value, TemporalType temporalType)	Sets a calendar parameter via a string name
setParameter(String name, Date value, TemporalType temporalType)	Sets a date parameter via a string name
setParameter(int position, Object value)	Sets parameter via a position
setParameter(int position, Calendar value, TemporalType temporalType)	Sets calendar parameter via a position
setParameter(int position, Date value, TemporalType temporalType)	Sets date parameter via a position
Object getOutputParameterValue(int position)	Retrieves an IN or OUT parameter that was passed back via position
Object getOutputParameterValue(String parameterName)	Retrieve an IN or OUT parameter that was passed back via a string
registerStoredProcedureParameter(String parameterName, Class type, ParameterMode mode)	Registers a stored procedure parameter
int getUpdateCount()	Retrieves the update count or –1 if there's no pending result
boolean execute()	Executes the query

PostgreSQL—it's very similar to PL/SQL. The language isn't important, but it highlights the fact that by using stored procedures, an Enterprise application becomes tied to a particular database, which may or may not be an issue.

Listing 11.10 Stored procedure for counting the bids for a particular user ID (pgSQL)

```
CREATE FUNCTION getQtyOrders(userId int) RETURNS int AS $$   <-- Defines a new PostgreSQL function taking one parameter
DECLARE
    qty int;
BEGIN
    SELECT COUNT(*) INTO qty FROM BID WHERE bazaaraccount_user_id = userId;
    RETURN qty;                                                <-- Returns a single integer result
END;
$$ LANGUAGE plpgsql;
```

The stored procedure in this listing defines a `getQtyOrders` method that accepts a user ID and returns the number of bids created by the particular user. Thus, the procedure has one parameter and one result. The input parameter is an integer and the result parameter is also an integer. The code in the next listing invokes this procedure.

Listing 11.11 Invoking a stored procedure using JPA

```
StoredProcedureQuery spq =                                     <-- 1 Creates a new StoredProcedureQuery
  entityManager.createStoredProcedureQuery("getQtyOrders");
spq.registerStoredProcedureParameter("param1", Integer.class,  <-- 2 Registers a parameter for stored procedure
  ParameterMode.IN);
spq.setParameter("param1",userID);                             <-- 3 Sets parameter
Object[] count = (Object[])spq.getSingleResult();
```

The code in this listing creates a `StoredProcedureQuery` ❶ and then registers a parameter that is an integer ❷. This parameter is named `param1`, which is then used for setting the value ❸. Finally, the stored procedure is executed just like any other query and the results retrieved. Thus, invoking a stored procedure isn't very different from invoking a regular query.

That concludes our survey of JPQL, the criteria API, and using native queries. Let's revisit the major topics of this chapter and then dive into CDI.

11.4 Summary

In this chapter we covered JPQL, the criteria API, and native SQL queries. The three approaches to querying data in JPA tackle different problems of querying O/R mapping data. JPQL is a query language with syntax very similar to that of SQL except you work in objects. It's still a string-based approach, and interacting with it is similar to working with JDBC's `PreparedStatements`. The criteria API is completely different—it uses a meta-model of your JPA entities, enabling you to construct queries using Java code that's type-safe. Although the code is verbose and not as easy to read, you won't have to worry about chasing syntax errors at runtime. The final query language support we covered was native queries. The native query support enables you to use native SQL queries. With the previous two approaches, JPA converts either the JPQL or criteria query into native SQL. With native SQL, you skip that step and can use database-specify features. With Java EE 7, you gained the ability to invoke stored procedures from JPA, which opens up even more opportunities.

In the next chapter we'll transition to CDI—a powerful dependency injection technology that was introduced with Java EE 6 and continues to be critical in Java EE 7.

12 Using CDI with EJB 3

This chapter covers

- Dependency injection for POJOs
- Scopes and bean lifecycles
- Core CDI constructs
- Long-running conversations

Context and Dependency Injection (CDI) is an exciting new feature that was introduced with Java EE 6 and further extended in Java EE 7. CDI brings full-fledged dependency injection and context support to the Java EE platform. In earlier chapters you saw examples of resource injection using `@PersistenceUnit`, `@Resource`, and `@EJB` to inject resources as well as other EJBs. We've also delved into interceptors that provide basic AOP support. These powerful features, along with other innovations including JPA, have greatly simplified Java EE development.

But the innovations that were introduced in Java EE 5 with EJB 3 were primarily limited to EJBs. Using EJBs from the web tier required a substantial amount of boilerplate code to retrieve instances from JNDI. JSF-backing beans were rudimentary and offered few services. Solutions such as JBoss Seam attempted to fill this gap by providing an advanced bean container that bridged the EJB and POJO world and also by providing additional services to non-EJB beans. The Java community took notice, and JBoss Seam served as the inspiration for CDI that was introduced as a core technology in Java EE 6 and expanded in Java EE 7.

This chapter will cover all of the fundamental concepts of CDI, as well as the basic constructs. Throughout this chapter you'll use CDI to build a robust front end to ActionBazaar and glue the JSF presentation layer to the EJBs. Let's start by looking at the genesis of CDI and the technologies that influenced its evolution.

12.1 Introducing CDI

CDI was originally developed via the Java Community Process (JCP) as JSR-299. Originally JSR-299 was called WebBeans, but it quickly became evident that the features encompassed within JSR-299 went far beyond replacing the oft-maligned JSF-managed beans. The progenitor of CDI was an open source project from JBoss called Seam. Seam attempted to simplify Java EE development by enabling JSF to directly use and invoke EJB, as well as by providing components—basically Java beans—that were defined using annotations and injected. Seam also included support for generating and sending emails, business process integration, and context. Seam's context feature included support for a conversational context, which greatly simplifies web application development for tabbed web browsers. When Seam was introduced, Java EE had negligible support for dependency injection (DI). At the same time, Spring was upending traditional Java EE development and challenging the standard Java EE containers. Spring demonstrated the power of dependency injection and the need for it in Java EE.

Although Seam greatly simplified Java EE development and made it possible to use EJBs easily from JSF, Seam was still an add-on. To use Seam you still had to download and configure it for your particular container. There were issues with some containers, so using Seam involved verifying that it would work with your specific container and possibly working around issues specific to your container. The value provided by Seam, combined with competition from Spring and Google Guice, made the capabilities provided by Seam too important to remain an external add-on. As a result, a JSR was initiated and many of the core features from Seam were pulled into Java EE 6 as CDI.

Integrating the core features of Seam required explicitly defining a bean within the context of Java EE. Prior to Java EE 6 there was no unified bean definition. At the time there were two types of beans: JSF-backing beans and Enterprise Java Beans. To provide a common definition, the concept of a managed bean was introduced with the managed bean specification. A managed bean is simply a POJO that's managed by a container, with the container providing a basic set of services including resource injection, lifecycle callbacks, and interceptors. A managed bean must have a no-argument constructor, not be serializable, and possess a unique name. Managed beans are defined using the `@ManagedBean` annotation with annotations for lifecycle callbacks: `@PostConstruct` and `@Destroy`. These requirements, such as the no-argument constructor, can be relaxed by managed bean extensions. EJBs, JSF-backing beans, and CDI beans are managed bean extensions.

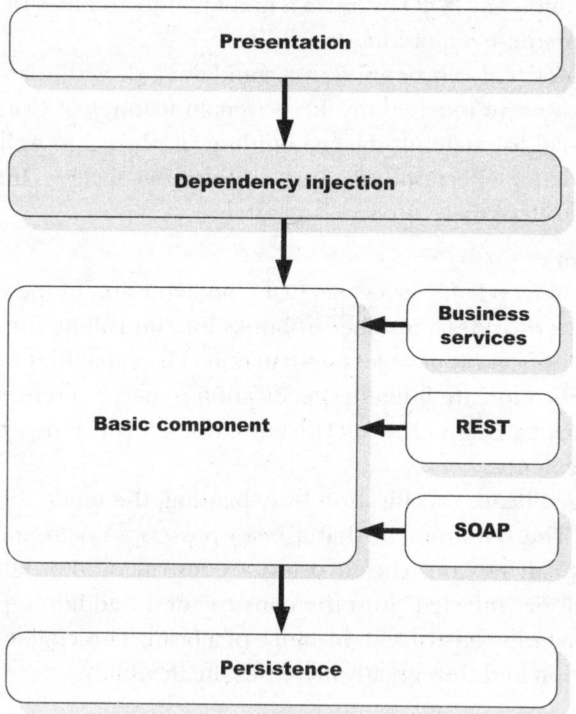

Figure 12.1 CDI in context of services

CDI is much more than an extension to managed beans. It's a full-fledged object container that can be used independently of Java EE. For example, CDI can be used in standalone desktop JavaFX applications. With CDI, practically any POJO can be a managed bean; this includes POJOs that lack no-argument constructors or require a special factory to be instantiated. CDI doesn't provide a component model of its own. More importantly, CDI unifies the JSF and EJB bean models, enabling JSF to use EJBs as backing beans. In some ways it's an integration framework that glues the front end to the back end. Figure 12.1 puts CDI in context with the other Java EE technologies.

As you can see in figure 12.1, CDI sits as the bridge layer between JSF and the managed beans. With the release of Java EE 7, CDI is now specified in JSR-346.

12.1.1 CDI services

CDI provides a core set of services that are built around the concepts of contexts and dependency injection. Contexts, which we'll define in more depth shortly, can be viewed as well-defined lifecycle scopes. You've already seen dependency injection in earlier chapters, but CDI takes DI to a new level. Earlier you used EJB 3 dependency injection to inject database connections, JPA persistence contexts, and references to other EJBs. This was accomplished via specific annotations such as `@Resource`, `@PersistenceContext`, and `@EJB`. EJB 3 dependency injection is limited to only EJBs;

you can't perform injection into any POJO or inject a non-EJB into an EJB. CDI's dependency injection doesn't have these limitations, as you'll see.

CDI is an object container that can be used as a standalone or within an existing Java EE container. Although we've touched on the two main features of CDI, the CDI container provides a lifecycle for stateful objects, binding of objects to well-defined contexts, type-safe dependency injection, an event notification facility, and robust interceptors. Let's look at each of these services separately.

LIFECYCLE FOR STATEFUL OBJECTS

CDI provides a well-defined lifecycle for its beans. CDI is an extension of the managed beans specification and thus provides a number of hooks for controlling the creation of new objects, as well as notification of object destruction. The capabilities specified in the managed bean specification are limited; specification is merely a reformulation of the limitations of JSF-backing beans. The specification doesn't preclude extensions and it encourages enhancements.

CDI extends the managed beans specification by expanding the modes by which a bean can be instantiated. The requirement that a bean possess a no-argument constructor is relaxed. Beans can be constructed using a constructor that takes arguments. The parameters will be "injected" into the constructor. In addition, producer methods can be defined that will construct an instance of a bean. This enables the factory pattern for bean creation and thus greatly increases the flexibility.

CONTEXTS

The concept of context is easiest to understand by looking at your typical e-commerce web application. Most web applications have at least two contexts or scopes: application and session. The data stored in the *application scope* is shared—it isn't tied to one particular user. An example of this would be data that cached for a website landing page. This page is accessible to all users, and it doesn't make sense to access the database for the same information for each visitor. *Session scope*, on the other hand, is associated with a specific user—typically a browser window. A typical example of a session scope is a virtual shopping cart. The shopping cart contains the items specific to each visitor. The application state associated with the user is associated/tracked using either cookies or IDs appended to the URL. Application and session scopes are different types of contexts.

We've just looked at two different contexts that you have in your typical web application. But if you step back, you'll realize that there's more than one context in your application—there are actually many. With the advent of tabbed web browsers, a user may be browsing two different parts of your website. In the case of a travel website, a user might have two tabs open and be comparing flights to Rome on two different days or comparing two different hotels. The user thus has two different contexts that must be tracked separately. In addition, the user may have created a nested context by launching a wizard in one window to not only pick a hotel but also book a car at the same time. As you can see, application scope and session scope are suddenly not enough; you need additional contexts with which to build your applications.

This is where CDI comes into play. It introduces additional contexts and provides a simple mechanism by which you can define additional contexts. Because CDI is also a container, it manages your objects being fully aware of the context the object is associated with. Objects are bound to contexts and their lifecycle is tied to the context. This is extremely powerful; the container is now doing a lot of the heavy lifting that used to be the responsibility of the application.

CDI comes with four built-in contexts or scopes:

- Application
- Conversation
- Request
- Session

Besides these four scopes, there are also two pseudo-scopes: singleton and dependent. The singleton scope handles the special case of singleton beans. The dependent scope is the scope that a bean is assigned to by default if the bean isn't assigned explicitly to a scope. An object that belongs to the dependent scope is created when the object it belongs to is created and is destroyed when its owning object is destroyed. This might seem a little confusing, but it'll be clarified as you move through this chapter.

You're not limited to the six scopes or contexts we just discussed. CDI has a pluggable architecture and with a little code, you can develop your own contexts. For example, you might port support for JSF's view scope into CDI.

TYPE-SAFE DEPENDENCY INJECTION

Unlike other DI frameworks, CDI doesn't use string-based identifiers to determine what object should be injected. Instead, CDI uses type information provided by the Java object model to determine what object should be injected. In situations where the determination is ambiguous because multiple Java objects match the type, qualifier annotations are used to select the correct candidate. Because CDI uses the Java type system and annotations, there's never any doubt as to what will be injected and the types always match.

EVENT NOTIFICATION

One of the dangers with large feature-rich applications is tight coupling. There's the danger that as the application grows it'll increasingly become a tangled mess. Injection will be performed just so a listener can be registered. Registration of listeners is fraught with many challenges, because this is server-side development where objects may be serialized and new sessions initiated. Although injection simplifies the process of acquiring a reference to an object, it isn't quite enough. What you want to be able to do is declare that a bean listens for certain events and then lets the framework handle the event routing. This is accomplished by placing an annotation on the method that receives the event, and the container handles the rest. This would be analogous in Swing to marking a method that processes an `ActionListenerEvent` and having the listener registration performed automatically.

INTERCEPTORS

You've already seen the interceptor support provided by EJB. Interceptor support in both EJB and CDI is specified in JSR-381 Interceptors 1.1. With CDI, interceptors aren't limited to EJBs and can be used on any bean managed by CDI. With CDI, interceptors can be used with business methods on a bean, as well as lifecycle and timeout callbacks. When we dive into implementation details, you'll see how CDI has used annotations for marking classes and methods that should be intercepted.

Related to interceptors, CDI also introduces a new construct called *decorators*. A decorator is an interceptor that's tied to a specific interface. The decorator implements the interface it will be intercepting. Thus, a decorator is an interceptor that provides interception that's tied to the specific business logic. A decorator, unlike an interceptor, has intimate knowledge of the class it's intercepting. An interceptor is a generic solution for crosscutting across disparate classes, whereas a decorator is for crosscutting on a specific inheritance hierarchy.

Now that you have a basic handle on the major features of CDI, it's time to turn your attention to the relationship between CDI and EJB 3. After all, this is a book on EJB, so we know you're interested in how the two technologies complement each other.

12.1.2 Relationship between CDI and EJB 3

The relationship between EJB and CDI can be confusing at first. Both are object containers and so there's some overlap in terms of functionality. EJB beans are still managed by the EJB container. Thus, the EJB container handles transactions and concurrency and provides all of the supporting functionality that we covered in earlier chapters. CDI manages its own beans but also provides services to EJBs. The two aren't competing technologies but are instead complementary. You can think of CDI beans as object containers that provide injection, events, interceptors, and scoping support to objects that don't need the full set of services provided by the EJB container. Throughout this book we've delineated the situations where you should use an EJB—where you need transaction support, security, and so on. CDI is the container for your POJOs.

CDI and EJB are fully integrated. This means that EJBs can use all of the services we just discussed including dependency injection, event notification, interceptors, and decorators. These services are available to all EJB types: singleton, stateless, stateful, and message-driven beans. Because there's an overlap in services, you might be wondering when you should use the EJB services (injection, interceptors, and so on) versus their CDI counterparts. The simple answer is to use the CDI variant because they're more powerful, generic, and not limited to just EJBs. As you'll see, you can safely use the `@Inject` instead of the `@EJB`.

The interoperability between the two technologies makes it much easier to call singleton, stateless, and stateful session beans. CDI's DI will support the injection of EJBs into CDI beans. This eliminates the need to write code that will retrieve beans from JNDI. Just add the `@Inject` annotation and CDI will take care of the rest. Thus, using EJBs has never been easier—you can treat an EJB bean just like any other POJO.

Furthermore, if a CDI bean takes on additional functionality, you can simply add a `@Stateless`, `@Singleton`, and `@Stateful` annotation and make your bean an EJB.

CDI isn't a replacement technology for EJBs but a powerful enhancement. CDI not only empowers EJB, it also greatly augments JSF.

12.1.3 Relationship between CDI and JSF 2

We've already touched on the key aspects of the relationship between CDI and JSF 2. CDI provides a robust replacement for JSF-backing beans. The enhanced beans provided by CDI are much more feature-rich as compared to JSF-backing beans. CDI beans are much more flexible—you don't need to define your beans in faces-config.xml. With CDI, practically any Java object can be a bean, and you have several different methods of instantiating a bean. CDI beans can be used as a drop-in replacement for JSF-managed beans.

Although we've already covered the relationship between CDI and EJB, CDI has a big impact on the use of EJBs from JSF. With CDI, JSF can directly invoke methods on EJBs. You no longer have to write glue code to connect JSF with EJBs. Thus, from a JSF page you can directly invoke a method on a singleton, stateless, or stateful session bean. EJBs can be directly resolved from Expression Language (EL) expressions.

We emphasize the strong interoperability between CDI and JSF, but CDI isn't tied to JSF. JSF benefits from the services provided by CDI, but CDI itself is agnostic to the web framework. Going forward, CDI support will undoubtedly be supported by other web frameworks. Already there's a plug-in enabling CDI and Struts 2 to interoperate. Because CDI is now a core part of Java EE 6 and 7 and is also mandated by the web profile, support for CDI will only continue to grow. Now that you have a conceptual understanding of CDI, let's take a quick look at the basics of CDI beans.

12.2 CDI beans

Unlike EJB, CDI doesn't have its own component model. A bean within CDI can be a managed bean (JSF), Enterprise Java Bean, or POJO. All of these types of objects can use the full range of services provided by CDI. In this chapter, when we refer to a CDI bean we usually mean a POJO unless stated otherwise. CDI beans are thus very flexible and not a distinct class of beans like JSF-managed beans or EJBs.

Although CDI is in no way tied to JSF, CDI beans (POJOs) should be used instead of JSF-managed beans. This means that you should no longer be defining beans with faces-config.xml or using the `@ManagedBean` annotation.

A CDI bean is associated with a context, has a type, and may be qualified. The context determines the lifecycle of the bean, whether it lives for only one request or it's a part of a conversation or workflow. One of the features of CDI is the fact that DI uses the type system. As a result, whereas other object containers use a string name, CDI uses the Java type as the name of the bean. Because a bean can only have one type, CDI includes something call a qualifier, which is type-safe, to distinguish between different instances of the same type. With this basic understanding of what constitutes a CDI bean, let's look at how you can use CDI beans.

12.2.1 How to use CDI beans

The creators of CDI took the approach of convention over configuration. This means that you can start using it immediately. If your application container supports CDI, which it does if it's at least compliant with Java EE 6, then all you have to do is place a beans.xml file in your application. The beans.xml file serves two purposes: it's a configuration file for CDI and it's a marker file so that CDI knows whether it needs to scan the JAR file for beans. The following listing shows an empty configuration file. This file should be placed in the META-INF directory of any archive containing the beans.

Listing 12.1 Empty beans.xml configuration file

```
<?xml version="1.0" encoding="UTF-8"?>
<beans xmlns="http://java.sun.com/xml/ns/javaee"
       xmlns:xsi="http://www.w3.org/2001/XMLSchema-instance"
       xsi:schemaLocation="http://java.sun.com/xml/ns/javaee
       http://java.sun.com/xml/ns/javaee/beans_1_0.xsd">
</beans>
```

Any POJO contained within the JAR archive can be a CDI bean. Generally you create an instance of a bean by either injecting an instance or referencing a bean from a JSF page. CDI will take care of acquiring an instance of the bean. One important feature to be aware of is that CDI is much more flexible than either JSF-managed beans or EJBs. With POJO beans you may have a constructor that takes arguments. Only one no-argument constructor may be provided, and its parameters must be other CDI beans (POJOs, JSF-managed beans, or EJBs). In addition, CDI supports producer methods for creating beans in situations where you either need to keep a reference to the original bean or have complete control over the instantiation of the bean. We'll examine these different techniques for creating beans as we proceed through the chapter. But first, let's examine the important concept of component naming.

12.2.2 Component naming and EL resolution

Unlike other DI frameworks, CDI doesn't use string-based identifiers for beans. Instead it relies on the Java type system so that DI is type-safe.

With unified EL expressions, there's no type information available. To solve this problem, CDI provides an annotation, `@Named`, which must be placed on classes or producer methods (covered later). This annotation defines the name that can then be used in unified EL expressions. The annotation is defined as follows:

```
package javax.inject;
@Qualifier
@Documented
@Retention(RUNTIME)
public @interface Named {
  String value() default "";
}
```

This annotation can optionally take a value, which will be used as the name of the bean. If no value is provided, the name of the class will be used instead. The `@Named` annotation doesn't mark the class as being a CDI bean; it merely defines a name for the class so that it can be called from a unified EL expression, as shown in the following listing..

Listing 12.2 `Employee` class marked for use with unified EL

```
@Named
@RequestScoped
public class Employee extends User implements Serializable {

    public String getTitle() {
        return title;
    }

    public void setTitle(String title) {
        this.title = title;
    }
    ...
}
```

❶ Assigns string-based name to be assigned to Employee (`@Named`)

Defines scope of class as being request (`@RequestScoped`)

This listing contains the `Employee` class from ActionBazaar. The `@Named` annotation has been placed on the class ❶. The class will thus be available for use in unified EL expressions. The `Employee` class is marked as being request-scoped; each request will get a new instance. In the next listing, an employee instance is referenced from the editEmployee.xhtml file.

Listing 12.3 Referencing employee instance from editEmployee.xhtml

```
<!DOCTYPE html>
<HTML
    xmlns:f="http://java.sun.com/jsf/core"
    xmlns:h="http://java.sun.com/jsf/html">
    <h:head>
        <title>Edit Employee</title>
    </h:head>
    <h:body>
        <h:form id="accountForm">
            <h:panelGrid columns="2">
                <h:outputLabel for="title" value="Title"/>
                <h:inputText id="title" value="#{employee.title}"/>
                <h:outputLabel for="username" value="User name"/>
                <h:inputText id="username" value="#{employee.username}"/>
        ...
            </h:panelGrid>
        ...
        </h:form>
</h:body>
</HTML>
```

Unified EL expression for accessing Employee's title property (`#{employee.title}`)

Unified EL expression for accessing Employee's username property (`#{employee.username}`)

As you can see in this listing, the name of the `Employee` bean is `employee` per the bean-naming conventions in Java. As a result, the first letter is lowercase. Without the `@Named` annotation, JSF would have been unable to resolve `employee`.

Let's next look at scoping. We've discussed contexts and scoping earlier in the chapter. Listing 12.2 contained a `@RequestScoped` annotation that may have seemed a little mysterious.

12.2.3 Bean scoping

Earlier we discussed the concept of contexts and scopes; both terms are used interchangeably. CDI comes with four scopes and two pseudo-scopes. Every bean is associated with a scope and the scope determines the lifecycle of the bean. When the scope is destroyed, so is the bean. The scope of a bean is configured using annotations that are placed on the class or a producer method (we'll cover this shortly). The annotations for the different scopes are documented in table 12.1.

Table 12.1 Scopes/contexts in CDI

Scope	Description
`@ApplicationScoped`	An instance is created only once for the duration of the application and is destroyed once the application is terminated.
`@Dependent`	An instance is created each time an injection is performed. This is the default scope of a bean and is used the vast majority of the time.
`@ConversationScoped`	This is a new scope type that was introduced with CDI but existed in JBoss's Seam. It's a scope that's programmatically controlled by the application. It spans multiple requests but is shorter than the session scope. In a web application, conversations are used for a task that spans multiple page requests. For example, this is how you'd handle the situations where a user is booking two different vacations in two different browser tabs.
`@RequestScoped`	This scope corresponds to the standard HTTP request. It begins when a request arrives and is discarded when the response is rendered.
`@SessionScoped`	This scope corresponds to the HTTP session. References live for the duration of the session.

If no annotation is placed on a bean, the bean is automatically assigned to the dependent scope. This means that a new instance of the bean will be created each time the bean is injected. The vast majority of the beans in an application will probably be dependent-scoped. For web applications, JSF-backing beans should be in either the request or the conversation scope.

Dependent scope and CDI

A common CDI mistake is to use a bean with the dependent scope as a backing bean for a JSF page. The problem with this approach is that each invocation will result in a new bean being created. When the user then submits the form, a new instance will be created, and it will appear as if the user never entered anything and the validation rules were skipped. Always use at least `@RequestScoped` or the stereotype `@Model`.

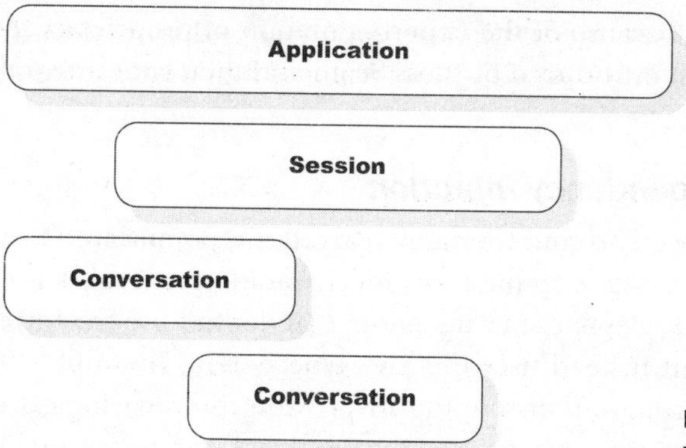

Figure 12.2 Conversation scope versus session and application

When using CDI, each bean is associated with a scope. The scope determines the lifecycle of the bean.

CONVERSATION SCOPE

The conversation scope deserves its own section. Unlike the other scopes, the conversation scope is a completely new beast. If you've used the forerunner to CDI, JBoss Seam (versions 1 or 2), you're probably familiar with the concept of a conversation. A conversation is a scope that's shorter than a session but longer than a request. This is shown in figure 12.2. A conversation is controlled programmatically; code determines when a conversation begins and ends.

The easiest way to think of a conversation is to look at how users interact with web applications using the current breed of web browsers. A bidder on ActionBazaar might open two tabs for viewing two items that they're interested in bidding on. Although they're viewing two separate items on two tabs, as far as ActionBazaar is concerned there's one session for this user. As a result, the current item the user is viewing can't be tracked using the user's session because the session is shared between the browser tabs. Imagine what would happen if the user were viewing a kayak on one tab and then opened up another tab to view a five-carat diamond. When the user switched back to the kayak and clicked Place Bid, there would be panic if the confirmation page showed a bid for the five-carat diamond. The concept of a conversation addresses this problem.

A bean is marked as belonging to a conversation by adding the `@ConversationScoped` annotation to the bean definition. By default, a conversation is associated with the current request scope and is terminated when the current request is destroyed. To make a conversation survive beyond the current request, it must be promoted to a *long-running conversation*. The promotion to a long-running conversation is done programmatically. For this to be done, the current conversation must be acquired via injection and the `begin` method invoked. A conversation can then either be programmatically terminated or expire after a fixed time period. The timeout is thus less than that of a session.

We'll revisit conversations later in this chapter once we've covered the basics of CDI. Conversations are one of the more advanced features. Conversations are an example of how the EE standard grows because of the experimentation of proprietary technologies. Conversations were first introduced by JBoss Seam and then later integrated into Java EE 6 and later.

12.3 Next generation of dependency injection

Dependency injection has been around for many years. It was popularized by proprietary frameworks. CDI looks to these frameworks for inspiration and takes it one step further by providing type-safe dependency injection. CDI doesn't use freeform strings to resolve dependencies but instead uses the Java type system. It couples this with component lifecycles and component scoping to provide the next logical step for dependency injection. Let's start off by looking at the `@Inject` annotation that you'll use extensively.

12.3.1 Injection with @Inject

The `@Inject` annotation is the heart of CDI. This annotation marks a point where an instance of a bean needs to be injected. It can be placed either on an instance variable or on a constructor. When the CDI container goes to instantiate a class containing fields marked with `@Inject`, it checks to see if an instance already exists; if not, it creates a new instance and sets the value. It's important to note that if a bean isn't annotated with a scoping annotation (`@Conversation`, `@RequestScoped`, or `@SessionScoped`, among others) then it falls under the *dependent* scope, which can be explicitly marked using the `@Dependent` annotation. CDI looks at the type on the injection point, as well as any qualifier annotations, to figure out what object needs to be injected or created and then injected. All of this resolution is performed when a bean is first instantiated.

Let's look at an example of using the `@Inject` annotation in ActionBazaar. Within ActionBazaar, the `LandingController` bean backs the homepage. It's an application-scoped bean that caches the newest items to be featured on the homepage. The newest items are cached because it doesn't make sense to hit the database for each page request. Retrieving data from the database on each request would dramatically decrease the scalability of the site with needless I/O. The code for the `LandingController` is shown in the following listing.

Listing 12.4 Backing bean for homepage

```
@Named                                          <- Makes LandingController to JSF
@ApplicationScoped                              <- Only one instance of LandingController will be created
public class LandingController {

  @Inject                                       <- (1) Injects itemManager
  private ItemManager itemManager;

  private List<Item> newestItems;

  @PostConstruct                                <- (2) Invoked after injection
  public void init() {
    newestItems = itemManager.getNewestItems();
  }
```

```
  public List<Item> getNewestItems() {
    return newestItems;
  }
}
```

The main focus in this code sample is the `@Inject` annotation on the `itemManager` ❶. When the `LandingController` is instantiated, CDI will retrieve an instance of the `itemManager` from the EJB container; `itemManager` is a stateless session bean. After injection, the CDI container will then invoke the method annotated with `@PostConstruct` ❷. Note that in this case you could easily have used the `@EJB` annotation instead. But you could have injected almost any other POJO, and you'll see this as the chapter proceeds. The next listing illustrates another permutation of the `@Inject` annotation using constructor injection.

Listing 12.5 Constructor using dependency injection

```
@Named
@ApplicationScoped
public class LandingController {

  private ItemManager itemManager;               ❶ Annotation removed from instance variable

  private List<Item> newestItems;

  protected LandingController() {}               ❷ Default constructor provided for container (serialization and the like)

  @Inject                                        ❸ Constructor marked with @Inject
  public LandingController( ItemManager itemManager) {     Constructor accepts ItemManager
    this.itemManager = itemManager;
  }
  ...
}
```

Using injection with a constructor gives you another approach for controlling the instantiation of a bean ❸. Only one constructor can be annotated for injection; if multiple constructors were annotated, the container would have no idea which one to use. In the case of the `LandingController`, the annotation is removed from the member variable ❶ and a parameter is added to the constructor. A default constructor ❷ is provided; that's often required by the container because the container usually wraps the object in a proxy to support method interceptors.

In the first example you could have easily used the `@EJB` annotations. The real power of the `@Inject` annotation is apparent when you annotate the constructor. This is a more natural approach—you don't need to use the `@PostConstruct` annotation to do setup operations after the bean is created and injection is performed. Using injection with constructors enables the beans to behave like regular POJOs—parameters are passed in via the constructor and the object initializes itself like any other object. You don't have to do injection and then use a callback to initialize the bean.

Up to this point, you've been letting the container instantiate the beans. But there are many situations where you want to control the creation of a bean and perform cleanup logic when the bean is to be destroyed. Let's take a look at producer methods.

12.3.2 Producer methods

In the last section you saw how you could use dependency injection with constructors to create a more natural approach to instantiating beans that was akin to how POJOs are constructed and used. But there are many situations where you need total control over the instantiation of a bean. For example, the bean instance might be derived from a record in a database or require some custom logic that prepares the bean instance or chooses the type that will be instantiated. To accommodate this requirement, CDI has the concept of a *producer method.* A producer is a method or instance variable that's consulted by CDI to create a bean instance. The method or instance variable is marked with the `@Producer` annotation. Because CDI is type-safe, it'll use the instance or return type to determine what type of bean the producer creates. A producer can also be annotated with a qualifier, but we'll defer discussion of qualifiers to later in the chapter. To better understand producers, let's look at an example from the ActionBazaar application in the following listing.

Listing 12.6 Producer providing a "currentUser" user instance

```
@Named
public class CurrentUserBean implements Serializable {

  @EJB
  private UserService userService;

  private User user;

  @Produces                                  <- (1) Marks method as a producer
  @SessionScoped                             <- (2) Instance that's being created is a session scoped
  @Named("currentUser")                      <- (3) Instance will be made available to JSF
  public User getCurrentUser() {
    if(user == null || user.isAnonymous()) {
      user = userService.getAuthenticatedUser();
    }
    return user;
  }

  public boolean isAuthenticated() {
    return userService.isAuthenticated();
  }
}
```

This listing has a producer method that's responsible for returning a `User` bean representing the current user visiting the ActionBazaar website. This method is annotated with the `@Produces` annotation (1). The `@SessionScoped` (2) annotation informs the CDI container that you want the instance stored in the current session. As a result, this method will be invoked only once for each session instance; the instance will be cached in the session. The `@Named` annotation (3) makes the instance available to JSF, giving JSF a string name that can be referenced from an EL expression. The next listing shows how the JSF page might look when using this `User` bean.

Listing 12.7 Invoking the producer from index.xhtml

```
<HTML xmlns:f="http://java.sun.com/jsf/core"
  xmlns:h="http://java.sun.com/jsf/html">
  <h:body>
    <h:form id="itemForm">
      Hi! <h:outputText rendered="#{currentUserBean.authenticated}"
        value="#{currentUser.username}"/>
      <h:link rendered="#{!currentUserBean.authenticated}"
        value="Sign in" outcome="login"/>
      <h:commandLink rendered="#{currentUserBean.authenticated}"
        immediate="true"
        action="#{logoutController.logout()}">Log-out</h:commandLink>
    </h:form>
  </h:body>
</HTML>
```

❶ Checks to see if user has authenticated

❷ Personalizes page with user's name

❸ Renders a link to login if user isn't authenticated

In this listing the producer method is invoked indirectly. Because the producer method is generating an instance which will be cached in the session, you want to invoke the producer method only when the user has authenticated and you have a principal object with the role of seller or bidder. So you first check to see if the user is authenticated ❶. If the user is authenticated ❷, then you evaluate the expression to display the username that results in either the current user instance being retrieved from the session object or the producer method invoked with the resulting value being cached in the session. If the visitor hasn't authenticated yet, you render a link to authenticate ❸.

With this code example, it's important to remember that CDI will scan all of the classes in a JAR file—the JAR file containing a beans.xml file. It'll keep track of all producer methods it discovers while analyzing the classes in the JAR file. When an instance of the bean is requested—a user as in the case of this example—CDI will invoke the producer method if an instance of the bean doesn't already exist in the current scope.

> **Producer methods and JPA**
>
> You might be wondering how CDI performs all of its magic. To provide these features, CDI wraps your bean in a proxy object. If you perform an `instanceof` on a bean that has been injected, comparing it against its type, it will return true. Most of the time, the fact that the injected bean is a proxy object isn't an issue. But JPA implementations often do care. If you try to pass a bean instance created by CDI to JPA, JPA will claim that the bean can't be persisted and that it isn't a known type. To solve this problem, you'll need to use a producer method and keep a reference to the original POJO. Anyone who gets a reference via injection will be working with a proxy.

In any bean in the application, you can now use the following code to get a reference to the current user:

```
@Inject
private User currentUser;
```

When looking at this code, remember to focus on the type. The name of the field is irrelevant as far as CDI is concerned. CDI does injection based on the type, which is therefore type-safe injection. But you may want to inject different instances of the `User` object—perhaps the `User` object is someone a customer service representative is currently servicing. In the next section you'll see how you can use qualifiers to add an additional layer of specificity beyond just the type of the injection point.

12.3.3 Using qualifiers

Dependency injection using just the type information is very powerful, but at this point you might be wondering whether you're limited to one instance of a given type. In the case of the current user example in the last section, what if you wanted to inject another instance representing the user a customer service representative is helping? CDI has a solution for this problem called a *qualifier.* A qualifier enables you to qualify certain injection points as using different instances of a bean. It enables you to mark a `User` object as being either the *current user* or the *current user being helped* and so on. A qualifier is specified using a custom annotation.

To define a qualifier, you define a new annotation and annotate the annotation with `@Qualifier`. The reason you're defining a new annotation and annotating, as opposed to passing a string name to a qualifier annotation, is so that you have strong typing. This is one of the differentiating features of CDI and reduces errors at runtime. The new annotation is then placed on both the injection points and the producer methods.

Building on the example of injecting the current authenticated user, you'll define a qualifier for the current authenticated user. This improves the readability of the code and also enables you to inject other user instances. The following code snippet defines the `@AuthenticatedUser` and `@Seller` qualifiers:

```
@Qualifier
@Retention(RUNTIME)
@Target({METHOD, FIELD, PARAMETER, TYPE})
public @interface AuthenticatedUser {}

@Qualifier
@Retention(RUNTIME)
@Target({METHOD, FIELD, PARAMETER, TYPE})
public @interface Seller {}
```

After defining the qualifier, you need to add the qualifier to the producer method:

```
@Produces @SessionScoped @AuthenticatedUser @Named("currentUser")
public User getCurrentUser() {
   ...
}
```

Once the qualifier has been defined, you can use it to tell CDI which instance you want injected, as shown in the next listing.

Listing 12.8 Controlling instance being injected via a qualifier

```
@Named
@RequestScoped
public class BidController implements Serializable {

  @Inject @Seller
  private User seller;

  @Inject @AuthenticatedUser
  private User user;

  public String placeOrder() {
    ...
  }
}
```

❶ Injects seller of item you're bidding

❷ Injects authenticated user who's bidding

In this listing you can see the qualifiers in action. You inject two `User` object instances. In the first instance ❶, you inject the seller of the item you're bidding on. In the second case you inject the authenticated user who's doing the bidding ❷. In both cases you've provided additional information so that the CDI container can figure out which instance to use.

The example shows only one qualifier, but it's possible to use multiple qualifiers. Multiple qualifiers provide an extra level of specification. Now that you have a handle on qualifiers, let's take a look at disposers.

12.3.4 Disposer methods

A *disposer* method is responsible for handling the destruction of a bean. Although it's conceptually similar to a C++ destructor or Java finalizer, it's uniquely different. First, a disposer method is placed in the same class as the producer, not on the class being disposed. Second, it's invoked when the context expires and the container is releasing the bean for destruction. For example, if a bean is session-scoped, the disposer method will not be invoked until the session has timed out.

Implementing a disposer method involves adding the `@Disposes` annotation to a method parameter. Qualifiers may also be used. Additional parameters can be specified; CDI will attempt to resolve the additional parameters as beans using qualifiers if provided. When the disposer method is invoked, the code can close database connections and so on. Let's see just how easy it is to use the `@Disposes` annotation, as shown in the next listing.

Listing 12.9 Disposer method handling destruction of an authenticated user instance

```
@Named
@SessionScoped
public class CurrentUserBean implements Serializable {
  ...
  @Produces @SessionScoped @AuthenticatedUser @Named("currentUser")
  public User getCurrentUser() {
    ...
  }
```

❶ Producer method must be in same class as disposer

```
    public void logout(
        @Disposes
        @AuthenticatedUser
        User user) {
        // Clean-up and record log-out
    }
}
```

❷ **Disposer method must be in same class as producer**

This listing demonstrates the disposer method in action. As mentioned, the disposer method must appear in the same class as the producer, but unlike the producer, it doesn't take additional parameters ❶. The disposer ❷ handles the destruction of the authenticated `User` object when the session inactivity timer expires. Within this method you can do whatever cleanup is needed.

You've seen how you can use qualifiers and producers in tandem to create different instances of an object that you can then inject. But there are times when you want to override the instance that's to be injected. Let's discuss that next.

12.3.5 Specifying alternatives

Applications often have multiple deployment scenarios. A deployment scenario might be different back ends such as MySQL database versus Oracle database, or content management systems such as Alfresco versus Documentum. In each of these scenarios you need different code deployed. In the coverage of injection so far, the bean that's being injected is determined at development time. But with different deployment scenarios, you need a mechanism at runtime to configure an *alternative* for an injection point. Obviously this mechanism must use a configuration file and not require code changes.

To solve this problem, CDI has the concept of *alternatives*. An alternative is an additional implementation of a bean, on the same inheritance hierarchy, that can be optionally used instead. To mark a bean as being an alternative, add the `@Alternative` annotation to the class. To use the alternative, enable it in the beans.xml configuration file. Depending on the target environment for the build, you'd optionally use a different beans.xml file or dynamically generate one.

ActionBazaar has several different deployment scenarios including production, development, and QA. When ActionBazaar is deployed to a container, it has a bean that automatically executes and preps the system with some initial data. This is the system startup bean. In a development scenario, the database is regenerated with each build and some test data is loaded into the database along with an initial set of users. For QA, the existing database is upgraded to the current version and a test set of users is loaded, if not already present, so that QA can run their test scripts. In a production environment, the bootstrap bean does nothing—a DBA will update the database if necessary and no changes to accounts or live data are made.

The hierarchy of the startup classes is shown in figure 12.3. The `SystemStartup` base class is the class that is used in production and the default bean. The two subclasses, both annotated with `@Alternative`, are used in development and QA, respectively.

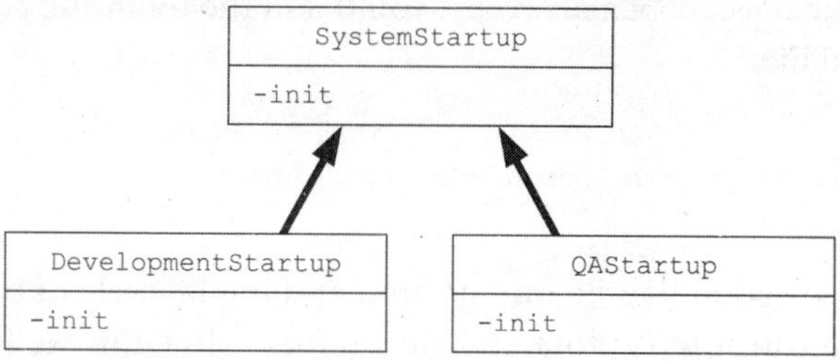

Figure 12.3 Startup class hierarchy

In the listing that follows, the `SystemStartup` bean instance is injected and calls from the method are annotated with `@PostConstruct`. The default implementation, `System-Startup`, will be injected for a production deployment.

Listing 12.10 Bootstrap class

```
@Singleton
@Startup
public class Bootstrap {

  @Inject
  private SystemStartup systemStartup;

  @PostConstruct
  public void postConstruct() {
    systemStartup.init();
  }
}
```

- **Bootstrap is a singleton instance created on startup**
- **SystemStartup instance is injected**
- **SystemStartup instance is invoked in postConstruct**

In the next listing you see the alternate implementation of `SystemStartup` that's used during development.

Listing 12.11 Alternate `SystemStartup` class providing a different implementation

```
@Alternativec
public class DevelopmentStartup extends SystemStartup {

  @Inject
  private UserService userService;

  @Inject
  private ItemManager itemManager;

  @Override
  public void init() {
    // load test users & data
  }
}
```

- **Class marked as an alternative implementation**
- **Extends base SystemStartup**

In this listing, the class is annotated with the `@Alternative` annotation and extends the base `SystemStartup` class. `DevelopmentStartup` will be used only if it's enabled. To enable an alternative, the class must be specified in the beans.xml file. As mentioned, you'll either package using a different beans.xml file or dynamically generate one at build time. To enable `DevelopmentStartup`, you'd add the following configuration entry to the beans.xml file:

```
<alternatives>
  <class>com.actionbazaar.setup.DevelopmentStartup</class>
</alternatives>
```

You now should have a pretty good handle on injection and the lifecycle of beans. It's time to turn your attention to interceptors and decorators. After this we'll look at using stereotypes to reduce the annotation explosion.

12.4 Interceptor and decorators

Earlier in this book we delved into the support for interceptors added in EJB 3. While EJB 3's interceptor support is useful, it's limited to EJBs. With CDI, interceptors can be used with any bean, not just an EJB. Like EJB 3, CDI uses annotations to drive its interceptor implementation. Although CDI's approach isn't as powerful as AspectJ's, it's much easier to use and with fewer complications.

CDI's support for interceptors comes in two flavors: traditional interceptors and decorators. A traditional interceptor can be applied to any method on any bean. The interceptor isn't specific to the bean or method it's intercepting. A traditional interceptor is what we usually think of when we see the term *interceptors.* CDI also includes a new type of interceptor called a *decorator.* A decorator implements the interface of the class it's intercepting—it's thus coupled to that class and intimately tied to its implementation or business function. Thus, a decorator knows its implementation.

A decorator is used to implement specific business functionality for an interface that's abstracting into a crosscutting concern. A traditional interceptor, on the other hand, provides generic crosscutting logic. This may appear confusing at first, but as you read through the subsequent sections and code, it'll crystalize. Let's begin by looking at traditional interceptors.

12.4.1 Interceptor bindings

Creating an interceptor with CDI involves four different coding tasks. Although these tasks aren't nearly as elegant as defining a point cut with AspectJ, they do provide you with a strong degree of predictability at runtime. The tasks are as follows:

1. Create an interceptor annotation.
2. Create an interceptor implementation annotated with the interceptor annotation.
3. Annotate targeted instances with the interceptor annotation.
4. Enable the interceptor with the beans.xml file.

There are three different kinds of interceptors, depending on the type of method and whether the interceptor is on an EJB timeout method, as documented in table 12.2. In this chapter we'll focus on a business method interceptor, but the other two are straightforward and no different.

Table 12.2 Interceptor types

Interceptor type	Annotation	Description
Business method	`@AroundInvoke`	Intercepts business method invocations
Lifecycle callback	`@PostConstruct/@PreDestroy`	Intercepts lifecycle callbacks
EJB timeout	`@AroundTimeout`	Intercepts EJB timeout methods

To define an interceptor, you need to first define an interceptor annotation. The interceptor annotation is used to associate the class or method to be intercepted with the interceptor implementation. Thus, the annotation is placed on both the interceptor implementation and the class or method you want intercepted. The interceptor isn't enabled by default; you must enable it via the beans.xml file. To get a better grasp of this, let's look at an example in ActionBazaar.

As with any important application, performance is an important consideration. During QA testing, you'll want to collect performance information on key interfaces so that you can establish a benchmark for the application. Thus, as in the last section, you'll use a separate beans.xml file for QA versus actual application production. The performance interceptor will track the execution time and write the statistics out to a flat file on the hard drive of the server. Here you'll focus on using this interceptor on the `LandingController`. The `LandingController` class backs the welcome page for ActionBazaar. If this page is slow, users might not continue browsing the rest of the site.

The `PerformanceMonitor` annotation is defined as follows:

```
@InterceptorBinding
@Retention(RUNTIME)
@Target({TYPE})
public @interface PerformanceMonitor {}
```

This annotation is itself annotated with the `@InterceptorBinding`. When CDI reflects on this annotation, it'll discover that you're requesting the method or methods to be wrapped with an interceptor. CDI will then create an instance of the inceptor. After defining the interceptor annotation, you need to define the interceptor implementation, as shown in the following listing.

Listing 12.12 Performance interceptor implementation

```
@PerformanceMonitor
@Interceptor
public class PerformanceInterceptor {

  @AroundInvoke
  public Object monitor(InvocationContext ctx) throws Exception {
    long start = new Date().getTime();
    try {
      return ctx.proceed();
    } finally {
      long elapsed = new Date().getTime() - start;
```

(1) Associates @PerformanceMonitor with PerformanceInterceptor

(2) …class …ng an …eptor

Identifies method that will intercept method invocation

InvocationContext contains context information

Invokes proceed method to invoke actual method

```
            Logger.getLogger("PerformanceInterceptor").log(Level.INFO,
              "Elapsed time: {0}", elapsed);
        }
    }
}
```

In this listing the interceptor implementation is defined. The interceptor must be annotated with the annotation ❶ to associate the interceptor with the annotation. The implementation must also be annotated with the `@Interceptor` annotation to mark this class as an interceptor ❷. The `@AroundInvoke` annotation marks the method that will actually handle the interception. Within this method, you can get information about the method you're intercepting along with its parameters via the `InvocationContext`. Using the proceed method, you can invoke the method you're wrapping or you can choose not to invoke the method if you want.

Documentation on the `InvocationContext` methods is shown in table 12.3. This class provides a wealth of information about the method you're intercepting along with each method's parameters and other context information.

Table 12.3 Methods on `InvocationContext`

Method	Description
`Object getTarget();`	Returns the object instance you're performing interception on
`Object getTimer();`	Returns the timer object associated with the timeout
`Method getMethod();`	Returns the method on which you're performing interception
`Object[] getParameters();`	Returns the parameters that are to be passed to the method
`void setParameters(Object[] os);`	A setter enabling you to change the parameters used to invoke the target method
`Map<String, Object> getContextData();`	Returns context data associated with this invocation—information from the annotation
`Object proceed() throws Exception;`	Proceeds with invoking the method

Once you've defined the interceptor, the next step is to actually use it. You can annotate either the class or individual methods within a class. To use it on the `LandingController`, you'd add it as follows:

```
@Named
@ApplicationScoped
@PerformanceMonitor
public class LandingController {
    ...
}
```

Adding the annotation to the LandingController doesn't enable it by default. Interceptors must be enabled in the beans.xml file. The following snippet enables this interceptor:

```
<interceptors>
  <class>com.actionbazaar.util.PerformanceInterceptor</class>
</interceptors>
```

With the interceptor enabled, each method invocation on the LandingController is tracked. You can annotate other classes as needed. If you're using multiple interceptors, the order in which they appear within the beans.xml file will determine the order in which they're executed. Additional interceptors are configured by adding additional <class></class> elements.

Now that you have a handle on traditional interceptors, let's examine CDI's decorators. Unlike interceptors, decorators are tied to a specific interface.

12.4.2 Decorators

A decorator is very similar to an interceptor. With a decorator you're once again intercepting method invocations on a bean. But unlike an interceptor, you're overriding the methods you want to intercept. A decorator extends or implements the interface of the bean it's intercepting. As a result, a decorator is tightly coupled to the bean and can implement business logic. Because you're overriding methods, you have easy access to method parameters.

To better understand decorators, let's focus on the bidding in ActionBazaar. One of the major concerns with a bidding site is fraud. When you're bidding against another user, you don't want to be bidding against the seller who has created a fake account to drive up the price of the item. To protect against this, you need rudimentary fraud detection. Although fraud detection is a part of the bidding process, it isn't core to the logic handling the bid. It's a crosscutting concern similar to logging but more specific. Consequently, you'll implement it using a decorator, as shown in the next listing.

Listing 12.13 Decorator that implements BidManager and intercepts methods

```
@Decorator
public abstract class BidManagerFraudDetector implements BidManager {

  @Inject
  @Delegate
  @BidManagerQualifier
  private BidManager bidManager;

  @Override
  public void placeBid(Bid bid) {
    ...
  }
}
```

1. arks this class as being a ecorator
2. Decorator is abstract
3. Injects BidManager instance you're wrapping
4. Marks this as delegate instance
5. Qualifier for identifying BidManager instances
6. Implements method you want to intercept

This listing has the code for the decorator. Creating a decorator involves annotating the class with the `@Decorator` annotation ❶ and implementing or extending the class you wish to decorate ❷. Then you inject ❸ the class you're decorating and mark it as the delegate instance ❹. You use a qualifier to ensure you get the correct instance ❺. Finally, you override the method you're interested in intercepting ❻. Because you're interested only in intercepting the `placeBid` method, you mark the class as being abstract.

Once again, decorators are disabled by default. To enable the preceding decorator, you'll need to add the following snippet to the beans.xml file:

```
<decorators>
  <class>com.actionbazaar.buslogic.BidManagerFraudDetector</class>
</decorators>
```

Just as with interceptors, you can have multiple decorators on a given class. The order of the decorators in the beans.xml file determines the order in which they'll be invoked. Now that you have a handle on interceptors and decorators, let's see how you can reduce the number of annotations convoluting your code.

12.5 Component stereotypes

As you've progressed through the features of CDI, you've been amassing an incredible number of annotations. On some methods the annotations are longer than the method prototype. If you look at many of these methods, you'll notice that in many cases you're repeating the same annotations over and over. This is quite a bit of redundant code to support. Luckily, the developers behind CDI foresaw this problem and added something called a *stereotype* to CDI.

It shouldn't be surprising that a stereotype is another annotation. But unlike the annotations you've seen so far, it consolidates a set of annotations into one annotation. You create a new annotation and add the annotations you want to consolidate into one to it. Let's start by considering the annotations on the `getCurrentUser()` method in the `CurrentUserBean` class. The method prototype in this case is shorter than the annotations applied to it:

```
@Named @SessionScoped
public class CurrentUserBean implements Serializable {
  @Produces @SessionScoped @AuthenticatedUser @Named
  public User getCurrentUser() {
    ...
  }
}
```

You can dramatically reduce the number of annotations on the method with a stereotype. It's defined as follows:

```
@SessionScoped
@AuthenticatedUser
@Named
@Stereotype
```

```
@Target( { TYPE, METHOD, FIELD })
@Retention(RUNTIME)
public @interface CurrentUser {}
```

With this new annotation, you've consolidated `@SessionScoped`, `@AuthenticatedUser`, and `@Named` down to `@CurrentUser`. You can see this annotation in action in the simplified code for the `CurrentUserBean`:

```
@Named @SessionScoped
public class CurrentUserBean implements Serializable {
  @Produces @CurrentUser
  public User getCurrentUser() {
    ...
  }
}
```

There are some ground rules for defining stereotypes. Stereotypes can encapsulate the following CDI annotations:

- Scope
- Interceptor bindings
- Named annotation for JSF integration
- Alternative annotation

You can't include other annotations such as those from JPA or EJB within a stereotype. You also can't include `@Produces` and other lifecycle annotations within a stereotype.

CDI ships with a built-in stereotype, `@Model`, for beans that are intended for the model component of the model-view-controller pattern. The `@Model` annotation is defined as follows:

```
@Named
@RequestScoped
@Documented
@Stereotype
@Target(value = {ElementType.TYPE, ElementType.METHOD, ElementType.FIELD})
@Retention(value = RetentionPolicy.RUNTIME)
public @interface Model {}
```

With this annotation, you replace `@Named` and `@RequestScoped` with `@Model`, as shown in the following snippet:

```
@Model
public class ItemController implements Serializable {
  ...
}
```

Stereotypes make CDI beans much easier to read. In the next section we'll take a look at CDI's support for events.

12.6 Injecting events

Dependency injection is extremely useful for acquiring references to other beans. But CDI has a slight twist on dependency injection with support for *injecting* events. This enables events to be delivered to other beans without any compile-time dependencies. The genius of this approach is that you can use an annotation to mark a method as being a recipient of the event and you're finished. The event will be delivered to your bean without any further work. You don't need to implement an interface or register your class as a listener to receive events. The container takes care of everything. Raising an event is similarly as easy; the object responsible for dispatching events is also injected into the class that needs to send the event.

The `@Observes` annotation is placed on one or more parameters of the method that's to receive an event. The type of the parameter is the type of the event. For example, if the type of the event were an `ActionEvent`, then the method would receive all `ActionEvents` that are fired. Attaching qualifiers to the method injection points provides additional specificity beyond just the type. Additional parameters are treated as beans that the container will either look up or instantiate.

To fire an event, the bean that will send the event uses an `Event` object that's typed for the object that's to be fired. It's injected using the `@Inject` annotation and can optionally possess qualifier annotations that will narrow the list of potential targets for the event. The `Event` object has a fire method that's used to send an event.

To better understand how events work in CDI, turn your attention to an example from ActionBazaar. In ActionBazaar, when a new item is listed, multiple beans need to be notified. The beans that need to be notified may change over time and a new module might be added to the application—obviously you don't want to edit the `BidController` each time. The `ItemController` therefore fires an event, which other beans, including `LandingController` and `TwitterNotifier`, are listening to and waiting to act upon. Using CDI's form of the observer pattern results in code with low coupling—`ItemController` doesn't have a reference to these other beans, and the other beans that are listening don't need to acquire a reference to `ItemController` to receive events. Figure 12.4 illustrates the event-delivery process.

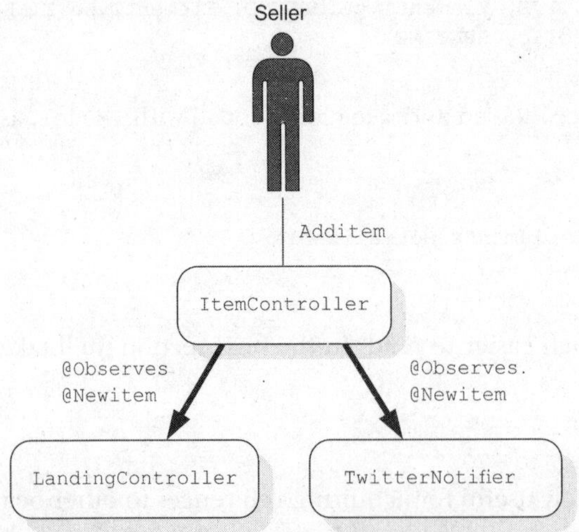

Figure 12.4 Events triggered by `addItem`

Let's start with the addItem method in ItemController. The relevant code for firing events is shown in the following listing.

Listing 12.14 ItemController and firing events

```
@Model
public class ItemController implements Serializable {

  @Inject
  @NewItem
  private Event<Item> itemNotifier;

  public String add() {
    // First save item then broadcast
    itemNotifier.fire(item);
    ...
    return NavigationRules.HOME.getRule();
  }
}
```

❶ Injects event object for broadcasting an event

❷ Qualifier to object being broadcast

Injected event object, typed for broadcasting a new item

❸ Broadcasts event to all listeners

In this listing the ItemController broadcasts new items. The event object is first injected into the bean ❶. It's qualified with the @NewItem ❷ qualifier so that you can target listeners who are specifically interested in a new item that has just been listed. The event object itself makes use of Java's Generics to ensure that you only call fire with the right type of object. Firing is relatively straightforward—you just call fire on the event object, passing in the item ❸. The code for processing an event is shown in the next listing.

Listing 12.15 LandingController updating its cache on a NewItem event

```
@Named
@ApplicationScoped
@PerformanceMonitor
public class LandingController {

  public void onNewItem(@Observes
                        @NewItem Item item) {
    newestItems.add(0,item);
  }

}
```

❶ Marks this method as an observer (listener)

❷ Method only processes new items

As you can see from this listener, CDI handled event registration for you. You didn't need to implement an interface or acquire a reference to the ItemController to register this class as a listener. The onNewItem method is a listener because the item parameter is annotated with @Observes ❶. The instances of item that you'll receive are restricted to only new items with the @NewItem qualifier ❷.

We've covered all the basic features of CDI. With your full understanding of CDI, it's time to revisit conversations to better understand how they work and are used.

12.7 Using conversations

Earlier in the chapter we touched briefly on conversations. CDI has the concept of scopes to which the lifecycle of a bean is tied. If a bean is tied to the request scope, it will exist only for the request—it won't be available on a subsequent request. A conversation-scoped bean will exist for the duration of a conversation, which is less than that of a session but greater than that of a request. Thus, a conversation spans multiple page requests and represents a subunit of work.

Conversations are central to how most users interact with their web browsers. It's now common for a user to have multiple tabs open in the web browser. The tabs may be pointed at the same web application. Consequently, the tabs will share the same session. For a travel site, the user might be planning a vacation in one tab and booking a business trip on another tab. It's critical for the web application to isolate each tab so that when the user clicks Submit on the tab for booking the business trip, the vacation isn't booked instead, or, worse yet, the business flights are booked but the hotel for the vacation is booked instead of the business accommodations. It's either last page visit wins or a messy situation in which the state between the tabs is mixed. One way to avoid this problem is to use an abstraction on top of the session with its own unique ID tracked in each tab. This is essentially what CDI is providing, but it's managing the life-cycle, thus enabling you to focus on the business logic.

To mark a bean as belonging to a conversation you annotate it with `@ConversationScoped`. But by default, a conversation will last for only one request unless you *promote* the current conversation. A conversation that hasn't been promoted is termed a *transient* conversation. The explicit promotion is necessary because the container needs to know when a long-running conversation is starting versus a short chat. The container also needs to know when the conversation ends. Both the explicit start and stop are used to manage resources. To start and stop a conversation, you interact with a `javax.enterprise.context.Conversation` object. It's acquired via injection. The methods on this interface are documented in table 12.4.

Table 12.4 Methods on conversation

Method	Description
`void begin()`	Converts the current transient conversation into a long-running conversation
`void begin(String id)`	Converts the current transient conversation into a long-running conversation with a custom ID
`void end()`	Terminates the conversation and converts it to a transient conversation
`String getId()`	Returns the ID of the current conversation
`long getTimeout()`	Returns the timeout of the current conversation in milliseconds

Table 12.4 Methods on conversation *(continued)*

Method	Description
`boolean isTransient()`	Returns true if the current conversation is transient and will be lost at the end of the request
`void setTimeout(long timeout)`	Sets a custom timeout for the current conversation; only applicable if the conversation isn't transient

To better understand conversations, let's look at a relatively simple use case from ActionBazaar. This use case will leverage most of the CDI skills you've acquired throughout the chapter, including producer methods and qualifiers. We'll look at how a user goes from viewing a list of items to actually placing a bid, as shown in sequence in figure 12.5.

The user starts off on the welcome page viewing a list of items—sailboats, in this case. This page has a picture of the item along with a short description. The user clicks an item that they're interested in, which opens up a detail page with more information on the item and a field for placing a bid. When opening the detail page, the user can right-click and choose Open Link in New Tab, which is commonly done if the user is checking out or comparing multiple items. If the user places a bid, they're brought to the Place Bid page, where the user can confirm the bid before committing. After the user has committed, they're brought back to the main page, which displays a short message confirming that the bid request has been processed.

For the purposes of this example, the user will open the items in two additional tabs, resulting in three tabs open: the welcome page (index.xhtml), the item page for J30 Sailboat (item.xhtml), and the item page for Hobie Wild Cat (item.xhtml). The two tabs displaying information for the selected boats should stay true to the boat they're displaying. Each tab thus represents a conversation.

The code in listing 12.16 displays the simplified welcome page that renders the list of new items. A bidder can click one of these items to display the item page. The link is a JSF command link, which will trigger a post request. The post request results

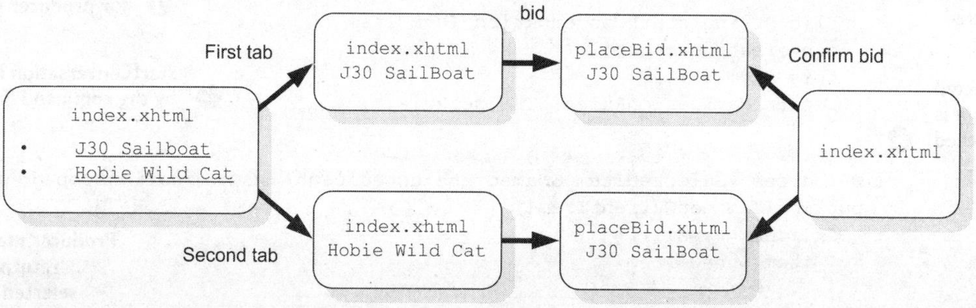

Figure 12.5 Sequence for placing a bid in ActionBazaar

in the startConversation method on the ItemController being invoked with the selected item.

Listing 12.16 Welcome page rendering links for items

```
<!DOCTYPE html>
<HTML
  xmlns:f="http://java.sun.com/jsf/core"
  xmlns:h="http://java.sun.com/jsf/html">
  <h:head>
    <title>Welcome to Action Bazaar</title>
  </h:head>
  <h:body>
    <h:form id="itemForm">
      <h:dataTable value="#{landingController.newestItems}" var="itr">   <- Data table rendering list of items for bid
        <h:column>
          <h:commandLink                                                 <- Command to open item page
            action="#{itemController.startConversation(itr)}">          <- Action method that initiates conversation
              #{itr.itemName}
          </h:commandLink>
        </h:column>
      </h:dataTable>
      <h:button outcome="addItem" value="Add Item"/>
    </h:form>
  </h:body>
</HTML>
```

The next listing shows the code that kicks off the long-running conversation.

Listing 12.17 ItemController—starting a conversation

```
@Model                                                     <- ❶ ItemController is request scoped
public class ItemController implements Serializable {

  @Inject
  private Conversation conversation;                       <- ❷ Conversation object injected

  private BigDecimal bidAmount;

  private Item item;                                       <- ❸ Selected item is cached for producer method

  public String startConversation(Item item) {            <- ❹ startConversation is invoked by the command link
    conversation.begin();                                  <- ❺ Conversation is started
    this.item = item;                                      <- ❻ Selected item is cached
    return NavigationRules.ITEM.getRule();
  }

  @Produces @SelectedItem @Named("selectedItem") @ConversationScoped   <- ❼ Producer method returns the selected item
  public Item getCurrentItem() {
    if(item == null) {
      item = new Item();
    }
    return item;
  }
}
```

This listing contains the code for the `ItemController` and specifically the `startConversation` method ❹ referenced in listing 12.16. There are a couple of important things to recognize:

- It is accessible to JSF EL expressions, as you saw in listing 12.16.
- It operates on an injected `Conversation` object.
- It "produces" the current selected item that then lives in the conversation.

The `@Model` annotation ❶ marks that this bean is accessible from JSF and that it has a request-scoped lifecycle. The `@Model` annotation is a stereotype and is shorthand for `@RequestScoped` and `@Named`. This is a common combination. Prior to the `startConversation` method being invoked from the command link, the CDI container injects a conversation object ❷. To start the conversation, you must explicitly tell the container that you're starting a conversation, which is done in the `startConversation` method ❺. At the same time, you cache the item the user has selected ❻ in property `item` ❸. You've now started a conversation and have also cached the item the user has selected.

The final responsibility of the `startConversation` method is to transition to the item page. The response is rendered within the current request so the cached item is still available. The page displaying the selected item is shown in listing 12.18. When this page is rendered, the `selectedItem` is retrieved from the `getCurrentItem` method ❼. This is a producer method, and it returns a selected item that's conversationally scoped and thus survives until the conversation is ended. The conversation can be ended either programmatically or through expiration from inactivity.

Listing 12.18 Item page—view and bid

```
<!DOCTYPE html>
<HTML
  xmlns:f="http://java.sun.com/jsf/core"
  xmlns:h="http://java.sun.com/jsf/html">
  <h:body>
    <h:form>
      Item Name: #{selectedItem.itemName}<br/>                    ❶
      Bid: <h:inputText value="#{currentBid.bidPrice}" size="5"/><br/>   ❷
      <h:commandButton value="Bid"
        action="#{bidController.placeOrder()}"/>                  ❸
    </h:form>
  </h:body>
</HTML>
```

❶ Displays name of selected item
❷ Amount of bid
❸ Command link for bidding on item

In this listing the name of the selected item is displayed ❶. This requests the selected item from the producer method in the `ItemController` shown in listing 12.17. The amount of the bid is captured using an input field ❷. Clicking the Command button ❸ causes the amount to be recorded and a confirmation page to be displayed. The `placeOrder` method call causes the placeBid.xhtml page to be displayed, which summarizes the bid and has a button for confirming the details and finalizing the bid. The code for `placeOrder` is contained within the `BidController`, as shown in the next listing.

Listing 12.19 placeBid.xhtml—confirms the bid

```
<HTML
  xmlns:f="http://java.sun.com/jsf/core"
  xmlns:h="http://java.sun.com/jsf/html">
  <h:body>
    <h:form>
      Confirm Item: #{selectedItem.itemName}<br/>     <-- 1 Displayed conversationally scoped selected item
       Amount: #{currentBid.bidPrice}<br/>
       <h:commandButton value="Confirm Bid"
         action="#{bidController.confirmBid()}"/>     <-- 2 Confirms bid
    </h:form>
  </h:body>
</HTML>
```

The code shown in this listing displays a page confirming the bid. The currently selected item is rendered again ❶; it's pulled from the conversation. A button then enables the bidder to place the bid ❷, which invokes the `confirmBid` method on the `BidController`. The code shown in the following listing concludes the bid.

Listing 12.20 `BidController`—concludes placing a bid

```
@Model
public class BidController implements Serializable {

  @Inject @SelectedItem                              <-- 1 Injects selected item from conversation
  private Item item;
  @Inject
  private Conversation conversation;                 <-- 2 Injects conversations

  public String confirmBid() {
    logger.log(Level.INFO, "Conversation ID: {0}",
    conversation.getId());                           <-- 3 Logs current conversation ID
    bidManager.placeBid(currentBid);
    conversation.end();                              <-- 4 Ends conversation
    return NavigationRules.HOME.getRule();
  }

  public String placeOrder() {
    // do some processing
    return NavigationRules.PLACE_BID.getRule();
  }
}
```

The selected item is injected into this controller ❶. The conversation is also injected ❷. The `confirmBid` method prints out the conversation ID for debugging purposes ❸. It also terminates the conversation ❹ once the bid has been successfully persisted. Objects residing in this conversation will be released.

In this example from ActionBazaar, the selected item has been stored in the conversational scope using a producer method. It's then accessed from two pages: the item page, which enables the user to view the item and make a bid, and the place bid page, where the user can review the bid and give final approval. This is just one example using the conversational scope—this is much easier than attempting to roll your own solution.

We've explored the major features of CDI. It's now time to wrap up our discussion on CDI with pointers on how to use it effectively with EJB 3.

12.8 Using CDI effectively with EJB 3

After reading this chapter about all of the exciting new features of CDI, you may be wondering where EJBs fit into the picture and how CDI can be effectively paired with EJB 3. You might also be questioning the relevance of EJBs and whether CDI is an EJB replacement. In this section we'll attempt to answer these questions and provide guidance with regard to architecting a Java EE application.

As mentioned earlier, CDI was added in Java EE 6 and its integration has continued to grow with Java EE 7. EJB and CDI are complementary technologies that enable one another and enable robust Java EE apps to be built relatively easily. CDI greatly simplifies the amount of work necessary to use EJBs—there's no need to access JNDI or write a custom JNDI abstraction layer. CDI introduces dependency injection and context features as well as some extensions to POJOs. CDI isn't a replacement for EJBs—EJBs are necessary when security, transactions, remoting, scheduling, asynchronous support, and locking are required. Don't forget, however, that EJBs are beans within CDI, so you can approach the problem as if everything is a CDI bean, and you upgrade a CDI bean to an EJB when you require the Enterprise services provided by the EJB container.

To effectively use CDI and EJB, it's best to examine the sample code in this chapter. Although ActionBazaar is a tiny application with some sections contrived and compressed for succinct code examples, it illustrates some of the best practices for integrating the two technologies. CDI is used in lieu of JSF-backing beans and support, the JSF interface. Note that CDI isn't tied to JSF—CDI is agnostic to the web framework. CDI beans keep the business layer clean by isolating UI functionality in a distinct layer. This is also good to do with both SOAP and RESTful web services—an EJB shouldn't be coded to support a SOAP-based web service or return JSON data for a RESTful service. A good architecture for your application, which isolates responsibility into separate layers, is made easier with CDI because CDI makes the integration between layers seamless.

Because EJBs are also CDI beans, one very important practice is to use `@Inject` instead of `@EJB`. The configurability provided by CDI makes testing an application much easier. Using the beans.xml configuration file, the instances injected can be changed for the purposes of unit and integration testing. A mock object can be injected so that a layer can be tested for its resilience to database exceptions or other types of errors that are difficult to simulate. Furthermore, the `@Inject` makes it irrelevant whether a bean is an EJB or simply a POJO—at any point in the future, you can upgrade the bean from a POJO to an EJB as the application evolves.

The support for decorators in CDI enables a highly tailored form of crosscutting that's much more powerful than what's available with EJB interceptors. This type of interceptor enables you to extract logic that's tied to the implementation of business logic but is distinctly separate. The example of a fraud detector in ActionBazaar is a good example. Although this is definitely related to placing a bid, it's logic that's distinct from the actual mechanism of registering the bid and will obviously evolve in sophistication. It needs to be separate—if you go in to implement a new fraud detector, you don't want that code comingled with the logic that processes the bid. An enhancement in fraud detection shouldn't destabilize the bid code and require a full QA regression of such a critical function for a crosscutting concern.

CDI events are extremely powerful and useful for reducing coupling in code—both in the replacements of JSF-backing beans and EJBs. CDI events should be used to decouple beans so that each bean doesn't have a reference to every other bean in the system. Highly coupled systems can be a nightmare where one change has an unintended ripple effect or requires an inordinate number of code changes. CDI events can thus be used for objects to fire events without needing to know who is receiving them or the receiver needing to have a reference for the sender. This dramatically reduces spaghetti code. One caveat, however, is that this functionality can be abused—events don't cross the JVM boundary. This means that if your application is load-balanced across multiple servers, you have to be careful. In the example here where events to notify the `LandingController` about a new item are used, this wouldn't scale in a multiserver environment. Each server would have a different list of new items. In this situation, JMS is thus a more appropriate solution. But CDI events can be used with JMS. A message-driven bean could receive a new listing and then send out a CDI event to all beans within the server, thereby solving the problem.

There's one area where a CDI supplants EJBs and that's with stateful session beans. Conversationally, scoped beans are much easier to use and more appropriate for most applications. In the past, most stateful session beans were being used to implement a long-running business process, or what we'd now term a conversation. Conversations are only the start; CDI supports the creation of custom scopes, which are much more flexible and lend themselves to creative and elegant solutions that are much easier to maintain.

12.9 Summary

In this chapter we examined the basics of CDI, and you learned what constitutes a CDI bean and the relationship between CDI beans, EJBs, and JSF-backing beans. We covered the various CDI scopes, including request, session, and conversation. Although it was beyond the scope of this chapter, CDI supports custom scopes, which are useful for implementing specific business processes. We covered in depth one of the most important features: dependency injection. Dependency injection in CDI uses Java type information, not freeform text strings. You learned that CDI's dependency injection was much more expansive than that of EJB—it can be used by constructors, for example. We delved into producer methods with an important side note about the interaction between CDI and JPA. Both interceptors and decorators were covered. Decorators are a specialized type of interceptor tied to an interface. We also looked at qualifiers and how qualifiers are used to distinguish between different instances of the same type—for example, a new item versus the current item you're bidding on. CDI uses qualifiers to figure out what instance you want injected. We then built on these concepts with a detailed overview of events and a complex example of conversations.

There are a couple of important points that we must emphasize. CDI isn't a replacement for EJBs, and is agnostic when it comes to web frameworks. Although CDI replaces JSF-backing beans, it isn't tied to JSF, nor is there anything JSF-specific in CDI. The `@Named` annotation is used to expose a CDI bean using a string name to other technologies such as JSF, so the framework will require a minimal inter-opt layer for CDI.

Part 4

Putting EJB into action

In this part you'll be shown guidelines for putting EJB 3 into action in your company. We'll first discuss packaging EJBs and entities for deployment to a server in chapter 13. You'll also learn about the Java EE module system and class loading in EE applications. Chapter 14 introduces web sockets, their relationship to EJBs, and asynchronous business logic execution using the EJB concurrency utilities. You'll be introduced to different testing strategies in chapter 15, which covers unit and integration testing without the need for deployment to a running server.

13 Packaging EJB 3 applications

This chapter covers

- The Java EE module system
- Class loading in EE applications
- Packaging EJBs and MDBx
- Packaging JPA
- Packaging CDI

In the previous chapters you learned how to build a business logic tier with session and message-driven beans, and you used entities to support the persistence tier. But now that you have all this code, what do you do with it?

This chapter begins with a discussion of application packaging and deployment—the fundamentals needed to get your Enterprise application running. We'll explore how the various modules (JAR, EJB-JAR, WAR, CDI, and EAR) of an EE application fit together and interact when deployed to the EE server. We'll discuss how EE applications are configured both through annotations and XML. Finally, we'll cover best practices and some common deployment issues, especially when deploying the same application across different EE server implementations. Let's start by looking at the EE modules and how they're packaged together.

13.1 Packaging your applications

Your Enterprise Java application may contain hundreds of custom-developed Java classes. The code you develop will be of different types, such as EJBs, Servlets, and JSF managed beans, and persistence, helper, and utility classes. This code, in turn, will also be supported by dozens of external libraries, resulting in hundreds more classes. All of these classes are part of your application. In addition, applications will also typically contain non-Java code, such as JSPs, HTML, CSS, JavaScript, and images. At some point, everything needs to come together and be put on the EE server. This is known as *deployment*.

Recall from chapter 1 that the EJB container is part of the EE server and it's responsible for managing EJBs and MDBs. An EJB-JAR module must be created for deployment to the EE server. To understand how to package EJB-JAR modules, you must consider how it fits into the bigger picture of Java EE packaging and understand what constitutes a complete Enterprise Java application.

Up to this point, we've focused on using EJB components like session beans and MDBs to build business logic and JPA entities to implement database persistence code. But your application won't be complete without a presentation tier that accesses the business logic you built with EJBs. For example, the EJBs you built for ActionBazaar don't make sense unless you have a client application accessing them. Most likely, you've used standard technologies such as JSF to build the web tier of your applications. These web applications, together with EJBs, constitute an Enterprise application you can deploy to an application server.

To deploy and run an application, you have to package the EJB-JAR and WAR modules together into an EAR and deploy the EAR to an application server. Java EE defines a standard way of packaging these modules using the JAR file format. One of the advantages of having this format defined as part of the specification is that modules are portable across application servers.

Table 13.1 lists the modules supported by an EE server. Each module usually groups similar pieces of the application together. For instance, you may have multiple EJB-JAR modules, each responsible for different parts of your business logic. Similarly, you may have multiple WAR modules providing unique user interfaces into the business. The EAR is intended to be the über module containing all the other modules, so in the end you're deploying only one file. The application server will scan the contents of the EAR and deploy it. We'll discuss how an EAR is loaded by the server in section 13.1.2.

Table 13.1 Modules supported by an EE server

Description	Descriptor	Contents
EJB Java Archive (EJB-JAR)	`META-INF/ejb-jar.xml` or `WEB-INF/ejb-jar.xml`	Session and message-driven beans. Optionally JPA and CDI may be included as well.

Table 13.1 Modules supported by an EE server *(continued)*

Description	Descriptor	Contents
Web Application Archive (WAR)	`WEB-INF/web.xml`	Web application artifacts such as Servlets, JSPs, JSF, static images, and so on. Optionally EJBs, JPA, and CDI may be included as well.
Enterprise Application Archive (EAR)	`META-INF/application.xml`	Other Java EE modules such as EJB-JARs and WARs.
Resource Adapter Archive (RAR)	`META-INF/ra.xml`	Resource adapters.
Client Application Archives (CAR)	`META-INF/application-client.xml`	Standalone Java client for EJBs.
Java Persistence Archive (JPA)	`META-INF/persistence.xml` or `WEB-INF/persistence.xml`	Java EE standard ORM between applications and databases. May be included as part of the following archives: EJB-JAR, WAR, EAR, and CAR.
Context Dependency and Injection Bean Archive (CDI)	`META-INF/bean.xml` or `WEB-INF/bean.xml`	Java EE standard dependency injection. May be included as part of the following archives: EJB-JAR, WAR, EAR, and CAR.

Enterprise Java applications need to be assembled into specific types of modules. Then a master EAR module is assembled that can be deployed to an application server. These are the available module types as specified by Java EE.

All of these files are in the basic JDK-JAR file format. You can use the `jar` utility that comes with the JDK to build them. In reality, either your IDE or your build tool (Maven or ANT) will do the monotonous work of building the module for you. But for each module, you must still supply the code and the deployment descriptor to configure it. Once all the modules are assembled, the final step is to assemble the master module (that is, the EAR) for deployment.

Deployment descriptors versus annotations

For many cases, deployment descriptors in EE archives are optional. Convention-over-configuration as well as in-code annotation has taken over the heavy lifting that deployment descriptors used to do when it came to configuring EE modules. But there are still cases where deployment descriptors are not only useful but are required. For example, when using CDI, your archive must contain a META-INF/beans.xml or WEB-INF/beans.xml, even if the file is empty, to indicate that your application uses CDI. So this is a case where a deployment descriptor is required. Another example is wiring up remote EJBs in different environments to different servers. Sure, you can hard-code remote server information in an annotation, but it's easier to have different deployment descriptors for your archives for different environments.

In this chapter, we focus primarily on the EJB-JAR module and the EAR modules as well as JPA and CDI. JPA entities are special. They don't have a specific module type of their own. Instead, entities can be packaged as part of most module types. For example, the ability to package entities in WARs allows you to use the EJB 3 JPA in web applications. Entities can also be packaged inside EJB-JAR modules allowing business logic to retrieve and alter business data. Standalone EJB Java clients can also contain entities, though use of entities in EJB Java clients is usually limited to the standalone client's runtime and configuration data, not core business data—that's what the EJBs are for. Entities aren't supported in RARs.

If entities are special, why doesn't Java EE have a different module type to package entities? After all, JBoss has the Hibernate Archive (HAR) to package persistence objects with Hibernate's O/R framework. You may know the answer to this question if you've followed the evolution of the EJB 3 specification. For those who haven't, we now regale you with "Tales from the Expert Group" (cue spooky music).

During the evolution of the EJB 3 public draft, the Persistence Archive (PAR) was introduced, which mysteriously vanished in the proposed final draft. The EJB and Java EE expert groups fought a huge, emotional battle over whether to introduce a module type for a persistence module at the Java EE level, and they sought suggestions from the community at large, as well as from various developer forums. Many developers think a separate persistence module is a bad idea because entities are supported both outside and inside the container. Considering that persistence is inherently a part of any application, it makes sense to support packaging entities with most module types, instead of introducing a new module type specialized for packaging entities. Now that you know what modules are supported and a little about how they were arrived at, shall we take a quick peek under the hood of an EAR module?

13.1.1 Dissecting the Java EE module system

The Java EE module system is based on the EAR file, which is the top-level module containing all other Java EE modules for deployment. So to understand how deployment works, let's take a closer look at the EAR file. We'll start with an example from ActionBazaar.

The ActionBazaar application contains an EJB-JAR module, a web module, a JAR containing helper classes, and an application client module. The file structure of the EAR module for ActionBazaar looks like this:

```
META-INF/application.xml
actionBazaar-ejb.jar
actionBazaar.war
actionBazaar-client.jar
lib/actionBazaar-commons.jar
```

Here application.xml is the deployment descriptor that describes the standard Java EE modules packaged in each EAR file. The contents of application.xml look something like the following listing.

Listing 13.1 ActionBazaar EAR module deployment descriptor

```
<application>
  <module>
    <ejb>actionBazaar-ejb.jar</ejb>                    ❶ EJB module
  </module>
  <module>
    <web>
      <web-uri>actionBazaar.war</web-uri>              ❷ Web module
      <context-root>ab</context-root>
    </web>
  </module>
  <module>
    <java>actionBazaar-client.jar</java>               ❸ Application client module
  </module>
</application>
```

If you review the EAR module deployment descriptor in this listing, you'll see that it explicitly identifies each of the artifacts as a specific type of module. The EJB module ❶ has the EJBs with your application's business logic. The web module ❷ is the web-based version your application. The application client module ❸ is another version of your application, such as a thick-client GUI. When you deploy this EAR to an application server, the application server uses the information in the deployment descriptor to deploy each of the module types.

Java EE 5.0 made the deployment descriptor optional, even in the EAR. This is a departure from previous versions of Java EE, where it was mandatory. The Java EE 5.0–compliant application servers deploy by performing automatic detection based on a standard naming convention or reading the content of archives. For more information on these conventions, see http://www.oracle.com/technetwork/java/namingconventions-139351.html. Next, we'll take a look at how application servers deploy an EAR module.

13.1.2 Loading a Java EE module

During the deployment process, the application server determines the module types, validates them, and takes appropriate steps so that the application is available to users. Although all application servers have to accomplish these goals, it's up to the individual vendor as to exactly how to implement it. One area where server implementations stand out is in how fast they can deploy the archive.

Although vendors are free to optimize their specific implementation, they all follow the specification's rules when it comes to what is required to be supported and in what order the loading occurs. This means that your application server will use the algorithm from figure 13.1 when attempting to load the EAR file that contains modules or archives from table 13.1.

When deploying an EAR containing multiple EJB-JARs, WARs, RARs, and other modules, the EAR module may easily contain thousands of individual classes. All these classes need to be resolved, loaded, and managed by the EE server, which isn't an easy

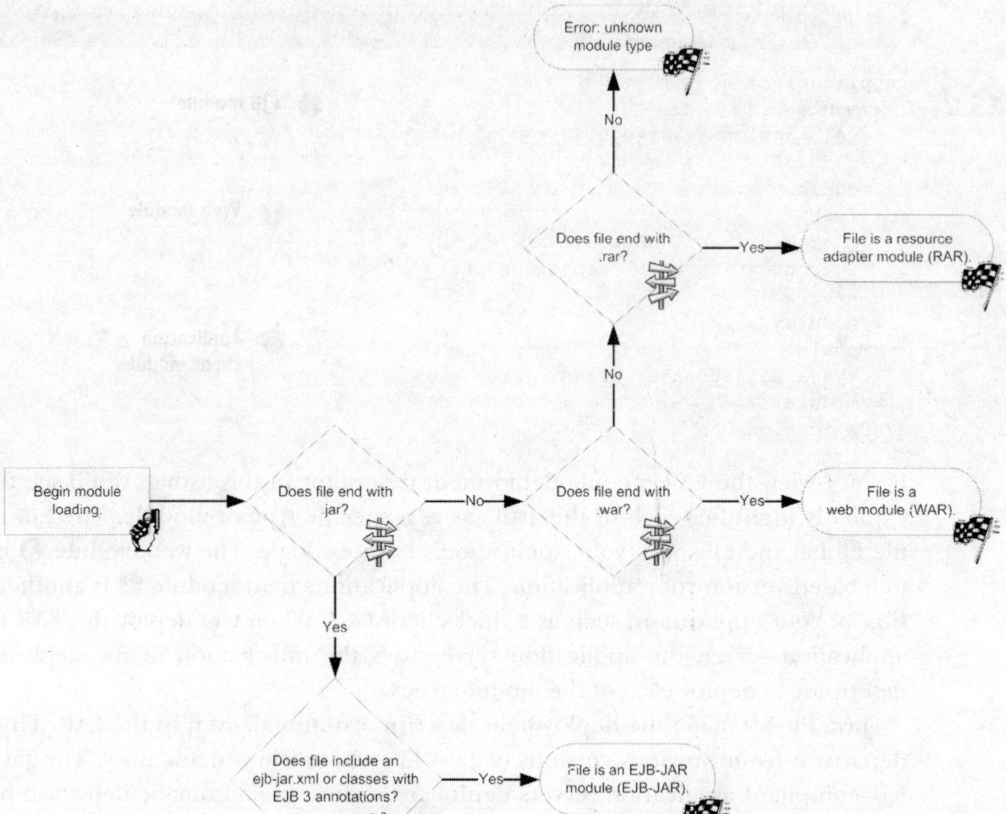

Figure 13.1 Rules followed by application servers to deploy an EAR module. Java EE doesn't require a deployment descriptor in the EAR module to identify the types of modules packaged. It's the responsibility of the Java EE server to determine the type of module based on its naming conventions (extension) and its content. It does so by following this algorithm.

task when different WARs may contain different versions of the same classes. We'll discuss next how an EE server handles this "JAR hell."

13.2 Exploring class loading

To explore EE server class loading, we'll first briefly review how Java class loaders work, and then we'll give a concise explanation of typical EE server class-loading strategies. Finally, we'll finish up by reviewing the EE specifications for dependencies between common EE modules.

13.2.1 Class-loading basics

Class loading in Java works based on a hierarchical structure of class loaders, with each class loader responsible for loading certain classes and each loader building on top of the previous one. This basic structure is depicted in figure 13.2.

Class loaders in Java follow a parent-first model when attempting to resolve a class. This means no matter what class loader you're in, the class loader will first ask its parent if it can load the class. If the parent can't load the class, the parent will ask its parent and so on until the bootstrap class loader is reached. If the bootstrap class loader can't

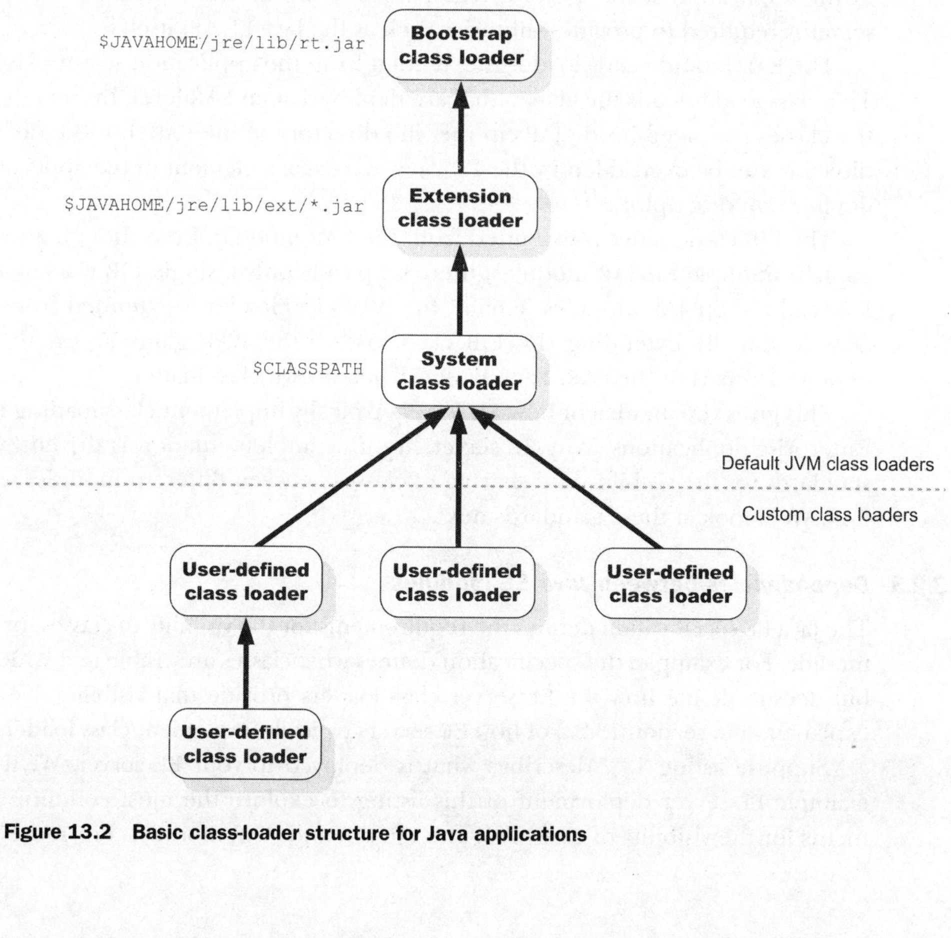

Figure 13.2 Basic class-loader structure for Java applications

load the class, you get a `java.lang.ClassNotFoundException`. Once a class is found and loaded, the class loader stores it in a local cache for quick reference. Now that you've had a quick refresher on basic class loading, let's look at how class loading gets a bit more complicated in Java EE applications.

13.2.2 Class loading in Java EE applications

An EAR module consisting of multiple EJB-JARs, WARs, and RARs, as well as supporting third-party libraries, will contain thousands of classes. It's up to the Java EE server to provide a class-loading strategy that ensures all the applications can resolve the classes they need.

Despite the importance of class loading, the Java EE specification doesn't provide implementation standards for EE server class loaders. The implementation is largely up to the EE server provider. What the Java EE specification does provide is the standards for the visibility and sharing of classes between different modules within an EAR. We'll look at these standards in the next section, but first, take a look at figure 13.3 to see the typical strategy most EE servers use to implement class loading.

As illustrated in figure 13.3, the application server class loader loads all of the JARs in the application server's /lib directory. These are all the libraries the application server is required to provide—libraries such as the Java EE API itself.

The EAR module class loader is extended from the application server class loader. This class loader loads the classes that are deployed at an EAR level. By default, they're the classes packaged inside JARs in the /lib directory of the EAR, but the default /lib directory can be overridden by the `library-directory` element in the application.xml deployment descriptor.

The EJB class loader is extended from the EAR module. Even though an EAR may contain multiple EJB-JAR modules, there's typically only a single EJB class loader that loads all the EJB-JAR modules. Finally, the WAR class loader is extended from the EJB class loader. By extending the EJB class loader, the WAR gains access to all EJBs deployed as part of the EAR. Each WAR will get its own class loader.

This gives you an idea of how EE servers typically implement class loading for their Enterprise applications. Why EE servers use this implementation is driven by the EE standards for the visibility and sharing of classes between different modules within an EAR. We'll look at these standards next.

13.2.3 Dependencies between Java EE modules

The Java EE specification defines the requirements for the visibility of classes for each EE module. For example, the specification defines what classes are visible to a WAR module but doesn't define how the EE server class loaders provide that visibility. We have an explanation in section 13.2.2 of how EE servers typically implement class loaders.

Suppose listing 13.2 describes what is deployed to your EE server. We'll use the example EE server deployment of this listing to explore the most common requirements for the visibility of classes for the EJB-JAR and WAR modules. For more visibility

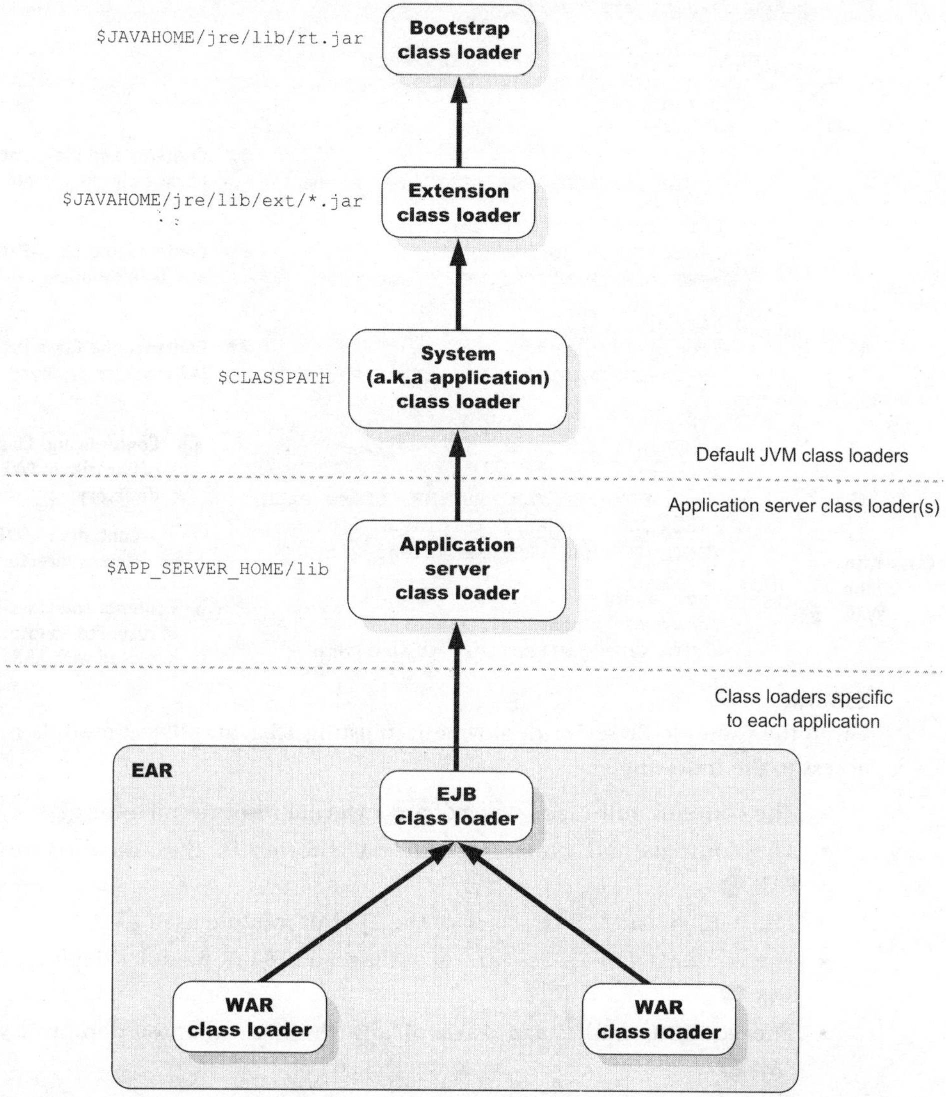

Figure 13.3 Typical class-loader structure for Java EE applications

requirements, or visibility requirements of other modules, refer to the Java EE platform specification.

Listing 13.2 Example EE server deployment

```
EE Server:
    resource-adapter1.rar:
        /com/**/*.class
        /META-INF/MANIFEST.MF  Class-Path:
```

❶ **Contents and Class-Path of external resource adaptors**

```
resource-adapter2.rar:
   /com/**/*.class
   /META-INF/MANIFEST.MF  Class-Path:

action-bazaar.ear:
   /lib/*.jar
       /com/**/*.class
       /META-INF/MANIFEST.MF  Class-Path:

       ejb-jar1.jar
       /com/**/*.class
       /META-INF/MANIFEST.MF  Class-Path:

   ejb-jar2.jar
       /com/**/*.class
       /META-INF/MANIFEST.MF  Class-Path:

   web-app1.war
       /WEB-INF/lib/*.jar
       /com/**/*.class
           /META-INF/MANIFEST.MF  Class-Path:
       /WEB-INF/classes/**/*.class
       /META-INF/MANIFEST.MF  Class-Path:

   resource-adaptor-3.rar
       /com/**/*.class
       /META-INF/MANIFEST.MF  Class-Path:
```

2 Contents and Class-Path of libraries in /lib directory

3 Contents and Class-Path of EJB-JAR module

4 Contents and Class-Path of EJB-JAR modules deployed with EAR

5 Contents and Class-Path of libraries in /WEB-INF/lib directory

6 Contents of /WEB-INF/ classes directory

7 Class-Path of the WAR

8 Contents and Class-Path of resource adaptors deployed with EAR

EJB-JAR

Given the example EE server deployment in listing 13.2, an EJB-JAR module must have access to the following:

- The contents and `Class-Path` of any external resource adaptor **1**
- The contents and `Class-Path` of each library in the /lib directory of the EAR **2**
- The contents and `Class-Path` of the EJB-JAR module itself **3**
- The contents and `Class-Path` of additional EJB-JAR modules deployed with the EAR **4**
- The contents and `Class-Path` of any resource adaptor deployed with the EAR **8**

WAR

Given the example EE server deployment in listing 13.2, a WAR module must have access to the following:

- The contents and `Class-Path` of any external resource adaptor **1**
- The contents and `Class-Path` of each library in the /lib directory of the EAR **2**
- The contents and `Class-Path` of each library in the /WEB-INF/lib directory of the WAR **5**
- The contents of the /WEB-INF/classes directory of the WAR **6**
- The `Class-Path` of the WAR **7**

- The contents and `Class-Path` of all EJB-JAR modules deployed with the EAR ❸, ❹
- The contents and `Class-Path` of any resource adaptor deployed with the EAR ❽

As you can see, the EE server class loader has a big job to do. With so many classes at so many different levels, class version conflicts become inevitable. Understanding the visibility requirements and remembering the parent-first delegation model that class loaders use to find classes will help you package your applications effectively. Next, let's take a look at how to package session and message-driven beans.

13.3 Packaging session and message-driven beans

Before creating an EAR to deploy your application to the EE server, you must create the modules the EAR will contain. Now that you understand class visibility between the different modules of your application, you're ready to look at how to package these modules and get them ready for deployment. Specifically, we're going to look at how to package session and message-driven beans. The Java EE specification allows session and message-driven beans to be packaged in an EJB-JAR module or the WAR module. When packaged in the EJB-JAR module, the beans will run in a full EJB container. When packaged inside a WAR module, the beans will run in an EJB Lite container, which has most but not all of the features of a full EJB container. We'll now look at packaging EJB-JAR and WAR modules, comment on the pros and cons of deployment descriptors versus annotations, and then finish by looking at configuring default interceptors.

13.3.1 Packaging EJB-JAR

An EJB-JAR module is really nothing more than a Java JAR archive. With Java EE's emphasis on convention-over-configuration and its use of annotations, the EJB-JAR module doesn't even need to include the META-INF/ejb-jar.xml deployment descriptor. When the EE server deploys an EAR, it'll automatically scan through the JAR and look for either EJB 3 annotations or the META-INF/ejb.jar.xml file to determine if the JAR is an EJB-JAR module (refer back to section 13.1.2 for more information on this scanning process). So to create an EJB-JAR module, create a normal Java JAR archive with the following structure:

```
ActionBazaar.jar:
  com/actionbazaar/ejb/BidServiceEjb.class
  com/actionbazaar/mdb/BidServiceMdb.class
  META-INF/ejb.jar.xml
```

Session bean (BidServiceEjb.class)
Message-driven bean (BidServiceMdb.class)
Deployment descriptor (optional) (META-INF/ejb.jar.xml)

How you create this JAR file is really a question of what technology you're using. For Java development, there are a lot of options when it comes to technology, so there's something out there to fit your needs. Let's explore options using NetBeans and Maven.

NETBEANS

Using NetBeans, create a new EJB module and add the source code for your session and message-driven beans. Figure 13.4 shows what the Projects tab view of the module may look like.

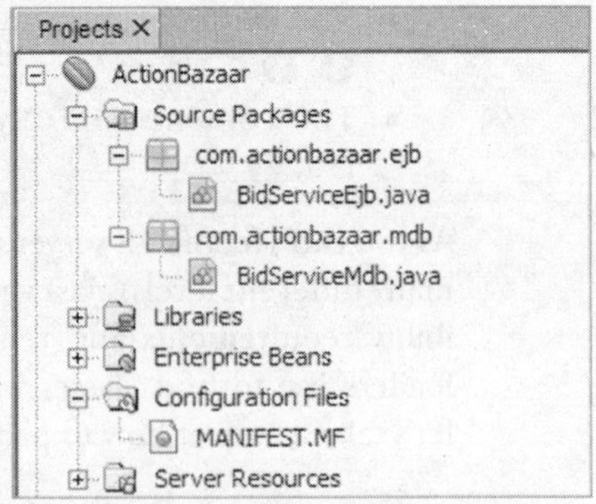

Figure 13.4 NetBeans Projects view of an EJB module

Once you've coded your beans, right-click on the project and choose Build. NetBeans will automatically compile the source code and generate the EJB-JAR module. Find the EJB-JAR module in the project's /dist directory. Looking inside the JAR file (figure 13.5), you'll see the classes and configuration files in the right places.

```
c:\>jar -tf ActionBazaar.jar
META-INF/
META-INF/MANIFEST.MF
com/
com/actionbazaar/
com/actionbazaar/ejb/
com/actionbazaar/mdb/
com/actionbazaar/ejb/BidServiceEjb.class
com/actionbazaar/mdb/BidServiceMdb.class
```

Figure 13.5 Contents of EJB-JAR module

You may notice that there's no META-INF/ejb-jar.xml. This is because the project doesn't have one yet. To add one, right-click the project, choose New, and then choose Standard Deployment Descriptor. NetBeans will then add an empty ejb-jar.xml file to the project. When you rebuild the project, the META-INF/ejb-jar.xml file will be automatically added to the EJB-JAR module.

MAVEN

When using Maven to create an EJB-JAR module, use `<packaging>ejb</packaging>` as the POM packaging type. To customize the configuration of the EJB-JAR module, use the `maven-ejb-plugin` to set options to change how Maven creates the JAR. The following listing shows a minimal POM file that will create an EJB-JAR module.

Listing 13.3 POM file to build an EJB-JAR

```
<project xmlns="http://maven.apache.org/POM/4.0.0"
  xmlns:xsi="http://www.w3.org/2001/XMLSchema-instance"
  xsi:schemaLocation="http://maven.apache.org/POM/4.0.0
  http://maven.apache.org/xsd/maven-4.0.0.xsd">
  <modelVersion>4.0.0</modelVersion>
  <groupId>com.actionbazaar</groupId>
  <artifactId>actionbazzar-ejb</artifactId>
  <version>1.0.0</version>
  <packaging>ejb</packaging>
  <build>
    <plugins>
      <plugin>
        <groupId>org.apache.maven.plugins</groupId>
        <artifactId>maven-ejb-plugin</artifactId>
        <version>2.3</version>
```

Packaging type as "ejb" will create an EJB-JAR module.

Use maven-ejb-plugin to configure creation of EJB-JAR module.

```
        <configuration>
          <ejbVersion>3.1</ejbVersion>
          <archive>
            <addMavenDescriptor>false</addMavenDescriptor>
            <manifest>
              <addClasspath>true</addClasspath>
            </manifest>
          </archive>
        </configuration>
      </plugin>
    </plugins>
  </build>
  <dependencies>
    <dependency>
      <groupId>javax</groupId>
      <artifactId>javaee-api</artifactId>
      <version>6.0</version>
      <type>jar</type>
      <scope>provided</scope>
    </dependency>
  </dependencies>
</project>
```

This option will add Class-Path: to META-INF/MANIFEST.MF.

Maven will create the EJB-JAR module in the /target directory. This will create an EJB-JAR module with no META-INF/ejb-jar.xml. To include the deployment descriptor, you can create /src/main/resources/META-INF/ejb-jar.xml. By putting the deployment descriptor in the standard Maven resources directory, Maven will automatically include it when the EJB-JAR module is built.

These are two options for building an EJB-JAR module. Now we'll look at packaging session and message-driven beans inside a WAR module.

13.3.2 Packaging EJB in WAR

The Java EE 6 specification allows for session and message-driven beans to be included inside a WAR module instead of having to deploy them separately in an EJB-JAR module. When included in a WAR module, the beans run in the EJB Lite container. This means that not all functionality of a full EJB container is available, but simple applications or prototypes will find this sufficient.

A WAR module is a Java JAR archive with contents conforming to the requirements of a WAR module specified by the Java EE specification. Typically, a WAR module will contain classes and other resources in a /classes subdirectory, third-party dependencies in a /lib subdirectory, and the configuration in /WEB-INF/web.xml. A WEB module's structure may look like this:

```
ActionBazaar.war:
  classes/
    com/actionbazaar/web/ejb/BidServiceEjb.class
    com/actionbazaar/web/mdb/BidServiceMdb.class
  WEB-INF/web.xml
```

Session bean inside a WAR

Message-driven bean inside a WAR

WAR deployment descriptor (optional)

Similar to creating EJB-JAR modules, how you actually create a WAR module is a question of what technology your development team is using. Next we'll look at examples using NetBeans and Maven.

NETBEANS

Using NetBeans, create a new Web Application module and add the source code for your session and message-driven beans. Figure 13.6 shows what the Projects view of the module may look like.

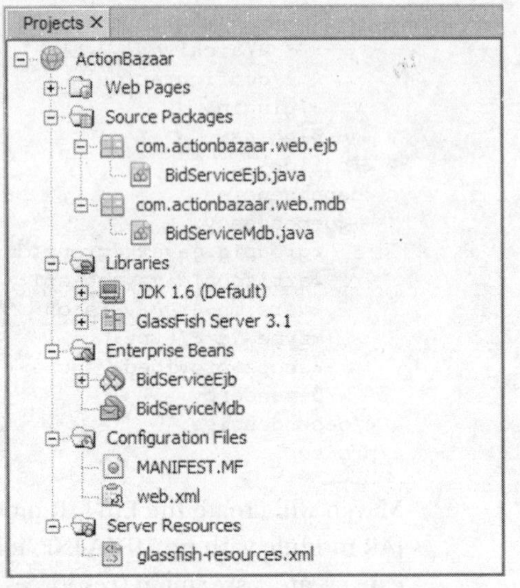

Figure 13.6 NetBeans Projects view of a Web Application module

This ActionBazaar WEB module contains a session bean and a message-driven bean. To build the project, right-click it and choose Build. NetBeans will create the WAR module for you and put it in the /dist subdirectory. You can see the structure of the WAR module in figure 13.7.

Similar to creating an EJB-JAR module with NetBeans, you'll notice there's no ejb-jar.xml. This is because the project doesn't have one yet. To add one, right-click the project, choose New, and then choose Standard Deployment Descriptor. NetBeans will then add an empty ejb-jar.xml file to the project. Unlike the EJB-JAR module, for a WEB module, NetBeans will create WEB-INF/ejb-jar.xml. When packaging session and message-driven beans in a WAR module, the ejb-jar.xml deployment descriptor goes in the WEB-INF subdirectory, not META-INF.

MAVEN

When using Maven to create a WAR module, use `<packaging>war</packaging>` as the POM packaging type. Use the `maven-war-plugin` to customize how Maven creates the WAR. The next listing shows a minimal POM file that will create a WAR module.

```
c:\>jar -tf ActionBazaar.war
META-INF/
META-INF/MANIFEST.MF
WEB-INF/
WEB-INF/classes/
WEB-INF/classes/com/
WEB-INF/classes/com/actionbazaar/
WEB-INF/classes/com/actionbazaar/web/
WEB-INF/classes/com/actionbazaar/web/ejb/
WEB-INF/classes/com/actionbazaar/web/mdb/
WEB-INF/classes/com/actionbazaar/web/ejb/BidServiceEjb.class
WEB-INF/classes/com/actionbazaar/web/mdb/BidServiceMdb.class
WEB-INF/web.xml
index.xhtml

c:\>
```

Figure 13.7 Contents of WAR module

Listing 13.4 POM file to build a WAR

```
<project xmlns="http://maven.apache.org/POM/4.0.0"
  xmlns:xsi="http://www.w3.org/2001/XMLSchema-instance"
  xsi:schemaLocation="http://maven.apache.org/POM/4.0.0
  http://maven.apache.org/xsd/maven-4.0.0.xsd">
  <modelVersion>4.0.0</modelVersion>
  <groupId>com.actionbazaar</groupId>
  <artifactId>actionbazzar-web</artifactId>
  <version>1.0.0</version>
  <packaging>web</packaging>
  <build>
    <plugins>
      <plugin>
        <groupId>org.apache.maven.plugins</groupId>
        <artifactId>maven-war-plugin</artifactId>
        <version>2.1</version>
        <configuration>
          <warName>ActionBazaar</warName>
          <archive>
            <addMavenDescriptor>false</addMavenDescriptor>
          </archive>
        </configuration>
      </plugin>
    </plugins>
  </build>
  <dependencies>
    <dependency>
      <groupId>javax</groupId>
      <artifactId>javaee-api</artifactId>
      <version>6.0</version>
      <type>jar</type>
      <scope>provided</scope>
    </dependency>
  </dependencies>
</project>
```

Packaging type as "war" will create a WAR module.

Use maven-war-plugin to configure creation of WAR module.

This option will set the name of the WAR module to ActionBazaar.war.

Maven will create the WAR module in the /target directory. The WAR module will contain a WEB-INF/web.xml but no ejb-jar.xml. To include ejb-jar.xml, you can create /src/main/webapp/WEB-INF/ejb-jar.xml. By putting it here, Maven will automatically include it when the EJB-JAR module is built.

> **Using remote EJBs in WAR modules**
>
> Although including EJBs directly inside a WAR module is a great convenience started with the Java EE 6 spec, it's not the only way to include EJBs inside a WAR module. It's very typical (particularly in high-use and high-availability applications) to need much more business rules processing power than web front-end display power. Therefore, the architecture of the application is divided into a small cluster of web front-end servers running the WAR module and a much larger cluster of back-end servers running the EJB modules. With two separate clusters, the WAR modules on the front end talk to the EJB modules on the back end remotely through `@Remote` EJBs.

> ***(continued)***
>
> If your application is architected like this, the Maven configuration of the maven-ejb-plugin can include the `<generateClient>true</generateClient>` option. With this option, Maven will package up all interfaces for the EJBs into its own JAR file. Your WAR modules can then include this dependency, which has only the interfaces instead of the entire EJB-JAR.

These are two options for building a WAR module. Now we'll look at whether deployment descriptors are even needed.

13.3.3 XML versus annotations

An EJB deployment descriptor (ejb-jar.xml) describes the contents of an EJB module, any resources used by it, and security transaction settings. The deployment descriptor is written in XML, and because it's external to the Java byte code, it allows you to separate concerns for development and deployment.

The deployment descriptor is optional and you could use annotations instead, but we don't advise using annotations in all cases for several reasons. Annotations are great for development but may not be well suited for deployments where settings may change frequently. During deployment it's common in large companies for different people to be involved for each environment (development, test, production, and so on). For instance, your application requires such resources as DataSource or JMS objects, and the JNDI names for these resources change between these environments. It doesn't make sense to hardcode these names in the code using annotations. The deployment descriptor allows the deployers to understand the contents and take appropriate action. Keep in mind that even if the deployment descriptor is optional, certain settings, such as default interceptors for an EJB-JAR module, require a deployment descriptor (see section 13.3.5). An EJB-JAR module may contain

- A deployment descriptor (ejb-jar.xml)
- A vendor-specific deployment descriptor, which is required to perform certain configuration settings in a particular EJB container

The good news is that you can mix and match annotations with descriptors by specifying some settings in annotations and others in the deployment descriptor. Be aware that the deployment descriptor is the final source and overrides settings provided through metadata annotations. To clarify, you could set the `TransactionAttribute` for an EJB method as `REQUIRES_NEW` using an annotation, and if you set it to `REQUIRED` in the deployment descriptor, the final effect will be `REQUIRED`.

Let's look at some quick examples to see what deployment descriptors look like so that you can package a deployment descriptor in your EJB module if you need to. The following listing shows a simple example of a deployment descriptor for the BazaarAdmin EJB.

> **Nonstandard deployment descriptors**
>
> In addition to the standard deployment descriptor (ejb-jar.xml), most application servers also have extensions that provide application server–specific configuration options. For example, GlassFish has the glassfish-ejb-jar.xml file and WebLogic has weblogic-ejb-jar.xml. It's important to remember that these aren't part of the Java EE specification standards. They'll work only on their respective application servers. These application-specific configuration files usually give you direct access to features of the server that are nonstandard and extend the default behavior of an EE server in some way. Although these extensions are sometimes useful, they make your application less portable between servers. In some cases, portability may become impossible.

Listing 13.5 A simple ejb-jar.xml

```
<ejb-jar version="3.2">                                   ← ❶ EJB specification version, in this case 3.2
  <enterprise-beans>
    <session>
      <ejb-name>BazaarAdmin</ejb-name>                    ← ❷ Identifier for EJB
      <remote>actionbazaar.buslogic.BazaarAdmin</remote>
      <ejb-class>actionbazaar.buslogic.BazaarAdminBean</ejb-class>
      <session-type>stateless</session-type>              ← ❸ Type of bean
      <transaction-type>Container</transaction-type>      ← ❹ Transaction type for bean
    </session>
  </enterprise-beans>
...
  <assembly-descriptor>
    <container-transaction>                               ← ❺ Contains settings for container-based transactions
      <method>
        <ejb-name>BazaarAdmin</ejb-name>
        <method-name>*</method-name>
      </method>
      <trans-attribute>Required</trans-attribute>
    </container-transaction>
    <security-role>
      <role-name>users</role-name>                        ← ❻ Specifies which roles are able to access BazaarAdmin bean
    </security-role>
  </assembly-descriptor>
</ejb-jar>
```

If you're using deployment descriptors for your EJBs, make sure that you set the `ejb-jar` version to 3.2 ❶ because this will be used by the Java EE server to determine the version of the EJBs being packaged in an archive. The `name` element ❷ identifies an EJB and is the same as the `name` element in the `@Stateless` annotation. These must match if you're overriding any values specified in the annotation with a descriptor. The `session-type` element ❸ determines the type of session bean. This value can be either stateless or stateful. You can use `transaction-type` ❹ to specify whether the bean uses CMT (`Container`) or BMT (`Bean`). The transaction, security, and other assembly details are set using the `assembly-descriptor` tag of the deployment descriptor ❺ ❻.

Table 13.2 lists commonly used annotations and their corresponding descriptor tags. Note that as we mentioned earlier there's an element for every annotation. You'll need only those that make sense for your development environment. Some of the descriptor elements you'll probably need are for resource references, interceptor binding, and declarative security. We encourage you to explore these on your own.

Table 13.2 One-to-one mapping between annotations and XML descriptor elements

Annotation	Type	Annotation element	Corresponding descriptor element
@Stateless	EJB type		<session-type>Stateless
		name	ejb-name
@Stateful	EJB type		<session-type>Stateful
		name	ejb-name
@MessageDriven	EJB type		message-driven
		name	ejb-name
@Remote	Interface type		remote
@Local	Interface type		Local
@Transaction-Management	Transaction management type at bean level		transaction-type
@Transaction-Attribute	Transaction settings method		container-transaction trans-attribute
@Interceptors	Interceptors		interceptor-binding interceptor-class
@ExcludeClass-Interceptors	Interceptors		exclude-classinterceptor
@ExcludeDefault-Interceptors	Interceptors		exclude-defaultinterceptors
@AroundInvoke	Custom interceptor		around-invoke
@PostActivate	Lifecycle method		post-activate
@PrePassivate	Lifecycle method		pre-passivate
@DeclareRoles	Security setting		security-role
@RolesAllowed	Security setting		method-permission
@PermitAll	Security setting		unchecked
@DenyAll	Security setting		exclude-list

Table 13.2 One-to-one mapping between annotations and XML descriptor elements *(continued)*

Annotation	Type	Annotation element	Corresponding descriptor element
`@RunAs`	Security setting		`security-identity` `run-as`
`@Resource`	Resource references (`DataSource`, JMS, environment, mail, and so on)		`resource-ref` `resource-env-ref` `message-destination-ref` `env-ref`
	Resource injection	Setter/field injection	`injection-target`
`@EJB`	EJB references		`ejb-ref` `ejb-local-ref`
`@Persistence-Context`	Persistence context reference		`persistence-context-ref`
`@PersistenceUnit`	Persistence unit reference		`persistence-unit-ref`

You can find the XML schema for the EJB 3 deployment descriptor at http://java.sun.com/xml/ns/javaee/ejb-jar_3_0.xsd.

13.3.4 Overriding annotations with XML

As we explained, you can mix and match deployment descriptors with annotations and use descriptors to override settings originally specified using annotations. Keep in mind that the more you mix the two, the more likely you are to make mistakes and create a debugging nightmare.

> **NOTE** The basic rule to remember is that the `name` element in stateless, stateful, and message-driven annotations is the same as the `ejb-name` element in the descriptor. If you don't specify the `name` element with these annotations, the name of the bean class is understood to be the `ejb-name` element. This means that when you're overriding an annotation setting with your deployment descriptor, the `ejb-name` element must match the bean class name.

Suppose you have a stateless session bean that uses these annotations:

```
@Stateless(name = "BazaarAdmin")
public class BazaarAdminBean implements BazaarAdmin {
  ...
  @TransactionAttribute(TransactionAttributeType.REQUIRES_NEW)
  public Item addItem() {...}
}
```

The value for the name element specified is BazaarAdmin, which is the same as the value of the ejb-name element specified in the deployment descriptor:

```
<ejb-name>BazaarAdmin</ejb-name>
```

If you don't specify the name element, the container will use the name BazaarAdminBean as the name of the bean class, and to override annotations you'll have to use that name in the deployment descriptor:

```
<ejb-name>BazaarAdminBean</ejb-name>
```

You used @TransactionAttribute to specify that the transaction attribute for a bean method be REQUIRES_NEW. If you want to override it to use REQUIRED, then use the following descriptor:

```
<assembly-descriptor>
  <container-transaction>
    <method>
      <ejb-name>BazaarAdmin</ejb-name>                          ❶ Identifier for EJB
      <method-name>getUserWithItems</method-name>
      <method-params></method-params>
    </method>
    <trans-attribute>Required</trans-attribute>                 ❷ Specify transaction level
  </container-transaction>
</assembly-descriptor>
```

In this example, the assembly-descriptor element is used to specify a transaction attribute ❷. In addition, the ejb-name element ❶ in the assembly descriptor matches the original name specified with the @Stateless annotation in the bean class.

13.3.5 Specifying default interceptors

Interceptors (as you'll recall from chapter 5) allow you to implement crosscutting code in an elegant manner. An interceptor can be defined at the class or method level, or a default interceptor can be defined at the module level for all EJB classes in the EJB-JAR. We mentioned that default interceptors for an EJB module can only be defined in the ejb-jar.xml deployment descriptor. The following listing shows how to specify default interceptors for an EJB module.

Listing 13.6 Default interceptor setting in ejb-jar.xml

```
<interceptor-binding>                                           ❶ Defines interceptor binding
  <ejb-name>*</ejb-name>                                        ❷ Applies binding to all EJBs
  <interceptor-class>
    actionbazaar.buslogic.CheckPermissionInterceptor
  </interceptor-class>
  <interceptor-class>
    actionbazaar.buslogic.ActionBazaarDefaultInterceptor
  </interceptor-class>
</interceptor-binding>
```

The interceptor-binding ❶ tag defines the binding of interceptors to a particular EJB with the ejb-name element. If you want to define the default interceptor or an interceptor binding for all EJBs in the EJB module, then you can specify `*` as the value for `ejb-name` ❷. You specify a class to use as the interceptor with the `<interceptor-class>` tag. As is evident from the listing, you can specify multiple interceptors in the same binding, and the order in which they're specified in the deployment descriptor determines the order of execution for the interceptor. In the example, `CheckPermissionInterceptor` will be executed prior to `ActionBazaarDefaultInterceptor` when any EJB method is executed.

If you want a refresher on how interceptors work, make a quick detour back to chapter 5 and then rejoin us here. We'll wait.

13.4 JPA packaging

The Java Persistence Architecture (JPA) was part of the EJB 3 specification, but as of EJB 3.2, it has been spun off into its own specification (http://jcp.org/en/jsr/detail?id=317). The main reason for this is JPA isn't limited to Java EE. It can be used in a Java Standard application as well. Because JPA is now its own specification, we'll highlight the most important parts as they relate to EJBs. Refer back to chapter 9 for more details about JPA.

13.4.1 Persistence module

Because the specification allows it to be used in any Java application, when it comes to Java Enterprise application development, JPA entities are simply part of the EJB-JAR or WAR modules. JPA entities may also be packaged as a regular JAR archive and deployed in the root of the EAR module. The key is the META-INF/persistence.xml file that designates the JAR archive, EJB-JAR module, or WAR module as containing one or more persistence units. We'll take a quick look at how to properly package JPA classes and the persistence.xml file.

JAR

The following listing shows how to package JPA inside a plain JAR archive.

Listing 13.7 Structure of a JAR containing JPA entities

```
ActionBazaar.jar:
  META-INF/
    persistence.xml          <-  ❶ JPA configuration file
  actionbazaar/
    persistence/             <-  ❷ JPA entity classes in persistence package
      Category.class
      Item.class
```

The configuration file exists as META-INF/persistence.xml ❶ and the entity classes are in their package subdirectory ❷.

EJB-JAR

If you want to include JPA entities in your EJB-JAR module, packaging is identical to how it's done for a plain JAR archive. The following listing shows how to package JPA inside an EJB-JAR module.

Listing 13.8 Structure of an EJB-JAR containing JPA entities

```
ActionBazaar-ejb.jar:
  META-INF/
    persistence.xml
  actionbazaar/
    buslogic/
      BazaarAdminBean.class
    persistence/
      Category.class
      Item.class
      BazaarAdmin.class
```

❶ JPA configuration file
❷ JPA entity classes in persistence package

The configuration file exists as META-INF/persistence.xml ❶ and the entity classes are in their package subdirectory ❷.

WAR

Packaging JPA entities in a WAR module can be a bit tricky. There are two ways to do it. The first and easiest way is to put the JAR containing your JPA entities into the WAR module WEB-INF/lib directory. The next listing shows how to package JPA inside an EAR module (assuming the JAR file from listing 13.7 is used).

Listing 13.9 Structure of a WAR containing JPA entities in JARs

```
ActionBazaar-web.war:
  WEB-INF/
    classes/
      ...
    lib/
      ActionBazaar.jar
    web.xml
  ...
```

But if the JPA entities aren't in a separate JAR but are instead directly part of the WAR module itself, the following listing shows how this should be done.

Listing 13.10 Structure of a WAR containing JPA entities

```
ActionBazaar-web.war:
  WEB-INF/
    classes/
      META-INF/
        persistence.xml
      persistence/
        Category.class
        Item.class
        BazaarAdmin.class
    lib/
      ...
    web.xml
```

❶ JPA configuration file
❷ JPA entity classes in persistence package

The persistence.xml file must go under /classes/META-INF/ ❶. The JPA entities are copied as *.class files in the subdirectory of their package ❷ as they usually are for a

WAR. Now that you know the structure of a persistence module, we'll teach you a little more about persistence.xml.

> **Persistence unit scoping**
>
> You can define a persistence unit in a WAR, EJB-JAR, or JAR at the EAR level. If you define a persistence unit in a module, it's visible only to that specific module. But if you define the unit by placing a JAR file in the root or lib directory of the EAR, the persistence unit will automatically be visible to all modules in the EAR. For this to work, you must remember the restriction that if the same name is used by a persistence unit in the EAR level and at the module level, the persistence unit in the module level will win.
>
> Assume you have an EAR file structure like this:
>
> ```
> lib/actionBazaar-common.jar
> actionBazaar-ejb.jar
> actionBazaar-web.war
> ```
>
> The actionBazaar-common.jar has a persistence unit with the name `actionBazaar` and actionBazaar-ejb.jar also has a persistence unit with the name `actionBazaar`.
>
> The `actionBazaar` persistence unit is automatically visible to the web module, and you can use it as follows:
>
> ```
> @PersistenceUnit(unitName = "actionBazaar")
> private EntityManagerFactory emf;
> ```
>
> But if you use this code in the EJB module, the local persistence unit will be accessed because the local persistence unit has precedence. If you want to access the persistence unit defined at the EAR level, you have to reference it with the specific name as follows:
>
> ```
> PersistenceUnit(unitName ="lib/actionBazaar-common.jar#actionBazaar")
> private EntityManagerFactory emf;
> ```

13.4.2 Describing the persistence module with persistence.xml

In chapter 9 we showed you how to group entities as a persistence unit and how to configure that unit using persistence.xml. Now that you know how to package entities, it's time to learn more about persistence.xml, the descriptor that transforms any JAR module into a persistence module. It's worth mentioning that persistence.xml is the only mandatory deployment descriptor that you have to deal with.

The following listing is an example of a simple persistence.xml that can be used with the ActionBazaar application. It'll successfully deploy to any Java EE container that supports JPA.

Listing 13.11 An example persistence.xml

```
<persistence>
  <persistence-unit name = "actionBazaar" transaction-type = "JTA">   ❶ Defines a JPA persistence unit
    <provider>
```

```
        oracle.toplink.essentials.PersistenceProvider
      </provider>
      <jta-data-source>jdbc/ActionBazaarDS</jta-data-source>
      <mapping-file>secondORMap.xml</mapping-file>
      <class>ejb3inaction.persistence.Category</class>
      <class>ejb3inaction.persistence.Bid</class>
      ...
      <jar-file>entities/ShippingEntities.jar</jar-file>
      <properties>
        <property name = "toplink.ddl-generation"
              value = "drop-and-create-tables"/>
      </properties>
    </persistence-unit>
  </persistence>
```

2 Fully qualified name of persistence provider

3 JNDI lookup name of JDBC data source

4 List of entities managed by this persistence unit

5 List of JAR files containing entities managed by this persistence unit

6 Persistence provider specific configuration options

Let's run through a quick review of the code. You define a persistence unit by using the `<persistence-unit>` element **1**. You can specify an optional factory class for the persistence provider **2**. If a persistence provider isn't specified, the default provider for the Enterprise server will be used. You specify the data source for the persistence provider **3** so JPA knows how to connect to the database. If you have multiple persistence units in a single archive, you may want to identify the entity classes that compose the persistence unit **4**. If you have entities in another JAR file that you want to include in this persistence unit, use `<jar-file>` **5** with a path to the JAR that's relative to this JAR file. Optionally, you can specify vendor-specific configuration using the `properties` element **6**.

> **JPA O/R mapping**
>
> Typically, JPA uses annotations for all of its O/R mappings. Sometimes annotations aren't a sufficient solution. An example is if the details of your object model change in different environments. In this case, JPA has orm.xml for specifying O/R mappings outside of code. When packaging your EE application, orm.xml goes side by side with persistence.xml. It can also be packaged with a location and name specified by `<mapping-file>` in persistence.xml. As with all deployment descriptors, if it exits, its configuration takes precedence over any annotations.

Because JPA is now its own specification, we won't go into any more detail here. We've given the requirements of packaging JPA entities in an EE application and described the basics of a persistence.xml file. Refer to the JPA specification or another Manning book for more information on JPA.

13.5 CDI packaging

Similar to JPA, CDI doesn't define any special deployment module because dependency injection isn't limited to a Java EE environment. CDI 1.1 for Java EE 7 is defined in JSR 346 (http://jcp.org/en/jsr/detail?id=346), which extends JSR 299 and JSR 330. CDI 1.1 adds specific requirements for dependency injection in a Java EE environment. But dependency injection may also be used in a Java Standard application.

Therefore, like JPA, CDI doesn't have its own EE module but is simply included as a part of other modules. In this section we'll quickly review how CDI is packaged as part of other EE modules, specifically JAR archives, EJB-JAR modules, and WAR modules. Refer to chapter 12 for more details about CDI.

13.5.1 CDI modules

When an EE application is deployed, CDI goes through bean discovery. Bean discovery is a process of determining which artifacts inside the EE application use CDI. These artifacts contain beans that the EE server must manage. An artifact may be a regular JAR archive or any of the Enterprise module types (see table 13.1). Bean discovery is simply looking for the beans.xml file in the following locations:

- META-INF/beans.xml in any JAR, EJB-JAR, application client JAR, or RAR in the EAR or in any JAR archive or directory referred to by any of them by the `Class-Path` of their META-INF/MANIFEST.MF
- WEB-INF/beans.xml of a WAR
- Any directory on the JVM class path with META-INF/beans.xml

If any of these locations has the beans.xml file, the EE server will scan all the classes in the archive and manage any managed beans it finds.

13.5.2 Using the beans.xml deployment descriptor

Chapter 12 covered CDI and the beans.xml file in detail so we won't cover it again here. But we'll quickly look at how to use the beans.xml file to package CDI in JAR archives, EJB-JAR modules, and WAR.

JAR

Suppose you're working on a non-EE application, or you're working on a supporting utility project to an EE application. In either case, you'll probably be creating a regular JAR archive to distribute your code. For the classes in your archive to use CDI, add the META-INF/beans.xml file. The following listing shows an example.

Listing 13.12 Structure of a JAR archive marked for CDI bean discovery

```
ActionBazaar-Utils.jar:
  META-INF/
    beans.xml                                          ❶ Marker/Config file for CDI in a JAR
  com/actionbazaar/util/BidServiceUtil.class           ❷ Classes in JAR scanned by CDI
```

The beans.xml ❶ marks the archive for CDI bean discovery; ❷ is a class scanned by CDI, and if it contains CDI annotations, it becomes a bean managed by CDI.

EJB-JAR

EJB-JAR modules are exactly the same as JAR archives. In the module, add the META-INF/beans.xml file. The next listing shows an example.

Listing 13.13 Structure of an EJB-JAR marked for CDI bean discovery

```
ActionBazaar.jar:
  META-INF/
    bean.xml
  com/actionbazaar/ejb/BidServiceEjb.class
  com/actionbazaar/dao/BidDao.class
  com/actionbazaar/dao/BidDaoJdbc.class
```

(1) Marker/Config file for CDI in an EJB-JAR
(2) Classes in EJB-JAR scanned by CDI
(3) Classes in EJB-JAR scanned by CDI
(4) Classes in EJB-JAR scanned by CDI

The beans.xml (1) marks the module for CDI bean discovery; (2)–(4) are classes scanned by CDI, and if they contain CDI annotations, they're managed by CDI.

WAR

For WAR modules, add the WEB-INF/beans.xml file. The following listing shows an example.

Listing 13.14 Structure of a WAR marked for CDI bean discovery

```
ActionBazaar-web.war:
  WEB-INF/
    beans.xml
    classes/
      persistence/
        Category.class
        Item.class
        BazaarAdmin.class
```

(1) Marker/Config file for CDI in a WAR
(2) Classes in WAR scanned by CDI
(3) Classes in WAR scanned by CDI
(4) Classes in WAR scanned by CDI

The beans.xml (1) marks the module for CDI bean discovery; (2)–(4) are classes scanned by CDI, and if they contain CDI annotations, they're managed by CDI. A WAR module also contains a WEB-INF/lib/ directory, which may contain any number of JAR archives. Remember, those JAR archives themselves may be marked for CDI by following the example of listing 13.12.

The beans.xml file has been vital to CDI up until Java EE 7. Now the Java EE 7 specification has made the beans.xml file optional. It's been replaced with the `bean-discovery-mode` annotation in the deployment descriptor. We'll look at this annotation next.

13.5.3 Using the bean-discovery-mode annotation

Once the beans.xml file could remain empty, and it served only as a marker for CDI; requests have been made to remove it altogether. The Java EE 7 specification has done just that. The `bean-discovery-mode` annotation has defined three modes that CDI uses to scan your classes in Java EE 7 applications. Table 13.3 describes these modes.

Table 13.3 Values for the bean-discovery-mode annotation

Value	Description
`ALL`	All types are processed. This behavior is the same as including the beans.xml in a Java EE 6 application.

Table 13.3 Values for the bean-discovery-mode annotation *(continued)*

Value	Description
ANNOTATED	Only types with bean-defining annotations are processed. This is the default Java EE 7 behavior.
NONE	All types in the archive (JAR) will be ignored.

In a Java EE 7 application, there's no need to include a beans.xml file. With no beans.xml file, CDI 1.1 will default to a beans discovery mode of ANNOTATED as described in table 13.3. This default behavior can be overridden by including a beans.xml and specifying a value for `bean-discovery-mode`, as shown in the following listing.

Listing 13.15 Specifying a value for `bean-discovery-mode`

```
<?xml version="1.0" encoding="UTF-8"?>
<beans xmlns="http://xmlns.jcp.org/xml/ns/javaee"
       xmlns:xsi="http://www.w3.org/2001/XMLSchema-instance"
       xsi:schemaLocation="http://xmlns.jcp.org/xml/ns/javaee
       http://xmlns.jcp.org/xml/ns/javaee/beans_1_1.xsd"
       bean-discovery-mode="all">                          <-- 1 Change value for bean-discovery-mode
</beans>
```

In this listing the value of `bean-discovery-mode` is set to `"all"` ❶, overriding the default Java EE 7 behavior and allowing all types to be processed as in Java EE 6.

Packaging your CDI code inside of JAR archives or EE modules is pretty easy. Next we'll go over some best practices for packaging and common problems you may run into.

13.6 Best practices and common deployment issues

After reading this chapter, it may appear that a lot of little pieces are required to deploy EJB 3 components. That may not be far from the truth. The reality, though, is that you don't have to keep track of all the pieces yourself; tools provided by the application servers help, and much of the glue code can be automated. You need to keep in mind some key principles, regardless of which components your application makes use of and which server you plan to deploy it to.

13.6.1 Packaging and deployment best practices

The following list of best practices can make your life easier while you're building and deploying your applications:

- *Start small.* Even if you're an experienced EE developer, start small when working on packaging your application and deploying it. Don't work for a month, generate hundreds of beans, and then try to package and deploy your application for the first time. If there are problems with the packaging, it's easier to solve them on a small deployment than a larger one.

- *Use a constant server environment.* For many, GlassFish is the choice for EE servers, but there are a lot of other options out there. When at all possible, make sure everyone on the team and all of your development environments are consistently using the same version of the same EE server. If EE servers must be different, avoid packaging problems by separating code from packaging.
- *Separate code from configuration packaging.* It's common for your applications to contain both your code and your configuration. It's also common for this to cause problems because packaging for development, test, and production environments may all differ. Avoid this headache by creating separate projects for packaging and move the packaging configuration (deployment descriptors!) to those projects. If you're using a build tool like Maven, declaring dependencies and combining projects is made easier. You may think it's overkill to have different projects for packaging to different environments, but it'll save you from packaging problems in the long run.
- *Understand your application and its dependencies.* Make sure that resources are configured before you deploy the application in your target environment. If an application requires a lot of resources, it's a good idea to use the deployment descriptor to communicate the dependencies for the deployer to resolve before attempting to deploy the application. Improper packaging of classes and libraries causes a lot of class-loading issues. You also need to understand the dependency of your applications on helper classes and third-party libraries and package them accordingly. Avoid duplication of libraries in multiple places. Instead, find a way to package your applications, and configure your application server so that you can share common libraries from multiple modules within the same application.
- *Avoid using proprietary APIs and annotations.* Don't use vendor-specific tags or annotations unless it's the only way to accomplish your task. Weigh doing so against the disadvantages, such as making your code less portable. If you're depending on proprietary behavior, check whether you can take advantage of a proprietary deployment descriptor.
- *Leverage your database administrator (DBA).* Work with your DBA to automate the creation of any database schemas for your application. Avoid depending on the automatic table creation feature for entities, because it may not meet your production deployment requirement. Make sure that the database is configured properly and that it doesn't become a bottleneck for your application. Past experience indicates that making friends with the DBA assigned to your project really helps! If your application requires other resources such as a JMS provider or LDAP-compliant security provider, then work with the appropriate administrators to configure them correctly. Again, using O/R mapping with XML and resource dependencies with XML descriptors can help you troubleshoot configuration issues without having to fiddle with the code.

- *Use your build tools.* Most likely you'll be using Maven to build your applications, but whatever tools you use, make sure you understand how to use them well and take complete advantage of them. Avoid any manual intervention to package your application. If you find yourself with manual steps, you're either not using the tool to its full potential or your tool of choice isn't adequate and you should replace it with something that will better suit your needs.

Now that you have some best practices in place, what do you do when that's still not enough? We'll let you in on a few secrets from the trenches that will make solving those packaging problems easier.

13.6.2 Troubleshooting common deployment problems

This section examines some common deployment problems that you may run into. Most can be addressed by properly assembling your application:

- `ClassNotFoundException` occurs when you're attempting to dynamically load a resource that can't be found. The reason for this exception can be a missing library at the correct loader level—you know, the JAR file containing the class that can't be found. If you're loading a resource or property file in your application, make sure you use `Thread.currentThread().getContextClassLoader().getResourceAsStream()`.
- `NoClassDefFoundException` is thrown when code tries to instantiate an object or when dependencies of a previously loaded class can't be resolved. Typically you run into this issue when all dependent libraries aren't at the same classloader level.
- `ClassCastException` normally is the result of duplication of classes at different levels. This occurs in the same-class, different-loader situation; that is, you try to cast a class loaded by class loader L1 with another class instance loaded by class loader L2.
- `NamingException` is typically thrown when a JNDI lookup fails, because the container tries to inject a resource for an EJB that doesn't exist. The stack trace for this exception gives the details about which lookup is failing. Make sure that your dependencies on data sources, EJBs, and other resources resolve properly.
- `NotSerializableException` is thrown when an object needs to be moved from in-memory to some kind of `byte[]` form but the object doesn't support this conversion. This can happen if stateful session beans need to be passivated and saved to disk to free up memory, or it can happen if session beans are accessed remotely and the objects they return need to be transferred over the network. Whatever the reason, if the object isn't serializable, you'll get this exception. The best way to avoid this is to add a JUnit test to assert the object is serializable. Typically objects start life with the ability to be serialized, but as time goes on and the objects are updated, nonserializable stuff creeps in.

- Your deployment may fail due to an invalid XML deployment descriptor. Make sure that your descriptors comply with the schema. You can do this by using an IDE to build your applications instead of manually editing XML descriptor files.

13.7 Summary

At the heart of Java EE applications lies the art of assembling and packaging Enterprise applications. This chapter briefly introduced the concepts of class loading and how the dependencies between classes in an EE application are specified by the Java Enterprise specification. We looked at how to properly package an EJB-JAR module as both a standalone module and inside a WAR, making sure the deployment descriptor for the EJB-JAR module gets packaged in the proper location. After that we covered packaging JPA and CDI, which don't have their own specific EE module but instead are packed inside of existing EE modules. Finally, we looked at some best practices and common errors and how to avoid them.

14 Using WebSockets with EJB 3

This chapter covers

- The basics of WebSockets
- Integrating WebSockets with Java EE
- Using annotated and programmatic endpoints

In this chapter we'll delve into an exciting new technology that was added to Java EE 7 to support HTML5: WebSockets. WebSockets are raw sockets that support true full-duplex communication between the web browser and back-end server. With WebSockets, you can push data to the web browser from the server without depending on hacks or having the client poll the server.

14.1 Limits of request–response

In the traditional HTTP model, the client browser opens a connection to an HTTP server and requests an operation to be performed, such as GET, POST, PUT, DELETE, and so on. The HTTP server performs the operation and returns a result, usually HTML content. The connection to the server may be kept open for additional requests so that if multiple resources from the server are being retrieved, each request doesn't require an additional socket to open and close. If you look at the complexity of some of the current web pages, this makes sense—pages with lots of content, such as eBay.com, would be extremely slow if each image had to endure a full socket opening and closing. In each case, however, the client is the initiator—the client makes a request and the server responds. The server never pushes data back to the client without the client making a request.

The request–response model works perfectly for websites that produce content, such as newspapers, online encyclopedias, academic journals, file sharing, and so on. But the request–response model breaks down for uses on sites such as gaming, instant messaging, stock updates, and anything else where content/data needs to be pushed from the server to the client asynchronously. The request–response paradigm is a hindrance for these sites—the client must always make the initial request. There are different approaches you can take to get around this problem.

One approach to get around the limitations of HTTP request–response is to use browser plug-ins like Java Applets, Flash, ActiveX, and so on. With these plug-ins, you can do practically anything because you can open up raw sockets to stream data back asynchronously. But they have several major drawbacks. End users must have the plug-in installed in their browser, and certain plug-ins, such as ActiveX, aren't cross-platform. In addition, many mobile browsers have limited support or no support for plug-ins; for example, Flash isn't available in the standard browser on iOS devices. The plug-ins often take a significant amount of time to initialize and load. Although fast computers and high-speed internet connections have made this less of an issue, it's still noticeable. Integrating plug-ins into a page isn't always clean and can be buggy. The biggest drawback, though, is that these technologies aren't using standard web protocols and the back-end server must be custom-written. Many corporate networks use proxies that are paired with authentication and port blocking as a part of corporate security. Non-HTTP traffic out of the company is thus completely blocked, meaning that an Applet couldn't communicate directly with a back-end server via a non-HTTP port. These are only a few of the problems that plague the browser plug-in approach.

Two other approaches taken to get around the limitations of the HTTP request–response model in the browser are AJAX and Comet. We'll compare each in the following section to WebSockets, but they aren't a complete solution. AJAX enables asynchronous calls from the web browser after the page has been loaded to retrieve either a partial page or data without a full page reload. Data is often returned in JSON (JavaScript Object Notation) format. AJAX is still a pull—the browser has to initiate the request. To create the impression of server push, many pre-HTML5 web applications coupled polling with AJAX, which is fine for email applications but not completely acceptable when near-real-time behavior is expected.

Comet does support server push. It leaves the HTTP connection open, or open as long as possible, so that data may be streamed back asynchronously from the server. Comet ties up a connection in the browser. Because this is a technique and not a standard, it doesn't have a standard server implementation, and the long-running socket connections can run into trouble with Enterprise firewalls.

Now that we've covered some of the limits of the request–response model, let's take a fresh look at the problem through the eyes of a new Java EE standard, WebSockets.

14.2 Introducing WebSockets

WebSockets are the solution to implementing truly asynchronous communication in web applications without using plug-ins, AJAX polling, or custom Comet solutions. It's standardized and part of HTML5, meaning that all browsers, including mobile browsers, must support it. Because it rests on top of HTTP and has a standard protocol, firewall and browser support is well defined. WebSockets also benefit from Web Worker, another part of HTML5. Web Workers for the first time give JavaScript rudimentary multithreading support, which is a necessity for asynchronous communication.

Let's dive into WebSockets further so that the Java EE 7 support will make more sense. If you've already mastered WebSockets, feel free to jump ahead to the next section.

To better understand WebSockets, we'll first examine the technology in the context of HTML5 without discussing the server component. We'll look at the basics of the protocol as well as how you interact with WebSockets from JavaScript. After you have a handle on the technology from a pure HTML5 perspective, we'll then compare it to AJAX and Comet. Although AJAX is still relevant and indeed useful, you'll see why WebSockets is a much better solution than Comet.

14.2.1 WebSockets basics

WebSockets are a new transport technology that uses HTTP. A connection starts out using HTTP or HTTPS and is then upgraded to a WebSocket connection using a handshake. WebSockets use HTTP/HTTPS so that existing infrastructure can be reused. Both HTTP and HTTPS are well understood by server-side software and intermediate infrastructure, such as firewalls and proxies. WebSockets are thus backward-compatible with existing network infrastructure. You don't have to have additional ports on a firewall opened or upgrade proxy firewalls.

Opening a WebSocket connection in the browser involves passing a URL using the WebSocket scheme to the WebSocket constructor. Here's an example JavaScript snippet to open a connection to the ActionBazaar support chat service:

```
var webSocket = new WebSocket('ws://127.0.0.1:8080/chapter14/chat');
```

The URL is prefixed with `ws:`, thus telling the browser that you want to use the WebSocket protocol. If you wanted the connection secured using SSL, you'd specify `wss:`, but to use SSL you'd need a signed certificate on the server. The request sent by the browser to the server is shown in the following listing.

Listing 14.1 HTTP handshake request

```
GET /chapter14/chat HTTP/1.1      ① Standard HTTP GET request header
Upgrade: websocket
Connection: Upgrade               ② Request upgrade to WebSocket protocol
Host: 127.0.0.1:8080
```

```
Origin: http://localhost:8040
Cookie: JSESSIONID=df1d67da4bc7eae66f50a05a9d05
Sec-WebSocket-Key: ddrh4Ti+hXSYfRS14HJodA==
Sec-WebSocket-Version: 13
Sec-WebSocket-Extensions: x-webkit-deflate-frame
HTTP Handshake Request
```

Identifier used to verify connection was upgraded

3 Java EE session management key associates connection with session

4 WebSocket specification version

5 Extended compression settings provided by web browser

As you can see, the client is requesting that the HTTP connection be upgraded to a WebSocket connection ❷. This is a standard HTTP request using the `GET` method ❶. The client provides a key that the server will use in the response ❸. This is used to verify that the connection was indeed upgraded. Additional parameters are provided to the server for the version ❹ and include a setting for optimizing the compression ❺.

The server responds to this request with a response affirming that the connection has been upgraded and that the client can begin transmitting additional data; the server can also begin transmitting data without any request from the client. The server's response is shown in the next listing.

Listing 14.2 HTTP handshake response

```
HTTP/1.1 101 Web Socket Protocol Handshake
X-Powered-By: Servlet/3.1 JSP/2.3 (GlassFish Server Open Source Edition 4.0
     Java/Oracle Corporation/1.7)
Server: GlassFish Server Open Source Edition 4.0
Connection: Upgrade
Sec-WebSocket-Accept: 5+Xng8HF5TYinHaBSIR1kt4n0vA=
Upgrade: websocket
```

HTTP 101 is returned denoting protocol switch

Special key returns confirming protocol change handled correctly

Successfully upgraded to WebSocket protocol

Once the connection has been upgraded, both the client and server can immediately begin transmitting messages back and forth. The content of the messages is application-dependent. The content can be binary data, XML, text, JSON, and so on. Currently, most applications use JSON because it's compact and easy to work with in JavaScript. XML, although self-documenting, is verbose and consumes significant overhead in both transmission and processing. The overhead can translate into performance problems, especially with mobile devices.

Sending data from JavaScript to the server involves invoking the `send` method on the `WebSocket` object. There are several different methods depending on the data type you want to transmit:

```
void send(DOMString data);
void send(Blob data);
void send(ArrayBuffer data);
void send(ArrayBufferView data);
```

In this chapter we'll focus primarily on sending text data, such as JSON, but you can also send binary and array data. The text method transmits the text as Unicode—text that isn't Unicode is converted to Unicode. The structure of the message can be anything—

you're free to format your messages however you see fit. Most of the time, though, you'll probably utilize JSON. JSON is compact and works well with JavaScript. In addition, with Java EE 7, you can marshal JSON directly into Java objects using the Java API for JSON processing (JSR-353). Let's look at a simple example of JSON plus WebSockets in the following listing.

Listing 14.3 Sending a JSON using WebSockets

```
var msg = {                                  <-- Create JavaScript
 type: "message",                                object and populate it
 text: "Hello World",
 date: Date.now()
};                                                        Send JavaScript
webSocket.send(JSON.stringify(msg));          <--         object
```

Here a JavaScript Object, `msg`, is created to which several properties are added: `type`, `text`, and `date`.

Sending binary data is useful in situations such as a file upload where you want to stream a large file to a server. The `send` method can transmit data only if the WebSocket connection has been opened; otherwise an error will be thrown. The error will be delivered the `onerror` callback, which we'll cover next.

In addition to sending data to the server, WebSockets can also receive data asynchronously. To accomplish this, WebSockets provide a number of callback hooks:

```
webSocket.onopen = function(evt) { /* Open Callback */};
webSocket.onclose = function(evt) { /* Close callback */};
webSocket.onmessage = function(evt) { /* Async message */ };
webSocket.onerror = function(evt) { /* Error callback */ };
```

These hooks cover the complete lifecycle of a WebSocket. The first callback, onopen, is invoked once the WebSocket connection to the server has successfully opened and can send and receive data. The `onclose` method is invoked when the WebSocket connection has been closed. Either the client or the server could have terminated the connection. The `onerror` callback is invoked when there's an error with the connection, such as when you attempt to transmit data on a closed connection. The `onmessage` callback is invoked when a message arrives from the server. The server can send a message back at any point—it doesn't have to be in response to a request from the client, like in the case of AJAX. The contents of the message can be an `ArrayBuffer`, `Blob`, or `String`. To retrieve the contents of the message, access the data property on the event.

Most of the time the data will be transmitted using JSON. JSON is much simpler and less verbose than XML. It's easier to parse and takes up less bandwidth; both are important attributes when dealing with mobile devices. The JSON format has two structures: name/value pairs and an ordered list of values. In the case of ActionBazaar, the next listing shows a simple chat message in JSON format.

Listing 14.4 Example ActionBazaar chat message

```
{
 "type": "ChatMessage",
 "user": "admin",
 "message", "I've forgotten my password"
}
```

The chat message in this listing is simple. It's an array of three properties or values. This message is much more compact than the equivalent XML message:

```
<chat-message>
 <type>ChatMessage</type>
 <user>admin</user><message>![CDATA[I've forgotten my password]]></message>
<chat-message>
```

The JSON message has only 79 characters versus 126 characters for the XML message. That is a 59% increase in the size of message going from JSON to XML and in the amount of data that must be transmitted and loaded into memory. Of course, the trade-off is that XML is self-documenting, and when combined with XML Schema, it can be validated. This isn't possible with JSON, although there are efforts to address this shortcoming.

In JavaScript the message in listing 14.4 can be converted into a JavaScript object and the properties easily accessed. The code in the following listing is an implementation of the `onMessage` callback.

Listing 14.5 Converting a JSON message into a JavaScript object

```
function onMessage(evt) {
 var msg = eval('(' + evt.data + ')');
 console.log('Type: ' + msg.type);
 console.log('User: ' + msg.user);
 console.log('Message: ' + msg.message);
}
```

❶ Callback method invoked by WebSockets (`function onMessage(evt) {`)
Convert JSON message to JavaScript object
Print out property on object

In this listing you receive a JSON message from a WebSocket callback ❶. You then evaluate the data payload of the message, thus converting it into a JavaScript object. Once the message is converted into a JavaScript object, you can access the properties with ease. Later in this chapter, you'll see how to marshal JSON into Java objects. Support for processing JSON was added in Java EE 7 via JSR-353.

You now have a fundamental understanding of WebSockets. Let's briefly contrast WebSockets with existing pre-HTML5 technologies. None of them are a complete or fully standardized solution.

14.2.2 WebSockets versus AJAX

AJAX (Asynchronous JavaScript and XML) is an older technique for exchanging between the client and server. Like WebSockets, the client initiates AJAX invocations. But unlike WebSockets, the invocations are synchronous—the client sends a message to the server and the server responds. After the client receives the server's message, the connection is closed. The communication is asynchronous from the perspective of the user because the AJAX call is performed on a separate thread so that the UI doesn't freeze.

AJAX is used in many common scenarios to avoid a full-page reload. Consider the example of the shipping page for ActionBazaar. The winning bidder must specify their address and select a shipping method, such as FedEx, UPS, or USPS. The shipping cost will depend on the ZIP code. To avoid a transition to another web page, thereby incurring a full-page load, an AJAX call to the server can retrieve the estimated shipping costs once a valid ZIP code has been entered. This reduces the load on the server, sends fewer pages to the server, and improves the overall usability of the shipping process.

Although the definition of AJAX includes XML, JSON can be used instead of XML. The data that's received from an AJAX call can be JSON, XML, or even HTML. All communication is done via HTTP or HTTPS. From the perspective of the server, an AJAX invocation looks like any other HTTP request.

At the heart of AJAX is the `XMLHttpRequest` object. This is a built-in JavaScript object with several methods for opening connections, sending data, and so on. An example of using this method is shown in the next listing.

Listing 14.6 AJAX method invocation from JavaScript

```
var request = new XMLHttpRequest();                 <-- 1 Instantiates an XMLHttpRequest object
request.onreadystatechange = function() {           <-- 2 Sets callback method
    if(request.readState == 4 &&
     request.status = 200) {                        <-- 3 Checks success of HTTP call
     // handle request.responseXML;
    }
}
request.open('GET',url);                            <-- 4 Opens HTTP GET request
request.send();                                     <-- 5 Invokes call on server
```

The code in this listing demonstrates the basic parts of an AJAX call. You first instantiate the `XMLHttpRequest` object ❶ and then set the callback function ❷. When the callback function is invoked, you check to see whether it was successful ❸. To initiate the call, you first open a connection ❹ and then send the request ❺.

> **Java server faces and AJAX**
>
> JSF provides wrapper methods to simplify AJAX calls. If you're using JSF as your presentation technology, you'll most likely use the `<f:ajax/>` tag to make AJAX calls, which invokes a method on a Java bean on the server. The JSF tag enables you to easily integrate AJAX into your application without having to build the plumbing. In addition, the JSF AJAX infrastructure will automatically update other JSF components, saving you the trouble of writing code that iterates through the DOM.

The JavaScript code in this listing isn't very different than the WebSocket code in listing 14.3. The major differences center on the functionality provided. AJAX uses a request–response model. There's no way to get server events back to the client asynchronously without an initial request from the server. For example, if you're implementing chat functionality, the client must repeatedly poll the server for chat messages if it's using AJAX. This extra network traffic increases the load on the server while making the chat service appear slow. AJAX is great for situations where the client needs to retrieve data from the server for validation or partial page updates. It's not suitable in situations where the server can generate data asynchronously or multiple messages need to be transmitted to the server before a response is received.

Related to AJAX is Comet, which attempts to use AJAX to provide WebSocket-like functionality prior to HTML5.

14.2.3 WebSockets versus Comet

The AJAX approach we discussed in the last section works perfectly for situations where the client needs to request information from the server, but it's not a good solution for situations where the server needs to push events back to the client. The client can use AJAX to poll the server, but this isn't an ideal solution for several reasons, including excessive network traffic and latency. Comet isn't a well-defined standard but rather a technique whereby existing web technologies are used to provide server-side push within the limitations of HTTP 1.1. The limitations of HTTP 1.1, of course, are the lack of support for long-lived connections whereby the server can push data back to the client. This is the problem that WebSockets solves.

There are several approaches to implementing Comet that can be grouped into either streaming or long-polling. This is nicely broken down in an article on IBM developerWorks.[1] This article describes how each approach works and provides code samples. We'll describe the two different approaches at a high level and contrast the technology with WebSockets. Actually implementing a Comet solution is beyond the scope of this section and you'll definitely want to use WebSockets.

Streaming is a technique whereby a long-lived HTTP request is created and messages are sent back over this connection. There are two approaches to creating this long-lived connection: Forever IFrames and multipart `XMLHttpRequests`.

With Forever IFrames, the page contains a hidden IFrame tag with an `src` attribute that requests content. When the server receives the request for IFrame, it keeps the connection open and transmits code embedded in `<script></script>` pairs containing the message. The browser executes the code, and the JavaScript snippet delivers the message it contains.

The other streaming approach, multipart `XMLHttpRequests`, has the client JavaScript code set the multipart flag on the `XMLHttpRequest`. The connection is left open and the server transmits each message as a multipart response. If you're familiar with multipart form submissions, this is analogous to multipart form submission in reverse.

---

1 Carbou, Mathieu. "Reverse Ajax, Part 1: Introduction to Comet." IBM developerWorks, July 19, 2011, http://www.ibm.com/developerworks/library/wa-reverseajax1/.

Forever IFrames and multipart `XMLHttpRequests` are both streaming approaches. The other approach to Comet is HTTP long-polling. With HTTP long-polling, the client opens an AJAX call to the server. The server hangs onto the connection until there's a response. Once it writes the response back to the client, the connection is closed. The client then initiates another AJAX call to the server to wait for another message.

Both streaming and long-polling are essentially hacks. With Forever IFrames there's no easy way to handle error detection and recovery. Multipart `XMLHttpRequests` aren't supported by all browsers. With long-polling there's the chance that you'll miss a message. What happens if a message arrives after a message has been delivered and closed but before the client is able to open the next connection? How does a server know when a client has disappeared so that it doesn't cache messages delivered on reconnect? Using `XMLHttpRequests` for either multipart responses or long-polling ties up a connection to the server, meaning that you can't issue AJAX calls elsewhere on the page. Additionally, issues arise with proxy firewalls and requests to subdomains.

WebSockets provides the functionality that drove the development of Comet without the complications. There's no need to use IFrames or generate JavaScript code to be passed back in a multipart response. With WebSockets both the client and server send data simultaneously, which can be text, JSON, XML, binary, and so on. There's a well-defined JavaScript API that's consistently supported across browsers.

One of the biggest differentiating factors between WebSockets and Comet is server-side support. Java EE 7 introduces standardized WebSockets to the Java platform. There's a well-defined API with essentially the same callbacks as you see on the JavaScript client. Comet doesn't have a standardized server-side API, partly because Comet isn't standardized itself. In the next couple of sections we'll dive into the Java EE WebSocket APIs.

14.3 WebSockets and Java EE

Now that you have a basic understanding of WebSockets and how they relate to other technologies, it's time to dive into the APIs. As we've already mentioned, WebSocket support for Java is defined in JSR-356. This JSR defines both client and server-side APIs. The client-side APIs can be used by any Java applications, thus giving JavaFX and command-line applications the ability to communicate with WebSocket endpoints. The server-side APIs are only available in Java EE containers.

The WebSocket API is defined in two Java packages: `javax.websocket.*` and `javax.websocket.server.*`. These packages correspond to client and server APIs, respectively. We'll focus most of our attention on the server APIs.

Before we dive into the server API, we need to spend a few minutes discussing threading and security. Unlike Servlets, a WebSocket endpoint is created for each client that initiates a connection. An endpoint is thus stateful and serves only one client. It's possible to override this behavior by supplying a `ServerEndpointConfi.Configurator` object that implements the `getEndPointInstance()` method. This method returns an instance of the WebSocket endpoint to be used for a new connection.

There are two immediate considerations with security and WebSockets: restricting access to authenticated users and encrypting traffic. A WebSocket endpoint is specified using a URL and is thus secured via a security constraint in web.xml. For example, the WebSocket endpoint for customer service representatives (CSRs) is secured using the security constraint in the following listing. The server endpoint is configured using the annotation `@ServerEndpoint(value="/support")`.

Listing 14.7 Securing a WebSocket endpoint

```
<security-constraint>
 <web-resource-collection>
 <web-resource-name>
 Limit CSR
 </web-resource-name>
 <url-pattern>/support/*</url-pattern>      ❶ Restrict connections under /support/*
 </web-resource-collection>
 <auth-constraint>
 <role-name>csr</role-name>                  ❷ Allow only CSR users to connect
 </auth-constraint>
</security-constraint>
```

The configuration in this listing restricts access to the WebSocket endpoint at `/support` ❶ to only authenticated CSRs ❷. This doesn't completely protect the endpoint. With the default settings, all WebSocket communication would be transmitted in clear text. Someone running a network sniffer could view the traffic and potentially even inject packets. For connections exchanging confidential communication, secure sockets should be used. With secure sockets, the client opens the connection using the `wss:` prefix instead of `ws:`. This will result in the connection being opened with HTTPS instead of HTTP. To enable secure sockets, the following snippet is added to the preceding security constraint:

```
<user-data-constraint>
 <transport-guarantee>CONFIDENTIAL</transport-guarantee>
</user-data-constraint>
```

Now that you have a basic understanding of WebSockets, let's look at the two types of endpoints.

14.3.1 WebSocket endpoints

WebSockets have two types of endpoints: programmatic and annotated.

PROGRAMMATIC ENDPOINTS

Programmatic endpoints split the responsibilities of handling the connection lifecycle events and message processing into separate classes. With a programmatic endpoint, you're responsible for extending `javax.websocket.Endpoint` to handle the initial connection request. There are also callbacks for handling errors, as well as connection close events. When a connection is opened, you can register `javax.websocket.MessageHandler` instances to process incoming messages.

Although programmatic endpoints are more complicated to construct than annotated endpoints, they're more versatile from an architectural perspective. Message handlers can be reused by multiple endpoints and thus aren't tied to a specific URI.

ANNOTATED ENDPOINTS

Annotated endpoints, as their name implies, use annotations to define and configure a WebSocket endpoint. An annotated endpoint can be any Java class; unlike programmatic endpoints, there's no class or interface from which you must inherit. There's no difference in message-handling capabilities, so the decision on whether to use programmatic or annotated endpoints depends solely on architectural considerations. With annotated endpoints you mark both lifecycle and messaging-handling methods with annotations.

USING WEBSOCKETS WITH EJB

There are two types of integration between WebSockets and EJBs to consider: exposing an EJB as a WebSocket endpoint and invoking an EJB from a WebSocket endpoint. The first approach isn't well defined in the Java EE 7 specification. Although a WebSocket endpoint could conceptually be a stateful session bean or a singleton bean, there's no explicit support for either case. Some containers, such as GlassFish 4.0 that uses the Tyrus WebSocket implementation, support exposing a singleton bean as a WebSocket endpoint, but this support isn't standardized yet. Your mileage may vary with other containers.

The second approach is supported. Using the `@EJB` annotation, you can inject references to EJBs into a WebSocket endpoint or message handler. This approach is better from an architectural point of view because WebSocket message handlers don't usually match granular business methods. WebSockets are fundamentally different from technologies such as JAX-WS that have well-defined messages and are usually used to expose business functionality to external systems.

Now that you've done some of the groundwork, we'll look at the `Session` interface before diving into the details of programmatic and annotated endpoints.

14.3.2 Session interface

The `javax.websocket.Session` interface is one of the most important WebSocket classes. You'll use this interface whether you're using programmatic or annotated endpoints. It represents a connection of a client to the server and is an abstract representation of the underlying socket connection. With WebSockets you're never able to access the underlying `java.net.Socket` instance; the `Session` interface is the closest you'll come to it.

An instance of the WebSocket interface is created when a client successfully initiates a connection to the server. A `Session` instance provides a number of useful methods, including those for sending messages back to the client, storing state, and obtaining more information about the connection. Depending on whether the endpoint is programmatic or annotated, you can acquire a reference to the session either in the `onOpen` handler or in the `onMessage` handler of an annotated endpoint. Several of the other callbacks can also optionally provide the `Session` interface.

SENDING A MESSAGE

The WebSocket interface contains two methods that you use to send messages back to the client:

- getAsyncRemote()—Sends asynchronous messages to the client
- getBasicRemote()—Sends synchronous messages to the client

Which method you choose depends on whether you want to send a message asynchronously or synchronously. The asynchronous method returns a RemoteEndpoint.Async instance, whereas the synchronous method returns a RemoteEndpoint.Basic. These both implement the RemoteEndpoint interface, as defined in the next listing.

Listing 14.8 RemoteEndpoint interface

```
public interface RemoteEndpoint {
public static interface Async extends RemoteEndpoint {
long getSendTimeout();
void setSendTimeout(long l);
void sendText(String string, SendHandler sh);
Future<Void> sendText(String string);
Future<Void> sendBinary(ByteBuffer bb);
void sendBinary(ByteBuffer bb, SendHandler sh);
Future<Void> sendObject(Object o);
void sendObject(Object o, SendHandler sh);
}
public static interface Basic extends RemoteEndpoint {
void sendText(String string) throws IOException;
void sendBinary(ByteBuffer bb) throws IOException;
void sendText(String string, boolean bln) throws IOException;
void sendBinary(ByteBuffer bb, boolean bln) throws IOException;
OutputStream getSendStream() throws IOException;
Writer getSendWriter() throws IOException;
void sendObject(Object o) throws IOException, EncodeException;
}
void setBatchingAllowed(boolean bln) throws IOException;
boolean getBatchingAllowed();
void flushBatch() throws IOException;
void sendPing(ByteBuffer bb) throws IOException,IllegalArgumentException;
void sendPong(ByteBuffer bb) throws IOException,IllegalArgumentException;
}
```

❶ Interface for sending asynchronous messages

❷ Interface for sending synchronous messages

Although we won't go into detail about each method, the asynchronous interface ❶ and the synchronous interface ❷ have the same basic capabilities. Both can send text as well as raw bytes and Java objects. When sending Java objects, the encoders registered on an endpoint will be used to convert the Java object into a representation that will be transmitted via a WebSocket.

The code in ActionBazaar using the asynchronous interface for sending out messages is as follows:

```
ChatMessage cm = new ChatMessage(username,message);
csrSession.getAsyncRemote().sendObject(cm);
```

> **Asynchronous versus synchronous messages**
> You might be wondering which message to use: synchronous or asynchronous. For most applications, it's better to go with asynchronous messages. Synchronous messages will result in your code slowing down and waiting on a slow client. If you're iterating over a list of `Session` objects and sending out a broadcast message, one slow client will slow messages to all clients. Furthermore, if you're in the middle of a transaction and send out a synchronous message, you'll lock that resource until the message is sent. You don't want to couple database table locking to slow WebSocket connections. This is a recipe to create a nonscalable application.
>
> Synchronous messages aren't a solution to concurrency issues. Design both your server and the client for asynchronous communication. Assume that connections will drop and the end user might be on a 2G cell network.

CLOSING WEBSOCKET CONNECTION

Once you're finished with a WebSocket connection, it's important to close it. WebSocket connections will live for a long time if you forget about them. They are expensive even if little data is being transmitted over them. The `Session` object provides two methods for closing a WebSocket connection:

```
close() throws IOException;
close(CloseReason closeReason) throws IOException;
```

The first `close` method, lacking a reason, closes the connection with a normal status code and no reason. The second `close` method enables you to provide a reason for closing the connection. In ActionBazaar if the web application is undeployed or the server is shut down (normally), all of the open WebSocket connections are closed and the following message is provided to the client so it may inform the user:

```
session.close(new CloseReason(CloseReason.CloseCodes.GOING_AWAY,
 "Server is going down for maintenance."));
```

ACQUIRING BASIC WEBSOCKET INFORMATION

The WebSocket `Session` interface also provides a wealth of information about the current client and type of connection. Some of the more useful methods are as follows:

- `getId()`—Returns a string with a unique identifier representing this session
- `getPathParameters()`—Returns parameters passed in as a part of the URL
- `getQueryString()`—Returns the query string of the URL `(?vacation=yes)`
- `getRequestParameterMap()`—Query string parsed and returned in a map
- `getRequestURI()`—URI under which this session was opened
- `isOpen()`—Returns `true` if the connection is still valid
- `isSecure()`—Returns `true` if the connection is using secure sockets
- `getUserPrincipal()`—Returns the authenticated user or null if none

- `getUserProperties()`—Returns a `Map<String,String>` that can be used to store data
- `addMessageHandler()`—registers a message handler used by programmatic endpoints

If the user has logged into the application via realm-based security, the `getUserPrincipal()` will return the principal object. This is used in the ActionBazaar example in the next section. The `getId()` method is useful to identify a specific session; remember that there may be multiple sessions open to one client (`getOpenSessions()` will provide a list), so don't assume there's one session for a client or attempt to use an IP address to identify an end user.

VALIDITY OF ISOPEN With the `isOpen()` call, remember that `isOpen()` is only valid the instant it's called. Just because it returns `true` doesn't mean the connection is still open and that your next call to send a message will succeed. The client may be in the process of closing the connection and a split millisecond later it'll actually be closed. `isOpen()` is useful only if it returns `false`. Don't make any assumptions with `isOpen()`!

In the next section we'll look at decoders and encoders, which you'll need to understand when processing messages.

14.3.3 Decoders and encoders

The WebSocket interfaces you'll see later in this chapter will allow you to register decoders and encoders. These are useful for converting incoming messages to Java objects and then converting Java objects into another representation when sending a message. You don't need to use the decoder/encoder functionality to implement a WebSocket endpoint. But unless you're processing just text messages with no structure or binary data, decoders and encoders will be invaluable in separating message processing from message encoding.

JAVA API FOR JSON Although it's beyond the scope of this section, encoders and decoders will most likely use SR-353, which is part of Java EE 7. This API provides a simple interface for generating and consuming JSON. The code examples for this book make extensive use of this API.

Let's start by taking a look at decoders.

DECODERS

A decoder is invoked prior to a message being handed off to your code. A decoder implements one of the subinterfaces of `javax.websocket.Decoder`. There are several different interfaces to choose from:

- `TextStream`—Works on a stream (`java.io.Reader`)
- `Text`—Works on a Java `String` that is fully loaded into memory
- `BinaryStream`—Processed using an `InputStream`
- `Binary`—Loaded into a `ByteBuffer` prior to being parsed

Which interface is picked depends on the data type you're transmitting. If it's JSON, you'd use either `TextStream` or `Text`. For binary data, such as an image, you'd choose `BinaryStream` or `Binary`. The `CommandMessage` decoder is shown in the following listing.

Listing 14.9 CommandMessage decoder

```
public class CommandMessageDecoder
 implements Decoder.Text<AbstractCommand> {          ❶ Extends Decoder.Text interface

 @Override
 public void init(EndpointConfig config) {}           ❷ Initializes decoder

 @Override
 public AbstractCommand decode(String message) throws DecodeException {
 ...
 }                                                    ❸ Converts text message into AbstractCommand

 @Override
 public boolean willDecode(String message) {          ❹ Returns true if decoder can parse text
 ...
 }

 @Override
 public void destroy() {}                             ❺ Cleans up any resources
}
```

The code in this listing is relatively straightforward. The class is declared as a decoder ❶ and parameterized with `AbstractCommand`—meaning that it'll convert the incoming text into an `AbstractCommand` object (data type in ActionBazaar). There are two lifecycle methods, `init()` ❷ and `destroy()` ❺. The `willDecode` message will be called first by the WebSocket implementation to find out if this decoder can handle the message ❹. If it can, the `decode` method will be invoked ❸.

ENCODERS

Encoders are similar to decoders. The interface and subinterfaces are defined in `javax.websocket.Endcoder`. The only difference is that the methods are named `encode` and the return type and method parameters are swapped. The `CommandMessage` encoder is shown in the following listing.

Listing 14.10 CommandMessage encoder

```
public class CommandMessageEncoder implements
 Encoder.Text<AbstractCommand>{                       ❶ Extends Encoder.Text interface

 @Override
 public void init(EndpointConfig config) {}           ❷ Initializes decoder

 @Override
 public void destroy() {}                             ❸ Invoked before decoder is released

 @Override
 public String encode(AbstractCommand commandMessage)
 throws EncodeException {                             ❹ Converts object to a String
```

```
StringWriter writer = new StringWriter();
...
return writer.toString();
}
}
```

The code in this listing is almost the same as the code in listing 14.9 except that instead of decoding the object, it's converted into text. The class extends `Encoder.Text` ❶ and is parameterized with `AbstractCommand`—meaning that this class will convert `AbstractCommand` instances into a `String`. The `initialize` method is invoked when the class is first instantiated ❷. When the encoder is destroyed, the `destroy` method ❸ enables it to clean up any references or resources. Finally, the `encode` method ❹ is responsible for converting the object to a `java.lang.String`. Now it's time to dive into ActionBazaar and see examples of WebSockets in action!

14.4 WebSockets in ActionBazaar

ActionBazaar uses WebSockets to provide online support to bidders and sellers, as well as to implement a support dashboard for CSRs. The online chat support enables CSRs to chat in real time with end users. The support dashboard provides near-real-time information on the number of users waiting for help and also the ability to post to a shared bulletin that is visible to all CSRs. With the shared bulletin, CSRs can check with each other on the status of the site. They can also verify with other CSRs whether the same issue is cropping up for multiple users.

The use of two different scenarios is shown here to demonstrate the two different approaches to implementing WebSocket endpoints with Java EE. The first, chat support, demonstrates the use of a programmatic endpoint where you have greater control. The second, the dashboard/bulletin, demonstrates the use of an annotated endpoint. There's also one more distinction between these two scenarios. In the first scenario, the WebSocket is being used to connect two users. In the second scenario, events are published out to all connected CSRs. Looking at the source code for these two examples will give you a template for implementing your own endpoints. Both examples will work in a load-balanced environment where there are multiple servers.

Figure 14.1 provides an overview of the chat-support implementation. A user, such as a bidder or seller, will navigate to the chat page. The JavaScript code on the page will automatically initiate a WebSocket connection with the `ClientChatEndpoint` (`/chat`). The `ClientChatEndpoint` will then call the `ChatServer`, which is a singleton bean. On the other end, when a CSR logs into the support page, the JavaScript code on that page will automatically initiate a WebSocket invocation with the `SupportChatEndpoint` (`/admin/support`). The `SupportChatEndpoint` then passes along the request to the `ChatServer` singleton bean. The `ChatServer` is thus the nexus and is responsible for routing the incoming messages. It caches the `javax.websocket.Session` for both the client and CSR endpoints. The code for the `ChatServer` bean is shown in the next listing.

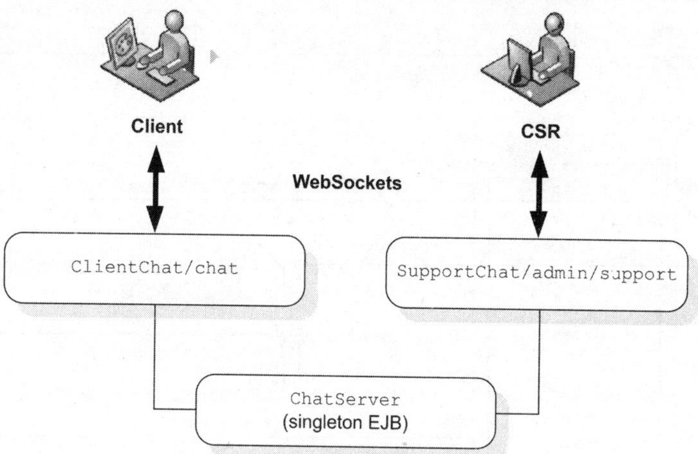

Figure 14.1 Chat support via WebSockets in ActionBazaar

Listing 14.11 ChatServer singleton bean—manages client and CSR chat sessions

```
@Singleton
public class ChatServer {
  private final Stack<Session> availableReps = new Stack<>();
  private final Stack<Session> waitingClients = new Stack<>();
  private final Set<Session> csrSessions;
  private final Set<Session> clientSessions;
  private final Map<String,SupportConversation> conversations;

  public void customServiceRepConnected(Session csrSession) {...}
  public void customServiceRepDisconnected(Session csrSession) {...}
  public void addClientSession(Session clientSession) {...}
  public void removeClientSession(Session clientSession) {...}
  public void sendMessage(Session sourceSession, String message) {...}
  public void shutdown() {...}
  public void performCommand(AbstractCommand command) {...}
}
```

❶ Waiting clients and CSRs
❷ All client and CSR WebSocket sessions
❸ ...upport ...sations ...rogress
❹ Support methods for a CSR
❺ Support methods for a client
❻ Sends ...essage
❼ Terminates all conversations
❽ Performs a command like ending a conversation

The code in this listing is relatively straightforward. The ChatServer tracks the list of CSRs and clients who aren't chatting yet ❶. It also tracks all of the sessions, regardless of whether they're engaged in a conversation or waiting to begin a conversation ❷. Finally, it maintains a list of clients and CSRs currently engaged in conversation ❸. It also has a method for either registering or disconnecting a CSR ❹ or a client ❺. When an endpoint onMessage is invoked, the endpoint calls the sendMessage ❻, which dispatches the message to both parties. If the server shuts down, detected via a ServletContextListener, the shutdown method then terminates all outstanding conversations, letting users know that the server is going down ❼. The last method, performCommand ❽, utilizes the command pattern to perform an operation for either the client or CSR. Currently, the operation is usually to end the chat, which happens when the client feels their question has been answered or the CSR gives up.

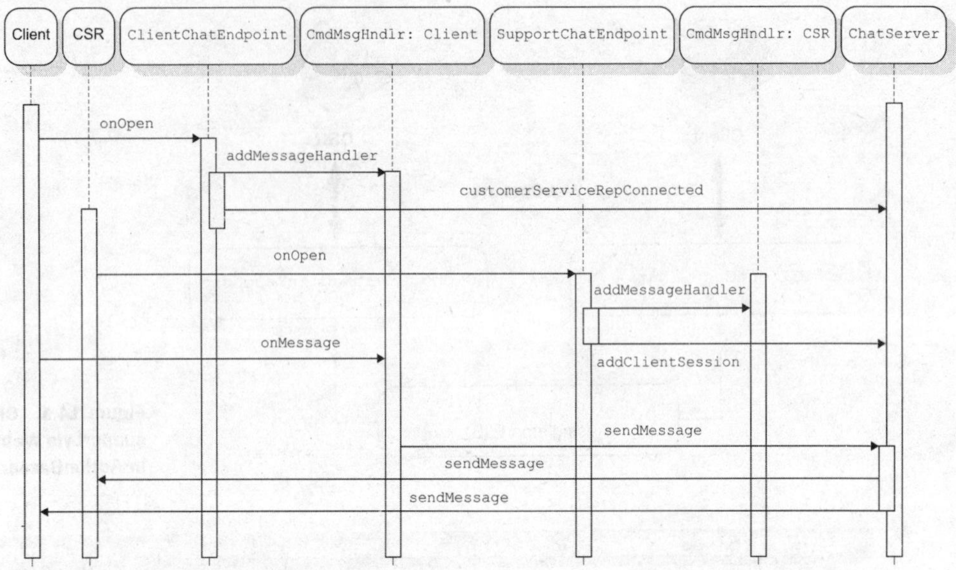

Figure 14.2 Interaction of the endpoint, message handler, and `ChatServer`

The sequence described here can be a little hard to fully conceptualize. Figure 14.2 illustrates the interaction between the various pieces. Although we haven't covered it yet, a programmatic endpoint uses a `MessageHandler` to process the incoming messages. In this sequence diagram, the client and CSR both initiate WebSocket instances that result in an `onOpen` being invoked on their respective endpoints. Two different instances of the same message handler class are instantiated. The message handler, shortened in the diagram from `CommandMessageHandler`, forwards messages to the `ChatServer`. The `ChatServer` then dispatches the message back to the client and also to the CSR. It should be noted that messages from the client and messages sent from the server back to the client are asynchronous. The client and server don't wait for their messages to be successfully sent and acknowledged before continuing. If there are any failures, the `onError` method (to be covered later) will be invoked.

JSON messages are exchanged between the client and server. On the server side, the `CommandMessageDecoder` and `CommandMessageEncoder` are responsible for decoding and encoding the chat messages. JAR-353 is used to implement both of these classes. JSON is much more compact than XML and is easier to work with in JavaScript.

Figure 14.3 illustrates the implementation of the bulletin WebSocket service. This service is much simpler than the customer service chat we just discussed. The bulletin service is used to implement a dashboard so that CSRs can see what's going on with the support queue and also send out broadcast messages to all of the other CSRs.

The bulletin endpoint is implemented using the annotation approach. This means that the lifecycle and message-handling functionality is handled by one object. Updates

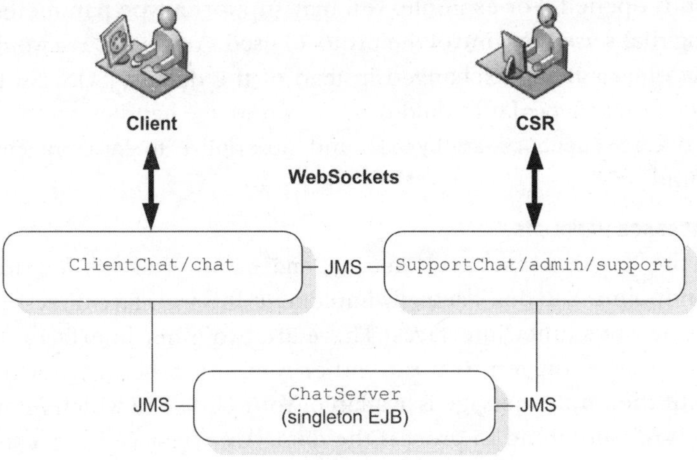

Figure 14.3 Overview of the support bulletin

from the `ChatServer` are published to all `BulletinService` endpoints using a JMS topic. Broadcast messages sent by one CSR to the bulletin are published to the same JMS topic. JMS is used instead of CDI events, because in a load-balanced environment, the `BulletinService` instances will be spread out across multiple servers. All messages sent via WebSockets use JSON. Now that you have a handle on how WebSockets are used in ActionBazaar, let's turn our attention to the chat service and see how it's implemented using a programmatic endpoint.

14.4.1 Using programmatic endpoints

As we've mentioned, there are two approaches to creating an endpoint: programmatic and annotated. In this section we'll discuss the programmatic endpoint. Although it sounds complicated, programmatic endpoints aren't more complicated than annotated endpoints. Programmatic endpoints simply give you control over the registration of message handlers. There are two reasons for using programmatic endpoints:

- Separate the message handler from the endpoint implementation.
- Register different message handlers depending on session information.

For the first reason, separating the endpoint implementation and message handler enables reuse of the message handler. There's not necessarily a one-to-one relationship between an endpoint and a message handler. An endpoint handles the lifecycle events and is bound to a URL. Consider the case of the ActionBazaar chat service—it makes use of two separate endpoints, one for the bidder/seller and another for the CSR. In both cases the message handler delegates the incoming message to the `SupportServer`. The `SupportServer` is a singleton bean that routes the message to the correct recipient. Because the message handler logic is the same for both endpoints, it doesn't make any sense to have two different implementations.

The second reason for using programmatic endpoints is more complicated. You may want to use different message handlers depending on parameters passed in when the session is opened. For example, you may support a type parameter on the connection string that's used to control the protocol used. A type of `Java` would result in serialized Java objects being exchanged instead of the default JSON. So the URL http://actionbazaar/chat?type=Java would result in a message handler being used that would accept `java.io.InputStream/byte[]` and deserialize to Java objects. Other possibilities abound.

UNDERSTANDING MESSAGE HANDLERS

Understanding the `javax.websocket.MessageHandler` interface is key for using programmatic endpoints. You don't actually implement this interface directly; instead you implement one of its inner interfaces. There are two inner interfaces: `Partial` or `Whole`. As their names suggest, you can either wait and process the whole message or defer until the whole message is available. Your choice of which interface to use depends on how you intend to process the data. Are you accepting a stream of data such as an image or video or a discrete message such as an update in an online video game? The definition of the `MessageHandler` interface is shown in the following listing.

Listing 14.12 `MessageHandler` interface

```
public interface MessageHandler {
 public static interface Partial<T extends Object>
 extends MessageHandler {
   public void onMessage(T partialMessage, boolean last);
 }
 public static interface Whole<T extends Object>
 extends MessageHandler {
   public void onMessage(T message);
 }
}
```

Interface for partial message processing

Interface for whole message processing

In this listing you can see the two subinterfaces that can be implemented. Both of these subinterfaces have an `onMessage` method. The interface uses Java's Generics so that you can be certain about the type to be passed to the implementation. If the type is a custom Java object or domain object from the application, then the decoder registered on the endpoint will be used. The partial handler interface includes a flag denoting whether the chunk of data passed in is complete.

There are some drawbacks to implementing the `MessageHandler` interface. Although we haven't covered the `@OnMessage` annotation yet, with the `@OnMessage` annotation you can optionally receive a `javax.websocket.Session` instance along with the data. You'd use the `Session` object to send data back to the client. Also, because a `MessageHandler` isn't a managed object, you can't inject references to EJBs, entity managers, and the like into it.

The code for the `ChatMessageHandler` is shown in the listing that follows. This message handler is used both by the endpoints bidder and seller and by the CSR.

Listing 14.13 ChatMessageHandler used in ActionBazaar

```
public class ChatMessageHandler implements MessageHandler.Whole<ChatMessage> {   ❶
 private final ChatServer chatServer;
 private final Session session;

 public ChatMessageHandler(ChatServer chatServer, Session session) {
 this.chatServer = chatServer;
 this.session = session;                                                        ❷
 }

 @Override
 public void onMessage(ChatMessage message) {
 chatServer.handleMessage(session, message.getMessage());                       ❸
 }
}
```

❶ Extend MessageHandler.Whole to process message block

❷ Cache WebSocket session and ChatServer singleton bean

❸ Route message to ChatServer bean for processing

The code shown in this listing implements the `MessageHandler.Whole` interface ❶ to process complete messages. The constructor caches references to the `ChatServer` singleton bean along with the WebSocket session ❷. You use these cached entities when you process the message ❸. There are a couple of things to remember when reading this code sample:

- Each WebSocket connection gets its own instance of the `ChatMessageHandler`.
- The `onMessage` takes a `ChatMessage`; WebSockets use a decoder, `ChatMessageDecoder`, to convert the JSON into a Java object.

In the next section you'll create endpoints and register the message handler.

USING PROGRAMMATIC WEBSOCKETS

Now that you have a message handler, it's time to define the endpoint. To define an endpoint, you must do four things:

1. Define a class that extends `javax.websocket.Endpoint`.
2. Provide an implementation of the `onOpen` method.
3. Register the message handler in the `onOpen` method.
4. Register the endpoint.

The class that you must extend, `javax.websocket.Endpoint`, is an abstract class. Its definition is as follows:

```
public abstract class Endpoint {
 public abstract void onOpen(Session session, EndpointConfig config);
 public void onClose(Session session, CloseReason closeReason) {
 // empty
 }
 public void onError(Session session, Throwable thr) {
 // empty
 }
}
```

An implementation must thus provide an implementation of the `onOpen` method. Within this method, registration of the message handler should be performed.

To create a programmatic WebSocket, extend javax.websocket.Endpoint and implement the onOpen method. To configure the endpoint so that it can receive connections, you need to annotate it with the @ServerEndpoint annotation, which we'll discuss in the next session when we cover annotated endpoints. Within the onMessage method, message handlers are registered via the addMessageHandler on the WebSocket session object. Only one message handler for each type of message can be registered. These message types are text, binary, and pong messages we discussed earlier. Once registered, you're ready to accept messages from the client.

14.4.2 Using annotated endpoints

Annotated endpoints are much easier but less flexible than programmatic endpoints. With an annotated endpoint, all configuration is performed via annotations. The annotations mark the class that's to be used as the endpoint, lifecycle callback methods, and methods that are to process messages. All of the functionality for the endpoint, lifecycle, and message processing is combined into a single Java object.

An annotated endpoint is instantiated by the WebSocket implementation. You don't have control over the creation of this class. An instance is created when a new connection is established and it's destroyed when the connection is closed. There are very few requirements for an endpoint class, but it must be a nonabstract concrete class with a public no-argument constructor. Dependency injection is performed after the class is created.

@SERVERENDPOINT

The @ServerEndpoint annotation is the annotation that marks a class as being a WebSocket endpoint. The container scans the class path at startup looking for classes with this annotation. Besides identifying the class as a WebSocket endpoint, it also configures the URI for the endpoint, as well as the encoders and decoders to be used when processing a message. The annotation is defined as follows:

```
@Retention(value = RetentionPolicy.RUNTIME)
@Target(value = {ElementType.TYPE})
public @interface ServerEndpoint {
 public String value();
 public String[] subprotocols() default {};
 public Class<? extends Decoder>[] decoders() default {};
 public Class<? extends Encoder>[] encoders() default {};
 public Class<? extends ServerEndpointConfig.Configurator> configurator()
 default ServerEndpointConfig.Configurator.class;
}
```

The parameters to the annotation configure the endpoint:

- value—The URI of the endpoint
- subprotocols—Ordered list of application-level protocols
- decoders—Ordered list of javax.websocket.Decoder subclasses
- encoders—Ordered list of javax.websocket.Encoder subclasses
- configurator—Custom to further configure the endpoint

Only the value parameter, specifying the URI of the endpoint, is required. All other parameters are optional. The URI is relative to the root of the WebSocket container. Because the WebSocket container is most often used from a web application container, the root is the same as the web application container. To get a better understanding of this annotation, let's look at an example from `BulletinService` from ActionBazaar in the next listing.

Listing 14.14 `BulletinService` endpoint configuration

```
@ServerEndpoint(
 value="/admin/bulletin",
 decoders = {BulletinMessageDecoder.class},
 encoders = {BulletinMessageEncoder.class})
public class BulletinService {
 ...
}
```

❶ Marks class as WebSocket endpoint
❷ Configures URI for BulletinService endpoint
❸ Decoder to be used for messages
❹ Encoder to be used for messages

In this listing the `BulletinService` class is annotated with `@ServerEndpoint` and will thus be exposed as a WebSocket endpoint ❶. The `value` parameter specifies the URI for the server ❷. Assuming the web application is deployed under the chapter 14 context, the full path to the service will be http://<address>:<port>/chapter14/admin/bulletin. An encoder is specified for the service that will encode methods being sent using the `BulletinMessadeEncoder` ❸. A decoder is also specified that will decode incoming messages ❹. Although multiple encoders and decoders can be specified, only the first decoder will be used.

@PathParam

The `@PathParam` annotation serves the same functional purpose as the `javax.ws.rs.PathParam` annotation you saw earlier when we covered RESTful web services in chapter 8. With it, you can map variables in the URI to parameters on methods annotated with `@OnMessage`, `@OnError`, `@OnOpen`, and `@OnClose`. This enables parameters to be passed in using the URL and can help to reduce the complexity of application messages exchanged via WebSockets. The annotation is defined as follows:

```
@Target(value = {ElementType.PARAMETER,
 ElementType.METHOD, ElementType.FIELD})
 @Retention(value = RetentionPolicy.RUNTIME)
 @Documented
 public @interface PathParam {
 public String value();
}
```

As you can see from this definition, there's only one parameter to the `@PathParam` annotation and that's the variable, which should also appear in the URI specified by the `@ServerEndpoint` annotation. The WebSocket implementation will attempt to convert the `String` in the URL to the data type of the parameter on the method. Only `String` and primitive types are supported. A failure to convert or an invalid parameter type will result in a `DecodeException` being thrown and passed to the method annotated with the `@OnError` annotation.

To better understand this annotation, let's consider how it's used in ActionBazaar. Because CSRs may access ActionBazaar from a multitude of clients, you need to know the type of client when a connection is opened. ActionBazaar makes the distinction between the following types of clients: desktop, mobile-web, and mobile-native. These client types are specific to ActionBazaar and are used by the application code to provide specialized messages for the different clients. The code is shown in the following listing.

Listing 14.15 Using path variables

```
@ServerEndpoint(value="/admin/bulletin/{clientType}",      ❶ Path variable defined
 decoders ={BulletinMessageDecoder.class},
 encoders = {BulletinMessageEncoder.class})
public class BulletinService {
 @OnOpen
 public void onOpen(                                       ❷ Path variable mapped to method parameter
 @PathParam("clientType") String clientType) {
 ...
 }
}
```

In this listing the variable `clientType` in the URI ❶ is mapped to a parameter in the `onOpen` method ❷. A native iPad ActionBazaar application, written in Objective-C, will thus construct the following URL: http://<address>:<port>/chapter14/admin/bulletin/mobile-native. The mobile-native portion of the URL will be passed into the `onOpen` method, where you can handle it and tailor subsequent responses.

@ONOPEN

The `@OnOpen` annotation marks a method on the endpoint that will be called when the connection is first opened. This annotation is defined as follows:

```
@Retention(value = RetentionPolicy.RUNTIME)
@Target(value = {ElementType.METHOD})
public @interface OnOpen {}
```

As you can see from this definition, this annotation is rather simple and has no properties. But looks can be deceiving, because the annotated method can accept several different parameters in any order. The WebSocket container will use Java reflection to examine the parameters and invoke the annotated method with the parameters you've requested. The types of parameters that the annotated method may accept are as follows:

- `javax.websocket.Session`—Newly created session for this connection
- `javax.websocket.EndpointConfig`—Configuration for the endpoint including the lists of decoders and encoders and also a map containing user properties
- `@PathParam` annotated parameters—Map variables from the URI to method parameters

The `@OnOpen` annotated method will be called only once when the connection is opened. If you accept a `Session` object, you can cache this object so that you can asynchronously send messages back to the client. In the case of the `BulletinService`, you cache the `Session` object and then use it from another method to send back updates to the client. This other method is monitoring a JMS queue for messages.

@OnClose

The `@OnClose` annotation is placed on a method that will be invoked when the connection is closed by either the client or the server. Like the method annotated with `@OnOpen`, the `@OnClose` method can take an optional set of parameters including the `Session`, `EndpointConfig`, and parameters annotated with `@PathParam`. This callback enables resources to be cleaned up and released. For example, in ActionBazaar the `BulletinService` endpoint is registered as a JMS consumer. The `onClose` annotated method is used to deregister the endpoint as a JMS consumer so that it can be garbage-collected. The code from ActionBazaar is shown in the following listing.

Listing 14.16 Using `@OnClose` annotation

```
@OnClose
public void cleanup() {          <-- ❶ Marked to handle close messages
...
}
```

In this listing the `cleanup()` method is marked to handle close events ❶. It's important to realize that when the method annotated with `@OnClose` is being invoked, messages can no longer be sent to the client. The connection has been indeed closed. Furthermore, if the `Session` has been cached and is being used asynchronously, invoking methods to send data may fail. Code might be in the process of sending data to the client when the connection is closed by the client or on the server. Be prepared to handle race conditions where the connection has been closed (on the remote side) but the `@OnClose` method has yet to be invoked. Liberal use of the `synchronized` keyword isn't the solution—only carefully handling errors and ensuring that code is thread-aware can ensure that the application functions correctly.

@OnMessage

The `@OnMessage` annotation is used to decorate the methods that will process incoming messages. Multiple methods in an endpoint can be decorated with the `@OnMessage` annotation. Each one must process a different data type. For example, you can't have two `@OnMessage` annotated methods that handle a `String`; how will the container know which method should be invoked?

The `@OnMessage` annotation is defined as follows:

```
@Retention(value = RetentionPolicy.RUNTIME)
@Target(value = {ElementType.METHOD})
public @interface OnMessage {
 public long maxMessageSize() default -1L;
}
```

As you can see from its definition, the annotation has only one parameter and that is the maximum message size. By default, there's no limit to a message size. But in practice, the maximum message size, set in bytes, should always be configured to guard against either bad client code or hacked clients that attempt to overwhelm the server with data. When a message arrives that exceeds the limit, the connection will be closed and a close code of 1009 (too big) returned to the client.

The data type the method can handle is broken down into three types: text data, binary data, and pong messages. These are broken out in table 14.1.

Table 14.1 `@OnMessage` parameter types

Type	Parameter type	Partial message	Notes
Text	`String`	No	
Text	`int`, `long`, `float`, `double`, etc.	No	
Text	`String`, `boolean`	Yes	If `boolean` true, message finished.
Text	Custom object	No	`Decoder.Text` must be registered.
Binary	`byte[]`	No	
Binary	`byte[]`, `boolean`	Yes	If `boolean` true, message finished.
Binary	`ByteBuffer`	No	
Binary	`ByteBuffer`, `boolean`	Yes	If `boolean` true, message finished.
Binary	`InputStream`	Yes	
Binary	Custom object	No	`Decover.Binary` must be registered.
Pong	`PongMessage`	No	

With the custom object types in table 14.1, custom decoders must be registered on the `@ServerEndpoint`. In addition to the parameters listed in the table, a message annotated with `@OnMessage` can accept the following parameters:

- `Session`—Session object associated with the client
- `@PathParam`—Maps URI variables to parameters

The parameters may appear in any order—the container will dynamically invoke the method using reflection.

Unlike the `MessageHandler` interface you saw earlier, methods decorated with `@OnMessage` can return data. If the return type is something other than a `String` or a Java primitive, an encoder must be registered on `@ServerEndpoint` for the type; otherwise an error will be generated.

Now that you have a theoretical handle on this annotation, let's look at an example of it from ActionBazaar in the next listing.

Listing 14.17 Message handlers from ActionBazaar `BulletinService`

```
@ServerEndpoint(value="/admin/bulletin/{clientType}",
 decoders = {BulletinCommandDecoder.class,BulletinMessageDecoder.class},
 encoders = {BulletinMessageEncoder.class,CommandResultEncoder.class})
public class BulletinService

 @OnMessage                                                    ❶ Marks method as a WebSocket message handler
 public void processMessage(String message, Session session) {  ❷ Accepts raw String and Session object
 ...
 }

 @OnMessage
 public CommandResult processCommand(                          ❸ WebSocket message handler with return type
 @PathParam("clientType") String clientType,                   ❹ Map URI variable to parameter
 BulletinCommand command,                                      ❺ Accept custom object—use decoder
 Session session) {
 ...
 }
}
```

This listing shows two methods from the `BulletinService` WebSocket endpoint ❶. The first method takes a `String` message and a WebSocket session as parameters ❷. This method essentially handles the bulletin board chat functionality. The second method is the more interesting of the two—it returns a `CommandResult` ❸ that will be converted to JSON by the `CommandResultEncoder` class. It also accepts the client type that's a variable from the URI ❹. Finally, it accepts a `BulletinCommand` object that's decoded from JSON using the `BulletinCommandDecoder` ❺.

As you can see from the example, processing messages is straightforward. The annotated API is much more flexible in terms of the parameters. Using the programmatic approach with the `MessageHandler` interface, it's not possible to get path parameters or a copy of the `Session` object.

@ONERROR

Error handling is very important for a WebSocket endpoint. At some point a connection to a remote client will be lost or there will be a bug in the logic. The `@OnError` annotation provides a mechanism for handling these unexpected situations. The annotation is defined as follows:

```
@Retention(value = RetentionPolicy.RUNTIME)
@Target(value = {ElementType.METHOD})
public @interface OnError {}
```

Only one method in a class can possess this annotation. The annotation itself has no parameters, but the method can optionally take any one of the following:

- `Throwable`—Exception representing the error
- `Session`—WebSocket session
- `@PathParam`—Annotated parameters

To get a better grasp of how this callback works, let's look at an example from the `BulletinService` in ActionBazaar in the following listing.

Listing 14.18 Handling WebSocket errors in `BulletinService`

```
@OnError                                                   ❶
public void handleFailure(Throwable t,                     ❷
Session session,                                           ❸
@PathParam("clientType") String clientType) {              ❹
...
}
```

❶ Marks handleFailure method as WebSocket error handler
❷ Accept throwable representing error
❸ Session encapsulating connection to client
❹ Map URI variable to method parameter

The `@OnError` annotation in the listing marks the `handleFailure` method as handling WebSocket errors ❶. It accepts three parameters. The first parameter ❷ is the exception and will contain the cause of the error. The second parameter is the WebSocket session ❸, and the third parameter is the client type as pulled from the URL used to invoke the WebSocket ❹.

You now have a handle on both programmatic endpoints and annotated endpoints. The next question is how you can use them in the context of EJB.

14.5 Using WebSockets effectively

WebSockets are a powerful addition to the Java EE stack and make it possible to develop applications that receive data from the server asynchronously. Clients no longer need to poll the server to check for updates—the server can now push messages back to the client. Unlike RESTful and SOAP-based web services, WebSocket endpoints are stateful. There are two elements of state here: there are objects that are kept in memory on the server (endpoint), and a socket connection is kept open to the client. If a given page opens two WebSocket connections to the server, as in the case of the ActionBazaar example with the chat and bulletin services, there are now two sets of objects and two expensive socket connections. WebSockets reduce the scalability of an application, but also makes it possible to provide push notifications from the server to the client in a standards-based approach that's superior to polling with AJAX or using nonstandard Comet.

To use WebSockets effectively, there are several important practices:

- Use WebSockets only when AJAX isn't a suitable solution.
- Store state in the user properties on the session, accessed via `Session.getUserProperties()`.
- Use EJBs for accessing transaction-based resources like databases.
- Use subprotocols to support versioning.
- Exchange data using JSON.
- Limit clients to one WebSocket connection.
- Set message size limits on WebSocket messages.

- Secure WebSocket endpoints using realm security.
- Use HTML5 WebSocket Security (WSS) whenever possible.

WebSockets are an exciting new HTML5 technology, but they aren't appropriate for every problem. WebSockets should be used only where push notifications from the server to the client are necessary. In the case of ActionBazaar, the chat service is one such case, because you don't want the client polling the server for new messages. But WebSockets wouldn't be an appropriate solution for performing web form validation, such as checking to make sure a username doesn't already exist when creating a new account. AJAX is still the appropriate solution for such situations. Also, in the case of ActionBazaar, it wouldn't be a good idea to use WebSockets from the main page to the application. You don't want every page view to result in a socket connection to the server.

State data for WebSockets should be stored in the user properties map on the session, accessed via `Session.getUserProperties()`. Only serializable objects should be stored in this map. Application state data shouldn't be stored in member variables, static variables, or on the local file system. In a load-balanced environment, the application container may roll over servicing of an endpoint to another node. Only data stored in the session would thus be available on the new node. While the application may work correctly in development on a single node, the behavior could change once the application is deployed to multiple nodes with a load balancer.

WebSocket endpoints should use EJBs for accessing transactional resources such as databases. Avoid injecting data sources into a WebSocket and accessing the database directly. First, you don't want WebSocket endpoints holding onto resources, such as a database connection, the entire time the WebSocket is in existence. Second, WebSockets shouldn't contain application logic. Logic should be implemented in either POJOs, if it doesn't touch transaction-based resources, or in EJBs.

WebSockets provide infrastructure for implementing your own communication protocol. WebSocket connections can be opened not only in web clients using JavaScript but also from iOS and Android applications. Supporting iOS and Android applications is different from supporting a web client. Because the JavaScript code is always downloaded from the server by the web browser, a web client usually has the most recent code. But in the case of native clients, the clients could be a couple of versions behind. Consequently, the subprotocol feature should be used from the outset for versioning. Unless the application is feature-complete with the first release, there will undoubtedly be revisions to the communication layer that won't be backward-compatible.

Currently, JSON is the favored format for data exchange, especially when dealing with mobile devices. Although JSON isn't self-documenting and lacks many of the more advanced features of XML, including validation with XML Schema, it's lightweight and suitable for situations where there are bandwidth and processing constraints. XML is verbose and requires a significant amount of overhead to process. On mobile devices this overhead affects battery life and application responsiveness.

WebSocket connections from the client should be used sparingly. The administrator example for ActionBazaar opened two WebSocket connections to the server. The use of two connections was done to demonstrate two different approaches to implementing endpoints, but only one connection should be used. Socket connection is expensive, and too many socket connections from each client will reduce application scalability.

Security should be a top concern when developing a WebSocket endpoint. Hacking can involve either breaking into a system or overwhelming it with a denial-of-service attack. It's important to set the maximum size on messages. A hacker may craft a script that attempts to stream gigabytes of invalid data to a WebSocket endpoint. This will have a net effect of starving resources to legitimate users. Additionally, unless an endpoint is meant to be publically available, it should be secured and require an authenticated session. Lastly, security WebSockets (wss) should be used to lock down and secure data. If wss isn't used, data is transmitted over the wire in plain text, meaning it can be easily intercepted, changed, and so on. Even if a page is requested using HTTPS, opening a WebSocket connection using ws: will result in an unencrypted socket connection being created. Now that you have a handle on best practices, it's time to wrap up the chapter.

14.6 Summary

This chapter began by introducing WebSockets and comparing them to AJAX and Comet. Unlike either AJAX or Comet, WebSockets provide full duplex bidirectional communication between the browser and server. WebSockets were introduced with HTML5 and, unlike Comet, which contorts existing technologies to enable the server to send messages without an initial request from the client, WebSockets are fully standardized and widely supported. WebSockets use the existing HTTP infrastructure and are thus compatible with existing firewalls.

Java EE 7 included standardized support for WebSockets via JSR-356. WebSockets can be defined either programmatically or via annotations. The programmatic approach is more flexible and enables control over the creation of the endpoint, as well as separation between the endpoint and the message handler. Annotated endpoints are easy to use. With annotated endpoints, just annotate a POJO with `@ServerEndpoint` and provide at least one method annotated with `@OnMessage`.

The WebSocket API supports the registration of message encoders and decoders. Encoders and decoders simplify development and allow for the message handler to receive Java objects instead of a raw stream. But a message handler can also receive plain text or an input stream of bytes. It can also optionally wait for the entire message or process the message in pieces. Using JSR-353, which was introduced with Java EE 7, it's easy to process and generate JSON within encoders and decoders.

The WebSocket specification is vague when it comes to the integration of WebSockets and Java EE. Some implementations, such as Tyrus (https://tyrus.java.net)

support beans as WebSocket endpoints or handlers. But given the special considerations of an endpoint, it's better to use an EJB from a WebSocket endpoint than to expose an EJB as a WebSocket endpoint.

WebSockets enable an entire new class of applications to be developed using Java EE. Previously, Java EE was primarily used to implement traditional web applications that used stateless EJBs. With the advent of WebSockets, Java EE 7 applications can now support single-page applications and talk directly with mobile applications running on iOS and Android.

15 Testing and EJB

This chapter covers

- Different testing strategies
- Unit testing EJBs
- Integration testing EJBs with the embedded `EJBContainer`
- Integration testing EJBs with Arquillian
- Using CDI in tests

In the previous chapters, we've focused on learning the different technologies EJB 3 has to offer and showcasing examples of those technologies so you understand how to use them and apply them in your own applications. But now that you know how to use the technologies, how do you guarantee they're going to fulfill your business requirements, operate securely and accurately, and give a positive user experience? You do this with testing.

This chapter covers some of the basics of testing EJB technologies. We'll start by discussing what the different testing strategies are and how they fit into testing EJBs. Next, we'll look at using technologies such as the embedded `EJBContainer` and Arquillian for more real-world tests. Finally, we'll present some common testing problems to avoid so your testing can be more effective. Let's start by introducing testing.

15.1 Introducing testing

Software testing is usually a heated topic because all developers agree testing is necessary and beneficial, but we disagree on the best way to do it. In this chapter we're going to look at the three general strategies for software testing: unit testing, integration testing, and functional testing. Each of these strategies will test your software in different ways, and each will have pros and cons associated with them. Finding a good balance among these three is usually the approach organizations take when developing a software testing strategy. So let's take a look at these testing strategies.

15.1.1 Testing strategies

In this section we're going to briefly introduce and give examples of testing your EJBs using the three different testing strategies: unit testing, integration testing, and functional testing. Each strategy has its specific purpose and exists to test your application in different ways. No testing strategy is 100% complete by itself, and not even the combination of all three strategies is guaranteed to find everything that may go wrong with your application. But combining all three will give you assurance that you application is working the way it's supposed to. So let's start with the first testing strategy, unit testing.

UNIT TESTING

The purpose of unit testing is to exercise the application's business logic by feeding it different input and examining the output to assert that the results are correct. Although this sounds simple and straightforward, unit testing can be very complicated and difficult to implement, especially with older code.

There are a wide variety of techniques for unit testing. All techniques, however, tend to have these fundamental principles in common:

1. No connections to outside resources are allowed (databases, web services, and so on).
2. Test only a single class at a time.
3. Test only a class's public contract (public methods or interface) and vary test input data to cover any private code.
4. Mock dependencies to return the data required to test the business logic of the class being tested.

JUnit is a popular testing framework for Java applications. Mockito is a powerful and easy-to-use framework for mocking a class's dependencies for unit tests. These two technologies, combined with the convention-over-configuration and POJO models of EJBs, have made unit testing EJBs much easier.

Although unit testing is a good start for ensuring code quality, it won't tell you the whole story. Once your application is deployed to a Java EE server, it gets turned into something else entirely. The Enterprise containers create and instantiate proxies for your EJBs, dependencies are injected, configuration files (`web.xml`, `ejb-jar.xml`) further configure the container, database connections are established, and much more. To make sure your code is still functioning properly after all this, you need to move beyond unit testing and into integration testing.

INTEGRATION TESTING

Integration testing is a strategy that tests your application's code in a way that closely mimics a real environment but isn't quite a real environment. Its primary purpose is to ensure that the interaction of your code with external resources is correct, and that when all of the different technologies used in the application actually come together, they can function as they're intended to. So what does this mean? Well, let's use a database as a simple example.

For your application to work properly, you need a database filled with the correct data. In an integration testing strategy, you don't mock the data as you do in a unit test. Instead, the test will most likely use an in-memory database that can be easily created and destroyed for the lifecycle of the integration tests. An in-memory database is a real database so it'll test your JPA entities and verify that they're working properly, but it's still not quite "real." The in-memory database mimic's the "real" external database for the purposes of the integration test.

How does this relate to EJBs? Just as the database is mimicked for integration tests, the EJB container needs to be mimicked for testing your EJBs. Just as there are in-memory databases like Derby to mimic "real" databases like MySQL or Oracle, there's an embedded `EJBContainer` that may be used to mimic a "real" Java EE server like GlassFish. Let's take a look at this embedded `EJBContainer`.

The embedded `EJBContainer` is part of the EJB specifications and is required in a full EJB implementation. We briefly introduced the embedded `EJBContainer` in chapter 5 as a way for EJBs to be used within Java SE applications. The embedded `EJBContainer` can also be utilized by integration tests for testing EJBs. The integration test can start the embedded `EJBContainer` in-memory, which will deploy all the EJBs it finds in the integration test's class path and then proceed with testing the EJBs. Although the embedded `EJBContainer` is a tremendous resource, using it can be quite a challenge. This is where technologies such as Arquillian come in.

Arquillian is a sophisticated integrated testing tool. Think of it as a wrapper around the embedded `EJBContainer`. It presents a simpler interface for configuring and running the embedded `EJBContainer`. This allows your integration testing to focus more on testing the EJBs than on resource management for running the integration tests.

Although integration testing takes the testing of your code a step further than unit testing, it still relies on mimicking the external resources your application depends on. To fully complete testing of your application, you need functional testing.

FUNCTIONAL TESTING

Functional testing is a testing strategy usually carried out by a separate testing team within the organization. At this level, the application is fully deployed into a real environment. The testing team will use a combination of automated and manual testing to check that the application is working properly. Because functional testing is typically outside the responsibility of the development team, we won't cover functional testing in any more detail. The remainder of this chapter will focus on unit testing and integration testing.

15.2 Unit testing EJBs

Let's dive into an example and see how to use JUnit and Mockito to unit test an EJB. Listing 15.1 is a simple stateless session bean in the ActionBazaar application. Its purpose is to determine what discount should be applied to a member's purchase. The discount to apply is determined by a simple business rule based on the membership level the member has purchased. Testing `DiscountManagerBean` is vital to ActionBazaar to prevent crazy discounts that may threaten the business.

If you download the code for this chapter, `DiscountManagerBean` is located in the `chapter15-ejb` Maven submodule. Let's take a look at the various parts of the bean so you'll know how to construct your unit tests.

Listing 15.1 DiscountManagerBean

```
@Stateless
public class DiscountManagerBean implements DiscountManager {    ❶ Class dependency that needs to be mocked

  @EJB
  MembershipLevelManager membershipLevelManager;

  public DiscountManagerBean() {}                                 ❷ Constructor needed by unit test to inject mocks

  public DiscountManagerBean(MembershipLevelManager mock) {
    this.membershipLevelManager = mock;
  }

  @Override                                                       ❸ Method that needs to be tested
  public double findDiscount(Member member) {
    double discount = 0.0;
    MembershipLevel ml
      = membershipLevelManager.findByMemberId(member.getId());    ❹ Method call needs to return mocked data when unit testing
    if (ml != null) {
      switch (ml.getType()) {
        case SILVER:
          discount = 0.05;
          break;
        case GOLD:
          discount = 0.10;
          break;
        case PLATINUM:
          discount = 0.12;
          break;
      }
    }                                                             ❺ Value returned by business method must be asserted by unit test
    return discount;
  }
}
```

`DiscountManagerBean` has a dependency on the `MembershipLevelManager` EJB ❶. Following the fundamental principles of writing unit tests, you'll need to mock this dependency. Mocking ensures that you avoid any external resources that `MembershipLevelManager` may need, and mocking ensures that the focus of the unit test is only on `DiscountManagerBean`. To get mocks into `DiscountManagerBean`, a constructor ❷ is provided that the unit test may use. The `findDiscount()` method ❸ contains the business logic to test. You can clearly see that the output of the method (that is, what the method returns) ❺ depends on a couple of different inputs. The first input is the `Member member` parameter passed to the method. The second is the `MembershipLevel` object ❹ returned by the `MembershipLevelManager` EJB. Full unit test coverage of this method will depend on providing all the different combinations of input to verify all the possible outputs.

Because unit testing is supposed to run quickly to verify the correct execution of individual classes, unit tests are typically included in the same project as the classes they're testing. The `DiscountManagerBeanTest` shown in the following listing can be found in the `chapter15-ejb` Maven submodule of this chapter's code. Now let's see how to write the unit test.

Listing 15.2 DiscountManagerBeanTest

```
public class DiscountManagerBeanTest {

  private Member member;
  private MembershipLevel membershipLevel;
  private MembershipLevelManager membershipLevelManagerMock;
  private DiscountManagerBean bean;

  @Before
  public void setUp() {
    member = new Member();
    member.setId(11L);
    member.setUsername("junit123");

    membershipLevel = new MembershipLevel();
    membershipLevel.setId(44L);
    membershipLevel.setMember(member);

    membershipLevelManagerMock = mock(MembershipLevelManager.class);
    when(membershipLevelManagerMock.findByMemberId(
      member.getId())).thenReturn(membershipLevel);

    bean = new DiscountManagerBean(membershipLevelManagerMock);
  }

  @Test
  public void userGetsGoldDiscount() {
    membershipLevel.setType(MembershipLevelType.GOLD);
    double discount = bean.findDiscount(member);
    assertEquals(0.10, discount, 0.0);
  }

  // other tests omitted for brevity

  @Test
  public void userGetsNoDiscountBecauseNotAMember() {
    when(membershipLevelManagerMock.findByMemberId(
      member.getId())).thenReturn(null);
    double discount = bean.findDiscount(member);
```

❶ Class-level properties used by all tests
❷ Creates Member for use in tests
❸ Creates MembershipLevel for use in tests
❹ Mocks MembershipLevelManager using Mockito
❺ Defines what input data the mocked object should respond to
❻ Defines what response the mocked object should return
❼ Creates an instance of the bean to test
❽ Unit test
❾ Defines test-specific input data for this test
❿ Asserts that the response is correct
⓫ Changes what mock returns for this test

```
    assertEquals(0.0, discount, 0.0);
  }
}
```

The first thing you see in this unit test is that it has a number of class-level properties ❶. These properties will have similar values for all the unit tests so they're pushed to the class level to avoid a lot of repeated code.

Next is the annotated `@Before` method responsible for setting these class-level properties before a test is run. `Member` is created ❷ with static data for the test. The same is also done for `MembershipLevel` ❸. `MembershipLevelManager` gets some special treatment because it's mocked using `Mockito.mock()` ❹. Mocking allows you to easily define how the object is to behave during the unit test. The `Mockito.when()` method is used ❺ to set behavior for the unit test so that when `findByMemberId()` is called with `member.getId()` ❻ as the method parameter, the mocked `MembershipLevelManager` object will return the `MembershipLevel` object instance. Once the mock is created, you can create an instance of `DiscountManagerBean` ❼, which is the class you want to unit test.

> **Test only one class at a time**
>
> You may be wondering how you'll know if `MembershipLevelManager` is working when you mock it. After all, if you mock `MembershipLevelManager`, you're not executing its code.
>
> Remember, this is okay because the focus of this unit test is on the `DiscountManagerBean`. The unit test should focus only on `DiscountManagerBean` and mock any dependencies the `DiscountManagerBean` uses with the assumption that those dependencies will work properly. But how do you know if they'll work properly?
>
> The answer is more unit tests! Just as this example is a unit test for `DiscountManagerBean`, you'll also want to create a unit test for `MembershipLevelBean`. A good rule to follow is if you mock one of your application's classes for a unit test, then whatever class you mocked should have its own unit test too.

Next is one of the `@Test` methods, specifically the `userGetsGoldDiscount()` unit test method ❽. The name of the test method should indicate the goal of the test, and by this method's name it's clear it's going to test that the `DiscountManagerBean` returns the appropriate discount if the member has a gold membership level. Inside this unit test method, the membership level is set to `GOLD` ❾. The `DiscountManagerBean.findDiscount()` method is called and the results are checked against what was expected for this test to pass ❿. Because unit tests for the other membership levels are almost identical to `userGetsGoldDiscount()`, we won't look at them in more detail. You may download the code for this chapter to see them. But we'll look at one additional unit test, the `userGetsNoDiscountBecauseNotAMember()` method.

By the name of the method, you can determine that this unit test needs to verify that `DiscountManagerBean` behaves properly if there's no membership level. To handle this test case, you use `Mockito.when()` inside the unit test method ⓫ to define a new response for the mocked `MembershipLevelManager` class. The new response is to return `null`. By having the mocked `MembershipLevelManager` class return `null`, you can then verify that `DiscountManagerBean` is still working properly in this case.

Unit testing is very powerful. It provides some indication as to whether your application is going to work correctly, but it's not foolproof. Once real objects are created by the Java EE server and wired together, a lot can change that can't be accounted for in unit testing. This is especially the case when your application depends on an external resource such as a database. The `DiscountManagerBean` depends on a database to hold the membership-level data, but testing whether data can be successfully retrieved from a database is outside the responsibilities for a unit test. To ensure your entity classes are working with the database, you need to take testing to the next level. This next level is integration testing, and we'll talk about it next.

15.3 Integration testing using embedded EJBContainer

Let's take a look at how you'll integration test the same `DiscountManagerBean` from listing 15.1. In the previous section we covered unit testing `DiscountManagerBean`. Using JUnit and Mockito, you saw how easy it is to create data and mocks and use them in the unit test to verify the results from the business methods. For integration testing, you're going to verify the same results, but you're going to do it in a completely different way.

The most important aspect of integration testing is to mimic the real execution environment as much as possible so you get an idea from the integration test how your application will run in a real environment. There are a few different ways to do this. This section will focus on using the embedded `EJBContainer`, which is an in-memory container that's easily started by any Java SE application. You're going to start the embedded container at the beginning of the test with the help of the builder method on the `EJBContainer` object, as follows:

```
EJBContainer ejbContainer = EJBContainer.createEJBContainer();
```

Once you have an instance of `EJBContainer`, you can use it to get a `Context`:

```
Context ctx = ejbContainer.getContext();
```

After you have a `Context`, you're free to look up any bean bound in JNDI. Getting an instance of the bean means you're then free to call whatever methods you want for the test:

```
DiscountManager manager = (DiscountManager) ctx.lookup(
  "java:global/chapter15-ejb-1.0/DiscountManagerBean");
```

This has been a quick, high-level overview of using the embedded `EJBContainer`. Although starting and using the embedded container can be this simple, it rarely is. The setup and configuration needed to get the embedded container functioning properly to support all the EJBs in your application can be a difficult task. The effort is worth it, because integration testing provides valuable information about your application.

15.3.1 Project configuration

Before getting into the code for the integration test, you first need to set up and configure the project to run it. To do this, the first question you need to answer is where the code for the integration test will live. The convention for a unit test is to include it in the same project as the class it's testing, because unit tests are quick and easy to execute and are the first line of defense to check if code changes break anything. But where do you put integration tests?

Integration tests will usually require a lot more complex configuration, and because the tests will be running in an embedded container, they usually will require a lot longer to run. Because of their complexity and time needed to run, integration tests are typically put into their own projects. This is what you're going to do for this integration test example. The code for this chapter contains a Maven submodule named `chapter15-ejb-embedded-test`, which is where you'll put the integration tests that use the embedded `EJBContainer`.

> **Will my integration tests ever run?**
>
> If you put your project's integration tests in a separate project, a common concern is whether the tests will ever get run. Unit tests inside a project are executed by Maven by default. But if the integration tests are in a separate project, a developer will need to take an extra manual step to run the tests, and most of the time this step will be skipped.
>
> This is where tools like Bamboo, Jenkins, and other automatic build platforms come in. The best practice is to configure these tools to run the integration tests automatically once changes to the project have been detected. Alternatively, instead of doing them on demand, they can be scheduled to run off hours, typically in the evening.
>
> By using tools like this, you remove the responsibility of running the integration tests from the development team and put it onto the tool. But if integration tests fail, then it becomes the developer's responsibility again.

Now that you've decided that the integration test code will live in its own project, we'll look at how to configure the project. The EJBs you want to test are in the Maven submodule named `chapter15-ejb`, and they're relatively simple so the `EJBContainer` configuration won't be too difficult. But the example code is also not trivial, so it's worthwhile to demonstrate the use of `EJBContainer`. The first configuration we'll look at is the Maven pom.xml.

MAVEN

The /chapter15-ejb-embedded-test/pom.xml will need a number of changes to run the integration tests using the embedded `EJBContainer`. The first change you need to be aware of is a property defining what version of the `chapter15-ejb` project you want to test. Your EJB project will most likely have multiple versions because code is developed and pushed to production over the years. As this happens, testing must also change to keep pace with the code it's testing. This property defines what version of the EJB code is to be tested:

```
<properties>
  <chapter15-ejb.version>1.0</chapter15-ejb.version>
</properties>
```

The reason you define this as a property is because you're going to need the value in a couple of different places inside pom.xml. It's always bad to duplicate version numbers like this, so a property to hold the value will do nicely. The first use of this property will be to add a dependency on the `chapter15-ejb` project. Adding the dependency is just like adding any other Maven dependency, but you use the property to define the version:

```
<dependency>
  <groupId>com.actionbazaar<groupId>
  <artifactId>chapter15-ejb</artifactId>
  <version>${chapter15-ejb.version}</version>
  <scope>test</scope>
</dependency>
```

You need to use this property in one more configuration change in pom.xml. You need to configure `maven-surefire-plugin` and pass a module name to the integration test. You'll see why you need to do this in a moment, but for right now, this is the `maven-surefire-plugin` configuration:

```
<build>
  <plugins>
    <plugin>
      <groupId>org.apache.maven.plugins</groupId>
      <artifactId>maven-surefire-plugin</artifactId>
      <version>2.10</version>
      <configuration>
        <systemProperties>
          <property>
            <name>moduleName</name>
            <value>chapter15-ejb-${chapter15-ejb.version}</value>
          </property>
        </systemProperties>
      </configuration>
    </plugin>
  </plugins>
</build>
```

The last pom.xml change you want to look at is the dependency on `glassfish-embedded-all`, which is the GlassFish implementation of the embedded `EJBContainer`. This is a normal Maven dependency:

```
<dependency>
    <groupId>org.glassfish.extras</groupId>
    <artifactId>glassfish-embedded-all</artifactId>
    <version>3.1</version>
    <scope>test</scope>
</dependency>
```

After adding the GlassFish dependency to your project, you need to provide GlassFish the configuration it needs to integration test your project's EJBs.

GLASSFISH

Because you're configuring Maven to use the GlassFish implementation of the embedded `EJBContainer`, you'll need to add some GlassFish configuration to the project. This configuration will be in the `chapter15-ejb-embedded-test` Maven submodule in the /src/test/domain/config directory. The files in this directory come from the domain1/config directory of a basic GlassFish installation. They're then slightly modified for the integration test. All the changes are in domain.xml.

The domain.xml file has had a few changes. First, all of the port configurations have been prepended with the value 2 in hopes of preventing port collisions when the integration test runs. For example, the default HTTP listener runs on port 8080, but for the integration test it has been changed to port 28080. All ports have been changed similarly. Second, the `jdbc-connection-pool` configurations have all been updated to use `org.apache.derby.jdbc.EmbeddedDataSource` as the data source. Using this data source, Derby will automatically start an in-memory database for the integration test, relieving the need for an external database server to be running. Finally, a new `jdbc-connection-pool` has been created specifically for the integration test for JPA entity classes of your project. Now that the integration test has a database, let's look at configuring JPA to use it.

JPA

For the integration test, you're going to test the `DiscountManagerBean`, which has a dependency on membership-level data from the `MembershipLevel` JPA entity. JPA needs to be able to work with the embedded Derby database when the integration test runs. You do this by configuring /src/test/resources/META-INF/persistence.xml to use a data source pointing to an embedded Derby database connection pool:

```
<jta-data-source>jdbc/chapter15-ejb-embedded</jta-data-source>
```

This JDBC binding is the `jdbc-connection-pool` you created in domain.xml specifically for this integration test. GlassFish comes with a default connection pool you could have used for this integration test, but in general, using a default resource like this isn't advisable. It's much better from an integration test perspective to create a new resource and make sure your code can use that resource, whatever it may be. In this case you configured GlassFish with a data source connected to an in-memory Derby database just for the integration test and now you've configured JPA to use it.

We've covered project configuration. Now let's get to the good stuff. Let's look at the integration test code itself.

15.3.2 *Integration test*

Let's take a look at the integration test code shown in the following listing, which uses the embedded `EJBContainer` to execute your EJB.

Listing 15.3 Embedded `EJBContainer` `DiscountManagerBeanEmbeddedTest`

```
public class DiscountManagerBeanEmbeddedTest {

  private static Context ctx;
  private static EJBContainer ejbContainer;
  private static String moduleName = System.getProperty("moduleName");

  @BeforeClass
  public static void setUpClass() {
    Map<String, Object> properties = new HashMap<>();
    properties.put("org.glassfish.ejb.embedded.glassfish.instance.root",
      "./src/test/domain");
    ejbContainer = EJBContainer.createEJBContainer(properties);
    ctx = ejbContainer.getContext();
  }

  @AfterClass
  public static void tearDownClass() {
    if (ejbContainer != null) {
      ejbContainer.close();
    }
  }

  @Test
  public void userGetsGoldDiscount() throws NamingException {
    Member member = new Member();
    member.setId(1L);
    member.setUsername("junitGoldMember");
    lookupMemberManager().insert(member);

    MembershipLevel membershipLevel = new MembershipLevel();
    membershipLevel.setMember(member);
    membershipLevel.setType(MembershipLevelType.GOLD);
    lookupMembershipLevelManager().insert(membershipLevel);

    DiscountManager discountManager = lookupDiscountManager();
    double discount = discountManager.findDiscount(member);
    assertEquals(0.10, discount, 0.0);
  }

  static DiscountManager lookupDiscountManager()
  throws NamingException {
    return (DiscountManager)lookupEjb(EjbName.DiscountManagerBean);
  }

  static MemberManager lookupMemberManager()
  throws NamingException {
    return (MemberManager)lookupEjb(EjbName.MemberManagerBean);
  }

  static MembershipLevelManager lookupMembershipLevelManager()
  throws NamingException {
    return (MembershipLevelManager)lookupEjb(
      EjbName.MembershipLevelManagerBean);
  }

  /** Common method for all JNDI lookup */
  static enum EjbName {
```

1. Gets system property used to perform JNDI lookup
2. Starts embedded EJBContainer before testing starts
4. Configures where to find GlassFish domain.xml for test
4. Starts embedded EJBContainer
5. Integration test method
6. Inserts member data into database
7. Inserts membership-level data into database
8. Integration tests the findDiscount() method
9. Helper methods to look up EJBs in JNDI
10. Enum to hold names of EJBs to use in JNDI lookups

```
    DiscountManagerBean, MemberManagerBean, MembershipLevelManagerBean
  }
  static Object lookupEjb(EjbName ejbName) throws NamingException {
    try {
      return ctx.lookup("java:global/"+moduleName+"/"+ejbName);
    } catch (Throwable ignore) {
      moduleName = "classes";
      return ctx.lookup("java:global/"+moduleName+"/"+ejbName);
    }
  }
}
```

⓫ **Common JNDI lookup method**

For this integration test, the first thing to look at is a call to get the `moduleName` system property ❶. What is this property? This property is used to perform JNDI lookups of the EJBs after the embedded container is started. Where does this property come from? Recall the configuration change you made to `maven-surefire-plugin` in pom.xml. You use the `chapter15-ejb.version` property value in pom.xml to generate the `moduleName` for `maven-surefire-plugin`, and then `maven-surefire-plugin` passes `moduleName` to the integration test, which gets `moduleName` as a system property. You do this because `moduleName` depends on the version of the `chapter15-ejb` project. To prevent duplicating this version, you pass it to the integration test. This makes changing the value in the future much easier.

The next thing to look at in this integration test is the `setUpClass()` method annotated with `@BeforeClass` ❷. This method is called by JUnit before an instance of the test class is created to set up any static resources the test needs—in this case, it's going to start the embedded `EJBContainer`. To configure the embedded `EJBContainer`, a `Map` is created and the `org.glassfish.ejb.embedded.glassfish.instance.root` property is put in the `Map`. The value is set as `./src/test/domain` ❸. This configures the embedded container with the directory where the GlassFish configuration files are found. This configuration is nonportable and specific to only the GlassFish implementation of the embedded `EJBContainer`. Once the configuration is defined, the last thing the `setUpClass()` method does is call `EJBContainer.createEJBContainer(properties)` ❹ to start the embedded container.

At this point all of the hard work of the integration test is done. It's typically much harder to get the embedded container configured and running than it is to actually use it to perform tests.

Now we'll look at the `userGetsGoldDiscount()` test method ❺. Recall that the same test method is used in listing 15.2 in the unit test. Although both the unit test and the integration test will essentially be performing the same test, they each do it in drastically different ways. The unit test uses mocks, avoids the EJB container, and tests `DiscountManagerBean` as a POJO. The integration test will attempt to execute `DiscountManagerBean` in an embedded `EJBContainer`. Let's see what the integration test needs to do this.

We configured an in-memory Derby database in `domain.xml` and bound it to `jdbc/chapter15-ejb-embedded` in JNDI for the integration test. The embedded database is created every time an integration test is run, so you need to get data into the database. The `userGetsGoldDiscount()` test method creates a `Member` entity, sets its data, and inserts it in the database ❻. The same thing is done with the membership-level data using the `MembershipLevel` entity ❼. Now that the appropriate data is in the database for the test, the `DiscountManagerBean findDiscount()` method is called ❽ and the results are asserted against expected results.

It's important to remember when then `DiscountManagerBean findDiscount()` method is called you're not simply calling a POJO method with mocked dependencies like the unit test in listing 15.2. In this integration test, when the `findDiscount()` method is called, the test is executing a real EJB method from a real EJB container running against a real database. So the integration test helps to verify not only that the `DiscountManagerBean` is returning the correct value but that all the different technologies—CDI, EJB, JPA, Database—are working together as they should.

Now that you've started the embedded `EJBContainer` and have run the integration test, what's left in the test class? There are a few helper methods used to get the beans from the embedded `EJBContainer` ❾: `lookupDiscountManager()`, `lookupMemberManager()`, and `lookupMembershipLevelManager()`. They all work the same way. They use the `EjbName` enum ❿ to tell the `lookupEjb()` method ⓫ exactly which bean to look up. The `lookupEjb()` method performs the JNDI lookup by first using the `moduleName` value, and if that fails, then it tries to use a hard-coded `"classes"` value. It tries both ways, because depending on how you run the tests with Maven, both are valid.

This concludes our coverage of integration testing using the embedded `EJBContainer`. As you can tell from this brief example, the embedded `EJBContainer` is very powerful and brings testing of your application to the next level. Using the `EJBContainer` directly can be a little difficult, though. Its configuration is complex, which may discourage its use. To deal with this complexity, integration testing tools such as Arquillian are available to help make integration testing easier. Let's take a look at Arquillian next.

15.4 Integration testing using Arquillian

In the previous section we talked about integration testing using the embedded `EJBContainer`. Now we're going to look at doing basically the same thing but using an integration testing framework named Arquillian. Why would you want to even use Arquillian if you can use the embedded `EJBContainer`? Simply put, Arquillian makes integration testing with embedded containers a little easier so you're able to concentrate more on the integration tests itself and not on all the plumbing needed to get it working. Arquillian also makes more complicated integration testing scenarios easier. For example, Arquillian has shrink-wraps for multiple Enterprise application servers, which may be very useful if your organization is in the middle of switching from one Enterprise server to another, or if you want to say your product supports multiple Enterprise servers to allow for sales to a wider range of clients.

Arquillian also supports remote integration testing. In some cases, integration testing with in-memory containers and resources isn't enough. In these cases an enterprise may have a special environment setup just for integration testing. Arquillian can connect to this environment and run your integration tests. These are just some of the reasons you may choose to use Arquillian. Let's assume ActionBazaar made this choice and wants to perform its integration testing using Arquillian. First, we'll look at how to set up the project to use Arquillian.

15.4.1 Project configuration

The code for this chapter contains a Maven submodule named `chapter15-ejb-arquillian-test`. This project contains the Arquillian integration tests for the `chapter15-ejb` EJBs.

As discussed in the previous section on integration testing with the embedded `EJBContainer`, you need to decide where the integration test code will live. The Arquillian integration tests will be in their own external project for the same reasons that the embedded `EJBContainer` integration tests are put in their own project. Integration tests are typically more complex, require external resources, and take much longer to run than unit tests. So it's best practice to put the Arquillian integration tests in their own project. A continuous integration testing tool, such as Bamboo or Jenkins, can be configured to run the integration test in case the development team forgets to do so before code changes are committed.

Configuring the project to run Arquillian integration tests is similar to the configuration for the embedded `EJBContainer` integration tests. Maven, Arquillian, GlassFish, and Derby all need to be configured to run the tests. You'll be using Arquillian's shrink-wrap over the GlassFish implementation of the embedded `EJBContainer`, which is why you still need to configure GlassFish. Before you do that, let's dive into the Maven configuration.

Maven

We'll start the configuration changes for Maven by adding the Arquillian dependencies to pom.xml. The first one you add tells Maven which version of Arquillian you want to get:

```
<dependencyManagement>
  <dependencies>
    <dependency>
      <groupId>org.jboss.arquillian</groupId>
      <artifactId>arquillian-bom</artifactId>
      <version>1.1.0.Final</version>
      <scope>import</scope>
      <type>pom</type>
    </dependency>
  </dependencies>
</dependencyManagement>
```

Next, you want to get the Arquillian project that integrates Arquillian with JUnit. This allows you to utilize the Maven test lifecycle to run the integration tests as if they were unit tests. But be aware. Just because you're using JUnit doesn't mean you'll be writing unit tests. JUnit will simply be a technology to basically bootstrap Arquillian and run the integration tests:

```
<dependency>
  <groupId>org.jboss.arquillian.junit</groupId>
  <artifactId>arquillian-junit-container</artifactId>
  <scope>test</scope>
</dependency>
```

Finally, you want to get the Arquillian wrappers over GlassFish because you'll be using the GlassFish implementation of the embedded `EJBContainer` for the integration tests:

```
<dependency>
  <groupId>org.jboss.arquillian.container</groupId>
  <artifactId>arquillian-glassfish-embedded-3.1</artifactId>
  <version>1.0.0.CR3</version>
</dependency>
```

We've covered the Arquillian dependencies in pom.xml. Two additional dependencies we need to look at are the dependencies to get the EJBs from the `chapter15-ejb` project (which you need to test) and `glassfish-embedded-all` for GlassFish. These two dependencies are the same as the `chapter15-ejb-embedded-test` project discussed in the previous section:

```
<dependency>
  <groupId>com.actionbazaar</groupId>
  <artifactId>chapter15-ejb</artifactId>
  <version>1.0</version>
  <scope>test</scope>
</dependency>
<dependency>
  <groupId>org.glassfish.extras</groupId>
  <artifactId>glassfish-embedded-all</artifactId>
  <version>3.1</version>
  <scope>test</scope>
</dependency>
```

This covers the configuration changes you need to make for Maven. Basically all you needed to do was add the dependencies to pom.xml. Now that the dependencies are added, you need to configure the rest of the technologies used during the integration test: Arquillian, Derby, and GlassFish. We'll start with Arquillian and then move on to configuring GlassFish and Derby.

ARQUILLIAN

Arquillian needs some configuration. Arquillian is a feature-rich integration testing tool, and going through its entire configuration is out of scope for this book. Instead we'll look at the simple configuration Arquillian needs for integration testing the `chapter15-ejb` EJBs. Arquillian's configuration file is src/test/resources/arquillian.xml. Because you want to run the integration tests with GlassFish, you need to tell Arquillian where to find the GlassFish resource configuration for the integration test. This is a simple property in arquillian.xml pointing to the glassfish-resources.xml file:

```
<arquillian xmlns="http://jboss.org/schema/arquillian"
            xmlns:xsi="http://www.w3.org/2001/XMLSchema-instance"
            xsi:schemaLocation="
        http://jboss.org/schema/arquillian
        http://jboss.org/schema/arquillian/arquillian_1_0.xsd">
  <container qualifier="glassfish-embedded" default="true">
    <configuration>
      <property name="resourcesXml">
      src/test/glassfish/glassfish-resources.xml
      </property>
    </configuration>
  </container>
</arquillian>
```

Simple enough, right? Believe it or not, that's all you need to do for Arquillian. Now let's see what's needed to configure GlassFish and Derby.

GLASSFISH AND DERBY

Just like section 15.3 on integration testing using the embedded `EJBContainer` directly, you need to configure GlassFish because it's the GlassFish implementation of `EJBContainer` that you'll be using. For the Arquillian integration test, you need to provide the src/test/glassfish/glassfish-resources.xml file. This file defines a `jdbc-connection-pool` for GlassFish and binds it in JNDI to `jdbc/chapter15-ejb-arquillian`:

```
<!DOCTYPE resources PUBLIC
   "-//GlassFish.org//DTD GlassFish Application Server 3.1
    Resource Definitions//EN"
   "http://glassfish.org/dtds/glassfish-resources_1_5.dtd">
<resources>
  <jdbc-resource pool-name="ArquillianEmbeddedDerbyPool"
    jndi-name="jdbc/chapter15-ejb-arquillian"/>
  <jdbc-connection-pool name="ArquillianEmbeddedDerbyPool"
    res-type="javax.sql.DataSource"
    datasource-classname="org.apache.derby.jdbc.EmbeddedDataSource"
    is-isolation-level-guaranteed="false">
    <property name="databaseName"
      value="target/derby/arquillian-integration-test"/>
    <property name="createDatabase" value="create"/>
  </jdbc-connection-pool>
</resources>
```

Notice that configuring GlassFish when using Arquillian is much different than when directly using the embedded `EJBContainer`. Using `EJBContainer`, you basically brought in the configuration for an entire GlassFish domain. Using Arquillian, you're specifying only the resources you want, which in this case is only a database connection pool to Derby. The last technology you need to configure is JPA. Let's take a look at the JPA configuration now.

JPA

JPA is configured with src/test/resources/META-INF/persistence.xml. It's basically identical to its configuration in section 15.3 on integration testing using the embedded `EJBContainer` directly. The only difference is the JNDI lookup value for the data source. The Arquillian integration test binds it in JNDI to `jdbc/chapter15-ejb-arquillian`, so persistence.xml reflects this:

```
<persistence version="2.1" xmlns="http://xmlns.jcp.org/xml/ns/persistence"
  xmlns:xsi="http://www.w3.org/2001/XMLSchema-instance"
  xsi:schemaLocation="http://xmlns.jcp.org/xml/ns/persistence
  http://xmlns.jcp.org/xml/ns/persistence/persistence_2_1.xsd">
  <persistence-unit name="ActionBazaar" transaction-type="JTA">
    <provider>org.eclipse.persistence.jpa.PersistenceProvider</provider>
    <jta-data-source>jdbc/chapter15-ejb-arquillian</jta-data-source>
    <exclude-unlisted-classes>false</exclude-unlisted-classes>
    <properties>
      <property
        name="eclipselink.ddl-generation" value="drop-and-create-tables"/>
    </properties>
  </persistence-unit>
</persistence>
```

We didn't need to set different JNDI lookup values for the data source between the `chapter15-ejb-embedded-test` project and the `chapter15-ejb-arquillian-test` project. Leaving them the same may have been easier, but easier isn't always better. It's good practice to make these values specific. By doing so, you're more likely to get the configuration right and you gain a better understanding of how the different technologies of your application work together.

This concludes the configuration you need to do for the `chapter15-ejb-arquillian-test` project. As you can see, it's similar to the configuration for the `chapter15-ejb-embedded-test` project in that the basic technologies still need to be configured: Maven, GlassFish, Derby, and JAP. But doing so is a bit different in each project. Now that you have the project configured, we can move on to the Arquillian integration test itself.

15.4.2 *Integration test*

The Arquillian integration test is much simpler and more streamlined than its embedded `EJBContainer` container counterpart. This makes the test easier to develop and maintain. The code for the Arquillian integration test of the `DiscountManager` EJB is shown in the following listing.

Listing 15.4 Arquillian `DiscountManagerBeanEmbeddedTest`

```
@RunWith(Arquillian.class)
public class DiscountManagerBeanArquillianTest {

  @Deployment
  public static JavaArchive createDeployment() {
    JavaArchive jar = ShrinkWrap.create(JavaArchive.class)
```

1 Tells JUnit to delegate running this test to Arquillian

2 Arquillian annotation to build the JavaArchive you want to test

3 Specifies a Java-Archive is being built

```
        .addPackage(DiscountManagerBean.class.getPackage())
        .addPackage(Member.class.getPackage())
        .addAsResource("META-INF/persistence.xml");
    System.out.println(jar.toString(true));
    return jar;
  }

  @EJB
  MemberManager memberManager;
  @EJB
  MembershipLevelManager membershipLevelManager;
  @EJB
  DiscountManager discountManager;

  @Before
  public void insertTestData() {
    Member member = new Member();
    member.setId(1L);
    member.setUsername("junitGoldMember");
    memberManager.insert(member);

    MembershipLevel membershipLevel = new MembershipLevel();
    membershipLevel.setMember(member);
    membershipLevel.setType(MembershipLevelType.GOLD);
    membershipLevelManager.insert(membershipLevel);
  }

  @Test
  public void userGetsGoldDiscount() {
    Member member = memberManager.find(1L);
    double discount = discountManager.findDiscount(member);
    assertEquals(0.10, discount, 0.0);
  }
}
```

4 Adds all classes in com.actionbazaar.ejb to JavaArchive
5 Adds all classes in com.actionbazaar.entity to JavaArchive
6 Adds [pers]istence.xml [to J]avaArchive
7 Injects EJBs for use in test
8 Inserts member data to database
9 Inserts membership level data into database
10 Calls the method you want to test
11 Asserts the integration test succeeds

Because you're using Arquillian to run this unit test, it allows you to use more advanced Java technologies like dependency injection that you're not able to use in the embedded `EJBContainer` test. This is great for you as a developer, because using these technologies allows you to concentrate more on the test itself and not on the plumbing to get it working.

Let's start by looking at `@RunWith(Arquillian.class)` **1**. `@RunsWith` is a JUnit feature that allows JUnit to hand off execution of the test. In this case, you're telling JUnit you want Arquillian to run the test. By doing this, you get access to the powerful features that Arquillian has, like `@Deployment`.

The `@Deployment` annotation comes next, and this annotation belongs to Arquillian, not JUnit. By having JUnit hand off execution of the test to Arquillian, you're able to use these Arquillian-specific features in the test. `@Deployment` annotates the `public static JavaArchive createDeployment()` method **2**. You include the method's full signature here, because unlike the JUnit annotations, the `@Deployment` annotation expects the method to return an implementation of `JavaArchive`. Think of a `JavaArchive` as an Arquillian representation of a JAR, EJB-JAR, WAR, or EAR. In chapter 5 we discussed the structures of these Enterprise archives. In an Arquillian integration test, the method annotated with `@Deployment` is responsible for creating a `JavaArchive` and putting inside of it the classes and resources (`.properties`, `.xml`, and the like) that would typically be in your project's final artifact. Because `chapter15-ejb` is an EJB-JAR project and its final artifact is a .jar file, in the integration test you specify `JavaArchive.class` ❸ as the type you're building. You add all classes from the `com.actionbazaar.ejb` package ❹ and the `com.actionbazaar.entity` package ❺ to the `JavaArchive`. You also add the persistence.xml file ❻ to the `JavaArchive` for JPA. Once the archive is built, the method returns it to Arquillian.

Under the covers, after Arquillian gets the `JavaArchive`, it starts the embedded container you've chosen to use (in this case you configured the GlassFish implementation) and deploys the `JavaArchive` to the container. Remember, `JavaArchive` is an abstraction. In this integration test you built an EJB-JAR, but you can also build a plain-old JAR, WAR, RAR, or EAR. Because Arquillian is running the container, your integration test can take advantage of Java EE technologies. You see this in the test with the use of the `@EJB` annotation to inject the `MemberManager`, `MembershipLevelManager`, and `DiscountManager` EJBs ❼. Contrast this with the JNDI lookups needed for the embedded `EJBContainer` integration tests. Developers can concentrate more on the test itself instead of getting JNDI lookups to work. The Arquillian integration test is easier to understand and more streamlined because it can take advantage of these advanced Java technologies. After the Arquillian has started the embedded container and performed any dependency injection on the test class, it's ready to run your tests—well, almost. Before the tests can run, the JUnit lifecycle methods must still be run.

In ❽ you see member data being inserted into the database, and in ❾ you see the same thing for membership-level data. Both of these actions are performed in a method annotated with JUnit `@Before`. When JUnit hands off responsibility for running the test to Arquillian, Arquillian interrupts the standard JUnit test lifecycle to call its own `@Deployment` method. Now that that's complete, Arquillian needs to come back to the JUnit test lifecycle, and this is what you see here. You need the database filled with the correct data to run the integration tests. You do this for member data and for membership-level data in the `@Before` method. At this point, the embedded container is up, dependencies have been injected into the test, and data has been added to the database (so you already know the embedded `EJBContainer` is working). Now all you have to do is run the tests.

The method annotated with `@Test` is `userGetsGoldDiscount()`. From the name of this test, it's obvious what the integration test will be trying to verify; given the data in the database for a gold-level member, will the member actually get the gold-level discount expected? In ❿ you call the `findDiscount(member)` method. Remember that this is a real EJB method call that will use real JPA classes to talk to a real database. The integration test mimics the real environment as closely as it can to make sure the integration of all these technologies is working properly. After the `findDiscount(member)` method is called, the response is asserted against the expected value ⓫. If all goes well, you'll get the green bar for the integration test.

That's it! You've successfully performed an integration test of the `chapter15-ejb` EJBs using Arquillian. In this example you showed only a single `@Test` method that covers only one use case that the `findDiscount(member)` method handles. The question is whether you should add more `@Test` methods to handle the other test cases. Answering this question really brings up the passions of the testing community. In general, the answer would be no, because that isn't the responsibility of the integration test. A unit test should handle all possible inputs and outputs and verify that the business logic is working properly. An integration test should verify that the integration of all the technologies (for example, EJB, JPA, and Database) is working properly. There are different kinds of tests with different goals, and you'll need to decide for yourself what works best for your projects in your organization.

This finishes our coverage of testing EJBs. We've covered how to unit test your EJB using JUnit and Mockito. We've also covered how you may integration test your EJBs, either by using the embedded `EJBContainer` directly or by using a integration testing tool such as Arquillian. Along the way we highlighted some best practices to make your code testing most effective. We'll review these best practices next.

15.5 Testing effectively

To test your code effectively, you'll need multiple levels of testing. Each level is focused on testing a specific aspect of your code. As long as you keep the tests at a particular level focused, you'll have an effective testing strategy.

The first level of testing is unit testing. The focus of unit testing is to verify that all of the business logic of all of your classes is working as expected. The strategy for doing this is to write tests to focus only on one class, mock whatever dependencies the class has, and vary both the data input to the class and the data returned by the mock to cover all possible business rules. Assert results returned from the class being tested against expected results. Whenever you mock a class that's also part of your application, you need to make sure you provide unit tests for that class as well so all of the classes in your application are covered. Unit tests shouldn't require a lot of setup and should be run quickly so broken business rules will be discovered immediately. Unit tests shouldn't rely on any external resources (database, web service, naming directory, and so on) to execute; all interaction with external services like this should be mocked returning appropriate data for the unit test. Keeping unit testing focused like this can result in a 100% covered green bar suite of tests on code that's completely undeployable to any Java EE server. But that's OK, because that isn't the focus of unit testing. Getting your code deployed is the focus of the next level of testing—integration testing.

The focus of integration testing is to verify that all of the different technologies used in the application can actually come together and function properly as a whole. Integration testing answers questions like these: Does the data persist to the database? Will the EJB be deployed? Will the interceptors fire in the order I expect them? During unit testing you verify that individual classes are functioning properly on their own. Now during integration testing you verify that the individual classes can come together (inside a container) as a whole and function as you expect them to. To perform integration testing, the Java EE specification defines the `EJBContainer`, which is an embedded container that can be started in-memory by any Java SE code. The `EJBContainer` may be used directly or it may be used indirectly by an integration testing tool that wraps it, such as Arquillian. In either case, the project configuration and configuration of all the different technologies used by your application may become very complex. As such, unlike unit tests that should remain in the projects containing the code the unit tests cover, integration tests are best put into their own project. Maven dependency injection can get all the code that needs to be integration tested, and continuous build tools like Bamboo or Jenkins ensure the integration tests get run. Although integration testing is a big step, it still can't cover all scenarios. The final level of testing is functional testing.

We didn't cover functional testing in this chapter except to mention it as a level of an effective testing strategy. Functional testing typically falls on a team of individuals whose job is to use the application and verify that it's working properly. At this level, your application is fully deployed to some testing environment that hopefully closely matches a production environment. Unit testing can tell you if the business rules are all working properly, and integration testing can tell you if the pieces of the application are integrating properly. Functional testing is the last line of defense for logical problems with your application. Unit and integration tests may all pass without any technical issues, but that doesn't necessarily mean that what the tests are checking is correct. For example, for the ActionBazaar auction application, it may have been decided at some point to give gold members an 80% discount. All unit and integration tests can verify that the application is doing this correctly, but (hopefully) the functional testing done by members of the testing team will look at the result and raise a concern.

Testing will never be 100% accurate, but combining all three of these testing strategies effectively will result in a well-performing application. This is all we're going to cover on testing of EJBs. Let's review what you've learned.

15.6 Summary

This chapter has been a brief introduction to testing EJBs. The first topic we covered was the different types of testing strategies, specifically unit testing, integration testing, and functional testing. We defined unit testing as a testing strategy designed to exercise the application's business logic by feeding it different input and examining the output to assert that the results are correct. It does this by concentrating tests on one class at a time and using a mocking tool such as Mockito to mock any dependencies to return responses appropriate for the test. Unit tests should be quick and easy to run with little or no setup and no access to external resources.

We defined integration testing as a testing strategy whose purpose is to verify that all of the different technologies and resources used in the application can actually come together and function properly as a whole. Integration tests typically use embedded technologies to start whatever resources are needed in memory to avoid having to rely on external resources to be up and running. We showed how Derby can be used as an embedded database. We also showed how the GlassFish implementation of the embedded `EJBContainer` can be used to test EJBs. The embedded `EJBContainer` can either be used directly or by a more advanced integration testing tool like Arquillian. Using Arquillian gives the test writer access to more advanced Java technology, such as CDI, which allows for injecting resources from the embedded container directly into the test. This allows more of the focus to be put on writing the test.

Finally, we defined functional testing as a testing strategy whose purpose is to be the last line of defense for logical problems with your application. Typically functional testing is performed by members of a testing team who can make intelligent decisions on the correctness of the application.

No testing will ever catch everything that can possibly go wrong. But a good testing strategy will minimize the risk and aid in the diagnosis when things do happen.

appendix A Deployment descriptor reference

In this appendix we'll summarize the tags of the EJB 3 descriptor. The appendix is designed to be a quick reference you can consult when you plan to use a descriptor in your Enterprise application. Each descriptor is defined by an XML schema, and we describe the elements of the schema.

As we've explained throughout the book, you have a choice of using annotations, XML descriptors, or both to configure your Enterprise application. We've mainly used annotations throughout this book, so here we also list what annotation is overridden by the descriptor when applicable.

This appendix provides a reference to ejb-jar.xml, which is the descriptor for session and message-driven beans. Although this book has a brief introduction to JPA, this appendix will not describe the persistence.xml in any more detail. We invite you to explore more about JPA on your own.

The schema for EJB 3.2 is referenced at http://xmlns.jcp.org/xml/ns/javaee/ejb-jar_3_2.xsd. This is the schema file we'll be discussing in this appendix. But the ejb-jar_3_2.xsd schema file references other schemas as part of its definition. All the schema files for EE 7 are available for download from Oracle at http://www.oracle.com/webfolder/technetwork/jsc/xml/ns/javaee/index.html#7.

A.1 ejb-jar.xml

ejb-jar.xml is the optional deployment descriptor that's packaged in an EJB module. ejb-jar.xml has two primary elements: `enterprise-beans` is used to define beans, resources, and services used by the beans, and `assembly-descriptor` is used to declare security roles, method permissions, declarative transaction settings, and interceptors. In this section we provide references only to the elements relevant to

EJB 3, and we don't discuss any elements in the schema that are for the sole purpose of backward compatibility with EJB 2. You can refer to the schema for ejb-jar.xml at http://xmlns.jcp.org/xml/ns/javaee/ejb-jar_3_2.xsd.

When creating a new ejb-jar.xml document, start by declaring the `ejb-jar` root element as follows:

```
<ejb-jar
  xmlns="http://xmlns.jcp.org/xml/ns/javaee"
  xmlns:xsi="http://www.w3.org/2001/XMLSchema-instance"
  xsi:schemaLocation="http://xmlns.jcp.org/xml/ns/javaee
                      http://xmlns.jcp.org/xml/ns/javaee/ejb-jar_3_2.xsd"
  version="3.2">
```

After declaring the root element, start filling in the document with the configuration that will override your annotations. Remember that ejb-jar.xml is optional. Using annotations is the preferred development method. If you do use annotations, any matching configuration you have in ejb-jar.xml will override the annotation. You may, however, not use annotations and put all of your configuration in ejb-jar.xml, but this isn't recommended. We'll now briefly summarize the child tags of the `<ejb-jar...>` root document.

A.1.1 <module-name>

`<module-name>` is used to define the name of the EJB module when deployed to the Enterprise server:

```
<ejb-jar...>
    <module-name>action-bazaar-ejb</module-name>
</ejb-jar>
```

It's only applicable to standalone EJB-JARS or EJB-JARS packaged in an EAR. It's ignored if used within a .war file, in which case standard .war file module name rules apply.

Though optional, `<module-name>` is quite useful, especially when build systems like Maven are used to construct your artifacts. Maven adds version numbers to the names of artifacts (action-bazaar-ejb-1.1.0.17.jar), and although visually this is beneficial because you can quickly see what version of artifacts are in your Enterprise application, from the point of view of deployment, version numbers make JNDI lookup names (if needed) extremely difficult because all lookup names need to change to include the version number. Using `<module-name>` can standardize the name of your module when deployed, no matter the version number.

A.1.2 <enterprise-beans>

The `<enterprise-beans>` tag is used to define EJBs in an EJB-JAR module. You can use `<session>` or `<message-driven>` subtags to define session or message-driven beans.

<SESSION>

The `<session>` tag is used to define a session bean:

```
<ejb-jar...>
    <enterprise-beans>
```

```
    <session>...</session>
  </enterprise-beans>
</ejb-jar>
```

The corresponding annotation is `@Session`. Table A.1 describes the tags to configure `<session>`.

Table A.1 Tags to configure `<session>`

Tag name	Description
`ejb-name`	A logical name for the session bean. Property `"name"` of `@Stateless` or `@Stateful` annotation.
`mapped-name`	A vendor-specific name for the bean. Property `"mapped-Name"` of the `@Stateless` or `@Stateful` annotation.
`remote`	Remote interface for the EJB: `@Remote`.
`local`	Local interface of the EJB: `@Local`.
`service-endpoint`	Web service endpoint interface for the EJB. Applies only to stateless beans: `@WebService`.
`ejb-class`	Fully qualified name of the bean class.
`session-type`	Type of session bean: `@Stateless` `@Stateful` `@Singleton`.
`stateful-timeout`	The amount of time a stateful bean can be idle before eligible for cleanup by the container: `@StatefulTimeout`.
`timeout-method`	The callback method for programmatically created timers: `@Timeout`.
`timer`	An EJB timer. Created by the container on deployment. Callbacks made to the `timeout-method`.
`init-on-startup`	Singleton bean should be created at deployment: `@Startup`.
`concurrency-management-type`	Specifies concurrency for singleton and stateful beans. May be either `Bean` or `Container`: `@Concurrency-Management`.
`concurrent-method`	Configures the container managed concurrency for a method.
`depends-on`	A list of one of more singleton beans that must be initialized before this singleton bean. Applies only to singleton beans. Use the `ejb-link` syntax to specify the dependencies: `@DependsOn`.
`init-method`	EJB 2-style create method for EJB 3 stateful EJBs: `@Init`.
`remove-method`	EJB 2-style remove method for EJB 3 stateful beans: `@Remove`.
`async-method`	Specifies method for asynchronous execution: `@Asynchronous`.
`transaction-type`	Specifies transaction for an EJB. May either `Bean` or `Container`: `@TransactionManagement`.

Table A.1 Tags to configure <session> *(continued)*

Tag name	Description
after-begin-method	Transaction callback method for a stateful bean to inform it that a new transaction has started: @AfterBegin.
before-completion-method	Transaction callback method for a stateful bean to inform it that a transaction is about to be committed: @BeforeCompletion.
after-completion-method	Transaction callback method for a stateful bean to inform it that a transaction has finished committing. Both commit and rollback will call this method: @AfterCompletion.
around-invoke	The method name on a class to be called during the around-invoke portion of an EJB invocation: @AroundInvoke.
around-timeout	The method name on a class to be called during the around-timeout portion of an EJB invocation: @AroundTimeout.
post-activate	Lifecycle callback method after activation: @PostActivate.
pre-passivate	Lifecycle callback method before passivation: @PrePassivate.
security-role-ref	References internal roles to external roles.
security-identity	Use the caller's security identity to enforce security or override the caller's identity for the specified "run-as" identity.
passivation-capable	Is the stateful bean able to be passivated?

<MESSAGE-DRIVEN>

The <message-driven> tag is used to define a message-driven bean (MDB):

```
<ejb-jar...>
    <enterprise-beans>
        <message-driven>...</message-driven>
    </enterprise-beans>
</ejb-jar>
```

The corresponding annotation is @MessageDriven. Table A.2 describes the tags to configure <message-driven>.

Table A.2 Tags to configure <message-driven>

Tag name	Description
ejb-name	The logical name for the MDB. Property "name" of @MessageDriven.
mapped-name	A vendor-specific name for the bean. Property "mappedName" of @MessageDriven.

Table A.2 Tags to configure <message-driven> *(continued)*

Tag name	Description
`ejb-class`	Fully qualified name of the bean class.
`messaging-type`	Messaging type supported—that is, the message listener interface of the MDB. Property `"messageListenerInterface"` of `@MessageDriven`.
`timeout-method`	The callback method for programmatically created timers: `@Timeout`.
`timer`	An EJB timer. Created by the container on deployment. Callbacks made to the `timeout-method`.
`transaction-type`	Specifies transaction for an EJB. May be either `Bean` or `Container`. `@TransactionManagement`
`message-destination-type`	Expected type of the destination—that is, `javax.jms.Queue`.
`message-destination-link`	A vendor-specific mapping of a logical destination with the actual destination.
`activation-config`	Name/value pairs to configure the MDB when running in the EJB container. Property `"activationConfig"` of `@MessageDriven`.
`around-invoke`	The method name on a class to be called during the around-invoke portion of an EJB invocation: `@AroundInvoke`.
`around-timeout`	The method name on a class to be called during the around-timeout portion of an EJB invocation: `@AroundTimeout`.
`security-role-ref`	References internal roles to external roles.
`security-identity`	Use the caller's security identity to enforce security or override the caller's identity for the specified "run-as" identity.

A.1.3 *Interceptors*

The `<interceptors>` tag is used to define interceptors for your EJB module:

```
<ejb-jar...>
    <interceptors>
        <interceptor>...</interceptor>
    </interceptors>
</ejb-jar>
```

Typically, you'd create an EJB interceptor by creating a new Java class and annotating a method of the new class with `@AroundInvoke` and `@AroundTimeout`. The `<interceptor>` tag corresponds to these annotations. In addition, the `<interceptor>` tag is required to configure a global interceptor, because no corresponding annotation exists for global interceptors. Table A.3 describes the tags to configure `<interceptor>`.

Table A.3 Tags to configure `<interceptor>`

Tag name	Description
description	Description of this interceptor.
interceptor-class	The fully qualified name of the class to serve as your interceptor.
around-invoke	The method name on a class to be called during the around-invoke portion of an EJB invocation: @AroundInvoke.
around-timeout	The method name on a class to be called during the around-timeout portion of an EJB invocation: @AroundTimeout.
around-construct	The method name on a class to be called during an object's construction: @AroundConstruct.
post-activate	Lifecycle callback method after activation: @PostActivate.
pre-passivate	Lifecycle callback method before passivation: @PrePassivate.

A.1.4 *<assembly-descriptor>*

The `<assembly-descriptor>` tag is used to define declarative transactions, security role and method permissions, and interceptor bindings:

```
<ejb-jar...>
    <assembly-descriptor>...</assembly-descriptor>
</ejb-jar>
```

<SECURITY-ROLE>

The `<security-role>` tag is used to define security roles used in the application:

```
<ejb-jar...>
    <assembly-descriptor>
        <security-role>...</security-role>
    </assembly-descriptor>
</ejb-jar>
```

The corresponding annotation is `@DeclareRoles`. Table A.4 describes the tag to configure `<security-role>`.

Table A.4 Tag to configure `<security-role>`

Tag name	Description
role-name	The name of the security role. Example: @DeclareRoles({"Admin", "User"}).

<METHOD-PERMISSION>

The `<method-permission>` tag is used to define what roles are allowed to execute which EJB methods:

```
<ejb-jar...>
    <assembly-descriptor>
        <method-permission>...</method-permission>
```

```
    </assembly-descriptor>
</ejb-jar>
```

The corresponding annotation is `@RolesAllowed`. Table A.5 describes the tags to configure `<method-permission>`.

Table A.5 Tags to configure `<method-permission>`

Tag name	Description
`role-name`	Name of the roll allowed to execute the method. This or `unchecked` may be used but not both.
`unchecked`	Specifies that all roles are allowed to execute the method. This or `role-name` may be used but not both.
`method`	Specifies the name of the EJB (as specified in `<session><ebj-name>`) and the name of the method to secure.

<CONTAINER-TRANSACTION>

The `<container-transaction>` tag is used to define transaction settings for EJB methods:

```
<ejb-jar...>
    <assembly-descriptor>
        <container-transaction>...</container-transaction>
    </assembly-descriptor>
</ejb-jar>
```

The corresponding annotation is `@TransactionAttribute`. Table A.6 describes the tags to configure `<container-transaction>`.

Table A.6 Tags to configure `<container-transaction>`

Tag name	Description
`trans-attribute`	Specifies the transaction attribute of the method. Valid values are `Required`, `RequiresNew`, `NotSupported`, `Supports`, `Never`, `Mandatory`.
`method`	Specifies the name of the EJB (as specified in `<session><ebj-name>`) and the name of the method to secure.

<INTERCEPTOR-BINDING>

The `<interceptor-binding>` tag is used to bind interceptors to EJBs at either a class level or a method level:

```
<ejb-jar...>
    <assembly-descriptor>
        <interceptor-binding>...</interceptor-binding>
    </assembly-descriptor>
</ejb-jar>
```

This tag is similar to the @Interceptors annotation. Table A.7 describes the tags to configure <interceptor-binding>.

Table A.7 Tags to configure <interceptor-binding>

Tag name	Description
ejb-name	Specifies the name of the EJB, as specified in <session><ebj-name> or the "name" element of @Stateless or @Stateful. This will apply the interceptor to all methods of the class. A value of "*" will create a default interceptor and bind to all EJB and MDB in the ejb-jar.xml file or .war file.
<interceptor-order> <interceptor-class>..</> </interceptor-order>	A list of interceptor classes that are bound to the contents of the ejb-name element. The interceptor-order is optional, and if used specifies the order in which the interceptors are to be called. No corresponding annotation for specifying order.
exclude-default-interceptors	Specifies that default interceptors aren't to be applied to the EJB class or method: @ExcludeDefaultInterceptors.
exclude-class-interceptors	Specifies that class interceptors aren't to be applied to the EJB class or method: @ExcludeClassInterceptors.
method	Specifies which method.

<MESSAGE-DESTINATION>

The <message-destination> tag specifies a logical destination name that's later mapped to a physical destination by the deployer:

```
<ejb-jar...>
    <assembly-descriptor>
        <message-destination>...</message-destination>
    </assembly-descriptor>
</ejb-jar>
```

Table A.8 describes the tags to configure <message-destination>.

Table A.8 Tags to configure <message-destination>

Tag name	Description
message-destination-name	Specifies a name for a message destination. This name must be unique among the names of message destinations within the ejb-jar.xml or .war file.
mapped-name	An application-specific, nonportable (not required to be supported) name that this destination should be mapped to.
lookup-name	The JNDi name to be looked up to resolve the message destination. This is typically the location in JNDI where your application server has put the destination.

<EXCLUDE-LIST>

The <exclude-list> tag specifies a list of methods that are denied permission to execute:

```
<ejb-jar...>
    <assembly-descriptor>
        <exclude-list>...</exclude-list>
    </assembly-descriptor>
</ejb-jar>
```

This tag is equivalent to the @DenyAll annotation. Table A.9 describes the tag to configure <exclude-list>.

Table A.9 Tags to configure <exclude-list>

Tag Name	Description
method	Specifies the name of the EJB (as specified in <session><ebj-name>) and the name of the method to secure.

APPLICATION-EXCEPTION

The <application-exception> tag specifies a list of application-specific exceptions that may be thrown by your EJBs and MDBs:

```
<ejb-jar...>
    <assembly-descriptor>
        <application-exception>...</application-exception>
    </assembly-descriptor>
</ejb-jar>
```

By listing application exceptions, you can configure whether the exception will cause a rollback of the current transaction. By default, an EJBException will trigger a rollback but application exceptions do not. This tag corresponds to the @ApplicationException annotation. Table A.10 describes the tags to configure <application-exception>.

Table A.10 Tags to configure <application-exception>

Tag name	Description
exception-class	Specifies the fully qualified name of the exception class.
rollback	Specifies if the container should roll back the transaction before throwing the exception up to the client.

appendix B Getting started with Java EE 7 SDK

This appendix is a general guide for the installation of the Java EE 7 SDK. We'll provide the basic instructions for installing the software and give a very brief introduction to the GlassFish Administration Console. We won't go into much more detail because documentation on any Java EE server can be an entire book on its own. We suggest you check out the GlassFish home page (https://glassfish.java.net/) for additional information on how to use and configure GlassFish.

The ActionBazaar code examples for this book are all Maven-based and generate artifacts that may be deployed to GlassFish. This appendix will show you how to build and deploy the "Hello World" application from chapter 1.

B.1 Installing the Java EE 7 SDK

Oracle offers a Java EE 7 development kit bundle that includes a JDK installation as well. This is the quickest and easiest way to get everything you need to start working with EJB 3 applications. The bundle includes:

- JDK 7
- GlassFish
- EE 7 code samples
- EE 7 API Javadocs
- Oracle's EE 7 tutorial

The bundle is downloadable from Oracle's website at http://www.oracle.com/technetwork/java/javaee/downloads/index.html. Your download options are the Java EE 7 SDK with and without a JDK and the Java EE 7 Web Profile SDK with and without a JDK. The easiest download to start with is the Java EE 7 SDK with a JDK. This

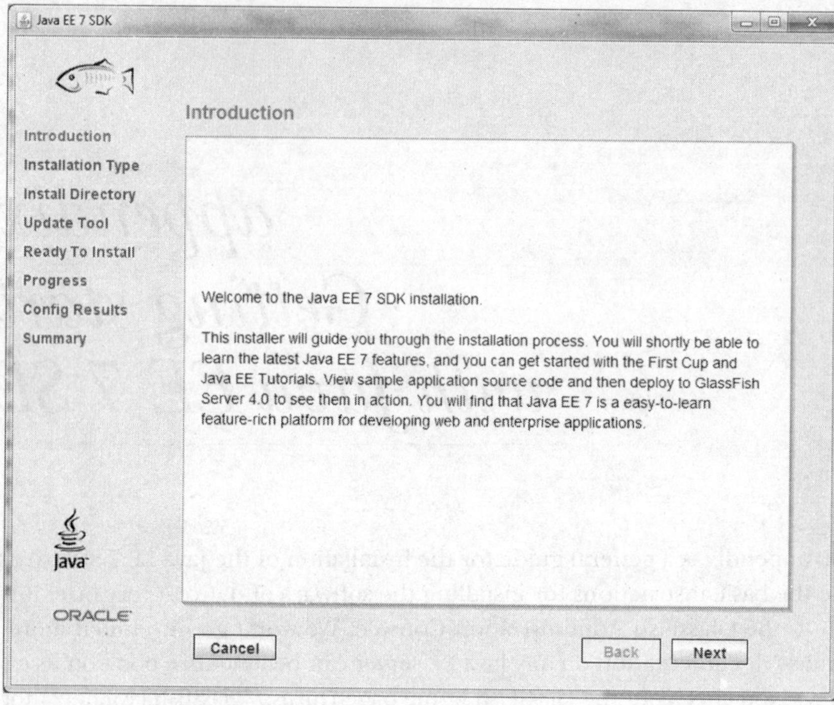

Figure B.1 Java EE 7 SDK welcome screen

will give you a complete EE server installation with the appropriate JDK to run it. The Web Profile SDK download is not a complete EE server, and although it's very useful, you should use a complete EE server until you're comfortable with the technology and are able to make an informed decision between the two. As of this writing, the most up-to-date and complete download is Java EE 7 SDK with JDK 7 Update 45, and the file downloaded is java_ee_sdk-7-jdk7-windows.exe. Downloads for all major platforms are available as well.

Once you have the installer downloaded, follow these steps:

1. Double-click the java_ee_sdk-7-jdk7-windows.exe executable. You'll see the welcome screen (figure B.1).
2. Click Next on this screen to start the installation process.
3. The next screen asks you for the installation type (figure B.2). Choose the Typical Installation option and click Next.
4. The next screen asks you for the install directory for GlassFish (figure B.3). Accept the default and install it into C:\glassfish4. Click Next.
5. The next screen asks you to install the update tool (figure B.4). The update tool is like any other online software update tool. When updates to GlassFish become available, you have the option to download and install them. If you're behind a firewall, you may need to enter the host name and port of your proxy. Get these

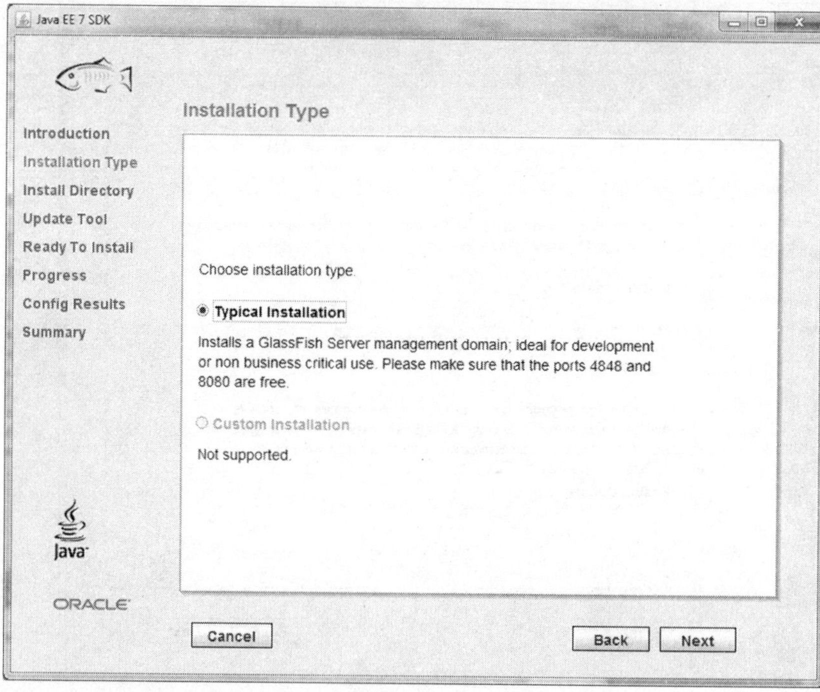

Figure B.2 Java EE 7 SDK installation type screen

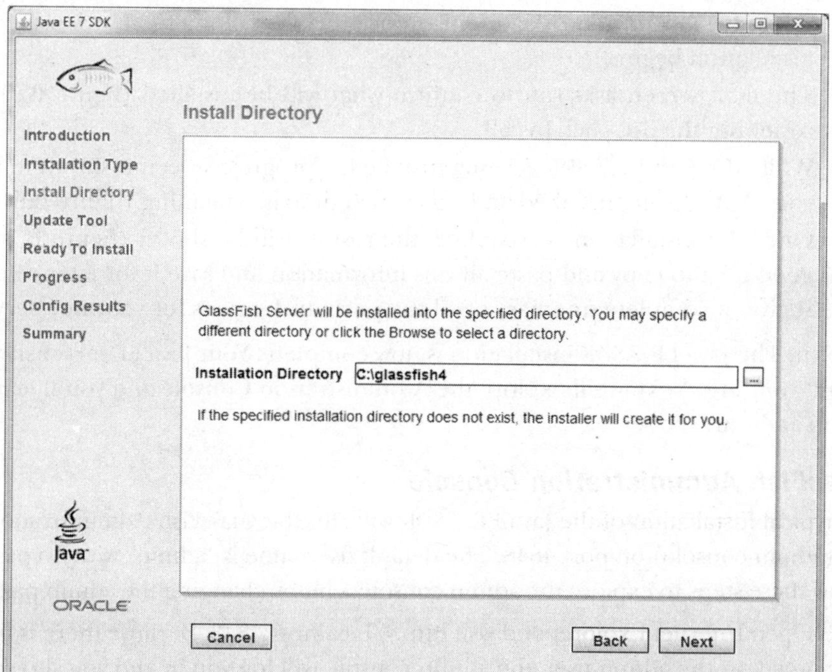

Figure B.3 Java EE 7 SDK install directory for GlassFish

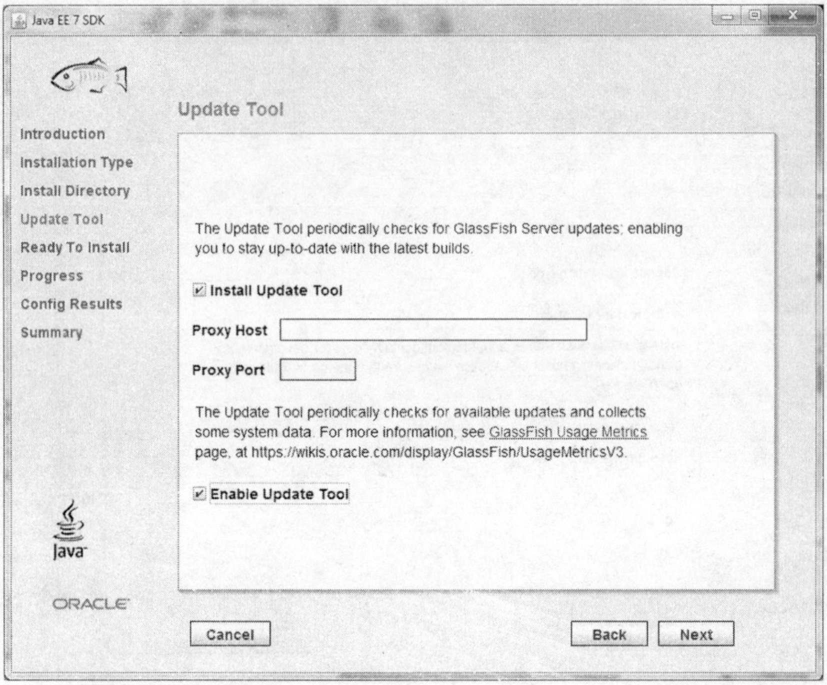

Figure B.4 Java EE 7 SDK update tool options

values from your network administrator. Click Next for a final review before the installation begins.

6. The next screen asks you to confirm what will be installed (figure B.5). After reviewing the list, click Install.
7. While the Java EE 7 SDK is being installed, a progress screen is shown to inform you what is being installed and how much time is remaining (figure B.6).
8. Once the installation is complete, the results will be shown (figure B.7). It's a good idea to copy and paste all this information and save it for later reference. It gives a complete summary of all the ports and servers for your new server.

That's it. The Java EE 7 SDK installation is now complete. Your Java EE server should be up and running. Next, we'll explore the Administration Console and you'll learn how to stop and start the server.

B.2 GlassFish Administration Console

The typical installation of the Java EE 7 SDK will run the GlassFish Administration Console (admin console) on port 4848. The default username is "admin" with no password. Follow these steps to explore the admin console a bit by changing the admin password:

1. Open Internet Explorer and visit http://localhost:4848. Because there is no password on the admin user, the admin console will log you in and you should see a page similar to figure B.8.

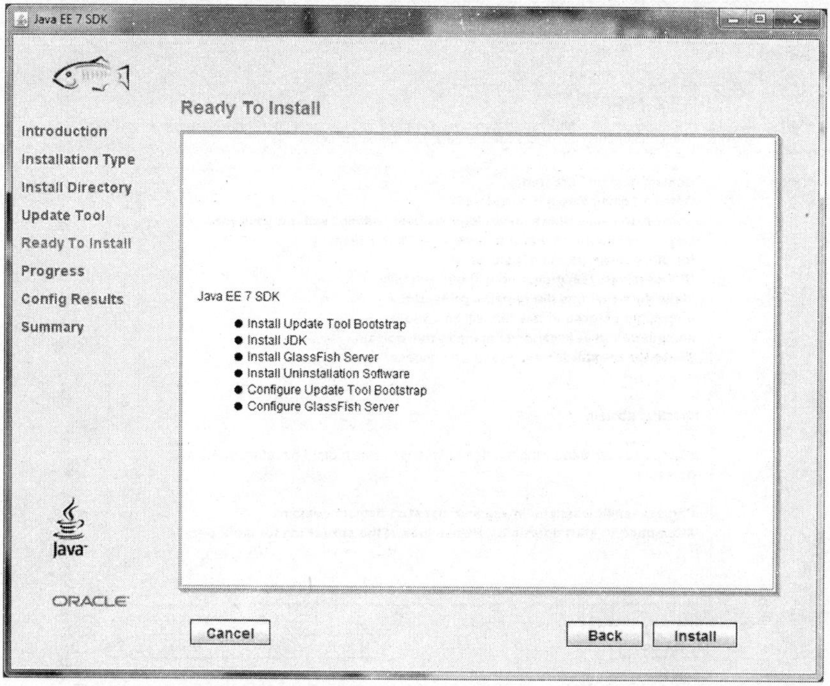

Figure B.5 Java EE 7 SDK ready to install confirmation

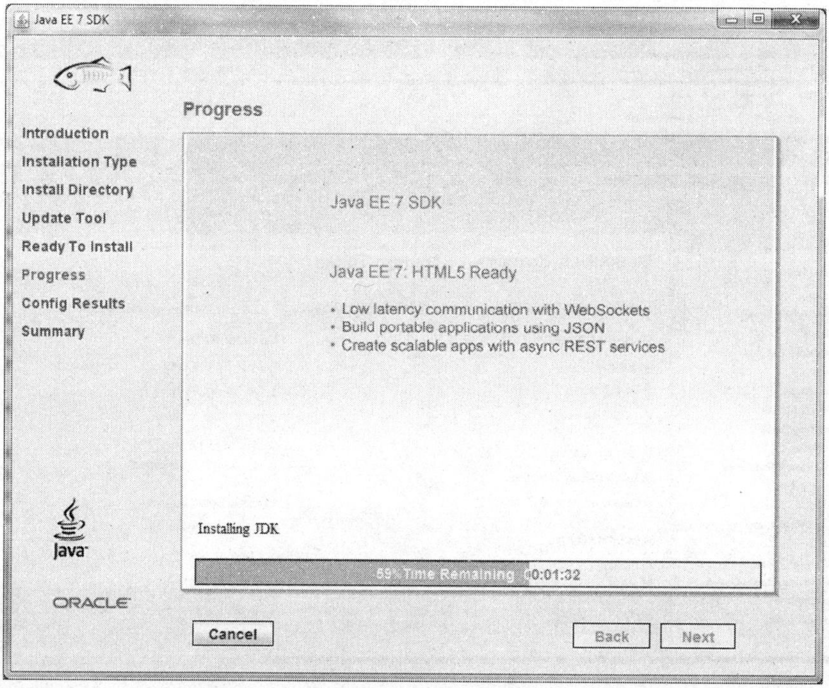

Figure B.6 Java EE 7 SDK installation progress

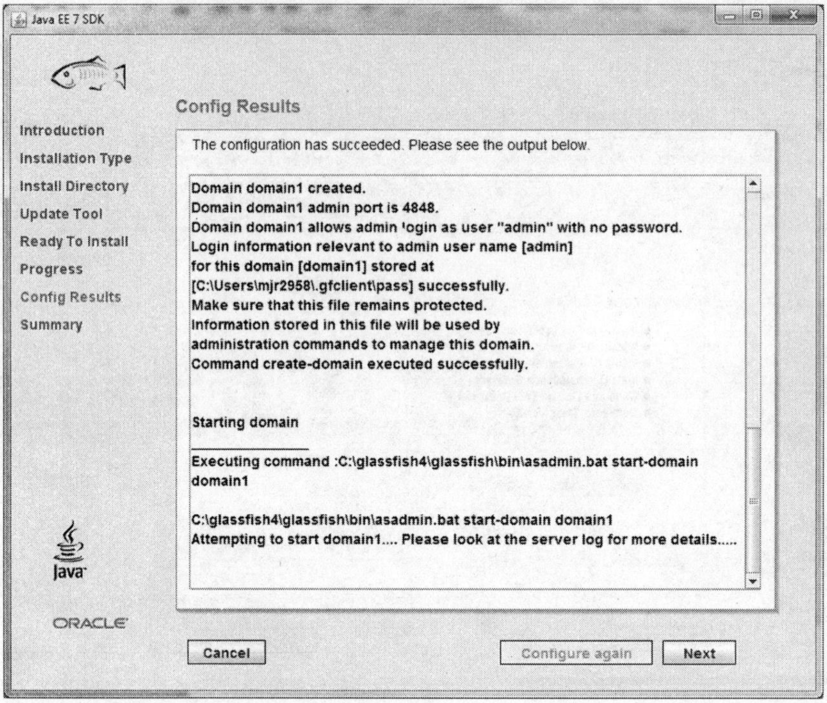

Figure B.7 Java EE 7 SDK installation results

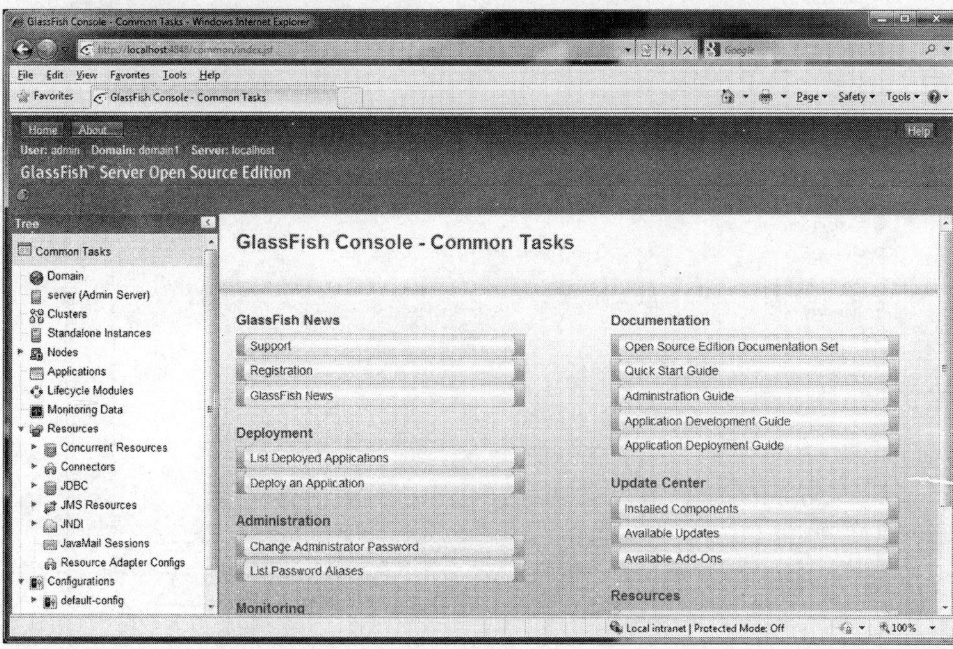

Figure B.8 GlassFish Administration Console application

2 Navigate the tree on the left to Configurations > server-config > Security > Realms > admin-realm (figure B.9). Click admin-realm.
3 You can now edit the admin-realm and manage its users. Click Manage Users (figure B.10); then click admin to edit the admin user (figure B.11).
4 Change the password for the admin user to something like adminadmin (figure B.12). Click Save.
5 Now click the Logout button. You'll get the login page for the admin console (figure B.13).

This was just a very small taste of the Administration Console. GlassFish is a full-featured Java EE 7 and its admin console can encompass an entire book on its own, so we won't go into any more detail here. The final topic we need to look at is how to start and stop your GlassFish application server.

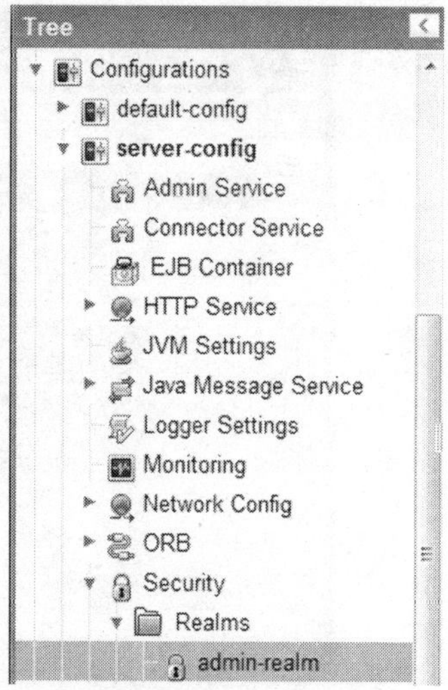

Figure B.9 The admin-realm for managing administrative access to the admin console

Figure B.10 Click to manage users for the realm.

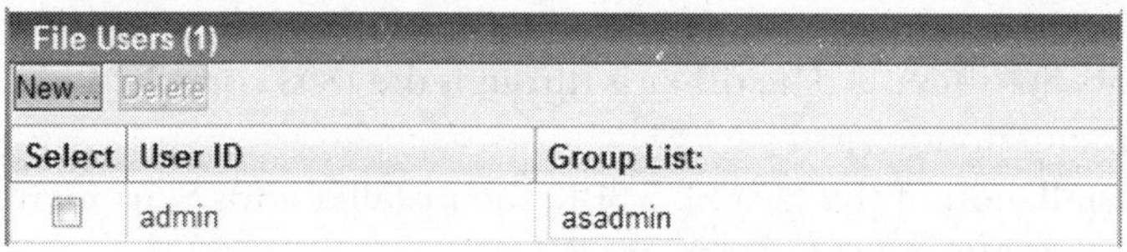

Figure B.11 Click admin to manage the admin user.

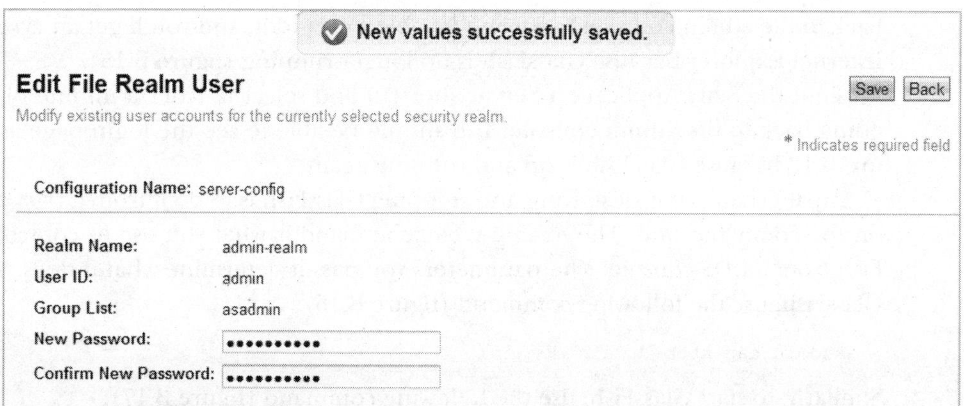

Figure B.12 Change the password for the admin user.

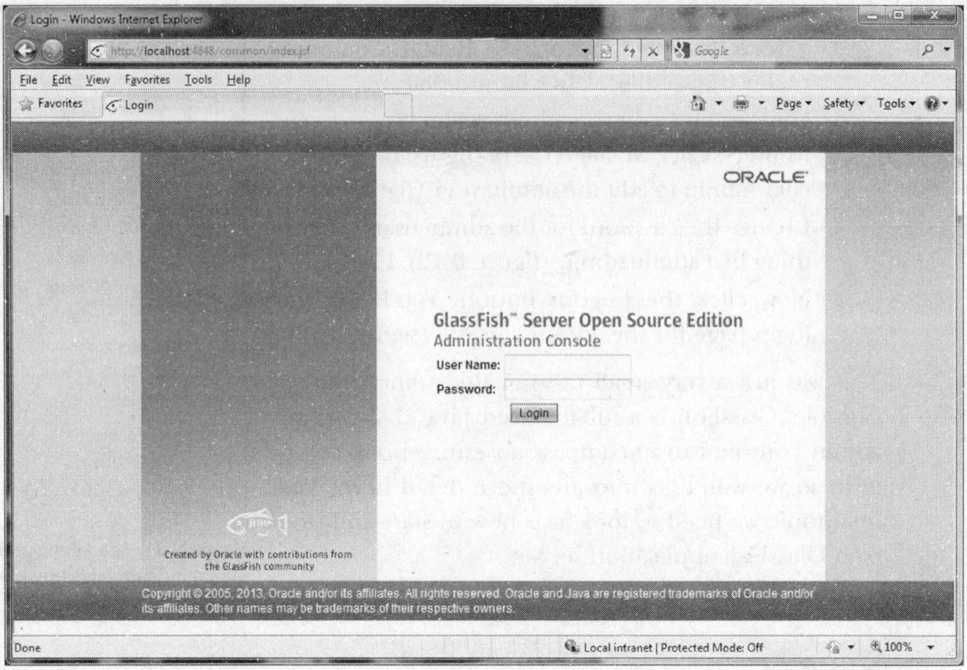

Figure B.13 GlassFish Administration Console login page after changing the password for the admin user

B.3 Starting and stopping GlassFish

In general, there are two ways to start and stop the GlassFish application. The first is through the Windows Start menu. The other is through the DOS console. Let's look at the Windows Start menu option first.

With a typical installation of the Java EE 7 SDK, the installer adds Start menu shortcuts for starting and stopping GlassFish (figure B.14).

Find the Stop Application Server shortcut and select it. After doing this, try going back to the admin console. You won't be able to get to it, and you'll get an error from Internet Explorer because GlassFish is no longer running (figure B.15).

Find the Start Application Server shortcut and select it. After a minute or so, try going back to the admin console. You should be able to see the login page as in figure B.13 because GlassFish is up and running again.

An alternative way of starting and stopping GlassFish is to do it from a DOS console on the command line. The `asadmin.bat` command is what you use to control GlassFish from a DOS console. The parameters you pass it determine what it does. To stop GlassFish, use the following command (figure B.16):

```
> asadmin.bat stop-domain domain1
```

Similarly, to start GlassFish, use the following command (figure B.17):

```
> asadmin.bat start-domain domain1
```

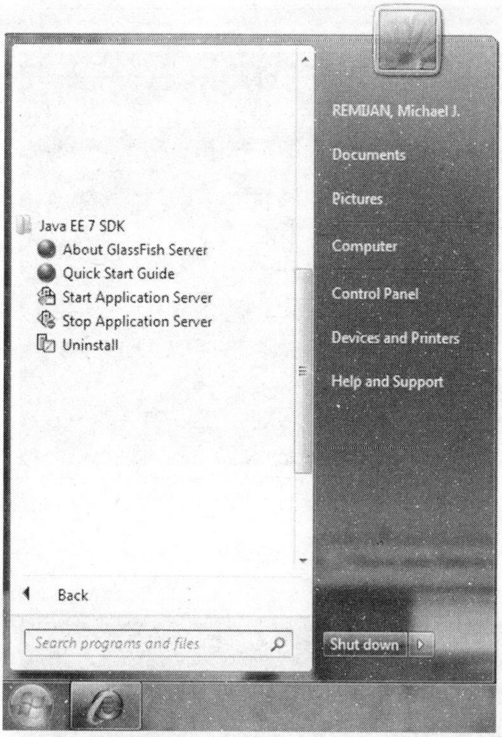

Figure B.14 Start menu shortcuts to start and stop GlassFish

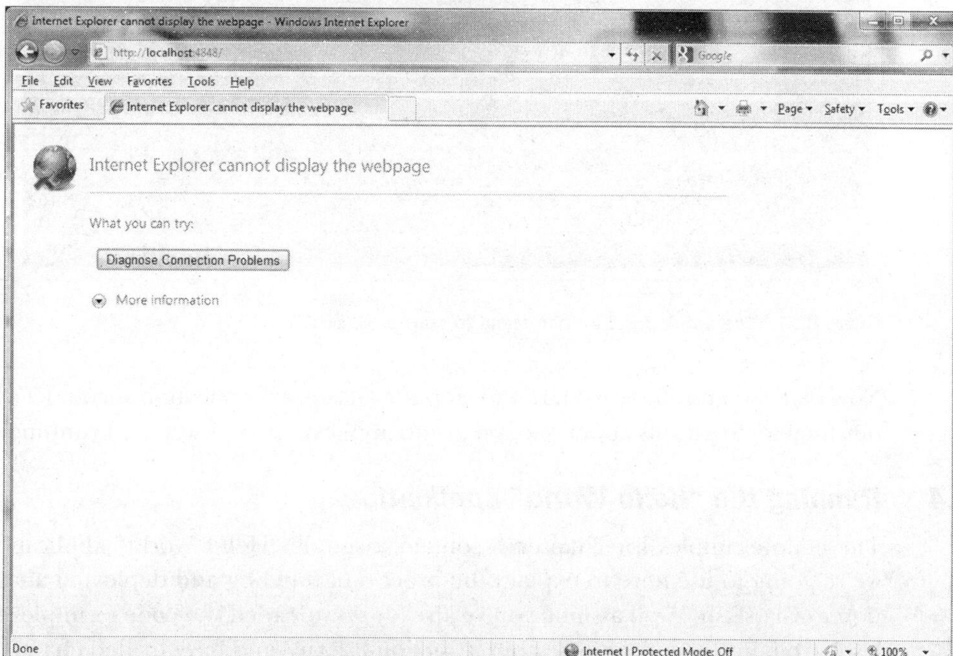

Figure B.15 Administration Console is not available because GlassFish has stopped

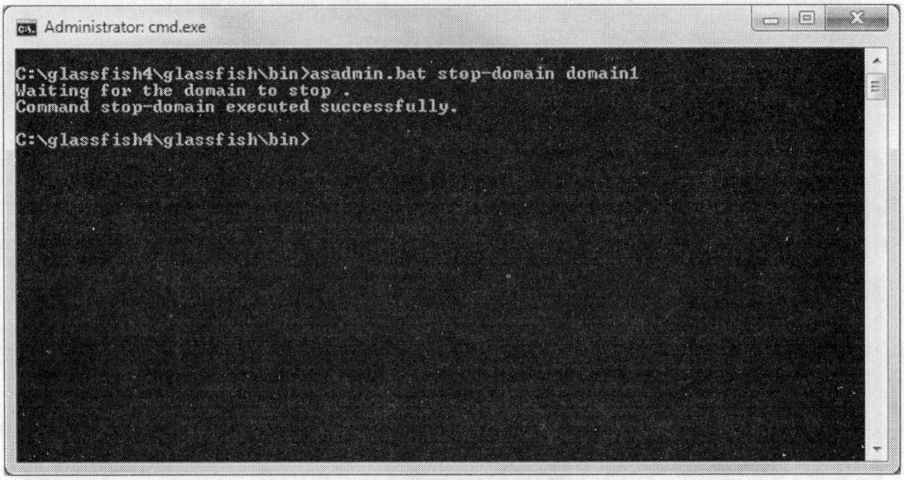

Figure B.16 The `asadmin.bat` command to stop `domain1`

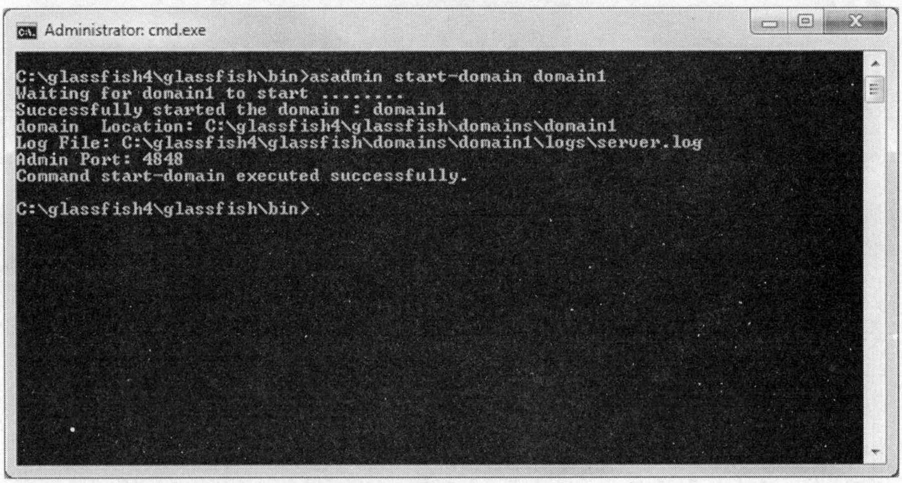

Figure B.17 The `asadmin.bat` command to start `domain1`

Now that you know how to start and stop the GlassFish application server, let's look at our final topic for this appendix and get an application deployed and running.

B.4 Running the "Hello World" application

The code examples for chapter 1 contain a simple "Hello World" application that we're going to use here to explain the process of building and deploying an application to GlassFish. We'll assume you've already downloaded the code examples for this book from http://code.google.com/p/action-bazaar/ and have loaded chapter 1 into NetBeans (figure B.18).

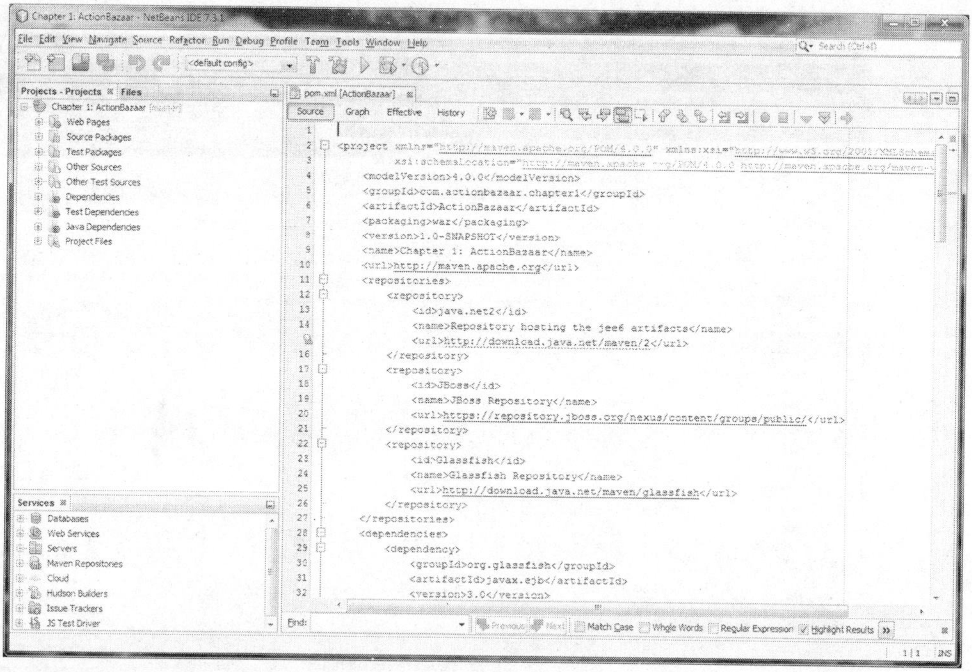

Figure B.18 Chapter 1 code examples open in NetBeans

To build and deploy the "Hello World" application from chapter 1, follow these steps:

1. Stop the GlassFish application server by following the instructions in section B.3.
2. Right-click the project and select Clean and Build. Verify that the build executed successfully by looking for `BUILD SUCCESS` from the Maven output.
3. Start the GlassFish application server by following the instructions in section B.3.
4. Navigate to Applications in the admin console and click Deploy (figure B.19).
5. Click Browse, navigate to the action-bazaar/chapter1/target directory, select the ActionBazaar.war file, and then click Open (figure B.20).
6. Verify that the Context Root value is ActionBazaar and the Application Name value is also ActionBazaar. Click the OK button to deploy the application to GlassFish (figure B.21).
7. If everything goes well, you'll see the ActionBazaar application successfully deployed to GlassFish (figure B.22).
8. Now open a new browser window to http://localhost:8080/ActionBazaar. You'll see the "Hello World" application in action (figure B.23)!

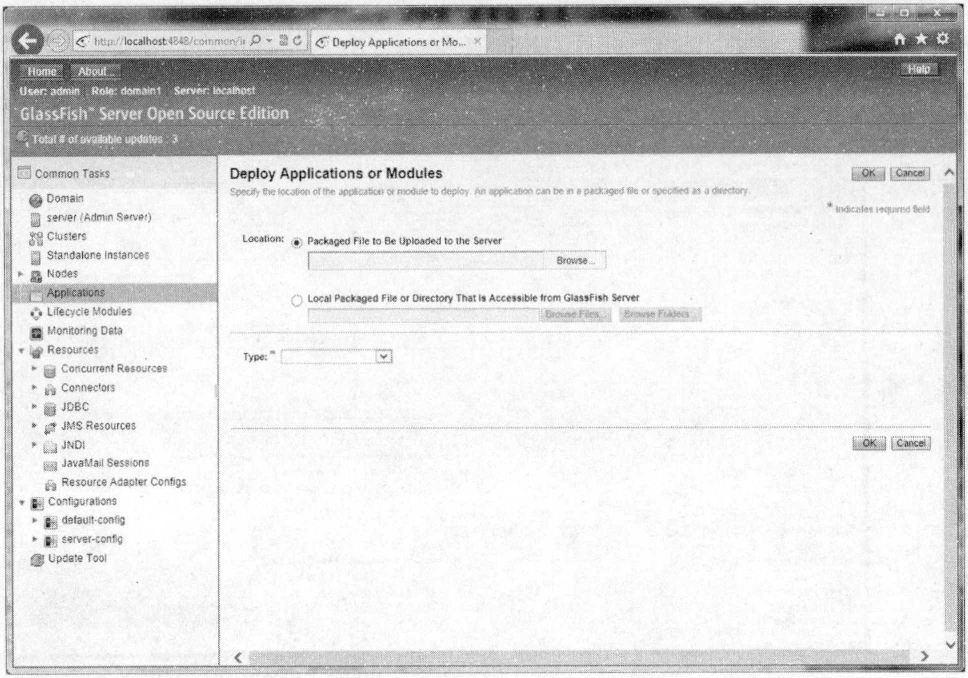

Figure B.19 GlassFish deploy application or module

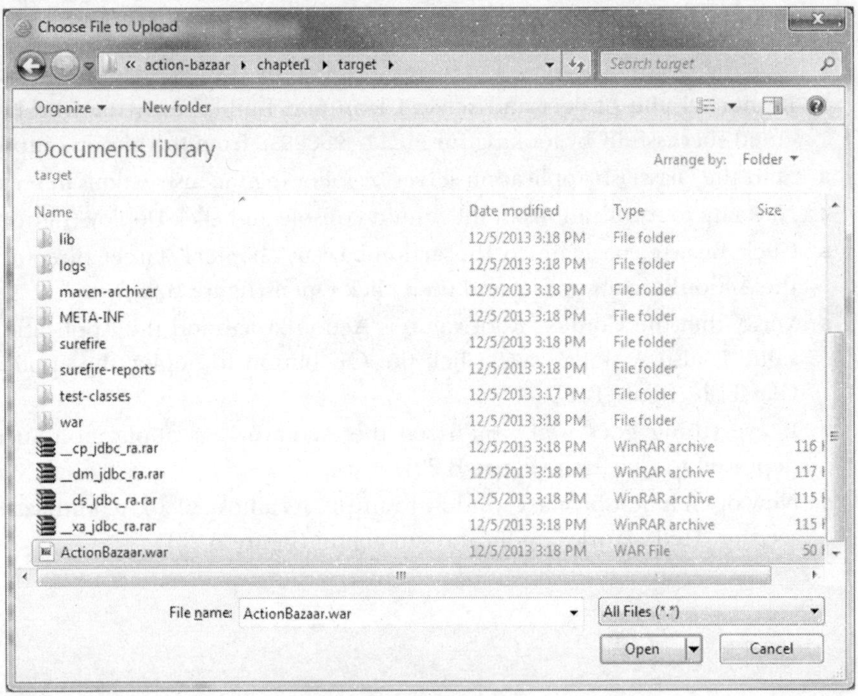

Figure B.20 Select ActionBazaar.war file to upload

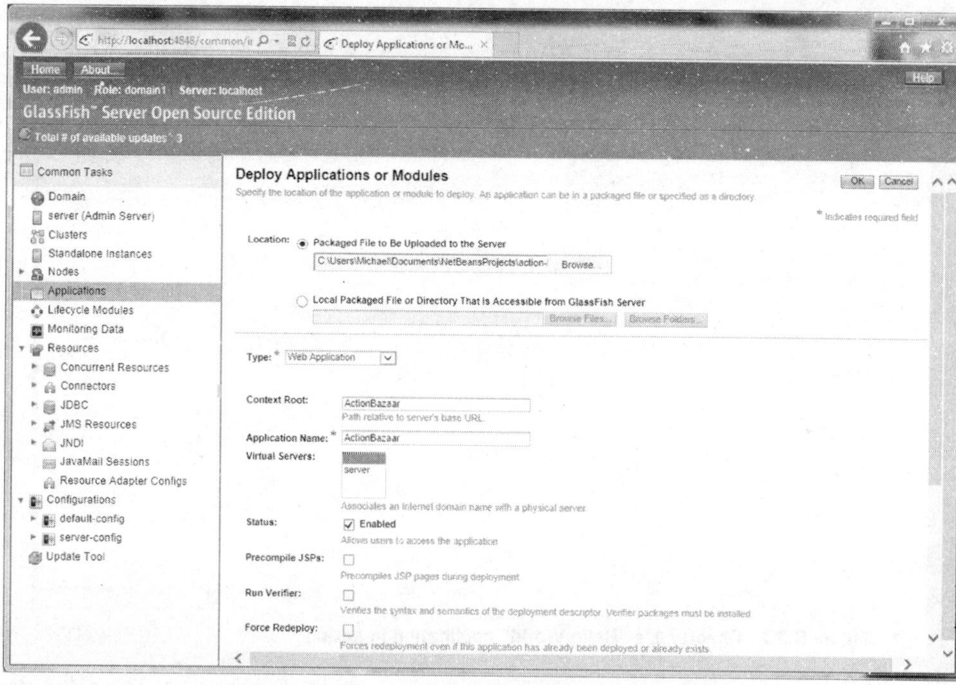

Figure B.21 Verify values for the application before deploying to GlassFish

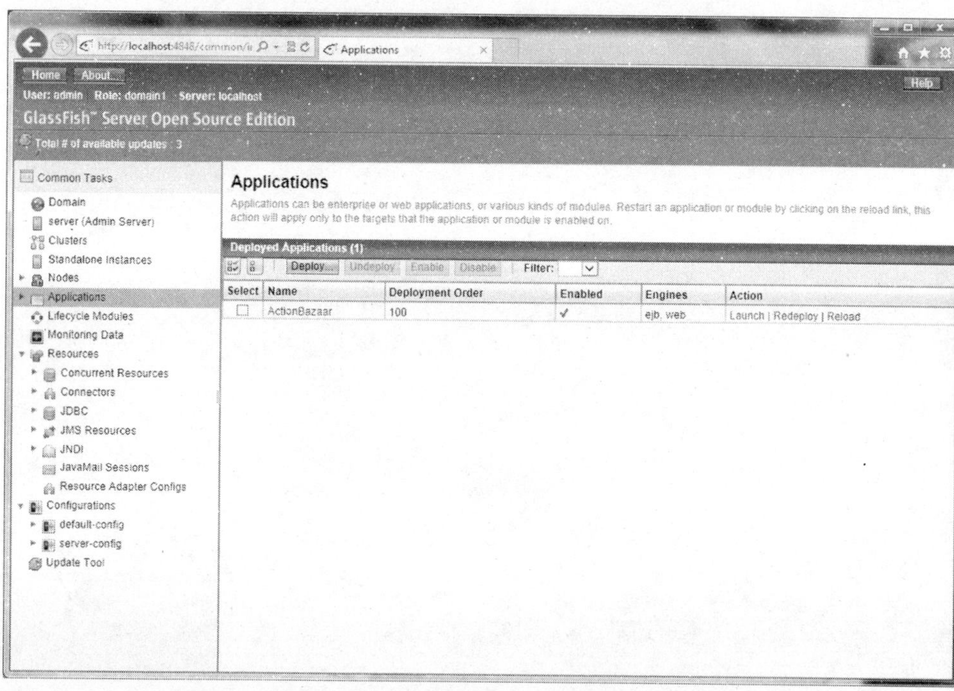

Figure B.22 ActionBazaar application successfully deployed to GlassFish

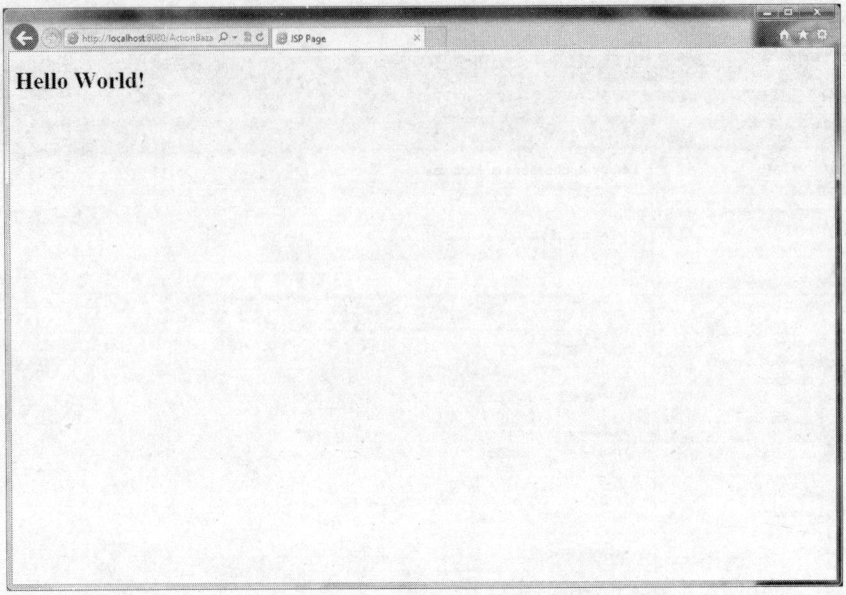

Figure B.23 Chapter 1's "Hello World" application in action

appendix C
EJB 3 developer certification exam

This appendix provides some general information on Oracle's Java certification process with focus on the EJB 3 certification exam. Oracle's EJB certification page sums up the exam as follows:

> *The Sun Certified EJB Developer for the Java EE6 Platform should have the knowledge required to build robust back-end functionality using Enterprise JavaBeans (EJB) version 3.1 technology. Through careful exam preparation, the candidate should gain practical experience with the EJB technology coding experience of session beans and message-driven beans. This candidate should also be familiar with EJB design, best practices, transaction management, messaging fundamentals, and security.* (Retrieved 12/22/2013 from http://education.oracle.com/pls/web_prod-plq-dad/db_pages.getpage?page_id=458&get_params=p_track_id:JEE6JPE.)

Certification is a great way for a Java software professional to enhance their skill set for their career. Studying for the certification gives you the opportunity to learn new technologies, techniques, and development processes you wouldn't normally be exposed to in your day-to-day work environment. After studying and learning, you can go on to take the certification exam that demonstrates basic competency in the subject matter. Finally, you can be an evangelist in the workplace and hopefully help steer your projects and infrastructure toward Java EE technologies that are better suited for your company's technical needs.

This EJB 3 book is an excellent source of information to study in preparation for the EJB 3 developer certification exam. What follows here is a general description of the Oracle Java certification process with the eventual goal of reaching and completing the EJB 3 developer certification exam. We'll cover

- How to get started with the certification process
- What path you need to take to get to the EJB 3 developer certification exam
- What topics are covered in the exam
- What the exam is like
- What to expect on exam day

Let's get started and see what Oracle's certification process is all about.

C.1 Getting started with the certification process

Oracle's certification process is a series of exams Java developers can take to demonstrate general competency and knowledge of both standard and Enterprise Java technology. The certification process starts with the basics of the Java Standard Edition (Java SE) and gradually builds in complexity as different paths take you to certifications on various Java Enterprise Edition (Java EE) technologies.

The exam process isn't complicated. Just like college courses, some exams have prerequisites you need to complete before getting the certification you may be interested in. By taking these prerequisite exams, you build your portfolio of Java certifications. The more certifications you have, the more you demonstrate your expertise with Java technology. This lets employers and colleagues know just how serious you are about Java and demonstrates your commitment to learning and independent study, which many employers value. We'll talk more about the prerequisites for the EJB certification exam in section C.2.

The certification exams are mostly multiple-choice questions. When you feel you're ready to take the exam, go online, schedule a time at a qualifying exam center in your area, show up, take the exam, and that's it. You'll be given your score at the end of the exam so you'll know instantly whether you passed. If you passed, you'll receive your certification in the mail a short time later.

Some certifications also have a development component to them. These are much like a home project or a homework assignment. The details of the project are sent to you along with a deadline. You then work at home on the project, and when you feel it's complete, you turn it in (hopefully before the deadline is up). After this, there's usually a follow-up at a qualifying exam center in your area that asks questions about the decisions you made on your project. For these exam components, you won't know your score when you've finished and you'll have to wait for your exam to be graded.

In all cases, you start your journey through the Oracle Java certification process by visiting http://java.sun.com. This will redirect you to Oracle's main page for Java technology. Once there, you'll want to look for the Certification Paths link, as shown in figure C.1.

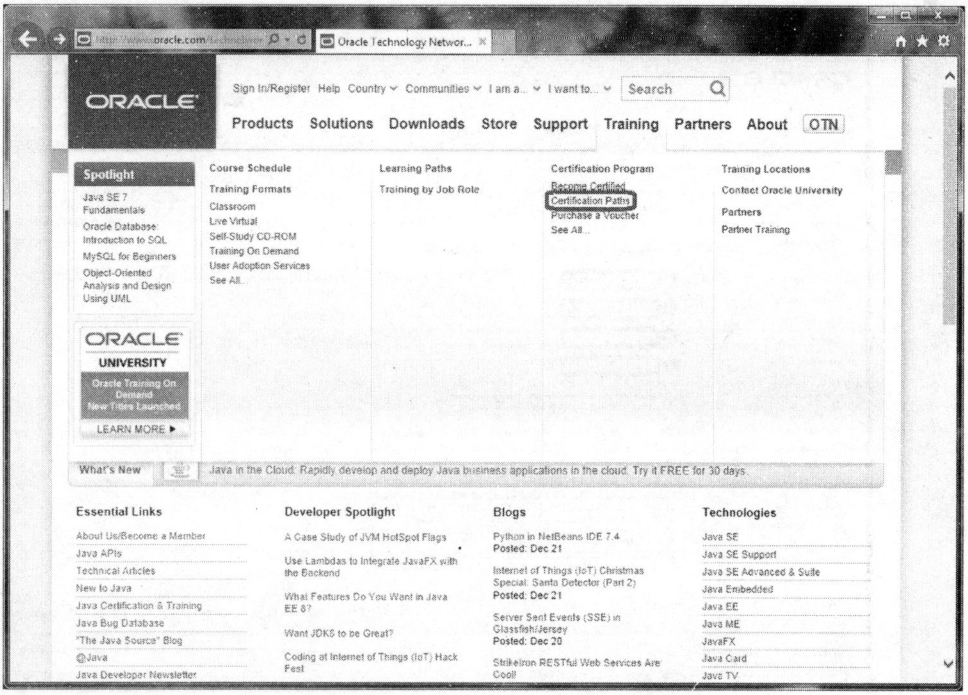

Figure C.1 Certification Paths link on Oracle's Java technology main page

Once at the Certification Paths page, you select from the drop-down boxes to narrow the list of exams. Figure C.2 shows the selections a typical Java EE developer will make:

1. Java EE Developer
2. Java and Middleware
3. Java
4. Java EE

The list of certifications will vary over time. Figure C.2 shows certifications for Java EE 5 and Java EE 6. But Java EE 7 is the most current release (as of this writing) with work already starting on Java EE 8. As new releases of Java EE come out, certifications for the older releases will drop and be replaced by the new ones. For an EJB developer, the Oracle Certified Expert, Java EE 6 Enterprise JavaBeans Developer is the certification you'll want to take. Next we're going to look at the path through the certification process to take this exam.

C.2 *Path to EJB 3 developer certification exam*

The Oracle Certified Expert, Java EE 6 Enterprise JavaBeans Developer is an advanced certification on Java EE technology. As such, it has some prerequisite certifications you'll need to get first. Section C.1 shows how to get started with the certification process and navigate through the Oracle website to the list of Java EE certification exams. If you click the Oracle Certified Expert, Java EE 6 Enterprise JavaBeans Developer link

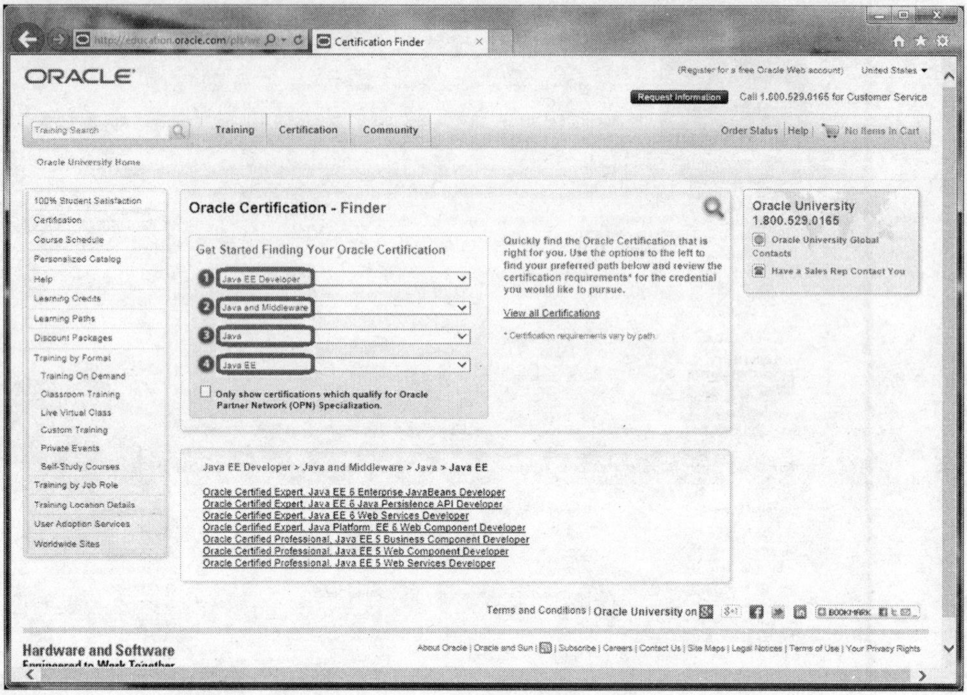

Figure C.2 List of Java EE certifications

shown in figure C.2, you'll get an overview description of the exam and its certification path, as shown in figure C.3.

The Oracle Certified Expert, Java EE 6 Enterprise JavaBeans Developer exam has one prerequisite: you must have the Oracle Certified Professional, Java SE (5, 6, or 7) Programmer or the older Sun Certified Java Programmer certification for any Java version.

Oracle has specific definitions for certification titles. The Oracle Certified Professional title is reserved for technologies on a broad scale such as Java SE. Java SE has a very large number of technologies that it encompasses—JDBC, I/O, threading, networking, data structures, and so on—but the Oracle Certified Professional certification title is for Java SE as a whole, not for a particular technology.

The Oracle Certified Expert title, on the other hand, is reserved for specific technologies. EJBs are a specific technology within Java EE, so the EJB certification is given the Oracle Certified Expert title. Because this book deals mainly with EJB technology, this is the certification we're focusing on, but there are other Oracle Certified Expert certifications available for other Java EE technologies. Use the Oracle certification website to search for them.

Before we start looking at the topics covered in the Oracle Certified Expert, Java EE 6 Enterprise JavaBeans Developer exam, there's one more point to make about the certification path. For you to get the certification, all the steps of the certification path must be completed, but they don't need to be completed in order. You can register for

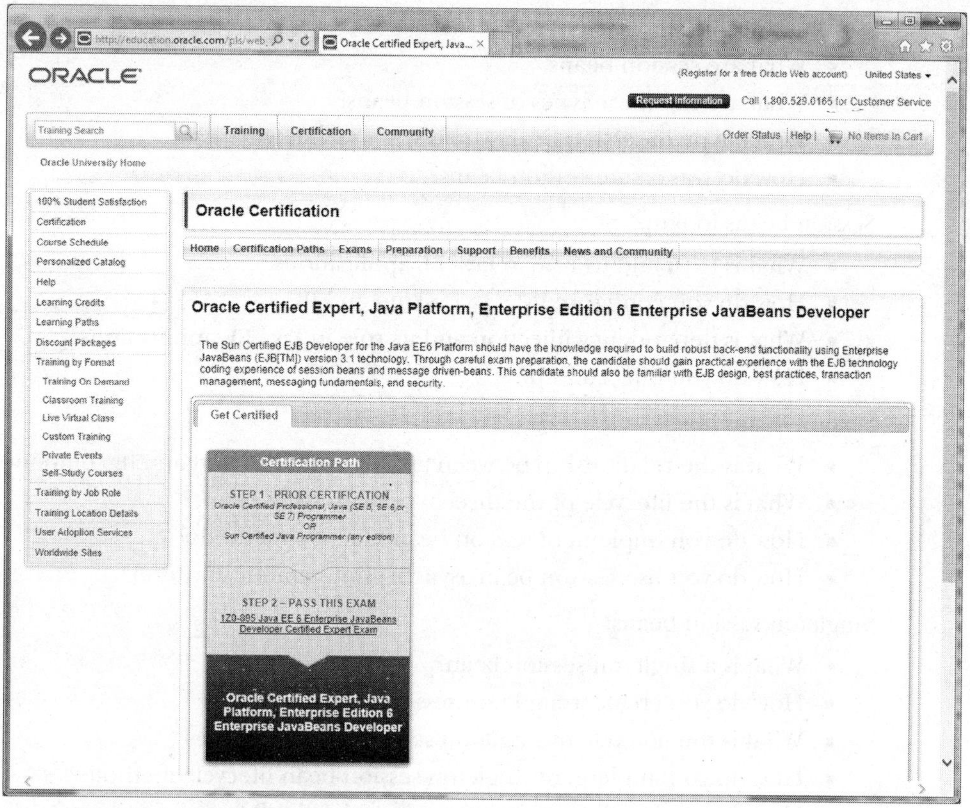

Figure C.3 Overview of EJB certification exam

and take the Oracle Certified Expert, Java EE 6 Enterprise JavaBeans Developer exam before the Oracle Certified Professional, Java SE 7 Programmer exam if you choose to do so. But you won't get the EJB certification until both exams are completed. Now let's take a look at what's in the EJB certification exam.

C.3 Topics covered in the exam

The topics covered in the Oracle Certified Expert, Java EE 6 Enterprise JavaBeans Developer exam are quite extensive, but that's because EJB technology is so feature-rich. What follows is a summary of the list of topics for the exam. In case you haven't guessed it by now, this book is an excellent resource to study for the exam.

Java EE:

- What is Java Platform Enterprise Edition (Java EE)?
- How does Java EE development differ?
- What are the Java EE application layers/tiers?
- What services do Java EE containers provide?
- What are the different Java EE component types (EJB, MDB, Servlet, and so on)?
- Compare and contrast the full versus EJB Lite containers.

Session beans:

- What are session beans?
- What are the three types of session beans?
- Which type of session bean would you use and why?
- How do you create session beans?

Session beans lookup:

- What is JNDI and its role in Java EE applications?
- How do you configure JNDI to look up an EJB?
- What is dependency injection and its role in Java EE applications?
- How do you inject an EJB?

Session beans lifecycle:

- What is the relationship between an EJB container and an EJB component?
- What is the lifecycle of the three types of session beans?
- How do you implement session bean lifecycle methods?
- How do you use session bean asynchronous communication?

Singleton session beans:

- What is a singleton session bean?
- How do you create a singleton session bean?
- What is the lifecycle of singleton session beans?
- How do you implement singleton session bean lifecycle methods?
- How do you handle concurrent access on a singleton session bean?

JMS:

- What is JMS?
- What are the roles of the JMS participants?

MDB:

- Why do session beans make bad message consumers?
- What is the lifecycle of message-driven beans?
- How do you create a JMS message-driven bean?

Timer services:

- What are timer services?
- How do you create a timer notification callback?

Interceptors:

- What are interceptors?
- How do you create an interceptor class?
- How do you apply an interceptor to methods on an EJB?
- What is the lifecycle of interceptors?
- How do you implement interceptor lifecycle methods?

Transactions:

- What are container-managed transactions (CMTs)?
- How do you join a CMT transaction?
- What are bean-managed transactions (BMT)?
- How do you start and end a BMT transaction?
- How do you apply transaction management to EJBs?
- How do you apply transaction management to MDBs?

Security:

- What is the Java EE security architecture?
- What is declarative authorization?
- What is programmatic authorization?

EJB best practices:

- What are EJBs best used for?
- What are best design patterns for web-based applications and application clients?
- What is the best way to handle exceptions?

This list of topics is comprehensive, but you should always look online for any changes or additional information. This is especially true if you plan on taking an EJB certification exam other than Oracle Certified Expert, Java EE 6 Enterprise JavaBeans Developer. You'll usually want to take whatever exam is most current. Now that we've looked at what topics you'll need to learn for the exam, crack open this book and start studying!

C.4 Studying for the exam

You have a few options to study for this exam:

- Self-study
- Guided self-study
- Online class
- Classroom

Self-study is the simplest and most cost effective option. Since you're reading this, you're already on your way! Go through all the topics in this book at your own pace and you should be in good shape for the exam.

Guided self-study is offered through Oracle University. It's essentially the same as self-study, but you pay Oracle for all the study materials. You study at your own pace and register for the exam when you're ready.

Online classes are also available through Oracle University. As the name implies, online classes are taken at home online. But they're structured just like classroom classes. Typically they're about eight hours a day for three days. This is a good option if you don't think you can study the topics on your own but are unable to travel to take a class.

Classroom classes are exactly what you'd expect. You must travel to some location (hopefully near you) and attend class for three days, eight hours a day. This option provides you the best environment for studying if your mind tends to wander and you lose focus easily. It also provides the best interaction with the instructor and is the easiest environment for asking questions and getting additional help.

Now that you have all of your studying done, let's look at what exam day will be like.

C.5 Exam day

Prior to exam day, you'll need to follow the steps in section C.1 to find the Certified Expert, Java EE 6 Enterprise JavaBeans Developer exam and register. There are many registration options. You may register at either a Pearson VUE testing center or an Oracle testing center. The exam you choose may be proctored, meaning you'll need to go to the testing center to take the exam, or unproctored, meaning the exam is online. It's best to explore all these options and pick the one that best fits your needs.

Whichever way you choose to take the exam, the exam itself should always be the same. Table C.1 lists the details of the exam. You have 110 minutes to take the exam, it's 60 multiple-choice questions, and you need at least a 73% to pass the exam. That's it—very simple.

Table C.1 Certification exam details

Exam number	1Z0-895
Associated certifications	Oracle Certified Expert, Java EE 6 Enterprise JavaBeans Developer
Exam product version	Java EE
Exam price	U.S.$245
Duration	110 minutes
Number of questions	60
Format	Multiple choice
Passing score	73%
Validated against	EE 6

Although highly unlikely, there's a possibility you won't pass the exam. If that happens, what do you do? Luckily, Oracle allows you to retake any failed exam with a few caveats. If you initially registered for a proctored exam, you must wait 14 days before taking the exam again whether you choose to register for another proctored exam or for the online exam. If you originally registered for the online exam, you can retake it at any time. You can never retake a beta version of an exam. And finally, don't try to pass yourself off as different people by registering yourself multiple times and getting multiple Oracle testing IDs.

index

B

C

E

P

X

Y